CRITICAL SURVEY OF
Poetry
Fourth Edition

Cumulative Indexes

CRITICAL SURVEY OF

Poetry

Fourth Edition

Cumulative Indexes

Resources
Indexes

Editor, Fourth Edition
Rosemary M. Canfield Reisman
Charleston Southern University

SALEM PRESS
Pasadena, California
Hackensack, New Jersey

Editor in Chief: Dawn P. Dawson

Editorial Director: Christina J. Moose	*Research Supervisor:* Jeffry Jensen
Development Editor: Tracy Irons-Georges	*Research Assistant:* Keli Trousdale
Project Editor: Rowena Wildin	*Production Editor:* Andrea E. Miller
Manuscript Editor: Desiree Dreeuws	*Page Desion:* James Hutson
Acquisitions Editor: Mark Rehn	*Layout:* Mary Overell
Editorial Assistant: Brett S. Weisberg	*Photo Editor:* Cynthia Breslin Beres

Cover photo (pictured left to right, top to bottom): Margaret Atwood (Bernd Thissen/dpa/LANDOV); Henry Wadsworth Longfellow (Time & Life Pictures/Getty Images); Lawrence Ferlinghetti (Getty Images); Breyten Breytenbach (Ulf Andersen/Getty Images); Thomas Hardy (The Granger Collection, New York); Rainer Maria Rilke (The Granger Collection, New York); Petrarch (The Granger Collection, New York), Ernesto Cardenal (AFP/Getty Images), Dorothy Parker (The Granger Collection, New York); Carl Sandburg (The Granger Collection, New York); Lord Byron (Archive Photos/Getty Images)

Some of the essays in this work, which have been updated, originally appeared in the following Salem Press publications, *Critical Survey of Poetry, English Language Series* (1983), *Critical Survey of Poetry: Foreign Language Series* (1984), *Critical Survey of Poetry, Supplement* (1987), *Critical Survey of Poetry, English Language Series, Revised Edition*, (1992; preceding volumes edited by Frank N. Magill), *Critical Survey of Poetry, Second Revised Edition* (2003; edited by Philip K. Jason).

∞ The paper used in these volumes conforms to the American National Standard for Permanence of Paper for Printed Library Materials, X39.48-1992 (R1997).

Library of Congress Cataloging-in-Publication Data

Critical survey of poetry. — 4th ed. / editor, Rosemary M. Canfield Reisman.
    v. cm.
Includes bibliographical references and index.
ISBN 978-1-58765-582-1 (set : alk. paper) — ISBN 978-1-58765-767-2 (cumulative indexes)
1. Poetry—History and criticism—Dictionaries. 2. Poetry—Bio-bibliography. 3. Poets—Biography—Dictionaries. I. Reisman, Rosemary M. Canfield.
PN1021.C7 2011
809.1'003--dc22

2010045095

First Printing

PRINTED IN THE UNITED STATES OF AMERICA

PUBLISHER'S NOTE

Cumulative Indexes is part of Salem Press's greatly expanded and redesigned *Critical Survey of Poetry* Series. The *Critical Survey of Poetry, Fourth Edition*, presents profiles of major poets, with sections on other literary forms, achievements, biography, general analysis, and analysis of the poet's most important poems or collections. Although the profiled authors may have written in other genres as well, sometimes to great acclaim, the focus of this set is on their most important works of poetry.

The *Critical Survey of Poetry* was originally published in 1983 and 1984 in separate English- and foreign-language series, a supplement in 1987, a revised English-language series in 1992, and a combined revised series in 2003. The *Fourth Edition* includes all poets from the previous edition and adds 145 new ones, covering 843 writers in total. The poets covered in this set represent more than 40 countries and their poetry dates from the eighth century B.C.E. to the present. The set also offers 72 informative overviews; 20 of these essays were added for this edition, including all the literary movement essays. In addition, 7 resources are provided, 2 of them new. More than 500 photographs and portraits of poets have been included.

For the first time, the material in the *Critical Survey of Poetry* has been organized into five subsets by geography and essay type: a 4-volume subset on *American Poets*, a 3-volume subset on *British, Irish, and Commonwealth Poets*, a 3-volume subset on *European Poets*, a 1-volume subset on *World Poets*, and a 2-volume subset of *Topical Essays*. Each poet appears in only one subset. *Topical Essays* is organized under the categories "Poetry Around the World," "Literary Movements," and "Criticism and Theory." *Cumulative Indexes* covers all five subsets and is free with purchase of more than one subset.

CUMULATIVE INDEXES

Cumulative Indexes functions as both a compilation of materials from the five subsets that make up *Critical Survey of Poetry* and a reference guide that simplifies finding material in the five subsets. It begins with a list of Contents. The Resources section contains comprehensive versions of the Bibliography, Guide to Online Resources, Time Line, Major Awards, and Chronological List of Poets found in the first four subsets of *Critical Survey of Poetry*. The Guide to Online Resources and Time Line were created for this edition.

All poet profiles and topical essays appear in the Geographical Index of Poets and Essays and the Categorized Index of Poets and Essays. The geographical index groups them by country or areas and the categorized index groups all profiles and essays by culture or group identities, literary movement, historical periods, and poetic forms and themes. The *Critical Survey of Poetry* Series: Master List of Contents lists all poets profiled in the complete series. The Subject Index is a comprehensive index, combining all subject indexes in the *Critical Survey of Poetry*.

ONLINE ACCESS

Salem Press provides access to its award-winning content both in traditional, printed form and online. Any school or library that purchases any subset is entitled to free, complimentary access to Salem's fully supported online version of that content. Features include a simple intuitive interface, user profile areas for students and patrons, sophisticated search functionality, and complete context, including appendixes. Access is available through a code printed on the inside cover of the first volume, and that access is unlimited and immediate. Our online customer service representatives, at (800) 221-1592, are happy to help with any questions. E-books are also available.

ACKNOWLEDGMENTS

Salem Press is grateful for the efforts of the original contributors of these essays and those of the outstanding academicians who took on the task of updating or

writing new material for the set. Their names and affiliations are listed in the "Contributors" section that follows. Finally, we are indebted to our editor, Professor Rosemary M. Canfield Reisman of Charleston Southern University, for her development of the table of contents for the *Critical Survey of Poetry, Fourth Edition* and her advice on updating the original articles to make this comprehensive and thorough revised edition an indispensable tool for students, teachers, and general readers alike.

CONTRIBUTORS

Claude Abraham
University of California, Davis

Paul Acker
Brown University

Robert Acker
University of Montana

Karley K. Adney
University of Wisconsin, Marathon County

Sidney Alexander
Virginia Commonwealth University

James Lovic Allen
University of Hawaii at Hilo

John Alspaugh
Richmond, Virginia

Nicole Anae
Charles Sturt University

Phillip B. Anderson
University of Central Arkansas

Andrew J. Angyal
Elon University

Stanley Archer
Texas A&M University

Rosemary Ascherl
Colchester, Connecticut

James R. Aubrey
United States Air Force Academy

Jane Augustine
Stuyvesant Station, New York

Charles Lewis Avinger, Jr.
Washtenaw Community College

Linda C. Badley
Middle Tennessee State University

L. Michelle Baker
The Catholic University of America

Peter Baker
Southern Connecticut State University

William Baker
Northern Illinois University

Angela Ball
University of Southern Mississippi

Lowell A. Bangerter
University of Wyoming

James John Baran
Louisiana State University-Shreveport

Stanisław Barańczak
Harvard University

Paula C. Barnes
Hampton University

Theodore Baroody
American Psychological Foundation

David Barratt
Montreat College

Jean-Pierre Barricelli
University of California, Riverside

Melissa E. Barth
Appalachian State University

Larry David Barton
Bemidgi, Minnesota

Enikő Molnár Basa
Library of Congress

Fiora A. Bassanese
University of Massachusetts, Boston

Sharon Bassett
California State University, Los Angeles

Robert Bateman
Concord College

Angela Bates
University of Cincinnati Writing Center

Walton Beacham
Beacham Publishing Corp.

Cynthia S. Becerra
Humphreys College

Kirk H. Beetz
Davis, California

Kate Begnal
Utah State University

Elizabeth J. Bellamy
Winthrop College

Todd K. Bender
University of Wisconsin-Madison

Robert Bensen
Hartwick College

Richard P. Benton
Trinity College

Donna Berliner
University of Texas at Dallas

Eleanor von Auw Berry
Milwaukee, Wisconsin

Dorothy M. Betz
Georgetown University

Peter Bien
University of Massachusetts, Dartmouth

M. D. Birnbaum
University of California, Los Angeles

Nicholas Birns
Eugene Lang College,
The New School

Richard Bizot
University of North Florida

Patrick Bizzaro
East Carolina University

Franz G. Blaha
University of Nebraska-Lincoln

Robert G. Blake
Elon University

Lynn Z. Bloom
University of Connecticut

Patricia J. Boehne
Eastern College

Robert E. Boenig
Texas A&M University

Allyson Booth
United States Naval Academy

András Boros-Kazai
Beloit College

Neal Bowers
Iowa State University

Kevin Boyle
Elon University

Harold Branam
Savannah State University

Gerhard Brand
California State University,
Los Angeles

Marie J. K. Brenner
Bethel College

Anne Kelsch Breznau
Kellogg Community College

Jeanie R. Brink
Arizona State University

J. R. Broadus
University of North Carolina

David Bromige
Sonoma State University

Steven Brown
University of Rhode Island, Kingston

Mary Hanford Bruce
Monmouth College

Joseph Bruchac
Greenfield Center, New York

Mitzi M. Brunsdale
Mayville State College

Amy Burnette
Appalachian State University

Alvin G. Burstein
University of Tennessee, Knoxville

Edward Butscher
Briarwood, New York

Susan Butterworth
Salem State College

Joseph P. Byrne
Belmont University

Richard J. Calhoun
Clemson University

Glauco Cambon
University of Connecticut

Ann M. Cameron
Indiana University, Kokomo

Edmund J. Campion
University of Tennessee

David Cappella
Boston University

H. W. Carle
St. Joseph, Missouri

David A. Carpenter
Eastern Illinois University

John Carpenter
University of Michigan

Peter Carravetta
Queens College, City University of
New York

Henry L. Carrigan, Jr.
Northwestern University

Joseph Carroll
Community College of Rhode Island

Caroline Carvill
Rose-Hulman Institute of Technology

Michael Case
Arizona State University

Leonard R. Casper
Boston College

Mary LeDonne Cassidy
South Carolina State University

Donald Cellini
Adrian College

Francisco J. Cevallos
Orono, Maine

G. A. Cevasco
St. John's University

Carole A. Champagne
University of Maryland-Eastern
Shore

Allan Chavkin
Southwest Texas State University

Chih-Ping Chen
Alma College

Diana Arlene Chlebek
The University of Akron Libraries

Luisetta Elia Chomel
University of Houston

Balance Chow
San Jose State University

Paul Christensen
Texas A&M University

Lindsay Christopher
University of Denver

C. L. Chua
California State University, Fresno

John R. Clark
University of South Florida

Kevin Clark
California Polytechnic State University

Patricia Clark
Grand Valley State University

Douglas Clouatre
North Platte, Nebraska

Peter Cocozzella
State University of New York at Binghamton

Steven E. Colburn
Largo, Florida

David W. Cole
University of Wisconsin Colleges

Caroline Collins
Quincy University

Richard Collins
Xavier University of Louisiana

Robert Colucci
Pittsburgh, Pennsylvania

John J. Conlon
University of South Florida, St. Petersburg

Julian W. Connolly
University of Virginia

Peter Constantine
New York, New York

Victor Contoski
University of Kansas

Joseph Coulson
Southwest Texas State University

Carrie Cowherd
Howard University

John W. Crawford
Henderson State University

Galbraith M. Crump
Kenyon College

Heidi K. Czerwiec
University of North Dakota

Diane D'Amico
Allegheny College

Dolores A. D'Angelo
American University

Robert Darling
Keuka College

Reed Way Dasenbrock
New Mexico State University

Anita Price Davis
Converse College

Delmer Davis
Andrews University

J. Madison Davis
Pennsylvania State College-Behrend College

Todd F. Davis
Goshen College

William V. Davis
Baylor University

Frank Day
Clemson University

Dennis R. Dean
University of Wisconsin-Parkside

Andonis Decavalles
Fairleigh Dickinson University

Paul J. deGrategno
Wesleyan College

Mary De Jong
Pennsylvania State University

Bill Delaney
San Diego, California

Lloyd N. Dendinger
University of South Alabama

K. Z. Derounian
University of Arkansas-Little Rock

Mary de Shazer
University of Oregon

Mark DeStephano
Saint Peter's College

Joseph Dewey
University of Pittsburgh-Johnstown

Marcia B. Dinneen
Bridgewater State College

Robert DiYanni
Pace University

Margaret A. Dodson
Boise, Idaho

Lillian Doherty
University of Maryland

Georgie L. Donovan
Appalachian State University

David C. Dougherty
Loyola College in Maryland

Lee Hunt Dowling
University of Houston

Theresa E. Dozier
Prince George's Community College

Paul A. Draghi
Indiana University

Desiree Dreeuws
Sunland, California

John Drury
University of Cincinnati

Doris Earnshaw
University of California, Davis

Robert Eddy
Fayetteville State University

K Edgington
Towson University

Cliff Edwards
Fort Hays State University

Richard A. Eichwald
St. Louis, Missouri

Robert P. Ellis
Worcester State College

Richard Kenneth Emmerson
Walla Walla College

Ann Willardson Engar
University of Utah

Bernard F. Engel
Michigan State University

David L. Erben
University of South Florida

Thomas L. Erskine
Salisbury University

Clara Estow
University of Massachusetts

Welch D. Everman
University of Maine

Jack Ewing
Boise, Idaho

Christoph Eykman
Boston College

Robert Faggen
Claremont McKenna College

Rodney Farnsworth
Indiana University

Nettie Farris
University of Louisville

Massud Farzan
Boston University

Howard Faulkner
Washburn University

Sarah Fedirka
Arizona State University

William L. Felker
Yellow Springs, Ohio

Thomas R. Feller
Nashville, Tennessee

Lydia E. Ferguson
Clemson University

Sandra K. Fischer
State University of New York at Albany

Rebecca Hendrick Flannagan
Francis Marion University

John Miles Foley
University of Missouri

Lydia Forssander-Song
Trinity Western University

Thomas C. Foster
University of Michigan-Flint

Margot K. Frank
Randolph-Macon Women's College

Walter B. Freed, Jr.
State University of New York at Geneseo

Kenneth Friedenreich
Dana Point, California

Lawrence S. Friedman
Indiana University

Jean C. Fulton
Landmark College

Kenneth E. Gadomski
University of Delaware

Ann D. Garbett
Averett University

Elaine Gardiner
Topeka, Kansas

Daniel H. Garrison
Northwestern University

Katherine Gyékényesi Gatto
Richmond Heights, Ohio

Edward V. Geist
Forest Hills, New York

Donna Gerstenberger
University of Washington

Jay A. Gertzman
Mansfield University

Scott Giantvalley
California State University, Dominguez Hills

Kenneth Gibbs
Sturbridge, Massachusetts

Keiko Matsui Gibson
Kanda University of International Studies

Morgan Gibson
Urbana, Illinois

Richard F. Giles
Wilfrid Laurier University

Ronald K. Giles
East Tennessee State University

C. Herbert Gilliland
United States Naval Academy

Dennis Goldsberry
College of Charleston

Vincent F. A. Golphin
The Writing Company

Lois Gordon
Fairleigh Dickinson University

Sidney Gottlieb
Sacred Heart University

Robert Edward Graalman, Jr.
Oklahoma State University

Ronald Gray
Grand Junction, Colorado

William H. Green
*Chattahoochee Valley State
    College*

John R. Griffin
University of Southern Colorado

John L. Grigsby
*Appalachian Research & Defense
    Fund of Kentucky, Inc.*

Daniel L. Guillory
Millikin University

Jeff Gundy
Bluffton College

Stephen I. Gurney
Bemidji State University

R. S. Gwynn
Lamar University

Tasha Haas
University of Kansas

Donald P. Haase
Wayne State University

Kenneth Hada
East Central University

Steven L. Hale
Georgia Perimeter College

Elsie Galbreath Haley
Metropolitan State College of Denver

Shelley P. Haley
Howard University

William T. Hamilton
Metropolitan State College of Denver

Katherine Hanley
St. Bernard's Institute

Todd C. Hanlin
University of Arkansas

Michele Hardy
Prince George's Community College

Maryhelen Cleverly Harmon
University of South Florida

John Harty III
University of Florida

Nelson Hathcock
Saint Xavier University

Robert Hauptman
St. Cloud State University

Robert W. Haynes
Texas A&M University

David M. Heaton
Ohio University

William J. Heim
University of South Florida

Michael Heller
Stuyvesant Station, New York

Michael Hennessy
Southwest Texas State University

Sarah Hilbert
Pasadena, California

Ann R. Hill
Randolph-Macon Woman's College

KaaVonia Hinton
Old Dominion University

Jeffrey D. Hoeper
Arkansas State University

Hilary Holladay
University of Massachusetts, Lowell

Daryl Holmes
Nicholls State University

John R. Holmes
*Franciscan University of
    Steubenville*

Elizabeth A. Holtze
Metropolitan State College of Denver

Donald D. Hook
Trinity College

Gregory D. Horn
*Southwest Virginia Community
    College*

Wm. Dennis Horn
Clarkson University

David Harrison Horton
Patten College

William Howard
Chicago State University

Kenneth A. Howe
Michigan State University

Anne Howells
Occidental College

John F. Hudson
West Concord Union Church

Mary Hurd
East Tennessee State University

Ramona L. Hyman
Loma Linda University

Earl G. Ingersoll
SUNY College at Brockport

Tracy Irons-Georges
Glendale, California

Teresa Ishigaki
California State University, Fresno

Miglena Ivanova
Coastal Carolina University

Maura Ives
Texas A&M University

Karen Jaehne
Washington, D.C.

Gerald Janecek
University of Kentucky

Helen Jaskoski
*California State University,
    Fullerton*

Philip K. Jason
United States Naval Academy

Lesley Jenike
*Columbus College of Art
    and Design*

Alfred W. Jensen
University of Idaho-Moscow

Jeffry Jensen
Pasadena, California

Ed Jewinski
Wilfrid Laurier University

Juan Fernández Jiménez
Pennsylvania State University

Christopher D. Johnson
Francis Marion University

Mark A. Johnson
Central Missouri State University

Sheila Golburgh Johnson
Santa Barbara, California

Judith L. Johnston
Rider College

William Jolliff
George Fox University

Ginger Jones
Lincoln University-Missouri

Leslie Ellen Jones
Pasadena, California

Robert C. Jones
Warrensburg, Missouri

Paul Kane
Vassar College

Leela Kapai
Prince George's Community College

Irma M. Kashuba
Chestnut Hill College

Theodore L. Kassier
University of Texas-San Antonio

Richard Keenan
*University of Maryland-Eastern
    Shore*

James M. Kempf
United States Air Force Academy

Claire Keyes
Salem State College

Karen A. Kildahl
South Dakota State University

Sue L. Kimball
Methodist College

Arthur Kincaid
Glenn Mills, Pennsylvania

Frederick Kirchhoff
Fort Wayne, Indiana

B. G. Knepper
Sioux City, Iowa

Jürgen Koppensteiner
University of Northern Iowa

Philip Krummrich
University of Georgia

Pam Fox Kuhlken
San Diego State University

Katherine C. Kurk
Northern Kentucky University

Vera M. Kutzinski
Yale University

Rebecca Kuzins
Pasadena, California

Norris J. Lacy
University of Kansas

Wendy Alison Lamb
South Pasadena, California

Mary Lang
Wharton County Junior College

Jeanne Larsen
Hollins College

Susan T. Larson
Clemson University

Patricia Ondek Laurence
*City College, City University of
    New York*

John Richard Law
Auburn University

William T. Lawlor
*University of Wisconsin-Stevens
    Point*

Carolina D. Lawson
Kent State University

Linda Ledford-Miller
University of Scranton

John M. Lee
James Madison University

L. L. Lee
Western Washington University

Raymond LePage
George Mason University

Robert W. Leutner
University of Iowa

Michael M. Levy
University of Wisconsin-Stout

Leon Lewis
Appalachian State University

Marie-Noëlle D. Little
Clinton, New York

James Livingston
Northern Michigan University

Archie K. Loss
Pennsylvania State University, Erie

Rick Lott
Arkansas State University

Dieter P. Lotze
Allegheny College

Michael Loudon
Eastern Illinois University

Bernadette Flynn Low
*Community College of Baltimore
    County-Dundalk*

Perry D. Luckett
United States Air Force Academy

Steven R. Luebke
University of Wisconsin-River Falls

Carol J. Luther
Pellissippi State Community College

R. C. Lutz
CII Group

John D. Lyons
University of Massachusetts, Dartmouth

Sara McAulay
California State University, Hayward

Janet McCann
Texas A&M University

Joanne McCarthy
Tacoma Community College

Dennis McCormick
University of Montana

John F. McDiarmid
New College of Florida

Gina Macdonald
Nicholls State University

Roxanne McDonald
Wilmot, New Hampshire

Fred R. McFadden
Coppin State College

Ron McFarland
University of Idaho

Richard D. McGhee
Arkansas State University

Arthur E. McGuinness
University of California, Davis

S. Thomas Mack
University of South Carolina-Aiken

Joseph McLaren
Hofstra University

Kevin McNeilly
University of British Columbia

Magdalena Mączyńska
The Catholic University of America

Mary E. Mahony
Wayne County Community College

Cherie R. Maiden
Furman University

David Maisel
Wellesley, Massachusetts

Joseph Maltby
University of Hawaii at Manoa

John Marney
Oakland University

Bruce K. Martin
Drake University

Richard Peter Martin
Princeton University

Linda K. Martinez
Independent Scholar

Richard E. Matlak
College of the Holy Cross

Anne Laura Mattrella
Southeastern University

Richard A. Mazzara
Oakland University

Laurence W. Mazzeno
Alvernia College

Richard E. Meyer
Western Oregon State College

Julia M. Meyers
Duquesne University

Michael R. Meyers
Pfeiffer University

Vasa D. Mihailovich
University of North Carolina

Edmund Miller
Long Island University

Jane Ann Miller
University of Massachusetts, Dartmouth

Jim Wayne Miller
Western Kentucky University

P. Andrew Miller
Northern Kentucky University

Paula M. Miller
Biola University

Mark Minor
Westmar College

Modrea Mitchell-Reichert
Texas State University-San Marcos

Leslie B. Mittleman
California State University, Long Beach

Thomas Moisan
Saint Louis University

Melissa Molloy
Rhode Island College and University of Rhode Island

Gene M. Moore
Virginia Commonwealth University

Michael D. Moore
Wilfrid Laurier University

Christina J. Moose
Pasadena, California

Ronald Moran
Clemson University

Bernard E. Morris
Modesto, California

Claire Clements Morton
Rock Hill, South Carolina

Gerald W. Morton
Auburn University-Montgomery

Charmaine Allmon Mosby
Western Kentucky University

Carole Moses
Lycoming College

C. L. Mossberg
Lycoming College

Adriano Moz
Spring Hill College

C. Lynn Munro
Belton, Missouri

Donna Munro
Bee & Flower Press

Russell Elliott Murphy
University of Arkansas at Little Rock

Monique Nagem
McNeese State University

Károly Nagy
Middlesex County College

Moses M. Nagy
University of Dallas

Joseph Natoli
Irvine, California

David Nerkle
Washington, D.C.

Caryn E. Neumann
Miami University of Ohio

Evelyn S. Newlyn
*Virginia Polytechnic Institute and
    State University*

Cynthia Nichols
North Dakota State University

Edward A. Nickerson
University of Delaware

Emma Coburn Norris
Troy State University

Leslie Norris
Brigham Young University

Holly L. Norton
University of Northwestern Ohio

Michael Paul Novak
Saint Mary College

Hermine J. van Nuis
*Indiana University-Purdue
    University, Fort Wayne*

George O'Brien
Georgetown University

James O'Brien
University of Wisconsin

Mahmoud Omidsalar
University of California, Los Angeles

Arsenio Orteza
WORLD Magazine

Elizabeth Spalding Otten
Manchester, New Hampshire

Robert M. Otten
Marymount University

Cóilín Owens
George Mason University

Shannon Oxley
University of Leeds

Edward F. Palm
Maryville University of St. Louis

Richard J. Panofsky
Las Vegas, Nevada

Robert J. Paradowski
Rochester Institute of Technology

Makarand Paranjape
Indian Institute of Technology

David J. Parent
Normal, Illinois

Michael P. Parker
United States Naval Academy

Ward Parks
Louisiana State University

Jay Paul
Christopher Newport University

John P. Pauls
Cincinnati, Ohio

La Verne Pauls
Cincinnati, Ohio

David Peck
Laguna Beach, California

Margaret T. Peischl
Virginia Commonwealth University

Charles A. Perrone
University of Florida

Peter Petro
University of British Columbia

Alice Hall Petry
Rhode Island School of Design

Chapel Louise Petty
Stillwater, Oklahoma

Allene Phy-Olsen
Austin Peay State University

Carol Lawson Pippen
Goucher College

Janet Polansky
University of Wisconsin

Susan G. Polansky
Carnegie Mellon University

Francis Poole
University of Delaware

Laurence M. Porter
Michigan State University

Stanley Poss
California State University, Fresno

John Povey
University of California, Los Angeles

Verbie Lovorn Prevost
*University of Tennessee at
    Chattanooga*

Rado Pribic
Lafayette College

Norman Prinsky
Augusta State University

Charles H. Pullen
Queen's University

Thomas Rankin
Concord, California

Honora Rankine-Galloway
University of Southern Denmark

Jed Rasula
University of California, Santa Cruz

John Raymer
Holy Cross College

Ralph Reckley, Sr.
Morgan State University

James Reece
University of Idaho

Rosemary M. Canfield Reisman
Charleston Southern University

Mark Rich
Cashton, Wisconsin

Sylvie L. F. Richards
Northwest Missouri State University

Kelly-Anne Riess
University of Regina

David Rigsbee
Virginia Tech

Helene M. Kastinger Riley
Clemson University

J. Thomas Rimer
University of Pittsburgh

Dorothy Dodge Robbins
Louisiana Tech University

Danny Robinson
Bloomsburg University

Nancy Weigel Rodman
Minneapolis, Minnesota

Richard E. Rogal
Illinois State University

Samuel J. Rogal
Illinois State University

Jill Rollins
Trafalgar School

Carl Rollyson
Baruch College, City University of New York

Joseph Rosenblum
Greensboro, North Carolina

Diane M. Ross
Lake Forest College

Robert L. Ross
University of Texas-Austin

Sven H. Rossel
University of Vienna

Patrizio Rossi
University of California, Santa Barbara

Norman Roth
University of Wisconsin

Victor Anthony Rudowski
Clemson University

Kathy Rugoff
University of North Carolina-Wilmington

Jay Ruud
Northern State University

Gregory M. Sadlek
University of Nebraska-Omaha

Ruth Salvaggio
Virginia Tech

Todd Samuelson
Cushing Memorial Library & Archives

Mark Sanders
College of the Mainland

Stephanie Sandler
Amherst College

Alexa L. Sandmann
University of Toledo

Minas Savvas
San Diego State University

Richard Sax
Lake Erie College

Elizabeth D. Schafer
Loachapoka, Alaska

William J. Scheick
University of Texas at Austin

John F. Schell
University of Arkansas at Little Rock

Paul Schlueter
Easton, Pennsylvania

Richard J. Schneider
Wilson, North Carolina

Beverly Schneller
Millersville University

Joachim Scholz
Washington College

Steven P. Schultz
Loyola University of Chicago

Paul J. Schwartz
Grand Forks, North Dakota

Robert W. Scott
American University

James Scruton
Bethel College

Roy Seeger
University of South Carolina, Aiken

Paul Serralheiro
Dawson College

Roberto Severino
Georgetown University

Emily Carroll Shearer
Middle Tennessee State University

Nancy E. Sherrod
Georgia Southern University

John C. Shields
Illinois State University

Anne Shifrer
Utah State University

Jack Shreve
Allegany Community College

R. Baird Shuman
University of Illinois at Urbana-Champaign

Paul Siegrist
Fort Hays State University

Thomas J. Sienkewicz
Monmouth College

Linda Simon
Atlanta, Georgia

Carl Singleton
Fort Hays State University

William Skaff
Baltimore, Maryland

Katherine Snipes
Eastern Washington University

Jean M. Snook
Memorial University of Newfoundland

Robert Lance Snyder
Georgia Institute of Technology

Janet L. Solberg
Kalamazoo College

Sherry G. Southard
Oklahoma State University

Madison U. Sowell
Brigham Young University

Charlotte Spivack
University of Massachusetts, Amherst

Richard Spuler
Rice University

Vivien Stableford
Reading, United Kingdom

Kenneth A. Stackhouse
Virginia Commonwealth University

Tuula Stark
Hermosa Beach, California

Virginia Starrett
California State University, Fullerton

Christine Steele
Independent Scholar

Karen F. Stein
University of Rhode Island

Shelby Stephenson
Pembroke State University

L. Robert Stevens
North Texas State University

Eve Walsh Stoddard
St. Lawrence University

Stefan Stoenescu
Ithaca, New York

James Stone
Shaker Heights, Ohio

Laura M. Stone
Milwaukee, Wisconsin

Michael L. Storey
Baltimore, Maryland

Gerald H. Strauss
Bloomsburg University

Ann Struthers
Coe College

Ryan D. Stryffeler
Ivy Tech Community College

Christopher J. Stuart
University of Tennessee at Chattanooga

Ernest Suarez
The Catholic University of America

Alan Sullivan
Fargo, North Dakota

James Sullivan
California State University, Los Angeles

Judith K. Taylor
Northern Kentucky University

Betty Taylor-Thompson
Texas Southern University

Christopher J. Thaiss
George Mason University

George Thaniel
University of Toronto

John Thomson
United States Air Force Academy

Jonathan Thorndike
Belmont University

Shelley Thrasher
Lamar State College-Orange

John H. Timmerman
Calvin College

Rogelio A. de la Torre
Indiana University at South Bend

John Clendenin Townsend
Kalamazoo, Michigan

Andy K. Trevathan
University of Arkansas

Janet G. Tucker
University of Arkansas

Thomas A. Van
University of Louisville

Karen Van Dyck
Columbia University

Nance Van Winckel
Lake Forest College

Paul Varner
Oklahoma Christian University

Martha Modena Vertreace-Doody
Kennedy-King College

Albert Wachtel
Pitzer College

Edward E. Waldron
Yankton College

Sue Walker
University of South Alabama

Catharine E. Wall
University of California, Riverside

Lisa M. Wallace
Sheffield, United Kingdom

Gary F. Waller
Wilfrid Laurier University

Marie Michelle Walsh
College of Notre Dame of Maryland

Gordon Walters
DePauw University

John Chapman Ward
Kenyon College

Shawncey Webb
Taylor University

Klaus Weissenberger
Rice University

Twyla R. Wells
Lima, Ohio

Craig Werner
University of Wisconsin

David Allen White
United States Naval Academy

James Whitlark
Texas Tech University

Bruce Wiebe
Lakeville, Minnesota

Barbara Wiedemann
Auburn University at Montgomery

Thomas Willard
University of Arizona

Edwin W. Williams
East Tennessee State University

Patricia A. R. Williams
Amherst College

Tyrone Williams
Xavier University

Judith Barton Williamson
Sauk Valley Community College

Rosemary Winslow
The Catholic University of America

Donald E. Winters, Jr.
Minneapolis Community College

Michael Witkoski
University of South Carolina

Chester L. Wolford
Penn State Erie, The Behrend College

Cynthia Wong
Western Illinois University

Philip Woodard
National University

Eugene P. Wright
North Texas State University

Scott D. Yarbrough
Charleston Southern University

Pauline Yu
University of Minnesota

Gary Zacharias
Palomar College

Gay Pitman Zieger
Santa Fe College

Harry Zohn
Brandeis University

CONTENTS

Publisher's Note v
Contributors vii
Contents xix

RESOURCES
Bibliography 3
Guide to Online Resources 31
Time Line 36
Major Awards 45
Chronological List of Poets 71

INDEXES
Geographical Index of Poets
    and Essays 85
Categorized Index of Poets and Essays 97
Critical Survey of Poetry Series:
    Master List of Contents 133
Subject Index 145

CRITICAL SURVEY OF
Poetry
Fourth Edition

Cumulative Indexes

RESOURCES

BIBLIOGRAPHY

CONTENTS

About This Bibliography 4

General Reference Sources 4
Biographical sources 4
Criticism 4
Poetry dictionaries and
    handbooks 5
Indexes of primary works 5
Poetics, poetic forms,
    and genres 5

English-Language Poetry 6
General reference sources 6
Biographical sources 6
Criticism 6
Dictionaries, histories, and
    handbooks 6
Index of primary works 7
Poetics 7
Postcolonial Anglophone
    poetry 7
Women writers 7
Africa and the Caribbean 7
General 7
Africa 7
Caribbean and West Indian 8
Australia 8
Aboriginal poets 8
Bibliographies 8
Biographical sources 8
Dictionaries, histories, and
    handbooks 8
Women writers 9
Canada 9
Biographical sources 9
Criticism 9
Dictionaries, histories, and
    handbooks 9
Indexes of primary works 10
England 10
Bibliographies 10
Biographical sources 10
Criticism 10
Dictionaries, histories, and
    handbooks 10
History: Old and Middle
    English 11
History: Renaissance
    to 1660 11

History: Restoration (1660)
    through eighteenth
    century 11
History: Nineteenth century 12
History: Twentieth century
    and contemporary 12
Women writers 13
India and South Asia 13
Irish poetry in English 13
Biographical sources 13
Dictionaries, histories, and
    handbooks 13
Women writers 13
New Zealand 13
Scottish poetry in English 14
United States 14
Biographical sources 14
Criticism 14
Dictionaries, histories, and
    handbooks 14
Indexes of primary works 14
History: Colonial to 1800 15
History: Nineteenth century 15
History: Twentieth century
    and contemporary 15
African American:
    Biographical sources 16
African American: Indexes of
    primary works 16
African American: Dictionaries,
    histories, and handbooks 16
African American: Women
    writers 16
Asian American 16
Latino 16
Native American 17
Regional poetry 17
Women writers 17
Welsh poetry in English 17

Foreign-Language Poetry 18
General reference sources 18
Biographical sources 18
Criticism 18
Dictionaries, histories, and
    handbooks 18
Index of primary works 18
Poetics 18
African languages 19
Arabic 19

Caribbean 19
Catalan 19
Celtic languages 19
Irish Gaelic 19
Scottish Gaelic 19
Welsh 19
Chinese 20
Classical Greek and Latin 20
Dutch and Flemish 20
Francophone 21
General 21
Africa and the Caribbean 21
France: Bibliography 21
France: Biographical
    sources 21
France: Criticism 21
France: Dictionaries, histories,
    and handbooks 21
France: Women writers 22
French Canadian 22
German 22
Biographical sources 22
Dictionaries, histories, and
    handbooks 22
Women writers 23
Greek 23
Hebrew and Yiddish 23
Hungarian 24
Indian and South Asian
    languages 24
Italian 24
Biographical sources 24
Dictionaries, histories, and
    handbooks 24
Women writers 24
Japanese 25
Biographical sources 25
Dictionaries, histories, and
    handbooks 25
Korean 25
Persian (Farsi) 25
Scandinavian languages 26
General 26
Danish 26
Icelandic 26
Norwegian 26
Swedish 26
Slavic languages 26
General 26
Albanian 26

Bulgarian 26
Croatian 26
Czech 26
Macedonian 27
Polish 27
Russian 27
Serbian 27

Slovak 27
Slovene 28
Ukrainian 28
Spanish and Portuguese 28
General 28
Africa 28
Caribbean 28

Mexico and Central
America 28
South America 29
Spain and Portugal 29
Tibetan 30
Turkish 30
Vietnamese 30

ABOUT THIS BIBLIOGRAPHY

This bibliography contains three main sections. The first, "General Reference Sources," lists books that treat poetry of all or several languages and countries. The section "English-Language Poetry" includes sources primarily relevant to poetry written in English; it is subdivided into general and country-specific materials, sometimes further grouped by type (biographical, indexes, etc.). The section headed "Foreign-Language Poetry" contains sources primarily relevant to poetry in languages other than English; it is also further subdivided into "General Reference Sources" and then language- or region-specific sources, and again, where appropriate, further subdivided by type of source. Materials that treat bilingual poetry written by U.S. writers are placed in the section on the United States. Sources treating poetry of multilingual geographical areas, such as the Caribbean, Africa, and Latin America, are listed in more than one section, as appropriate. Section headings also indicate, by means of "see also" cross-references, when more than one section is likely to contain relevant sources.

GENERAL REFERENCE SOURCES

BIOGRAPHICAL SOURCES

Colby, Vineta, ed. *World Authors, 1975-1980*. Wilson Authors Series. New York: H. W. Wilson, 1985.

_____. *World Authors, 1980-1985*. Wilson Authors Series. New York: H. W. Wilson, 1991.

_____. *World Authors, 1985-1990*. Wilson Authors Series. New York: H. W. Wilson, 1995.

Cyclopedia of World Authors. 4th rev. ed. 5 vols. Pasadena, Calif.: Salem Press, 2003.

Dictionary of Literary Biography. 254 vols. Detroit: Gale Research, 1978- .

International Who's Who in Poetry and Poets' Encyclopaedia. Cambridge, England: International Biographical Centre, 1993.

Seymour-Smith, Martin, and Andrew C. Kimmens, eds. *World Authors, 1900-1950*. Wilson Authors Series. 4 vols. New York: H. W. Wilson, 1996.

Thompson, Clifford, ed. *World Authors, 1990-1995*. Wilson Authors Series. New York: H. W. Wilson, 1999.

Wakeman, John, ed. *World Authors, 1950-1970*. New York: H. W. Wilson, 1975.

_____. *World Authors, 1970-1975*. Wilson Authors Series. New York: H. W. Wilson, 1991.

Willhardt, Mark, and Alan Michael Parker, eds. *Who's Who in Twentieth Century World Poetry*. New York: Routledge, 2000.

CRITICISM

Brooks, Cleanth, and Robert Penn Warren. *Understanding Poetry*. 4th ed. Reprint. Fort Worth, Tex.: Heinle & Heinle, 2003.

Classical and Medieval Literature Criticism. Detroit: Gale Research, 1988- .

Contemporary Literary Criticism. Detroit: Gale Research, 1973- .

Day, Gary. *Literary Criticism: A New History*. Edinburgh, Scotland: Edinburgh University Press, 2008.

Draper, James P., ed. *World Literature Criticism 1500 to the Present: A Selection of Major Authors from Gale's Literary Criticism Series*. 6 vols. Detroit: Gale Research, 1992.

Habib, M. A. R. *A History of Literary Criticism: From*

Plato to the Present. Malden, Mass.: Wiley-Blackwell, 2005.

Jason, Philip K., ed. *Masterplots II: Poetry Series, Revised Edition*. 8 vols. Pasadena, Calif.: Salem Press, 2002.

Literature Criticism from 1400 to 1800. Detroit: Gale Research, 1984-   .

Lodge, David, and Nigel Wood. *Modern Criticism and Theory*. 3d ed. New York: Longman, 2008.

Magill, Frank N., ed. *Magill's Bibliography of Literary Criticism*. 4 vols. Englewood Cliffs, N.J.: Salem Press, 1979.

MLA International Bibliography. New York: Modern Language Association of America, 1922-   .

Nineteenth-Century Literature Criticism. Detroit: Gale Research, 1981-   .

Twentieth-Century Literary Criticism. Detroit: Gale Research, 1978-   .

Vedder, Polly, ed. *World Literature Criticism Supplement: A Selection of Major Authors from Gale's Literary Criticism Series*. 2 vols. Detroit: Gale Research, 1997.

Young, Robyn V., ed. *Poetry Criticism: Excerpts from Criticism of the Works of the Most Significant and Widely Studied Poets of World Literature*. 29 vols. Detroit: Gale Research, 1991.

POETRY DICTIONARIES AND HANDBOOKS

Carey, Gary, and Mary Ellen Snodgrass. *A Multicultural Dictionary of Literary Terms*. Jefferson, N.C.: McFarland, 1999.

Deutsch, Babette. *Poetry Handbook: A Dictionary of Terms*. 4th ed. New York: Funk & Wagnalls, 1974.

Drury, John. *The Poetry Dictionary*. Cincinnati, Ohio: Story Press, 1995.

Kinzie, Mary. *A Poet's Guide to Poetry*. Chicago: University of Chicago Press, 1999.

Lennard, John. *The Poetry Handbook: A Guide to Reading Poetry for Pleasure and Practical Criticism*. New York: Oxford University Press, 1996.

Matterson, Stephen, and Darryl Jones. *Studying Poetry*. New York: Oxford University Press, 2000.

Packard, William. *The Poet's Dictionary: A Handbook of Prosody and Poetic Devices*. New York: Harper & Row, 1989.

Preminger, Alex, et al., eds. *The New Princeton Encyclopedia of Poetry and Poetics*. 3d rev. ed. Princeton, N.J.: Princeton University Press, 1993.

Shipley, Joseph Twadell, ed. *Dictionary of World Literary Terms, Forms, Technique, Criticism*. Rev. ed. Boston: George Allen and Unwin, 1979.

INDEXES OF PRIMARY WORKS

Frankovich, Nicholas, ed. *The Columbia Granger's Index to Poetry in Anthologies*. 11th ed. New York: Columbia University Press, 1997.

_____. *The Columbia Granger's Index to Poetry in Collected and Selected Works*. New York: Columbia University Press, 1997.

Guy, Patricia. *A Women's Poetry Index*. Phoenix, Ariz.: Oryx Press, 1985.

Hazen, Edith P., ed. *Columbia Granger's Index to Poetry*. 10th ed. New York: Columbia University Press, 1994.

Hoffman, Herbert H., and Rita Ludwig Hoffman, comps. *International Index to Recorded Poetry*. New York: H. W. Wilson, 1983.

Kline, Victoria. *Last Lines: An Index to the Last Lines of Poetry*. 2 vols. Vol. 1, *Last Line Index, Title Index*; Vol. 2, *Author Index, Keyword Index*. New York: Facts On File, 1991.

Marcan, Peter. *Poetry Themes: A Bibliographical Index to Subject Anthologies and Related Criticisms in the English Language, 1875-1975*. Hamden, Conn.: Linnet Books, 1977.

Poem Finder. Great Neck, N.Y.: Roth, 2000.

POETICS, POETIC FORMS, AND GENRES

Attridge, Derek. *Poetic Rhythm: An Introduction*. New York: Cambridge University Press, 1995.

Brogan, T. V. F. *Verseform: A Comparative Bibliography*. Baltimore: Johns Hopkins University Press, 1989.

Fussell, Paul. *Poetic Meter and Poetic Form*. Rev. ed. New York: McGraw-Hill, 1979.

Hollander, John. *Rhyme's Reason*. 3d ed. New Haven, Conn.: Yale University Press, 2001.

Jackson, Guida M. *Traditional Epics: A Literary Companion*. New York: Oxford University Press, 1995.

Padgett, Ron, ed. *The Teachers and Writers Handbook*

of Poetic Forms. 2d ed. New York: Teachers & Writers Collaborative, 2000.

Pinsky, Robert. *The Sounds of Poetry: A Brief Guide.* New York: Farrar, Straus and Giroux, 1998.

Preminger, Alex, and T. V. F. Brogan, eds. *New Princeton Encyclopedia of Poetry and Poetics.* 3d ed. Princeton, N.J.: Princeton University Press, 1993.

Spiller, Michael R. G. *The Sonnet Sequence: A Study of*

Its Strategies. Studies in Literary Themes and Genres 13. New York: Twayne, 1997.

Turco, Lewis. *The New Book of Forms: A Handbook of Poetics.* Hanover, N.H.: University Press of New England, 1986.

Williams, Miller. *Patterns of Poetry: An Encyclopedia of Forms.* Baton Rouge: Louisiana State University Press, 1986.

ENGLISH-LANGUAGE POETRY

GENERAL REFERENCE SOURCES

Biographical sources

Bold, Alan. *Longman Dictionary of Poets: The Lives and Works of 1001 Poets in the English Language.* Harlow, Essex: Longman, 1985.

Riggs, Thomas, ed. *Contemporary Poets.* Contemporary Writers Series. 7th ed. Detroit: St. James Press, 2001.

Criticism

Alexander, Harriet Semmes, comp. *American and British Poetry: A Guide to the Criticism, 1925-1978.* Manchester, England: Manchester University Press, 1984.

_____. *American and British Poetry: A Guide to the Criticism, 1979-1990.* 2 vols. Athens, Ohio: Swallow Press, 1995.

Annual Bibliography of English Language and Literature. Cambridge, England: Modern Humanities Research Association, 1920-   .

Childs, Peter. *The Twentieth Century in Poetry: A Critical Survey.* New York: Routledge, 1999.

Cline, Gloria Stark, and Jeffrey A. Baker. *An Index to Criticism of British and American Poetry.* Metuchen, N.J.: Scarecrow Press, 1973.

Coleman, Arthur. *Epic and Romance Criticism: A Checklist of Interpretations, 1940-1972.* New York: Watermill Publishers, 1973.

Donow, Herbert S., comp. *The Sonnet in England and America: A Bibliography of Criticism.* Westport, Conn.: Greenwood Press, 1982.

Jason, Philip K., ed. *Masterplots II: Poetry Series, Revised Edition.* 8 vols. Pasadena, Calif.: Salem Press, 2002.

Kuntz, Joseph M., and Nancy C. Martinez. *Poetry Explication: A Checklist of Interpretation Since 1925 of British and American Poems Past and Present.* 3d ed. Boston: Hall, 1980.

Roberts, Neil, ed. *A Companion to Twentieth-Century Poetry.* Malden, Mass.: Blackwell Publishers, 2001.

Walcutt, Charles Child, and J. Edwin Whitesell, eds. *Modern Poetry.* Vol. 1 in *The Explicator Cyclopedia.* Chicago: Quadrangle Books, 1968.

_____. *Traditional Poetry: Medieval to Late Victorian.* Vol. 2 in *The Explicator Cyclopedia.* Chicago: Quadrangle Books, 1968.

The Year's Work in English Studies. London: Blackwell, 1921-   .

Dictionaries, histories, and handbooks

Draper, Ronald P. *An Introduction to Twentieth-Century Poetry in English.* New York: St. Martin's Press, 1999.

Gingerich, Martin E. *Contemporary Poetry in America and England, 1950-1975: A Guide to Information Sources.* American Literature, English Literature, and World Literatures in English: An Information Guide Series 41. Detroit: Gale Research, 1983.

Hamilton, Ian, ed. *The Oxford Companion to Twentieth-Century Poetry in English.* New York: Oxford University Press, 1994.

Perkins, David. *From the 1890's to the High Modernist Mode.* Vol. 1 in *A History of Modern Poetry.* Cambridge, Mass.: Belknap-Harvard University Press, 1976.

_____. *Modernism and After*. Vol. 2 in *A History of Modern Poetry*. 2 vols. Cambridge, Mass.: Belknap-Harvard University Press, 1987.

Index of primary works

Poetry Index Annual: A Title, Author, First Line, Keyword, and Subject Index to Poetry in Anthologies. Great Neck, N.Y.: Poetry Index, 1982-   .

Poetics

Brogan, T. V. F. *English Versification, 1570-1980: A Reference Guide with a Global Appendix*. Baltimore: Johns Hopkins University Press, 1981.

Malof, Joseph. *A Manual of English Meters*. Bloomington: Indiana University Press, 1970.

Shapiro, Karl, and Robert Beum. *A Prosody Handbook*. New York: Harper, 1965.

Postcolonial Anglophone poetry (see also Australia; Irish poetry in English; Scottish poetry in English; Welsh poetry in English)

Benson, Eugene, and L. W. Connolly. *Encyclopedia of Post-Colonial Literatures in English*. 2 vols. London: Routledge, 1994.

Bery, Ashok. *Cultural Translation and Postcolonial Poetry*. New York: Palgrave Macmillan, 2007.

Keown, Michelle. *Pacific Islands Writing: The Postcolonial Literatures of Aotearoa/New Zealand and Oceania*. New York: Oxford University Press, 2007.

Lawson, Alan, et al. *Post-Colonial Literatures in English: General, Theoretical, and Comparative, 1970-1993*. A Reference Publication in Literature. New York: G. K. Hall, 1997.

Mohanram, Radhika, and Gita Rajan, eds. *English Postcoloniality: Literatures from Around the World*. Contributions to the Study of World Literature 66. Westport, Conn.: Greenwood Press, 1996.

Patke, Rajeev S. *Postcolonial Poetry in English*. New York: Oxford University Press, 2006.

Ramazani, Jahan. *The Hybrid Muse: Postcolonial Poetry in English*. Chicago: University of Chicago Press, 2001.

Williams, Mark. *Post-Colonial Literatures in English: Southeast Asia, New Zealand, and the Pacific, 1970-1992*. Reference Publications in Literature. New York: G. K. Hall, 1996.

Women writers

Davis, Gwenn, and Beverly A. Joyce, comps. *Poetry by Women to 1900: A Bibliography of American and British Writers*. Toronto: University of Toronto Press, 1991.

Mark, Alison, and Deryn Rees-Jones. *Contemporary Women's Poetry: Reading, Writing, Practice*. New York: St. Martin's Press, 2000.

AFRICA AND THE CARIBBEAN (*see also in the foreign-language section:* AFRICAN LANGUAGES; CARIBBEAN; FRANCOPHONE; SPANISH AND PORTUGUESE)

General

Lindfors, Bernth, and Reinhard Sander, eds. *Twentieth-Century Caribbean and Black African Writers: First Series*. Dictionary of Literary Biography 117. Detroit: Gale Research, 1992.

_____. *Twentieth-Century Caribbean and Black African Writers: Second Series*. Dictionary of Literary Biography 125. Detroit: Gale Research, 1993.

_____. *Twentieth-Century Caribbean and Black African Writers: Third Series*. Dictionary of Literary Biography 157. Detroit: Gale Research, 1996.

Africa

Fraser, Robert. *West African Poetry: A Critical History*. Cambridge, England: Cambridge University Press, 1986.

Killam, Douglas, and Ruth Rowe, eds. *The Companion to African Literatures*. Bloomington: Indiana University Press, 2000.

Lindfors, Bernth. *Black African Literature in English: A Guide to Information Sources*. American Literature, English Literature, and World Literatures in English: An Information Guide Series 23. Detroit: Gale Research, 1979.

_____. *Black African Literature in English, 1977-1981 Supplement*. New York: Africana, 1986.

_____. *Black African Literature in English, 1982-1986*. New York: Zell, 1989.

_____. *Black African Literature in English, 1987-1991*. Bibliographical Research in African Literature 3. London: Zell, 1995.

Ojaide, Tanure. *Poetic Imagination in Black Africa:*

Essays on African Poetry. Durham, N.C.: Carolina Academic Press, 1996.

Ojaide, Tanure, and Tijan M. Sallah, eds. *The New African Poetry: An Anthology*. Boulder, Colo.: Lynne Rienner, 1999.

Parekh, Pushpa Naidu, and Siga Fatima Jagne. *Postcolonial African Writers: A Bio-Bibliographical Critical Sourcebook*. Westport, Conn.: Greenwood Press, 1998.

Scanlon, Paul A., ed. *South African Writers*. Dictionary of Literary Biography 225. Detroit: Gale Group, 2000.

Caribbean and West Indian

Allis, Jeannette B. *West Indian Literature: An Index to Criticism, 1930-1975*. Reference Publication in Latin American Studies. Boston: Hall, 1981.

Arnold, A. James, ed. *A History of Literature in the Caribbean*. 3 vols. Philadelphia: J. Benjamins, 1994.

Bloom, Harold, ed. *Caribbean Women Writers*. Women Writers of English and Their Work. Philadelphia: Chelsea House, 1997.

Breiner, Laurence A. *An Introduction to West Indian Poetry*. Cambridge, England: Cambridge University Press, 1998.

Brown, Stewart, and Mark McWatt, eds. *The Oxford Book of Caribbean Verse*. New York: Oxford University Press, 2005.

Burnett, Paula, ed. *The Penguin Book of Caribbean Verse in English*. London: Penguin Global, 2006.

Dance, Daryl Cumber, ed. *Fifty Caribbean Writers: A Bio-Bibliographical Critical Sourcebook*. New York: Greenwood Press, 1986.

Dawes, Kwame, ed. *Talk Yuh Talk: Interviews with Anglophone Caribbean Poets*. Charlottesville: University Press of Virginia, 2001.

Fenwick, M. J. *Writers of the Caribbean and Central America: A Bibliography*. Garland Reference Library of the Humanities 1244. New York: Garland, 1992.

Herdeck, Donald E., ed. *Caribbean Writers: A Bio-Bibliographical-Critical Encyclopedia*. Washington, D.C.: Three Continents Press, 1979.

Hughes, Roger, comp. *Caribbean Writing: A Checklist*. London: Commonwealth Institute Library Services, 1986.

Jenkins, Lee M. *The Language of Caribbean Poetry: Boundaries of Expression*. Gainesville: University Press of Florida, 2004.

Jordan, Alma, and Barbara Comissiong. *The English-Speaking Caribbean: A Bibliography of Bibliographies*. Reference Publication in Latin American Studies. Boston: Hall, 1984.

Miller, Kei, ed. *New Caribbean Poetry: An Anthology*. Manchester, England: Carcanet, 2007.

Narain, Denise DeCaires. *Contemporary Caribbean Women's Poetry: Making Style*. New York: Routledge, 2002.

AUSTRALIA

Aboriginal poets

Healy, John Joseph. *Literature and the Aborigine in Australia, 1770-1975*. New York: St. Martin's Press, 1978.

Schurmann-Zeggel, Heinz. *Black Australian Literature: A Bibliography of Fiction, Poetry, Drama, Oral Traditions and Non-Fiction, Including Critical Commentary, 1900-1991*. New York: Peter Lang, 1997.

Shoemaker, Adam. *Black Words, White Page*. UQP Studies in Australian Literature. St. Lucia: University of Queensland Press, 1989.

Bibliographies

Hergenhan, Laurie, and Martin Duwell, eds. *The ALS Guide to Australian Writers: A Bibliography*. UQP Studies in Australian Literature. Queensland: University of Queensland Press, 1992.

Webby, Elizabeth. *Early Australian Poetry: An Annotated Bibliography of Original Poems Published in Australian Newspapers, Magazines, and Almanacks Before 1850*. Sydney: Hale, 1982.

Biographical sources

Samuels, Selina, ed. *Australian Literature, 1788-1914*. Dictionary of Literary Biography 230. Detroit: Gale Group, 2001.

Who's Who of Australian Writers. 2d ed. Clayton: National Centre for Australian Studies, 1995.

Dictionaries, histories, and handbooks

Andrews, B. G., and William H. Wilde. *Australian Literature to 1900: A Guide to Information Sources*. American Literature, English Literature, and World Literatures in English: An Information Guide Series 22. Detroit: Gale Research, 1980.

Brins, Nicholas, and Rebecca McNeer, eds. *A Companion to Australian Literature Since 1900*. Rochester, N.Y.: Camden House, 2007.

Elliott, Brian Robinson. *The Landscape of Australian Poetry*. Melbourne: Cheshire, 1967.

Gray, Robert, and Geoffrey Lehmann, eds. *Australian Poetry in the Twentieth Century*. Port Melbourne: William Heinemann Australia, 1991.

Green, H. M. *A History of Australian Literature: Pure and Applied—A Critical Review of All Forms of Literature Produced in Australia from the First Books Published After the Arrival of the First Fleet Until 1950*. Revised by Dorothy Green. 2 vols. London: Angus & Robertson, 1984.

Hergenhan, Laurie. *The Penguin New Literary History of Australia*. New York: Penguin, 1988.

Hooton, Joy, and Harry Heseltine. *Annals of Australian Literature*. 2d ed. Melbourne: Oxford University Press, 1992.

Jaffa, Herbert C. *Modern Australian Poetry, 1920-1970: A Guide to Information Sources*. American Literature, English Literature, and World Literatures in English: An Information Guide Series 24. Detroit: Gale Research, 1979.

Lever, Richard, James Wieland, and Scott Findlay. *Post-colonial Literatures in English: Australia, 1970-1992*. A Reference Publication in Literature. New York: G. K. Hall, 1996.

Lock, Fred, and Alan Lawson. *Australian Literature: A Reference Guide*. 2d ed. Australian Bibliographies. New York: Oxford University Press, 1980.

Pierce, Peter, ed. *The Cambridge History of Australian Literature*. New York: Cambridge University Press, 2009.

Wilde, W. H., Joy Hooton, and Barry Andrews. *The Oxford Companion to Australian Literature*. 2d ed. New York: Oxford University Press, 1994.

Women writers

Adelaide, Debra. *Bibliography of Australian Women's Literature, 1795-1990: A Listing of Fiction, Poetry, Drama, and Non-fiction Published in Monograph Form Arranged Alphabetically by Author*. Port Melbourne: Thorpe with National Centre for Australian Studies, 1991.

Hampton, Susan, and Kate Llewellyn, eds. *The Penguin Book of Australian Women Poets*. New York: Penguin Ringwood, 1986.

CANADA (*see also in the foreign-language section:* FRANCOPHONE)

Biographical sources

Lecker, Robert, Jack David, and Ellen Quigley, eds. *Canadian Writers and Their Works: Poetry Series*. Downsview, Ont.: ECW Press, 1983.

McLeod, Donald, ed. *Canadian Writers and Their Works Cumulated Index Volume: Poetry Series*. Toronto, Ont.: ECW Press, 1993.

New, W. H., ed. *Canadian Writers Before 1890*. Dictionary of Literary Biography 99. Detroit: Gale Research, 1990.

_____. *Canadian Writers, 1890-1920*. Dictionary of Literary Biography 92. Detroit: Gale Research, 1990.

_____. *Canadian Writers, 1920-1959: First Series*. Dictionary of Literary Biography 68. Detroit: Gale Research, 1988.

_____. *Canadian Writers, 1920-1959: Second Series*. Dictionary of Literary Biography 88. Detroit: Gale Research, 1989.

_____. *Canadian Writers Since 1960: First Series*. Dictionary of Literary Biography 53. Detroit: Gale Research, 1986.

_____. *Canadian Writers Since 1960: Second Series*. Dictionary of Literary Biography 60. Detroit: Gale Research, 1987.

Criticism

Platnick, Phyllis. *Canadian Poetry: Index to Criticisms, 1970-1979*. Ontario: Canadian Library Association, 1985.

Dictionaries, histories, and handbooks

Brandt, Di, and Barbara Godard, eds. *Wider Boundaries of Daring: The Modernist Impulse in Canadian Women's Poetry*. Waterloo, Ont.: Wilfrid Laurier University Press, 2009.

Marshall, Tom. *Harsh and Lovely Land: The Major Canadian Poets and the Making of a Canadian Tradition*. Vancouver: University of British Columbia Press, 1979.

Starnino, Carmine, ed. *The New Canon: An Anthology of Canadian Poetry*. Montreal: Véhicule Press, 2006.

Stevens, Peter. *Modern English-Canadian Poetry: A Guide to Information Sources*. American Literature, English Literature, and World Literatures in English: An Information Guide Series 15. Detroit: Gale Research, 1978.

Indexes of primary works

Fee, Margery, ed. *Canadian Poetry in Selected English-Language Anthologies: An Index and Guide*. Halifax, N.S.: Dalhousie University, University Libraries, School of Library Service, 1985.

McQuarrie, Jane, Anne Mercer, and Gordon Ripley, eds. *Index to Canadian Poetry in English*. Toronto: Reference Press, 1984.

ENGLAND (*see also* IRISH POETRY IN ENGLISH; SCOTTISH POETRY IN ENGLISH; WELSH POETRY IN ENGLISH)

Bibliographies

Case, Arthur E. *A Bibliography of English Poetical Miscellanies, 1521-1750*. London: Oxford University Press for the Bibliographical Society, 1935.

Dyson, A. E., ed. *English Poetry: Select Bibliographical Guides*. London: Oxford University Press, 1971.

Biographical sources

Fredeman, William E., and Ira B. Nadel, eds. *Victorian Poets Before 1850*. Dictionary of Literary Biography 32. Detroit: Gale Research, 1984.

_____. *Victorian Poets After 1850*. Dictionary of Literary Biography 35. Detroit: Gale Research, 1985.

Greenfield, John R., ed. *British Romantic Poets, 1789-1832: First Series*. Dictionary of Literary Biography 93. Detroit: Gale Research, 1990.

_____, ed. *British Romantic Poets, 1789-1832: Second Series*. Dictionary of Literary Biography 96. Detroit: Gale Research, 1990.

Hester, M. Thomas, ed. *Seventeenth-Century British Nondramatic Poets: First Series*. Dictionary of Literary Biography 121. Detroit: Gale Research, 1992.

Quinn, Patrick, ed. *British Poets of the Great War: Brooke, Rosenberg, Thomas: A Documentary Volume*. Dictionary of Literary Biography 216. Detroit: Gale Group, 2000.

Sherry, Vincent B., Jr., ed. *Poets of Great Britain and Ireland, 1945-1960*. Dictionary of Literary Biography 27. Detroit: Gale Research, 1984.

_____. *Poets of Great Britain and Ireland, Since 1960*. Dictionary of Literary Biography 40. Detroit: Gale Research, 1985.

Sitter, John, ed. *Seventeenth-Century British Nondramatic Poets: Second Series*. Dictionary of Literary Biography 126. Detroit: Gale Research, 1993.

_____. *Seventeenth-Century British Nondramatic Poets: Third Series*. Dictionary of Literary Biography 131. Detroit: Gale Research, 1993.

_____. *Eighteenth-Century British Poets: First Series*. Dictionary of Literary Biography 95. Detroit: Gale Research, 1990.

_____. *Eighteenth-Century British Poets: Second Series*. Dictionary of Literary Biography 109. Detroit: Gale Research, 1991.

Stanford, Donald E., ed. *British Poets, 1880-1914*. Dictionary of Literary Biography 19. Detroit: Gale Research, 1983.

_____. *British Poets, 1914-1945*. Dictionary of Literary Biography 20. Detroit: Gale Research, 1983.

Thesing, William B., ed. *Late Nineteenth- and Early Twentieth-Century British Women Poets*. Dictionary of Literary Biography 240. Detroit: Gale Group, 2001.

_____. *Victorian Women Poets*. Dictionary of Literary Biography 199. Detroit: Gale Research, 1999.

Criticism

Guide to British Poetry Explication. 4 vols. Boston: G. K. Hall, 1991.

Dictionaries, histories, and handbooks

Courthope, W. J. *A History of English Poetry*. New York: Macmillan, 1895-1910.

Garrett, John. *British Poetry Since the Sixteenth Century: A Student's Guide*. Totowa, N.J.: Barnes & Noble Books, 1987.

Mell, Donald Charles, Jr. *English Poetry, 1660-1800: A Guide to Information Sources*. American Literature, English Literature, and World Literatures in English: An Information Guide Series 40. Detroit: Gale Research, 1982.

Smith, Eric. *A Dictionary of Classical Reference in English Poetry*. Totowa, N.J.: Barnes & Noble, 1984.

Woodring, Carl, and James Shapiro, eds. *The Colum-*

bia History of British Poetry. New York: Columbia University Press, 1993.

History: Old and Middle English

Aertsen, Hank, and Rolf H. Bremmer, eds. *Companion to Old English Poetry*. Amsterdam: VU University Press, 1994.

Beale, Walter H. *Old and Middle English Poetry to 1500: A Guide to Information Sources*. American Literature, English Literature, and World Literatures in English: An Information Guide Series 7. Detroit: Gale Research, 1976.

Brown, Carleton, and Rossell Hope Robbins. *The Index of Middle English Verse*. New York: Columbia University Press for the Index Society, 1943.

Cooney, Helen, ed. *Nation, Court, and Culture: New Essays on Fifteenth Century Poetry*. Dublin: Four Courts Press, 2001.

Hirsh, John C., ed. *Medieval Lyric: Middle English Lyrics, Ballads, and Carols*. Annotated ed. Malden, Mass.: Blackwell, 2005.

Jost, Jean E. *Ten Middle English Arthurian Romances: A Reference Guide*. Boston: G. K. Hall, 1986.

Martinez, Nancy C., and Joseph G. R. Martinez. *Old English-Medieval*. Vol. 1 in *Guide to British Poetry Explication*. Boston: G. K. Hall, 1991.

O'Keeffe, Katherine O'Brien, ed. *Old English Shorter Poems: Basic Readings*. Garland Reference Library of the Humanities 1432. New York: Garland, 1994.

Palmer, R. Barton, ed. and trans. *Medieval Epic and Romance: An Anthology of English and French Narrative*. Glen Allen, Va.: College Publishing, 2007.

Pearsall, Derek. *Old English and Middle English Poetry*. Vol. 1 in *The Routledge History of English Poetry*. London: Routledge, 1977.

Scanlon, Larry, ed. *The Cambridge Companion to Medieval Literature, 1100-1500*. New York: Cambridge University Press, 2009.

History: Renaissance to 1660

Cheney, Patrick, Andrew Hadfield, and Garrett A. Sullivan, Jr., eds. *Early Modern English Poetry: A Critical Companion*. New York: Oxford University Press, 2006.

Frank, Joseph. *Hobbled Pegasus: A Descriptive Bibliography of Minor English Poetry, 1641-1660*.

Albuquerque: University of New Mexico Press, 1968.

Gutierrez, Nancy A. *English Historical Poetry, 1476-1603: A Bibliography*. Garland Reference Library of the Humanities 410. New York: Garland, 1983.

Martinez, Nancy C., and Joseph G. R. Martinez. *Renaissance*. Vol. 2 in *Guide to British Poetry Explication*. Boston: G. K. Hall, 1991.

Post, Jonathan F. S., ed. *Green Thoughts, Green Shades: Essays by Contemporary Poets on the Early Modern Lyric*. Berkeley: University of California Press, 2002.

Ringler, William A., Jr. *Bibliography and Index of English Verse Printed 1476-1558*. New York: Mansell, 1988.

Ringler, William A., Michael Rudick, and Susan J. Ringler. *Bibliography and Index of English Verse in Manuscript, 1501-1558*. New York: Mansell, 1992.

Rivers, Isabel. *Classical and Christian Ideas in English Renaissance Poetry: A Student's Guide*. 2d ed. New York: Routledge, 1994.

History: Restoration (1660) through eighteenth century

Fairer, David. *English Poetry of the Eighteenth Century, 1700-1789*. Annotated ed. Harlow, Essex, England: Longman, 2003.

Foxon, D. F. *English Verse 1701-1750: A Catalogue of Separately Printed Poems with Notes on Contemporary Collected Editions*. 2 vols. Cambridge, England: Cambridge University Press, 1975.

Jackson, J. R. de J. *Annals of English Verse, 1770-1835: A Preliminary Survey of the Volumes Published*. Garland Reference Library of the Humanities 535. New York: Garland, 1985.

Martinez, Nancy C., Joseph G. R. Martinez, and Erland Anderson. *Restoration-Romantic*. Vol. 3 in *Guide to British Poetry Explication*. Boston: G. K. Hall, 1991.

Nokes, David, and Janet Barron. *An Annotated Critical Bibliography of Augustan Poetry*. Annotated Critical Bibliographies. New York: St. Martin's Press, 1989.

Rothstein, Eric. *Restoration and Eighteenth-Century Poetry, 1660-1780*. Vol. 3 in *The Routledge History of English Poetry*. Boston: Routledge & Kegan Paul, 1981.

Sitter, John, ed. *The Cambridge Companion to Eighteenth-Century Poetry*. New York: Cambridge University Press, 2001.

Starr, G. Gabrielle. *Lyric Generations: Poetry and the Novel in the Long Eighteenth Century*. Baltimore: Johns Hopkins University Press, 2004.

History: Nineteenth century

Blyth, Caroline, ed. *Decadent Verse: An Anthology of Late-Victorian Poetry, 1872-1900*. London: Anthem Press, 2009.

Bristow, Joseph, ed. *The Cambridge Companion to Victorian Poetry*. New York: Cambridge University Press, 2000.

Chapman, Alison, ed. *Victorian Women Poets*. Cambridge, England: D. S. Brewer, 2003.

Faverty, Frederic E., ed. *The Victorian Poets: A Guide to Research*. 2d ed. Cambridge, Mass.: Harvard University Press, 1968.

Jackson, J. R. de J. *Poetry of the Romantic Period*. Vol. 4 in *The Routledge History of English Poetry*. Boston: Routledge & Kegan Paul, 1980.

Jordan, Frank, ed. *The English Romantic Poets: A Review of Research and Criticism*. 4th ed. New York: MLA, 1985.

McLane, Maureen N., and James Chandler, eds. *The Cambridge Companion to British Romantic Poetry*. New York: Cambridge University Press, 2008.

Martinez, Nancy C., Joseph G. R. Martinez, and Erland Anderson. *Victorian-Contemporary*. Vol. 4 in *Guide to British Poetry Explication*. Boston: G. K. Hall, 1991.

O'Gorman, Francis, ed. *Victorian Poetry: An Annotated Anthology*. Malden, Mass.: Wiley-Blackwell, 2004.

O'Neill, Michael, and Charles Mahoney, eds. *Romantic Poetry: An Annotated Anthology*. Malden, Mass.: Wiley-Blackwell, 2008.

Reilly, Catherine W. *Late Victorian Poetry, 1880-1899: An Annotated Biobibliography*. New York: Mansell, 1994.

_____. *Mid-Victorian Poetry, 1860-1879: An Annotated Biobibliography*. New York: Mansell, 2000.

Reiman, Donald H. *English Romantic Poetry, 1800-1835: A Guide to Information Sources*. American Literature, English Literature, and World Literature in English: An Information Guide Series 27. Detroit: Gale Research, 1979.

Richards, Bernard Arthur. *English Poetry of the Victorian Period, 1830-1890*. 2d ed. New York: Longman, 2001.

Roberts, Adam. *Romantic and Victorian Long Poems: A Guide*. Brookfield, Vt.: Ashgate, 1999.

History: Twentieth century and contemporary

Anderson, Emily Ann. *English Poetry, 1900-1950: A Guide to Information Sources*. American Literature, English Literature, and World Literatures in English: An Information Guide Series 33. Detroit: Gale Research, 1982.

Bradley, Jerry. *The Movement: British Poets of the 1950's*. New York: Twayne, 1993.

Broom, Sarah. *Contemporary British and Irish Poetry: An Introduction*. Illustrated ed. New York: Palgrave Macmillan, 2006.

Corcoran, Neil, ed. *The Cambridge Companion to Twentieth-Century English Poetry*. New York: Cambridge University Press, 2007.

Davie, Donald. *Under Briggflatts: A History of Poetry in Great Britain, 1960-1988*. Chicago: University of Chicago Press, 1989.

Dowson, Jane, and Alice Entwistle. *A History of Twentieth-Century British Women's Poetry*. New York: Cambridge University Press, 2005.

Lehmann, John. *The English Poets of the First World War*. New York: Thames and Hudson, 1982.

Martinez, Nancy C., Joseph G. R. Martinez, and Erland Anderson. *Victorian-Contemporary*. Vol. 4 in *Guide to British Poetry Explication*. Boston: G. K. Hall, 1991.

Persoon, James. *Modern British Poetry, 1900-1939*. Twayne's Critical History of Poetry Studies. New York: Twayne, 1999.

Reilly, Catherine W. *English Poetry of the Second World War: A Biobibliography*. Boston: G. K. Hall, 1986.

Schmidt, Michael. *A Reader's Guide to Fifty Modern British Poets*. New York: Barnes & Noble, 1979.

Shields, Ellen F. *Contemporary English Poetry: An Annotated Bibliography of Criticism to 1980*. Garland Reference Library of the Humanities 460. New York: Garland, 1984.

Thwaite, Anthony. *Poetry Today: A Critical Guide to British Poetry, 1960-1992*. New York: Longman with the British Council, 1996.

Tuma, Keith, ed. *Anthology of Twentieth-Century British and Irish Poetry*. Annotated ed. New York: Oxford University Press, 2001.

Women writers

Chapman, Alison, ed. *Victorian Women Poets*. Cambridge, England: D. S. Brewer, 2003.

Dowson, Jane, and Alice Entwistle. *A History of Twentieth-Century British Women's Poetry*. New York: Cambridge University Press, 2005.

Gray, F. Elizabeth. *Christian and Lyric Tradition in Victorian Women's Poetry*. New York: Routledge, 2009.

Jackson, J. R. de J. *Romantic Poetry by Women: A Bibliography, 1770-1835*. Oxford: Clarendon-Oxford University Press, 1993.

INDIA AND SOUTH ASIA

Agrawal, K. A. *Toru Dutt: The Pioneer Spirit of Indian English Poetry—A Critical Study*. New Delhi: Atlantic, 2009.

De Souza, Eunice, ed. *Early Indian Poetry in English: An Anthology, 1829-1947*. New Delhi: Oxford University Press, 2005.

King, Bruce. *Modern Indian Poetry in English*. Rev. ed. New Delhi: Oxford University Press, 2001.

Naik, M. K. *A History of Indian English Literature*. New Delhi: Sahitya Akademi, 1989.

Rama, Atma. *Indian Poetry and Fiction in English*. New Delhi: Bahri Publications, 1991.

Singh, Amritjit, Rajiav Verma, and Irene M. Johsi. *Indian Literature in English, 1827-1979: A Guide to Information Sources*. American Literature, English Literature, and World Literatures in English: An Information Guide Series 36. Detroit: Gale Research, 1981.

Singh, Kanwar Dinesh. *Contemporary Indian English Poetry: Comparing Male and Female Voices*. New Delhi: Atlantic, 2008.

Sinha, R. P. N. *Indo-Anglican Poetry: Its Birth and Growth*. New Delhi: Reliance Publishing House, 1987.

Thayil, Jeet, ed. *The Bloodaxe Book of Contemporary Indian Poets*. Cambridge, Mass.: Bloodaxe, 2008.

IRISH POETRY IN ENGLISH (*see also in the foreign-language section:* CELTIC LANGUAGES)

Biographical sources

Sherry, Vincent B., Jr., ed. *Poets of Great Britain and Ireland, 1945-1960*. Dictionary of Literary Biography 27. Detroit: Gale Research, 1984.

_____. *Poets of Great Britain and Ireland Since 1960*. Dictionary of Literary Biography 40. Detroit: Gale Research, 1985.

Dictionaries, histories, and handbooks

Broom, Sarah. *Contemporary British and Irish Poetry: An Introduction*. Illustrated ed. New York: Palgrave Macmillan, 2006.

Hogan, Robert, ed. *Dictionary of Irish Literature*. Rev. ed. 2 vols. Westport, Conn.: Greenwood Press, 1996.

Schirmer, Gregory A. *Out of What Began: A History of Irish Poetry in English*. Ithaca, N.Y.: Cornell University Press, 1998.

Tuma, Keith, ed. *Anthology of Twentieth-Century British and Irish Poetry*. Annotated ed. New York: Oxford University Press, 2001.

Women writers

Colman, Anne Ulry. *Dictionary of Nineteenth-Century Irish Women Poets*. Galway: Kenny's Bookshop, 1996.

McBreen, Joan, ed. *The White Page = An Bhileog Bhán: Twentieth-Century Irish Women Poets*. Cliffs of Moher, Ireland: Salmon, 1999.

Weekes, Ann Owens. *Unveiling Treasures: The Attic Guide to the Published Works of Irish Women Literary Writers: Drama, Fiction, Poetry*. Dublin: Attic Press, 1993.

NEW ZEALAND

Keown, Michelle. *Pacific Islands Writing: The Postcolonial Literatures of Aotearoa/New Zealand and Oceania*. New York: Oxford University Press, 2007.

Marsack, Robyn, and Andrew Johnstone, eds. *Twenty Contemporary New Zealand Poets: An Anthology*. Manchester, England: Carcaret Press, 2009.

Sturm, Terry, ed. *The Oxford History of New Zealand Literature in English*. Auckland: Oxford University Press, 1991.

Thomson, John. *New Zealand Literature to 1977: A*

Guide to Information Sources. American Literature, English Literature, and World Literatures in English: An Information Guide Series 30. Detroit: Gale Research, 1980.

SCOTTISH POETRY IN ENGLISH (*see also in the foreign-language section:* CELTIC LANGUAGES)

Glen, Duncan. *The Poetry of the Scots: An Introduction and Bibliographical Guide to Poetry in Gaelic, Scots, Latin, and English*. Edinburgh: Edinburgh University Press, 1991.

Mapstone, Sally, ed. *Older Scots Literature*. Edinburgh: John Donald, 2005.

Martin, Joanna. *Kingship and Love in Scottish Poetry, 1424-1540*. Farnham, Surrey, England: Ashgate, 2008.

Scottish Poetry Index: An Index to Poetry and Poetry-Related Material in Scottish Literary Magazines, 1952- . Edinburgh: Scottish Poetry Library, 1994-2000.

UNITED STATES

Biographical sources

Alfonsi, Ferdinando. *Dictionary of Italian-American Poets*. American University Studies. Series II, Romance Languages and Literature 112. New York: Peter Lang, 1989.

Baughman, Ronald, ed. *American Poets*. Vol. 3 in *Contemporary Authors: Bibliographical Series*. Detroit: Gale Research, 1986.

Conte, Joseph, ed. *American Poets Since World War II: Fourth Series*. Dictionary of Literary Biography 165. Detroit: Gale Research, 1996.

_____. *American Poets Since World War II: Fifth Series*. Dictionary of Literary Biography 169. Detroit: Gale Research, 1996.

_____. *American Poets Since World War II: Sixth Series*. Dictionary of Literary Biography 193. Detroit: Gale Research, 1998.

Greiner, Donald J., ed. *American Poets Since World War II*. Dictionary of Literary Biography 5. Detroit: Gale Research, 1980.

Gwynn, R. S., ed. *American Poets Since World War II: Second Series*. Dictionary of Literary Biography 105. Detroit: Gale Research, 1991.

_____. *American Poets Since World War II: Third Series*. Dictionary of Literary Biography 120. Detroit: Gale Research, 1992.

Quartermain, Peter, ed. *American Poets, 1880-1945: First Series*. Dictionary of Literary Biography 45. Detroit: Gale Research, 1986.

_____. *American Poets, 1880-1945: Second Series*. Dictionary of Literary Biography 48. Detroit: Gale Research, 1986.

_____. *American Poets, 1880-1945: Third Series*. Dictionary of Literary Biography 54. Detroit: Gale Research, 1987.

Criticism

Guide to American Poetry Explication. Reference Publication in Literature. 2 vols. Boston: G. K. Hall, 1989.

Dictionaries, histories, and handbooks

Kamp, Jim, ed. *Reference Guide to American Literature*. 3d ed. Detroit: St. James Press, 1994.

Parini, Jay, ed. *The Columbia History of American Poetry*. New York: Columbia University Press, 1993.

Perkins, George, Barbara Perkins, and Phillip Leininger, eds. *Benét's Reader's Encyclopedia of American Literature*. New York: HarperCollins, 1991.

Shucard, Alan. *American Poetry: The Puritans Through Walt Whitman*. Twayne's Critical History of Poetry Series. Boston: Twayne, 1988.

Waggoner, Hyatt H. *American Poets from the Puritans to the Present*. Rev. ed. Baton Rouge: Louisiana University Press, 1984.

Indexes of primary works

American Poetry Index: An Author, Title, and Subject Guide to Poetry by Americans in Single-Author Collections. Great Neck, N.Y.: Granger, 1983-1988.

Annual Index to Poetry in Periodicals. Great Neck, N.Y.: Poetry Index Press, 1985-1988.

Caskey, Jefferson D., comp. *Index to Poetry in Popular Periodicals, 1955-1959*. Westport, Conn.: Greenwood Press, 1984.

Index of American Periodical Verse. Lanham, Md.: Scarecrow Press, 1971.

Index to Poetry in Periodicals: American Poetic Renaissance, 1915-1919: An Index of Poets and Poems Published in American Magazines and Newspapers. Great Neck, N.Y.: Granger, 1981.

Index to Poetry in Periodicals, 1920-1924: An Index of Poets and Poems Published in American Magazines and Newspapers. Great Neck, N.Y.: Granger, 1983.

Index to Poetry in Periodicals, 1925-1992: An Index of Poets and Poems Published in American Magazines and Newspapers. Great Neck, N.Y.: Granger, 1984.

History: Colonial to 1800

Lemay, J. A. Leo. *A Calendar of American Poetry in the Colonial Newspapers and Magazines and in the Major English Magazines Through 1765.* Worcester, Mass.: American Antiquarian Society, 1972.

Scheick, William J., and JoElla Doggett. *Seventeenth-Century American Poetry: A Reference Guide.* Reference Guides in Literature 14. Boston: G. K. Hall, 1977.

Wegelin, Oscar. *Early American Poetry: A Compilation of the Titles of Volumes of Verse and Broadsides by Writers Born or Residing in North America, North of the Mexican Border, 1650-1820.* 2d ed. 2 vols. New York: Smith, 1930.

History: Nineteenth century

Bennett, Paula, Karen L. Kilcup, and Philipp Schweighauser. *Teaching Nineteenth-Century American Poetry.* New York: Modern Language Association of America, 2007.

Haralson, Eric L., ed. *Encyclopedia of American Poetry: The Nineteenth Century.* Chicago: Fitzroy Dearborn, 1998.

Jason, Philip K. *Nineteenth Century American Poetry: An Annotated Bibliography.* Pasadena, Calif.: Salem Press, 1989.

Lee, A. Robert, ed. *Nineteenth-Century American Poetry.* Critical Studies Series. Totowa, N.J.: Barnes & Noble, 1985.

Olson, Steven. *The Prairie in Nineteenth Century American Poetry.* Norman: University of Oklahoma Press, 1995.

Ruppert, James. *Colonial and Nineteenth Century.* Vol. 1 in *Guide to American Poetry Explication.* Boston: G. K. Hall, 1989.

Sorby, Angela. *Schoolroom Poets: Childhood and the Place of American Poetry, 1865-1917.* Durham: University of New Hampshire Press, 2005.

History: Twentieth century and contemporary

Altieri, Charles. *The Art of Twentieth-Century American Poetry: Modernism and After.* Malden, Mass.: Blackwell, 2006.

Axelrod, Steven Gould, and Camille Roman, eds. *Modernisms, 1900-1950.* Vol. 2 in *The New Anthology of American Poetry.* New Brunswick, N.J.: Rutgers University Press, 2005.

Beach, Christopher. *The Cambridge Introduction to Twentieth-Century American Poetry.* New York: Cambridge University Press, 2003.

Davis, Lloyd, and Robert Irwin. *Contemporary American Poetry: A Checklist.* Metuchen, N.J.: Scarecrow Press, 1975.

Gioia, Dana, David Mason, and Meg Schoerke, eds. *Twentieth-Century American Poetics: Poets on the Art of Poetry.* Boston: McGraw-Hill, 2004.

_____. *Twentieth-Century American Poetry.* Boston: McGraw-Hill, 2003.

Green, Scott E. *Contemporary Science Fiction, Fantasy, and Horror Poetry: A Resource Guide and Biographical Directory.* New York: Greenwood Press, 1989.

Haralson, Eric L., ed. *Encyclopedia of American Poetry: The Twentieth Century.* Chicago: Fitzroy Dearborn, 2001.

Kane, Daniel. *All Poets Welcome: The Lower East Side Poetry Scene in the 1960's.* Berkeley: University of California Press, 2003.

Kirsch, Adam. *The Wounded Surgeon: Confession and Transformation in Six American Poets.* New York: W. W. Norton, 2005.

Leo, John R. *Modern and Contemporary.* Vol. 2 in *Guide to American Poetry Explication.* Boston: G. K. Hall, 1989.

McPheron, William. *The Bibliography of Contemporary American Poetry, 1945-1985: An Annotated Checklist.* Westport, Conn.: Meckler, 1986.

Moramarco, Fred, and William Sullivan. *Containing Multitudes: Poetry in the United States Since 1950.* Critical History of Poetry Series. New York: Twayne, 1998.

Rasula, Jed. *This Compost: Ecological Imperatives in American Poetry.* Athens: University of Georgia Press, 2002.

Shucard, Alan, Fred Moramarco, and William Sullivan. *Modern American Poetry, 1865-1950*. Boston: Twayne, 1989.

Ward, Geoffrey. *Statutes of Liberty: The New York School of Poets*. New York: Palgrave Macmillan, 2001.

African American: Biographical sources

Harris, Trudier, ed. *Afro-American Writers Before the Harlem Renaissance*. Dictionary of Literary Biography 50. Detroit: Gale Research, 1986.

_____. *Afro-American Writers from the Harlem Renaissance to 1940*. Dictionary of Literary Biography 51. Detroit: Gale Research, 1987.

Harris, Trudier, and Thadious M. Davis, eds. *Afro-American Poets Since 1955*. Dictionary of Literary Biography 41. Detroit: Gale Research, 1985.

African American: Indexes of primary works

Chapman, Dorothy Hilton, comp. *Index to Black Poetry*. Boston, G. K. Hall, 1974.

Frankovich, Nicholas, and David Larzelere, eds. *The Columbia Granger's Index to African-American Poetry*. New York: Columbia University Press, 1999.

African American: Dictionaries, histories, and handbooks

French, William P., et al. *Afro-American Poetry and Drama, 1760-1975: A Guide to Information Sources*. American Literature, English Literature, and World Literatures in English: An Information Guide Series 17. Detroit: Gale Research, 1979.

Major, Clarence, ed. *The Garden Thrives: Twentieth Century African-American Poetry*. New York: HarperPerennial, 1996.

Rampersad, Arnold, and Hilary Herbold, eds. *The Oxford Anthology of African-American Poetry*. New York: Oxford University Press, 2005.

Sherman, Joan R. *Invisible Poets: Afro-Americans of the Nineteenth Century*. 2d ed. Urbana: University of Illinois Press, 1989.

Wagner, Jean, and Kenneth Douglas, trans. *Black Poets of the United States: From Paul Laurence Dunbar to Langston Hughes*. Urbana: University of Illinois Press, 1973.

African American: Women writers

Chapman, Dorothy Hilton, comp. *Index to Poetry by Black American Women*. Bibliographies and Indexes in Afro-American and African Studies 15. New York: Greenwood Press, 1986.

Lee, Valerie, ed. *The Prentice Hall Anthology of African American Women's Literature*. Upper Saddle River, N.J.: Pearson Prentice Hall, 2006.

Asian American

Chang, Juliana, ed. *Quiet Fire: A Historical Anthology of Asian American Poetry, 1892-1970*. New York: Asian American Writers' Workshop, 1996.

Chang, Victoria, ed. *Asian American Poetry: The Next Generation*. Urbana: University of Illinois Press, 2004.

Cheung, King-Kok, ed. *An Interethnic Companion to Asian American Literature*. New York: Cambridge University Press, 1997.

Cheung, King-Kok, and Stan Yogi. *Asian American Literature: An Annotated Bibliography*. New York: MLA, 1988.

Huang, Guiyou, ed. *Asian American Poets: A Bio-Bibliographical Critical Sourcebook*. Westport, Conn.: Greenwood Press, 2002.

Yu, Timothy. *Race and the Avant-Garde: Experimental and Asian American Poetry Since 1965*. Stanford, Calif.: Stanford University Press, 2009.

Zhou, Xiaojing. *The Ethics and Poetics of Alterity in Asian American Poetry*. Iowa City: University of Iowa Press, 2006.

Latino

Aragón, Francisco, ed. *The Wind Shifts: New Latino Poetry*. Tucson: University of Arizona Press, 2007.

Bleznick, Donald William. *A Sourcebook for Hispanic Literature and Language: A Selected, Annotated Guide to Spanish, Spanish-American, and United States Hispanic Bibliography, Literature, Linguistics, Journals, and Other Source Materials*. 3d ed. Lanham, Md.: Scarecrow Press, 1995.

Candelaria, Cordelia. *Chicano Poetry: A Critical Introduction*. Westport, Conn.: Greenwood Press, 1986.

Dick, Bruce Allen, ed. *A Poet's Truth: Conversations with Latino/Latina Poets*. Tucson: University of Arizona Press, 2003.

Eger, Ernestina N. *A Bibliography of Criticism of Contemporary Chicano Literature*. Berkeley: Chicano Library Publications, University of California, 1982.

Kanellos, Nicolás, ed. *Biographical Dictionary of Hispanic Literature in the United States: The Literature of Puerto Ricans, Cuban Americans, and Other Hispanic Writers*. New York: Greenwood Press, 1989.

Lomelí, Francisco A., and Carl R. Shirley, eds. *Chicano Writers: First Series*. Dictionary of Literary Biography 82. Detroit: Gale Research, 1989.

_____. *Chicano Writers: Second Series*. Dictionary of Literary Biography 122. Detroit: Gale Research, 1992.

_____. *Chicano Writers: Third Series*. Dictionary of Literary Biography 209. Detroit: Gale Group, 1999.

Martínez, Julio A., and Francisco A. Lomelí, eds. *Chicano Literature: A Reference Guide*. Westport, Conn.: Greenwood Press, 1985.

Native American

Fast, Robin Riley. *The Heart as a Drum: Continuance and Resistance in American Indian Poetry*. Ann Arbor: University of Michigan Press, 1999.

Howard, Helen Addison. *American Indian Poetry*. Twayne's United States Authors Series 334. Boston: Twayne, 1979.

Littlefield, Daniel F., Jr., and James W. Parins. *A Biobibliography of Native American Writers, 1772-1924*. Native American Bibliography Series 2. Metuchen, N.J.: Scarecrow Press, 1981.

_____. *A Biobibliography of Native American Writers, 1772-1924: Supplement*. Native American Bibliography Series 5. Metuchen, N.J.: Scarecrow Press, 1985.

Lundquist, Suzanne Evertsen. *Native American Literatures: An Introduction*. New York: Continuum, 2004.

Porter, Joy, and Kenneth M. Roemer, eds. *The Cambridge Companion to Native American Literature*. New York: Cambridge University Press, 2005.

Rader, Dean, and Janice Gould, eds. *Speak to Me Words: Essays on Contemporary American Indian Poetry*. Tucson: University of Arizona Press, 2003.

Roemer, Kenneth M., ed. *Native American Writers of the United States*. Dictionary of Literary Biography 175. Detroit: Gale Research, 1997.

Ruoff, A. LaVonne Brown. *American Indian Literatures: An Introduction, Bibliographic Review, and Selected Bibliography*. New York: Modern Language Association, 1990.

Wiget, Andrew. *Native American Literature*. Twayne's United States Authors Series 467. Boston: Twayne, 1985.

_____, ed. *Dictionary of Native American Literature*. Garland Reference Library of the Humanities 1815. New York: Garland, 1994.

Wilson, Norma. *The Nature of Native American Poetry*. Albuquerque: University of New Mexico Press, 2000.

Regional poetry

Bain, Robert, and Joseph M. Flora, eds. *Contemporary Poets, Dramatists, Essayists, and Novelists of the South: A Bio-bibliographical Sourcebook*. Westport, Conn.: Greenwood Press, 1994.

Jantz, Harold S. *The First Century of New England Verse*. Worcester, Mass.: American Antiquarian Society, 1944.

Women writers

Davidson, Phebe, ed. *Conversations with the World: American Women Poets and Their Work*. Pasadena, Calif.: Trilogy Books, 1998.

Drake, William. *The First Wave: Women Poets in America, 1915-1945*. New York: Macmillan, 1987.

Gray, Janet, ed. *She Wields a Pen: American Women Poets of the Nineteenth Century*. Iowa City: University of Iowa Press, 1997.

Reardon, Joan, and Kristine A. Thorsen. *Poetry by American Women, 1900-1975: A Bibliography*. Metuchen, N.J.: Scarecrow Press, 1979.

_____. *Poetry by American Women, 1975-1989: A Bibliography*. Metuchen, N.J.: Scarecrow Press, 1990.

WELSH POETRY IN ENGLISH (*see also in the foreign-language section:* CELTIC LANGUAGES)

Conran, Anthony. *Frontiers in Anglo-Welsh Poetry*. Cardiff: University of Wales Press, 1997.

FOREIGN-LANGUAGE POETRY

GENERAL REFERENCE SOURCES
Biographical sources
Jackson, William T. H., ed. *European Writers*. 14 vols. New York: Scribner, 1983-1991.

Kunitz, Stanley, and Vineta Colby, eds. *European Authors, 1000-1900: A Biographical Dictionary of European Literature*. New York: Wilson, 1967.

Magill, Frank N., ed. *Critical Survey of Poetry: Foreign Language Series*. 5 vols. Englewood Cliffs, N.J.: Salem Press, 1984.

_____. *Critical Survey of Poetry: Supplement*. Englewood Cliffs, N.J.: Salem Press, 1987.

Serafin, Steven, ed. *Encyclopedia of World Literature in the Twentieth Century*. 3d ed. 4 vols. Detroit: St. James Press, 1999.

_____. *Twentieth-Century Eastern European Writers: First Series*. Dictionary of Literary Biography 215. Detroit: Gale Group, 1999.

_____. *Twentieth-Century Eastern European Writers: Second Series*. Dictionary of Literary Biography 220. Detroit: Gale Group, 2000.

_____. *Twentieth-Century Eastern European Writers: Third Series*. Dictionary of Literary Biography 232. Detroit: Gale Group, 2001.

Solé, Carlos A., ed. *Latin American Writers*. 3 vols. New York: Scribner, 1989.

Criticism
Coleman, Arthur. *A Checklist of Interpretation, 1940-1973, of Classical and Continental Epics and Metrical Romances*. Vol. 2 in *Epic and Romance Criticism*. 2 vols. New York: Watermill, 1974.

Jason, Philip K., ed. *Masterplots II: Poetry Series, Revised Edition*. 8 vols. Pasadena, Calif.: Salem Press, 2002.

Krstovic, Jelena, ed. *Hispanic Literature Criticism*. Detroit: Gale Research, 1994.

The Year's Work in Modern Language Studies. London: Oxford University Press, 1931.

Dictionaries, histories, and handbooks
Auty, Robert, et al. *Traditions of Heroic and Epic Poetry*. 2 vols. Vol. 1, *The Traditions*; Vol. 2, *Characteristics and Techniques*. Publications of the Modern Humanities Research Association 9, 13. London: Modern Humanities Research Association, 1980, 1989.

Bede, Jean-Albert, and William B. Edgerton, eds. *Columbia Dictionary of Modern European Literature*. 2d ed. New York: Columbia University Press, 1980.

France, Peter, ed. *The Oxford Guide to Literature in English Translation*. New York: Oxford University Press, 2000.

Henderson, Lesley, ed. *Reference Guide to World Literature*. 2d ed. 2 vols. New York: St. James Press, 1995.

Oinas, Felix, ed. *Heroic Epic and Saga: An Introduction to the World's Great Folk Epics*. Bloomington: Indiana University Press, 1978.

Ostle, Robin, ed. *Modern Literature in the Near and Middle East, 1850-1970*. Routledge/SOAS Contemporary Politics and Culture in the Middle East Series. New York: Routledge, 1991.

Prusek, Jaroslav, ed. *Dictionary of Oriental Literatures*. 3 vols. Vol. 1, *East Asia*, edited by Z. Shupski; Vol. 2, *South and South-East Asia*, edited by D. Zbavitel; Vol. 3, *West Asia and North Africa*, edited by J. Becka. New York: Basic Books, 1974.

Pynsent, Robert B., ed. *Reader's Encyclopedia of Eastern European Literature*. New York: HarperCollins, 1993.

Weber, Harry B., George Gutsche, and P. Rollberg, eds. *The Modern Encyclopedia of East Slavic, Baltic, and Eurasian Literatures*. 10 vols. Gulf Breeze, Fla.: Academic International Press, 1977.

Index of primary works
Hoffman, Herbert H. *Hoffman's Index to Poetry: European and Latin American Poetry in Anthologies*. Metuchen, N.J.: Scarecrow Press, 1985.

Poetics
Gasparov, M. L. *A History of European Versification*. Translated by G. S. Smith and Marina Tarlinskaja. New York: Oxford University Press, 1996.

Wimsatt, William K., ed. *Versification: Major Language Types: Sixteen Essays*. New York: Modern Language Association, 1972.

AFRICAN LANGUAGES (*see also in the English-language section:* GENERAL REFERENCE SOURCES (POSTCOLONIAL); AFRICA AND THE CARIBBEAN; *in the Foreign-language section:* FRANCOPHONE; SPANISH AND PORTUGUESE)

Elimimian, Isaac Irabor. *Theme and Style in African Poetry*. Lewiston, N.Y.: E. Mellen, 1991.

Herdeck, Donald E., ed. *African Authors: A Companion to Black African Writing, 1300-1973*. Dimensions of the Black Intellectual Experience. Washington, D.C.: Black Orpheus Press, 1973.

Killam, Douglas, and Ruth Rowe, eds. *The Companion to African Literatures*. Bloomington: Indiana University Press, 2000.

Limb, Peter, and Jean-Marie Volet. *Bibliography of African Literatures*. Lanham, Md.: Scarecrow Press, 1996.

ARABIC

Allen, Roger. *An Introduction to Arabic Literature*. Cambridge, England: Cambridge University Press, 2001.

Badawi, M. M. *A Critical Introduction to Modern Arabic Poetry*. New York: Cambridge University Press, 1975.

_____. *Modern Arabic Literature*. New York: Cambridge University Press, 1992.

Frolov, D. V. *Classical Arabic Verse: History and Theory of 'Arūd*. Boston: Brill, 2000.

Meisami, Julie Scott, and Paul Starkey, eds. *Encyclopedia of Arabic Literature*. New York: Routledge, 1998.

CARIBBEAN (*see also in the English-language section:* AFRICA AND THE CARIBBEAN; *in the Foreign-language section:* DUTCH AND FLEMISH; FRANCOPHONE; SPANISH AND PORTUGUESE)

Arnold, A. James, ed. *A History of Literature in the Caribbean*. 3 vols. Vol. 1, *Hispanic and Francophone Regions*; Vol. 2, *English and Dutch-Speaking Countries*; Vol. 3, *Cross-Cultural Studies*. Comparative History of Literatures in European Languages 10. Philadelphia: J. Benjamins, 1994.

Berrian, Brenda F., and Aart Broek. *Bibliography of Women Writers from the Caribbean, 1831-1986*. Washington, D.C.: Three Continents Press, 1989.

Fenwick, M. J. *Writers of the Caribbean and Central America: A Bibliography*. Garland Reference Library of the Humanities 1244. New York: Garland, 1992.

Goslinga, Marian. *Caribbean Literature: A Bibliography*. Scarecrow Area Bibliographies 15. Lanham, Md.: Scarecrow Press, 1998.

Herdeck, Donald E., ed. *Caribbean Writers: A Bio-Bibliographical-Critical Encyclopedia*. Washington, D.C.: Three Continents Press, 1979.

CATALAN

Barkan, Stanley H., ed. *Four Postwar Catalan Poets*. Rev. ed. Translated by David H. Rosenthal. Merrick, N.Y.: Cross-Cultural Communications, 1994.

Crowe, Anna, ed. *Light off Water: Twenty-five Catalan Poems, 1978-2002*. Translated by Iolanda Pelegri. Manchester, England: Carcanet Press, 2007.

Rosenthal, David H. *Postwar Catalan Poetry*. Lewisburg, Pa.: Bucknell University Press, 1991.

CELTIC LANGUAGES (*see also in the English-language section:* IRISH POETRY IN ENGLISH; SCOTTISH POETRY IN ENGLISH; WELSH POETRY IN ENGLISH)

Irish Gaelic

McBreen, Joan, ed. *The White Page = An Bhileog Bhán: Twentieth-Century Irish Women Poets*. Cliffs of Moher, Ireland: Salmon, 1999.

Scottish Gaelic

Gifford, Douglas, and Dorothy McMillan. *A History of Scottish Women's Writing*. Edinburgh: Edinburgh University Press, 1997.

Glen, Duncan. *The Poetry of the Scots: An Introduction and Bibliographical Guide to Poetry in Gaelic, Scots, Latin, and English*. Edinburgh: Edinburgh University Press, 1991.

Thomson, Derick S. *An Introduction to Gaelic Poetry*. 2d ed. Edinburgh: Edinburgh University Press, 1989.

Welsh

Jarman, A. O. H., and Gwilym Rees Hughes, eds. *A Guide to Welsh Literature*. 6 vols. Cardiff: University of Wales Press, 1992-2000.

Lofmark, Carl. *Bards and Heroes: An Introduction to Old Welsh Poetry*. Felinfach, Wales: Llanerch, 1989.

Williams, Gwyn. *An Introduction to Welsh Poetry, from the Beginnings to the Sixteenth Century*. London: Faber and Faber, 1953.

CHINESE

Barnstone, Tony, and Chou Ping, eds. *The Anchor Book of Chinese Poetry: From Ancient to Contemporary, the Full 3,000-Year Tradition*. New York: Anchor Books, 2004.

Cai, Zong-qi, ed. *How to Read Chinese Poetry: A Guided Anthology*. Bilingual ed. New York: Columbia University Press, 2007.

Chang, Kang-i Sun, and Haun Saussy, eds. *Women Writers of Traditional China: An Anthology of Poetry and Criticism*. Stanford, Calif.: Stanford University Press, 1999.

Haft, Lloyd, ed. *The Poem*. Vol. 3 in *A Selective Guide to Chinese Literature, 1900-1949*. New York: E. J. Brill, 1989.

Lin, Julia C., trans. and ed. *Twentieth-Century Chinese Women's Poetry: An Anthology*. Armonk, N.Y.: M. E. Sharpe, 2009.

Lupke, Christopher, ed. *New Perspectives on Contemporary Chinese Poetry*. New York: Palgrave Macmillan, 2008.

Lynn, Richard John. *Guide to Chinese Poetry and Drama*. 2d ed. Boston, Mass.: G. K. Hall, 1984.

Nienhauser, William, Jr., ed. *The Indiana Companion to Traditional Chinese Literature*. Bloomington: Indiana University Press, 1986.

Owen, Stephen. *The Making of Early Chinese Classical Poetry*. Cambridge, Mass.: Harvard University Asia Center, 2006.

Wu-chi, Liu. *An Introduction to Chinese Literature*. Bloomington: Indiana University Press, 1966.

Yip, Wai-lim, ed. and trans. *Chinese Poetry: An Anthology of Major Modes and Genres*. 2d ed. Durham, N.C.: Duke University Press, 1997.

CLASSICAL GREEK AND LATIN

Albrecht, Michael von. *Roman Epic: An Interpretive Introduction*. Boston: Brill, 1999.

Braund, Susanna Morton. *Latin Literature*. New York: Routledge, 2002.

Briggs, Ward W. *Ancient Greek Authors*. Dictionary of Literary Biography 176. Detroit: Gale Research, 1997.

_____. *Ancient Roman Writers*. Dictionary of Literary Biography 211. Detroit: Gale Group, 1999.

Budelmann, Felix, ed. *The Cambridge Companion to Greek Lyric*. New York: Cambridge University Press, 2009.

Constantine, Peter, et al., eds. *The Greek Poets: Homer to the Present*. New York: W. W. Norton, 2009.

David, A. P. *The Dance of the Muses: Choral Theory and Ancient Greek Poetics*. New York: Oxford University Press, 2006.

Dihle, Albrecht, and Clare Krojzl, trans. *A History of Greek Literature: From Homer to the Hellenistic Period*. New York: Routledge, 1994.

Green, Ellen, ed. *Women Poets in Ancient Greece and Rome*. Norman: University of Oklahoma Press, 2005.

Harrison, Stephen, ed. *A Companion to Latin Literature*. Malden, Mass.: Blackwell, 2004.

Kessels, A. H. M., and W. J. Verdenius, comps. *A Concise Bibliography of Ancient Greek Literature*. 2d ed. Apeldoorn, Netherlands: Administratief Centrum, 1982.

King, Katherine Callen. *Ancient Epic*. Hoboken, N.J.: Wiley-Blackwell, 2009.

Lefkowitz, Mary R. *The Lives of the Greek Poets*. Baltimore: The Johns Hopkins University Press, 1981.

Lyne, R. O. *Collected Papers on Latin Poetry*. Edited by S. J. Harrison. New York: Oxford University Press, 2007.

Raffel, Burton, trans. *Pure Pagan: Seven Centuries of Greek Poems and Fragments*. New York: Random House, 2004.

West, M. L., trans. *Greek Lyric Poetry*. 1993. Reprint. New York: Oxford University Press, 2008.

DUTCH AND FLEMISH

Meijer, Reinder P. *Literature of the Low Countries: A Short History of Dutch Literature in the Netherlands and Belgium*. New ed. Boston: Nijhoff, 1978.

Nieuwenhuys, Robert. *Mirror of the Indies: A History of Dutch Colonial Literature*. Translated by Frans van Rosevelt, edited by E. M. Beekman. Library of

the Indies. Amherst: University of Massachusetts Press, 1982.

Vermij, Lucie, and Martje Breedt Bruyn. *Women Writers from the Netherlands and Flanders*. Amsterdam: International Feminist Book Fair Press/Dekker, 1992.

Weevers, Theodoor. *Poetry of the Netherlands in Its European Context, 1170-1930*. London: University of London-Athlone Press, 1960.

FRANCOPHONE
General
Gilroy, James P., ed. *Francophone Literatures of the New World*. Denver, Colo.: Dept. of Foreign Languages and Literatures, University of Denver, 1982.

Africa and the Caribbean
Blair, Dorothy S. *African Literature in French: A History of Creative Writing in French from West and Equatorial Africa*. New York: Cambridge University Press, 1976.

Brown, Stewart, and Mark McWatt, eds. *The Oxford Book of Caribbean Verse*. New York: Oxford University Press, 2005.

D'Almeida, Irène Assiba, ed. *A Rain of Words: A Bilingual Anthology of Women's Poetry in Francophone Africa*. Translated by Janis A. Mayes. Charlottesville: University of Virginia Press, 2009.

Haigh, Sam, ed. *An Introduction to Caribbean Francophone Writing: Guadeloupe and Martinique*. New York: Berg, 1999.

Hurley, E. Anthony. *Through a Black Veil: Readings in French Caribbean Poetry*. Trenton, N.J.: Africa World Press, 2000.

Larrier, Renée Brenda. *Francophone Women Writers of Africa and the Caribbean*. Gainesville: University Press of Florida, 2000.

Moore, Gerald, and Ulli Beier, eds. *The Penguin Book of Modern African Poetry*. 4th ed. New York: Penguin, 2007.

Ojaide, Tanure. *Poetic Imagination in Black Africa: Essays on African Poetry*. Durham, N.C.: Carolina Academic Press, 1996.

Parekh, Pushpa Naidu, and Siga Fatima Jagne. *Postcolonial African Writers: A Bio-bibliographical Critical Sourcebook*. Westport, Conn.: Greenwood Press, 1998.

France: Bibliography
Kempton, Richard. *French Literature: An Annotated Guide to Selected Bibliographies*. New York: Modern Language Association of America, 1981.

France: Biographical sources
Beum, Robert, ed. *Nineteenth-Century French Poets*. Dictionary of Literary Biography 217. Detroit: Gale Group, 2000.

Sinnreich-Levi, Deborah, and Ian S. Laurie, eds. *Literature of the French and Occitan Middle Ages: Eleventh to Fifteenth Centuries*. Dictionary of Literary Biography 208. Detroit: Gale Group, 1999.

France: Criticism
Coleman, Kathleen. *Guide to French Poetry Explication*. New York: G. K. Hall, 1993.

France: Dictionaries, histories, and handbooks
Acquisto, Joseph. *French Symbolist Poetry and the Idea of Music*. Burlington, Vt.: Ashgate, 2006.

Aulestia, Gorka. *The Basque Poetic Tradition*. Translated by Linda White. Reno: University of Nevada Press, 2000.

Banks, Kathryn. *Cosmos and Image in the Renaissance: French Love Lyric and Natural-Philosophical Poetry*. London: Legenda, 2008.

Bishop, Michael. *Nineteenth-Century French Poetry*. Twayne's Critical History of Poetry Series. New York: Twayne, 1993.

Brereton, Geoffrey. *An Introduction to the French Poets, Villon to the Present Day*. 2d rev. ed. London: Methuen, 1973.

Caws, Mary Ann, ed. *The Yale Anthology of Twentieth-Century French Poetry*. New Haven, Conn.: Yale University Press, 2004.

Dolbow, Sandra W. *Dictionary of Modern French Literature: From the Age of Reason Through Realism*. New York: Greenwood Press, 1986.

France, Peter, ed. *The New Oxford Companion to Literature in French*. New York: Clarendon Press, 1995.

Gaunt, Simon, and Sarah Key, eds. *The Cambridge Companion to Medieval French Literature*. New York: Cambridge University Press, 2008.

_____. *The Troubadours: An Introduction*. New York: Cambridge University Press, 1999.

Levi, Anthony. *Guide to French Literature*. 2 vols. Chicago: St. James Press, 1992-1994.

Moss, Ann. *Poetry and Fable: Studies in Mythological Narrative in Sixteenth-Century France*. New York: Cambridge University Press, 2009.

Palmer, R. Barton, ed. and trans. *Medieval Epic and Romance: An Anthology of English and French Narrative*. Glen Allen, Va.: College Publishing, 2007.

Shaw, Mary Lewis. *The Cambridge Introduction to French Poetry*. New York: Cambridge University Press, 2003.

Switten, Margaret Louise. *Music and Poetry in the Middle Ages: A Guide to Research on French and Occitan Song, 1100-1400*. New York: Garland, 1995.

Thomas, Jean-Jacques, and Steven Winspur. *Poeticized Language: The Foundations of Contemporary French Poetry*. University Park: Pennsylvania State University Press, 1999.

Willett, Laura, trans. *Poetry and Language in Sixteenth-Century France: Du Bellay, Ronsard, Sébillet*. Toronto: Centre for Reformation and Renaissance Studies, Victoria University, 2004.

France: Women writers

Sartori, Eva Martin, and Dorothy Wynne Zimmerman. *French Women Writers: A Bio-bibliographical Source Book*. New York: Greenwood Press, 1991.

Shapiro, Norman R., ed. and trans. *French Women Poets of Nine Centuries: The Distaff and the Pen*. Baltimore: Johns Hopkins University Press, 2008.

French Canadian (see also in the English-language section: Canada)

Blouin, Louise, Bernard Pozier, and D. G. Jones, eds. *Esprit de Corps: Québec Poetry of the Late Twentieth Century in Translation*. Winnipeg, Man.: Muses, 1997.

Platnick, Phyllis. *Canadian Poetry: Index to Criticisms, 1970-1979 = Poésie canadienne: Index de critiques, 1970-1979*. Ontario: Canadian Library Association, 1985.

GERMAN

Biographical sources

Hardin, James, ed. *German Baroque Writers, 1580-1660*. Dictionary of Literary Biography 164. Detroit: Gale Research, 1996.

_____. *German Baroque Writers, 1661-1730*. Dictionary of Literary Biography 168. Detroit: Gale Research, 1996.

Hardin, James, and Will Hasty, eds. *German Writers and Works of the Early Middle Ages, 800-1170*. Dictionary of Literary Biography 148. Detroit: Gale Research, 1995.

Hardin, James, and Siegfried Mews, eds. *Nineteenth-Century German Writers to 1840*. Dictionary of Literary Biography 133. Detroit: Gale Research, 1993.

_____. *Nineteenth-Century German Writers, 1841-1900*. Dictionary of Literary Biography 129. Detroit: Gale Research, 1993.

Hardin, James, and Max Reinhart, eds. *German Writers and Works of the High Middle Ages, 1170-1280*. Dictionary of Literary Biography 138. Detroit: Gale Research, 1994.

_____. *German Writers of the Renaissance and Reformation, 1280-1580*. Dictionary of Literary Biography 179. Detroit: Gale Group, 1997.

Hardin, James, and Christoph E. Schweitzer, eds. *German Writers from the Enlightenment to Sturm und Drang, 1720-1764*. Dictionary of Literary Biography 97. Detroit: Gale Research, 1990.

_____. *German Writers in the Age of Goethe, Sturm und Drang to Classicism*. Dictionary of Literary Biography 94. Detroit: Gale Research, 1990.

_____. *German Writers in the Age of Goethe, 1789-1832*. Dictionary of Literary Biography 90. Detroit: Gale Research, 1989.

Dictionaries, histories, and handbooks

Appleby, Carol. *German Romantic Poetry: Goethe, Novalis, Heine, Hölderlin*. Maidstone, Kent, England: Crescent Moon, 2008.

Baird, Jay W. *Hitler's War Poets: Literature and Politics in the Third Reich*. New York: Cambridge University Press, 2008.

Browning, Robert M. *German Poetry from 1750 to 1900*. New York: Continuum, 1984.

_____. *German Poetry in the Age of the Enlightenment: From Brockes to Klopstock*. University Park: Pennsylvania State University Press, 1978.

Dobozy, Maria. *Re-membering the Present: The Medieval German Poet-Minstrel in Cultural Context*. Turnhout, Belgium: Brepois, 2005.

Faulhaber, Uwe K., and Penrith B. Goff. *German Liter-*

ature: An Annotated Reference Guide. New York: Garland, 1979.

Hanak, Miroslav John. *A Guide to Romantic Poetry in Germany*. New York: Peter Lang, 1987.

Hofmann, Michael, ed. *Twentieth-Century German Poetry: An Anthology*. New York: Farrar, Straus and Giroux, 2008.

Hutchinson, Peter, ed. *Landmarks in German Poetry*. New York: Peter Lang, 2000.

Leeder, Karen J. *Breaking Boundaries: A New Generation of Poets in the GDR, 1979-1989*. New York: Oxford University Press, 1996.

Mathiew, Gustave, and Guy Stern, eds. *Introduction to German Poetry*. New York: Dover Publications, 1991.

Nader, Andrés José, ed. *Traumatic Verses: On Poetry in German from the Concentration Camps, 1933-1945*. Rochester, N.Y.: Camden House, 2007.

Owen, Ruth J. *The Poet's Role: Lyric Responses to German Unification by Poets from the GDR*. Amsterdam: Rodopi, 2001.

Women writers

Boland, Eavan, ed. and trans. *After Every War: Twentieth-Century Women Poets*. Princeton, N.J.: Princeton University Press, 2004.

Classen, Albrecht, ed. and trans. *Late-Medieval German Women's Poetry: Secular and Religious Songs*. Rochester, N.Y.: D. S. Brewer, 2004.

Harper, Anthony, and Margaret C. Ives. *Sappho in the Shadows: Essays on the Work of German Women Poets of the Age of Goethe, 1749-1832*. New York: Peter Lang, 2000.

GREEK (*see also* CLASSICAL GREEK AND LATIN)

Bien, Peter, et al., eds. *A Century of Greek Poetry, 1900-2000*. Bilingual ed. Westwood, N.J.: Cosmos, 2004.

Constantine, Peter, et al., eds. *The Greek Poets: Homer to the Present*. New York: W. W. Norton, 2009.

Demaras, Konstantinos. *A History of Modern Greek Literature*. Translated by Mary P. Gianos. Albany: State University of New York Press, 1972.

Saïd, Suzanne, and Monique Trédé. *A Short History of Greek Literature*. Translated by Trista Selous et al. New York: Routledge, 1999.

Valaoritis, Nanos, and Thanasis Maskaleris, eds. *An Anthology of Modern Greek Poetry*. Jersey City, N.J.: Talisman House, 2003.

Van Dyck, Karen. *Kassandra and the Censors: Greek Poetry Since 1967*. Ithaca, N.Y.: Cornell University Press, 1998.

HEBREW AND YIDDISH

Alonso Schokel, Luis. *A Manual of Hebrew Poetics*. Subsidia Biblica 11. Rome: Editrice Pontificio Istituto Biblico, 1988.

Alter, Robert. *The Art of Biblical Poetry*. New York: Basic Books, 1985.

Burnshaw, Stanley, T. Carmi, and Ezra Spicehandler, eds. *The Modern Hebrew Poem Itself: From the Beginnings to the Present, Sixty-nine Poems in a New Presentation*. With new afterword, "Hebrew Poetry from 1965 to 1988." Cambridge, Mass.: Harvard University Press, 1989.

Gevirtz, Stanley. *Patterns in the Early Poetry of Israel*. Chicago: University of Chicago Press, 1963.

Kugel, James L. *The Great Poems of the Bible: A Reader's Companion with New Translations*. New York: Free Press, 1999.

Liptzin, Solomon. *A History of Yiddish Literature*. Middle Village, N.Y.: Jonathan David, 1985.

Madison, Charles Allan. *Yiddish Literature: Its Scope and Major Writers*. New York: F. Ungar, 1968.

O'Connor, M. *Hebrew Verse Structure*. Winona Lake, Ind.: Eisenbrauns, 1980.

Pagis, Dan. *Hebrew Poetry of the Middle Ages and the Renaissance*. Berkeley: University of California Press, 1991.

Petersen, David L., and Kent Harold Richards. *Interpreting Hebrew Poetry*. Minneapolis: Fortress Press, 1992.

Watson, Wilfred G. E. *Classical Hebrew Poetry: A Guide to Its Techniques*. 2d ed. Sheffield, England: JSOT Press, 1986.

Wiener, Leo. *The History of Yiddish Literature in the Nineteenth Century*. 2d ed. New York: Hermon Press, 1972.

Zinberg, Israel. *Old Yiddish Literature from Its Origins to the Haskalah Period*. Translated and edited by Bernard Martin. Cincinnati: Hebrew Union College Press, 1975.

HUNGARIAN

Gömöri, George, and George Szirtes, eds. *The Colonnade of Teeth: Modern Hungarian Poetry*. Chester Springs, Pa.: Dufour Editions, 1996.

Kolumban, Nicholas, ed. and trans. *Turmoil in Hungary: An Anthology of Twentieth Century Hungarian Poetry*. St. Paul, Minn.: New Rivers Press, 1996.

Makkai, Adam, ed. *In Quest of the "Miracle Stag": The Poetry of Hungary, an Anthology of Hungarian Poetry in English Translation from the Thirteenth Century to the Present*. Foreword by Árpád Göncz. Urbana: University of Illinois Press, 1996.

Suleiman, Susan Rubin, and Éva Forgács, eds. *Contemporary Jewish Writing in Hungary: An Anthology*. Lincoln: University of Nebraska Press, 2003.

Szirtes, George, ed. *Leopard V: An Island of Sound—Poetry and Fiction Before and Beyond the Iron Curtain*. New York: Random House, 2004.

INDIAN AND SOUTH ASIAN LANGUAGES (*see also* ARABIC; PERSIAN; VIETNAMESE)

Dimock, Edward C., Jr., et al. *The Literatures of India: An Introduction*. Chicago: University of Chicago Press, 1974.

Gerow, Edwin. *Indian Poetics*. Wiesbaden: Harrassowitz, 1977.

Lienhard, Siegfried. *A History of Classical Poetry: Sanskrit, Pali, Prakrit*. Wiesbaden, Germany: Harrassowitz, 1984.

Mahmud, Shabana. *Urdu Language and Literature: A Bibliography of Sources in European Languages*. New York: Mansell, 1992.

Natarajan, Nalini, ed. *Handbook of Twentieth-Century Literatures of India*. Westport, Conn.: Greenwood Press, 1996.

Rajan, P. K., and Swapna Daniel, eds. *Indian Poetics and Modern Texts: Essays in Criticism*. New Delhi: S. Chand, 1998.

Sadiq, Mohammed. *A History of Urdu Literature*. Delhi: Oxford University Press, 1984.

Saran, Saraswiti. *The Development of Urdu Poetry*. New Delhi: Discovery Publishing House, 1990.

ITALIAN

Biographical sources

De Stasio, Giovanna Wedel, Glauco Cambon, and Antonio Illiano, eds. *Twentieth-Century Italian Poets: First Series*. Dictionary of Literary Biography 114. Detroit: Gale Research, 1992.

_____. *Twentieth-Century Italian Poets: Second Series*. Dictionary of Literary Biography 128. Detroit: Gale Research, 1993.

Dictionaries, histories, and handbooks

Bohn, Willard, ed. and trans. *Italian Futurist Poetry*. Toronto: University of Toronto Press, 2005.

Bondanella, Peter, and Julia Conaway Bondanella, eds. *Dictionary of Italian Literature*. Rev. ed. Westport, Conn.: Greenwood Press, 1996.

Cavallo, Jo Ann. *The Romance Epics of Boiardo, Ariosto, and Tasso: From Public Duty to Private Pleasure*. Toronto: University of Toronto Press, 2004.

Condini, Ned, ed. and trans. *An Anthology of Modern Italian Poetry in English Translation, with Italian Text*. New York: Modern Language Association of America, 2009.

Dombroski, Robert S. *Italy: Fiction, Theater, Poetry, Film Since 1950*. Middle Village, N.Y.: Council on National Literatures, 2000.

Holmes, Olivia. *Assembling the Lyric Self: Authorship from Troubador Song to Italian Poetry Book*. Minneapolis: University of Minnesota Press, 2000.

Italian Poets of the Twentieth Century. Florence, Italy: Casalini Libri, 1997.

Kleinhenz, Christopher. *The Early Italian Sonnet: The First Century, 1220-1321*. Collezione di Studi e Testi n.s. 2. Lecce, Italy: Milella, 1986.

Payne, Roberta L., ed. *Selection of Modern Italian Poetry in Translation*. Montreal: McGill-Queen's University Press, 2004.

Zatti, Sergio. *The Quest for Epic: From Ariosto to Tasso*. Translated by Sally Hill with Dennis Looney, edited by Looney. Toronto: University of Toronto Press, 2006.

Women writers

Blum, Cinzia Sartini, and Lara Trubowitz, eds. and trans. *Contemporary Italian Women Poets: A Bilingual Anthology*. New York: Italica Press, 2001.

Frabotta, Biancamaria, ed. *Italian Women Poets*. Translated by Corrado Federici. Toronto: Guernica Editions, 2002.

Stortoni, Laura A., and Mary P. Lillie, eds. *Women Poets of the Italian Renaissance: Courtly Ladies and Courtesans*. New York: Italica, 1997.

JAPANESE
Biographical sources

Carter, Steven D., ed. *Medieval Japanese Writers*. Dictionary of Literary Biography 203. Detroit: Gale Group, 1999.

Hisamatsu, Sen'ichi, ed. *Biographical Dictionary of Japanese Literature*. New York: Harper & Row, 1976.

Dictionaries, histories, and handbooks

Bownas, Geoffrey, and Anthony Thwaite, eds. and trans. *The Penguin Book of Japanese Verse*. Rev. ed. London: Penguin Books, 2009.

Brower, Robert, and Earl Miner. *Japanese Court Poetry*. 1961. Reprint. Stanford, Calif.: Stanford University Press, 1988.

Carter, Steven D., trans. *Traditional Japanese Poetry: An Anthology*. Stanford, Calif.: Stanford University Press, 1991.

_____. *Waiting for the Wind: Thirty-six Poets of Japan's Late Medieval Age*. Reprint. New York: Columbia University Press, 1994.

Miner, Earl Roy, Hiroko Odagiri, and Robert E. Morrell. *The Princeton Companion to Classical Japanese Literature*. Princeton, N.J.: Princeton University Press, 1985.

Morton, Leith. *Modernism in Practice: An Introduction to Postwar Japanese Poetry*. Honolulu: University of Hawaii Press, 2004.

Ooka, Makoto. *The Poetry and Poetics of Ancient Japan*. Translated by Thomas Fitzsimmons. Santa Fe, N.Mex.: Katydid Books, 1997.

Rimer, J. Thomas. *A Reader's Guide to Japanese Literature*. 2d ed. New York: Kodansha International, 1999.

Rimer, J. Thomas, and Van C. Gessel, eds. *The Columbia Anthology of Modern Japanese Literature*. 2 vols. New York: Columbia University Press, 2005-2007.

Rimer, J. Thomas, and Robert E. Morrell. *Guide to Japanese Poetry*. Asian Literature Bibliography Series. 2d ed. Boston, Mass.: G. K. Hall, 1984.

Sato, Hiroaki, ed. and trans. *Japanese Women Poets: An Anthology*. Armonk, N.Y.: M. E. Sharpe, 2007.

Shirane, Haruo. *Traditional Japanese Literature: An Anthology, Beginnings to 1600*. Rev. ed. Translated by Sonja Arntzen et al. New York: Columbia University Press, 2007.

_____, ed. *Early Modern Japanese Literature: An Anthology, 1600-1900*. Translated by James Brandon et al. New York: Columbia University Press, 2002.

KOREAN

Kim, Jaihiun. *Modern Korean Poetry*. Fremont, Calif.: Asian Humanities Press, 1994.

_____. *Traditional Korean Verse Since the 1900's*. Seoul, South Korea: Hanshin, 1991.

Korean Poetry: An Anthology with Critical Essays. Seoul, South Korea: Korean Culture & Arts Foundation, 1984.

Lee, Young-gul. *The Classical Poetry of Korea*. Seoul, South Korea: Korean Culture and Arts Foundation, 1981.

McCann, David R. *Form and Freedom in Korean Poetry*. New York: Brill, 1988.

Who's Who in Korean Literature. Korean Culture & Arts Foundation. Elizabeth, N.J.: Hollym, 1996.

PERSIAN (FARSI)

Husain, Iqbal. *The Early Persian Poets of India (A.H. 421-670)*. Patna, India: Patna University, 1937.

Jackson, A. V. Williams. *Early Persian Poetry, from the Beginnings Down to the Time of Firdausi*. New York: Macmillan, 1920.

Meisami, Julie Scott. *Medieval Persian Court Poetry*. Princeton, N.J.: Princeton University Press, 1987.

Thackston, W. M. *A Millennium of Classical Persian Poetry: A Guide to the Reading and Understanding of Persian Poetry from the Tenth to the Twentieth Century*. Bethesda, Md.: Iranbooks, 1994.

Thiesen, Finn. *A Manual of Classical Persian Prosody: With Chapters on Urdu, Karakhanidic, and Ottoman Prosody*. Wiesbaden, Germany: O. Harrassowitz, 1982.

SCANDINAVIAN LANGUAGES

General

Sjåvik, Jan. *Historical Dictionary of Scandinavian Literature and Theater*. Lanham, Md.: Scarecrow Press, 2006.

Sumari, Anni, and Nicolaj Stochholm, eds. *The Other Side of Landscape: An Anthology of Contemporary Nordic Poetry*. New York: Slope Editions, 2006.

Zuck, Virpi, ed. *Dictionary of Scandinavian Literature*. New York: Greenwood Press, 1990.

Danish

Borum, Poul. *Danish Literature: A Short Critical Survey*. Copenhagen: Det Danske Selskab, 1979.

Rossel, Sven H., ed. *A History of Danish Literature*. Lincoln: University of Nebraska Press, 1992.

Stecher-Hansen, Marianne, ed. *Twentieth-Century Danish Writers*. Dictionary of Literary Biography 214. Detroit: Gale Group, 1999.

Icelandic

Beck, Richard. *History of Icelandic Poets, 1800-1940*. Ithaca, N.Y.: Cornell University Press, 1950.

McTurk, Rory, ed. *A Companion to Old Norse-Icelandic Literature and Culture*. Malden, Mass.: Blackwell, 2005.

Neijman, Daisy, ed. *A History of Icelandic Literature*. Vol. 5 in *A History of Scandinavian Literatures*, edited by Sven H. Rossel. Lincoln: University of Nebraska Press, 2006.

Norwegian

McTurk, Rory, ed. *A Companion to Old Norse-Icelandic Literature and Culture*. Malden, Mass.: Blackwell, 2005.

Naess, Harald S. *A History of Norwegian Literature*. Lincoln: University of Nebraska Press, 1993.

Swedish

Scobbie, Irene. *Aspects of Modern Swedish Literature*. 2d ed. Norwich, England: Norvik Press, 1999.

Forsås-Scott, Helena. *Swedish Women's Writing, 1850-1995*. Atlantic Highlands, N.J.: Athlone, 1997.

Page, Edita, ed. *The Baltic Quintet: Poems from Estonia, Finland, Latvia, Lithuania, and Sweden*. Hamilton, Ont.: Wolsak and Wynn, 2008.

Warme, Lars G., ed. *A History of Swedish Literature*. Vol. 3 in *A History of Scandinavian Literatures*, edited by Sven H. Rossel. Lincoln: University of Nebraska Press, 1996.

SLAVIC LANGUAGES

General

Jakobson, Roman, C. H. van Schooneveld, and Dean S. Worth, eds. *Slavic Poetics: Essays in Honor of Kiril Taranovsky*. Slavistic Printings and Reprintings 267. The Hague: Mouton, 1973.

Mihailovich, Vasa D., comp. and ed. *Modern Slavic Literatures*. 2 vols. Vol. 1, *Russian Literature*; Vol. 2, *Bulgarian, Czechoslovak, Polish, Ukrainian, and Yugoslav Literatures*. New York: F. Ungar, 1972.

Tschizewskij, Dmitrij. *Comparative History of Slavic Literatures*. Translated by Richard Noel Porter and Martin P. Rice, edited by Serge A. Zenkovsky. Nashville, Tenn.: Vanderbilt University Press, 1971.

Albanian

Elsie, Robert. *Dictionary of Albanian Literature*. Westport, Conn.: Greenwood Press, 1986.

_____. *Studies in Modern Albanian Literature and Culture*. East European Monographs 455. New York: Distributed by Columbia University Press, 1996.

Pipa, Arshi. *Contemporary Albanian Literature*. East European Monographs 305. New York: Distributed by Columbia University Press, 1991.

Ressuli, Namik. *Albanian Literature*. Edited by Eduard Lico. Boston: Pan-Albanian Federation of America Vatra, 1987.

Bulgarian

Matejic, Mateja, et al. *A Biobibliographical Handbook of Bulgarian Authors*. Translated by Predrag Matejic, edited by Karen L. Black. Columbus, Ohio: Slavica, 1981.

Croatian

Miletich, John S. *Love Lyric and Other Poems of the Croatian Renaissance: A Bilingual Anthology*. Bloomington, Ind.: Slavica, 2009.

Czech

French, Alfred. *The Poets of Prague: Czech Poetry Between the Wars*. New York: Oxford University Press, 1969.

Kovtun, George J. *Czech and Slovak Literature in English: A Bibliography*. 2d ed. Washington, D.C.: Library of Congress, 1988.

Lodge, Kirsten, ed. and trans. *Solitude, Vanity, Night: An Anthology of Czech Decadent Poetry*. Prague: Charles University, 2007.

Novák, Arne. *Czech Literature*. Translated by Peter Kussi, edited by William E. Harkins. Joint Committee on Eastern Europe Publication Series 4. Ann Arbor: Michigan Slavic Publications, 1976.

Volkova, Bronislava, and Clarice Cloutier, eds. and trans. *Up the Devil's Back: A Bilingual Anthology of Twentieth-Century Czech Poetry*. Bloomington, Ind.: Slavica, 2008.

Macedonian

Osers, Ewald, ed. *Contemporary Macedonian Poetry*. Translated by Eward Osers. London: Kultura/Forest Books, 1991.

Polish

Barańczak, Stanisław, and Clare Cavanagh, eds. and trans. *Polish Poetry of the Last Two Decades of Communist Rule: Spoiling Cannibals' Fun*. Foreword by Helen Vendler. Evanston, Ill.: Northwestern University Press, 1991.

Carpenter, Bogdana, ed. *Monumenta Polonica: The First Four Centuries of Polish Poetry, a Bilingual Anthology*. Ann Arbor: Michigan Slavic Publications, 1989.

Czerniawski, Adam, ed. *The Mature Laurel: Essays on Modern Polish Poetry*. Chester Springs, Pa.: Dufour Editions, 1991.

Czerwinski, E. J., ed. *Dictionary of Polish Literature*. Westport, Conn.: Greenwood Press, 1994.

Grol, Regina, ed. *Ambers Aglow: An Anthology of Contemporary Polish Women's Poetry*. Austin, Tex.: Host, 1996.

Mengham, Rod, et al., trans. *Altered State: The New Polish Poetry*. Ottawa, Ont.: Arc, 2003.

Miłosz, Czesław, ed. *Postwar Polish Poetry: An Anthology*. 3d ed. Berkeley: University of California Press, 1983.

Russian

Blok, Aleksandr. *Us Four Plus Four: Eight Russian Poets Conversing*. New Orleans, La.: UNO Press, 2008.

Bunimovitch, Evgeny, and J. Kates, eds. *Contemporary Russian Poetry: An Anthology*. Translated by Kates. Champaign: Dalkey Archive Press, University of Illinois, 2008.

Cornwell, Neil, ed. *Reference Guide to Russian Literature*. Chicago: Fitzroy Dearborn, 1998.

Kates, J., ed. *In the Grip of Strange Thoughts: Russian Poetry in a New Era*. Brookline, Mass.: Zephyr Press, 2000.

Nabokov, Vladimir Vladimirovich, comp. and trans. *Verses and Versions: Three Centuries of Russian Poetry*. Edited by Brian Boyd and Stanislav Shvabrin. Orlando, Fla.: Harcourt, 2008.

Poggioli, Renato. *The Poets of Russia, 1890-1930*. Cambridge, Mass.: Harvard University Press, 1960.

Polukhina, Valentina, and Daniel Weissbort, eds. *An Anthology of Contemporary Russian Women Poets*. Iowa City: University of Iowa Press, 2005.

Rydel, Christine A., ed. *Russian Literature in the Age of Pushkin and Gogol: Poetry and Drama*. Dictionary of Literary Biography 205. Detroit: Gale Group, 1999.

Tschizewskij, Dmitrij. *History of Nineteenth-Century Russian Literature*. Translated by Richard Noel Porter. Edited by Serge A. Zenkovsky. Nashville, Tenn.: Greenwood Press, 1974.

Wachtel, Michael. *The Cambridge Introduction to Russian Poetry*. New York: Cambridge University Press, 2004.

_____. *The Development of Russian Verse: Meter and Its Meanings*. New York: Cambridge University Press, 1998.

Serbian

Holton, Milne, and Vasa D. Mihailovich, eds. and trans. *Serbian Poetry from the Beginnings to the Present*. New Haven, Conn.: Yale Center for International and Area Studies, 1988.

Simic, Charles, ed. and trans. *The Horse Has Six Legs: An Anthology of Serbian Poetry*. St. Paul, Minn.: Graywolf Press, 1992.

Slovak

Kovtun, George J. *Czech and Slovak Literature in English: A Bibliography*. 2d ed. Washington, D.C.: Library of Congress, 1988.

Kramoris, Ivan Joseph, ed. *An Anthology of Slovak Po-*

etry: A Selection of Lyric and Narrative Poems and Folk Ballads in Slovak and English. Scranton, Pa.: Obrana Press, 1947.

Petro, Peter. *A History of Slovak Literature*. Montreal: McGill-Queen's University Press, 1995.

Smith, James Sutherland, Pavol Hudik, and Jan Bajanek, eds. *In Search of Beauty: An Anthology of Contemporary Slovak Poetry in English*. Translated by Bajanek. Mundelein, Ill.: Bolchazy-Carducci, 2004.

Slovene

Cooper, Henry R., ed. *A Bilingual Anthology of Slovene Literature*. Bloomington, Ind.: Slavica, 2003.

Jurkovič, Tina, ed. *Contemporary Slovenian Literature in Translation*. Translated by Lili Potpara. Ljubljana, Slovenia: Študentska založba, 2002.

Mokrin-Pauer, Vida. *Six Slovenian Poets*. Translated by Ana Jeinika, edited by Brane Mozetič. Todmorden, Lancashire, England: Arc, 2006.

Zawacki, Andrew, ed. *Afterwards: Slovenian Writing, 1945-1995*. Buffalo, N.Y.: White Pine Press, 1999.

Ukrainian

Cyzevkyj, Dmytro. *A History of Ukrainian Literature: From the Eleventh to the End of the Nineteenth Century*. Translated by Dolly Ferguson, Doreen Gorsline, and Ulana Petyk. Edited by George S. N. Luckyi. 2d ed. New York: Ukrainian Academic Press, 1997.

Piaseckyj, Oksana. *Bibliography of Ukrainian Literature in English and French: Translations and Critical Works, 1950-1986*. University of Ottawa Ukrainian Studies 10. Ottawa: University of Ottawa Press, 1989.

SPANISH AND PORTUGUESE
General

Bleznick, Donald William. *A Sourcebook for Hispanic Literature and Language: A Selected, Annotated Guide to Spanish, Spanish-American, and United States Hispanic Bibliography, Literature, Linguistics, Journals, and Other Source Materials*. 3d ed. Lanham, Md.: Scarecrow Press, 1995.

Newmark, Maxim. *Dictionary of Spanish Literature*. Westport, Conn.: Greenwood Press, 1972.

Sefami, Jacobo, comp. *Contemporary Spanish American Poets: A Bibliography of Primary and Secondary Sources*. Bibliographies and Indexes in World Literature 33. Westport, Conn.: Greenwood Press, 1992.

Woodbridge, Hensley Charles. *Guide to Reference Works for the Study of the Spanish Language and Literature and Spanish American Literature*. 2d ed. New York: Modern Language Association of America, 1997.

Africa

Ojaide, Tanure. *Poetic Imagination in Black Africa: Essays on African Poetry*. Durham, N.C.: Carolina Academic Press, 1996.

Parekh, Pushpa Naidu, and Siga Fatima Jagne. *Postcolonial African Writers: A Bio-bibliographical Critical Sourcebook*. Westport, Conn.: Greenwood Press, 1998.

Caribbean

Brown, Stewart, and Mark McWatt, eds. *The Oxford Book of Caribbean Verse*. New York: Oxford University Press, 2005.

Fenwick, M. J. *Writers of the Caribbean and Central America: A Bibliography*. Garland Reference Library of the Humanities 1244. New York: Garland, 1992.

James, Conrad, and John Perivolaris, eds. *The Cultures of the Hispanic Caribbean*. Gainesville: University Press of Florida, 2000.

Martinez, Julia A., ed. *Dictionary of Twentieth-Century Cuban Literature*. Westport, Conn.: Greenwood Press, 1990.

Mexico and Central America

Agosín, Marjorie, and Roberta Gordenstein, eds. *Miriam's Daughters: Jewish Latin American Women Poets*. Foreword by Agosín. Santa Fe, N.Mex.: Sherman Asher, 2001.

Cortes, Eladio. *Dictionary of Mexican Literature*. Westport, Conn.: Greenwood Press, 1992.

Dauster, Frank N. *The Double Strand: Five Contemporary Mexican Poets*. Louisville: University Press of Kentucky, 1987.

Foster, David William. *Mexican Literature: A Bibliography of Secondary Sources*. 2d ed. Metuchen, N.J.: Scarecrow Press, 1992.

_____, ed. *Mexican Literature: A History*. Austin: University of Texas Press, 1994.

González Peña, Carlos. *History of Mexican Literature*. Translated by Gusta Barfield Nance and Florence Johnson Dunstan. 3d rev. ed. Dallas: Southern Methodist University Press, 1968.

Nicholson, Irene. *A Guide to Mexican Poetry, Ancient and Modern*. Mexico: Editorial Minutiae Mexicana, 1968.

Vicuña, Cecilia, and Ernesto Livon-Grosman, eds. *The Oxford Book of Latin American Poetry: A Bilingual Anthology*. New York: Oxford University Press, 2009.

Washbourne, Kelly, ed. *An Anthology of Spanish American Modernismo: In English Translation, with Spanish Text*. Translated by Washbourne with Sergio Waisman. New York: Modern Language Association of America, 2007.

South America

Agosín, Marjorie, and Roberta Gordenstein, eds. *Miriam's Daughters: Jewish Latin American Women Poets*. Foreword by Agosín. Santa Fe, N.Mex.: Sherman Asher, 2001.

Brotherston, Gordon. *Latin American Poetry: Origins and Presence*. New York: Cambridge University Press, 1975.

Perrone, Charles A. *Seven Faces: Brazilian Poetry Since Modernism*. Durham, N.C.: Duke University Press, 1996.

Rowe, William. *Poets of Contemporary Latin America: History and the Inner Life*. New York: Oxford University Press, 2000.

Smith, Verity, ed. *Encyclopedia of Latin American Literature*. Chicago: Fitzroy Dearborn, 1997.

Stern, Irwin, ed. *Dictionary of Brazilian Literature*. Westport, Conn.: Greenwood Press, 1988.

Vicuña, Cecilia, and Ernesto Livon-Grosman, eds. *The Oxford Book of Latin American Poetry: A Bilingual Anthology*. New York: Oxford University Press, 2009.

Washbourne, Kelly, ed. *An Anthology of Spanish American Modernismo: In English Translation, with Spanish Text*. Translated by Washbourne with Sergio Waisman. New York: Modern Language Association of America, 2007.

Spain and Portugal

Bellver, Catherine G. *Absence and Presence: Spanish Women Poets of the Twenties and Thirties*. Lewisburg, Pa.: Bucknell University Press, 2001.

_____. *Dictionary of the Literature of the Iberian Peninsula*. Cranbury, N.J.: Associated University Presses, 2001.

Florit, Eugenio, ed. *Introduction to Spanish Poetry*. New York: Dover Publications, 1991.

Foster, David Williams, Daniel Altamiranda, and Carmen de Urioste, eds. *Spanish Literature: 1700 to the Present*. Spanish Literature 3. New York: Garland, 2000.

Fox, Gwyn. *Subtle Subversions: Reading Golden Age Sonnets by Iberian Women*. Washington, D.C.: Catholic University of America Press, 2008.

McNerny, Kathleen, and Cristina Enriques de Salamanca, eds. *Double Minorities of Spain: A Bio-bibliographic Guide to Women Writers of the Catalan, Galician, and Basque Countries*. New York: Modern Language Association of America, 1994.

Merwin, W. S., ed. and trans. *Spanish Ballads*. Port Townsend, Wash.: Copper Canyon Press, 2008.

Mudrovic, W. Michael. *Mirror, Mirror on the Page: Identity and Subjectivity in Spanish Women's Poetry, 1975-2000*. Bethlehem, Pa.: Lehigh University Press, 2009.

Penna, Michael L., ed. *Twentieth-Century Spanish Poets: First Series*. Dictionary of Literary Biography 108. Detroit: Gale Research, 1991.

Pérez, Janet. *Modern and Contemporary Spanish Women Poets*. New York: Prentice Hall International, 1996.

St. Martin, Hardie, ed. *Roots and Wings: Poetry from Spain, 1900-1975*. Buffalo, N.Y.: White Pine Press, 2004.

Walters, Gareth. *The Cambridge Introduction to Spanish Poetry*. New York: Cambridge University Press, 2003.

West-Settle, Cecile, and Sylvia Sherno, eds. *Contemporary Spanish Poetry: The Word and the World*. Madison, N.J.: Fairleigh Dickinson University Press, 2005.

Wilcox, John. *Women Poets of Spain, 1860-1990: To-*

ward a Gynocentric Vision. Urbana: University of Illinois Press, 1997.

Winfield, Jerry Phillips. *Twentieth-Century Spanish Poets: Second Series*. Dictionary of Literary Biography 134. Detroit: Gale Research, 1994.

TIBETAN

Cabezon, Jose I., and Roger R. Jackson. *Tibetan Literature: Studies in Genre*. Ithaca, N.Y.: Snow Lion, 1995.

Hartley, Lauran R., and Patricia Schiaffini-Vedani, eds. *Modern Tibetan Literature and Social Change*. Durham, N.C.: Duke University Press, 2008.

Jinpa, Thupten, and Jas Elsner. *Songs of Spiritual Experience: Tibetan Buddhist Poems of Insight and Awakening*. Boston: Shambhala, 2000.

TURKISH

Andrews, Walter G., Jr. *An Introduction to Ottoman Poetry*. Minneapolis: Bibliotheca Islamica, 1976.

Gibb, E. J. W. *A History of Ottoman Poetry*. 6 vols. Cambridge, England: Published and distributed by the Trustees of the "E. J. W. Gibb Memorial," 1963-1984.

VIETNAMESE

Thông, Huynh Sanh, ed. and trans. *An Anthology of Vietnamese Poems: From the Eleventh Through the Twentieth Centuries*. New Haven, Conn.: Yale University Press, 1996.

"Vietnamese Poetry and History." Special issue of *Crossroads: An Interdisciplinary Journal of Southeast Asian Studies* 7, no. 2 (1992).

Maura Ives; updated by Tracy Irons-Georges

Guide to Online Resources

Web Sites

The following sites were visited by the editors of Salem Press in 2010. Because URLs frequently change, the accuracy of these addresses cannot be guaranteed; however, long-standing sites, such as those of colleges and universities, national organizations, and government agencies, generally maintain links when their sites are moved.

Academy of American Poets

http://www.poets.org

The mission of the Academy of American Poets is to "support American poets at all stages of their careers and to foster the appreciation of contemporary poetry." The academy's comprehensive Web site features information on poetic schools and movements; a Poetic Forms Database; an Online Poetry Classroom, with educator and teaching resources; an index of poets and poems; essays and interviews; general Web resources; links for further study; and more.

African Literature and Writers on the Internet

http://www-sul.stanford.edu/depts/ssrg/africa

This page is included in the Africa South of the Sahara site created by Karen Fung of Stanford University. It provides an alphabetical list of links to numerous resources about African poets and writers, online journals and essays, association Web sites, and other materials.

Australian Literature

http://www.middlemiss.org/lit/lit.html

Perry Middlemiss, a Melbourne-based blogger, created this useful resource about Australian writers, including poets, and their works. It features an alphabetical list of authors that links to biographies and lists of their works. The site also provides, for some of the listed works, links to synopses and excerpts.

The Cambridge History of English and American Literature

http://www.bartleby.com/cambridge

This site provides an exhaustive examination of the development of all forms of literature in Great Britain and the United States. The multivolume set on which this site is based was published in 1907-1921 but remains a relevant, classic work. It offers "a wide selection of writing on orators, humorists, poets, newspaper columnists, religious leaders, economists, Native Americans, song writers, and even non-English writing, such as Yiddish and Creole."

The Canadian Literature Archive

http://www.umanitoba.ca/canlit

Created and maintained by the English Department at the University of Manitoba, this site is a comprehensive collection of materials for and about Canadian writers. It includes an alphabetical listing of authors with links to additional Web-based information. Users also can retrieve electronic texts, announcements of literary events, and videocasts of author interviews and readings.

A Celebration of Women Writers

http://digital.library.upenn.edu/women

This site is an extensive compendium on the contributions of women writers throughout history. The "Local Editions by Authors" and "Local Editions by Category" pages include access to electronic texts of the works of numerous writers. Users can also access biographical and bibliographical information by browsing lists arranged by writers' names, countries of origin, ethnicities, and the centuries in which they lived.

Contemporary British Writers

http://www.contemporarywriters.com/authors

Created by the British Council, this site offers profiles of living writers of the United Kingdom, the Republic of Ireland, and the Commonwealth. Information includes biographies, bibliographies, critical reviews, and news about literary prizes. Photographs are also featured. Users can search the site by author, genre, nationality, gender, publisher, book title, date of publication, and prize name and date.

Internet Public Library: Native American Authors

http://www.ipl.org/div/natam

The Internet Public Library, a Web-based collection of resource materials, includes this informational index to writers of Native American heritage. An alphabetical list of authors features links to biographies, lists of works, electronic texts, tribal Web sites, and other online resources. The majority of the writers covered are contemporary Indian authors, but some historical authors also are featured. Users also can retrieve information by browsing lists of titles and tribes. In addition, the site contains a bibliography of print and online materials about Native American literature.

LiteraryHistory.com

http://www.literaryhistory.com

This site is an excellent source of academic, scholarly, and critical literature about eighteenth, nineteenth, and twentieth century American and English writers. It provides numerous pages about specific eras and genres, including individual pages for eighteenth, nineteenth, and twentieth century literature and for African American and postcolonial literatures. These pages contain alphabetical lists of authors that link to articles, reviews, overviews, excerpts of works, teaching guides, podcasts, and other materials.

Literary Resources on the Net

http://andromeda.rutgers.edu/~jlynch/Lit

Jack Lynch of Rutgers University maintains this extensive collection of links to Web sites that are useful to researchers, including numerous sites about American and English literature. This collection is a good place to begin online research about poetry, as it links to other sites with broad ranges of literary topics. The site is organized chronologically, with separate pages about the Middle Ages, the Renaissance, the eighteenth century, the Romantic and Victorian eras, and twentieth century British and Irish literature. It also has separate pages providing links to Web sites about American literature and to women's literature and feminism.

LitWeb

http://litweb.net

LitWeb provides biographies of hundreds of world authors throughout history that can be accessed through an alphabetical listing. The pages about each writer contain a list of his or her works, suggestions for further reading, and illustrations. The site also offers information about past and present winners of major literary prizes.

The Modern Word: Authors of the Libyrinth

http://www.themodernword.com/authors.html

The Modern Word site, although somewhat haphazard in its organization, provides a great deal of critical information about writers. The "Authors of the Libyrinth" page is very useful, linking author names to essays about them and other resources. The section of the page headed "The Scriptorium" presents "an index of pages featuring writers who have pushed the edges of their medium, combining literary talent with a sense of experimentation to produce some remarkable works of modern literature."

Outline of American Literature

http://www.america.gov/publications/books/outline
-of-american-literature.html

This page of the America.gov site provides access to an electronic version of the ten-chapter volume *Outline of American Literature*, a historical overview of poetry and prose from colonial times to the present published by the Bureau of International Information Programs of the U.S. Department of State.

Poetry Foundation

http://www.poetryfoundation.org

The Poetry Foundation, publisher of *Poetry* magazine, is an independent literary organization. Its Web site offers links to essays; news; events; online poetry resources, such as blogs, organizations, publications, and references and research; a glossary of literary terms; and a Learning Lab that includes poem guides and essays on poetics.

Poetry in Translation

http://poetryintranslation.com

This independent resource provides modern translations of classic texts by famous poets and also provides original poetry and critical works. Visitors can choose from several languages, including English, Spanish, Chinese, Russian, Italian, and Greek. Original text is available as well. Also includes links to further literary resources.

Poetry International Web

http://international.poetryinternationalweb.org

Poetry International Web features information on poets from countries such as Indonesia, Zimbabwe, Iceland, India, Slovenia, Morocco, Albania, Afghanistan, Russia, and Brazil. The site offers news, essays, interviews and discussion, and hundreds of poems, both in their original languages and in English translation.

Poet's Corner

http://theotherpages.org/poems

The Poet's Corner, one of the oldest text resources on the Web, provides access to about seven thousand works of poetry by several hundred different poets from around the world. Indexes are arranged and searchable by title, name of poet, or subject. The site also offers its own resources, including "Faces of the Poets"—a gallery of portraits—and "Lives of the Poets"—a growing collection of biographies.

Representative Poetry Online

http://rpo.library.utoronto.ca

This award-winning resource site, maintained by Ian Lancashire of the Department of English at the University of Toronto in Canada, has several thousand English-language poems by hundreds of poets. The collection is searchable by poet's name, title of work, first line of a poem, and keyword. The site also includes a time line, a glossary, essays, an extensive bibliography, and countless links organized by country and by subject.

The Victorian Web

http://www.victorianweb.org

One of the finest Web sites about the nineteenth century, the Victorian Web provides a wealth of information about Great Britain during the reign of Queen Victoria, including information about the era's literature. The section "Genre & Technique" includes poetry.

Voice of the Shuttle

http://vos.ucsb.edu

One of the most complete and authoritative places for online information about literature, Voice of the Shuttle is maintained by professors and students in the English Department at the University of California, Santa Barbara. The site provides countless links to electronic books, academic journals, literary association Web sites, sites created by university professors, and many other resources.

Voices from the Gaps

http://voices.cla.umn.edu/

Voices from the Gaps is a site of the English Department at the University of Minnesota, dedicated to providing resources on the study of women artists of color, including writers. The site features a comprehensive index searchable by name, and it provides biographical information on each writer or artist and other resources for further study.

Western European Studies

http://wess.lib.byu.edu

The Western European Studies Section of the Association of College and Research Libraries maintains this collection of resources useful to students of Western European history and culture. It also is a good place to find information about non-English-language litera-

ture. The site includes separate pages about the literatures and languages of the Netherlands, France, Germany, Iberia, Italy, and Scandinavia, in which users can find links to electronic texts, association Web sites, journals, and other materials, the majority of which are written in the languages of the respective countries.

ELECTRONIC DATABASES

Electronic databases usually do not have their own URLs. Instead, public, college, and university libraries subscribe to these databases, provide links to them on their Web sites, and make them available to library card holders or other specified patrons. Readers can visit library Web sites or ask reference librarians to check on availability.

Bloom's Literary Reference Online

Facts On File publishes this database of thousands of articles by renowned scholar Harold Bloom and other literary critics, examining the lives and works of great writers worldwide. The database also includes information on more than forty-two thousand literary characters, literary topics, themes, movements, and genres, plus video segments about literature. Users can retrieve information by browsing writers' names, titles of works, time periods, genres, or writers' nationalities.

Canadian Literary Centre

Produced by EBSCO, the Canadian Literary Centre database contains full-text content from ECW Press, a Toronto-based publisher, including the titles in the publisher's Canadian fiction studies, Canadian biography, and Canadian writers and their works series; *ECW's Biographical Guide to Canadian Novelists*; and *George Woodcock's Introduction to Canadian Fiction*. Author biographies, essays and literary criticism, and book reviews are among the database's offerings.

Literary Reference Center

EBSCO's Literary Reference Center (LRC) is a comprehensive full-text database designed primarily to help high school and undergraduate students in English and the humanities with homework and research assignments about literature. The database contains massive amounts of information from reference works,

books, literary journals, and other materials, including more than 31,000 plot summaries, synopses, and overviews of literary works; almost 100,000 essays and articles of literary criticism; about 140,000 author biographies; more than 605,000 book reviews; and more than 5,200 author interviews. It contains the entire contents of Salem Press's MagillOnLiterature Plus. Users can retrieve information by browsing a list of authors' names or titles of literary works; they can also use an advanced search engine to access information by numerous categories, including author name, gender, cultural identity, national identity, and the years in which he or she lived, or by literary title, character, locale, genre, and publication date. The Literary Reference Center also features a literary-historical time line, an encyclopedia of literature, and a glossary of literary terms.

Literary Resource Center

Published by Gale, this comprehensive literary database contains information on the lives and works of more than 130,000 authors in all genres, in all time periods, and throughout the world. In addition, the database offers more than 70,000 full-text critical essays and reviews from some of Gale's reference publications, including *Contemporary Literary Criticism*, *Literature Criticism from 1400-1800*, *Nineteenth-Century Literature Criticism*, and *Twentieth-Century Literary Criticism*; more than 7,000 overviews of frequently studied works; more than 650,000 full-text articles, critical essays, and reviews from about three hundred scholarly journals and literary magazines; more than 4,500 interviews; and about five hundred links to selected Web sites. Users can retrieve information by browsing author name, ethnicity, nationality, and years of birth and death; titles of literary works; genres; selected literary movements or time periods; keywords; and themes of literary works. Literary Resource Center also features a literary-historical time line and an encyclopedia of literature.

MagillOnLiterature Plus

MagillOnLiterature Plus is a comprehensive, integrated literature database produced by Salem Press and available on the EBSCOhost platform. The data-

base contains the full text of essays in Salem's many literature-related reference works, including *Masterplots*, *Cyclopedia of World Authors*, *Cyclopedia of Literary Characters*, *Cyclopedia of Literary Places*, *Critical Survey of Poetry, Critical Survey of Long Fiction*, *Critical Survey of Short Fiction*, *World Philosophers and Their Works*, *Magill's Literary Annual*, and *Magill's Book Reviews*. Among its contents are articles on more than 35,000 literary works and more than 8,500 poets, writers, dramatists, essayists, and philosophers; more than 1,000 images; and a glossary of more than 1,300 literary terms. The biographical essays include lists of authors' works and secondary bibliographies, and hundreds of overview essays examine and discuss literary genres, time periods, and national literatures.

Rebecca Kuzins; updated by Desiree Dreeuws

TIME LINE

c. 2000 B.C.E.	The main portion of *Gilgamesh* (*Gilgamesh Epic*, 1917) is written on cuneiform clay tablets. This epic, which is the oldest surviving poem, recounts the exploits of Gilgamesh, the legendary king of Uruk and the first literary hero.
c. 750 B.C.E.	Homer composes the *Iliad* (English translation, 1611), a Greek epic poem that recounts the fall of Troy. This work and Homer's subsequent poem the *Odyssey* (c. 725 B.C.E.; English translation, 1614) will establish the epic poem as a genre in Western literature and will influence European literature and culture for centuries.
c. 700 B.C.E.	The Greek poet Hesiod writes *Erga kai Emerai* (*Works and Days*, 1618), in which the poet instructs his wastrel brother Perses about the virtues of hard work and provides advice about farming techniques.
c. 630 B.C.E.	Sappho, one of the most admired poets of the ancient world, is born on the Greek island of Lesbos.
c. 500 B.C.E.	Vālmīki, whom Indian tradition credits with having invented poetry, composes *Rāmāyaṇa* (*The Ramayana*, 1870-1874). Written in Sanskrit, this poem is the national epic of India and will continue to influence poetry, art, drama, and religion in South and Southeast Asia into the twenty-first century.
c. 498-446 B.C.E.	Pindar produces *Epinikia* (*Odes*, 1656), a collection of odes celebrating the victories of athletes in the Panhellenic festival games.
c. 400 B.C.E.-400 C.E.	The *Mahābhārata* (*The Mahabharata*, 1834), the longest surviving poem in any language, is written in Sanskrit. This epic records political, ethical, mythological, and philosophical thought in ancient India. The *Bhagavadgītā* (*The Bhagavad Gita,* 1785), a Hindu devotional text composed between c. 200 B.C.E. and 200 C.E., is preserved as an interlude in the *Mahābhārata*.
c. 334-323 B.C.E.	Aristotle writes *De poetica* (*Poetics*, 1705), an early work of literary criticism in which he analyzes the essence of poetry and distinguishes its various forms, including the epic, comic, and tragic.
October 15, 70 B.C.E.	Vergil, whom many consider the greatest poet of ancient Rome, is born in Andes, Cisalpine Gaul, near Mantua (now in Italy).
c. 17 B.C.E.	Horace, the premier Roman lyric poet, analyzes the poetic genre in *Ars poetica* (*The Art of Poetry*, 1567), which is included in *Epistles* (c. 20-15 B.C.E.; English translation, 1567). Among his literary theories, Horace praises consistency as the highest virtue of poetry and advises poets to carefully choose each word and incident, as well as the meter of their compositions.
c. 8 C.E.	The Roman poet Ovid composes *Metamorphoses* (English translation, 1567), an epic recounting more than two hundred stories from Greek and Roman mythology, legend, and history.
c. 103 C.E.	Martial, the Roman writer who perfected the genre of epigrammatic poetry, dies in Hispania (now in Spain).
210	Ruan Ji is born in Weishi, China. He will compose eighty-two verses designated as *yonghuai shi* (poems singing of my emotions), which will be studied and imitated by subsequent Chinese poets.
c. 670	Cædmon, the first English poet, composes "Hymn," which combines the meters of Nordic heroic poetry with the subject matter of the Scriptures.

689	Meng Haoran, the first great poet of the Tang Dynasty, is born in Xianyang, China.
701	Li Bo, one of the two greatest poets in Chinese literature, is born in what is now Chinese Turkistan.
712	Du Fu, one of the two greatest poets in Chinese literature, is born in Gongxian, China.
mid-eighth century	*Manyōshū* (*The Collections of Ten Thousand Leaves*, also as *The Ten Thousand Leaves*, pb. 1981, and as *The Manyoshu*, 1940), an anthology of more than 4,500 Japanese poems, is compiled.
c. 1000	*Beowulf*, an Old English epic heroic poem, is composed by an anonymous writer.
c. 1010	The Persian poet Firdusi creates the Iranian national epic, *Shahnamah* (*Sah-name*, 1906), or "the book of kings." Later translations of this epic will influence the work of Western poets.
ninth-twelfth centuries	Anonymous writers compose the Old Norse poems that are collected in the *Poetic Edda*. These poems are primarily preserved in the Icelandic *Codex Regius*, a manuscript written in the thirteenth century. The *Poetic Edda* is the most important source of information on Norse mythology and Germanic heroic legends.
twelfth century	Omar Khayyám, a Persian poet, composes *Rubā'īyāt* (*True Translation of Hakim Omar Khayyam's "Robaiyat,"* 1994; commonly known as *Rubáiyát of Omar Khayyám*). The work is a series of *ruba'i*, or individual quatrains.
twelfth century	*Chanson de Roland* (*The Song of Roland*, 1880), the oldest surviving French medieval epic poem, is written. This epic, recounting the defeat of Count Roland, Charlemagne's nephew, by a Saracen army in 877, is one of about one hundred surviving French *chansons de geste* (songs of heroic action).
c. 1200	*Nibelungenlied* (English translation, 1848) is written in Middle High German by an unknown Austrian monk. This epic poem explores Germanic conceptions of the true values of knighthood.
early thirteenth century	The oldest surviving Spanish epic poem, *Cantar de mío Cid* (*Chronicle of the Cid*, 1846), is composed. This work describes the exploits of the Spanish hero El Cid.
c. 1205	Layamon composes *Brut*, the first major literary work written in Middle English and the first English-language version of the stories of King Arthur and King Lear.
July 20, 1304	Petrarch is born in Arezzo, Tuscany (now in Italy). His work will include vernacular poems in which he celebrates his everlasting love for a woman named Laura.
1320	Hafiz, the master of the *ghazal*, or lyric poem, is born in Shīrāz, Persia (now in Iran).
c. 1320	Dante creates his masterpiece, the three-volume *La divina commedia* (*The Divine Comedy*, 1802). This work describes the poet's journey through the three realms of the Christian otherworld—Hell, Purgatory, and Paradise.
1387-1400	Geoffrey Chaucer writes *The Canterbury Tales*, a collection of comic stories told by a group of pilgrims.
c. 1400	The Pearl-Poet composes *Sir Gawain and the Green Knight*, one of many medieval poems concerning King Arthur and his knights.
1570	Scottish writer Robert Henryson publishes *The Morall Fabillis of Esope, the Phyrgian* (also known as *Fables*, twelve shorter poems of uncertain attribution). These didactic poems retell thirteen of Aesop's animal fables.
1572	*Os Lusíadas* (*The Lusiads*, 1655), Luís de Camões's epic poem about Portugal's expansion, is published.

1572	John Donne is born in London. He will become the best-known of the Metaphysical poets, a group of seventeenth century English writers that includes George Herbert, Andrew Marvell, Thomas Traherne, Henry Vaughan, Richard Crashaw, Abraham Cowley, Sir William Davenant, Sir John Suckling, and Thomas Carew.
1590	Edmund Spencer creates *The Faerie Queene*, his allegorical tribute to Queen Elizabeth I.
1595	*Defence of Poesie* by Sir Philip Sidney is published. In this work of Renaissance literary criticism, Sidney argues for the superiority of poetry over any other aesthetic pursuit.
1609	William Shakespeare's *Sonnets* are published. In addition to being one of the world's greatest dramatists, Shakespeare wrote some of the greatest love poems in the English language.
August 6, 1637	Ben Jonson, the founder of English neoclassical poetry, dies in London. Jonson's verse imitates Roman classical forms and subject matters, foreshadowing a style that would be more commonly employed by eighteenth century British poets.
1644	Matsuo Bashō, considered by many to be the greatest of the haiku poets, is born in Ueno, Igo Province, Japan.
November, 1648	Sor Juana Inés de la Cruz, the major writer of colonial Spanish America, is born in New Spain (now Mexico). She will write more than four hundred poems, as well as plays and prose works.
1650	Anne Bradstreet's *The Tenth Muse Lately Sprung Up in America: Or, Several Poems Compiled with Great Variety of Wit and Learning, Full of Delight* is published. Bradstreet is one of America's foremost colonial poets and the first female poet to be published in America.
1660-1700	During "The Age of Dryden," the prolific John Dryden writes and translates numerous works of literature. His two hundred poems are composed in a variety of genres, including odes, verse epistles, satires, and religious poetry.
1667	The first books of John Milton's *Paradise Lost* are published, with the remaining volumes released in 1674. This work is arguably the greatest epic poem in English.
1712	Alexander Pope publishes his mock-epic poem *The Rape of the Lock*.
June 24, 1729	Edward Taylor, an English-born minister and one of the premier American colonial poets, dies in Westfield, Massachusetts.
1751	Thomas Gray's poem "Elegy Written in a Country Churchyard," one of the most popular works of British literature, is published.
1770	Johann Wolfgang von Goethe publishes *Neue Lieder* (*New Poems*, 1853), his first volume of poetry. In his lyric poetry, Goethe mastered the use of diverse meters, techniques, and styles as had no other German writer before him.
1773	Phillis Wheatley's *Poems on Various Subjects, Religious and Moral* is published. Wheatley is America's first black poet and the second female poet to be published in America, after Anne Bradstreet.
1786	The Kilmarnock edition of Robert Burns's *Poems, Chiefly in the Scottish Dialect*, is published. The poetic works of Burns, who is regarded as the national poet of Scotland, include more than three hundred songs about eighteenth century life in that country.

January 22, 1788	Lord Byron is born in London. His creation of the defiant and brooding "Byronic hero" would exert a profound influence on nineteenth century Romantic sensibility.
1794	William Blake publishes *Songs of Innocence and of Experience*. Blake was one of the earliest English Romantic poets.
1798	William Wordsworth and Samuel Taylor Coleridge anonymously publish *Lyrical Ballads*, a collection of their Romantic poetry that includes the first appearance of Coleridge's poem *The Rime of the Ancient Mariner*. In his preface to the collection, Wordsworth argues that primitivism—the belief that there is an intrinsic "state of nature" from which humankind has fallen into wickedness—is the basis of Romanticism.
1800	German writer Friedrich Schiller composes his best-known poem, "Das Lied von der Glocke" ("The Song of the Bell"), a philosophical ballad in which he projects humankind's mortal existence against the background of the bell's creation.
December 17, 1807	John Greenleaf Whittier is born in Haverhill, Massachusetts. He and several other Americans—Henry Wadsworth Longfellow, James Russell Lowell, Oliver Wendell Holmes, and William Cullen Bryant—would later be known as the Fireside Poets because nineteenth century Americans often gathered around the fireside to hear a family member read these writers' works.
1817	John Keats publishes his first volume of poetry. Keats would die before his twenty-sixth birthday, but in that brief time he would produce some of the greatest Romantic poetry in the English language.
1820	*Ruslan i Lydumila* (*Ruslan and Liudmila*, 1936), the first long poem by Alexander Pushkin, is published. Pushkin is the first poet to write in a purely Russian style.
1820	*Méditations poétiques* (*Poetical Meditations*, 1839), by Alphonse de Lamartine, hailed as the first masterpiece of French Romantic poetry, is published.
July 8, 1822	Percy Bysshe Shelley drowns in a boating accident in Italy, less than one month before his thirtieth birthday. One of the premier English Romantic poets, Shelley used a wide variety of stanzaic patterns and poetic forms in his work.
1827	*Buch der Lieder* (*Book of Songs*, 1856), by the German poet Heinrich Heine, is published. The most controversial poet of his time, Heine is renowned for his love poetry.
December 10, 1830	Emily Dickinson is born in Amherst, Massachusetts. Although she gained little recognition for her work during her lifetime, Dickinson would later be considered one of America's greatest lyric poets.
1831	French Romantic poet Victor Hugo attains lyrical maturity with the publication of *Les Feuilles d'automne*, in which he treats themes of childhood, nature, and love.
1842	Robert Browning publishes *Dramatic Lyrics*, which includes "My Last Duchess," one of his best dramatic monologues.
October 7, 1849	Edgar Allan Poe dies in Baltimore, Maryland, at the age of forty. Poe's poetry would influence many British poets and writers. He also wrote literary criticism in which he maintained that critics should protect readers from bad poetry and encourage poets to live up to their potential.

1850	The first of the four versions of "The Blessed Damozel" is published in a British magazine. The ballad's author, Dante Gabriel Rossetti, is also a painter and a member of the Pre-Raphaelite Brotherhood of artists. Rossetti's poetry, with its use of medieval settings and painterly detail, exemplifies the Pre-Raphaelite style of art and literature.
1850	Elizabeth Barrett Browning publishes *Poems: New Edition*, which includes *Sonnets from the Portuguese*.
November 5, 1850	Prince Albert selects Alfred, Lord Tennyson, to replace William Wordsworth as England's poet laureate. The appointment is announced after *In Memorium* (1850), Tennyson's elegy upon the death of his friend Arthur Henry Hallem, was published and became an instant best seller. Tennyson will hold the position of poet laureate for the next forty-two years.
1855	Henry Wadsworth Longfellow, the most popular English-language poet of the nineteenth century, publishes *The Song of Hiawatha*.
1855	The first edition of Walt Whitman's *Leaves of Grass* is published. Whitman radically alters conventional poetry by using free verse and ordinary diction.
1857	The first edition of French poet Charles Baudelaire's *Les Fleurs du mal* (*Flowers of Evil*, 1931) is published. The poems in this collection are characterized by their bold metaphors and bizarre juxtapositions of beauty and ugliness.
1867	Matthew Arnold publishes "Dover Beach," which makes reference to the Victorian debate between religion and science.
1873	*Une Saison en enfer* (*A Season in Hell*, 1932), by Arthur Rimbaud, is published. Rimbaud will become one of the most influential of the French Symbolist poets.
1876	*L'Après-midi d'un faune* (*The Afternoon of a Faun*, 1936), by French Symbolist poet Stéphane Mallarmé, is published. Mallarmé's work influenced younger poets, who hailed him as an exemplar of Symbolism.
1877	Jacint Verdaguer publishes *La Atlántida*, written in the Catalan language. Verdaguer's works exemplify the religious, patriotic, and epic characteristics of the nineteenth century Renaixença, a period of rebirth for Catalan literature and art.
1888	*Azul*, a collection of works by Nicaraguan poet Rubén Darío, is published, receiving praise from both South American and European critics. Darío is one of the founders of the *Modernismo* literary movement, and his poetry features innovative themes, language, meters, and rhymes.
1889	Anna Akhmatov is born near Odessa, Ukraine. She will become one of the leading poets of the Russian Acmeist movement.
1898	Thomas Hardy publishes the first of his eight volumes of poetry, *Wessex Poems, and Other Verses*.
1907	Rudyard Kipling receives the Nobel Prize in Literature.
1908	*A Lume Spento*, the first volume of poetry by Ezra Pound, is published. In the first two decades of the twentieth century, Pound and T. S. Eliot will create the idiom that will characterize modern American and English poetry.

1912	Harriet Monroe founds *Poetry* magazine, which will continue to be issued into the twenty-first century. The magazine will publish works by many of the world's leading poets, including Ezra Pound, T. S. Eliot, Marianne Moore, Carl Sandburg, and Rabindranath Tagore, and will discover such poets as Gwendolyn Brooks, John Ashbery, and James Merrill.
1913	*Alcools: Poèmes, 1898-1913 (Alcools: Poems, 1898-1913*, 1964), by Guilluame Apollinaire, is published. Apollinaire was one of the first French poets to describe the discontinuity and disorientation of modern society.
1913	Indian poet Rabindranath Tagore receives the Nobel Prize in Literature.
1913-1930	Robert Bridges is poet laureate of the United Kingdom.
April 23, 1915	Rupert Brooke dies while performing his military service during World War I. During this year, Brooke's collection *1914, and Other Poems*, which features five sonnets glamorizing the fate of martyred soldiers, is published.
1918	Sara Teasdale receives the Pulitzer Prize in Poetry for *Love Songs*.
1919-1935	The Harlem Renaissance produces some of the finest African-American literature, music, and art of the twentieth century. Poets associated with this movement include Langston Hughes, Countée Cullen, and Claude McKay.
1922	T. S. Eliot's *The Waste Land* is published. In this influential work, Eliot describes human alienation in the years following World War I.
1923	Irish poet William Butler Yeats is awarded the Nobel Prize in Literature.
1924	*Haru to shura (Spring and Asura*, 1973), by Japanese poet Kenji Miyazawa, is released. This collection is the only volume of Miyazawa's poetry published during his lifetime.
1930	*The Bridge*, by Hart Crane, is published. In this lengthy poem, Crane seeks to provide a synthesis of the American identity.
1930	Conrad Aiken receives the Pulitzer Prize in Poetry for *Selected Poems*.
1936	The publication of *Twenty-five Poems* establishes Welsh writer Dylan Thomas as a significant poet.
1936	Patrick Kavanagh publishes his collection *Ploughman, and Other Poems*. Kavanagh will become a major figure in the second generation of the Irish literary revival.
August 19, 1936	Federico García Lorca is executed by members of the Spanish fascist party during the Spanish Civil War. His poetry is characterized by startling images and metaphors drawn from traditional Spanish culture.
October 17, 1938	Les A. Murray is born in Nabiac, New South Wales, Australia. His work will earn him the distinction of being Australia's major poet and also one of the finest poets of his generation writing in English.
1941	Robert Frost receives the Frost Medal from the Poetry Society of America for distinguished lifetime service to American poetry.
1945	Gabriela Mistral is the first Latin American writer to receive the Nobel Prize in Literature.
1945-1946	Louise Bogan serves as America's poet laureate.
1947-1948	Robert Lowell serves as America's poet laureate.
1950	E. E. Cummings receives the Academy of American Poets Fellowship.
1950	Wallace Stevens receives the Bollingen Prize in Poetry.

1951	Gottfried Benn receives the Georg Büchner Prize, the most important literary prize in Germany.
1952	Frank O'Hara's first collection, *A City Winter, and Other Poems*, is published. O'Hara, Kenneth Koch, James Schuyler, and John Ashbery were the central members of the New York School of poets, an influential group of writers during the late 1950's.
1953	Archibald MacLeish and William Carlos Williams receive the Bollingen Prize in Poetry.
1956	"Howl," by Allen Ginsberg, is published. This poem is the best-known work by one of the Beat writers, a group whose other members include poets Kenneth Rexroth, Lawrence Ferlinghetti, Michael McClure, Gregory Corso, and Philip Whalen.
1956	Spanish poet Juan Ramón Jiménez is awarded the Nobel Prize in Literature.
1956	Elizabeth Bishop receives the Pulitzer Prize in Poetry for *Poems: North and South*.
1958	Irish poet Thomas Kinsella receives the Guinness Poetry Award for *Another September*.
1959	Gary Snyder publishes his first collection, *Riprap*. Snyder's environmentally conscious poetry will later make him a member of the Green movement, a group of writers who advocate the need to repair and sustain the damaged environment.
1960	*The Colossus, and Other Poems*, Sylvia Plath's first poetry collection, is published.
1960	Donald Allen's anthology *The New American Poetry: 1945-1960*, is published. This collection contains the work of several poets associated with the Black Mountain School, including Charles Olson, Robert Creeley, Robert Duncan, Edward Dorn, Denise Levertov, Paul Blackburn, Joel Oppenheimer, and Hilda Morley.
1960	Delmore Schwartz receives the Bollingen Prize in Poetry.
1961	"Babii Yar," Yevgeny Yevtushenko's poem castigating Soviet anti-Semitism, is published.
1961	X. J. Kennedy receives the Lamont Poetry Selection (now the James Laughlin Award) for *Nude Descending a Staircase*.
1961	Randall Jarrell receives the National Book Award in Poetry for *The Woman at the Washington Zoo*.
1963	Hans Magnus Enzensberger receives the Georg Büchner Prize, the most important literary prize in Germany.
1964	*Rediscovery, and Other Poems*, the first book by Ghanaian writer Kofi Awoonor, is published.
1965	Philip Larkin receives the Queen's Gold Medal for Poetry.
1965	Marianne Moore is awarded the Academy of American Poets Fellowship.
1965	Henri Coulette receives the Lamont Poetry Selection (now the James Laughlin Award) for *The War of the Secret Agents*.
1965	Theodore Roethke receives the National Book Award in Poetry for *The Far Field*.
1966	*The Circle Game*, a collection of poems and the first critically acclaimed work by Canadian writer Margaret Atwood, is published.
1966	German-born poet Nelly Sachs is awarded the Nobel Prize in Literature.
1967	Anne Sexton is awarded the Pulitzer Prize in Poetry for *Live or Die*.
1968	Nikki Giovanni's first book of poetry, *Black Feeling, Black Talk*, is published to critical acclaim, with some praising her as the "Princess of Black Poetry."

1969	Stevie Smith receives the Queen's Gold Medal for Poetry.
1969	John Berryman receives the National Book Award in Poetry for *His Toy, His Dream, His Rest*.
1971	Chilean poet Pablo Neruda receives the Nobel Prize in Literature.
1972-1984	John Betjeman is poet laureate of the United Kingdom.
1973	Nigerian writer Chinua Achebe publishes *Christmas in Biafra, and Other Poems*.
1974-1976	Stanley Kunitz serves as America's poet laureate. He will hold this position again in 2000-2001.
1975	French-Canadian poet Anne Hèbert receives the Governor-General's Award for *Les Enfants du sabbat* (*Children of the Black Sabbath*, 1977).
1976	Jorge Guillén receives the Miguel de Cervantes Prize, which honors the lifetime achievement of an outstanding writer in the Spanish language.
1976	Australian poet A. D. Hope receives the Christopher Brennan Award in recognition of his lifetime literary achievement.
1978	Josephine Miles receives the Academy of American Poets Fellowship.
1978	Howard Nemerov is awarded the Pulitzer Prize in Poetry for *Collected Poems*.
1979	W. S. Merwin is awarded the Bollingen Prize in Poetry.
1980	Polish writer Czesław Miłosz is awarded the Nobel Prize in Literature.
1981	Carolyn Forché receives the Lamont Poetry Selection (now the James Laughlin Award) for *The Country Between Us*.
1985-1986	Gwendolyn Brooks serves as America's poet laureate.
1986	Wole Soyinka of Nigeria receives the Nobel Prize in Literature.
1986	Yves Bonnefoy is awarded the Goncourt Prize in Poetry by the Goncourt Literary Society of France.
1987	Joseph Brodsky, a Soviet writer exiled in the United States, receives the Nobel Prize in Literature. Brodsky wrote his poetry in Russian, and it was translated into many languages, with the English translations earning him high regard in the West.
1987	Philip Levine receives the Ruth Lilly Poetry Prize, awarded by the Poetry Foundation in recognition of lifetime achievement im English-language poetry.
1990	Mexican writer Octavio Paz is awarded the Nobel Prize in Literature.
1991	Donald Hall receives the Frost Medal from the Poetry Society of America for distinguished lifetime service to American poetry.
1992	West Indian writer Derek Walcott receives the Nobel Prize in Literature.
1992	Mary Oliver receives the National Book Award in Poetry for *New and Selected Poems*.
1993	Thom Gunn receives the Lenore Marshall Poetry Prize from the Academy of American Poets for *The Man with Night Sweats*.
January 20, 1993	Maya Angelou reads her poem "On the Pulse of Morning" during the inauguration of President Bill Clinton.
1994	*Poetry Canada Review* ceases publication. The magazine was founded in 1978 by Clifton Whiten in order to publish and review poetry from across Canada.
1994	Paul Muldoon receives the T. S. Eliot Prize for *The Annals of Chile*. The annual award is given to the best new poetry collection published in the United Kingdom or the Republic of Ireland.

1994	Irish poet Eavan Boland and American poets Linda Hogan and Jack Gilbert are among the five recipients of the Lannan Literary Award for Poetry.
1994	Brigit Pegeen Kelley receives the Lamont Poetry Selection (now the James Laughlin Award) for *Song*.
1995	Irish writer Seamus Heaney receives the Nobel Prize in Literature.
1995	Denise Levertov receives the Academy of American Poets Fellowship.
1997-2000	Robert Pinsky serves as America's poet laureate.
1998	Ted Hughes receives the T. S. Eliot Prize for *Birthday Letters*. The annual award is given to the best new poetry collection published in the United Kingdom or the Republic of Ireland.
1999	Maxine Kumin receives the Ruth Lilly Poetry Prize, awarded by the Poetry Foundation in recognition of lifetime achievement in English-language poetry.
2001	Louise Glück receives the Bollingen Prize in Poetry.
2001	Sonia Sanchez receives the Frost Medal from the Poetry Society of America for distinguished lifetime service to American poetry.
2001	Canadian poet Anne Carson receives the Griffin Poetry Prize for *Men in the Off Hours*.
September 15, 2001	Scott Simon of National Public Radio reads W. H. Auden's poem "September 1, 1939" (with many lines omitted). The poem is relevant to the terrorist attacks on September 11, 2001, and will be widely circulated and discussed.
2002	Sharon Olds receives the Academy of American Poets Fellowship.
2003	Li-Young Lee receives the Academy of American Poets Fellowship.
2003	Eamon Grennan receives the Lenore Marshall Poetry Prize from the Academy of American Poets for *Still Life with Waterfall*.
2006	Nicaraguan writer Claribel Alegría is awarded the Neustadt International Prize for her body of work.
2007	Robert Haas receives the National Book Award in Poetry for *Time and Materials*.
2007-2008	Charles Simic is America's poet laureate.
2009	Harryette Mullen receives the Academy of American Poets Fellowship.
2009	Allen Grossman receives the Bollingen Prize in Poetry.
2009	Linda Gregg receives the Lenore Marshall Poetry Prize from the Academy of American Poets for *All of It Singing: New and Selected Poems*.
January 20, 2009	Elizabeth Alexander reads her poem "Praise Song for the Day" at the inauguration of President Barack Obama.
July 1, 2010	The Library of Congress announces that W. S. Merwin will replace Kay Ryan as the seventeenth poet laureate of the United States. Merwin is the recipient of two Pulitzer Prizes, the National Book Award, and the Bollingen Prize in Poetry.

Rebecca Kuzins

MAJOR AWARDS

ACADEMY OF AMERICAN POETS FELLOWSHIP

The Academy of American Poets awards American poets with fellowships for distinguished poetic achievement. No awards were given between 1938 and 1945, or in 1949 and 1951.

1937: Edwin Markham
1946: Edgar Lee Masters
1947: Ridgely Torrence
1948: Percy MacKaye
1950: E. E. Cummings
1952: Padraic Colum
1953: Robert Frost
1954: Louise Townsend Nicholl and Oliver St. John Gogarty
1955: Rolfe Humphries
1956: William Carlos Williams
1957: Conrad Aiken
1958: Robinson Jeffers
1959: Louise Bogan
1960: Jesse Stuart
1961: Horace Gregory
1962: John Crowe Ransom
1963: Ezra Pound and Allen Tate
1964: Elizabeth Bishop
1965: Marianne Moore
1966: Archibald MacLeish and John Berryman
1967: Mark Van Doren
1968: Stanley Kunitz
1969: Richard Eberhart
1970: Howard Nemerov
1971: James Wright
1972: W. D. Snodgrass
1973: W. S. Merwin
1974: Léonie Adams
1975: Robert Hayden
1976: J. V. Cunningham
1977: Louis Coxe

1978: Josephine Miles
1979: May Swenson and Mark Strand
1980: Mona Van Duyn
1981: Richard Hugo
1982: John Frederick Nims and John Ashbery
1983: James Schuyler and Philip Booth
1984: Richmond Lattimore and Robert Francis
1985: Amy Clampitt and Maxine Kumin
1986: Irving Feldman and Howard Moss
1987: Josephine Jacobsen and Alfred Corn
1988: Donald Justice
1989: Richard Howard
1990: William Meredith
1991: J. D. McClatchy
1992: Adrienne Rich
1993: Gerald Stern
1994: David Ferry
1995: Denise Levertov
1996: Jay Wright
1997: John Haines
1998: Charles Simic
1999: Gwendolyn Brooks
2000: Lyn Hejinian
2001: Ellen Bryant Voigt
2002: Sharon Olds
2003: Li-Young Lee
2004: Jane Hirschfield
2005: Claudia Rankine
2006: Carl Phillips
2007: James McMichael
2008: Brigit Pegeen Kelly
2009: Harryette Mullen

ADONAIS PRIZE FOR POETRY

The Adonais Prize for Poetry, or Premio Adonáis de Poesía, is awarded annually in Spain to an unpublished Spanish-language poem from any country. Created in 1943 by the publishing house Biblioteca Hispánica, the prize was placed in the hands of Ediciones RIALP in 1946.

1943: José Suárez Carreño (Spain)—"Edad del hombre"; Vicente Gaos (Spain)—"Arcángel de mi noche"; Alfonso Moreno (Spain)—"El vuelo de la carne"

1944: no award

1945: no award

1946: no award

1947: José Hierro (Spain)—"Alegría"

1948: no award

1949: Ricardo Molina (Spain)—"Corimbo"

1950: José García Nieto (Spain)—"Dama de soledad"

1951: Lorenzo Gomis (Spain)—"El caballo"

1952: Antonio Fernández Spencer (Dominican Republic)—"Bajo la luz del día"

1953: Claudio Rodríguez (Spain)—"Don de la ebriedad"

1954: José Angel Valente (Spain)—"A modo de esperanza"

1955: Javier de Bengoechea (Spain)—"Hombre en forma de elegía"

1956: María Elvira Lacaci (Spain)—"Humana voz"

1957: Carlos Sahagún (Spain)—"Profecías del agua"

1958: Rafael Soto Verges (Spain)—"La agorera"

1959: Francisco Brines (Spain)—"Las brasas"

1960: Mariano Roldán (Spain)—"Hombre nuevo"

1961: Luis Feria (Spain)—"Conciencia"

1962: Jesús Hilario Tundidor (Spain)—"Junto a mi silencio"

1963: Félix Grande (Spain)—"Las piedras"

1964: Diego Jesús Jiménez (Spain)—"La ciudad"

1965: Joaquín Caro Romero (Spain)—"El tiempo en el espejo"

1966: Miguel Fernández (Spain)—"Sagrada materia"

1967: Joaquín Benito de Lucas (Spain)—"Materia de olvido"

1968: Roberto Sosa (Honduras)—"Los pobres"

1969: Angel García López (Spain)—"A flor de piel"

1970: Pureza Canelo (Spain)—"Lugar común"

1971: José Infante (Spain)—"Elegía y no"

1972: José Luis Alegre Cudos (Spain)—"Abstracción de Mío Cid con Cid Mío"

1973: José Antonio Moreno Jurado (Spain)—"Ditirambos para mi propia burla"

1974: Julia Castillo (Spain)—"Urgencias de un río interior"

1975: Angel Sánchez Pascual (Spain)—"Ceremonia de la inocencia"

1976: Jorge G. Aranguren (Spain)—"De fuegos, tigres, ríos"

1977: Eloy Sánchez Rosillo (Spain)—"Maneras de estar solo"

1978: Arcadio López-Casanova (Spain)—"La oscura potestad"

1979: Laureano Albán (Costa Rica)—"Herencia del otoño"

1980: Blanca Andreu (Spain)—"De una niña de provincias que vino a vivir en un Chagall"

1981: Miguel Velasco (Spain)—"Las berlinas del sueño"

1982: Luis García Montero (Spain)—"El jardín extranjero"

1983: Javier Peñas Navarro (Spain)—"Adjetivos sin agua, adjetivos con agua"

1984: Amalia Iglesias Serna (Spain)—"Un lugar para el fuego"

1985: Juan Carlos Mestre (Spain)—"Antífona de otoño en el valle del Bierzo"

1986: Juan María Calles (Spain)—"Silencio celeste"

1987: Francisco Serradilla (Spain)—"El bosque insobornable"

1988: Miguel Sánchez Gatell (Spain)—"La soledad absoluta de la tierra"

1989: Juan Carlos Marset (Spain)—"Puer profeta"

1990: Diego Doncel (Spain)—"El único umbral"

1991: Jesús Javier Lázaro Puebla (Spain)—"Canción para una amazona dormida"

1992: Juan Antonio Marín Alba (Spain)—"El horizonte de la noche"

1993: María Luisa Mora Alameda (Spain)—"Busca y captura"

1994: Ana Merino (Spain)—"Preparativos para un viaje"

1995: Eduardo Moga (Spain)—"La luz oída"

1996: Rosario Neira (Spain)—"No somos ángeles"

1997: Luis Martínez-Falero (Spain)—"Plenitud de la materia"

1998: Luis Enrique Belmonte (Venezuela)—"Inútil registro"

1999: Irene Sánchez Carrón (Spain)—"Escenas principales de actor secundario"

2000: Joaquín Pérez Azaústre (Spain)—"Una interpretación"

2001: José Antonio Gómez-Coronado (Spain)—"El triunfo de los días"

2002: Adrián González da Costa (Spain)—"Rua dos douradores"

2003: Javier Vela (Spain)—"La hora del crepúsculo"

2004: José Martínez Ros (Spain)—"La enfermedad"

2005: Carlos Vaquerizo (Spain)—"Fiera venganza del tiempo"

2006: Jorge Galán (pseudonym of George Alexander Portillo; El Salvador)—"Breve historia del Alba"

2007: Teresa Soto González (Spain)—"Un poemario (Imitación de Wislawa)"

2008: Rogelio Guedea (Mexico)—"Kora"

2009: Rubén Martín Díaz (Spain)—"El minuto interior"

ANDREI BELY PRIZE

The Andrei Bely Prize in Russian Literature was founded in 1978 and honors literature in various categories, such as poetry, prose, criticism, and humanitarian investigations. The prize is one ruble, a bottle of vodka, and an apple. The poetry winners are listed below.

1978: Victor Krivulin

1979: Elena Shwartz

1980: Vladimir Aleinikov

1981: Alexander Mironov

1982: no award

1983: Olga Sedakova

1984: no award

1985: Alexei Parschikov

1986: no award

1987: Genady Aigi

1988: Ivan Zhdanov

1989: no award

1990: no award

1991: Alexander Gornon

1992: no award

1993: no award

1994: Shamshad Abdulayev

1995: no award

1996: no award

1997: Victor Letsev

1998: Mikhail Eremin

1999: Elena Fanailova

2000: Yaroslav Mogutin

2001: Vasily Filipov

2002: Mikhail Gronas

2003: Mikhail Eisenberg

2004: Elizabeth Mnatsakonova

2005: Maria Stepanova

2006: Alexander Skidan

2007: Aleksei Tvetkov

2008: Vladimir Aristov and Sergei Kruglov

2009: Nikolai Kononov

BOLLINGEN PRIZE IN POETRY

Administered by Yale University Library, this award is given to an American poet. Awarded every two years since 1963.

1949: Ezra Pound

1950: Wallace Stevens

1951: John Crowe Ransom

1952: Marianne Moore

1953: Archibald MacLeish and William Carlos
    Williams
1954: W. H. Auden
1955: Léonie Adams and Louise Bogan
1956: Conrad Aiken
1957: Allen Tate
1958: E. E. Cummings
1959: Theodore Roethke
1960: Delmore Schwartz
1961: Yvor Winters
1962: John Hall Wheelock and Richard Eberhart
1963: Robert Frost
1965: Horace Gregory
1967: Robert Penn Warren
1969: John Berryman and Karl Shapiro
1971: Richard Wilbur and Mona Van Duyn
1973: James Merrill
1975: A. R. Ammons

1977: David Ignatow
1979: W. S. Merwin
1981: Howard Nemerov and May Swenson
1983: Anthony Hecht and John Hollander
1985: John Ashbery and Fred Chappell
1987: Stanley Kunitz
1989: Edgar Bowers
1991: Laura Riding Jackson and Donald Justice
1993: Mark Strand
1995: Kenneth Koch
1997: Gary Snyder
1999: Robert Creeley
2001: Louise Glück
2003: Adrienne Rich
2005: Jay Wright
2007: Frank Bidart
2009: Allen Grossman

CHRISTOPHER BRENNAN AWARD

First awarded in 1974, the Christopher Brennan Award (formerly the Robert Frost Prize) recognizes an Australian poet for lifetime achievement. The Fellowship of Australian Writers sponsors the award, which is named after the poet Christopher Brennan.

1974: R. D. Fitzgerald
1976: A. D. Hope
    Judith Wright
1977: Gwen Harwood
1979: Rosemary Dobson
1980: John Blight
1982: Vincent Buckley
1983: Bruce Dawe
    Les A. Murray
1988: Roland Robinson
1991: Elizabeth Riddell
1992: R. A. Simpson

1993: Geoffrey Dutton
1994: Judith Rodriguez
1995: Robert Adamson
    Thomas Shapcott
1996: Dorothy Hewett
1998: Jennifer Maiden
1999: Kevin Hart
2001: Dorothy Porter
2003: Philip Salom
2004: Kris Hemensley
2006: Geoff Page
2008: John Kinsella

GEORG BÜCHNER PRIZE

Given yearly by the Deutsche Akademie für Sprache und Dichtung to German-language authors, the Georg Büchner Prize is the most important literary prize in Germany. Created in 1923 to be given to visual artists, poets, actors, and singers, in 1951 it became a general literary prize. The list below includes only poets who have received the award.

1929: Carl Zuckmayer
1932: Albert H. Rausch
1945: Hans Schiebelhuth
1946: Fritz Usinger
1948: Hermann Heiss
1950: Elisabeth Langgässer
1951: Gottfried Benn
1954: Martin Kessel
1955: Marie Luise Kaschnitz
1956: Karl Krolow
1957: Erich Kästner
1959: Günter Eich
1960: Paul Celan
1963: Hans Magnus Enzensberger
1964: Ingeborg Bachmann
1965: Günter Grass
1969: Helmut Heissenbüttel

1970: Thomas Bernhard
1976: Heinz Piontek
1977: Reiner Kunze
1979: Ernst Meister (posthumous)
1984: Ernst Jandl
1985: Heiner Müller
1987: Erich Fried
1991: Wolf Biermann
1993: Peter Rühmkorf
1995: Durs Grünbein
1996: Sarah Kirsch
1997: Hans Carl Artmann
2000: Volker Braun
2001: Friederike Mayröcker
2002: Wolfgang Hilbig
2006: Oskar Pastior (posthumous)

MIGUEL DE CERVANTES PRIZE

Spain's ministry of culture awards its prize to honor the lifetime achievement of an outstanding writer in the Spanish language. Recipients, nominated by the language academies of Spanish-speaking countries, can be of any nationality. The list below includes only poets who have received the award.

1976: Jorge Guillén (Spain)
1978: Dámaso Alonso (Spain)
1979: Jorge Luis Borges (Argentina) and Gerardo
    Diego (Spain)
1981: Octavio Paz (Mexico)
1982: Luis Rosales (Spain)
1983: Rafael Alberti (Spain)
1990: Adolfo Bioy Casares (Argentina)
1992: Dulce María Loynaz (Cuba)

1996: José García Nieto (Spain)
1998: José Hierro (Spain)
2001: Álvaro Mutis (Colombia)
2002: José Jiménez Lozano (Spain)
2003: Gonzalo Rojas (Chile)
2005: Sergio Pitol (Mexico)
2006: Antonio Gamoneda (Spain)
2007: Juan Gelman (Argentina)
2009: José Emilio Pacheco (Mexico)

T. S. ELIOT PRIZE

Administered by the Poetry Book Society, this annual award is given to the best new poetry collection published in the United Kingdom or the Republic of Ireland.

1993: Ciaran Carson—*First Language*
1994: Paul Muldoon—*The Annals of Chile*
1995: Mark Doty—*My Alexandria*
1996: Les A. Murray—*Subhuman Redneck Poems*
1997: Don Paterson—*God's Gift to Women*
1998: Ted Hughes—*Birthday Letters*
1999: Hugo Williams—*Billy's Rain*
2000: Michael Longley—*The Weather in Japan*
2001: Anne Carson—*The Beauty of the Husband*

2002: Alice Oswald—*Dart*
2003: Don Paterson—*Landing Light*
2004: George Szirtes—*Reel*
2005: Carol Ann Duffy—*Rapture*
2006: Seamus Heaney—*District and Circle*
2007: Sean O'Brien—*The Drowned Book*
2008: Jen Hadfield—*Nigh-No-Place*
2009: Philip Gross—*The Water Table*

FLAIANO PRIZE

The Flaiano Prize (Premio Flaiano) is an Italian international award recognizing achievement in the fields of theater, cinema, television, and literature (novels, poetry, and literary criticism). Below are the winners of the Poetry Prize.

1986: Maria Luisa Spaziani
1987: Luciano Luisi
1988: Elio Filippo Accrocca
1989: Pietro Cimatti, Vivian Lamarque, Benito Sablone
1990: Edoardo Albinati, Dario Bellezza, Vico Faggi
1991: Renzo Barsacchi, Isabella Scalfaro, Massimo Scrignòli
1992: Marco Guzzi, Luciano Roncalli, Mario Trufelli
1993: Attilio Bertolucci, Cesare Vivaldi

1994: Piero Bigongiari
1995: Seamus Heaney
1996: Yves Bonnefoy
1997: Miroslav Holub
1998: Lawrence Ferlinghetti
1999: Yang Lian
2000: Derek Walcott
2001: Charles Tomlinson
2002: Adonis

FROST MEDAL

Awarded by the Poetry Society of America to a poet for distinguished lifetime service to American poetry. Awarded annually since 1984.

1930: Jessie Rittenhouse
1941: Robert Frost
1942: Edgar Lee Masters
1943: Edna St. Vincent Millay
1947: Gustav Davidson
1951: Wallace Stevens
1952: Carl Sandburg
1955: Leonora Speyer
1967: Marianne Moore

1971: Melville Cane
1974: John Hall Wheelock
1976: A. M. Sullivan
1984: Jack Stadler
1985: Robert Penn Warren
1986: Allen Ginsberg and Richard Eberhart
1987: Robert Creeley and Sterling Brown
1988: Carolyn Kizer
1989: Gwendolyn Brooks

1990: Denise Levertov and James Laughlin
1991: Donald Hall
1992: Adrienne Rich and David Ignatow
1993: William Stafford
1994: A. R. Ammons
1995: John Ashbery
1996: Richard Wilbur
1997: Josephine Jacobsen
1998: Stanley Kunitz
1999: Barbara Guest
2000: Anthony Hecht

2001: Sonia Sanchez
2002: Galway Kinnell
2003: Lawrence Ferlinghetti
2004: Richard Howard
2005: Marie Ponsot
2006: Maxine Kumin
2007: John Hollander
2008: Michael S. Harper
2009: X. J. Kennedy
2010: Lucille Clifton

GOLDEN WREATH AWARD

Struga Poetry Evenings, a major international poetry festival in Macedonia, presents its award to living poets for lifetime achievement.

1966: Robert Rozhdestvensky (Soviet Union)
1967: Bulat Okudzhava (Soviet Union)
1968: László Nagy (Hungary)
1969: Mak Dizdar (Bosnia and Herzegovina)
1970: Miodrag Pavlović (Serbia)
1971: W. H. Auden (United States)
1972: Pablo Neruda (Chile)
1973: Eugenio Montale (Italy)
1974: Fazıl Hüsnü Dağlarca (Turkey)
1975: Léopold Senghor (Senegal)
1976: Eugène Guillevic (France)
1977: Artur Lundkvist (Sweden)
1978: Rafael Alberti (Spain)
1979: Miroslav Krleža (Croatia)
1980: Hans Magnus Enzensberger (Germany)
1981: Blaže Koneski (Macedonia)
1982: Nichita Stănescu (Romania)
1983: Sachchidananda Hirananda Vatsyayan Agyey (India)
1984: Andrey Voznesensky (Soviet Union)
1985: Yannis Ritsos (Greece)
1986: Allen Ginsberg (United States)
1987: Tadeusz Różewicz (Poland)

1988: Desanka Maksimović (Serbia)
1989: Thomas W. Shapcott (Australia)
1990: Justo Jorge Padrón (Spain)
1991: Joseph Brodsky (United States)
1992: Ferenc Juhász (Hungary)
1993: Gennadiy Aygi (Chuvash Republic)
1994: Ted Hughes (England)
1995: Yehuda Amichai (Israel)
1996: Makoto Ooka (Japan)
1997: Adunis (Syria)
1998: Lu Yuan (China)
1999: Yves Bonnefoy (France)
2000: Edoardo Sanguineti (Italy)
2001: Seamus Heaney (Northern Ireland)
2002: Slavko Mihalić (Croatia)
2003: Tomas Tranströmer (Sweden)
2004: Vasco Graça Moura (Portugal)
2005: W. S. Merwin (United States)
2006: Nancy Morejón (Cuba)
2007: Mahmoud Darwish (Palestine)
2008: Fatos Arapi (Albania)
2009: Tomaž Šalamun (Slovenia)
2010: Ljabomir Levčev (Bulgaria)

GONCOURT PRIZE IN POETRY

The Goncourt Literary Society of France, also known as the Goncourt Academy, has awarded its prize in poetry since 1985.

1985: Claude Roy
1986: Yves Bonnefoy
1987: no award
1988: Eugène Guillevic
1989: Alain Bosquet
1990: Charles Le Quintrec
1991: Jean-Claude Renard
1992: Georges-Emmanuel Clancier
1993: no award
1994: no award
1995: Lionel Ray
1996: André Velter
1997: Maurice Chappaz

1998: Lorand Gaspar
1999: Jacques Réda
2000: Liliane Wouters
2001: Claude Esteban
2002: Andrée Chedid
2003: Philippe Jaccottet
2004: Jacques Chessex
2005: Charles Dobzynski
2006: Alain Jouffroy
2007: Marc Alyn
2008: Claude Vigée
2009: Abdellatif Laabi

GOVERNOR GENERAL'S LITERARY AWARDS

Presented by the Canada Council for the Arts annually to the best English-language and French-language books in seven categories, including poetry. This list comprises works published in English.

1981: F. R. Scott—*The Collected Poems of F. R. Scott*
1982: Phyllis Webb—*The Vision Tree: Selected Poems*
1983: David Donnell—*Settlements*
1984: Paulette Jiles—*Celestial Navigation*
1985: Fred Wah—*Waiting for Saskatchewan*
1986: Al Purdy—*The Collected Poems of Al Purdy*
1987: Gwendolyn MacEwen—*Afterworlds*
1988: Erin Mouré—*Furious*
1989: Heather Spears—*The Word for Sand*
1990: Margaret Avison—*No Time*
1991: Don McKay—*Night Field*
1992: Lorna Crozier—*Inventing the Hawk*
1993: Don Coles—*Forests of the Medieval World*
1994: Robert Hilles—*Cantos from a Small Room*
1995: Anne Szumigalski—*Voice*
1996: E. D. Blodgett—*Apostrophes: Woman at a Piano*

1997: Dionne Brand—*Land to Light On*
1998: Stephanie Bolster—*White Stone: The Alice Poems*
1999: Jan Zwicky—*Songs for Relinquishing the Earth*
2000: Don McKay—*Another Gravity*
2001: George Elliott Clarke—*Execution Poems*
2002: Roy Miki—*Surrender*
2003: Tim Lilburn—*Kill-Site*
2004: Roo Borson—*Short Journey Upriver Toward Oishida*
2005: Anne Compton—*Processional*
2006: John Pass—*Stumbling in the Bloom*
2007: Don Domanski—*All Our Wonder Unavenged*
2008: Jacob Scheier—*More to Keep Us Warm*
2009: David Zieroth—*The Fly in Autumn*

This list comprises works published in French.

1981: Michel Beaulieu—*Visages*
1982: Michel Savard—*Forages*

1983: Suzanne Paradis—*Un Goût de sel*
1984: Nicole Brossard—*Double Impression*

1985: André Roy—*Action writing*
1986: Cécile Cloutier—*L'Écouté*
1987: Fernand Ouellette—*Les Heures*
1988: Marcel Labine—*Papiers d'épidémie*
1989: Pierre DesRuisseaux—*Monème*
1990: Jean-Paul Daoust—*Les Cendres bleues*
1991: Madeleine Gagnon—*Chant pour un Québec lointain*
1992: Gilles Cyr—*Andromède attendra*
1993: Denise Desautels—*Le Saut de l'ange*
1994: Fulvio Caccia—*Aknos*
1995: Émile Martel—*Pour orchestre et poète seul*
1996: Serge Patrice—*Le Quatuor de l'errance,* followed by *La Traversée du désert*
1997: Pierre Nepveu—*Romans-fleuves*
1998: Suzanne Jacob—*La Part de feu,* preceded by *Le Deuil de la rancune*
1999: Herménégilde Chiasson—*Conversations*
2000: Normand de Bellefeuille—*La Marche de l'aveugle sans son chien*
2001: Paul Chanel Malenfant—*Des Ombres portées*
2002: Robert Dickson—*Humains paysages en temps de paix relative*
2003: Pierre Nepveu—*Lignes aériennes*
2004: André Brochu—*Les jours à vif*
2005: Jean-Marc Desgent—*Vingtièmes siècles*
2006: Hélène Dorion—*Ravir: Les lieux*
2007: Serge Patrice Thibodeau—*Seul on est*
2008: Michel Pleau—*La Lenteur du monde*
2009: Hélène Monette—*Thérèse pour joie et orchestre*

THE GRIFFIN POETRY PRIZE

The Griffin Poetry Prize is given by Canada each year, beginning in 2001, to collections by one living Canadian poet and one living international poet writing in the English language. Lifetime Recognition Awards to poets from all countries and languages were added in 2006.

2001: Anne Carson—*Men in the Off Hours* (Canada); Nikolai Popov and Heather McHugh, translation of *Glottal Stop: 101 Poems by Paul Celan* (international)
2002: Christian Bök—*Eunoia* (Canada); Alice Notley—*Disobedience* (international)
2003: Margaret Avison—*Concrete and Wild Carrot* (Canada); Paul Muldoon—*Moy Sand and Gravel* (international)
2004: Anne Simpson—*Loop* (Canada); August Kleinzahler—*The Strange Hours Travelers Keep* (international)
2005: Roo Borson—*Short Journey Upriver Toward Oishida* (Canada); Charles Simic—*Selected Poems, 1963-2003* (international)
2006: Sylvia Legris—*Nerve Squall* (Canada); Kamau Brathwaite—*Born to Slow Horses* (international); Lifetime Recognition Award, Robin Blaser
2007: Don McKay—*Strike/Slip* (Canada); Charles Wright—*Scar Tissue* (international); Lifetime Recognition Award, Tomas Tranströmer
2008: Robin Blaser—*The Holy Forest: Collected Poems of Robin Blaser* (Canada); John Ashbery—*Notes from the Air: Selected Later Poems* (international); Lifetime Recognition Award, Ko Un
2009: A. F. Moritz—*The Sentinel* (Canada); C. D. Wright—*Rising, Falling, Hovering* (international); Lifetime Recognition Award, Hans Magnus Enzensberger
2010: Karen Solie—*Pigeon* (Canada); Eilean Ni Chuilleanain—*The Sun-fish* (international); Lifetime Recognition Award, Adrienne Rich

JNANPITH AWARD

The Indian literary and research organization Bharatiya Jnanpith presents its annual award for lifetime achievement in literature, including poetry, written by an Indian citizen in any of several Indian languages.

1965: G. Sankara Kurup
1966: Tarashankar Bandopadhyaya
1967: Kuppali V. Puttappa and Umashankar Joshi
1968: Sumitranandan Pant
1969: Firaq Gorakhpuri
1970: Viswanatha Satyanarayana
1971: Bishnu Dey
1972: Ramdhari Singh Dinkar
1973: Dattatreya R. Bendre and Gopinath Mohanty
1974: Vishnu S. Khandekar
1975: P. V. Akilandam
1976: Ashapurna Devi
1977: K. Shivaram Karanth
1978: Sachchidananda H. V. Ajneya
1979: Birendra K. Bhattacharya
1980: S. K. Pottekkatt
1981: Amrita Pritam
1982: Mahadevi Varma
1983: Maasti V. Ayengar
1984: Thakazhi S. Pillai
1985: Pannalal Patel
1986: Sachidananda Routroy

1987: V. V. S. Kusumagraj
1988: C. Narayana Reddy
1989: Qurratulain Hyder
1990: V. K. Gokak
1991: Subhash Mukhopadhyaya
1992: Naresh Mehta
1993: Sitakant Mahapatra
1994: U. R. Anantha Murthy
1995: M. T. Vasudevan Nair
1996: Mahasweta Devi
1997: Ali Sardar Jafri
1998: Girish Karnad
1999: Nirmal Verma and Gurdial Singh
2000: Indira Goswami
2001: Rajendra Shah
2002: D. Jayakantan
2003: Vinda Karandikar
2004: Rahman Rahi
2005: Kunwar Narain
2006: Ravindra Kelekar and Satya Vrat Shasti
2007: Akhlaq Mohammed Khan (Shahryar)
2008: O. N. V. Kurap

LANNAN LITERARY AWARD FOR POETRY

The Lannan Literary Awards are a series of awards and literary fellowships given out in various fields by the Lannan Foundation. Established in 1989, the awards "honor both established and emerging writers whose work is of exceptional quality."

1989: Cid Corman, George Evans, Peter Levitt
1990: Derek Mahon, Seamus Heaney
1991: William Bronk, Chrystos, Pattiann Rogers, Herbert Morris
1992: A. R. Ammons, Thomas Centolella, Killarney Clary, Suzanne Gardinier, Susan Mitchell, Luis J. Rodriguez
1993: Cyrus Cassells, Denise Levertov, Benjamin Alire Saenz
1994: Simon Armitage, Eavan Boland, Linda Hogan, Jack Gilbert, Richard Kenney

1995: Hayden Carruth, Carol Ann Duffy, Arthur Sze, Li-Young Lee
1996: Anne Carson, Lucille Clifton, William Trevor, Donald Justice
1997: Ken Smith
1998: Frank Bidart, Jon Davis, Mary Oliver
1999: Dennis O'Driscoll, C. D. Wright, Louise Glück
2000: Herbert Morris, Jay Wright
2001: no award
2002: Alan Dugan, Peter Dale Scott
2003: no award

2004: Peter Reading
2005: Pattiann Rogers
2006: Bruce Weigl

2007: no award
2008: August Kleinzahler
2009: no award

JAMES LAUGHLIN AWARD

The Academy of American Poets gives this annual award to a poet for the publication of an outstanding second poetry collection. Originally known as the Lamont Poetry Selection, the name was changed in 1995 to honor poet and publisher James Laughlin.

1954: Constance Carrier—*The Middle Voice*
1955: Donald Hall—*Exiles and Marriages*
1956: Philip Booth—*Letter from a Distant Land*
1957: Daniel Berrigan, S. J.—*Time Without Number*
1958: Ned O'Gorman—*The Night of the Hammer*
1959: Donald Justice—*The Summer Anniversaries*
1960: Robert Mezey—*The Lovemaker*
1961: X. J. Kennedy—*Nude Descending a Staircase*
1962: Edward Field—*Stand Up, Friend, with Me*
1963: no award
1964: Adrien Stoutenberg—*Heroes, Advise Us*
1965: Henri Coulette—*The War of the Secret Agents*
1966: Kenneth O. Hanson—*The Distance Anywhere*
1967: James Scully—*The Marches*
1968: Jane Cooper—*The Weather of Six Mornings*
1969: Marvin Bell—*A Probable Volume of Dreams*
1970: William Harmon—*Treasury Holiday*
1971: Stephen Dobyns—*Concurring Beasts*
1972: Peter Everwine—*Collecting the Animals*
1973: Marilyn Hacker—*Presentation Piece*
1974: John Balaban—*After Our War*
1975: Lisel Mueller—*The Private Life*
1976: Larry Levis—*The Afterlife*
1977: Gerald Stern—*Lucky Life*
1978: Ai—*Killing Floor*
1979: Frederick Seidel—*Sunrise*
1980: Michael Van Walleghen—*More Trouble with the Obvious*
1981: Carolyn Forché—*The Country Between Us*
1982: Margaret Gibson—*Long Walks in the Afternoon*
1983: Sharon Olds—*The Dead and the Living*

1984: Philip Schultz—*Deep Within the Ravine*
1985: Cornelius Eady—*Victims of the Latest Dance Craze*
1986: Jane Shore—*The Minute Hand*
1987: Garrett Kaoru Hongo—*The River of Heaven*
1988: Mary Jo Salter—*Unfinished Painting*
1989: Minnie Bruce Pratt—*Crime Against Nature*
1990: Li-Young Lee—*The City in Which I Love You*
1991: Susan Wood—*Campo Santo*
1992: Kathryn Stripling Byer—*Wildwood Flower*
1993: Rosanna Warren—*Stained Glass*
1994: Brigit Pegeen Kelly—*Song*
1995: Ralph Angel—*Neither World*
1996: David Rivard—*Wise Poison*
1997: Tony Hoagland—*Donkey Gospel*
1998: Sandra Alcosser—*Except by Nature*
1999: Tory Dent—*HIV, Mon Amour*
2000: Liz Waldner—*A Point Is That Which Has No Point*
2001: Peter Johnson—*Miracles and Mortifications*
2002: Karen Volkman—*Spar*
2003: Vijay Seshadri—*The Long Meadow*
2004: Jeff Clark—*Music and Suicide*
2005: Barbara Jane Reyes—*Poeta en San Francisco*
2006: Tracy K. Smith—*Duende*
2007: Brenda Shaughnessy—*Human Dark with Sugar*
2008: Rusty Morrison—*the true keeps calm biding its story*
2009: Jennifer K. Sweeney—*How to Live on Bread and Music*

GRACE LEVEN PRIZE FOR POETRY

The Grace Leven Prize for Poetry was established in 1947 by William Baylebridge in the name of his benefactor. The award is given to "the best volume of poetry published in the preceding twelve months by a writer either Australian-born, or naturalised in Australia and resident in Australia for not less than ten years."

1947: Nan McDonald—*Pacific Sea*

1948: Francis Webb—*A Drum for Ben Boyd*

1949: Judith Wright—*Woman to Man*

1951: Rex Ingamells—*The Great South Land*

1952: R. D. Fitzgerald—*Between Two Tides*

1953: Roland Robinson—*Tumult of the Swans*

1954: John Thompson—*Thirty Poems*

1955: A. D. Hope—*The Wandering Islands*

1957: Leonard Mann—*Elegaic, and Other Poems*

1958: Geoffrey Dutton—*Antipodes in Shoes*

1959: R. D. Fitzgerald—*The Wind at Your Door: A Poem*

1960: Colin Thiele—*Man in a Landscape*

1961: Thomas Shapcott—*Time on Fire*

1962: R. D. Fitzgerald—*South-most Tree*

1963: Ian Mudie—*The North-Bound Rider*

1964: David Rowbotham—*All the Room*

1965: Les Murray and Geoffrey Lehmann—*The Ilex Tree*

1966: William Hart-Smith—*The Talking Clothes: Poems*

1967: Douglas Stewart—*Collected Poems, 1936-1967*

1968: David Campbell—*Selected Poems, 1942-1968*

1969: Randolph Stow—*A Counterfeit Silence: Selected Poems*

1970: Bruce Beaver—*Letters to Live Poets*

1971: James McAuley—*Collected Poems, 1936-1970*; Judith Wright—*Collected Poems, 1942-1970*

1972: Peter Skrzynecki—*Head-waters*

1973: Rodney Hall—*A Soapbox Omnibus*

1974: David Malouf—*Neighbours in a Thicket: Poems*

1975: Gwen Harwood—*Selected Poems* (1975)

1976: John Blight—*Selected Poems, 1939-1975*

1977: Robert Adamson—*Selected Poems*

1978: Bruce Dawe—*Sometimes Gladness: Collected Poems, 1954-1978*

1979: David Campbell—*The Man in the Honeysuckle*

1980: Les Murray—*The Boys Who Stole the Funeral*

1981: Geoffrey Lehmann—*Nero's Poems: Translations of the Public and Private Poems of the Emperor Nero*

1982: Vivian Smith—*Tide Country*

1983: Peter Porter—*Collected Poems*

1984: Rosemary Dobson—*The Three Fates, and Other Poems*

1985: Robert Gray—*Selected Poems, 1963-1983* Chris Wallace-Crabbe—*The Amorous Cannibal*

1986: Rhyll McMaster—*Washing the Money: Poems with Photographs*

1987: Elizabeth Riddell—*Occasions of Birds, and Other Poems*

1988: John Tranter—*Under Berlin*

1989: Dorothy Hewett—*A Tremendous World in Her Head*

1990: Les Murray—*Dog Fox Field*

1992: Kevin Hart—*Peniel* Gary Catalano—*Empire of Grass*

1993: Philip Hodgins—*The End of the Season*

1995: Kevin Hart—*New and Selected Poems*; Jemal Sharah—*Path of Ghosts: Poems, 1986-93*

1997: John Kinsella—*The Undertow: New and Selected Poems*

2001: Geoff Page—*Darker and Lighter*

2002: Kate Lilley—*Versary*

2003: Stephen Edgar—*Lost in the Foreground*

2004: Luke Davies—*Totem*

2005: Noel Rowe—*Next to Nothing*

2006: Alan Gould—*The Past Completes Me: Selected Poems, 1973-2003*

2007: Robert Adamson—*The Goldfinches of Baghdad*

2008: Alan Wearne—*The Australian Popular Song Book*

2010: Judith Beveridge—*Storm and Honey*

RUTH LILLY POETRY PRIZE

This annual prize, awarded by the Poetry Foundation, recognizes lifetime achievement in English-language poetry.

1986: Adrienne Rich
1987: Philip Levine
1988: Anthony Hecht
1989: Mona Van Duyn
1990: Hayden Carruth
1991: David Wagoner
1992: John Ashbery
1993: Charles Wright
1994: Donald Hall
1995: A. R. Ammons
1996: Gerald Stern
1997: William Matthews
1998: W. S. Merwin

1999: Maxine Kumin
2000: Carl Dennis
2001: Yusef Komunyakaa
2002: Lisel Mueller
2003: Linda Pastan
2004: Kay Ryan
2005: C. K. Williams
2006: Richard Wilbur
2007: Lucille Clifton
2008: Gary Snyder
2009: Fanny Howe
2010: Eleanor Ross Taylor

LENORE MARSHALL POETRY PRIZE

Awarded by the Academy of American Poets annually to a poet for the publication in the United States of an outstanding poetry collection.

1975: Cid Corman—*O/I*
1976: Denise Levertov—*The Freeing of the Dust*
1977: Philip Levine—*The Names of the Lost*
1978: Allen Tate—*Collected Poems, 1919-1976*
1979: Hayden Carruth—*Brothers, I Loved You All*
1980: Stanley Kunitz—*The Poems of Stanley Kunitz, 1928-1978*
1981: Sterling A. Brown—*The Collected Poems of Sterling A. Brown*
1982: John Logan—*The Bridge of Chance: Poems, 1974-1980*
1983: George Starbuck—*The Argot Merchant Disaster*
1984: Josephine Miles—*Collected Poems, 1930-1983*
1985: John Ashbery—*A Wave*
1986: Howard Moss—*New Selected Poems*
1987: Donald Hall—*The Happy Man*
1988: Josephine Jacobsen—*The Sisters: New and Selected Poems*
1989: Thomas McGrath—*Selected Poems, 1938-1988*
1990: Michael Ryan—*God Hunger*
1991: John Haines—*New Poems, 1980-1988*
1992: Adrienne Rich—*An Atlas of the Difficult World*

1993: Thom Gunn—*The Man with Night Sweats*
1994: W. S. Merwin—*Travels*
1995: Marilyn Hacker—*Winter Numbers*
1996: Charles Wright—*Chickamauga*
1997: Robert Pinsky—*The Figured Wheel: New and Collected Poems, 1966-1996*
1998: Mark Jarman—*Questions for Ecclesiastes*
1999: Wanda Coleman—*Bathwater Wine*
2000: David Ferry—*Of No Country I Know: New and Selected Poems and Translations*
2001: Fanny Howe—*Selected Poems*
2002: Madeline DeFrees—*Blue Dusk*
2003: Eamon Grennan—*Still Life with Waterfall*
2004: Donald Revell—*My Mojave*
2005: Anne Winters—*The Displaced of Capital*
2006: Eleanor Lerman—*Our Post-Soviet History Unfolds*
2007: Alice Notley—*Grave of Light: New and Selected Poems, 1970-2005*
2008: Henri Cole—*Blackbird and Wolf*
2009: Linda Gregg—*All of It Singing: New and Selected Poems*

MASAOKA SHIKI INTERNATIONAL HAIKU PRIZE

Beginning in 2000, the Haiku Grand Prize and several Haiku Prizes have been given every two years at the International Haiku Symposium to raise international awareness of the poet Masaoka Shiki and his chosen form, the haiku. Ehime Prefecture, birthplace of the poet, sponsors the award.

2000: Grand Prize — Yves Bonnefoy (France); Haiku Prize — Li Mang (China), Bart Mesotten (Belgium), Robert Speiss (United States), Kazuo Sato (Japan)

2002: Grand Prize — Cor van den Neuvel (United States); Haiku Prize — Satya Bhushan Verma (India), Shigeki Wada (Japan)

2004: Grand Prize — Gary Snyder (United States);

Haiku Prize — Hidekazu Masuda (Brazil), Ko Reishi (Taiwan), Bansei Tsukushi (Japan)

2006: No awards

2008: Grand Prize — Tota Kaneko (Japan); Haiku Prize — Biwao Kawahara (Japan); Sweden Award: Sonoo Uchida (Japan), O-Young Lee (South Korea)

NATIONAL BOOK AWARD IN POETRY

Awarded by the National Book Foundation to an American poet for the publication of the best book of poetry during the year. Not awarded from 1984 to 1990.

1950: William Carlos Williams—*Paterson: Book III and Selected Poems*

1951: Wallace Stevens—*The Auroras of Autumn*

1952: Marianne Moore—*Collected Poems*

1953: Archibald MacLeish—*Collected Poems, 1917-1952*

1954: Conrad Aiken—*Collected Poems*

1955: Wallace Stevens—*The Collected Poems of Wallace Stevens*

1956: W. H. Auden—*The Shield of Achilles*

1957: Richard Wilbur—*Things of the World*

1958: Robert Penn Warren—*Promises: Poems, 1954-1956*

1959: Theodore Roethke—*Words for the Wind*

1960: Robert Lowell—*Life Studies*

1961: Randall Jarrell—*The Woman at the Washington Zoo*

1962: Alan Dugan—*Poems*

1963: William Stafford—*Traveling Through the Dark*

1964: John Crowe Ransom—*Selected Poems*

1965: Theodore Roethke—*The Far Field*

1966: James Dickey—*Buckdancer's Choice: Poems*

1967: James Merrill—*Nights and Days*

1968: Robert Bly—*The Light Around the Body*

1969: John Berryman—*His Toy, His Dream, His Rest*

1970: Elizabeth Bishop—*The Complete Poems*

1971: Mona Van Duyn—*To See, to Take*

1972: Frank O'Hara—*The Collected Poems of Frank O'Hara* and Howard Moss—*Selected Poems*

1973: A. R. Ammons—*Collected Poems, 1951-1971*

1974: Allen Ginsberg—*The Fall of America: Poems of These States* and Adrienne Rich—*Diving into the Wreck: Poems, 1971-1972*

1975: Marilyn Hacker—*Presentation Piece*

1976: John Ashbery—*Self-Portrait in a Convex Mirror*

1977: Richard Eberhart—*Collected Poems, 1930-1976*

1978: Howard Nemerov—*The Collected Poems of Howard Nemerov*

1979: James Merrill—*Mirabell: Book of Numbers*

1980: Philip Levine—*Ashes*

1981: Lisel Mueller—*The Need to Hold Still*

1982: William Bronk—*Life Supports: New and Collected Poems*

1983: Galway Kinnell—*Selected Poems* and Charles Wright—*Country Music: Selected Early Poems*

1991: Philip Levine—*What Work Is*

1992: Mary Oliver—*New and Selected Poems*

1993: A. R. Ammons—*Garbage*

1994: James Tate—*A Worshipful Company of Fletchers*

1995: Stanley Kunitz—*Passing Through: The Later Poems*

1996: Hayden Carruth—*Scrambled Eggs and Whiskey: Poems, 1991-1995*

1997: William Meredith—*Effort at Speech: New and Selected Poems*

1998: Gerald Stern—*This Time: New and Selected Poems*

1999: Ai—*Vice: New and Selected Poems*

2000: Lucille Clifton—*Blessing the Boats: New and Selected Poems, 1988-2000*

2001: Alan Dugan—*Poems Seven: New and Complete Poetry*

2002: Ruth Stone—*In the Next Galaxy*

2003: C. K. Williams—*The Singing*

2004: Jean Valentine—*Door in the Mountain: New and Collected Poems, 1965-2003*

2005: W. S. Merwin—*Migration: New and Selected Poems*

2006: Nathaniel Mackey—*Splay Anthem*

2007: Robert Hass—*Time and Materials*

2008: Mark Doty—*Fire to Fire: New and Collected Poems*

2009: Keith Waldrop—*Transcendental Studies: A Trilogy*

Neustadt International Prize for Literature

Awarded biennially since 1970, this award sponsored by the University of Oklahoma honors writers for a body of work. The list below includes only poets who have received the award.

1970: Giuseppe Ungaretti (Italy)

1974: Francis Ponge (France)

1976: Elizabeth Bishop (United States)

1978: Czesław Miłosz (Poland)

1980: Josef Škvorecky (Czechoslovakia/Canada)

1982: Octavio Paz (Mexico)

1984: Paavo Haavikko (Finland)

1990: Tomas Tranströmer (Sweden)

1992: João Cabral de Melo Neto (Brazil)

1994: Edward Kamau Brathwaite (Barbados)

2000: David Malouf (Australia)

2002: Alvaro Mutis (Colombia)

2004: Adam Zagajewski (Poland)

2006: Claribel Alegría (Nicaragua/El Salvador)

2010: Duo Duo (China)

New South Wales Premier's Literary Awards

Established in 1979, the New South Wales Premier's Literary Awards includes the Kenneth Slessor Prize for poetry.

1980: David Campbell—*Man in the Honeysuckle*

1981: Alan Gould—*Astral Sea*

1982: Fay Zwicky—*Kaddish, and Other Poems*

1983: Vivian Smith—*Tide Country*

1984: Les A. Murray—*The People's Other World*

1985: Kevin Hart—*Your Shadow*

1986: Robert Gray—*Selected Poems, 1963-83*

1987: Philip Hodgins—*Blood and Bone*

1988: Judith Beveridge—*The Domesticity of Giraffes*

1989: John Tranter—*Under Berlin*

1990: Robert Adamson—*The Clean Dark*

1991: Jennifer Maiden—*The Winter Baby*

1992: Elizabeth Riddell—*Selected Poems*

1993: Les A. Murray—*Translations from the Natural World*

1994: Barry Hill—*Ghosting William Buckley*

1995: Peter Boyle—*Coming Home from the World*

1996: Eric Beach—*Weeping for Lost Babylon*; J. S. Harry—*Selected Poems*

1997: Anthony Lawrence—*The Viewfinder*

1999: Lee Cataldi—*Race Against Time*

2000: Jennifer Maiden—*Mines*

2001: Ken Taylor—*Africa*
2002: Alan Wearne—*The Lovemakers*
2003: Jill Jones—*Screens Jets Heaven: New and Selected Poems*
2004: Pam Brown—*Dear Deliria: New and Selected Poems*

2005: Samuel Wagan Watson—*Smoke Encrypted Whispers*
2006: Jaya Savige—*Latecomers*
2007: John Tranter—*Urban Myths: 210 Poems*
2008: Kathryn Lomer—*Two Kinds of Silence*
2009: L. K. Holt—*Man Wolf Man*

NIKE AWARD

Established in 1997 and sponsored by the Polish newspaper Gazeta Wyborcza *and the consulting company NICOM, the NIKE Literary Award (Nagroda Literacka NIKE) is given to the best book by a single living author writing in Polish published the previous year. It is open to works in all literary genres. Only poetry collections that have received the jury award are listed below.*

1998: Czesław Miłosz—*Piesek przydrożny* (Road-side Dog)
1999: Stanisław Barańczak—*Chirurgiczna precyzja* (surgical precision)
2000: Tadeusz Różewicz—*Matka odchodzi* (mother is leaving)

2003: Jarosław Marek Rymkiewicz—*Zachód słonca w Milanówku* (sunset in Milanówek)
2009: Eugeniusz Tkaczyszyn—*Dycki for Piosenka o zaleznosciach i uzaleznieniach* (song of dependency and addiction)

NOBEL PRIZE IN LITERATURE

Awarded annually since 1901, this prize is given to an author for his or her entire body of literary work. The list below includes only the poets who have been so honored.

1901: Sully Prudhomme
1906: Giosuè Carducci
1907: Rudyard Kipling
1913: Rabindranath Tagore
1923: William Butler Yeats
1945: Gabriela Mistral
1946: Hermann Hesse
1948: T. S. Eliot
1956: Juan Ramón Jiménez
1958: Boris Pasternak
1959: Salvatore Quasimodo
1960: Saint-John Perse
1963: George Seferis
1966: Nelly Sachs
1969: Samuel Beckett

1971: Pablo Neruda
1974: Harry Martinson
1975: Eugenio Montale
1977: Vicente Aleixandre
1979: Odysseus Elytis
1980: Czesław Miłosz
1984: Jaroslav Seifert
1986: Wole Soyinka
1987: Joseph Brodsky
1990: Octavio Paz
1992: Derek Walcott
1995: Seamus Heaney
1996: Wisława Szymborska
2005: Harold Pinter
2009: Herta Müller

PEN/VOELCKER AWARD FOR POETRY

The PEN/Voelcker Award for Poetry is given biennially to an American poet whose distinguished body of work represents a notable and accomplished presence in U.S. literature.

1994: Martín Espada
1996: Franz Wright
1998: C. K. Williams
2000: Heather McHugh

2002: Frederick Seidel
2004: Robert Pinsky
2006: Linda Gregg
2008: Kimiko Hahn

POET LAUREATE CONSULTANT IN POETRY

An appointment is given through the Library of Congress to a poet who then serves as the United States' official poet, or poet laureate.

1937-1941: Joseph Auslander
1943-1944: Allen Tate
1944-1945: Robert Penn Warren
1945-1946: Louise Bogan
1946-1947: Karl Shapiro
1947-1948: Robert Lowell
1948-1949: Léonie Adams
1949-1950: Elizabeth Bishop
1950-1952: Conrad Aiken
1952: William Carlos Williams (did not serve)
1956-1958: Randall Jarrell
1958-1959: Robert Frost
1959-1961: Richard Eberhart
1961-1963: Louis Untermeyer
1963-1964: Howard Nemerov
1964-1965: Reed Whittemore
1965-1966: Stephen Spender
1966-1968: James Dickey
1968-1970: William Jay Smith
1970-1971: William Stafford
1971-1973: Josephine Jacobsen
1973-1974: Daniel Hoffman
1974-1976: Stanley Kunitz
1976-1978: Robert Hayden
1978-1980: William Meredith
1981-1982: Maxine Kumin

1982-1984: Anthony Hecht
1984-1985: Robert Fitzgerald (limited by health) and Reed Whittemore (interim consultant)
1985-1986: Gwendolyn Brooks
1986-1987: Robert Penn Warren (first poet to be designated Poet Laureate Consultant in Poetry)
1987-1988: Richard Wilbur
1988-1990: Howard Nemerov
1990-1991: Mark Strand
1991-1992: Joseph Brodsky
1992-1993: Mona Van Duyn
1993-1995: Rita Dove
1995-1997: Robert Hass
1997-2000: Robert Pinsky
1999-2000: Rita Dove, Louise Glück, and W. S. Merwin (special consultants for Library of Congress bicentennial)
2000-2001: Stanley Kunitz
2001-2003: Billy Collins
2003-2004: Louise Glück
2004-2006: Ted Kooser
2006-2007: Donald Hall
2007-2008: Charles Simic
2008-2010: Kay Ryan
2010-   : W. S. Merwin

POET LAUREATE OF THE UNITED KINGDOM OF GREAT BRITAIN AND NORTHERN IRELAND

The British Poet Laureate, originally an appointment for life, is now a ten-year term. John Dryden was the first official laureate. Carol Ann Duffy, in 2009, became the first woman appointed to the position.

1591-1599: Edmund Spenser
1599-1619: Samuel Daniel
1619-1637: Ben Jonson
1638-1668: William Davenant
1668-1689: John Dryden
1689-1692: Thomas Shadwell
1692-1715: Nahum Tate
1715-1718: Nicholas Rowe
1718-1730: Laurence Eusden
1730-1757: Colley Cibber
1757-1785: William Whitehead
1785-1790: Thomas Warton

1790-1813: Henry James Pye
1813-1843: Robert Southey
1843-1850: William Wordsworth
1850-1892: Alfred, Lord Tennyson
1896-1913: Alfred Austin
1913-1930: Robert Bridges
1930-1967: John Masefield
1967-1972: Cecil Day Lewis
1972-1984: Sir John Betjeman
1984-1998: Ted Hughes
1999-2009: Andrew Motion
2009-   : Carol Ann Duffy

PULITZER PRIZE IN POETRY

Awarded by Columbia University's Graduate School of Journalism to honor an American poet who has published a distinguished collection of poetry.

1918: Sara Teasdale—*Love Songs*
1919: Margaret Widdemer—*Old Road to Paradise* and Carl Sandburg—*Cornhuskers*
1920: no award
1921: no award
1922: Edwin Arlington Robinson—*Collected Poems*
1923: Edna St. Vincent Millay—*The Ballad of the Harp-Weaver*
1924: Robert Frost—*New Hampshire: A Poem with Notes and Grace Notes*
1925: Edwin Arlington Robinson—*The Man Who Died Twice*
1926: Amy Lowell—*What's O'Clock*
1927: Leonora Speyer—*Fiddler's Farewell*
1928: Edwin Arlington Robinson—*Tristram*
1929: Stephen Vincent Benét—*John Brown's Body*
1930: Conrad Aiken—*Selected Poems*
1931: Robert Frost—*Collected Poems*
1932: George Dillon—*The Flowering Stone*
1933: Archibald MacLeish—*Conquistador*
1934: Robert Hillyer—*Collected Verse*
1935: Audrey Wurdemann—*Bright Ambush*

1936: Robert P. Tristram Coffin—*Strange Holiness*
1937: Robert Frost—*A Further Range*
1938: Marya Zaturenska—*Cold Morning Sky*
1939: John Gould Fletcher—*Selected Poems*
1940: Mark Van Doren—*Selected Poems*
1941: Leonard Bacon—*Sunderland Capture*
1942: William Rose Benet—*The Dust Which Is God*
1943: Robert Frost—*A Witness Tree*
1944: Stephen Vincent Benét—*Western Star*
1945: Karl Shapiro—*V-Letter and Other Poems*
1946: no award
1947: Robert Lowell—*Lord Weary's Castle*
1948: W. H. Auden—*The Age of Anxiety*
1949: Peter Viereck—*Terror and Decorum*
1950: Gwendolyn Brooks—*Annie Allen*
1951: Carl Sandburg—*Complete Poems*
1952: Marianne Moore—*Collected Poems*
1953: Archibald MacLeish—*Collected Poems, 1917-1952*
1954: Theodore Roethke—*The Waking*
1955: Wallace Stevens—*Collected Poems*
1956: Elizabeth Bishop—*Poems: North and South*

1957: Richard Wilbur—*Things of This World*

1958: Robert Penn Warren—*Promises: Poems, 1954-1956*

1959: Stanley Kunitz—*Selected Poems, 1928-1958*

1960: W. D. Snodgrass—*Heart's Needle*

1961: Phyllis McGinley—*Times Three: Selected Verse from Three Decades*

1962: Alan Dugan—*Poems*

1963: William Carlos Williams—*Pictures from Breughel*

1964: Louis Simpson—*At the End of the Open Road*

1965: John Berryman—*Seventy-seven Dream Songs*

1966: Richard Eberhart—*Selected Poems*

1967: Anne Sexton—*Live or Die*

1968: Anthony Hecht—*The Hard Hours*

1969: George Oppen—*Of Being Numerous*

1970: Richard Howard—*Untitled Subjects*

1971: W. S. Merwin—*The Carrier of Ladders*

1972: James Wright—*Collected Poems*

1973: Maxine Kumin—*Up Country*

1974: Robert Lowell—*The Dolphin*

1975: Gary Snyder—*Turtle Island*

1976: John Ashbery—*Self-Portrait in a Convex Mirror*

1977: James Merrill—*Divine Comedies*

1978: Howard Nemerov—*Collected Poems*

1979: Robert Penn Warren—*Now and Then*

1980: Donald Justice—*Selected Poems*

1981: James Schuyler—*The Morning of the Poem*

1982: Sylvia Plath—*The Collected Poems*

1983: Galway Kinnell—*Selected Poems*

1984: Mary Oliver—*American Primitive*

1985: Carolyn Kizer—*Yin*

1986: Henry Taylor—*The Flying Change*

1987: Rita Dove—*Thomas and Beulah*

1988: William Meredith—*Partial Accounts: New and Selected Poems*

1989: Richard Wilbur—*New and Collected Poems*

1990: Charles Simic—*The World Doesn't End*

1991: Mona Van Duyn—*Near Changes*

1992: James Tate—*Selected Poems*

1993: Louise Glück—*The Wild Iris*

1994: Yusef Komunyakaa—*Neon Vernacular: New and Selected Poems*

1995: Philip Levine—*The Simple Truth*

1996: Jorie Graham—*The Dream of the Unified Field*

1997: Lisel Mueller—*Alive Together: New and Selected Poems*

1998: Charles Wright—*Black Zodiac*

1999: Mark Strand—*Blizzard of One*

2000: C. K. Williams—*Repair*

2001: Stephen Dunn—*Different Hours*

2002: Carl Dennis—*Practical Gods*

2003: Paul Muldoon—*Moy Sand and Gravel*

2004: Franz Wright—*Walking to Martha's Vineyard*

2005: Ted Kooser—*Delights and Shadows*

2006: Claudia Emerson—*Late Wife*

2007: Natasha Trethewey—*Native Guard*

2008: Robert Hass—*Time and Materials*

2009: W. S. Merwin—*The Shadow of Sirius*

2010: Rae Armantrout—*Versed*

QUEEN'S GOLD MEDAL FOR POETRY

A special committee, selected and chaired by the British poet laureate, selects for this medal a poet from any nation or realm of the British Commonwealth.

1934: Laurence Whistler

1937: W. H. Auden

1940: Michael Thwaites

1952: Andrew Young

1953: Arthur Waley

1954: Ralph Hodgson

1955: Ruth Pitter

1956: Edmund Blunden

1957: Siegfried Sassoon

1959: Frances Cornford

1960: John Betjeman

1962: Christopher Fry

1963: William Plomer

1964: R. S. Thomas

1965: Philip Larkin

1967: Charles Causley

1968: Robert Graves

1969: Stevie Smith

1970: Roy Fuller
1971: Stephen Spender
1973: John Heath-Stubbs
1974: Ted Hughes
1977: Norman Nicholson
1981: D. J. Enright
1986: Norman MacCaig
1988: Derek Walcott
1989: Allen Curnow
1990: Sorley Maclean
1991: Judith Wright

1992: Kathleen Raine
1996: Peter Redgrove
1998: Les Murray
2000: Edwin Morgan
2001: Michael Longley
2002: Peter Porter
2003: U. A. Fanthorpe
2004: Hugo Williams
2006: Fleur Adcock
2007: James Fenton
2010: Don Paterson

QUEENSLAND PREMIER'S LITERARY AWARDS

Inaugurated in 1999, the Queensland Premier's Literary Awards are a leading literary awards program within Australia, with prizes in more than fourteen categories. The Arts Queensland Judith Wright Calanthe Award is given each year for the best poetry collection.

2004: Judith Beveridge—*Wolf Notes*
2005: Sarah Day—*The Ship*
2006: John Kinsella—*The New Arcadia*
2007: Laurie Duggan—*The Passenger*

2008: David Malouf—*Typewriter Music*
2009: Emma Jones—*The Striped World*
2010: Peter Boyle—*Apo crypha*

JUAN RULFO PRIZE FOR LATIN AMERICAN AND CARIBBEAN LITERATURE

The Guadalajara International Book Fair in Mexico presents its annual literary award to a writer from the Americas who writes in Spanish, Portuguese, French, or English. Award organizers include Mexico's National Council for Culture and Arts and the University of Guadalajara. The list below includes only poets who have received the award.

1991: Nicanor Parra (Chile)
1993: Eliseo Diego (Cuba)
1998: Olga Orozco (Argentina)
2000: Juan Gelman (Argentina)
2002: Cintio Vitier (Cuba)

2004: Juan Goytisolo (Spain)
2005: Tomás Segovia (Mexico)
2007: Fernando del Paso (Mexico)
2009: Rafael Cadenas (Venezuela)

SHELLEY MEMORIAL AWARD

Awarded by the Poetry Society of America to an American poet on the basis of genius and need.

1929: Conrad Aiken
1930: Lizette Woodworth Reese
1931: Archibald MacLeish
1932: no award
1933: Lola Ridge and Frances Frost

1934: Lola Ridge and Marya Zaturenska
1935: Josephine Miles
1936: Charlotte Wilder and Ben Belitt
1937: Lincoln Fitzell
1938: Robert Francis and Harry Brown

1939: Herbert Bruncken and Winfield T. Scott
1940: Marianne Moore
1941: Ridgely Torrence
1942: Robert Penn Warren
1943: Edgar Lee Masters
1944: E. E. Cummings
1945: Karl Shapiro
1946: Rolfe Humphries
1947: Janet Lewis
1948: John Berryman
1949: Louis Kent
1950: Jeremy Ingalls
1951: Richard Eberhart
1952: Elizabeth Bishop
1953: Kenneth Patchen
1954: Leonie Adams
1955: Robert Fitzgerald
1956: George Abbe
1957: Kenneth Rexroth
1958: Rose Garcia Villa
1959: Delmore Schwartz
1960: Robinson Jeffers
1961: Theodore Roethke
1962: Eric Barker
1963: William Stafford
1964: Ruth Stone
1965: David Ignatow
1966: Anne Sexton
1967: May Swenson
1968: Anne Stanford
1969: X. J. Kennedy and Mary Oliver
1970: Adrienne Rich and Louise Townsend Nicholl
1971: Galway Kinnell
1972: John Ashbery and Richard Wilbur
1973: W. S. Merwin
1974: Edward Field

1975: Gwendolyn Brooks
1976: Muriel Rukeyser
1977: Jane Cooper and William Everson
1978: Hayden Carruth
1979: Julia Randall
1980: Robert Creeley
1981: Alan Dugan
1982: Jon Anderson and Leo Connellan
1983: Denise Levertov and Robert Duncan
1984: Etheridge Knight
1986: Gary Snyder
1987: Mona Van Duyn
1988: Dennis Schmitz
1989: no award
1990: Thomas McGrath and Theodore Weiss
1991: Shirley Kaufman
1992: Lucille Clifton
1993: Josephine Jacobsen
1994: Kenneth Koch and Cathy Song
1995: Stanley Kunitz
1996: Robert Pinsky and Anne Waldman
1997: Frank Bidart
1998: Eleanor Ross Taylor
1999: Tom Sleigh
2000: Jean Valentine
2001: Alice Notley and Michael Palmer
2002: Angela Jackson and Marie Ponsot
2003: James McMichael
2004: Yusef Komunyakaa
2005: Lyn Hejinian
2006: George Stanley
2007: Kimiko Hahn
2008: Ed Roberson
2009: Ron Padgett and Gary Young
2010: Kenneth Irby and Eileen Myles

WALLACE STEVENS AWARD

Awarded by the Academy of American Poets to a poet for outstanding and proven mastery of the art of poetry.

1994: W. S. Merwin
1995: James Tate

1996: Adrienne Rich
1997: Anthony Hecht

1998: A. R. Ammons
1999: Jackson MacLow
2000: Frank Bidart
2001: John Ashbery
2002: Ruth Stone
2003: Richard Wilbur

2004: Mark Strand
2005: Gerald Stern
2006: Michael Palmer
2007: Charles Simic
2008: Louise Glück
2009: Jean Valentine

KINGSLEY TUFTS POETRY AWARD

Claremont Graduate University presents the annual Kingsley Tufts Poetry Award for a single collection of a poet's work.

1993: Susan Mitchell—*Rapture*
1994: Yusef Komunyakaa—*Neon Vernacular*
1995: Thomas Lux—*Split Horizon*
1996: Deborah Digges—*Rough Music*
1997: Campbell McGrath—*Spring Comes to Chicago*
1998: John Koethe—*Falling Water*
1999: B. H. Fairchild—*The Art of the Lathe*
2000: Robert Wrigley—*Reign of Snakes*
2001: Alan Shapiro—*The Dead Alive and Busy*

2002: Carl Phillips—*The Tether*
2003: Linda Gregerson—*Waterborne*
2004: Henri Cole—*Middle Earth*
2005: Michael Ryan—*New and Selected Poems*
2006: Lucia Perillo—*Luck Is Luck*
2007: Rodney Jones—*Salvation Blues*
2008: Tom Sleigh—*Space Walk*
2009: Matthea Harvey—*Modern Life*
2010: D. A. Powell—*Chronic*

TIN UJEVIĆ AWARD

The Tin Ujević Award is an award given for contributions to Croatian poetry. Founded in 1980 and awarded by the Croatian Writers' Society, it is considered the most prestigious such award in Croatia.

1981: Nikica Petrak—"Tiha knjiga"
1982: Slavko Mihalić—"Pohvala praznom džepu"
1983: Irena Vrkljan—"U koži moje sestre"
1984: Nikola Milićević—"Nepovrat"
1985: Branimir Bošnjak—"Semanti ka gladovanja"
1986: Igor Zidić—"Strijela od stakla"
1987: Dragutin Tadijanović—"Kruh svagdanji"
1988: Tonko Maroević—"Trag roga ne bez vraga"
1989: Tonći Petrasov Marović—"Moći ne govoriti"
1990: Luko Paljetak—"Snižena vrata"
1991: Vlado Gotovac—"Crna kazaljka"
1992: Zvonimir Golob—"Rana"
1993: Mate Ganza—"Knjiga bdjenja"
1994: Dražen Katunarić—"Nebo/Zemlja"
1995: Vladimir Pavlović—"Gral"

1996: Dubravko Horvatić—"Ratnoa noć"
1997: Boris Domagoj Biletić—"Radovi na nekropoli"
1998: Gordana Benić—"Laterna magica"
1999: Andrijana Škunca—"Novaljski svjetlopis"
2000: Mario Suško—"Versus axsul"
2001: Ivan Slamnig—"Ranjeni tenk" (posthumous)
2002: Petar Gudelj—"Po zraku i po vodi"
2003: Vesna Parun—"Suze putuju"
2004: Alojzije Majetić—"Odmicanje pau ine"
2005: Borben Vladović—"Tijat"
2006: Željko Knežević—"Kopito trajnoga konja"
2007: Ante Stamać—"Vrijeme, vrijeme"
2008: Miroslav Slavko Mađer—"Stihovi dugih naziva"
2009: Tomislav Marijan Bilosnić—"Molitve"

WALT WHITMAN AWARD

Awarded by the Academy of American Poets to a poet for the publication of a distinguished first collection of poetry.

1975: Reg Saner—*Climbing into the Roots*
1976: Laura Gilpin—*The Hocus-Pocus of the Universe*
1977: Lauren Shakely—*Guilty Bystander*
1978: Karen Snow—*Wonders*
1979: David Bottoms—*Shooting Rats at the Bibb County Dump*
1980: Jared Carter—*Work, for the Night Is Coming*
1981: Alberto Ríos—*Whispering to Fool the Wind*
1982: Anthony Petrosky—*Jurgis Petraskas*
1983: Christopher Gilbert—*Across the Mutual Landscape*
1984: Eric Pankey—*For the New Year*
1985: Christianne Balk—*Bindweed*
1986: Chris Llewellyn—*Fragments from the Fire*
1987: Judith Baumel—*The Weight of Numbers*
1988: April Bernard—*Blackbird Bye Bye*
1989: Martha Hollander—*The Game of Statues*
1990: Elaine Terranova—*The Cult of the Right Hand*
1991: Greg Glazner—*From the Iron Chair*
1992: Stephen Yenser—*The Fire in All Things*

1993: Alison Hawthorne Deming—*Science and Other Poems*
1994: Jan Richman—*Because the Brain Can Be Talked into Anything*
1995: Nicole Cooley—*Resurrection*
1996: Joshua Clover—*Madonna anno domini*
1997: Barbara Ras—*Bite Every Sorrow*
1998: Jan Heller Levi—*Once I Gazed at You in Wonder*
1999: Judy Jordan—*Carolina Ghost Woods*
2000: Ben Doyle—*Radio, Radio*
2001: John Canaday—*The Invisible World*
2002: Sue Kwock Kim—*Notes from the Divided Country*
2003: Tony Tost—*Invisible Bride*
2004: Geri Doran—*Resin*
2005: Mary Rose O'Reilley—*Half Wild*
2006: Anne Pierson Wiese—*Floating City*
2007: Sally Van Doren—*Sex at Noon Taxes*
2008: Jonathan Thirkield—*The Walker's Corridor*
2009: J. Michael Martinez—*Heredities*
2010: Carl Adamshick—*Curses and Wishes*

YALE SERIES OF YOUNGER POETS

This annual event of Yale University Press aims to publish the first collection of a promising American poet. Founded in 1919, it is the oldest annual literary award in the United States. Judges have included Stephen Vincent Benét (1933-1942), Archibald MacLeish (1944-1946), W. H. Auden (1947-1959), Stanley Kunitz (1969-1977), W. S. Merwin (1998-2003), Louise Glück (2003-2010), and Carl Phillips (2011-). Years reflect publication dates.

1919: John Chipman—*Farrar Forgotten Shrines*
1919: Howard Buck—*The Tempering*
1920: Darl MacLeod Boyle—*Where Lilith Dances*
1920: Thomas Caldecot Chubb—*The White God, and Other Poems*
1920: David Osborne Hamilton—*Four Gardens*
1920: Alfred Raymond Bellinger—*Spires and Poplars*
1921: Hervey Allen—*Wampum and Old Gold*
1921: Viola C. White—*Horizons*
1921: Oscar Williams—*Golden Darkness*

1921: Theodore H. Banks, Jr.—*Wild Geese*
1922: Bernard Raymund—*Hidden Waters*
1922: Medora C. Addison—*Dreams and a Sword*
1922: Paul Tanaquil—*Attitudes*
1922: Harold Vinal—*White April*
1923: Marion M. Boyd—*Silver Wands*
1923: Amos Niven Wilder—*Battle-Retrospect*
1923: Beatrice E. Harmon—*Mosaics*
1923: Dean B. Lyman, Jr.—*The Last Lutanist*
1924: Elizabeth Jessup—*Blake Up and Down*

1925: Dorothy E. Reid—*Coach into Pumpkin*

1926: Eleanor Slater—*Quest*

1926: Thomas Hornsby Ferril—*High Passage*

1927: Lindley Williams Hubbell—*Dark Pavilion*

1928: Ted Olson—*A Stranger and Afraid*

1928: Francis Claiborne Mason—*This Unchanging Mask*

1928: Mildred Bowers—*Twist o' Smoke*

1929: Frances M. Frost—*Hemlock Wall*

1929: Henri Faust—*Half-Light and Overture*

1930: Louise Owen—*Virtuosa*

1931: Dorothy Belle Flanagan—*Dark Certainty*

1932: Paul Engle—*Worn Earth*

1933: Shirley Barker—*The Dark Hills Under*

1934: James Agee—*Permit Me Voyage*

1935: Muriel Rukeyser—*Theory of Flight*

1936: Edward Weismiller—*The Deer Come Down*

1937: Margaret Haley—*The Gardener Mind*

1938: Joy Davidman—*Letter to a Comrade*

1939: Reuel Denney—*The Connecticut River, and Other Poems*

1940: Norman Rosten—*Return Again, Traveler*

1941: Jeremy Ingalls—*The Metaphysical Sword*

1942: Margaret Walker—*For My People*

1944: William Meredith—*Love Letters from an Impossible Land*

1945: Charles E. Butler—*Cut Is the Branch*

1946: Eve Merriam—*Family Circle*

1947: Joan Murray—*Poems*

1948: Robert Horan—*A Beginning*

1949: Rosalie Moore—*The Grasshopper's Man, and Other Poems*

1951: Adrienne Rich—*A Change of World*

1952: W. S. Merwin—*A Mask for Janus*

1953: Edgar Bogardus—*Various Jangling Keys*

1954: Daniel Hoffman—*An Armada of Thirty Whales*

1956: John Ashbery—*Some Trees*

1957: James Wright—*The Green Wall*

1958: John Hollander—*A Crackling of Thorns*

1959: William Dickey—*Of the Festivity*

1960: George Starbuck—*Bone Thoughts*

1961: Alan Dugan—*Poems*

1962: Jack Gilbert—*Views of Jeopardy*

1963: Sandra Hochman—*Manhattan Pastures*

1964: Peter Davison—*The Breaking of the Day*

1965: Jean Valentine—*Dream Barker*

1967: James Tate—*The Lost Pilot*

1968: Helen Chasin—*Coming Close, and Other Poems*

1969: Judith Johnson—*Sherwin Uranium Poems*

1970: Hugh Seidman—*Collecting Evidence*

1971: Peter Klappert—*Lugging Vegetables to Nantucket*

1972: Michael Casey—*Obscenities*

1973: Robert Hass—*Field Guide*

1974: Michael Ryan—*Threats Instead of Trees*

1975: Maura Stanton—*Snow on Snow*

1976: Carolyn Forché—*Gathering the Tribes*

1977: Olga Broumas—*Beginning with O*

1978: Bin Ramke—*The Difference Between Night and Day*

1979: Leslie Ullman—*Natural Histories*

1980: William Virgil Davis—*One Way to Reconstruct the Scene*

1981: John Bensko—*Green Soldiers*

1982: David Wojahn—*Icehouse Lights*

1983: Cathy Song—*Picture Bride*

1984: Richard Kenney—*The Evolution of the Flightless Bird*

1985: Pamela Alexander—*Navigable Waterways*

1986: George Bradley—*Terms to Be Met*

1987: Julie Agoos—*Above the Land*

1988: Brigit Pegeen Kelly—*To the Place of Trumpets*

1989: Thomas Bolt—*Out of the Woods*

1990: Daniel Hall—*Hermit with Landscape*

1991: Christiane Jacox Kyle—*Bears Dancing in the Northern Air*

1992: Nicholas Samaras—*Hands of the Saddlemaker*

1993: Jody Gladding—*Stone Crop*

1994: Valerie Wohlfeld—*Thinking the World Visible*

1995: Tony Crunk—*Living in the Resurrection*

1996: Ellen Hinsey—*Cities of Memory*

1997: Talvikki Ansel—*My Shining Archipelago*

1999: Craig Arnold—*Shells*

2000: Davis McCombs—*Ultima Thule*

2001: Maurice Manning—*Laurence Booth's Book of Visions*

2002: Sean Singer—*Discography*

2003: Loren Goodman—*Famous Americans*

2004: Peter Streckfus—*The Cuckoo*

2005: Richard Siken—*Crush*

2006: Jay Hopler—*Green Squall*

2007: Jessica Fisher—*Frail-Craft*

2008: Fady Joudah—*The Earth in the Attic*

2009: Arda Collins—*It Is Daylight*

2010: Ken Chen—*Juvenilia*

2011: Katherine Larson—*Radial Symmetry*

CHRONOLOGICAL LIST OF POETS

This chronology of the poets covered in the Critical Survey of Poetry, Fourth Edition, *serves as a time line for students interested in the development of poetry from its earliest days to modern times. The arrangement is chronological on the basis of birth years, and the proximity of writers provides students with some insights into potential influences and contemporaneous developments.*

BORN BEFORE 1000

Homer (c. early eighth century B.C.E.)
Hesiod (fl. c. 700 B.C.E.)
Theognis (c. seventh century B.C.E.)
Archilochus (c. 680 B.C.E.)
Sappho (c. 630 B.C.E.)
Anacreon (c. 571 B.C.E.)
Pindar (c. 518 B.C.E.)
Vālmīki (fl. c. 500 B.C.E.)
Theocritus (c. 308 B.C.E.)
Leonidas of Tarentum (fl. early third century B.C.E.)
Apollonius Rhodius (between 295 and 260 B.C.E.)
Meleager (c. 140 B.C.E.)
Lucretius (c. 98 B.C.E.)
Catullus (c. 85 B.C.E.)
Vergil (October 15, 70 B.C.E.)
Horace (December 8, 65 B.C.E.)
Propertius, Sextus (c. 57-48 B.C.E.)
Ovid (March 20, 43 B.C.E.)
Persius (December 4, 34 C.E.)
Martial (March 1, c. 38-41 C.E.)
Lucan (November 3, 39 C.E.)
Statius (between 40 and 45 C.E.)
Juvenal (c. 60 C.E.)
Ruan Ji (210)
Callimachus (c. 305)
Tao Qian (365)
Xie Lingyun (385)
Cædmon (early seventh century)
Meng Haoran (689)
Li Bo (701)
Wang Wei (701)
Du Fu (712)
Cynewulf (757)
Firdusi (between 932 and 941)

BORN 1001-1500

Omar Khayyám (May 18, 1048?)
Judah ha-Levi (c. 1075)
Li Qingzhao (1084)
Marie de France (c. 1150)
Hartmann von Aue (c. 1160-1165)
Walther von der Vogelweide (c. 1170)
Wolfram von Eschenbach (c. 1170)
Layamon (c. 1200)
Saʿdi (c. 1200)
Rūmī, Jalāl al-Dīn (c. September 30, 1207)
Gottfried von Strassburg (fl. c. 1210)
Guillaume de Lorris (c. 1215)
Cavalcanti, Guido (c. 1259)
Dante (May or June, 1265)
Petrarch (July 20, 1304)
Boccaccio, Giovanni (June or July, 1313)
Hafiz (c. 1320)
Gower, John (c. 1330)
Langland, William (c. 1332)
Chaucer, Geoffrey (c. 1343)
Pearl-Poet (fl. latter half of the fourteenth century)
Christine de Pizan (c. 1365)
Lydgate, John (1370?)
Chartier, Alain (c. 1385)
Charles d'Orléans (November 24, 1394)
Henryson, Robert (c. 1425)
Villon, François (1431)
Manrique, Jorge (c. 1440)
Boiardo, Matteo Maria (May, 1440 or 1441)
Poliziano (July 14, 1454)
Dunbar, William (c. 1460)
Skelton, John (c. 1460)
Bembo, Pietro (May 20, 1470)
Ariosto, Ludovico (September 8, 1474)

Michelangelo (March 6, 1475)
Fracastoro, Girolamo (c. 1478)
Heywood, John (c. 1497)

BORN 1501-1600
Garcilaso de la Vega (1501)
Wyatt, Sir Thomas (1503)
Surrey, Henry Howard, earl of (1517)
Du Bellay, Joachim (c. 1522)
Stampa, Gaspara (c. 1523)
Camões, Luís de (c. 1524)
Ronsard, Pierre de (September 11, 1524)
León, Luis de (1527)
Sackville, Thomas (1536)
Gascoigne, George (c. 1539)
John of the Cross, Saint (June 24, 1542)
Tasso, Torquato (March 11, 1544)
Breton, Nicholas (c. 1545)
Ralegh, Sir Walter (c. 1552)
Spenser, Edmund (c. 1552)
Greville, Fulke (October 3, 1554)
Sidney, Sir Philip (November 30, 1554)
Malherbe, François de (1555)
Lodge, Thomas (1558?)
Greene, Robert (c. July, 1558)
Chapman, George (c. 1559)
Southwell, Robert (1561)
Góngora y Argote, Luis de (July 11, 1561)
Daniel, Samuel (1562?)
Constable, Henry (1562)
Vega Carpio, Lope de (November 25, 1562)
Drayton, Michael (1563)
Sidney, Sir Robert (November 19, 1563)
Marlowe, Christopher (February 6, 1564)
Shakespeare, William (April 23, 1564)
Campion, Thomas (February 12, 1567)
Nashe, Thomas (November, 1567)
Davies, Sir John (April, 1569)
Marino, Giambattista (October 18, 1569)
Dekker, Thomas (c. 1572)
Donne, John (between January 24 and
    June 19, 1572)
Jonson, Ben (June 11, 1573)
Drummond of Hawthornden, William (December 13,
    1585)

Herrick, Robert (August 24, 1591)
Quarles, Francis (1592)
King, Henry (January 16, 1592)
Herbert, George (April 3, 1593)
Carew, Thomas (1594)
Calderón de la Barca, Pedro (January 17, 1600)

BORN 1601-1700
Davenant, Sir William (February, 1606)
Waller, Edmund (March 3, 1606)
Fanshawe, Sir Richard (June, 1608)
Milton, John (December 9, 1608)
Suckling, Sir John (February 10, 1609)
Bradstreet, Anne (1612?)
Crashaw, Richard (c. 1612)
Butler, Samuel (February 8, 1612)
Cowley, Abraham (1618)
Lovelace, Richard (1618)
Marvell, Andrew (March 31, 1621)
La Fontaine, Jean de (July 8, 1621)
Vaughan, Henry (April 17, 1622)
Newcastle, Margaret Cavendish, duchess of
    (1623)
Cotton, Charles (April 28, 1630)
Dryden, John (August 19, 1631)
Etherege, Sir George (c. 1635)
Boileau-Despréaux, Nicolas (November 11, 1636)
Traherne, Thomas (c. 1637)
Sedley, Sir Charles (March, 1639)
Behn, Aphra (July?, 1640)
Matsuo Bashō (1644)
Taylor, Edward (c. 1645)
Rochester, John Wilmot, earl of (April 10, 1647)
Cruz, Sor Juana Inés de la (November, 1648)
Oldham, John (August 9, 1653)
Finch, Anne (April, 1661)
Prior, Matthew (July 21, 1664)
Swift, Jonathan (November 30, 1667)
Congreve, William (January 24, 1670)
Addison, Joseph (May 1, 1672)
Watts, Isaac (July 17, 1674)
Young, Edward (July 3, 1683)
Gay, John (June 30, 1685)
Pope, Alexander (May 21, 1688)
Thomson, James (September 7, 1700)

BORN 1701-1800

Johnson, Samuel (September 18, 1709)
Gray, Thomas (December 26, 1716)
Collins, William (December 25, 1721)
Smart, Christopher (April 11, 1722)
Goldsmith, Oliver (November 10, 1728 or 1730)
Cowper, William (November 26, 1731)
Goethe, Johann Wolfgang von (August 28, 1749)
Freneau, Philip (January 2, 1752)
Chatterton, Thomas (November 20, 1752)
Wheatley, Phillis (1753?)
Crabbe, George (December 24, 1754)
Blake, William (November 28, 1757)
Burns, Robert (January 25, 1759)
Schiller, Friedrich (November 10, 1759)
Bowles, William Lisle (September 24, 1762)
Issa (June 15, 1763)
Hölderlin, Friedrich (March 20, 1770)
Wordsworth, William (April 7, 1770)
Scott, Sir Walter (August 15, 1771)
Novalis (May 2, 1772)
Coleridge, Samuel Taylor (October 21, 1772)
Southey, Robert (August 12, 1774)
Landor, Walter Savage (January 30, 1775)
Lamb, Charles (February 10, 1775)
Foscolo, Ugo (February 6, 1778)
Tegnér, Esaias (November 13, 1782)
Hunt, Leigh (October 19, 1784)
Manzoni, Alessandro (March 7, 1785)
Byron, Lord (January 22, 1788)
Eichendorff, Joseph von (March 10, 1788)
Lamartine, Alphonse de (October 21, 1790)
Shelley, Percy Bysshe (August 4, 1792)
Clare, John (July 13, 1793)
Hemans, Felicia Dorothea (September 25, 1793)
Bryant, William Cullen (November 3, 1794)
Darley, George (1795)
Keats, John (October 31, 1795)
Horton, George Moses (c. 1797)
Vigny, Alfred de (March 27, 1797)
Heine, Heinrich (December 13, 1797)
Solomos, Dionysios (April 8, 1798)
Leopardi, Giacomo (June 29, 1798)
Mickiewicz, Adam (December 24, 1798)
Hood, Thomas (May 23, 1799)

Pushkin, Alexander (June 6, 1799)
Vörösmarty, Mihály (December 1, 1800)

BORN 1801-1850

Hugo, Victor (February 26, 1802)
Lönnrot, Elias (April 9, 1802)
Mangan, James Clarence (May 1, 1803)
Emerson, Ralph Waldo (May 25, 1803)
Beddoes, Thomas Lovell (June 30, 1803)
Mörike, Eduard (September 8, 1804)
Browning, Elizabeth Barrett (March 6, 1806)
Longfellow, Henry Wadsworth (February 27, 1807)
Whittier, John Greenleaf (December 17, 1807)
Nerval, Gérard de (May 22, 1808)
Poe, Edgar Allan (January 19, 1809)
FitzGerald, Edward (March 31, 1809)
Giusti, Giuseppe (May 12, 1809)
Tennyson, Alfred, Lord (August 6, 1809)
Holmes, Oliver Wendell (August 29, 1809)
Słowacki, Juliusz (September 4, 1809)
Musset, Alfred de (December 11, 1810)
Hallam, Arthur Henry (February 1, 1811)
Gautier, Théophile (August 30, 1811)
Browning, Robert (May 7, 1812)
Lear, Edward (May 12, 1812)
Very, Jones (August 28, 1813)
Lermontov, Mikhail (October 15, 1814)
Arany, János (March 2, 1817)
Thoreau, Henry David (July 12, 1817)
Brontë, Emily (July 30, 1818)
Clough, Arthur Hugh (January 1, 1819)
Lowell, James Russell (February 22, 1819)
Whitman, Walt (May 31, 1819)
Melville, Herman (August 1, 1819)
Tuckerman, Frederick Goddard (February 4, 1821)
Baudelaire, Charles (April 9, 1821)
Arnold, Matthew (December 24, 1822)
Petőfi, Sándor (January 1, 1823)
Patmore, Coventry (July 23, 1823)
Allingham, William (March 19, 1824)
Meredith, George (February 12, 1828)
Rossetti, Dante Gabriel (May 12, 1828)
Gezelle, Guido (May 1, 1830)

Rossetti, Christina (December 5, 1830)
Dickinson, Emily (December 10, 1830)
Carroll, Lewis (January 27, 1832)
Morris, William (March 24, 1834)
Hernández, José (November 10, 1834)
Thomson, James (November 23, 1834)
Carducci, Giosuè (July 27, 1835)
Bécquer, Gustavo Adolfo (February 17, 1836)
Castro, Rosalía de (February 24, 1837)
Swinburne, Algernon Charles (April 5, 1837)
Hardy, Thomas (June 2, 1840)
Lanier, Sidney (February 3, 1842)
Mallarmé, Stéphane (March 18, 1842)
Verlaine, Paul (March 30, 1844)
Hopkins, Gerard Manley (July 28, 1844)
Bridges, Robert (October 23, 1844)
Corbière, Tristan (July 18, 1845)
Riley, James Whitcomb (October 7, 1849)
Stevenson, Robert Louis (November 13, 1850)

BORN 1851-1870

Markham, Edwin (April 23, 1852)
Wilde, Oscar (October 16, 1854)
Rimbaud, Arthur (October 20, 1854)
Verhaeren, Émile (May 21, 1855)
Annensky, Innokenty (September 1, 1855)
Pascoli, Giovanni (December 31, 1855)
Reese, Lizette Woodworth (January 9, 1856)
Housman, A. E. (March 26, 1859)
Laforgue, Jules (August 16, 1860)
Tagore, Rabindranath (May 7, 1861)
D'Annunzio, Gabriele (March 12, 1863)
Cavafy, Constantine P. (April 17, 1863)
Holz, Arno (April 26, 1863)
Unamuno y Jugo, Miguel de (September 29, 1864)
Yeats, William Butler (June 13, 1865)
Kipling, Rudyard (December 30, 1865)
Darío, Rubén (January 18, 1867)
Æ (April 10, 1867)
George, Stefan (July 12, 1868)
Claudel, Paul (August 6, 1868)
Masters, Edgar Lee (August 23, 1868)
Mew, Charlotte (November 15, 1869)
Robinson, Edwin Arlington (December 22, 1869)
Belloc, Hilaire (July 27, 1870)

BORN 1871-1880

Dučić, Jovan (February 5, 1871)
González Martínez, Enrique (April 13, 1871)
Morgenstern, Christian (May 6, 1871)
Johnson, James Weldon (June 17, 1871)
Valéry, Paul (October 30, 1871)
Crane, Stephen (November 1, 1871)
Dunbar, Paul Laurence (June 27, 1872)
Péguy, Charles-Pierre (January 7, 1873)
De la Mare, Walter (April 25, 1873)
Service, Robert W. (January 16, 1874)
Hofmannsthal, Hugo von (February 1, 1874)
Stein, Gertrude (February 3, 1874)
Lowell, Amy (February 9, 1874)
Frost, Robert (March 26, 1874)
Kraus, Karl (April 28, 1874)
Machado, Antonio (July 26, 1875)
Rilke, Rainer Maria (December 4, 1875)
Hesse, Hermann (July 2, 1877)
Ady, Endre (November 22, 1877)
Sandburg, Carl (January 6, 1878)
Thomas, Edward (March 3, 1878)
Masefield, John (June 1, 1878)
Yosano Akiko (December 7, 1878)
Stevens, Wallace (October 2, 1879)
Lindsay, Vachel (November 10, 1879)
Apollinaire, Guillaume (August 26, 1880)
Blok, Aleksandr (November 28, 1880)

BORN 1881-1890

Neihardt, John G. (January 8, 1881)
Bynner, Witter (August 10, 1881)
Guest, Edgar A. (August 20, 1881)
Zweig, Stefan (November 28, 1881)
Colum, Padraic (December 8, 1881)
Jiménez, Juan Ramón (December 23, 1881)
Joyce, James (February 2, 1882)
Pratt, E. J. (February 4, 1882)
Loy, Mina (December 27, 1882)
Gibran, Kahlil (January 6, 1883)
Kazantzakis, Nikos (February 18, 1883)
Saba, Umberto (March 9, 1883)
Williams, William Carlos (September 17, 1883)
Babits, Mihály (November 26, 1883)

Teasdale, Sara (August 8, 1884)

Lawrence, D. H. (September 11, 1885)

Wylie, Elinor (September 17, 1885)

Untermeyer, Louis (October 1, 1885)

Pound, Ezra (October 30, 1885)

Benn, Gottfried (May 2, 1886)

Khodasevich, Vladislav (May 28, 1886)

Benét, William Rose (February 2, 1886)

Sassoon, Siegfried (September 8, 1886)

Wheelock, John Hall (September 9, 1886)

H. D. (Hilda Doolittle) (September 10, 1886)

Jeffers, Robinson (January 10, 1887)

Trakl, Georg (February 3, 1887)

Muir, Edwin (May 15, 1887)

Perse, Saint-John (May 31, 1887)

Brooke, Rupert (August 3, 1887)

Sitwell, Edith (September 7, 1887)

Arp, Hans (September 16, 1887)

Moore, Marianne (November 15, 1887)

Ungaretti, Giuseppe (February 8, 1888)

Ransom, John Crowe (April 30, 1888)

Pessoa, Fernando (June 13, 1888)

Seeger, Alan (June 22, 1888)

Eliot, T. S. (September 26, 1888)

Mistral, Gabriela (April 7, 1889)

Reyes, Alfonso (May 17, 1889)

Akhmatova, Anna (June 23, 1889)

Cocteau, Jean (July 5, 1889)

Aiken, Conrad (August 5, 1889)

Reverdy, Pierre (September 13, 1889)

McKay, Claude (September 15, 1889)

Pasternak, Boris (February 10, 1890)

Gurney, Ivor (August 28, 1890)

Rosenberg, Isaac (November 25, 1890)

BORN 1891-1900

Mandelstam, Osip (January 15, 1891)

Salinas, Pedro (November 27, 1891)

Sachs, Nelly (December 10, 1891)

Millay, Edna St. Vincent (February 22, 1892)

Vallejo, César (March 16, 1892)

Södergran, Edith (April 4, 1892)

MacLeish, Archibald (May 7, 1892)

Bishop, John Peale (May 21, 1892)

Aldington, Richard (July 8, 1892)

MacDiarmid, Hugh (August 11, 1892)

Tsvetayeva, Marina (October 8, 1892)

Guillén, Jorge (January 18, 1893)

Foix, J. V. (January 28, 1893)

Owen, Wilfred (March 18, 1893)

Mayakovsky, Vladimir (July 19, 1893)

Parker, Dorothy (August 22, 1893)

Van Doren, Mark (June 13, 1894)

Reznikoff, Charles (August 31, 1894)

Cummings, E. E. (October 14, 1894)

Toomer, Jean (December 26, 1894)

Hillyer, Robert (June 3, 1895)

Graves, Robert (July 24, 1895)

Esenin, Sergei (October 3, 1895)

Jones, David (November 1, 1895)

Słonimski, Antoni (November 15, 1895)

Éluard, Paul (December 14, 1895)

Breton, André (February 19, 1896)

Tzara, Tristan (April 4, 1896)

Clarke, Austin (May 9, 1896)

Miyazawa, Kenji (August 27, 1896)

Montale, Eugenio (October 12, 1896)

Blunden, Edmund (November 1, 1896)

Bogan, Louise (August 11, 1897)

Wheelwright, John (September 9, 1897)

Aragon, Louis (October 3, 1897)

Tolson, Melvin B. (February 6, 1898)

Brecht, Bertolt (February 10, 1898)

Gregory, Horace (April 10, 1898)

Aleixandre, Vicente (April 26, 1898)

García Lorca, Federico (June 5, 1898)

Benét, Stephen Vincent (July 22, 1898)

Cowley, Malcolm (August 24, 1898)

Ponge, Francis (March 27, 1899)

Michaux, Henri (May 24, 1899)

Crane, Hart (July 21, 1899)

Lewis, Janet (August 17, 1899)

Borges, Jorge Luis (August 24, 1899)

Tate, Allen (November 19, 1899)

Adams, Léonie (December 9, 1899)

Prévert, Jacques (February 4, 1900)

Bunting, Basil (March 1, 1900)

Seferis, George (March 13, 1900)

Winters, Yvor (October 17, 1900)

BORN 1901-1910

Riding, Laura (January 16, 1901)
Brown, Sterling A. (May 1, 1901)
Ausländer, Rose (May 11, 1901)
Manger, Itzik (May 28, 1901)
Quasimodo, Salvatore (August 20, 1901)
Seifert, Jaroslav (September 23, 1901)
Hikmet, Nazim (January 20, 1902)
Hughes, Langston (February 1, 1902)
Fearing, Kenneth (July 28, 1902)
Nash, Ogden (August 19, 1902)
Smith, Stevie (September 20, 1902)
Cernuda, Luis (September 21, 1902)
Bontemps, Arna (October 13, 1902)
Drummond de Andrade, Carlos (October 31, 1902)
Illyés, Gyula (November 2, 1902)
Alberti, Rafael (December 16, 1902)
Niedecker, Lorine (May 12, 1903)
Cullen, Countée (May 30, 1903)
Follain, Jean (August 29, 1903)
Rakosi, Carl (November 6, 1903)
Zukofsky, Louis (January 23, 1904)
Eberhart, Richard (April 5, 1904)
Day Lewis, Cecil (April 27, 1904)
Martinson, Harry (May 6, 1904)
Birney, Earle (May 13, 1904)
Neruda, Pablo (July 12, 1904)
Kavanagh, Patrick (October 21, 1904)
McGinley, Phyllis (March 21, 1905)
Warren, Robert Penn (April 24, 1905)
Kunitz, Stanley (July 29, 1905)
Ważyk, Adam (November 17, 1905)
Hein, Piet (December 16, 1905)
Rexroth, Kenneth (December 22, 1905)
Beckett, Samuel (April 13, 1906)
Still, James (July 16, 1906)
Betjeman, John (August 28, 1906)
Empson, William (September 27, 1906)
Senghor, Léopold (October 9, 1906)
Auden, W. H. (February 21, 1907)
Kirstein, Lincoln (May 4, 1907)
Char, René (June 14, 1907)
Hope, A. D. (July 21, 1907)
MacNeice, Louis (September 12, 1907)

Ekelöf, Gunnar (September 15, 1907)
Oppen, George (April 24, 1908)
Roethke, Theodore (May 25, 1908)
Jacobsen, Josephine (August 19, 1908)
Pavese, Cesare (September 9, 1908)
Pentzikis, Nikos (October 30, 1908)
Swir, Anna (February 7, 1909)
Spender, Stephen (February 28, 1909)
Radnóti, Miklós (May 5, 1909)
Ritsos, Yannis (May 14, 1909)
Rolfe, Edwin (September 7, 1909)
Barnard, Mary (December 6, 1909)
Scott, Winfield Townley (April 30, 1910)
Olson, Charles (December 27, 1910)

BORN 1911-1920

Bishop, Elizabeth (February 8, 1911)
Belitt, Ben (May 2, 1911)
Miles, Josephine (June 11, 1911)
Miłosz, Czesław (June 30, 1911)
Cunningham, J. V. (August 23, 1911)
Elytis, Odysseus (November 2, 1911)
Porter, Anne (November 6, 1911)
Patchen, Kenneth (December 13, 1911)
Fuller, Roy (February 11, 1912)
Durrell, Lawrence (February 27, 1912)
Layton, Irving (March 12, 1912)
Sarton, May (May 3, 1912)
Everson, William (September 10, 1912)
Prince, F. T. (September 13, 1912)
Thomas, R. S. (March 29, 1913)
Césaire, Aimé (June 26, 1913)
Hayden, Robert (August 4, 1913)
Shapiro, Karl (November 10, 1913)
Nims, John Frederick (November 20, 1913)
Schwartz, Delmore (December 8, 1913)
Rukeyser, Muriel (December 15, 1913)
Randall, Dudley (January 14, 1914)
Stafford, William (January 17, 1914)
Ignatow, David (February 7, 1914)
Reed, Henry (February 22, 1914)
Kees, Weldon (February 24, 1914)
Paz, Octavio (March 31, 1914)
Howes, Barbara (May 1, 1914)
Jarrell, Randall (May 6, 1914)

Villa, José García (August 5, 1914)
Parra, Nicanor (September 5, 1914)
Berryman, John (October 25, 1914)
Thomas, Dylan (October 27, 1914)
Dodson, Owen (November 28, 1914)
Merton, Thomas (January 31, 1915)
Walker, Margaret (July 7, 1915)
Gardner, Isabella (September 7, 1915)
Otero, Blas de (March 15, 1916)
Ciardi, John (June 24, 1916)
Hébert, Anne (August 1, 1916)
Viereck, Peter (August 5, 1916)
McGrath, Thomas (November 20, 1916)
Lowell, Robert (March 1, 1917)
Bobrowski, Johannes (April 9, 1917)
Brooks, Gwendolyn (June 7, 1917)
Bronk, William (February 17, 1918)
Coxe, Louis (April 15, 1918)
Smith, William Jay (April 22, 1918)
Duncan, Robert (January 7, 1919)
Meredith, William (January 9, 1919)
Ferlinghetti, Lawrence (March 24, 1919)
Swenson, May (May 28, 1919)
Whittemore, Reed (September 11, 1919)
Nemerov, Howard (March 1, 1920)
Clampitt, Amy (June 15, 1920)
Bukowski, Charles (August 16, 1920)
Guest, Barbara (September 6, 1920)
Celan, Paul (November 23, 1920)

BORN 1921-1930

Ponsot, Marie (1921)
Wilbur, Richard (March 1, 1921)
Berrigan, Daniel (May 9, 1921)
Van Duyn, Mona (May 9, 1921)
Emanuel, James A. (June 15, 1921)
Carruth, Hayden (August 3, 1921)
Różewicz, Tadeusz (October 9, 1921)
Moss, Howard (January 22, 1922)
Pasolini, Pier Paolo (March 5, 1922)
Davie, Donald (July 17, 1922)
Popa, Vasko (July 29, 1922)
Larkin, Philip (August 9, 1922)
Paley, Grace (December 11, 1922)
Hecht, Anthony (January 16, 1923)

Logan, John (January 23, 1923)
Dickey, James (February 2, 1923)
Dugan, Alan (February 12, 1923)
Simpson, Louis (March 27, 1923)
Hoffman, Daniel (April 3, 1923)
Bonnefoy, Yves (June 24, 1923)
Szymborska, Wisława (July 2, 1923)
Yamada, Mitsuye (July 5, 1923)
Evans, Mari (July 16, 1923)
Holub, Miroslav (September 13, 1923)
Abse, Dannie (September 22, 1923)
Whalen, Philip (October 20, 1923)
Levertov, Denise (October 24, 1923)
Schuyler, James (November 9, 1923)
Hugo, Richard (December 21, 1923)
Mueller, Lisel (February 8, 1924)
Bowers, Edgar (March 2, 1924)
Stryk, Lucien (April 7, 1924)
Amichai, Yehuda (May 3, 1924)
Alegría, Claribel (May 12, 1924)
Field, Edward (June 7, 1924)
Corman, Cid (June 29, 1924)
Haines, John Meade (June 29, 1924)
Miller, Vassar (July 19, 1924)
Herbert, Zbigniew (October 29, 1924)
Beer, Patricia (November 4, 1924)
Cardenal, Ernesto (January 20, 1925)
Gomringer, Eugen (January 20, 1925)
Spicer, Jack (January 30, 1925)
Gilbert, Jack (February 17, 1925)
Stern, Gerald (February 22, 1925)
Koch, Kenneth (February 27, 1925)
Kaufman, Bob (April 18, 1925)
Kumin, Maxine (June 6, 1925)
Justice, Donald (August 12, 1925)
Menashe, Samuel (September 16, 1925)
Booth, Philip (October 8, 1925)
Kizer, Carolyn (December 10, 1925)

BORN 1926-1930

Snodgrass, W. D. (January 5, 1926)
Ammons, A. R. (February 18, 1926)
Merrill, James (March 3, 1926)
Creeley, Robert (May 21, 1926)
Ginsberg, Allen (June 3, 1926)

Wagoner, David (June 5, 1926)
Middleton, Christopher (June 10, 1926)
Bachmann, Ingeborg (June 25, 1926)
O'Hara, Frank (June 27, 1926)
Logue, Christopher (November 23, 1926)
Blackburn, Paul (November 24, 1926)
Bly, Robert (December 23, 1926)
Tomlinson, Charles (January 8, 1927)
Kinnell, Galway (February 1, 1927)
Ashbery, John (July 28, 1927)
Merwin, W. S. (September 30, 1927)
Grass, Günter (October 16, 1927)
Coulette, Henri (November 11, 1927)
Wright, James (December 13, 1927)
Sissman, L. E. (January 1, 1928)
Levine, Philip (January 10, 1928)
Macdonald, Cynthia (February 2, 1928)
Angelou, Maya (April 4, 1928)
Kinsella, Thomas (May 4, 1928)
Davison, Peter (June 27, 1928)
Hall, Donald (September 20, 1928)
Feldman, Irving (September 22, 1928)
Sexton, Anne (November 9, 1928)
Pavlović, Miodrag (November 28, 1928)
Cassity, Turner (January 12, 1929)
Montague, John (February 28, 1929)
Dorn, Edward (April 2, 1929)
Sorrentino, Gilbert (April 27, 1929)
Rich, Adrienne (May 16, 1929)
Dana, Robert (June 2, 1929)
Garrett, George (June 11, 1929)
Kennedy, X. J. (August 21, 1929)
Gunn, Thom (August 29, 1929)
Howard, Richard (October 13, 1929)
Hollander, John (October 28, 1929)
Enzensberger, Hans Magnus (November 11, 1929)
Walcott, Derek (January 23, 1930)
Oppenheimer, Joel (February 18, 1930)
Corso, Gregory (March 26, 1930)
Williams, Miller (April 8, 1930)
Snyder, Gary (May 8, 1930)
Brathwaite, Edward Kamau (May 11, 1930)
Hughes, Ted (August 17, 1930)
Silverstein, Shel (September 25, 1930 or 1932)

Pinter, Harold (October 10, 1930)
Pagis, Dan (October 16, 1930)
Achebe, Chinua (November 16, 1930)
Silkin, Jon (December 2, 1930)

BORN 1931-1935

Haavikko, Paavo (January 25, 1931)
Bernhard, Thomas (February 10, 1931)
Tranströmer, Tomas (April 15, 1931)
Knight, Etheridge (April 19, 1931)
MacBeth, George (January 19, 1932)
Updike, John (March 18, 1932)
Pastan, Linda (May 27, 1932)
Hill, Geoffrey (June 18, 1932)
Okigbo, Christopher (August 16, 1932)
McClure, Michael (October 20, 1932)
Plath, Sylvia (October 27, 1932)
Meinke, Peter (December 29, 1932)
Ko Un (January 8, 1933)
Price, Reynolds (February 1, 1933)
Voznesensky, Andrei (May 12, 1933)
Yevtushenko, Yevgeny (July 18, 1933)
Kunze, Reiner (August 16, 1933)
Lorde, Audre (February 18, 1934)
Flint, Roland (February 27, 1934)
Momaday, N. Scott (February 27, 1934)
Strand, Mark (April 11, 1934)
Hollo, Anselm (April 12, 1934)
Valentine, Jean (April 27, 1934)
Soyinka, Wole (July 13, 1934)
McDonald, Walt (July 18, 1934)
Berry, Wendell (August 5, 1934)
Di Prima, Diane (August 6, 1934)
Cohen, Leonard (September 2, 1934)
Sanchez, Sonia (September 9, 1934)
Zimmer, Paul (September 18, 1934)
Baraka, Amiri (October 7, 1934)
Berrigan, Ted (November 15, 1934)
Brautigan, Richard (January 30, 1935)
Awoonor, Kofi (March 13, 1935)
Slavitt, David (March 23, 1935)
Wright, Jay (May 25, 1935)
Applewhite, James (August 8, 1935)
Wright, Charles (August 25, 1935)
Oliver, Mary (September 10, 1935)

Kelly, Robert (September 24, 1935)
Johnson, Ronald (November 25, 1935)
Rivera, Tomás (December 22, 1935)

BORN 1936-1940
Piercy, Marge (March 31, 1936)
Chappell, Fred (May 28, 1936)
Clifton, Lucille (June 27, 1936)
Jordan, June (July 9, 1936)
Williams, C. K. (November 4, 1936)
Biermann, Wolf (November 15, 1936)
Harrison, Tony (April 30, 1937)
Howe, Susan (June 10, 1937)
Bell, Marvin (August 3, 1937)
Wakoski, Diane (August 3, 1937)
Ostriker, Alicia Suskin (November 11, 1937)
Harrison, Jim (December 11, 1937)
Reed, Ishmael (February 22, 1938)
Harper, Michael S. (March 18, 1938)
Simic, Charles (May 9, 1938)
Carver, Raymond (May 25, 1938)
Oates, Joyce Carol (June 16, 1938)
Murray, Les A. (October 17, 1938)
Galvin, Brendan (October 20, 1938)
Heaney, Seamus (April 13, 1939)
Kooser, Ted (April 25, 1939)
Dacey, Philip (May 9, 1939)
Plumly, Stanley (May 23, 1939)
Bidart, Frank (May 27, 1939)
Young, Al (May 31, 1939)
Dunn, Stephen (June 24, 1939)
McMichael, James (July 19, 1939)
Breytenbach, Breyten (September 16, 1939)
Dennis, Carl (September 17, 1939)
Allen, Paula Gunn (October 24, 1939)
Atwood, Margaret (November 18, 1939)
Mitsui, James Masao (February 4, 1940)
Rogers, Pattiann (March 23, 1940)
Brodsky, Joseph (May 24, 1940)
Pinsky, Robert (October 20, 1940)
Heyen, William (November 1, 1940)
Welch, James (November 18, 1940)
Rodgers, Carolyn M. (December 14, 1940)

BORN 1941-1945
Hass, Robert (March 1, 1941)
Glancy, Diane (March 18, 1941)
Collins, Billy (March 22, 1941)
Derricotte, Toi (April 12, 1941)
Hejinian, Lyn (May 17, 1941)
Ortiz, Simon (May 27, 1941)
Grennan, Eamon (November 13, 1941)
Mora, Pat (January 19, 1942)
Madhubuti, Haki R. (February 23, 1942)
Taylor, Henry (June 21, 1942)
Gregg, Linda (September 9, 1942)
Fairchild, B. H. (October 17, 1942)
Matthews, William (November 11, 1942)
Olds, Sharon (November 19, 1942)
Hacker, Marilyn (November 27, 1942)
Smith, Dave (December 19, 1942)
Glück, Louise (April 22, 1943)
Voigt, Ellen Bryant (May 9, 1943)
Glenn, Mel (May 10, 1943)
Giovanni, Nikki (June 7, 1943)
Gallagher, Tess (July 21, 1943)
McPherson, Sandra (August 2, 1943)
Corn, Alfred (August 14, 1943)
Ondaatje, Michael (September 12, 1943)
Balaban, John (December 2, 1943)
Tate, James (December 8, 1943)
Shomer, Enid (February 2, 1944)
Walker, Alice (February 9, 1944)
Gibson, Margaret (February 17, 1944)
Lifshin, Lyn (July 12, 1944)
Williams, Sherley Anne (August 25, 1944)
Boland, Eavan (September 24, 1944)
Kirby, Davi (November 29, 1944)
Wallace, Ronald (February 18, 1945)
Waldman, Anne (April 2, 1945)
Dubie, Norman (April 10, 1945)
Zagajewski, Adam (April 21, 1945)
Notley, Alice (November 8, 1945)
Muske, Carol (December 17, 1945)

BORN 1946-1950
Hampl, Patricia (March 12, 1946)
Levis, Larry (September 30, 1946)
Bang, Mary Jo (October 22, 1946)

CHRONOLOGICAL LIST OF POETS

Critical Survey of Poetry

Cliff, Michelle (November 2, 1946)
Lum, Wing Tek (November 11, 1946)
Barańczak, Stanisław (November 13, 1946)
Codrescu, Andrei (December 20, 1946)
Orr, Gregory (February 3, 1947)
Shore, Jane (March 10, 1947)
Komunyakaa, Yusef (April 29, 1947)
Kenyon, Jane (May 23, 1947)
Peacock, Molly (June 30, 1947)
Hogan, Linda (July 16, 1947)
Scalapino, Leslie (July 25, 1947)
Norris, Kathleen (July 27, 1947)
Ai (October 21, 1947)
Mackey, Nathaniel (October 25, 1947)
Steele, Timothy (January 22, 1948)
Goldbarth, Albert (January 31, 1948)
Wormser, Baron (February 4, 1948)
Silko, Leslie Marmon (March 5, 1948)
McHugh, Heather (August 20, 1948)
Santos, Sherod (September 9, 1948)
Anderson, Maggie (September 23, 1948)
Ehrhart, W. D. (September 30, 1948)
Ackerman, Diane (October 7, 1948)
Wright, C. D. (January 6, 1949)
Weigl, Bruce (January 27, 1949)
Ali, Agha Shahid (February 4, 1949)
Cruz, Victor Hernández (February 6, 1949)
Fenton, James (April 25, 1949)
St. John, David (July 24, 1949)
Bottoms, David (September 11, 1949)
Hirsch, Edward (January 20, 1950)
Alvarez, Julia (March 27, 1950)
Bernstein, Charles (April 4, 1950)
Forché, Carolyn (April 28, 1950)
Zamora, Daisy (June 20, 1950)
Carson, Anne (June 21, 1950)
Gregerson, Linda (August 5, 1950)
Twichell, Chase (August 20, 1950)
Gioia, Dana (December 24, 1950)

BORN 1951-1960
Kelly, Brigit Pegeen (April 21, 1951)
Hudgins, Andrew (April 22, 1951)
Graham, Jorie (May 9, 1951)

Harjo, Joy (May 9, 1951)
Hongo, Garrett Kaoru (May 30, 1951)
Muldoon, Paul (June 20, 1951)
Baca, Jimmy Santiago (January 2, 1952)
Fulton, Alice (January 25, 1952)
Ní Dhomhnaill, Nuala (February 16, 1952)
Shapiro, Alan (February 18, 1952)
Ortiz Cofer, Judith (February 24, 1952)
Nye, Naomi Shihab (March 12, 1952)
Soto, Gary (April 12, 1952)
Jarman, Mark (June 5, 1952)
Mura, David (June 17, 1952)
Seth, Vikram (June 20, 1952)
Dove, Rita (August 28, 1952)
Ríos, Alberto (September 18, 1952)
Hirshfield, Jane (February 24, 1953)
Leithauser, Brad (February 27, 1953)
Wright, Franz (March 18, 1953)
Collier, Michael (May 25, 1953)
Mullen, Harryette (July 1, 1953)
Doty, Mark (August 10, 1953)
Wojahn, David (August 22, 1953)
Schnackenberg, Gjertrud (August 27, 1953)
Eady, Cornelius (January 7, 1954)
Moss, Thylias (February 27, 1954)
Erdrich, Louise (June 7, 1954)
Cervantes, Lorna Dee (August 6, 1954)
Cisneros, Sandra (December 20, 1954)
Baker, David (December 27, 1954)
Hunt, Erica (1955)
Swensen, Cole (1955)
Chin, Marilyn (January 14, 1955)
Karr, Mary (January 16, 1955)
Hahn, Kimiko (July 5, 1955)
Young, Dean (July 18, 1955)
Song, Cathy (August 20, 1955)
Cole, Henri (1956)
Gerstler, Amy (October 24, 1956)
Emerson, Claudia (January 13, 1957)
Espada, Martín (August 7, 1957)
Lee, Li-Young (August 19, 1957)
Lindsay, Sarah (December 31, 1958)
Phillips, Carl (July 23, 1959)

BORN 1961 AND LATER

Kasischke, Laura (1961)

Beatty, Paul (1962)

Alexander, Elizabeth (May 30, 1962)

Kasdorf, Julia (December 6, 1962)

Rankine, Claudia (1963)

Trethewey, Natasha (April 26, 1966)

Alexie, Sherman (October 7, 1966)

Fennelly, Beth Ann (May 22, 1971)

INDEXES

GEOGRAPHICAL INDEX OF POETS AND ESSAYS

The boldface letters that precede numbers in this index indicate the set in which the entry can be found: **AP** = American Poets, **BP** = British, Irish, and Commonwealth Poets, **EP** = European Poets, **WP** = World Poets, *and* **TE** = Topical Essays.

AFRICA. *See also* **GHANA; LIBYA; NIGERIA; SENEGAL; SOUTH AFRICA**
African Poetry, **TE:** 15
Postcolonial Criticism, **TE:** 769
Postcolonial Poetry, **TE:** 500

ARGENTINA
Borges, Jorge Luis, **WP:** 39
Hernández, José, **WP:** 114

ASIA. *See* **CHINA; INDIA; JAPAN; SOUTH KOREA; TIBET**

ASIA MINOR. *See also* **TURKEY**
Rūmī, Jalāl al-Dīn, **WP:** 255
Sappho, **EP:** 941

AUSTRALIA
Australian and New Zealand Poetry, **TE:** 30
Hope, A. D., **BP:** 660
Murray, Les A., **BP:** 946
Postcolonial Criticism, **TE:** 769
Postcolonial Poetry, **TE:** 500

AUSTRIA
Bachmann, Ingeborg, **EP:** 72
Bernhard, Thomas, **EP:** 112
Hofmannsthal, Hugo von, **EP:** 478
Kraus, Karl, **EP:** 563
Rilke, Rainer Maria, **EP:** 889
Trakl, Georg, **EP:** 1033

Walther von der Vogelweide, **EP:** 1119
Zweig, Stefan, **EP:** 1141

BARBADOS
Brathwaite, Edward Kamau, **AP:** 228

BELGIUM. *See also* **FLANDERS**
Gezelle, Guido, **EP:** 384
Michaux, Henri, **EP:** 688
Sarton, May, **AP:** 1714
Verhaeren, Émile, **EP:** 1089

BOHEMIA. *See also* **CZECH REPUBLIC**
Kraus, Karl, **EP:** 563

BOLIVIA
Gomringer, Eugen, **EP:** 405

BOSNIA AND HERZEGOVINA
Dučić, Jovan, **EP:** 292

BRAZIL
Drummond de Andrade, Carlos, **WP:** 76
Latin American Poetry, **TE:** 435

BUKOVINA
Manger, Itzik, **EP:** 650

CANADA
Atwood, Margaret, **BP:** 37
Birney, Earle, **BP:** 86

Canadian poetry, **TE:** 37
Carson, Anne, **BP:** 225
Cohen, Leonard, **BP:** 272
Hébert, Anne, **BP:** 605
Jacobsen, Josephine, **AP:** 950
Layton, Irving, **BP:** 808
Ondaatje, Michael, **BP:** 973
Postcolonial Criticism, **TE:** 769
Postcolonial Poetry, **TE:** 500
Pratt, E. J., **BP:** 1016
Service, Robert W., **BP:** 1099
Strand, Mark, **AP:** 1918

CARIBBEAN. *See* **JAMAICA; MARTINIQUE; ST. LUCIA; WEST INDIES**

CEYLON. *See* **SRI LANKA**

CHILE
Latin American Poetry, **TE:** 435
Mistral, Gabriela, **WP:** 185
Neruda, Pablo, **WP:** 196
Parra, Nicanor, **WP:** 216

CHINA
Chin, Marilyn, **AP:** 307
Chinese Poetry, **TE:** 54
Du Fu, **WP:** 84
Li Bo, **WP:** 150
Li Qingzhao, **WP:** 157
Meng Haoran, **WP:** 182
Ruan Ji, **WP:** 250
Tao Qian, **WP:** 288
Tibetan Poetry, **TE:** 604
Wang Wei, **WP:** 326
Xie Lingyun, **WP:** 334

CROATIA
Croatian Poetry, **TE:** 71

CZECH REPUBLIC. *See also*
BOHEMIA
Czech Poetry, **TE:** 78
Holub, Miroslav, **EP:** 492
Kraus, Karl, **EP:** 563
Rilke, Rainer Maria, **EP:** 889
Seifert, Jaroslav, **EP:** 961

DENMARK
Hein, Piet, **EP:** 447

EGYPT
Apollonius Rhodius, **EP:** 30
Callimachus, **EP:** 175
Cavafy, Constantine P., **EP:** 204
Ungaretti, Giuseppe, **EP:** 1056

EL SALVADOR
Alegría, Claribel, **WP:** 9
Latin American Poetry, **TE:** 435

ENGLAND
Addison, Joseph, **BP:** 7
Æ, **BP:** 13
Aldington, Richard, **BP:** 17
Allingham, William, **BP:** 23
Arnold, Matthew, **BP:** 30
Auden, W. H., **BP:** 47
Beddoes, Thomas Lovell, **BP:** 56
Beer, Patricia, **BP:** 60
Behn, Aphra, **BP:** 66
Belloc, Hilaire, **BP:** 73
Betjeman, John, **BP:** 80
Blake, William, **BP:** 91
Blunden, Edmund, **BP:** 104
Bowles, William Lisle, **BP:** 119
Bradstreet, Anne, **AP:** 223
Breton, Nicholas, **BP:** 124
Bridges, Robert, **BP:** 131
Brontë, Emily, **BP:** 137
Brooke, Rupert, **BP:** 144
Browning, Elizabeth Barrett, **BP:** 149

Browning, Robert, **BP:** 158
Bunting, Basil, **BP:** 168
Butler, Samuel, **BP:** 180
Byron, Lord, **BP:** 186
Cædmon, **BP:** 197
Campion, Thomas, **BP:** 202
Carew, Thomas, **BP:** 208
Carroll, Lewis, **BP:** 213
Chapman, George, **BP:** 228
Chatterton, Thomas, **BP:** 235
Chaucer, Geoffrey, **BP:** 243
Clare, John, **BP:** 254
Clough, Arthur Hugh, **BP:** 266
Coleridge, Samuel Taylor, **BP:** 276
Collins, William, **BP:** 287
Confessional Poets, **TE:** 668
Congreve, William, **BP:** 296
Constable, Henry, **BP:** 301
Cotton, Charles, **BP:** 306
Cowley, Abraham, **BP:** 312
Cowper, William, **BP:** 320
Crabbe, George, **BP:** 327
Crashaw, Richard, **BP:** 337
Cynewulf, **BP:** 344
Daniel, Samuel, **BP:** 352
Darley, George, **BP:** 359
Davenant, Sir William, **BP:** 362
Davie, Donald, **BP:** 367
Davies, Sir John, **BP:** 375
Day Lewis, Cecil, **BP:** 384
Dekker, Thomas, **BP:** 390
De la Mare, Walter, **BP:** 398
Donne, John, **BP:** 405
Drayton, Michael, **BP:** 417
Dryden, John, **BP:** 433
Durrell, Lawrence, **BP:** 451
Eliot, T. S., **BP:** 458
Empson, William, **BP:** 468
English and American Poetry in the Nineteenth Century, **TE:** 174
English and American Poetry in the Twentieth Century, **TE:** 185

English and Continental Poetry in the Fourteenth Century, **TE:** 98
English Poetry in the Eighteenth Century, **TE:** 160
English Poetry in the Fifteenth Century, **TE:** 120
English Poetry in the Seventeenth Century, **TE:** 144
English Poetry in the Sixteenth Century, **TE:** 130
Etherege, Sir George, **BP:** 476
Fanshawe, Sir Richard, **BP:** 481
Fenton, James, **BP:** 487
Finch, Anne, **BP:** 491
FitzGerald, Edward, **BP:** 495
Fuller, Roy, **BP:** 500
Gascoigne, George, **BP:** 505
Gay, John, **BP:** 512
Goldsmith, Oliver, **BP:** 520
Gower, John, **BP:** 525
Graves, Robert, **BP:** 534
Gray, Thomas, **BP:** 542
Green Movement Poets, **TE:** 690
Greene, Robert, **BP:** 548
Greville, Fulke, **BP:** 555
Guest, Edgar A., **AP:** 748
Gunn, Thom, **BP:** 560
Gurney, Ivor, **BP:** 568
Hallam, Arthur Henry, **BP:** 575
Hardy, Thomas, **BP:** 579
Harrison, Tony, **BP:** 588
Hemans, Felicia Dorothea, **BP:** 609
Herbert, George, **BP:** 617
Herrick, Robert, **BP:** 626
Heywood, John, **BP:** 635
Hill, Geoffrey, **BP:** 641
Hood, Thomas, **BP:** 650
Hopkins, Gerard Manley, **BP:** 666
Housman, A. E., **BP:** 677
Hughes, Ted, **BP:** 686
Hunt, Leigh, **BP:** 694
Imagists, **TE:** 644
Johnson, Samuel, **BP:** 700

Jones, David, **BP:** 707
Jonson, Ben, **BP:** 711
Keats, John, **BP:** 731
King, Henry, **BP:** 743
Kipling, Rudyard, **BP:** 760
Lamb, Charles, **BP:** 768
Landor, Walter Savage, **BP:** 774
Langland, William, **BP:** 780
Larkin, Philip, **BP:** 786
Lawrence, D. H., **BP:** 795
Layamon, **BP:** 803
Lear, Edward, **BP:** 812
Levertov, Denise, **AP:** 1111
Lodge, Thomas, **BP:** 817
Logue, Christopher, **BP:** 823
Lovelace, Richard, **BP:** 827
Lydgate, John, **BP:** 832
MacBeth, George, **BP:** 841
MacNeice, Louis, **BP:** 854
Manger, Itzik, **EP:** 650
Marie de France, **EP:** 666
Marlowe, Christopher, **BP:** 870
Marvell, Andrew, **BP:** 877
Masefield, John, **BP:** 885
Meredith, George, **BP:** 890
Merton, Thomas, **AP:** 1325
Metaphysical Poets, **TE:** 615
Mew, Charlotte, **BP:** 894
Middleton, Christopher, **BP:** 898
Milton, John, **BP:** 905
Modernists, **TE:** 650
Morris, William, **BP:** 924
Movement Poets, **TE:** 679
Muir, Edwin, **BP:** 933
Nashe, Thomas, **BP:** 953
Newcastle, Margaret Cavendish, duchess of, **BP:** 958
Ní Dhomhnaill, Nuala, **BP:** 964
Oldham, John, **BP:** 969
Owen, Wilfred, **BP:** 977
Patmore, Coventry, **BP:** 983
Pearl-Poet, **BP:** 991
Pinter, Harold, **BP:** 1001
Pope, Alexander, **BP:** 1005
Postcolonial Criticism, **TE:** 769

Prince, F. T., **BP:** 1021
Prior, Matthew, **BP:** 1026
Quarles, Francis, **BP:** 1031
Ralegh, Sir Walter, **BP:** 1037
Reed, Henry, **BP:** 1043
Restoration Poetry, **TE:** 620
Rochester, John Wilmot, earl of, **BP:** 1048
Romantic Poets, **TE:** 626
Rosenberg, Isaac, **BP:** 1055
Rossetti, Christina, **BP:** 1060
Rossetti, Dante Gabriel, **BP:** 1065
Sackville, Thomas, **BP:** 1074
Sassoon, Siegfried, **BP:** 1080
Scott, Sir Walter, **BP:** 1087
Sedley, Sir Charles, **BP:** 1094
Service, Robert W., **BP:** 1099
Shakespeare, William, **BP:** 1105
Shelley, Percy Bysshe, **BP:** 1112
Sidney, Sir Philip, **BP:** 1126
Sidney, Sir Robert, **BP:** 1135
Silkin, Jon, **BP:** 1141
Sitwell, Edith, **BP:** 1145
Skelton, John, **BP:** 1153
Smart, Christopher, **BP:** 1159
Smith, Stevie, **BP:** 1164
Southey, Robert, **BP:** 1171
Southwell, Robert, **BP:** 1178
Spender, Stephen, **BP:** 1183
Spenser, Edmund, **BP:** 1191
Suckling, Sir John, **BP:** 1206
Surrey, Henry Howard, earl of, **BP:** 1212
Swift, Jonathan, **BP:** 1218
Swinburne, Algernon Charles, **BP:** 1227
Taylor, Edward, **AP:** 1959
Tennyson, Alfred, Lord, **BP:** 1236
Thomas, Edward, **BP:** 1252
Thomson, James (1700-1748), **BP:** 1260
Thomson, James (1834-1882), **BP:** 1264
Tomlinson, Charles, **BP:** 1268
Traherne, Thomas, **BP:** 1277

Waller, Edmund, **BP:** 1290
Watts, Isaac, **BP:** 1297
Wilde, Oscar, **BP:** 1303
Wordsworth, William, **BP:** 1310
Wyatt, Sir Thomas, **BP:** 1322
Young, Edward, **BP:** 1349
Zweig, Stefan, **EP:** 1141

EUROPE
European Oral and Epic Traditions, **TE:** 214

FINLAND
Haavikko, Paavo, **EP:** 435
Hollo, Anselm, **AP:** 887
Lönnrot, Elias, **EP:** 617
Scandinavian Poetry, **TE:** 526
Södergran, Edith, **EP:** 981

FLANDERS
Gezelle, Guido, **EP:** 384

FRANCE
Apollinaire, Guillaume, **EP:** 22
Aragon, Louis, **EP:** 35
Arp, Hans, **EP:** 62
Baudelaire, Charles, **EP:** 80
Beckett, Samuel, **EP:** 87
Belloc, Hilaire, **BP:** 73
Boileau-Despréaux, Nicolas, **EP:** 138
Bonnefoy, Yves, **EP:** 142
Breton, André, **EP:** 157
Breytenbach, Breyten, **EP:** 162
Celan, Paul, **EP:** 214
Char, René, **EP:** 226
Charles d'Orléans, **EP:** 230
Chartier, Alain, **EP:** 236
Christine de Pizan, **EP:** 240
Claudel, Paul, **EP:** 244
Cocteau, Jean, **EP:** 253
Corbière, Tristan, **EP:** 260
Du Bellay, Joachim, **EP:** 289
Éluard, Paul, **EP:** 313
Follain, Jean, **EP:** 335

French Poetry Since 1700, **TE:** 254
French Poetry to 1700, **TE:** 232
French Symbolists, **TE:** 639
Gautier, Théophile, **EP:** 368
Guillame de Lorris, **EP:** 424
Heine, Heinrich, **EP:** 451
Hugo, Victor, **EP:** 518
Jean de Meung, **EP:** 424
La Fontaine, Jean de, **EP:** 577
Laforgue, Jules, **EP:** 584
Lamartine, Alphonse de, **EP:** 591
Malherbe, François de, **EP:** 639
Mallarmé, Stéphane, **EP:** 644
Marie de France, **EP:** 666
Marino, Giambattista, **EP:** 674
Merton, Thomas, **AP:** 1325
Michaux, Henri, **EP:** 688
Mickiewicz, Adam, **EP:** 702
Musset, Alfred de, **EP:** 736
Nerval, Gérard de, **EP:** 741
Péguy, Charles-Pierre, **EP:** 791
Perse, Saint-John, **EP:** 801
Ponge, Francis, **EP:** 848
Prévert, Jacques, **EP:** 861
Reverdy, Pierre, **EP:** 883
Rilke, Rainer Maria, **EP:** 889
Rimbaud, Arthur, **EP:** 897
Ronsard, Pierre de, **EP:** 912
Senghor, Léopold, **WP:** 264
Słowacki, Juliusz, **EP:** 972
Stein, Gertrude, **AP:** 1885
Tzara, Tristan, **EP:** 1044
Valéry, Paul, **EP:** 1065
Verlaine, Paul, **EP:** 1093
Vigny, Alfred de, **EP:** 1099
Villon, François, **EP:** 1106
Zagajewski, Adam, **EP:** 1137

GERMANY. *See also* SWABIA
Amichai, Yehuda, **WP:** 14
Arp, Hans, **EP:** 62
Ausländer, Rose, **AP:** 65
Benn, Gottfried, **EP:** 107
Biermann, Wolf, **EP:** 119
Bobrowski, Johannes, **EP:** 126

Brecht, Bertolt, **EP:** 149
East German Poetry, **TE:** 87
Eichendorff, Joseph von, **EP:** 299
Enzensberger, Hans Magnus, **EP:** 323
George, Stefan, **EP:** 377
German Poetry to 1800, **TE:** 283
German Poetry: 1800 to Reunification, **TE:** 298
German Poetry Since Reunification, **TE:** 315
Goethe, Johann Wolfgang von, **EP:** 396
Gomringer, Eugen, **EP:** 405
Gottfried von Strassburg, **EP:** 415
Grass, Günter, **EP:** 418
Hartmann von Aue, **EP:** 441
Heine, Heinrich, **EP:** 451
Hesse, Hermann, **EP:** 471
Hofmannsthal, Hugo von, **EP:** 478
Hölderlin, Friedrich, **EP:** 485
Holz, Arno, **EP:** 497
Kunze, Reiner, **EP:** 570
Morgenstern, Christian, **EP:** 727
Mörike, Eduard, **EP:** 732
Mueller, Lisel, **AP:** 1383
Novalis, **EP:** 748
Rakosi, Carl, **AP:** 1590
Rilke, Rainer Maria, **EP:** 889
Sachs, Nelly, **EP:** 930
Schiller, Friedrich, **EP:** 949
Trakl, Georg, **EP:** 1033
Walther von der Vogelweide, **EP:** 1119
Wolfram von Eschenbach, **EP:** 1130

GHANA
Awoonor, Kofi, **WP:** 25

GREAT BRITAIN. *See also* ENGLAND; IRELAND
Abse, Dannie, **BP:** 1
Addison, Joseph, **BP:** 7
Æ, **BP:** 13

Aldington, Richard, **BP:** 17
Allingham, William, **BP:** 23
Arnold, Matthew, **BP:** 30
Auden, W. H., **BP:** 47
Beddoes, Thomas Lovell, **BP:** 56
Beer, Patricia, **BP:** 60
Behn, Aphra, **BP:** 66
Belloc, Hilaire, **BP:** 73
Betjeman, John, **BP:** 80
Blake, William, **BP:** 91
Blunden, Edmund, **BP:** 104
Bowles, William Lisle, **BP:** 119
Bradstreet, Anne, **AP:** 223
Breton, Nicholas, **BP:** 124
Bridges, Robert, **BP:** 131
Brontë, Emily, **BP:** 137
Brooke, Rupert, **BP:** 144
Browning, Elizabeth Barrett, **BP:** 149
Browning, Robert, **BP:** 158
Bunting, Basil, **BP:** 168
Burns, Robert, **BP:** 173
Butler, Samuel, **BP:** 180
Byron, Lord, **BP:** 186
Cædmon, **BP:** 197
Campion, Thomas, **BP:** 202
Carew, Thomas, **BP:** 208
Carroll, Lewis, **BP:** 213
Chapman, George, **BP:** 228
Chatterton, Thomas, **BP:** 235
Chaucer, Geoffrey, **BP:** 243
Clare, John, **BP:** 254
Clough, Arthur Hugh, **BP:** 266
Coleridge, Samuel Taylor, **BP:** 276
Collins, William, **BP:** 287
Confessional Poets, **TE:** 668
Congreve, William, **BP:** 296
Constable, Henry, **BP:** 301
Cotton, Charles, **BP:** 306
Cowley, Abraham, **BP:** 312
Cowper, William, **BP:** 320
Crabbe, George, **BP:** 327
Crashaw, Richard, **BP:** 337
Cynewulf, **BP:** 344

Daniel, Samuel, **BP:** 352

Darley, George, **BP:** 359

Davenant, Sir William, **BP:** 362

Davie, Donald, **BP:** 367

Davies, Sir John, **BP:** 375

Day Lewis, Cecil, **BP:** 384

Dekker, Thomas, **BP:** 390

De la Mare, Walter, **BP:** 398

Donne, John, **BP:** 405

Drayton, Michael, **BP:** 417

Drummond of Hawthornden, William, **BP:** 424

Dryden, John, **BP:** 433

Dunbar, William, **BP:** 442

Durrell, Lawrence, **BP:** 451

Eliot, T. S., **BP:** 458

Empson, William, **BP:** 468

English and American Poetry in the Nineteenth Century, **TE:** 174

English and American Poetry in the Twentieth Century, **TE:** 185

English and Continental Poetry in the Fourteenth Century, **TE:** 98

English Poetry in the Eighteenth Century, **TE:** 160

English Poetry in the Fifteenth Century, **TE:** 120

English Poetry in the Seventeenth Century, **TE:** 144

English Poetry in the Sixteenth Century, **TE:** 130

Etherege, Sir George, **BP:** 476

Fanshawe, Sir Richard, **BP:** 481

Fenton, James, **BP:** 487

Finch, Anne, **BP:** 491

FitzGerald, Edward, **BP:** 495

Fuller, Roy, **BP:** 500

Gascoigne, George, **BP:** 505

Gay, John, **BP:** 512

Goldsmith, Oliver, **BP:** 520

Gower, John, **BP:** 525

Graves, Robert, **BP:** 534

Gray, Thomas, **BP:** 542

Green Movement Poets, **TE:** 690

Greene, Robert, **BP:** 548

Grennan, Eamon, **AP:** 741

Greville, Fulke, **BP:** 555

Guest, Edgar A., **AP:** 748

Gunn, Thom, **BP:** 560

Gurney, Ivor, **BP:** 568

Hallam, Arthur Henry, **BP:** 575

Hardy, Thomas, **BP:** 579

Harrison, Tony, **BP:** 588

Heaney, Seamus, **BP:** 594

Hemans, Felicia Dorothea, **BP:** 609

Henryson, Robert, **BP:** 612

Herbert, George, **BP:** 617

Herrick, Robert, **BP:** 626

Heywood, John, **BP:** 635

Hill, Geoffrey, **BP:** 641

Hood, Thomas, **BP:** 650

Hopkins, Gerard Manley, **BP:** 666

Housman, A. E., **BP:** 677

Hughes, Ted, **BP:** 686

Hunt, Leigh, **BP:** 694

Imagists, **TE:** 644

Johnson, Samuel, **BP:** 700

Jones, David, **BP:** 707

Jonson, Ben, **BP:** 711

Keats, John, **BP:** 731

King, Henry, **BP:** 743

Kipling, Rudyard, **BP:** 760

Lamb, Charles, **BP:** 768

Landor, Walter Savage, **BP:** 774

Langland, William, **BP:** 780

Larkin, Philip, **BP:** 786

Lawrence, D. H., **BP:** 795

Layamon, **BP:** 803

Lear, Edward, **BP:** 812

Levertov, Denise, **AP:** 1111

Lodge, Thomas, **BP:** 817

Logue, Christopher, **BP:** 823

Lovelace, Richard, **BP:** 827

Lydgate, John, **BP:** 832

MacBeth, George, **BP:** 841

MacDiarmid, Hugh, **BP:** 846

MacNeice, Louis, **BP:** 854

Manger, Itzik, **EP:** 650

Marie de France, **EP:** 666

Marlowe, Christopher, **BP:** 870

Marvell, Andrew, **BP:** 877

Masefield, John, **BP:** 885

Meredith, George, **BP:** 890

Merton, Thomas, **AP:** 1325

Metaphysical Poets, **TE:** 615

Mew, Charlotte, **BP:** 894

Middleton, Christopher, **BP:** 898

Milton, John, **BP:** 905

Modernists, **TE:** 650

Morris, William, **BP:** 924

Movement Poets, **TE:** 679

Muir, Edwin, **BP:** 933

Nashe, Thomas, **BP:** 953

Newcastle, Margaret Cavendish, duchess of, **BP:** 958

Ní Dhomhnaill, Nuala, **BP:** 964

Oldham, John, **BP:** 969

Owen, Wilfred, **BP:** 977

Patmore, Coventry, **BP:** 983

Pearl-Poet, **BP:** 991

Pinter, Harold, **BP:** 1001

Pope, Alexander, **BP:** 1005

Postcolonial Criticism, **TE:** 769

Prince, F. T., **BP:** 1021

Prior, Matthew, **BP:** 1026

Quarles, Francis, **BP:** 1031

Ralegh, Sir Walter, **BP:** 1037

Reed, Henry, **BP:** 1043

Restoration Poetry, **TE:** 620

Rochester, John Wilmot, earl of, **BP:** 1048

Romantic Poets, **TE:** 626

Rosenberg, Isaac, **BP:** 1055

Rossetti, Christina, **BP:** 1060

Rossetti, Dante Gabriel, **BP:** 1065

Sackville, Thomas, **BP:** 1074

Sassoon, Siegfried, **BP:** 1080

Scott, Sir Walter, **BP:** 1087

Sedley, Sir Charles, **BP:** 1094

Service, Robert W., **BP:** 1099

Shakespeare, William, **BP:** 1105

Shelley, Percy Bysshe, **BP:** 1112
Sidney, Sir Philip, **BP:** 1126
Sidney, Sir Robert, **BP:** 1135
Silkin, Jon, **BP:** 1141
Sitwell, Edith, **BP:** 1145
Skelton, John, **BP:** 1153
Smart, Christopher, **BP:** 1159
Smith, Stevie, **BP:** 1164
Southey, Robert, **BP:** 1171
Southwell, Robert, **BP:** 1178
Spender, Stephen, **BP:** 1183
Spenser, Edmund, **BP:** 1191
Suckling, Sir John, **BP:** 1206
Surrey, Henry Howard, earl of, **BP:** 1212
Swift, Jonathan, **BP:** 1218
Swinburne, Algernon Charles, **BP:** 1227
Taylor, Edward, **AP:** 1959
Tennyson, Alfred, Lord, **BP:** 1236
Thomas, Dylan, **BP:** 1245
Thomas, Edward, **BP:** 1252
Thomas, R. S., **BP:** 1257
Thomson, James (1700-1748), **BP:** 1260
Thomson, James (1834-1882), **BP:** 1264
Tomlinson, Charles, **BP:** 1268
Traherne, Thomas, **BP:** 1277
Vaughan, Henry, **BP:** 1284
Waller, Edmund, **BP:** 1290
Watts, Isaac, **BP:** 1297
Wilde, Oscar, **BP:** 1303
Wordsworth, William, **BP:** 1310
Wyatt, Sir Thomas, **BP:** 1322
Young, Edward, **BP:** 1349
Zweig, Stefan, **EP:** 1141

GREECE. *See also* **LESBOS**
Anacreon, **EP:** 17
Archilochus, **EP:** 50
Callimachus, **EP:** 175
Cavafy, Constantine P., **EP:** 204
Elytis, Odysseus, **EP:** 317
Foscolo, Ugo, **EP:** 340

Greek Poetry in Antiquity, **TE:** 320
Greek Poetry Since 1820, **TE:** 331
Hesiod, **EP:** 465
Hikmet, Nazim, **WP:** 117
Homer, **EP:** 502
Kazantzakis, Nikos, **EP:** 557
Leonidas of Tarentum, **EP:** 602
Macedonian Poetry, **TE:** 475
Meleager, **EP:** 685
Pentzikis, Nikos, **EP:** 797
Pindar, **EP:** 836
Ritsos, Yannis, **EP:** 904
Sappho, **EP:** 941
Seferis, George, **EP:** 957
Solomos, Dionysios, **EP:** 987
Theocritus, **EP:** 1023
Theognis, **EP:** 1029

GUADELOUPE
Perse, Saint-John, **EP:** 801

HONG KONG
Chin, Marilyn, **AP:** 307

HUNGARY
Ady, Endre, **EP:** 1
Arany, János, **EP:** 42
Babits, Mihály, **EP:** 68
Hungarian Poetry, **TE:** 352
Illyés, Gyula, **EP:** 528
Petőfi, Sándor, **EP:** 816
Radnóti, Miklós, **EP:** 879
Rakosi, Carl, **AP:** 1590
Vörösmarty, Mihály, **EP:** 1112

INDIA
Ali, Agha Shahid, **AP:** 24
Durrell, Lawrence, **BP:** 451
Indian English Poetry, **TE:** 365
Kipling, Rudyard, **BP:** 760
Postcolonial Poetry, **TE:** 500
Seth, Vikram, **WP:** 272
Tagore, Rabindranath, **WP:** 281
Vālmīki, **WP:** 308

INDONESIA
Lee, Li-Young, **AP:** 1102

IRAN
Firdusi, **WP:** 96
Hafiz, **WP:** 108
Omar Khayyám, **WP:** 208
Rūmī, Jalāl al-Dīn, **WP:** 255
Saʿdi, **WP:** 260

IRELAND. *See also* **NORTHERN IRELAND**
Æ, **BP:** 13
Allingham, William, **BP:** 23
Beckett, Samuel, **EP:** 87
Boland, Eavan, **BP:** 108
Clarke, Austin, **BP:** 261
Colum, Padraic, **BP:** 292
Darley, George, **BP:** 359
Goldsmith, Oliver, **BP:** 520
Grennan, Eamon, **AP:** 741
Heaney, Seamus, **BP:** 594
Joyce, James, **BP:** 719
Kavanagh, Patrick, **BP:** 726
Kinsella, Thomas, **BP:** 751
MacBeth, George, **BP:** 841
MacNeice, Louis, **BP:** 854
Mangan, James Clarence, **BP:** 866
Montague, John, **BP:** 914
Muldoon, Paul, **BP:** 937
Swift, Jonathan, **BP:** 1218
Wilde, Oscar, **BP:** 1303
Yeats, William Butler, **BP:** 1330

ISRAEL
Amichai, Yehuda, **WP:** 14
Manger, Itzik, **EP:** 650
Pagis, Dan, **WP:** 213

ITALY. *See also* **SICILY; TUSCANY**
Ariosto, Ludovico, **EP:** 56
Bembo, Pietro, **EP:** 101
Boccaccio, Giovanni, **EP:** 131
Boiardo, Matteo Maria, **EP:** 135

Carducci, Giosuè, **EP:** 185

Catullus, **EP:** 197

Cavalcanti, Guido, **EP:** 210

Christine de Pizan, **EP:** 240

D'Annunzio, Gabriele, **EP:** 264

Dante, **EP:** 270

Foscolo, Ugo, **EP:** 340

Fracastoro, Girolamo, **EP:** 345

Giusti, Giuseppe, **EP:** 391

Horace, **EP:** 510

Italian Poetry Since 1800, **TE:** 393

Italian Poetry to 1800, **TE:** 377

Juvenal, **EP:** 553

Landor, Walter Savage, **BP:** 774

Leonidas of Tarentum, **EP:** 602

Leopardi, Giacomo, **EP:** 607

Lucan, **EP:** 621

Lucretius, **EP:** 627

Manzoni, Alessandro, **EP:** 660

Marino, Giambattista, **EP:** 674

Michelangelo, **EP:** 694

Montale, Eugenio, **EP:** 721

Ovid, **EP:** 763

Pascoli, Giovanni, **EP:** 771

Pasolini, Pier Paolo, **EP:** 776

Pavese, Cesare, **EP:** 783

Persius, **EP:** 806

Petrarch, **EP:** 828

Poliziano, **EP:** 841

Pound, Ezra, **AP:** 1577

Propertius, Sextus, **EP:** 866

Quasimodo, Salvatore, **EP:** 873

Saba, Umberto, **EP:** 925

Stampa, Gaspara, **EP:** 993

Statius, **EP:** 998

Tasso, Torquato, **EP:** 1014

Ungaretti, Giuseppe, **EP:** 1056

Vergil, **EP:** 1080

JAMAICA

Cliff, Michelle, **WP:** 61

McKay, Claude, **AP:** 1234

Rankine, Claudia, **AP:** 1602

Simpson, Louis, **AP:** 1793

JAPAN

Issa, **WP:** 126

Japanese Poetry Since 1800, **TE:** 427

Japanese Poetry to 1800, **TE:** 412

Matsuo Bashō, **WP:** 170

Miyazawa, Kenji, **WP:** 191

Yamada, Mitsuye, **AP:** 2244

Yosano Akiko, **WP:** 349

LATIN AMERICA. *See also* **ARGENTINA; BOLIVIA; BRAZIL; CHILE; EL SALVADOR; MEXICO; NICARAGUA; PERU**

Latin American Poetry, **TE:** 435

LEBANON

Gibran, Kahlil, **AP:** 663

LESBOS

Sappho, **EP:** 941

LIBYA

Callimachus, **EP:** 175

LITHUANIA

Miłosz, Czesław, **EP:** 709

MARTINIQUE

Césaire, Aimé, **WP:** 56

MEXICO

Cernuda, Luis, **EP:** 220

Cruz, Sor Juana Inés de la, **WP:** 64

González Martínez, Enrique, **WP:** 101

Latin American Poetry, **TE:** 435

Paz, Octavio, **WP:** 230

Reyes, Alfonso, **WP:** 245

MIDDLE EAST. *See* **ASIA MINOR; EGYPT; IRAN; ISRAEL; OTTOMAN EMPIRE; PERSIA; SYRIA**

MONTENEGRO

Popa, Vasko, **EP:** 856

NEW ZEALAND

Australian and New Zealand Poetry, **TE:** 30

Postcolonial Criticism, **TE:** 769

NICARAGUA

Alegría, Claribel, **WP:** 9

Cardenal, Ernesto, **WP:** 52

Darío, Rubén, **WP:** 71

Latin American Poetry, **TE:** 435

Zamora, Daisy, **WP:** 354

NIGERIA

Achebe, Chinua, **WP:** 1

Okigbo, Christopher, **WP:** 205

Soyinka, Wole, **WP:** 276

NORTHERN IRELAND. *See also* **IRELAND**

Heaney, Seamus, **BP:** 594

Muldoon, Paul, **BP:** 937

OTTOMAN EMPIRE

Hikmet, Nazim, **WP:** 117

PERSIA

Firdusi, **WP:** 96

Hafiz, **WP:** 108

Omar Khayyám, **WP:** 208

Rūmī, Jalāl al-Dīn, **WP:** 255

Saʿdi, **WP:** 260

PERU

Latin American Poetry, **TE:** 435

Vallejo, César, **WP:** 300

PHILIPPINES

Villa, José García, **AP:** 2048

POLAND

Barańczak, Stanisław, **EP:** 77

Herbert, Zbigniew, **EP:** 458

Mandelstam, Osip, **WP:** 163
Mickiewicz, Adam, **EP:** 702
Miłosz, Czesław, **EP:** 709
Polish Poetry, **TE:** 489
Różewicz, Tadeusz, **EP:** 917
Słonimski, Antoni, **EP:** 968
Słowacki, Juliusz, **EP:** 972
Stryk, Lucien, **AP:** 1927
Swir, Anna, **EP:** 1004
Szymborska, Wisława, **EP:** 1007
Ważyk, Adam, **EP:** 1126
Zagajewski, Adam, **EP:** 1137

PORTUGAL
Camões, Luís de, **EP:** 180
Pessoa, Fernando, **EP:** 811

PUERTO RICO
Cruz, Victor Hernández, **AP:** 400

ROMAN EMPIRE. *See also*
   ASIA MINOR; BOHEMIA;
   EGYPT; GERMANY;
   GREECE; ITALY;
   SWABIA
Catullus, **EP:** 197
Horace, **EP:** 510
Juvenal, **EP:** 553
Latin Poetry, **TE:** 441
Lucan, **EP:** 621
Lucretius, **EP:** 627
Martial, **EP:** 678
Ovid, **EP:** 763
Persius, **EP:** 806
Propertius, Sextus, **EP:** 866
Statius, **EP:** 998
Theocritus, **EP:** 1023
Theognis, **EP:** 1029
Vergil, **EP:** 1080

ROMANIA. *See also*
   BUKOVINA
Ady, Endre, **EP:** 1
Ausländer, Rose, **AP:** 65
Celan, Paul, **EP:** 214

Codrescu, Andrei, **AP:** 331
Layton, Irving, **BP:** 808
Manger, Itzik, **EP:** 650
Pagis, Dan, **WP:** 213
Tzara, Tristan, **EP:** 1044

RUSSIA
Akhmatova, Anna, **WP:** 3
Annensky, Innokenty, **WP:** 21
Blok, Aleksandr, **WP:** 33
Brodsky, Joseph, **WP:** 44
Esenin, Sergei, **WP:** 90
Khodasevich, Vladislav, **WP:** 133
Lermontov, Mikhail, **WP:** 142
Mandelstam, Osip, **WP:** 163
Mayakovsky, Vladimir, **WP:** 176
Mickiewicz, Adam, **EP:** 702
Pasternak, Boris, **WP:** 222
Pushkin, Alexander, **WP:** 236
Russian Poetry, **TE:** 509
Södergran, Edith, **EP:** 981
Tsvetayeva, Marina, **WP:** 293
Voznesensky, Andrei, **WP:** 311
Yevtushenko, Yevgeny, **WP:** 339

ST. LUCIA
Walcott, Derek, **WP:** 317

SCANDINAVIA. *See*
   DENMARK; FINLAND;
   SWEDEN

SCOTLAND
Burns, Robert, **BP:** 173
Drummond of Hawthornden,
   William, **BP:** 424
Dunbar, William, **BP:** 442
Henryson, Robert, **BP:** 612
MacBeth, George, **BP:** 841
MacDiarmid, Hugh, **BP:** 846
Muir, Edwin, **BP:** 933
Scott, Sir Walter, **BP:** 1087
Service, Robert W., **BP:** 1099
Stevenson, Robert Louis, **BP:**
   1201

Thomson, James (1700-1748),
   BP: 1260
Thomson, James (1834-1882),
   BP: 1264

SENEGAL
Senghor, Léopold, **WP:** 264

SERBIA
Dučić, Jovan, **EP:** 292
Macedonian Poetry, **TE:** 475
Pavlović, Miodrag, **EP:** 786
Popa, Vasko, **EP:** 856
Serbian Poetry, **TE:** 566
Simic, Charles, **AP:** 1785

SICILY
Theocritus, **EP:** 1023

SLOVAKIA. *See also* **CZECH**
   REPUBLIC
Slovak Poetry, **TE:** 573

SLOVENIA
Slovenian Poetry, **TE:** 579

SOUTH AFRICA
Breytenbach, Breyten, **EP:** 162
Prince, F. T., **BP:** 1021

SOUTH KOREA
Ko Un, **WP:** 138

SOVIET UNION. *See* **RUSSIA;**
   UKRAINE

SPAIN
Alberti, Rafael, **EP:** 6
Aleixandre, Vicente, **EP:** 12
Bécquer, Gustavo Adolfo, **EP:** 95
Calderón de la Barca, Pedro, **EP:**
   170
Castro, Rosalía de, **EP:** 190
Catalan Poetry, **TE:** 48
Cernuda, Luis, **EP:** 220

Foix, J. V., **EP:** 329
García Lorca, Federico, **EP:** 355
Garcilaso de la Vega, **EP:** 362
Góngora y Argote, Luis de, **EP:** 410
Guillén, Jorge, **EP:** 430
Jiménez, Juan Ramón, **EP:** 533
John of the Cross, Saint, **EP:** 539
Judah ha-Levi, **EP:** 549
León, Luis de, **EP:** 597
Lucan, **EP:** 621
Machado, Antonio, **EP:** 633
Manrique, Jorge, **EP:** 657
Martial, **EP:** 678
Otero, Blas de, **EP:** 757
Salinas, Pedro, **EP:** 936
Spanish Poetry Since 1400, **TE:** 592
Spanish Poetry to 1400, **TE:** 583
Unamuno y Jugo, Miguel de, **EP:** 1051
Vallejo, César, **WP:** 300
Vega Carpio, Lope de, **EP:** 1073

SRI LANKA
Ondaatje, Michael, **BP:** 973

SWABIA
Hartmann von Aue, **EP:** 441

SWEDEN
Ekelöf, Gunnar, **EP:** 306
Martinson, Harry, **EP:** 681
Sachs, Nelly, **EP:** 930
Scandinavian Poetry, **TE:** 526
Södergran, Edith, **EP:** 981
Tegnér, Esaias, **EP:** 1020
Tranströmer, Tomas, **EP:** 1039

SWITZERLAND
Arp, Hans, **EP:** 62
Gomringer, Eugen, **EP:** 405

SYRIA
Gibran, Kahlil, **AP:** 663
Meleager, **EP:** 685

TIBET
Tibetan Poetry, **TE:** 604

TURKEY. *See also* **ASIA MINOR**
Hikmet, Nazim, **WP:** 117
Rūmī, Jalāl al-Dīn, **WP:** 255
Seferis, George, **EP:** 957

TUSCANY
Giusti, Giuseppe, **EP:** 391

UKRAINE
Akhmatova, Anna, **WP:** 3
Ausländer, Rose, **AP:** 65

UNITED STATES
Ackerman, Diane, **AP:** 1
Adams, Léonie, **AP:** 4
African American Poetry, **TE:** 3
Ai, **AP:** 8
Aiken, Conrad, **AP:** 12
Alexander, Elizabeth, **AP:** 17
Alexie, Sherman, **AP:** 21
Ali, Agha Shahid, **AP:** 24
Allen, Paula Gunn, **AP:** 27
Alvarez, Julia, **AP:** 31
Ammons, A. R., **AP:** 37
Anderson, Maggie, **AP:** 43
Angelou, Maya, **AP:** 46
Applewhite, James, **AP:** 51
Ashbery, John, **AP:** 55
Asian American Poetry, **TE:** 21
Auden, W. H., **BP:** 47
Ausländer, Rose, **AP:** 65
Baca, Jimmy Santiago, **AP:** 71
Baker, David, **AP:** 77
Balaban, John, **AP:** 81
Bang, Mary Jo, **AP:** 85
Baraka, Amiri, **AP:** 89
Barnard, Mary, **AP:** 100
Beat Poets, **TE:** 661
Beatty, Paul, **AP:** 107
Becker, Robin, **AP:** 110
Belitt, Ben, **AP:** 114

Bell, Marvin, **AP:** 119
Benét, Stephen Vincent, **AP:** 124
Benét, William Rose, **AP:** 128
Bernstein, Charles, **AP:** 132
Berrigan, Daniel, **AP:** 137
Berrigan, Ted, **AP:** 143
Berry, Wendell, **AP:** 146
Berryman, John, **AP:** 155
Bidart, Frank, **AP:** 162
Bishop, Elizabeth, **AP:** 169
Bishop, John Peale, **AP:** 177
Black Mountain School, **TE:** 684
Blackburn, Paul, **AP:** 180
Bly, Robert, **AP:** 188
Bogan, Louise, **AP:** 197
Bontemps, Arna, **AP:** 205
Booth, Philip, **AP:** 209
Bottoms, David, **AP:** 216
Bowers, Edgar, **AP:** 219
Bradstreet, Anne, **AP:** 223
Brautigan, Richard, **AP:** 239
Brodsky, Joseph, **WP:** 44
Bronk, William, **AP:** 243
Brooks, Gwendolyn, **AP:** 247
Brown, Sterling A., **AP:** 254
Bryant, William Cullen, **AP:** 259
Bukowski, Charles, **AP:** 264
Bynner, Witter, **AP:** 274
Carruth, Hayden, **AP:** 278
Carver, Raymond, **AP:** 284
Cassity, Turner, **AP:** 291
Cernuda, Luis, **EP:** 220
Cervantes, Lorna Dee, **AP:** 298
Chappell, Fred, **AP:** 303
Chin, Marilyn, **AP:** 307
Ciardi, John, **AP:** 312
Cisneros, Sandra, **AP:** 318
Clampitt, Amy, **AP:** 322
Cliff, Michelle, **WP:** 61
Clifton, Lucille, **AP:** 326
Codrescu, Andrei, **AP:** 331
Cole, Henri, **AP:** 333
Collier, Michael, **AP:** 336
Collins, Billy, **AP:** 341
Colum, Padraic, **BP:** 292

Confessional Poets, **TE:** 668
Corman, Cid, **AP:** 347
Corn, Alfred, **AP:** 352
Corso, Gregory, **AP:** 356
Coulette, Henri, **AP:** 362
Cowley, Malcolm, **AP:** 366
Coxe, Louis, **AP:** 375
Crane, Hart, **AP:** 379
Crane, Stephen, **AP:** 387
Creeley, Robert, **AP:** 392
Cruz, Victor Hernández, **AP:** 400
Cullen, Countée, **AP:** 404
Cummings, E. E., **AP:** 410
Cunningham, J. V., **AP:** 417
Dacey, Philip, **AP:** 425
Dana, Robert, **AP:** 430
Davison, Peter, **AP:** 437
Dennis, Carl, **AP:** 441
Derricotte, Toi, **AP:** 444
Dickey, James, **AP:** 448
Dickinson, Emily, **AP:** 455
Di Prima, Diane, **AP:** 464
Dodson, Owen, **AP:** 471
Dorn, Edward, **AP:** 474
Doty, Mark, **AP:** 481
Dove, Rita, **AP:** 486
Dubie, Norman, **AP:** 493
Dugan, Alan, **AP:** 498
Dunbar, Paul Laurence, **AP:** 502
Duncan, Robert, **AP:** 509
Dunn, Stephen, **AP:** 517
Eady, Cornelius, **AP:** 521
Eberhart, Richard, **AP:** 526
Ehrhart, W. D., **AP:** 532
Eliot, T. S., **BP:** 458
Emanuel, James A., **AP:** 538
Emerson, Claudia, **AP:** 541
Emerson, Ralph Waldo, **AP:** 544
English and American Poetry in the Nineteenth Century, **TE:** 174
English and American Poetry in the Twentieth Century, **TE:** 185
Erdrich, Louise, **AP:** 553

Espada, Martín, **AP:** 559
Evans, Mari, **AP:** 563
Everson, William, **AP:** 567
Fairchild, B. H., **AP:** 579
Fearing, Kenneth, **AP:** 582
Feldman, Irving, **AP:** 588
Fennelly, Beth Ann, **AP:** 591
Ferlinghetti, Lawrence, **AP:** 593
Field, Edward, **AP:** 602
Fireside Poets, **TE:** 633
Flint, Roland, **AP:** 607
Forché, Carolyn, **AP:** 611
Freneau, Philip, **AP:** 618
Frost, Robert, **AP:** 625
Fulton, Alice, **AP:** 633
Gallagher, Tess, **AP:** 639
Galvin, Brendan, **AP:** 644
Gardner, Isabella, **AP:** 653
Garrett, George, **AP:** 656
Gerstler, Amy, **AP:** 660
Gibran, Kahlil, **AP:** 663
Gibson, Margaret, **AP:** 670
Gilbert, Jack, **AP:** 673
Ginsberg, Allen, **AP:** 677
Gioia, Dana, **AP:** 688
Giovanni, Nikki, **AP:** 692
Glancy, Diane, **AP:** 702
Glenn, Mel, **AP:** 706
Glück, Louise, **AP:** 710
Goldbarth, Albert, **AP:** 719
Graham, Jorie, **AP:** 725
Green Movement Poets, **TE:** 690
Gregerson, Linda, **AP:** 732
Gregg, Linda, **AP:** 735
Gregory, Horace, **AP:** 738
Grennan, Eamon, **AP:** 741
Guest, Barbara, **AP:** 745
Guest, Edgar A., **AP:** 748
Gunn, Thom, **BP:** 560
H. D., **AP:** 754
Hacker, Marilyn, **AP:** 761
Hahn, Kimiko, **AP:** 768
Haines, John Meade, **AP:** 772
Hall, Donald, **AP:** 775
Hampl, Patricia, **AP:** 785

Harjo, Joy, **AP:** 789
Harlem Renaissance, **TE:** 655
Harper, Michael S., **AP:** 794
Harrison, Jim, **AP:** 802
Hass, Robert, **AP:** 814
Hayden, Robert, **AP:** 820
Hecht, Anthony, **AP:** 826
Hejinian, Lyn, **AP:** 836
Heyen, William, **AP:** 841
Hillyer, Robert, **AP:** 850
Hirsch, Edward, **AP:** 853
Hirshfield, Jane, **AP:** 858
Hoffman, Daniel, **AP:** 863
Hogan, Linda, **AP:** 871
Hollander, John, **AP:** 877
Hollo, Anselm, **AP:** 887
Holmes, Oliver Wendell, **AP:** 893
Hongo, Garrett Kaoru, **AP:** 900
Horton, George Moses, **AP:** 905
Howard, Richard, **AP:** 909
Howe, Susan, **AP:** 913
Howes, Barbara, **AP:** 921
Hudgins, Andrew, **AP:** 924
Hughes, Langston, **AP:** 927
Hugo, Richard, **AP:** 934
Hunt, Erica, **AP:** 938
Ignatow, David, **AP:** 941
Imagists, **TE:** 644
Jacobsen, Josephine, **AP:** 950
Jarman, Mark, **AP:** 953
Jarrell, Randall, **AP:** 957
Jeffers, Robinson, **AP:** 963
Johnson, James Weldon, **AP:** 972
Johnson, Ronald, **AP:** 976
Jordan, June, **AP:** 981
Justice, Donald, **AP:** 986
Karr, Mary, **AP:** 993
Kasdorf, Julia, **AP:** 996
Kasischke, Laura, **AP:** 999
Kaufman, Bob, **AP:** 1002
Kees, Weldon, **AP:** 1006
Kelly, Brigit Pegeen, **AP:** 1012
Kelly, Robert, **AP:** 1015
Kennedy, X. J., **AP:** 1020
Kenyon, Jane, **AP:** 1028

Kinnell, Galway, **AP:** 1033

Kirby, David, **AP:** 1039

Kirstein, Lincoln, **AP:** 1042

Kizer, Carolyn, **AP:** 1046

Knight, Etheridge, **AP:** 1053

Koch, Kenneth, **AP:** 1058

Komunyakaa, Yusef, **AP:** 1064

Kooser, Ted, **AP:** 1070

Kumin, Maxine, **AP:** 1073

Kunitz, Stanley, **AP:** 1083

Lanier, Sidney, **AP:** 1095

Latino Poetry, **TE:** 466

Lee, Li-Young, **AP:** 1102

Leithauser, Brad, **AP:** 1108

Levertov, Denise, **AP:** 1111

Levine, Philip, **AP:** 1120

Levis, Larry, **AP:** 1127

Lewis, Janet, **AP:** 1132

Lifshin, Lyn, **AP:** 1136

Lindsay, Sarah, **AP:** 1143

Lindsay, Vachel, **AP:** 1146

Logan, John, **AP:** 1153

Longfellow, Henry Wadsworth, **AP:** 1157

Lorde, Audre, **AP:** 1166

Lowell, Amy, **AP:** 1172

Lowell, James Russell, **AP:** 1180

Lowell, Robert, **AP:** 1187

Loy, Mina, **AP:** 1200

Lum, Wing Tek, **AP:** 1204

McClure, Michael, **AP:** 1207

Macdonald, Cynthia, **AP:** 1211

McDonald, Walt, **AP:** 1215

McGinley, Phyllis, **AP:** 1221

McGrath, Thomas, **AP:** 1225

McHugh, Heather, **AP:** 1230

McKay, Claude, **AP:** 1234

Mackey, Nathaniel, **AP:** 1241

MacLeish, Archibald, **AP:** 1244

McMichael, James, **AP:** 1255

McPherson, Sandra, **AP:** 1258

Madhubuti, Haki R., **AP:** 1265

Manger, Itzik, **EP:** 650

Markham, Edwin, **AP:** 1274

Masters, Edgar Lee, **AP:** 1278

Matthews, William, **AP:** 1284

Meinke, Peter, **AP:** 1290

Melville, Herman, **AP:** 1294

Menashe, Samuel, **AP:** 1302

Meredith, William, **AP:** 1308

Merrill, James, **AP:** 1317

Merton, Thomas, **AP:** 1325

Merwin, W. S., **AP:** 1331

Metaphysical Poets, **TE:** 615

Middleton, Christopher, **BP:** 898

Miles, Josephine, **AP:** 1340

Millay, Edna St. Vincent, **AP:** 1344

Miller, Vassar, **AP:** 1349

Miłosz, Czesław, **EP:** 709

Mitsui, James Masao, **AP:** 1354

Modernists, **TE:** 650

Momaday, N. Scott, **AP:** 1358

Montague, John, **BP:** 914

Moore, Marianne, **AP:** 1364

Mora, Pat, **AP:** 1371

Moss, Howard, **AP:** 1375

Moss, Thylias, **AP:** 1380

Mueller, Lisel, **AP:** 1383

Mullen, Harryette, **AP:** 1387

Mura, David, **AP:** 1390

Muske, Carol, **AP:** 1396

Nash, Ogden, **AP:** 1401

Native American Poetry, **TE:** 478

Neihardt, John G., **AP:** 1405

Nemerov, Howard, **AP:** 1409

New York School, **TE:** 674

Niedecker, Lorine, **AP:** 1415

Nims, John Frederick, **AP:** 1421

Norris, Kathleen, **AP:** 1428

Notley, Alice, **AP:** 1431

Nye, Naomi Shihab, **AP:** 1435

Oates, Joyce Carol, **AP:** 1443

O'Hara, Frank, **AP:** 1451

Olds, Sharon, **AP:** 1456

Oliver, Mary, **AP:** 1463

Olson, Charles, **AP:** 1469

Oppen, George, **AP:** 1477

Oppenheimer, Joel, **AP:** 1481

Orr, Gregory, **AP:** 1485

Ortiz, Simon, **AP:** 1493

Ortiz Cofer, Judith, **AP:** 1499

Ostriker, Alicia Suskin, **AP:** 1502

Paley, Grace, **AP:** 1506

Parker, Dorothy, **AP:** 1509

Pastan, Linda, **AP:** 1514

Patchen, Kenneth, **AP:** 1520

Peacock, Molly, **AP:** 1525

Phillips, Carl, **AP:** 1529

Piercy, Marge, **AP:** 1532

Pinsky, Robert, **AP:** 1538

Plath, Sylvia, **AP:** 1547

Plumly, Stanley, **AP:** 1556

Poe, Edgar Allan, **AP:** 1561

Ponsot, Marie, **AP:** 1569

Porter, Anne, **AP:** 1573

Postcolonial Criticism, **TE:** 769

Pound, Ezra, **AP:** 1577

Price, Reynolds, **AP:** 1586

Rakosi, Carl, **AP:** 1590

Randall, Dudley, **AP:** 1595

Rankine, Claudia, **AP:** 1602

Ransom, John Crowe, **AP:** 1605

Reed, Ishmael, **AP:** 1612

Reese, Lizette Woodworth, **AP:** 1616

Rexroth, Kenneth, **AP:** 1621

Reznikoff, Charles, **AP:** 1627

Rich, Adrienne, **AP:** 1633

Riding, Laura, **AP:** 1642

Riley, James Whitcomb, **AP:** 1645

Ríos, Alberto, **AP:** 1654

Rivera, Tomás, **AP:** 1657

Robinson, Edwin Arlington, **AP:** 1660

Rodgers, Carolyn M., **AP:** 1668

Roethke, Theodore, **AP:** 1671

Rogers, Pattiann, **AP:** 1679

Rolfe, Edwin, **AP:** 1682

Rukeyser, Muriel, **AP:** 1686

St. John, David, **AP:** 1693

Salinas, Pedro, **EP:** 936

Sanchez, Sonia, **AP:** 1698

Sandburg, Carl, **AP:** 1704

Santos, Sherod, **AP:** 1711
Sarton, May, **AP:** 1714
Scalapino, Leslie, **AP:** 1724
Schnackenberg, Gjertrud, **AP:** 1728
Schuyler, James, **AP:** 1732
Schwartz, Delmore, **AP:** 1738
Scott, Winfield Townley, **AP:** 1746
Seeger, Alan, **AP:** 1750
Service, Robert W., **BP:** 1099
Sexton, Anne, **AP:** 1753
Shapiro, Alan, **AP:** 1759
Shapiro, Karl, **AP:** 1764
Shomer, Enid, **AP:** 1769
Shore, Jane, **AP:** 1773
Silko, Leslie Marmon, **AP:** 1777
Silverstein, Shel, **AP:** 1781
Simic, Charles, **AP:** 1785
Simpson, Louis, **AP:** 1793
Sissman, L. E., **AP:** 1802
Slavitt, David, **AP:** 1809
Smith, Dave, **AP:** 1817
Smith, William Jay, **AP:** 1825
Snodgrass, W. D., **AP:** 1831
Snyder, Gary, **AP:** 1840
Song, Cathy, **AP:** 1853
Sorrentino, Gilbert, **AP:** 1858
Soto, Gary, **AP:** 1862
Spicer, Jack, **AP:** 1868
Stafford, William, **AP:** 1872
Steele, Timothy, **AP:** 1881
Stein, Gertrude, **AP:** 1885
Stern, Gerald, **AP:** 1893
Stevens, Wallace, **AP:** 1905
Still, James, **AP:** 1913
Strand, Mark, **AP:** 1918
Stryk, Lucien, **AP:** 1927
Swensen, Cole, **AP:** 1931
Swenson, May, **AP:** 1934
Tate, Allen, **AP:** 1941
Tate, James, **AP:** 1947
Taylor, Edward, **AP:** 1959
Taylor, Henry, **AP:** 1968
Teasdale, Sara, **AP:** 1974

Thoreau, Henry David, **AP:** 1977
Tolson, Melvin B., **AP:** 1984
Toomer, Jean, **AP:** 1988
Trethewey, Natasha, **AP:** 1995
Tuckerman, Frederick Goddard, **AP:** 1998
Twichell, Chase, **AP:** 2002
Untermeyer, Louis, **AP:** 2007
Updike, John, **AP:** 2016
Valentine, Jean, **AP:** 2024
Van Duyn, Mona, **AP:** 2032
Van Doren, Mark, **AP:** 2027
Very, Jones, **AP:** 2039
Viereck, Peter, **AP:** 2042
Villa, José García, **AP:** 2048
Voigt, Ellen Bryant, **AP:** 2054
Wagoner, David, **AP:** 2059
Wakoski, Diane, **AP:** 2068
Waldman, Anne, **AP:** 2076
Walker, Alice, **AP:** 2080
Walker, Margaret, **AP:** 2086
Wallace, Ronald, **AP:** 2090
Warren, Robert Penn, **AP:** 2094
Weigl, Bruce, **AP:** 2102
Welch, James, **AP:** 2107
Whalen, Philip, **AP:** 2111
Wheatley, Phillis, **AP:** 2114
Wheelock, John Hall, **AP:** 2123
Wheelwright, John, **AP:** 2126
Whitman, Walt, **AP:** 2130
Whittemore, Reed, **AP:** 2140
Whittier, John Greenleaf, **AP:** 2144
Wilbur, Richard, **AP:** 2151
Williams, C. K., **AP:** 2161
Williams, Miller, **AP:** 2168
Williams, Sherley Anne, **AP:** 2172
Williams, William Carlos, **AP:** 2175
Winters, Yvor, **AP:** 2184
Wojahn, David, **AP:** 2190
Wormser, Baron, **AP:** 2196
Wright, C. D., **AP:** 2203

Wright, Charles, **AP:** 2207
Wright, Franz, **AP:** 2217
Wright, James, **AP:** 2221
Wright, Jay, **AP:** 2231
Wylie, Elinor, **AP:** 2240
Yamada, Mitsuye, **AP:** 2244
Young, Al, **AP:** 2248
Young, Dean, **AP:** 2257
Zimmer, Paul, **AP:** 2261
Zukofsky, Louis, **AP:** 2265

WALES
Abse, Dannie, **BP:** 1
Hemans, Felicia Dorothea, **BP:** 609
Herbert, George, **BP:** 617
Jones, David, **BP:** 707
Thomas, Dylan, **BP:** 1245
Thomas, R. S., **BP:** 1257
Vaughan, Henry, **BP:** 1284

WEST INDIES. *See also*
GUADELOUPE
Brathwaite, Edward Kamau, **AP:** 228
Caribbean Poetry, **TE:** 43
Césaire, Aimé, **WP:** 56
Cliff, Michelle, **WP:** 61
McKay, Claude, **AP:** 1234
Perse, Saint-John, **EP:** 801
Postcolonial Poetry, **TE:** 500
Simpson, Louis, **AP:** 1793
Walcott, Derek, **WP:** 317

YUGOSLAVIA. *See also*
BOHEMIA; BOSNIA AND HERZEGOVINA; MONTENEGRO; SERBIA
Macedonian Poetry, **TE:** 475
Pavlović, Miodrag, **EP:** 786
Popa, Vasko, **EP:** 856
Simic, Charles, **AP:** 1785

CATEGORIZED INDEX OF POETS AND ESSAYS

The Categorized Index of Poets and Essays covers three primary subject areas: Culture/Group Identities, Historical Periods/Literary Movements, and Poetic Forms and Themes. The **boldface** *letters that precede numbers in this index indicate the set in which the entry can be found:* **AP** = American Poets, **BP** = British, Irish, and Commonwealth Poets, **EP** = European Poets, **WP** = World Poets, *and* **TE** = Topical Essays.

Cultural/Group Identities

African American culture 99
Asian American culture 100
Gay and lesbian culture. 107
Jewish culture. 110

Latino culture 111
Native American culture 117
Women poets 130

Historical Periods/Literary Movements

Acmeist poets 97
Aesthetic poets. 99
Alexandrian poets 99
American colonial poets 99
American early national poets 100
Augustan Age, English 100
Augustan Age, Roman 100
Avant-garde poets 100
Beat poets. 101
Black Arts movement 101
Black Mountain poets 101
Caroline Age 101
Cavalier poets. 101
Chicago Renaissance 102
Classical period, China 102
Classicism: seventeenth and eighteenth
    centuries. 102
Classicism: nineteenth century 102
Classicism: twentieth century 102
Commonwealth Interregnum 102
Confessional poets 103
Cubism 103
Dadaism 103
Decadent poets 103
Deep Image poets. 103
Dolce stil nuovo 103

Edwardian age 104
Elizabethan age. 105
Enlightenment 105
Experimental poets 106
Expressionism 107
Feminist poets 107
Fireside poets 107
Fugitive poets 107
Futurism 107
Generation of '98 108
Generation of '27 108
Generation of '68 108
Georgian poets 108
Goethe, age of 108
Golden Age, Latin 108
Golden Age, Roman 108
Golden Age, Spanish 108
Graveyard school 108
Gruppe 108
Harlem Renaissance 109
Harvard aesthetes. 109
Hellenistic poets 109
Hermeticism 109
Imagism 109
Impressionism 109
Irish Literary Revival. 109

Jacobean age 110
Jazz poets 110
Johnson, age of 110
Jugendstil 110
Lake poets 110
Language poetry 111
Lost Generation 111
Merry Gang 114
Metaphysical poets 114
Middle English period 114
Middle High German period 114
Modernism 114
Modernismo 115
Movement poets 115
Native American Renaissance 117
Naturalism 117
Naturalism, American 117
Negritude 118
Neoclassical poets 118
Neoplatonism 118
Neorealism 118
Neo-Romanticism 118
New Formalism 118
New York School 119
Objectivism 119
Oxford Movement 120
Parnassianism 120
Pastoral poets 120
Pattern poets 120

Pléiade poets 120
Political poets 120
Postconfessional poets 122
Postmodernism 122
Pre-Raphaelites 123
Pre-Romanticism 123
Realism 124
Renaissance 125
Renaissance, American 125
Renaissance, English 125
Renaissance, French 125
Renaissance, Italian 125
Renaissance, Scottish 126
Renaissance, Spanish 126
Restoration 126
Risorgimento 126
Romanticism 126
Romanticism, American 126
Socialist Realism 127
Southern Agrarians 129
Sturm und drang 129
Surrealist poets 129
Symbolist poets 129
Transcendentalism 129
Tudor age 130
Ultraism 130
Victorian era 130
War poets 130
Young Vienna Group 132

Poetic Forms and Themes

Ballads 100
Children's/young adult poetry 102
Concrete poetry 102
Dialect poetry 103
Dramatic monologues 103
Ecopoetry 104
Ekphrastic poetry 104
Elegies 104
Epics 105
Epigrams 106
Expansive poetry 106
Fables 107
Ghazals 108

Haiku 108
Hymns 109
Light verse 111
Love poetry 111
Lyric poetry 112
Minimalist poetry 114
Narrative poetry 116
Nature poetry 117
New narrative poetry 119
Occasional verse 119
Odes 119
Oral tradition 120
Performance poetry 120

Petrarchan sonnets 120
Prose poetry 123
Religious poetry 124
Satiric poetry 127
Songs 127

Sonnets 128
Topographical poetry 129
Verse dramatists 130
Visionary poetry 130

ACMEIST POETS

Akhmatova, Anna, **WP:** 3
Annensky, Innokenty, **WP:** 21
Mandelstam, Osip, **WP:** 163
Pasternak, Boris, **WP:** 222

AESTHETIC POETS

Baudelaire, Charles, **EP:** 80
Coleridge, Samuel Taylor, **BP:** 276
Emerson, Ralph Waldo, **AP:** 544
Gautier, Théophile, **EP:** 368
George, Stefan, **EP:** 377
Goethe, Johann Wolfgang von, **EP:** 396
Meredith, George, **BP:** 890
Poe, Edgar Allan, **AP:** 1561
Rossetti, Dante Gabriel, **BP:** 1065
Schiller, Friedrich, **EP:** 949
Swinburne, Algernon Charles, **BP:** 1227
Wilde, Oscar, **BP:** 1303
Yeats, William Butler, **BP:** 1330

AFRICAN AMERICAN CULTURE. *See also* BLACK ARTS MOVEMENT; HARLEM RENAISSANCE; JAZZ POETS

African American Poetry, **TE:** 3
Ai, **AP:** 8
Alexander, Elizabeth, **AP:** 17
Angelou, Maya, **AP:** 46
Baraka, Amiri, **AP:** 89
Beatty, Paul, **AP:** 107
Bontemps, Arna, **AP:** 205

Brathwaite, Edward Kamau, **AP:** 228
Brooks, Gwendolyn, **AP:** 247
Brown, Sterling A., **AP:** 254
Cliff, Michelle, **WP:** 61
Clifton, Lucille, **AP:** 326
Cruz, Victor Hernández, **AP:** 400
Cullen, Countée, **AP:** 404
Derricotte, Toi, **AP:** 444
Dodson, Owen, **AP:** 471
Dove, Rita, **AP:** 486
Dunbar, Paul Laurence, **AP:** 502
Eady, Cornelius, **AP:** 521
Emanuel, James A., **AP:** 538
Evans, Mari, **AP:** 563
Giovanni, Nikki, **AP:** 692
Harlem Renaissance, **TE:** 655
Harper, Michael S., **AP:** 794
Hayden, Robert, **AP:** 820
Horton, George Moses, **AP:** 905
Hughes, Langston, **AP:** 927
Hunt, Erica, **AP:** 938
Johnson, James Weldon, **AP:** 972
Jordan, June, **AP:** 981
Kaufman, Bob, **AP:** 1002
Knight, Etheridge, **AP:** 1053
Komunyakaa, Yusef, **AP:** 1064
Lorde, Audre, **AP:** 1166
McKay, Claude, **AP:** 1234
Mackey, Nathaniel, **AP:** 1241
Madhubuti, Haki R., **AP:** 1265
Moss, Thylias, **AP:** 1380
Mullen, Harryette, **AP:** 1387
Phillips, Carl, **AP:** 1529
Randall, Dudley, **AP:** 1595
Rankine, Claudia, **AP:** 1602
Reed, Ishmael, **AP:** 1612

Rodgers, Carolyn M., **AP:** 1668
Sanchez, Sonia, **AP:** 1698
Tolson, Melvin B., **AP:** 1984
Toomer, Jean, **AP:** 1988
Trethewey, Natasha, **AP:** 1995
Walker, Alice, **AP:** 2080
Walker, Margaret, **AP:** 2086
Wheatley, Phillis, **AP:** 2114
Williams, Sherley Anne, **AP:** 2172
Wright, Jay, **AP:** 2231
Young, Al, **AP:** 2248

AGE OF GOETHE. *See* GOETHE, AGE OF

AGE OF JOHNSON. *See* JOHNSON, AGE OF

AGRARIAN POETS. *See* SOUTHERN AGRARIANS

ALEXANDRIAN POETS

Apollonius Rhodius, **EP:** 30
Callimachus, **EP:** 175
Leonidas of Tarentum, **EP:** 602
Theocritus, **EP:** 1023

AMERICAN COLONIAL POETS

Bradstreet, Anne, **AP:** 223
English and American Poetry in the Nineteenth Century, **TE:** 174
Freneau, Philip, **AP:** 618
Taylor, Edward, **AP:** 1959
Wheatley, Phillis, **AP:** 2114

AMERICAN EARLY NATIONAL POETS

Bryant, William Cullen, **AP:** 259

Dickinson, Emily, **AP:** 455

Emerson, Ralph Waldo, **AP:** 544

English and American Poetry in the Nineteenth Century, **TE:** 174

Fireside Poets, **TE:** 633

Freneau, Philip, **AP:** 618

Holmes, Oliver Wendell, **AP:** 893

Horton, George Moses, **AP:** 905

Lanier, Sidney, **AP:** 1095

Longfellow, Henry Wadsworth, **AP:** 1157

Lowell, James Russell, **AP:** 1180

Melville, Herman, **AP:** 1294

Poe, Edgar Allan, **AP:** 1561

Riley, James Whitcomb, **AP:** 1645

Thoreau, Henry David, **AP:** 1977

Tuckerman, Frederick Goddard, **AP:** 1998

Very, Jones, **AP:** 2039

Whitman, Walt, **AP:** 2130

Whittier, John Greenleaf, **AP:** 2144

AMERICAN INDIAN CULTURE. *See* NATIVE AMERICAN CULTURE; NATIVE AMERICAN RENAISSANCE

AMERICAN NATURALISM. *See* NATURALISM, AMERICAN

AMERICAN RENAISSANCE. *See* RENAISSANCE, AMERICAN

AMERICAN ROMANTICISM. *See* ROMANTICISM, AMERICAN

ASIAN AMERICAN CULTURE

Ai, **AP:** 8

Ali, Agha Shahid, **AP:** 24

Asian American Poetry, **TE:** 21

Chin, Marilyn, **AP:** 307

Hahn, Kimiko, **AP:** 768

Hongo, Garrett Kaoru, **AP:** 900

Lee, Li-Young, **AP:** 1102

Lum, Wing Tek, **AP:** 1204

Mitsui, James Masao, **AP:** 1354

Mura, David, **AP:** 1390

Song, Cathy, **AP:** 1853

Villa, José García, **AP:** 2048

Yamada, Mitsuye, **AP:** 2244

AUGUSTAN AGE, ENGLISH

Addison, Joseph, **BP:** 7

Collins, William, **BP:** 287

Cowper, William, **BP:** 320

English Poetry in the Eighteenth Century, **TE:** 160

Finch, Anne, **BP:** 491

Gay, John, **BP:** 512

Gray, Thomas, **BP:** 542

Johnson, Samuel, **BP:** 700

Pope, Alexander, **BP:** 1005

Prior, Matthew, **BP:** 1026

Swift, Jonathan, **BP:** 1218

Thomson, James (1700-1748), **BP:** 1260

Watts, Isaac, **BP:** 1297

Young, Edward, **BP:** 1349

AUGUSTAN AGE, ROMAN

Horace, **EP:** 510

Ovid, **EP:** 763

Propertius, Sextus, **EP:** 866

Vergil, **EP:** 1080

AVANT-GARDE POETS

Apollinaire, Guillaume, **EP:** 22

Aragon, Louis, **EP:** 35

Ashbery, John, **AP:** 55

Berrigan, Ted, **AP:** 143

Breton, André, **EP:** 157

Celan, Paul, **EP:** 214

Cocteau, Jean, **EP:** 253

Crane, Stephen, **AP:** 387

Cummings, E. E., **AP:** 410

Ekelöf, Gunnar, **EP:** 306

Esenin, Sergei, **WP:** 90

Foix, J. V., **EP:** 329

Guest, Barbara, **AP:** 745

Herbert, Zbigniew, **EP:** 458

Joyce, James, **BP:** 719

Koch, Kenneth, **AP:** 1058

Laforgue, Jules, **EP:** 584

Lowell, Amy, **AP:** 1172

Loy, Mina, **AP:** 1200

Mallarmé, Stéphane, **EP:** 644

Notley, Alice, **AP:** 1431

O'Hara, Frank, **AP:** 1451

Pagis, Dan, **WP:** 213

Porter, Anne, **AP:** 1573

Reverdy, Pierre, **EP:** 883

Schuyler, James, **AP:** 1732

Schwartz, Delmore, **AP:** 1738

Seifert, Jaroslav, **EP:** 961

Stein, Gertrude, **AP:** 1885

Tzara, Tristan, **EP:** 1044

Vallejo, César, **WP:** 300

Waldman, Anne, **AP:** 2076

Ważyk, Adam, **EP:** 1126

Young, Dean, **AP:** 2257

BALLADS

Allingham, William, **BP:** 23

Arany, János, **EP:** 42

Auden, W. H., **BP:** 47

Benét, Stephen Vincent, **AP:** 124

Benét, William Rose, **AP:** 128

Biermann, Wolf, **EP:** 119

Brown, Sterling A., **AP:** 254

Cavalcanti, Guido, **EP:** 210

Coleridge, Samuel Taylor, **BP:** 276

Cruz, Sor Juana Inés de la, **WP:** 64

Dunbar, Paul Laurence, **AP:** 502

Finch, Anne, **BP:** 491

García Lorca, Federico, **EP:** 355

Goethe, Johann Wolfgang von,
   EP: 396

Gower, John, **BP:** 525

Graves, Robert, **BP:** 534

Hardy, Thomas, **BP:** 579

Hayden, Robert, **AP:** 820

Hoffman, Daniel, **AP:** 863

Hood, Thomas, **BP:** 650

Horton, George Moses, **AP:** 905

Hughes, Langston, **AP:** 927

Jeffers, Robinson, **AP:** 963

Jiménez, Juan Ramón, **EP:** 533

Kipling, Rudyard, **BP:** 760

Kirstein, Lincoln, **AP:** 1042

Longfellow, Henry Wadsworth,
   AP: 1157

McGrath, Thomas, **AP:** 1225

McKay, Claude, **AP:** 1234

Manger, Itzik, **EP:** 650

Masefield, John, **BP:** 885

Meredith, George, **BP:** 890

Prior, Matthew, **BP:** 1026

Randall, Dudley, **AP:** 1595

Rossetti, Dante Gabriel, **BP:** 1065

Schiller, Friedrich, **EP:** 949

Scott, Sir Walter, **BP:** 1087

Service, Robert W., **BP:** 1099

Słonimski, Antoni, **EP:** 968

Southey, Robert, **BP:** 1171

Stevenson, Robert Louis, **BP:**
   1201

Suckling, Sir John, **BP:** 1206

Swinburne, Algernon Charles,
   BP: 1227

Tasso, Torquato, **EP:** 1014

Tennyson, Alfred, Lord, **BP:** 1236

Villon, François, **EP:** 1106

Walker, Margaret, **AP:** 2086

Whittier, John Greenleaf, **AP:**
   2144

Wordsworth, William, **BP:** 1310

BEAT POETS

Beat Poets, **TE:** 661

Blackburn, Paul, **AP:** 180

Brautigan, Richard, **AP:** 239

Bukowski, Charles, **AP:** 264

Corso, Gregory, **AP:** 356

Di Prima, Diane, **AP:** 464

Duncan, Robert, **AP:** 509

Everson, William, **AP:** 567

Ferlinghetti, Lawrence, **AP:** 593

Gilbert, Jack, **AP:** 673

Ginsberg, Allen, **AP:** 677

Gunn, Thom, **BP:** 560

Hollo, Anselm, **AP:** 887

Kaufman, Bob, **AP:** 1002

Larkin, Philip, **BP:** 786

McClure, Michael, **AP:** 1207

Olson, Charles, **AP:** 1469

Patchen, Kenneth, **AP:** 1520

Ponsot, Marie, **AP:** 1569

Rexroth, Kenneth, **AP:** 1621

Snyder, Gary, **AP:** 1840

Sorrentino, Gilbert, **AP:** 1858

Spicer, Jack, **AP:** 1868

Wakoski, Diane, **AP:** 2068

Whalen, Philip, **AP:** 2111

BLACK ARTS MOVEMENT

African American Poetry, **TE:** 3

Baraka, Amiri, **AP:** 89

Brooks, Gwendolyn, **AP:** 247

Clifton, Lucille, **AP:** 326

Derricotte, Toi, **AP:** 444

Giovanni, Nikki, **AP:** 692

Jordan, June, **AP:** 981

Knight, Etheridge, **AP:** 1053

Madhubuti, Haki R., **AP:** 1265

Randall, Dudley, **AP:** 1595

Reed, Ishmael, **AP:** 1612

Rodgers, Carolyn M., **AP:** 1668

Sanchez, Sonia, **AP:** 1698

Walker, Alice, **AP:** 2080

BLACK MOUNTAIN POETS

Black Mountain School, **TE:** 684

Blackburn, Paul, **AP:** 180

Creeley, Robert, **AP:** 392

Dorn, Edward, **AP:** 474

Duncan, Robert, **AP:** 509

Kelly, Robert, **AP:** 1015

Levertov, Denise, **AP:** 1111

McClure, Michael, **AP:** 1207

Olson, Charles, **AP:** 1469

Oppenheimer, Joel, **AP:** 1481

Snyder, Gary, **AP:** 1840

CAROLINE AGE

Butler, Samuel, **BP:** 180

Carew, Thomas, **BP:** 208

Cowley, Abraham, **BP:** 312

Crashaw, Richard, **BP:** 337

Davenant, Sir William, **BP:** 362

Donne, John, **BP:** 405

Drummond of Hawthornden,
   William, **BP:** 424

English Poetry in the Seventeenth
   Century, **TE:** 144

Fanshawe, Sir Richard, **BP:** 481

Herbert, George, **BP:** 617

Herrick, Robert, **BP:** 626

Jonson, Ben, **BP:** 711

Lovelace, Richard, **BP:** 827

Milton, John, **BP:** 905

Quarles, Francis, **BP:** 1031

Suckling, Sir John, **BP:** 1206

CAVALIER POETS

Carew, Thomas, **BP:** 208

Davenant, Sir William, **BP:** 362

English Poetry in the Seventeenth
   Century, **TE:** 144

Herrick, Robert, **BP:** 626

Jonson, Ben, **BP:** 711

Lovelace, Richard, **BP:** 827

Milton, John, **BP:** 905

Waller, Edmund, **BP:** 1290

CELTIC REVIVAL. *See* **IRISH
LITERARY REVIVAL**

CHICAGO RENAISSANCE
Lindsay, Vachel, **AP:** 1146
Masters, Edgar Lee, **AP:** 1278
Sandburg, Carl, **AP:** 1704

CHILDREN'S/YOUNG ADULT POETRY
Ackerman, Diane, **AP:** 1
Allingham, William, **BP:** 23
Angelou, Maya, **AP:** 46
Belloc, Hilaire, **BP:** 73
Booth, Philip, **AP:** 209
Bowles, William Lisle, **BP:** 119
Brooks, Gwendolyn, **AP:** 247
Carroll, Lewis, **BP:** 213
Ciardi, John, **AP:** 312
Clifton, Lucille, **AP:** 326
De la Mare, Walter, **BP:** 398
Fuller, Roy, **BP:** 500
Giovanni, Nikki, **AP:** 692
Glenn, Mel, **AP:** 706
Graves, Robert, **BP:** 534
Hollander, John, **AP:** 877
Hughes, Ted, **BP:** 686
Jarrell, Randall, **AP:** 957
Kennedy, X. J., **AP:** 1020
Kipling, Rudyard, **BP:** 760
La Fontaine, Jean de, **EP:** 577
Lamb, Charles, **BP:** 768
Lear, Edward, **BP:** 812
Logue, Christopher, **BP:** 823
MacBeth, George, **BP:** 841
Mistral, Gabriela, **WP:** 185
Miyazawa, Kenji, **WP:** 191
Mora, Pat, **AP:** 1371
Moss, Howard, **AP:** 1375
Nash, Ogden, **AP:** 1401
Nye, Naomi Shihab, **AP:** 1435
Pasternak, Boris, **WP:** 222
Riley, James Whitcomb, **AP:** 1645
Roethke, Theodore, **AP:** 1671
Rossetti, Christina, **BP:** 1060
Sandburg, Carl, **AP:** 1704
Seifert, Jaroslav, **EP:** 961

Silverstein, Shel, **AP:** 1781
Smart, Christopher, **BP:** 1159
Smith, William Jay, **AP:** 1825
Snodgrass, W. D., **AP:** 1831
Soto, Gary, **AP:** 1862
Stein, Gertrude, **AP:** 1885
Stevenson, Robert Louis, **BP:** 1201
Swenson, May, **AP:** 1934
Watts, Isaac, **BP:** 1297
Wilbur, Richard, **AP:** 2151

CLASSICAL PERIOD, CHINA
Du Fu, **WP:** 84
Li Bo, **WP:** 150
Li Qingzhao, **WP:** 157
Meng Haoran, **WP:** 182
Ruan Ji, **WP:** 250
Tao Qian, **WP:** 288
Wang Wei, **WP:** 326
Xie Lingyun, **WP:** 334

CLASSICISM: SEVENTEENTH AND EIGHTEENTH CENTURIES. *See also* **NEOCLASSICAL POETS**
English Poetry in the Eighteenth Century, **TE:** 160
English Poetry in the Seventeenth Century, **TE:** 144
La Fontaine, Jean de, **EP:** 577

CLASSICISM: NINETEENTH CENTURY
Bridges, Robert, **BP:** 131
Carducci, Giosuè, **EP:** 185
English and American Poetry in the Nineteenth Century, **TE:** 174
Hölderlin, Friedrich, **EP:** 485
Landor, Walter Savage, **BP:** 774
MacLeish, Archibald, **AP:** 1244
Mickiewicz, Adam, **EP:** 702
Musset, Alfred de, **EP:** 736

Pushkin, Alexander, **WP:** 236
Vörösmarty, Mihály, **EP:** 1112

CLASSICISM: TWENTIETH CENTURY
Belloc, Hilaire, **BP:** 73
Bidart, Frank, **AP:** 162
Bridges, Robert, **BP:** 131
Cunningham, J. V., **AP:** 417
Glück, Louise, **AP:** 710
Hope, A. D., **BP:** 660
Jeffers, Robinson, **AP:** 963
Khodasevich, Vladislav, **WP:** 133
Kizer, Carolyn, **AP:** 1046
Martinson, Harry, **EP:** 681
Middleton, Christopher, **BP:** 898
Nims, John Frederick, **AP:** 1421
Reyes, Alfonso, **WP:** 245
Slavitt, David, **AP:** 1809
Viereck, Peter, **AP:** 2042

COLONIAL POETS. *See* **AMERICAN COLONIAL POETS**

COMMONWEALTH INTERREGNUM
Davenant, Sir William, **BP:** 362
English Poetry in the Seventeenth Century, **TE:** 144
King, Henry, **BP:** 743
Marvell, Andrew, **BP:** 877
Milton, John, **BP:** 905
Newcastle, Margaret Cavendish, duchess of, **BP:** 958
Vaughan, Henry, **BP:** 1284
Waller, Edmund, **BP:** 1290

CONCRETE POETRY
Apollinaire, Guillaume, **EP:** 22
Carroll, Lewis, **BP:** 213
Cummings, E. E., **AP:** 410
Gomringer, Eugen, **EP:** 405
Herbert, George, **BP:** 617
Hollander, John, **AP:** 877

Johnson, Ronald, **AP:** 976
Komunyakaa, Yusef, **AP:** 1064
Meinke, Peter, **AP:** 1290
Patchen, Kenneth, **AP:** 1520
Pound, Ezra, **AP:** 1577

CONFESSIONAL POETS. *See also* POSTCONFESSIONAL POETS

Berrigan, Ted, **AP:** 143
Berryman, John, **AP:** 155
Confessional Poets, **TE:** 668
Ginsberg, Allen, **AP:** 677
Hughes, Ted, **BP:** 686
Jarrell, Randall, **AP:** 957
Lowell, Robert, **AP:** 1187
Plath, Sylvia, **AP:** 1547
Roethke, Theodore, **AP:** 1671
Schwartz, Delmore, **AP:** 1738
Sexton, Anne, **AP:** 1753
Snodgrass, W. D., **AP:** 1831

CUBISM

Apollinaire, Guillaume, **EP:** 22
Cocteau, Jean, **EP:** 253
Cummings, E. E., **AP:** 410
Loy, Mina, **AP:** 1200
Reverdy, Pierre, **EP:** 883
Rexroth, Kenneth, **AP:** 1621
Stein, Gertrude, **AP:** 1885
Stevens, Wallace, **AP:** 1905
Ważyk, Adam, **EP:** 1126
Williams, William Carlos, **AP:** 2175
Winters, Yvor, **AP:** 2184
Zukofsky, Louis, **AP:** 2265

DADAISM

Aragon, Louis, **EP:** 35
Arp, Hans, **EP:** 62
Breton, André, **EP:** 157
Éluard, Paul, **EP:** 313
Illyés, Gyula, **EP:** 528
Loy, Mina, **AP:** 1200
Middleton, Christopher, **BP:** 898

Morgenstern, Christian, **EP:** 727
Seifert, Jaroslav, **EP:** 961
Tzara, Tristan, **EP:** 1044

DECADENT POETS

Baudelaire, Charles, **EP:** 80
Dučić, Jovan, **EP:** 292
Gautier, Théophile, **EP:** 368
Laforgue, Jules, **EP:** 584
Rimbaud, Arthur, **EP:** 897
Verlaine, Paul, **EP:** 1093
Wilde, Oscar, **BP:** 1303

DEEP IMAGE POETS

Bly, Robert, **AP:** 188
Ignatow, David, **AP:** 941
Kelly, Robert, **AP:** 1015
Kinnell, Galway, **AP:** 1033
Levis, Larry, **AP:** 1127
McPherson, Sandra, **AP:** 1258
Simpson, Louis, **AP:** 1793
Stafford, William, **AP:** 1872
Tate, James, **AP:** 1947
Wakoski, Diane, **AP:** 2068
Wright, James, **AP:** 2221

DIALECT POETRY

Brathwaite, Edward Kamau, **AP:** 228
Brown, Sterling A., **AP:** 254
Burns, Robert, **BP:** 173
Chappell, Fred, **AP:** 303
Cullen, Countée, **AP:** 404
Cummings, E. E., **AP:** 410
Dunbar, Paul Laurence, **AP:** 502
Dunbar, William, **BP:** 442
Frost, Robert, **AP:** 625
Harrison, Tony, **BP:** 588
Heaney, Seamus, **BP:** 594
Holmes, Oliver Wendell, **AP:** 893
Hughes, Langston, **AP:** 927
Johnson, Ronald, **AP:** 976
Kavanagh, Patrick, **BP:** 726
Lanier, Sidney, **AP:** 1095
Lowell, James Russell, **AP:** 1180

MacDiarmid, Hugh, **BP:** 846
McKay, Claude, **AP:** 1234
Mullen, Harryette, **AP:** 1387
Rankine, Claudia, **AP:** 1602
Riley, James Whitcomb, **AP:** 1645
Stevenson, Robert Louis, **BP:** 1201
Still, James, **AP:** 1913
Walcott, Derek, **WP:** 317
Williams, Sherley Anne, **AP:** 2172
Young, Al, **AP:** 2248

DOLCE STIL NUOVO

Boccaccio, Giovanni, **EP:** 131
Cavalcanti, Guido, **EP:** 210
Dante, **EP:** 270
Petrarch, **EP:** 828

DRAMATIC MONOLOGUES

Ai, **AP:** 8
Benét, Stephen Vincent, **AP:** 124
Bidart, Frank, **AP:** 162
Blackburn, Paul, **AP:** 180
Blok, Aleksandr, **WP:** 33
Bowers, Edgar, **AP:** 219
Brontë, Emily, **BP:** 137
Browning, Robert, **BP:** 158
Bunting, Basil, **BP:** 168
Byron, Lord, **BP:** 186
Carruth, Hayden, **AP:** 278
Catullus, **EP:** 197
Cavafy, Constantine P., **EP:** 204
Creeley, Robert, **AP:** 392
Fearing, Kenneth, **AP:** 582
Field, Edward, **AP:** 602
Gerstler, Amy, **AP:** 660
Glück, Louise, **AP:** 710
Gregory, Horace, **AP:** 738
Gunn, Thom, **BP:** 560
Hecht, Anthony, **AP:** 826
Hirsch, Edward, **AP:** 853
Hollander, John, **AP:** 877
Howard, Richard, **AP:** 909

Jones, David, **BP:** 707

Laforgue, Jules, **EP:** 584

Lowell, Robert, **AP:** 1187

MacBeth, George, **BP:** 841

Masters, Edgar Lee, **AP:** 1278

Mew, Charlotte, **BP:** 894

Millay, Edna St. Vincent, **AP:** 1344

Mora, Pat, **AP:** 1371

Morris, William, **BP:** 924

Paley, Grace, **AP:** 1506

Prince, F. T., **BP:** 1021

Reed, Henry, **BP:** 1043

Riley, James Whitcomb, **AP:** 1645

Ritsos, Yannis, **EP:** 904

Rossetti, Dante Gabriel, **BP:** 1065

Shapiro, Alan, **AP:** 1759

Snodgrass, W. D., **AP:** 1831

Swinburne, Algernon Charles, **BP:** 1227

Tennyson, Alfred, Lord, **BP:** 1236

Theocritus, **EP:** 1023

Tolson, Melvin B., **AP:** 1984

Vigny, Alfred de, **EP:** 1099

Wilbur, Richard, **AP:** 2151

Williams, Miller, **AP:** 2168

Wright, James, **AP:** 2221

EARLY NATIONAL POETS. *See* AMERICAN EARLY NATIONAL POETS

ECOPOETRY

Ammons, A. R., **AP:** 37

Berry, Wendell, **AP:** 146

Dorn, Edward, **AP:** 474

Emerson, Ralph Waldo, **AP:** 544

Galvin, Brendan, **AP:** 644

Green Movement Poets, **TE:** 690

Grennan, Eamon, **AP:** 741

Haines, John Meade, **AP:** 772

Harjo, Joy, **AP:** 789

Harrison, Jim, **AP:** 802

Heyen, William, **AP:** 841

Jeffers, Robinson, **AP:** 963

McClure, Michael, **AP:** 1207

Merwin, W. S., **AP:** 1331

Oliver, Mary, **AP:** 1463

Ortiz, Simon, **AP:** 1493

Rogers, Pattiann, **AP:** 1679

Silkin, Jon, **BP:** 1141

Snyder, Gary, **AP:** 1840

Stevens, Wallace, **AP:** 1905

Wagoner, David, **AP:** 2059

Waldman, Anne, **AP:** 2076

Whitman, Walt, **AP:** 2130

Wordsworth, William, **BP:** 1310

Wormser, Baron, **AP:** 2196

Yeats, William Butler, **BP:** 1330

EDWARDIAN AGE

Belloc, Hilaire, **BP:** 73

Hardy, Thomas, **BP:** 579

Kipling, Rudyard, **BP:** 760

Masefield, John, **BP:** 885

Yeats, William Butler, **BP:** 1330

EKPHRASTIC POETRY

Ariosto, Ludovico, **EP:** 56

Ashbery, John, **AP:** 55

Auden, W. H., **BP:** 47

Bang, Mary Jo, **AP:** 85

Bernstein, Charles, **AP:** 132

Bidart, Frank, **AP:** 162

Bishop, Elizabeth, **AP:** 169

Blake, William, **BP:** 91

Boland, Eavan, **BP:** 108

Bonnefoy, Yves, **EP:** 142

Bowles, William Lisle, **BP:** 119

Gautier, Théophile, **EP:** 368

Goldbarth, Albert, **AP:** 719

Graham, Jorie, **AP:** 725

Gunn, Thom, **BP:** 560

Haines, John Meade, **AP:** 772

Hampl, Patricia, **AP:** 785

Hayden, Robert, **AP:** 820

Hecht, Anthony, **AP:** 826

Hirsch, Edward, **AP:** 853

Hollander, John, **AP:** 877

Homer, **EP:** 502

Jonson, Ben, **BP:** 711

Keats, John, **BP:** 731

Kennedy, X. J., **AP:** 1020

Markham, Edwin, **AP:** 1274

Miłosz, Czesław, **EP:** 709

Mitsui, James Masao, **AP:** 1354

Ostriker, Alicia Suskin, **AP:** 1502

Ritsos, Yannis, **EP:** 904

St. John, David, **AP:** 1693

Schwartz, Delmore, **AP:** 1738

Song, Cathy, **AP:** 1853

Swensen, Cole, **AP:** 1931

Thomas, R. S., **BP:** 1257

ELEGIES

Adams, Léonie, **AP:** 4

Ali, Agha Shahid, **AP:** 24

Allingham, William, **BP:** 23

Applewhite, James, **AP:** 51

Arnold, Matthew, **BP:** 30

Bang, Mary Jo, **AP:** 85

Behn, Aphra, **BP:** 66

Berrigan, Ted, **AP:** 143

Berry, Wendell, **AP:** 146

Berryman, John, **AP:** 155

Blunden, Edmund, **BP:** 104

Bradstreet, Anne, **AP:** 223

Brecht, Bertolt, **EP:** 149

Brodsky, Joseph, **WP:** 44

Callimachus, **EP:** 175

Camões, Luís de, **EP:** 180

Carew, Thomas, **BP:** 208

Chaucer, Geoffrey, **BP:** 243

Cotton, Charles, **BP:** 306

Dodson, Owen, **AP:** 471

Donne, John, **BP:** 405

Doty, Mark, **AP:** 481

Drayton, Michael, **BP:** 417

Drummond of Hawthornden, William, **BP:** 424

Dunbar, Paul Laurence, **AP:** 502

Feldman, Irving, **AP:** 588

Finch, Anne, **BP:** 491

Garcilaso de la Vega, **EP:** 362

Gardner, Isabella, **AP:** 653

Gerstler, Amy, **AP:** 660

Gilbert, Jack, **AP:** 673

Goethe, Johann Wolfgang von, **EP:** 396

Hafiz, **WP:** 108

Hall, Donald, **AP:** 775

Hampl, Patricia, **AP:** 785

Harrison, Tony, **BP:** 588

Heaney, Seamus, **BP:** 594

Hirsch, Edward, **AP:** 853

Hölderlin, Friedrich, **EP:** 485

Jiménez, Juan Ramón, **EP:** 533

Johnson, Samuel, **BP:** 700

Justice, Donald, **AP:** 986

Keats, John, **BP:** 731

King, Henry, **BP:** 743

Leopardi, Giacomo, **EP:** 607

Lermontov, Mikhail, **WP:** 142

Lowell, Robert, **AP:** 1187

MacLeish, Archibald, **AP:** 1244

Manrique, Jorge, **EP:** 657

Milton, John, **BP:** 905

Miyazawa Kenji, **WP:** 191

Mörike, Eduard, **EP:** 732

Nerval, Gérard de, **EP:** 741

Newcastle, Margaret Cavendish, duchess of, **BP:** 958

Nims, John Frederick, **AP:** 1421

Okigbo, Christopher, **WP:** 205

Ovid, **EP:** 763

Plumly, Stanley, **AP:** 1556

Propertius, Sextus, **EP:** 866

Quarles, Francis, **BP:** 1031

Rexroth, Kenneth, **AP:** 1621

Rilke, Rainer Maria, **EP:** 889

Santos, Sherod, **AP:** 1711

Schnackenberg, Gjertrud, **AP:** 1728

Senghor, Léopold, **WP:** 264

Shapiro, Alan, **AP:** 1759

Southwell, Robert, **BP:** 1178

Stern, Gerald, **AP:** 1893

Surrey, Henry Howard, earl of, **BP:** 1212

Swinburne, Algernon Charles, **BP:** 1227

Theognis, **EP:** 1029

Tranströmer, Tomas, **EP:** 1039

Vaughan, Henry, **BP:** 1284

Wheatley, Phillis, **AP:** 2114

ELIZABETHAN AGE

Breton, Nicholas, **BP:** 124

Chapman, George, **BP:** 228

Constable, Henry, **BP:** 301

Daniel, Samuel, **BP:** 352

Davies, Sir John, **BP:** 375

Dekker, Thomas, **BP:** 390

Drayton, Michael, **BP:** 417

English Poetry in the Sixteenth Century, **TE:** 130

Gascoigne, George, **BP:** 505

Greene, Robert, **BP:** 548

Greville, Fulke, **BP:** 555

Heywood, John, **BP:** 635

Jonson, Ben, **BP:** 711

Lodge, Thomas, **BP:** 817

Marlowe, Christopher, **BP:** 870

Nashe, Thomas, **BP:** 953

Ralegh, Sir Walter, **BP:** 1037

Sackville, Thomas, **BP:** 1074

Shakespeare, William, **BP:** 1105

Sidney, Sir Philip, **BP:** 1126

Sidney, Sir Robert, **BP:** 1135

Southwell, Robert, **BP:** 1178

Spenser, Edmund, **BP:** 1191

ENGLISH AUGUSTAN AGE. *See* **AUGUSTAN AGE, ENGLISH**

ENGLISH PERIOD, MIDDLE. *See* **MIDDLE ENGLISH PERIOD**

ENGLISH RENAISSANCE. *See* **RENAISSANCE, ENGLISH**

ENLIGHTENMENT. *See also* **NEOCLASSICAL POETS**

English Poetry in the Seventeenth Century, **TE:** 144

Heine, Heinrich, **EP:** 451

Novalis, **EP:** 748

EPICS

Apollonius Rhodius, **EP:** 30

Arany, János, **EP:** 42

Archilochus, **EP:** 50

Ariosto, Ludovico, **EP:** 56

Baraka, Amiri, **AP:** 89

Benét, Stephen Vincent, **AP:** 124

Benét, William Rose, **AP:** 128

Blake, William, **BP:** 91

Boccaccio, Giovanni, **EP:** 131

Boiardo, Matteo Maria, **EP:** 135

Bradstreet, Anne, **AP:** 223

Browning, Elizabeth Barrett, **BP:** 149

Byron, Lord, **BP:** 186

Callimachus, **EP:** 175

Camões, Luís de, **EP:** 180

Cardenal, Ernesto, **WP:** 52

Chappell, Fred, **AP:** 303

Clarke, Austin, **BP:** 261

Corn, Alfred, **AP:** 352

Cowley, Abraham, **BP:** 312

Crane, Hart, **AP:** 379

Dante, **EP:** 270

Dorn, Edward, **AP:** 474

Dove, Rita, **AP:** 486

Drayton, Michael, **BP:** 417

Enzensberger, Hans Magnus, **EP:** 323

Ferlinghetti, Lawrence, **AP:** 593

Firdusi, **WP:** 96

Greek Poetry in Antiquity, **TE:** 320

Haavikko, Paavo, **EP:** 435

Hartmann von Aue, **EP:** 441

Heaney, Seamus, **BP:** 594

Hernández, José, **WP:** 114

Hesiod, **EP:** 465

Hikmet, Nazim, **WP:** 117
Homer, **EP:** 502
Hugo, Victor, **EP:** 518
Illyés, Gyula, **EP:** 528
Kazantzakis, Nikos, **EP:** 557
Ko Un, **WP:** 138
Koch, Kenneth, **AP:** 1058
Landor, Walter Savage, **BP:** 774
Layamon, **BP:** 803
Lermontov, Mikhail, **WP:** 142
Logue, Christopher, **BP:** 823
Longfellow, Henry Wadsworth,
    AP: 1157
Lönnrot, Elias, **EP:** 617
Lucan, **EP:** 621
Lucretius, **EP:** 627
Lydgate, John, **BP:** 832
MacLeish, Archibald, **AP:** 1244
Martinson, Harry, **EP:** 681
Masters, Edgar Lee, **AP:** 1278
Mickiewicz, Adam, **EP:** 702
Milton, John, **BP:** 905
Miyazawa, Kenji, **WP:** 191
Morris, William, **BP:** 924
Neihardt, John G., **AP:** 1405
Neruda, Pablo, **WP:** 196
Notley, Alice, **AP:** 1431
Pasternak, Boris, **WP:** 222
Perse, Saint-John, **EP:** 801
Petőfi, Sándor, **EP:** 816
Pope, Alexander, **BP:** 1005
Pushkin, Alexander, **WP:** 236
Rivera, Tomás, **AP:** 1657
Schwartz, Delmore, **AP:** 1738
Seth, Vikram, **WP:** 272
Słonimski, Antoni, **EP:** 968
Słowacki, Juliusz, **EP:** 972
Snyder, Gary, **AP:** 1840
Southey, Robert, **BP:** 1171
Southwell, Robert, **BP:** 1178
Spenser, Edmund, **BP:** 1191
Statius, **EP:** 998
Tasso, Torquato, **EP:** 1014
Tegnér, Esaias, **EP:** 1020
Tsvetayeva, Marina, **WP:** 293

Tzara, Tristan, **EP:** 1044
Vālmīki, **WP:** 308
Vega Carpio, Lope de, **EP:** 1073
Vergil, **EP:** 1080
Viereck, Peter, **AP:** 2042
Vörösmarty, Mihály, **EP:** 1112
Walcott, Derek, **WP:** 317
Waldman, Anne, **AP:** 2076
Whitman, Walt, **AP:** 2130
Williams, William Carlos, **AP:**
    2175
Wolfram von Eschenbach, **EP:**
    1130
Yevtushenko, Yevgeny, **WP:** 339
Zukofsky, Louis, **AP:** 2265

EPIGRAMS

Ammons, A. R., **AP:** 37
Apollonius Rhodius, **EP:** 30
Belloc, Hilaire, **BP:** 73
Callimachus, **EP:** 175
Cardenal, Ernesto, **WP:** 52
Catullus, **EP:** 197
Chappell, Fred, **AP:** 303
Coulette, Henri, **AP:** 362
Crashaw, Richard, **BP:** 337
Cunningham, J. V., **AP:** 417
Davies, Sir John, **BP:** 375
Donne, John, **BP:** 405
Goethe, Johann Wolfgang von,
    EP: 396
Hein, Piet, **EP:** 447
Herrick, Robert, **BP:** 626
Heywood, John, **BP:** 635
Jonson, Ben, **BP:** 711
Kraus, Karl, **EP:** 563
Kunze, Reiner, **EP:** 570
Landor, Walter Savage, **BP:** 774
Leithauser, Brad, **AP:** 1108
Leonidas of Tarentum, **EP:** 602
Machado, Antonio, **EP:** 633
Martial, **EP:** 678
Meleager, **EP:** 685
Nemerov, Howard, **AP:** 1409
Nims, John Frederick, **AP:** 1421

Prior, Matthew, **BP:** 1026
Pushkin, Alexander, **WP:** 236
Quarles, Francis, **BP:** 1031
Schiller, Friedrich, **EP:** 949
Southwell, Robert, **BP:** 1178
Steele, Timothy, **AP:** 1881
Theocritus, **EP:** 1023
Thoreau, Henry David, **AP:** 1977

EXPANSIVE POETRY

Alvarez, Julia, **AP:** 31
Baker, David, **AP:** 77
Dove, Rita, **AP:** 486
Gioia, Dana, **AP:** 688
Hacker, Marilyn, **AP:** 761
Hudgins, Andrew, **AP:** 924
Leithauser, Brad, **AP:** 1108
Peacock, Molly, **AP:** 1525
Schnackenberg, Gjertrud, **AP:**
    1728
Steele, Timothy, **AP:** 1881

EXPERIMENTAL POETS

Aiken, Conrad, **AP:** 12
Bang, Mary Jo, **AP:** 85
Bernstein, Charles, **AP:** 132
Birney, Earle, **BP:** 86
Breton, André, **EP:** 157
Celan, Paul, **EP:** 214
Chappell, Fred, **AP:** 303
Cummings, E. E., **AP:** 410
Darío, Rubén, **WP:** 71
Ekelöf, Gunnar, **EP:** 306
Elytis, Odysseus, **EP:** 317
Foix, J. V., **EP:** 329
García Lorca, Federico, **EP:** 355
Harrison, Jim, **AP:** 802
Hejinian, Lyn, **AP:** 836
Hollo, Anselm, **AP:** 887
Howe, Susan, **AP:** 913
Hunt, Erica, **AP:** 938
Komunyakaa, Yusef, **AP:** 1064
Lowell, Amy, **AP:** 1172
MacBeth, George, **BP:** 841
Mallarmé, Stéphane, **EP:** 644

Moss, Thylias, **AP:** 1380
Parra, Nicanor, **WP:** 216
Patchen, Kenneth, **AP:** 1520
Paz, Octavio, **WP:** 230
Rankine, Claudia, **AP:** 1602
Reverdy, Pierre, **EP:** 883
Rimbaud, Arthur, **EP:** 897
Scalapino, Leslie, **AP:** 1724
Seferis, George, **EP:** 957
Sexton, Anne, **AP:** 1753
Sitwell, Edith, **BP:** 1145
Stein, Gertrude, **AP:** 1885
Tomlinson, Charles, **BP:** 1268
Toomer, Jean, **AP:** 1988
Tsvetayeva, Marina, **WP:** 293
Valéry, Paul, **EP:** 1065
Villa, José García, **AP:** 2048
Voznesensky, Andrei, **WP:** 311
Whalen, Philip, **AP:** 2111
Williams, C. K., **AP:** 2161
Williams, William Carlos, **AP:** 2175
Winters, Yvor, **AP:** 2184
Wright, C. D., **AP:** 2203

EXPRESSIONISM
Benn, Gottfried, **EP:** 107
Biermann, Wolf, **EP:** 119
Brecht, Bertolt, **EP:** 149
Celan, Paul, **EP:** 214
García Lorca, Federico, **EP:** 355
Trakl, Georg, **EP:** 1033

FABLES
Archilochus, **EP:** 50
Chaucer, Geoffrey, **BP:** 243
Dryden, John, **BP:** 433
Finch, Anne, **BP:** 491
Gay, John, **BP:** 512
Henryson, Robert, **BP:** 612
Heywood, John, **BP:** 635
La Fontaine, Jean de, **EP:** 577
Marie de France, **EP:** 666

FEMINIST POETS
Alegría, Claribel, **WP:** 9
Allen, Paula Gunn, **AP:** 27
Atwood, Margaret, **BP:** 37
Beer, Patricia, **BP:** 60
Behn, Aphra, **BP:** 66
Boland, Eavan, **BP:** 108
Cervantes, Lorna Dee, **AP:** 298
Christine de Pizan, **EP:** 240
Cliff, Michelle, **WP:** 61
Cruz, Sor Juana Inés de la, **WP:** 64
Derricotte, Toi, **AP:** 444
Di Prima, Diane, **AP:** 464
Evans, Mari, **AP:** 563
Feminist Criticism, **TE:** 736
Finch, Anne, **BP:** 491
Forché, Carolyn, **AP:** 611
Fulton, Alice, **AP:** 633
H. D., **AP:** 754
Hacker, Marilyn, **AP:** 761
Hirshfield, Jane, **AP:** 858
Hogan, Linda, **AP:** 871
Howe, Susan, **AP:** 913
Kenyon, Jane, **AP:** 1028
Kizer, Carolyn, **AP:** 1046
Levertov, Denise, **AP:** 1111
Lorde, Audre, **AP:** 1166
Macdonald, Cynthia, **AP:** 1211
McPherson, Sandra, **AP:** 1258
Mew, Charlotte, **BP:** 894
Millay, Edna St. Vincent, **AP:** 1344
Mora, Pat, **AP:** 1371
Moss, Thylias, **AP:** 1380
Muske, Carol, **AP:** 1396
Notley, Alice, **AP:** 1431
Olds, Sharon, **AP:** 1456
Oliver, Mary, **AP:** 1463
Ostriker, Alicia Suskin, **AP:** 1502
Paley, Grace, **AP:** 1506
Piercy, Marge, **AP:** 1532
Queer Theory, **TE:** 774
Rich, Adrienne, **AP:** 1633
Rodgers, Carolyn M., **AP:** 1668
Rukeyser, Muriel, **AP:** 1686

Sarton, May, **AP:** 1714
Sexton, Anne, **AP:** 1753
Shomer, Enid, **AP:** 1769
Stein, Gertrude, **AP:** 1885
Swir, Anna, **EP:** 1004
Valentine, Jean, **AP:** 2024
Van Duyn, Mona, **AP:** 2032
Waldman, Anne, **AP:** 2076
Walker, Alice, **AP:** 2080
Walker, Margaret, **AP:** 2086
Yamada, Mitsuye, **AP:** 2244
Yosano Akiko, **WP:** 349
Zamora, Daisy, **WP:** 354

FIRESIDE POETS
Bryant, William Cullen, **AP:** 259
Fireside Poets, **TE:** 633
Holmes, Oliver Wendell, **AP:** 893
Longfellow, Henry Wadsworth, **AP:** 1157
Lowell, James Russell, **AP:** 1180
Whittier, John Greenleaf, **AP:** 2144

FRENCH RENAISSANCE. *See* **RENAISSANCE, FRENCH**

FUGITIVE POETS
Hecht, Anthony, **AP:** 826
Jarrell, Randall, **AP:** 957
Ransom, John Crowe, **AP:** 1605
Riding, Laura, **AP:** 1642
Tate, Allen, **AP:** 1941
Warren, Robert Penn, **AP:** 2094

FUTURISM
Loy, Mina, **AP:** 1200
Mayakovsky, Vladimir, **WP:** 176
Montale, Eugenio, **EP:** 721
Pasternak, Boris, **WP:** 222

GAY AND LESBIAN CULTURE
Allen, Paula Gunn, **AP:** 27
Ashbery, John, **AP:** 55

Becker, Robin, **AP:** 110
Bishop, Elizabeth, **AP:** 169
Cavafy, Constantine P., **EP:** 204
Cernuda, Luis, **EP:** 220
Cliff, Michelle, **WP:** 61
Cole, Henri, **AP:** 333
Corn, Alfred, **AP:** 352
Crane, Hart, **AP:** 379
Cullen, Countée, **AP:** 404
Doty, Mark, **AP:** 481
Duncan, Robert, **AP:** 509
Feminist Criticism, **TE:** 736
Field, Edward, **AP:** 602
George, Stefan, **EP:** 377
Ginsberg, Allen, **AP:** 677
Gunn, Thom, **BP:** 560
Hacker, Marilyn, **AP:** 761
Housman, A. E., **BP:** 677
Howard, Richard, **AP:** 909
Jordan, June, **AP:** 981
Lear, Edward, **BP:** 812
Logan, John, **AP:** 1153
Lorde, Audre, **AP:** 1166
Meleager, **EP:** 685
Merrill, James, **AP:** 1317
Mew, Charlotte, **BP:** 894
O'Hara, Frank, **AP:** 1451
Oliver, Mary, **AP:** 1463
Pasolini, Pier Paolo, **EP:** 776
Phillips, Carl, **AP:** 1529
Price, Reynolds, **AP:** 1586
Queer Theory, **TE:** 774
Rich, Adrienne, **AP:** 1633
Rimbaud, Arthur, **EP:** 897
Sappho, **EP:** 941
Sarton, May, **AP:** 1714
Sassoon, Siegfried, **BP:** 1080
Schuyler, James, **AP:** 1732
Spicer, Jack, **AP:** 1868
Stein, Gertrude, **AP:** 1885
Verlaine, Paul, **EP:** 1093
Walker, Alice, **AP:** 2080
Whitman, Walt, **AP:** 2130
Wilde, Oscar, **BP:** 1303

GENERATION OF '98
Machado, Antonio, **EP:** 633
Unamuno y Jugo, Miguel de, **EP:** 1051

GENERATION OF '27
Alberti, Rafael, **EP:** 6
Aleixandre, Vicente, **EP:** 12
Cernuda, Luis, **EP:** 220
García Lorca, Federico, **EP:** 355
Guillén, Jorge, **EP:** 430
Salinas, Pedro, **EP:** 936

GENERATION OF '68
Barańczak, Stanisław, **EP:** 77
Zagajewski, Adam, **EP:** 1137

GEORGIAN POETS
Blunden, Edmund, **BP:** 104
Brooke, Rupert, **BP:** 144
De la Mare, Walter, **BP:** 398
Graves, Robert, **BP:** 534
Housman, A. E., **BP:** 677
Lawrence, D. H., **BP:** 795
Rosenberg, Isaac, **BP:** 1055
Sassoon, Siegfried, **BP:** 1080

GERMAN PERIOD, MIDDLE HIGH. *See* **MIDDLE HIGH GERMAN PERIOD**

GHAZALS
Ali, Agha Shahid, **AP:** 24
Bly, Robert, **AP:** 188
Hafiz, **WP:** 108
Harrison, Jim, **AP:** 802
Judah ha-Levi, **EP:** 549
Rich, Adrienne, **AP:** 1633
Rūmī, Jalāl al-Dīn, **WP:** 255
Saʿdi, **WP:** 260

GOETHE, AGE OF
Eichendorff, Joseph von, **EP:** 299
Goethe, Johann Wolfgang von, **EP:** 396

Heine, Heinrich, **EP:** 451
Hölderlin, Friedrich, **EP:** 485
Novalis, **EP:** 748
Schiller, Friedrich, **EP:** 949

GOLDEN AGE, LATIN
Catullus, **EP:** 197
Horace, **EP:** 510
Lucretius, **EP:** 627
Ovid, **EP:** 763
Persius, **EP:** 806
Propertius, Sextus, **EP:** 866

GOLDEN AGE, ROMAN
Vergil, **EP:** 1080

GOLDEN AGE, SPANISH
Calderón de la Barca, Pedro, **EP:** 170
Góngora y Argote, Luis de, **EP:** 410
John of the Cross, Saint, **EP:** 539
León, Luis de, **EP:** 597
Vega Carpio, Lope de, **EP:** 1073

GRAVEYARD SCHOOL
Beddoes, Thomas Lovell, **BP:** 56
Chatterton, Thomas, **BP:** 235
Collins, William, **BP:** 287
Cowper, William, **BP:** 320
Goldsmith, Oliver, **BP:** 520
Gray, Thomas, **BP:** 542
Smart, Christopher, **BP:** 1159
Young, Edward, **BP:** 1349

GRUPPE
Bachmann, Ingeborg, **EP:** 72
Bobrowski, Johannes, **EP:** 126

HAIKU
Baraka, Amiri, **AP:** 89
Blackburn, Paul, **AP:** 180
Carruth, Hayden, **AP:** 278
Collins, Billy, **AP:** 341
Di Prima, Diane, **AP:** 464
Emanuel, James A., **AP:** 538

Ginsberg, Allen, **AP:** 677
Harrison, Jim, **AP:** 802
Issa, **WP:** 126
Jordan, June, **AP:** 981
McClure, Michael, **AP:** 1207
Matsuo Bashō, **WP:** 170
Merrill, James, **AP:** 1317
Muldoon, Paul, **BP:** 937
Sanchez, Sonia, **AP:** 1698
Seferis, George, **EP:** 957
Snyder, Gary, **AP:** 1840
Tranströmer, Tomas, **EP:** 1039

HARLEM RENAISSANCE
African American Poetry, **TE:** 3
Bontemps, Arna, **AP:** 205
Brown, Sterling A., **AP:** 254
Cullen, Countée, **AP:** 404
Harlem Renaissance, **TE:** 655
Hughes, Langston, **AP:** 927
Jarrell, Randall, **AP:** 957
Johnson, James Weldon, **AP:** 972
McKay, Claude, **AP:** 1234
Tolson, Melvin B., **AP:** 1984
Toomer, Jean, **AP:** 1988

HARVARD AESTHETES
Cowley, Malcolm, **AP:** 366
Cummings, E. E., **AP:** 410
Hillyer, Robert, **AP:** 850
Wheelwright, John, **AP:** 2126

HELLENISTIC POETS
Apollonius Rhodius, **EP:** 30
Callimachus, **EP:** 175
Leonidas of Tarentum, **EP:** 602
Meleager, **EP:** 685
Sappho, **EP:** 941
Theocritus, **EP:** 1023

HERMETICISM
Montale, Eugenio, **EP:** 721
Quasimodo, Salvatore, **EP:** 873
Ungaretti, Giuseppe, **EP:** 1056
Vaughan, Henry, **BP:** 1284

HISPANIC CULTURE. *See* LATINO CULTURE

HOMOSEXUAL CULTURE. *See* GAY AND LESBIAN CULTURE

HOUSEHOLD POETS. *See* FIRESIDE POETS

HYMNS
Addison, Joseph, **BP:** 7
Bryant, William Cullen, **AP:** 259
Callimachus, **EP:** 175
Chapman, George, **BP:** 228
Chatterton, Thomas, **BP:** 235
Cowper, William, **BP:** 320
Davies, Sir John, **BP:** 375
Drummond of Hawthornden, William, **BP:** 424
Dunbar, Paul Laurence, **AP:** 502
Dunbar, William, **BP:** 442
Foscolo, Ugo, **EP:** 340
Gezelle, Guido, **EP:** 384
Hemans, Felicia Dorothea, **BP:** 609
Hesiod, **EP:** 465
Hölderlin, Friedrich, **EP:** 485
Johnson, James Weldon, **AP:** 972
Judah ha-Levi, **EP:** 549
McClure, Michael, **AP:** 1207
Manzoni, Alessandro, **EP:** 660
Novalis, **EP:** 748
Ronsard, Pierre de, **EP:** 912
Sappho, **EP:** 941
Smart, Christopher, **BP:** 1159
Theocritus, **EP:** 1023
Unamuno y Jugo, Miguel de, **EP:** 1051
Very, Jones, **AP:** 2039
Watts, Isaac, **BP:** 1297
Wheatley, Phillis, **AP:** 2114
Whittier, John Greenleaf, **AP:** 2144

IMAGE WRITING. *See* PATTERN POETS

IMAGISM
Aldington, Richard, **BP:** 17
Belitt, Ben, **AP:** 114
Bunting, Basil, **BP:** 168
Corman, Cid, **AP:** 347
Crane, Stephen, **AP:** 387
Guest, Barbara, **AP:** 745
H. D., **AP:** 754
Imagists, **TE:** 644
Joyce, James, **BP:** 719
Lawrence, D. H., **BP:** 795
Lewis, Janet, **AP:** 1132
Lowell, Amy, **AP:** 1172
Moore, Marianne, **AP:** 1364
Plath, Sylvia, **AP:** 1547
Pound, Ezra, **AP:** 1577
Reznikoff, Charles, **AP:** 1627
Sandburg, Carl, **AP:** 1704
Simic, Charles, **AP:** 1785
Stevens, Wallace, **AP:** 1905
Tomlinson, Charles, **BP:** 1268
Wakoski, Diane, **AP:** 2068
Williams, William Carlos, **AP:** 2175
Winters, Yvor, **AP:** 2184

IMPRESSIONISM
Crane, Stephen, **AP:** 387
Hofmannsthal, Hugo von, **EP:** 478
Holz, Arno, **EP:** 497
Laforgue, Jules, **EP:** 584
Lowell, Amy, **AP:** 1172
Nerval, Gérard de, **EP:** 741
Verhaeren, Émile, **EP:** 1089
Verlaine, Paul, **EP:** 1093

IRISH LITERARY REVIVAL
Æ, **BP:** 13
Clarke, Austin, **BP:** 261
Colum, Padraic, **BP:** 292
Joyce, James, **BP:** 719
Kavanagh, Patrick, **BP:** 726
Yeats, William Butler, **BP:** 1330

IRISH RENAISSANCE. *See*
**IRISH LITERARY
REVIVAL**

ITALIAN RENAISSANCE. *See*
RENAISSANCE, ITALIAN

JACOBEAN AGE

Breton, Nicholas, **BP:** 124
Campion, Thomas, **BP:** 202
Chapman, George, **BP:** 228
Constable, Henry, **BP:** 301
Davies, Sir John, **BP:** 375
Dekker, Thomas, **BP:** 390
Donne, John, **BP:** 405
Drayton, Michael, **BP:** 417
Drummond of Hawthornden,
    William, **BP:** 424
English Poetry in the Seventeenth
    Century, **TE:** 144
Herbert, George, **BP:** 617
Jonson, Ben, **BP:** 711
Quarles, Francis, **BP:** 1031
Ralegh, Sir Walter, **BP:** 1037
Shakespeare, William, **BP:** 1105
Sidney, Sir Robert, **BP:** 1135

JAZZ POETS

Alexander, Elizabeth, **AP:** 17
Baraka, Amiri, **AP:** 89
Carruth, Hayden, **AP:** 278
Eady, Cornelius, **AP:** 521
Evans, Mari, **AP:** 563
Harjo, Joy, **AP:** 789
Harper, Michael S., **AP:** 794
Hughes, Langston, **AP:** 927
Kaufman, Bob, **AP:** 1002
Komunyakaa, Yusef, **AP:** 1064
Lindsay, Vachel, **AP:** 1146
Mackey, Nathaniel, **AP:** 1241
Patchen, Kenneth, **AP:** 1520
Williams, Sherley Anne, **AP:**
    2172
Young, Al, **AP:** 2248

JEWISH CULTURE

Abse, Dannie, **BP:** 1
Amichai, Yehuda, **WP:** 14
Ausländer, Rose, **AP:** 65
Becker, Robin, **AP:** 110
Bell, Marvin, **AP:** 119
Biermann, Wolf, **EP:** 119
Brodsky, Joseph, **WP:** 44
Celan, Paul, **EP:** 214
Codrescu, Andrei, **AP:** 331
Davison, Peter, **AP:** 437
Feldman, Irving, **AP:** 588
Ginsberg, Allen, **AP:** 677
Goldbarth, Albert, **AP:** 719
Hacker, Marilyn, **AP:** 761
Hecht, Anthony, **AP:** 826
Heine, Heinrich, **EP:** 451
Hirsch, Edward, **AP:** 853
Hollander, John, **AP:** 877
Ignatow, David, **AP:** 941
Judah ha-Levi, **EP:** 549
Kraus, Karl, **EP:** 563
Kumin, Maxine, **AP:** 1073
Kunitz, Stanley, **AP:** 1083
Layton, Irving, **BP:** 808
Levertov, Denise, **AP:** 1111
Levine, Philip, **AP:** 1120
Lifshin, Lyn, **AP:** 1136
Mandelstam, Osip, **WP:** 163
Manger, Itzik, **EP:** 650
Menashe, Samuel, **AP:** 1302
Nemerov, Howard, **AP:** 1409
Oppen, George, **AP:** 1477
Oppenheimer, Joel, **AP:** 1481
Ostriker, Alicia Suskin, **AP:** 1502
Pagis, Dan, **WP:** 213
Paley, Grace, **AP:** 1506
Pastan, Linda, **AP:** 1514
Piercy, Marge, **AP:** 1532
Pinsky, Robert, **AP:** 1538
Rakosi, Carl, **AP:** 1590
Reznikoff, Charles, **AP:** 1627
Rich, Adrienne, **AP:** 1633
Rolfe, Edwin, **AP:** 1682
Rosenberg, Isaac, **BP:** 1055

Rukeyser, Muriel, **AP:** 1686
Saba, Umberto, **EP:** 925
Sachs, Nelly, **EP:** 930
Sassoon, Siegfried, **BP:** 1080
Schwartz, Delmore, **AP:** 1738
Shapiro, Alan, **AP:** 1759
Shapiro, Karl, **AP:** 1764
Shore, Jane, **AP:** 1773
Silkin, Jon, **BP:** 1141
Słonimski, Antoni, **EP:** 968
Stein, Gertrude, **AP:** 1885
Stern, Gerald, **AP:** 1893
Tzara, Tristan, **EP:** 1044
Untermeyer, Louis, **AP:** 2007
Ważyk, Adam, **EP:** 1126
Zukofsky, Louis, **AP:** 2265
Zweig, Stefan, **EP:** 1141

JOHNSON, AGE OF

Burns, Robert, **BP:** 173
Chatterton, Thomas, **BP:** 235
Collins, William, **BP:** 287
Cowper, William, **BP:** 320
Crabbe, George, **BP:** 327
English Poetry in the Eighteenth
    Century, **TE:** 160
Goldsmith, Oliver, **BP:** 520
Gray, Thomas, **BP:** 542
Johnson, Samuel, **BP:** 700
Smart, Christopher, **BP:** 1159

JUGENDSTIL

George, Stefan, **EP:** 377
Hofmannsthal, Hugo von, **EP:** 478
Rilke, Rainer Maria, **EP:** 889

LAKE POETS

Coleridge, Samuel Taylor, **BP:**
    276
Southey, Robert, **BP:** 1171
Wordsworth, William, **BP:** 1310

LANDSCAPE POETRY. *See*
**TOPOGRAPHICAL
POETRY**

LANGUAGE POETRY

Bernstein, Charles, **AP:** 132
Hejinian, Lyn, **AP:** 836
Hollo, Anselm, **AP:** 887
Howe, Susan, **AP:** 913
Hunt, Erica, **AP:** 938
Scalapino, Leslie, **AP:** 1724
Swensen, Cole, **AP:** 1931
Wright, C. D., **AP:** 2203

LATIN GOLDEN AGE. *See*
GOLDEN AGE, LATIN

LATINO CULTURE

Alvarez, Julia, **AP:** 31
Baca, Jimmy Santiago, **AP:** 71
Cervantes, Lorna Dee, **AP:** 298
Cisneros, Sandra, **AP:** 318
Cruz, Victor Hernández, **AP:** 400
Espada, Martín, **AP:** 559
Latino Poetry, **TE:** 466
Mora, Pat, **AP:** 1371
Ortiz Cofer, Judith, **AP:** 1499
Ríos, Alberto, **AP:** 1654
Rivera, Tomás, **AP:** 1657
Silko, Leslie Marmon, **AP:** 1777
Soto, Gary, **AP:** 1862

LESBIAN CULTURE. *See*
GAY AND LESBIAN
CULTURE

LIGHT VERSE

Belloc, Hilaire, **BP:** 73
Chappell, Fred, **AP:** 303
Cohen, Leonard, **BP:** 272
Collins, Billy, **AP:** 341
Dacey, Philip, **AP:** 425
Davies, Sir John, **BP:** 375
Fenton, James, **BP:** 487
Hein, Piet, **EP:** 447
Hollander, John, **AP:** 877
Hood, Thomas, **BP:** 650
Hunt, Leigh, **BP:** 694
Kirby, David, **AP:** 1039

Logue, Christopher, **BP:** 823
McGinley, Phyllis, **AP:** 1221
Silverstein, Shel, **AP:** 1781
Taylor, Henry, **AP:** 1968
Updike, John, **AP:** 2016

LOST GENERATION

Bishop, John Peale, **AP:** 177
Cowley, Malcolm, **AP:** 366
Crane, Hart, **AP:** 379
Cummings, E. E., **AP:** 410
MacLeish, Archibald, **AP:** 1244
Pound, Ezra, **AP:** 1577
Stein, Gertrude, **AP:** 1885

LOVE POETRY

Ady, Endre, **EP:** 1
Alegría, Claribel, **WP:** 9
Amichai, Yehuda, **WP:** 14
Archilochus, **EP:** 50
Bécquer, Gustavo Adolfo, **EP:** 95
Berryman, John, **AP:** 155
Bradstreet, Anne, **AP:** 223
Brautigan, Richard, **AP:** 239
Browning, Elizabeth Barrett, **BP:** 149
Burns, Robert, **BP:** 173
Campion, Thomas, **BP:** 202
Carew, Thomas, **BP:** 208
Carson, Anne, **BP:** 225
Catullus, **EP:** 197
Cavafy, Constantine P., **EP:** 204
Charles d'Orléans, **EP:** 230
Chartier, Alain, **EP:** 236
Christine de Pizan, **EP:** 240
Ciardi, John, **AP:** 312
Cisneros, Sandra, **AP:** 318
Clough, Arthur Hugh, **BP:** 266
Cohen, Leonard, **BP:** 272
Colum, Padraic, **BP:** 292
Constable, Henry, **BP:** 301
Cotton, Charles, **BP:** 306
Cowley, Abraham, **BP:** 312
Crane, Hart, **AP:** 379
Crashaw, Richard, **BP:** 337

Cruz, Sor Juana Inés de la, **WP:** 64
Cullen, Countée, **AP:** 404
Cummings, E. E., **AP:** 410
Dante, **EP:** 270
Davies, Sir John, **BP:** 375
Donne, John, **BP:** 405
Drayton, Michael, **BP:** 417
Dučić, Jovan, **EP:** 292
Dunbar, Paul Laurence, **AP:** 502
Dunn, Stephen, **AP:** 517
Éluard, Paul, **EP:** 313
Emanuel, James A., **AP:** 538
Emerson, Claudia, **AP:** 541
Empson, William, **BP:** 468
Etherege, Sir George, **BP:** 476
Gallagher, Tess, **AP:** 639
Gardner, Isabella, **AP:** 653
Gibran, Kahlil, **AP:** 663
Gilbert, Jack, **AP:** 673
Giovanni, Nikki, **AP:** 692
Gottfried von Strassburg, **EP:** 415
Graves, Robert, **BP:** 534
Guillame de Lorris, **EP:** 424
Guillén, Jorge, **EP:** 430
Hall, Donald, **AP:** 775
Hallam, Arthur Henry, **BP:** 575
Hartmann von Aue, **EP:** 441
Heine, Heinrich, **EP:** 451
Herrick, Robert, **BP:** 626
Hongo, Garrett Kaoru, **AP:** 900
Hope, A. D., **BP:** 660
Horton, George Moses, **AP:** 905
Jean de Meung, **EP:** 424
John of the Cross, Saint, **EP:** 539
Jordan, June, **AP:** 981
Keats, John, **BP:** 731
King, Henry, **BP:** 743
Kinnell, Galway, **AP:** 1033
Kizer, Carolyn, **AP:** 1046
Knight, Etheridge, **AP:** 1053
Layton, Irving, **BP:** 808
Li Qingzhao, **WP:** 157
Lovelace, Richard, **BP:** 827
Loy, Mina, **AP:** 1200

Manrique, Jorge, **EP:** 657

Marvell, Andrew, **BP:** 877

Meinke, Peter, **AP:** 1290

Millay, Edna St. Vincent, **AP:** 1344

Montague, John, **BP:** 914

Mörike, Eduard, **EP:** 732

Neruda, Pablo, **WP:** 196

Oates, Joyce Carol, **AP:** 1443

Oppenheimer, Joel, **AP:** 1481

Ovid, **EP:** 763

Pasternak, Boris, **WP:** 222

Patchen, Kenneth, **AP:** 1520

Petőfi, Sándor, **EP:** 816

Petrarch, **EP:** 828

Pinter, Harold, **BP:** 1001

Poliziano, **EP:** 841

Prince, F. T., **BP:** 1021

Prior, Matthew, **BP:** 1026

Propertius, Sextus, **EP:** 866

Pushkin, Alexander, **WP:** 236

Radnóti, Miklós, **EP:** 879

Ralegh, Sir Walter, **BP:** 1037

Rexroth, Kenneth, **AP:** 1621

Rochester, John Wilmot, earl of, **BP:** 1048

Roethke, Theodore, **AP:** 1671

Ronsard, Pierre de, **EP:** 912

Rossetti, Christina, **BP:** 1060

Rossetti, Dante Gabriel, **BP:** 1065

Rūmī, Jalāl al-Dīn, **WP:** 255

Salinas, Pedro, **EP:** 936

Sappho, **EP:** 941

Sedley, Sir Charles, **BP:** 1094

Seifert, Jaroslav, **EP:** 961

Senghor, Léopold, **WP:** 264

Sexton, Anne, **AP:** 1753

Shakespeare, William, **BP:** 1105

Sidney, Sir Philip, **BP:** 1126

Sidney, Sir Robert, **BP:** 1135

Silkin, Jon, **BP:** 1141

Simpson, Louis, **AP:** 1793

Stampa, Gaspara, **EP:** 993

Steele, Timothy, **AP:** 1881

Suckling, Sir John, **BP:** 1206

Surrey, Henry Howard, earl of, **BP:** 1212

Swenson, May, **AP:** 1934

Swir, Anna, **EP:** 1004

Tasso, Torquato, **EP:** 1014

Teasdale, Sara, **AP:** 1974

Vallejo, César, **WP:** 300

Van Duyn, Mona, **AP:** 2032

Verhaeren, Émile, **EP:** 1089

Verlaine, Paul, **EP:** 1093

Villon, François, **EP:** 1106

Waldman, Anne, **AP:** 2076

Waller, Edmund, **BP:** 1290

Walther von der Vogelweide, **EP:** 1119

Wyatt, Sir Thomas, **BP:** 1322

Yosano Akiko, **WP:** 349

LYRIC POETRY

Ackerman, Diane, **AP:** 1

Adams, Léonie, **AP:** 4

Ady, Endre, **EP:** 1

Alberti, Rafael, **EP:** 6

Alexie, Sherman, **AP:** 21

Allingham, William, **BP:** 23

Anacreon, **EP:** 17

Anderson, Maggie, **AP:** 43

Annensky, Innokenty, **WP:** 21

Apollinaire, Guillaume, **EP:** 22

Applewhite, James, **AP:** 51

Arany, János, **EP:** 42

Ariosto, Ludovico, **EP:** 56

Arnold, Matthew, **BP:** 30

Arp, Hans, **EP:** 62

Auden, W. H., **BP:** 47

Awoonor, Kofi, **WP:** 25

Babits, Mihály, **EP:** 68

Bachmann, Ingeborg, **EP:** 72

Baker, David, **AP:** 77

Baudelaire, Charles, **EP:** 80

Bécquer, Gustavo Adolfo, **EP:** 95

Beddoes, Thomas Lovell, **BP:** 56

Behn, Aphra, **BP:** 66

Belitt, Ben, **AP:** 114

Belloc, Hilaire, **BP:** 73

Benn, Gottfried, **EP:** 107

Bernhard, Thomas, **EP:** 112

Berry, Wendell, **AP:** 146

Berryman, John, **AP:** 155

Biermann, Wolf, **EP:** 119

Blackburn, Paul, **AP:** 180

Blake, William, **BP:** 91

Blunden, Edmund, **BP:** 104

Bogan, Louise, **AP:** 197

Bradstreet, Anne, **AP:** 223

Breton, Nicholas, **BP:** 124

Bridges, Robert, **BP:** 131

Brodsky, Joseph, **WP:** 44

Brown, Sterling A., **AP:** 254

Burns, Robert, **BP:** 173

Bynner, Witter, **AP:** 274

Byron, Lord, **BP:** 186

Camões, Luís de, **EP:** 180

Campion, Thomas, **BP:** 202

Cardenal, Ernesto, **WP:** 52

Carducci, Giosuè, **EP:** 185

Carew, Thomas, **BP:** 208

Cassity, Turner, **AP:** 291

Catullus, **EP:** 197

Cavalcanti, Guido, **EP:** 210

Celan, Paul, **EP:** 214

Cernuda, Luis, **EP:** 220

Chaucer, Geoffrey, **BP:** 243

Christine de Pizan, **EP:** 240

Ciardi, John, **AP:** 312

Clare, John, **BP:** 254

Clough, Arthur Hugh, **BP:** 266

Cohen, Leonard, **BP:** 272

Cole, Henri, **AP:** 333

Coleridge, Samuel Taylor, **BP:** 276

Collins, William, **BP:** 287

Congreve, William, **BP:** 296

Constable, Henry, **BP:** 301

Cotton, Charles, **BP:** 306

Cowley, Abraham, **BP:** 312

Coxe, Louis, **AP:** 375

Crane, Hart, **AP:** 379

Cruz, Sor Juana Inés de la, **WP:** 64

Cummings, E. E., **AP:** 410

Cynewulf, **BP:** 344

Daniel, Samuel, **BP:** 352

D'Annunzio, Gabriele, **EP:** 264

Dante, **EP:** 270

Darío, Rubén, **WP:** 71

Darley, George, **BP:** 359

Davenant, Sir William, **BP:** 362

Davies, Sir John, **BP:** 375

Day Lewis, Cecil, **BP:** 384

Dekker, Thomas, **BP:** 390

De la Mare, Walter, **BP:** 398

Dickinson, Emily, **AP:** 455

Donne, John, **BP:** 405

Doty, Mark, **AP:** 481

Dove, Rita, **AP:** 486

Drayton, Michael, **BP:** 417

Drummond of Hawthornden, William, **BP:** 424

Dryden, John, **BP:** 433

Du Fu, **WP:** 84

Dučić, Jovan, **EP:** 292

Dunbar, Paul Laurence, **AP:** 502

Duncan, Robert, **AP:** 509

Durrell, Lawrence, **BP:** 451

Eberhart, Richard, **AP:** 526

Eichendorff, Joseph von, **EP:** 299

Elytis, Odysseus, **EP:** 317

Emerson, Claudia, **AP:** 541

Esenin, Sergei, **WP:** 90

Fairchild, B. H., **AP:** 579

Fanshawe, Sir Richard, **BP:** 481

Feldman, Irving, **AP:** 588

Ferlinghetti, Lawrence, **AP:** 593

Field, Edward, **AP:** 602

Foix, J. V., **EP:** 329

Foscolo, Ugo, **EP:** 340

Frost, Robert, **AP:** 625

García Lorca, Federico, **EP:** 355

Gascoigne, George, **BP:** 505

Goethe, Johann Wolfgang von, **EP:** 396

Góngora y Argote, Luis de, **EP:** 410

Gray, Thomas, **BP:** 542

Gregerson, Linda, **AP:** 732

Gregory, Horace, **AP:** 738

Greville, Fulke, **BP:** 555

Hardy, Thomas, **BP:** 579

Hartmann von Aue, **EP:** 441

Heaney, Seamus, **BP:** 594

Herbert, George, **BP:** 617

Hesse, Hermann, **EP:** 471

Hillyer, Robert, **AP:** 850

Hirsch, Edward, **AP:** 853

Hirshfield, Jane, **AP:** 858

Hölderlin, Friedrich, **EP:** 485

Holz, Arno, **EP:** 497

Homer, **EP:** 502

Horace, **EP:** 510

Housman, A. E., **BP:** 677

Howes, Barbara, **AP:** 921

Hugo, Victor, **EP:** 518

Ignatow, David, **AP:** 941

Illyés, Gyula, **EP:** 528

Jacobsen, Josephine, **AP:** 950

Jeffers, Robinson, **AP:** 963

John of the Cross, Saint, **EP:** 539

Jonson, Ben, **BP:** 711

Kasischke, Laura, **AP:** 999

Kavanagh, Patrick, **BP:** 726

Keats, John, **BP:** 731

Kenyon, Jane, **AP:** 1028

King, Henry, **BP:** 743

Kinsella, Thomas, **BP:** 751

Kipling, Rudyard, **BP:** 760

Kizer, Carolyn, **AP:** 1046

Ko Un, **WP:** 138

Kraus, Karl, **EP:** 563

Kumin, Maxine, **AP:** 1073

Kunze, Reiner, **EP:** 570

Laforgue, Jules, **EP:** 584

Lamartine, Alphonse de, **EP:** 591

Landor, Walter Savage, **BP:** 774

Lanier, Sidney, **AP:** 1095

Lee, Li-Young, **AP:** 1102

Leopardi, Giacomo, **EP:** 607

Lermontov, Mikhail, **WP:** 142

Levertov, Denise, **AP:** 1111

Li Bo, **WP:** 150

Li Qingzhao, **WP:** 157

Lodge, Thomas, **BP:** 817

Logan, John, **AP:** 1153

Lovelace, Richard, **BP:** 827

MacDiarmid, Hugh, **BP:** 846

Machado, Antonio, **EP:** 633

McHugh, Heather, **AP:** 1230

Malherbe, François de, **EP:** 639

Mandelstam, Osip, **WP:** 163

Manger, Itzik, **EP:** 650

Manzoni, Alessandro, **EP:** 660

Marlowe, Christopher, **BP:** 870

Martinson, Harry, **EP:** 681

Marvell, Andrew, **BP:** 877

Masefield, John, **BP:** 885

Meredith, George, **BP:** 890

Merrill, James, **AP:** 1317

Michelangelo, **EP:** 694

Mickiewicz, Adam, **EP:** 702

Miles, Josephine, **AP:** 1340

Millay, Edna St. Vincent, **AP:** 1344

Miller, Vassar, **AP:** 1349

Milton, John, **BP:** 905

Mistral, Gabriela, **WP:** 185

Montale, Eugenio, **EP:** 721

Morgenstern, Christian, **EP:** 727

Muir, Edwin, **BP:** 933

Musset, Alfred de, **EP:** 736

Nashe, Thomas, **BP:** 953

Neihardt, John G., **AP:** 1405

Neruda, Pablo, **WP:** 196

Nerval, Gérard de, **EP:** 741

Niedecker, Lorine, **AP:** 1415

Oliver, Mary, **AP:** 1463

Omar Khayyám, **WP:** 208

Orr, Gregory, **AP:** 1485

Ortiz, Simon, **AP:** 1493

Otero, Blas de, **EP:** 757

Parker, Dorothy, **AP:** 1509

Pasternak, Boris, **WP:** 222

Pavese, Cesare, **EP:** 783

Petőfi, Sándor, **EP:** 816

Petrarch, **EP:** 828

Pindar, **EP:** 836

Pinter, Harold, **BP:** 1001

Plath, Sylvia, **AP:** 1547

Poe, Edgar Allan, **AP:** 1561

Poliziano, **EP:** 841

Prior, Matthew, **BP:** 1026

Pushkin, Alexander, **WP:** 236

Quarles, Francis, **BP:** 1031

Quasimodo, Salvatore, **EP:** 873

Radnóti, Miklós, **EP:** 879

Reese, Lizette Woodworth, **AP:** 1616

Rilke, Rainer Maria, **EP:** 889

Robinson, Edwin Arlington, **AP:** 1660

Rochester, John Wilmot, earl of, **BP:** 1048

Ronsard, Pierre de, **EP:** 912

Rossetti, Christina, **BP:** 1060

Rossetti, Dante Gabriel, **BP:** 1065

Saba, Umberto, **EP:** 925

Sachs, Nelly, **EP:** 930

Salinas, Pedro, **EP:** 936

Sandburg, Carl, **AP:** 1704

Santos, Sherod, **AP:** 1711

Sappho, **EP:** 941

Sarton, May, **AP:** 1714

Schiller, Friedrich, **EP:** 949

Schnackenberg, Gjertrud, **AP:** 1728

Scott, Sir Walter, **BP:** 1087

Sedley, Sir Charles, **BP:** 1094

Seifert, Jaroslav, **EP:** 961

Senghor, Léopold, **WP:** 264

Shelley, Percy Bysshe, **BP:** 1112

Sidney, Sir Philip, **BP:** 1126

Słowacki, Juliusz, **EP:** 972

Smart, Christopher, **BP:** 1159

Smith, William Jay, **AP:** 1825

Song, Cathy, **AP:** 1853

Southey, Robert, **BP:** 1171

Soyinka, Wole, **WP:** 276

Spenser, Edmund, **BP:** 1191

Steele, Timothy, **AP:** 1881

Stern, Gerald, **AP:** 1893

Swinburne, Algernon Charles, **BP:** 1227

Tasso, Torquato, **EP:** 1014

Tate, Allen, **AP:** 1941

Teasdale, Sara, **AP:** 1974

Tennyson, Alfred, Lord, **BP:** 1236

Thomas, Dylan, **BP:** 1245

Tranströmer, Tomas, **EP:** 1039

Vallejo, César, **WP:** 300

Vaughan, Henry, **BP:** 1284

Vega Carpio, Lope de, **EP:** 1073

Very, Jones, **AP:** 2039

Vigny, Alfred de, **EP:** 1099

Villon, François, **EP:** 1106

Voigt, Ellen Bryant, **AP:** 2054

Vörösmarty, Mihály, **EP:** 1112

Voznesensky, Andrei, **WP:** 311

Walcott, Derek, **WP:** 317

Waller, Edmund, **BP:** 1290

Walther von der Vogelweide, **EP:** 1119

Wheelock, John Hall, **AP:** 2123

Wilde, Oscar, **BP:** 1303

Williams, Miller, **AP:** 2168

Wojahn, David, **AP:** 2190

Wolfram von Eschenbach, **EP:** 1130

Wordsworth, William, **BP:** 1310

Wright, Charles, **AP:** 2207

Wyatt, Sir Thomas, **BP:** 1322

Xie Lingyun, **WP:** 334

Zimmer, Paul, **AP:** 2261

Zweig, Stefan, **EP:** 1141

MERRY GANG

Etherege, Sir George, **BP:** 476

Rochester, John Wilmot, earl of, **BP:** 1048

Sedley, Sir Charles, **BP:** 1094

METAPHYSICAL POETS

Bradstreet, Anne, **AP:** 223

Bronk, William, **AP:** 243

Carew, Thomas, **BP:** 208

Cowley, Abraham, **BP:** 312

Crashaw, Richard, **BP:** 337

Cruz, Sor Juana Inés de la, **WP:** 64

Donne, John, **BP:** 405

Herbert, George, **BP:** 617

Khodasevich, Vladislav, **WP:** 133

King, Henry, **BP:** 743

Marvell, Andrew, **BP:** 877

Metaphysical Poets, **TE:** 615

Taylor, Edward, **AP:** 1959

Traherne, Thomas, **BP:** 1277

Vaughan, Henry, **BP:** 1284

MIDDLE ENGLISH PERIOD

Chaucer, Geoffrey, **BP:** 243

English Poetry in the Fifteenth Century, **TE:** 120

Gower, John, **BP:** 525

Langland, William, **BP:** 780

Lydgate, John, **BP:** 832

MIDDLE HIGH GERMAN PERIOD

Gottfried von Strassburg, **EP:** 415

Hartmann von Aue, **EP:** 441

Walther von der Vogelweide, **EP:** 1119

Wolfram von Eschenbach, **EP:** 1130

MINIMALIST POETRY

Bobrowski, Johannes, **EP:** 126

Brautigan, Richard, **AP:** 239

Bukowski, Charles, **AP:** 264

Cisneros, Sandra, **AP:** 318

Clifton, Lucille, **AP:** 326

Dana, Robert, **AP:** 430

Matthews, William, **AP:** 1284

Paley, Grace, **AP:** 1506

Valentine, Jean, **AP:** 2024

MODERNISM

Adams, Léonie, **AP:** 4

Aiken, Conrad, **AP:** 12

Aldington, Richard, **BP:** 17

Auden, W. H., **BP:** 47

Babits, Mihály, **EP:** 68

Barnard, Mary, **AP:** 100

Baudelaire, Charles, **EP:** 80
Beckett, Samuel, **EP:** 87
Benn, Gottfried, **EP:** 107
Berryman, John, **AP:** 155
Betjeman, John, **BP:** 80
Birney, Earle, **BP:** 86
Bishop, John Peale, **AP:** 177
Blunden, Edmund, **BP:** 104
Bogan, Louise, **AP:** 197
Booth, Philip, **AP:** 209
Brooke, Rupert, **BP:** 144
Brown, Sterling A., **AP:** 254
Bunting, Basil, **BP:** 168
Bynner, Witter, **AP:** 274
Cardenal, Ernesto, **WP:** 52
Carruth, Hayden, **AP:** 278
Corman, Cid, **AP:** 347
Cowley, Malcolm, **AP:** 366
Crane, Hart, **AP:** 379
Cullen, Countée, **AP:** 404
D'Annunzio, Gabriele, **EP:** 264
Day Lewis, Cecil, **BP:** 384
De la Mare, Walter, **BP:** 398
Dickey, James, **AP:** 448
Dučić, Jovan, **EP:** 292
Durrell, Lawrence, **BP:** 451
Eliot, T. S., **BP:** 458
Empson, William, **BP:** 468
Fearing, Kenneth, **AP:** 582
Frost, Robert, **AP:** 625
Fuller, Roy, **BP:** 500
Graves, Robert, **BP:** 534
Gregory, Horace, **AP:** 738
H. D., **AP:** 754
Haavikko, Paavo, **EP:** 435
Hall, Donald, **AP:** 775
Hayden, Robert, **AP:** 820
Hecht, Anthony, **AP:** 826
Hikmet, Nazim, **WP:** 117
Hofmannsthal, Hugo von, **EP:** 478
Hopkins, Gerard Manley, **BP:** 666
Hugo, Richard, **AP:** 934
Illyés, Gyula, **EP:** 528
Jacobsen, Josephine, **AP:** 950
Jarrell, Randall, **AP:** 957

Jeffers, Robinson, **AP:** 963
Jones, David, **BP:** 707
Joyce, James, **BP:** 719
Kazantzakis, Nikos, **EP:** 557
Kees, Weldon, **AP:** 1006
Kinsella, Thomas, **BP:** 751
Lawrence, D. H., **BP:** 795
Lindsay, Vachel, **AP:** 1146
Lowell, Robert, **AP:** 1187
McKay, Claude, **AP:** 1234
MacLeish, Archibald, **AP:** 1244
MacNeice, Louis, **BP:** 854
Masefield, John, **BP:** 885
Masters, Edgar Lee, **AP:** 1278
Meredith, William, **AP:** 1308
Merton, Thomas, **AP:** 1325
Mew, Charlotte, **BP:** 894
Middleton, Christopher, **BP:** 898
Millay, Edna St. Vincent, **AP:** 1344
Modernists, **TE:** 650
Montale, Eugenio, **EP:** 721
Moore, Marianne, **AP:** 1364
Moss, Howard, **AP:** 1375
Nash, Ogden, **AP:** 1401
Neruda, Pablo, **WP:** 196
Okigbo, Christopher, **WP:** 205
Ondaatje, Michael, **BP:** 973
Otero, Blas de, **EP:** 757
Owen, Wilfred, **BP:** 977
Parker, Dorothy, **AP:** 1509
Pascoli, Giovanni, **EP:** 771
Paz, Octavio, **WP:** 230
Pentzikis, Nikos, **EP:** 797
Pessoa, Fernando, **EP:** 811
Ponge, Francis, **EP:** 848
Pound, Ezra, **AP:** 1577
Pratt, E. J., **BP:** 1016
Radnóti, Miklós, **EP:** 879
Rakosi, Carl, **AP:** 1590
Ransom, John Crowe, **AP:** 1605
Reed, Henry, **BP:** 1043
Reznikoff, Charles, **AP:** 1627
Riding, Laura, **AP:** 1642
Rilke, Rainer Maria, **EP:** 889

Rosenberg, Isaac, **BP:** 1055
Różewicz, Tadeusz, **EP:** 917
St. John, David, **AP:** 1693
Sandburg, Carl, **AP:** 1704
Sarton, May, **AP:** 1714
Sassoon, Siegfried, **BP:** 1080
Scott, Winfield Townley, **AP:** 1746
Seferis, George, **EP:** 957
Senghor, Léopold, **WP:** 264
Sitwell, Edith, **BP:** 1145
Smith, Stevie, **BP:** 1164
Södergran, Edith, **EP:** 981
Spender, Stephen, **BP:** 1183
Stevens, Wallace, **AP:** 1905
Still, James, **AP:** 1913
Tate, Allen, **AP:** 1941
Teasdale, Sara, **AP:** 1974
Thomas, Dylan, **BP:** 1245
Tolson, Melvin B., **AP:** 1984
Toomer, Jean, **AP:** 1988
Trakl, Georg, **EP:** 1033
Ungaretti, Giuseppe, **EP:** 1056
Van Doren, Mark, **AP:** 2027
Wheelwright, John, **AP:** 2126
Yeats, William Butler, **BP:** 1330

MODERNISMO

Castro, Rosalía de, **EP:** 190
Darío, Rubén, **WP:** 71
Drummond de Andrade, Carlos, **WP:** 76
García Lorca, Federico, **EP:** 355
González Martínez, Enrique, **WP:** 101
Jiménez, Juan Ramón, **EP:** 533
Salinas, Pedro, **EP:** 936

MOVEMENT POETS

Davie, Donald, **BP:** 367
Gunn, Thom, **BP:** 560
Larkin, Philip, **BP:** 786
Movement Poets, **TE:** 679

NARRATIVE POETRY

Ai, **AP:** 8
Aiken, Conrad, **AP:** 12
Akhmatova, Anna, **WP:** 3
Alexander, Elizabeth, **AP:** 17
Alexie, Sherman, **AP:** 21
Allingham, William, **BP:** 23
Arany, János, **EP:** 42
Archilochus, **EP:** 50
Ariosto, Luovico, **EP:** 56
Baca, Jimmy Santiago, **AP:** 71
Benét, Stephen Vincent, **AP:** 124
Benét, William Rose, **AP:** 128
Bidart, Frank, **AP:** 162
Biermann, Wolf, **EP:** 119
Boccaccio, Giovanni, **EP:** 131
Bottoms, David, **AP:** 216
Brown, Sterling A., **AP:** 254
Browning, Elizabeth Barrett, **BP:** 149
Browning, Robert, **BP:** 158
Burns, Robert, **BP:** 173
Byron, Lord, **BP:** 186
Callimachus, **EP:** 175
Camões, Luís de, **EP:** 180
Carroll, Lewis, **BP:** 213
Cassity, Turner, **AP:** 291
Chapman, George, **BP:** 228
Chappell, Fred, **AP:** 303
Chaucer, Geoffrey, **BP:** 243
Ciardi, John, **AP:** 312
Clarke, Austin, **BP:** 261
Clifton, Lucille, **AP:** 326
Coleridge, Samuel Taylor, **BP:** 276
Collier, Michael, **AP:** 336
Collins, Billy, **AP:** 341
Corman, Cid, **AP:** 347
Corn, Alfred, **AP:** 352
Cotton, Charles, **BP:** 306
Cowley, Malcolm, **AP:** 366
Coxe, Louis, **AP:** 375
Crabbe, George, **BP:** 327
Crane, Hart, **AP:** 379
Creeley, Robert, **AP:** 392

Cullen, Countée, **AP:** 404
Cynewulf, **BP:** 344
Dacey, Philip, **AP:** 425
Daniel, Samuel, **BP:** 352
Dante, **EP:** 270
Dorn, Edward, **AP:** 474
Dove, Rita, **AP:** 486
Drummond de Andrade, Carlos, **WP:** 76
Dunbar, Paul Laurence, **AP:** 502
Dunbar, William, **BP:** 442
Eichendorff, Joseph von, **EP:** 299
Emerson, Ralph Waldo, **AP:** 544
Erdrich, Louise, **AP:** 553
Fairchild, B. H., **AP:** 579
Firdusi, **WP:** 96
FitzGerald, Edward, **BP:** 495
Forché, Carolyn, **AP:** 611
Fracastoro, Girolamo, **EP:** 345
Frost, Robert, **AP:** 625
Galvin, Brendan, **AP:** 644
Garrett, George, **AP:** 656
Gibson, Margaret, **AP:** 670
Gioia, Dana, **AP:** 688
Glancy, Diane, **AP:** 702
Glenn, Mel, **AP:** 706
Gottfried von Strassburg, **EP:** 415
Gregg, Linda, **AP:** 735
Gregory, Horace, **AP:** 738
Gurney, Ivor, **BP:** 568
Hall, Donald, **AP:** 775
Hartmann von Aue, **EP:** 441
Hayden, Robert, **AP:** 820
Heine, Heinrich, **EP:** 451
Hemans, Felicia Dorothea, **BP:** 609
Henryson, Robert, **BP:** 612
Hesiod, **EP:** 465
Heywood, John, **BP:** 635
Hikmet, Nazim, **WP:** 117
Homer, **EP:** 502
Hongo, Garrett Kaoru, **AP:** 900
Hudgins, Andrew, **AP:** 924
Hughes, Ted, **BP:** 686
Hugo, Victor, **EP:** 518

Jarman, Mark, **AP:** 953
Jeffers, Robinson, **AP:** 963
Justice, Donald, **AP:** 986
Kelly, Brigit Pegeen, **AP:** 1012
Kilping, Rudyard, **BP:** 760
Kirby, David, **AP:** 1039
Knight, Etheridge, **AP:** 1053
Kooser, Ted, **AP:** 1070
Laforgue, Jules, **EP:** 584
Lamartine, Alphonse de, **EP:** 591
Langland, William, **BP:** 780
Layamon, **BP:** 803
Leithauser, Brad, **AP:** 1108
Lermontov, Mikhail, **WP:** 142
Levertov, Denise, **AP:** 1111
Lodge, Thomas, **BP:** 817
Longfellow, Henry Wadsworth, **AP:** 1157
Lucan, **EP:** 621
Lucretius, **EP:** 627
Lydgate, John, **BP:** 832
McDonald, Walt, **AP:** 1215
MacLeish, Archibald, **AP:** 1244
McMichael, James, **AP:** 1255
Marie de France, **EP:** 666
Marlowe, Christopher, **BP:** 870
Martinson, Harry, **EP:** 681
Masefield, John, **BP:** 885
Masters, Edgar Lee, **AP:** 1278
Melville, Herman, **AP:** 1294
Meredith, George, **BP:** 890
Merrill, James, **AP:** 1317
Mickiewicz, Adam, **EP:** 702
Milton, John, **BP:** 905
Morris, William, **BP:** 924
Murray, Les A., **BP:** 946
Neihardt, John G., **AP:** 1405
Notley, Alice, **AP:** 1431
Nye, Naomi Shihab, **AP:** 1435
Oates, Joyce Carol, **AP:** 1443
Ortiz Cofer, Judith, **AP:** 1499
Ovid, **EP:** 763
Pascoli, Giovanni, **EP:** 771
Pearl-Poet, **BP:** 991
Péguy, Charles-Pierre, **EP:** 791

Petőfi, Sándor, **EP:** 816
Poe, Edgar Allan, **AP:** 1561
Pratt, E. J., **BP:** 1016
Prior, Matthew, **BP:** 1026
Rexroth, Kenneth, **AP:** 1621
Ríos, Alberto, **AP:** 1654
Ritsos, Yannis, **EP:** 904
Rivera, Tomás, **AP:** 1657
Robinson, Edwin Arlington, **AP:** 1660
Rossetti, Christina, **BP:** 1060
Rossetti, Dante Garbiel, **BP:** 1065
Rūmī, Jalāl al-Dīn, **WP:** 255
Saʿdi, **WP:** 260
Sandburg, Carl, **AP:** 1704
Scott, Sir Walter, **BP:** 1087
Scott, Winfield Townley, **AP:** 1746
Shakespeare, William, **BP:** 1105
Shapiro, Alan, **AP:** 1759
Sissman, L. E., **AP:** 1802
Sitwell, Edith, **BP:** 1145
Slavitt, David, **AP:** 1809
Słowacki, Juliusz, **EP:** 972
Smith, Dave, **AP:** 1817
Solomos, Dionysios, **EP:** 987
Southey, Robert, **BP:** 1171
Southwell, Robert, **BP:** 1178
Spenser, Edmund, **BP:** 1191
Taylor, Henry, **AP:** 1968
Tennyson, Alfred, Lord, **BP:** 1236
Theocritus, **EP:** 1023
Thomson, James (1834-1882), **BP:** 1264
Trethewey, Natasha, **AP:** 1995
Tsvetayeva, Marina, **WP:** 293
Tuckerman, Frederick, **AP:** 1998
Tzara, Tristan, **EP:** 1044
Van Doren, Mark, **AP:** 2027
Vega Carpio, Lope de, **EP:** 1073
Vergil, **EP:** 1080
Wakoski, Diane, **AP:** 2068
Warren, Robert Penn, **AP:** 2094
Watts, Isaac, **BP:** 1297
Whittier, John Greenleaf, **AP:** 2144

Wilde, Oscar, **BP:** 1303
Williams, C. K., **AP:** 2161
Williams, William Carlos, **AP:** 2175
Wolfram von Eschenbach, **EP:** 1130
Wordsworth, William, **BP:** 1310
Yeats, William Butler, **BP:** 1330
Young, Edward, **BP:** 1349

NATIVE AMERICAN CULTURE
Alexie, Sherman, **AP:** 21
Allen, Paula Gunn, **AP:** 27
Baca, Jimmy Santiago, **AP:** 71
Cervantes, Lorna Dee, **AP:** 298
Erdrich, Louise, **AP:** 553
Glancy, Diane, **AP:** 702
Harjo, Joy, **AP:** 789
Hogan, Linda, **AP:** 871
Momaday, N. Scott, **AP:** 1358
Native American Poetry, **TE:** 478
Ortiz, Simon, **AP:** 1493
Silko, Leslie Marmon, **AP:** 1777
Smith, William Jay, **AP:** 1825
Welch, James, **AP:** 2107
Wright, Jay, **AP:** 2231

NATIVE AMERICAN RENAISSANCE
Harjo, Joy, **AP:** 789
Hogan, Linda, **AP:** 871
Momaday, N. Scott, **AP:** 1358
Native American Poetry, **TE:** 478
Ortiz, Simon, **AP:** 1493
Silko, Leslie Marmon, **AP:** 1777

NATURALISM
English and American Poetry in the Nineteenth Century, **TE:** 174
Holz, Arno, **EP:** 497
Verhaeren, Émile, **EP:** 1089

NATURALISM, AMERICAN
Crane, Stephen, **AP:** 387
Masters, Edgar Lee, **AP:** 1278
Neihardt, John G., **AP:** 1405
Robinson, Edwin Arlington, **AP:** 1660

NATURE POETRY. *See also* ECOPOETRY
Ackerman, Diane, **AP:** 1
Aleixandre, Vicente, **EP:** 12
Allingham, William, **BP:** 23
Ammons, A. R., **AP:** 37
Applewhite, James, **AP:** 51
Barnard, Mary, **AP:** 100
Bell, Marvin, **AP:** 119
Benét, William Rose, **AP:** 128
Berry, Wendell, **AP:** 146
Betjeman, John, **BP:** 80
Blunden, Edmund, **BP:** 104
Bobrowski, Johannes, **EP:** 126
Bryant, William Cullen, **AP:** 259
Carver, Raymond, **AP:** 284
Castro, Rosalía de, **EP:** 190
Clare, John, **BP:** 254
Cotton, Charles, **BP:** 306
Cowley, Malcolm, **AP:** 366
Cowper, William, **BP:** 320
Darley, George, **BP:** 359
Davison, Peter, **AP:** 437
Du Fu, **WP:** 84
Dučić, Jovan, **EP:** 292
Eberhart, Richard, **AP:** 526
Emerson, Ralph Waldo, **AP:** 544
Finch, Anne, **BP:** 491
Frost, Robert, **AP:** 625
Galvin, Brendan, **AP:** 644
George, Stefan, **EP:** 377
Green Movement Poets, **TE:** 690
Grennan, Eamon, **AP:** 741
Gurney, Ivor, **BP:** 568
Haines, John Meade, **AP:** 772
Hardy, Thomas, **BP:** 579
Heyen, William, **AP:** 841
Hillyer, Robert, **AP:** 850

Hope, A. D., **BP:** 660
Hopkins, Gerard Manley, **BP:** 666
Horton, George Moses, **AP:** 905
Howes, Barbara, **AP:** 921
Kinnell, Galway, **AP:** 1033
Matsuo Bashō, **WP:** 170
Meng Haoran, **WP:** 182
Merton, Thomas, **AP:** 1325
Merwin, W. S., **AP:** 1331
Nemerov, Howard, **AP:** 1409
Niedecker, Lorine, **AP:** 1415
Nims, John Frederick, **AP:** 1421
Oliver, Mary, **AP:** 1463
Pasternak, Boris, **WP:** 222
Peacock, Molly, **AP:** 1525
Pessoa, Fernando, **EP:** 811
Porter, Anne, **AP:** 1573
Rexroth, Kenneth, **AP:** 1621
Swenson, May, **AP:** 1934
Tagore, Rabindranath, **WP:** 281
Tao Qian, **WP:** 288
Teasdale, Sara, **AP:** 1974
Thomas, Edward, **BP:** 1252
Thomson, James (1700-1748), **BP:** 1260
Thoreau, Henry David, **AP:** 1977
Verlaine, Paul, **EP:** 1093
Very, Jones, **AP:** 2039
Wagoner, David, **AP:** 2059
Walker, Alice, **AP:** 2080
Wang Wei, **WP:** 326
Wheatley, Phillis, **AP:** 2114
Whitman, Walt, **AP:** 2130
Whittier, John Greenleaf, **AP:** 2144
Wylie, Elinor, **AP:** 2240
Xie Lingyun, **WP:** 334

NEGRITUDE
Césaire, Aimé, **WP:** 56
Senghor, Léopold, **WP:** 264

NEOCLASSICAL POETS
Addison, Joseph, **BP:** 7
Boileau-Despréaux, Nicolas, **EP:** 138

Cotton, Charles, **BP:** 306
Cowper, William, **BP:** 320
Crabbe, George, **BP:** 327
Davenant, Sir William, **BP:** 362
Dryden, John, **BP:** 433
English Poetry in the Seventeenth Century, **TE:** 144
Fanshawe, Sir Richard, **BP:** 481
Finch, Anne, **BP:** 491
Foscolo, Ugo, **EP:** 340
Gay, John, **BP:** 512
Goethe, Johann Wolfgang von, **EP:** 396
Herrick, Robert, **BP:** 626
Johnson, Samuel, **BP:** 700
Milton, John, **BP:** 905
Newcastle, Margaret Cavendish, duchess, **BP:** 958
Oldham, John, **BP:** 969
Pope, Alexander, **BP:** 1005
Prior, Matthew, **BP:** 1026
Restoration Poetry, **TE:** 620
Schiller, Friedrich, **EP:** 949
Waller, Edmund, **BP:** 1290
Wheatley, Phillis, **AP:** 2114

NEOPLATONISM
Bembo, Pietro, **EP:** 101
Breton, Nicholas, **BP:** 124
Camões, Luís de, **EP:** 180
Chapman, George, **BP:** 228
Drummond of Hawthornden, William, **BP:** 424
Hayden, Robert, **AP:** 820
Keats, John, **BP:** 731
Michelangelo, **EP:** 694
Robinson, Edwin Arlington, **AP:** 1660
Shelley, Percy Bysshe, **BP:** 1112
Sidney, Sir Robert, **BP:** 1135
Spenser, Edmund, **BP:** 1191
Stampa, Gaspara, **EP:** 993
Thoreau, Henry David, **AP:** 1977

Traherne, Thomas, **BP:** 1277
Wordsworth, William, **BP:** 1310
Yeats, William Butler, **BP:** 1330

NEOREALISM
Pasolini, Pier Paolo, **EP:** 776
Pavese, Cesare, **EP:** 783
Quasimodo, Salvatore, **EP:** 873

NEO-ROMANTICISM
Benn, Gottfried, **EP:** 107
Carroll, Lewis, **BP:** 213
Hirsch, Edward, **AP:** 853
Hopkins, Gerard Manley, **BP:** 666
Housman, A. E., **BP:** 677
Hughes, Ted, **BP:** 686
Jiménez, Juan Ramón, **EP:** 533
Morris, William, **BP:** 924
Santos, Sherod, **AP:** 1711
Słonimski, Antoni, **EP:** 968
Thomas, Dylan, **BP:** 1245
Yeats, William Butler, **BP:** 1330

NEW FORMALISM
Alvarez, Julia, **AP:** 31
Corn, Alfred, **AP:** 352
Dacey, Philip, **AP:** 425
Gioia, Dana, **AP:** 688
Goldbarth, Albert, **AP:** 719
Hacker, Marilyn, **AP:** 761
Hollander, John, **AP:** 877
Hudgins, Andrew, **AP:** 924
Jarman, Mark, **AP:** 953
Kennedy, X. J., **AP:** 1020
Leithauser, Brad, **AP:** 1108
Peacock, Molly, **AP:** 1525
Schnackenberg, Gjertrud, **AP:** 1728
Seth, Vikram, **WP:** 272
Shapiro, Alan, **AP:** 1759
Steele, Timothy, **AP:** 1881
Wallace, Ronald, **AP:** 2090
Wilbur, Richard, **AP:** 2151
Winters, Yvor, **AP:** 2184

NEW NARRATIVE POETRY
Gioia, Dana, **AP:** 688
Jarman, Mark, **AP:** 953
Leithauser, Brad, **AP:** 1108

NEW NEGRO MOVEMENT.
See **HARLEM RENAISSANCE**

NEW YORK SCHOOL
Ashbery, John, **AP:** 55
Berrigan, Ted, **AP:** 143
Guest, Barbara, **AP:** 745
Koch, Kenneth, **AP:** 1058
New York School, **TE:** 674
Notley, Alice, **AP:** 1431
O'Hara, Frank, **AP:** 1451
Porter, Anne, **AP:** 1573
Schuyler, James, **AP:** 1732
Schwartz, Delmore, **AP:** 1738
Waldman, Anne, **AP:** 2076
Young, Dean, **AP:** 2257

OBJECTIVISM
Bunting, Basil, **BP:** 168
Corman, Cid, **AP:** 347
Niedecker, Lorine, **AP:** 1415
Oppen, George, **AP:** 1477
Pound, Ezra, **AP:** 1577
Rakosi, Carl, **AP:** 1590
Rexroth, Kenneth, **AP:** 1621
Reznikoff, Charles, **AP:** 1627
Williams, William Carlos, **AP:** 2175
Zukofsky, Louis, **AP:** 2265

OCCASIONAL VERSE
Apollonius Rhodius, **EP:** 30
Behn, Aphra, **BP:** 66
Bembo, Pietro, **EP:** 101
Berry, Wendell, **AP:** 146
Burns, Robert, **BP:** 173
Campion, Thomas, **BP:** 202
Chapman, George, **BP:** 228
Christine de Pizan, **EP:** 240

Clarke, Austin, **BP:** 261
Clough, Arthur Hugh, **BP:** 266
Cotton, Charles, **BP:** 306
Crashaw, Richard, **BP:** 337
Cruz, Sor Juana Inés de la, **WP:** 64
Davenant, Sir William, **BP:** 362
Davies, Sir John, **BP:** 375
Donne, John, **BP:** 405
Dryden, John, **BP:** 433
Du Fu, **WP:** 84
Ehrhart, W. D., **AP:** 532
Emerson, Ralph Waldo, **AP:** 544
Fenton, James, **BP:** 487
Finch, Anne, **BP:** 491
Góngora y Argote, Luis de, **EP:** 410
Harrison, Tony, **BP:** 588
Holmes, Oliver Wendell, **AP:** 893
Jonson, Ben, **BP:** 711
King, Henry, **BP:** 743
Kinsella, Thomas, **BP:** 751
Lamb, Charles, **BP:** 768
MacNeice, Louis, **BP:** 854
Meinke, Peter, **AP:** 1290
Milton, John, **BP:** 905
Moore, Marianne, **AP:** 1364
Morris, William, **BP:** 924
Nash, Ogden, **AP:** 1401
Prior, Matthew, **BP:** 1026
Ralegh, Sir Walter, **BP:** 1037
Riley, James Whitcomb, **AP:** 1645
Sandburg, Carl, **AP:** 1704
Schuyler, James, **AP:** 1732
Skelton, John, **BP:** 1153
Southey, Robert, **BP:** 1171
Spenser, Edmund, **BP:** 1191
Stampa, Gaspara, **EP:** 993
Statius, **EP:** 998
Stevenson, Robert Louis, **BP:** 1201
Traherne, Thomas, **BP:** 1277
Vaughan, Henry, **BP:** 1284
Waller, Edmund, **BP:** 1290

Wheatley, Phillis, **AP:** 2114
Whittier, John Greeleaf, **AP:** 2144
Winters, Yvor, **AP:** 2184
Young, Al, **AP:** 2248
Young, Edward, **BP:** 1349

ODES
Applewhite, James, **AP:** 51
Carducci, Giosuè, **EP:** 185
Claudel, Paul, **EP:** 244
Collins, William, **BP:** 287
Congreve, William, **BP:** 296
Cowley, Abraham, **BP:** 312
Davenant, Sir William, **BP:** 362
Drayton, Michael, **BP:** 417
Du Bellay, Joachim, **EP:** 289
Dunbar, Paul Laurence, **AP:** 502
Fanshawe, Sir Richard, **BP:** 481
Finch, Anne, **BP:** 491
Gray, Thomas, **BP:** 542
Hafiz, **WP:** 108
Hölderlin, Friedrich, **EP:** 485
Hollander, John, **AP:** 877
Hood, Thomas, **BP:** 650
Horace, **EP:** 510
Hugo, Victor, **EP:** 518
Jonson, Ben, **BP:** 711
Keats, John, **BP:** 731
Lowell, James Russell, **AP:** 1180
McClure, Michael, **AP:** 1207
Malherbe, François de, **EP:** 639
Manzoni, Alessandro, **EP:** 660
Marino, Giambattista, **EP:** 674
Meredith, George, **BP:** 890
Mora, Pat, **AP:** 1371
Mörike, Eduard, **EP:** 732
Neruda, Pablo, **WP:** 196
O'Hara, Frank, **AP:** 1451
Paley, Grace, **AP:** 1506
Patmore, Coventry, **BP:** 983
Pindar, **EP:** 836
Poliziano, **EP:** 841
Prior, Matthew, **BP:** 1026
Ronsard, Pierre de, **EP:** 912
Rukeyser, Muriel, **AP:** 1686

Sappho, **EP:** 941

Schiller, Friedrich, **EP:** 949

Southey, Robert, **BP:** 1171

Swinburne, Algernon Charles, **BP:** 1227

Thomson, James (1700-1748), **BP:** 1260

Thoreau, Henry David, **AP:** 1977

Tuckerman, Frederick, **AP:** 1998

Wright, C. D., **AP:** 2203

ORAL TRADITION

African Poetry, **TE:** 15

Anacreon, **EP:** 17

Archilochus, **EP:** 50

Awoonor, Kofi, **WP:** 25

Beatty, Paul, **AP:** 107

Cædmon, **BP:** 197

European Oral and Epic Traditions, **TE:** 214

Giovanni, Nikki, **AP:** 692

Greek Poetry in Antiquity, **TE:** 320

Harper, Michael S., **AP:** 794

Hesiod, **EP:** 465

Homer, **EP:** 502

Kaufman, Bob, **AP:** 1002

Lindsay, Vachel, **AP:** 1146

Marie de France, **EP:** 666

Ortiz, Simon, **AP:** 1493

Sappho, **EP:** 941

Silko, Leslie Marmon, **AP:** 1777

Theognis, **EP:** 1029

OXFORD MOVEMENT

Hopkins, Gerard Manley, **BP:** 666

Rossetti, Christina, **BP:** 1060

PARNASSIANISM

Annensky, Innokenty, **WP:** 21

Gautier, Théophile, **EP:** 368

Mallarmé, Stéphane, **EP:** 644

Słonimski, Antoni, **EP:** 968

Verlaine, Paul, **EP:** 1093

PASTORAL POETS

Boiardo, Matteo Maria, **EP:** 135

Breton, Nicholas, **BP:** 124

Chatterton, Thomas, **BP:** 235

Clare, John, **BP:** 254

Clough, Arthur Hugh, **BP:** 266

Crabbe, George, **BP:** 327

Drayton, Michael, **BP:** 417

Finch, Anne, **BP:** 491

Garcilaso de la Vega, **EP:** 362

Gay, John, **BP:** 512

Goldsmith, Oliver, **BP:** 520

Henryson, Robert, **BP:** 612

Herrick, Robert, **BP:** 626

Hesiod, **EP:** 465

Lodge, Thomas, **BP:** 817

Marino, Giambattista, **EP:** 674

Marvell, Andrew, **BP:** 877

Milton, John, **BP:** 905

Petrarch, **EP:** 828

Pope, Alexander, **BP:** 1005

Prior, Matthew, **BP:** 1026

Quarles, Francis, **BP:** 1031

Ronsard, Pierre de, **EP:** 912

Sidney, Sir Philip, **BP:** 1126

Spenser, Edmund, **BP:** 1191

Swift, Jonathan, **BP:** 1218

Tasso, Torquato, **EP:** 1014

Theocritus, **EP:** 1023

Vaughan, Henry, **BP:** 1284

Vergil, **EP:** 1080

PATTERN POETS

Apollinaire, Guillaume, **EP:** 22

Cummings, E. E., **AP:** 410

Goldsmith, Oliver, **BP:** 520

Herbert, George, **BP:** 617

Herrick, Robert, **BP:** 626

Hollander, John, **AP:** 877

Johnson, Ronald, **AP:** 976

Mallarmé, Stéphane, **EP:** 644

Swenson, May, **AP:** 1934

PERFORMANCE POETRY

Beatty, Paul, **AP:** 107

Mullen, Harryette, **AP:** 1387

Waldman, Anne, **AP:** 2076

PETRARCHAN SONNETS

Bembo, Pietro, **EP:** 101

Berryman, John, **AP:** 155

Browning, Elizabeth Barrett, **BP:** 149

Hacker, Marilyn, **AP:** 761

Keats, John, **BP:** 731

Michelangelo, **EP:** 694

Mickiewicz, Adam, **EP:** 702

Millay, Edna St. Vincent, **AP:** 1344

Petrarch, **EP:** 828

Ralegh, Sir Walter, **BP:** 1037

Reese, Lizette Woodworth, **AP:** 1616

Ronsard, Pierre de, **EP:** 912

Sidney, Sir Philip, **BP:** 1126

Sidney, Sir Robert, **BP:** 1135

Spenser, Edmund, **BP:** 1191

Stampa, Gaspara, **EP:** 993

Surrey, Henry Howard, earl of, **BP:** 1212

Wright, James, **AP:** 2221

Wyatt, Sir Thomas, **BP:** 1322

PLATONISM. *See* NEOPLATONISM

PLÉIADE POETS

Du Bellay, Joachim, **EP:** 289

Ronsard, Pierre de, **EP:** 912

POLITICAL POETS

Achebe, Chinua, **WP:** 1

Addison, Joseph, **BP:** 7

Ady, Endre, **EP:** 1

Æ, **BP:** 13

Alberti, Rafael, **EP:** 6

Alegría, Claribel, **WP:** 9

Aragon, Louis, **EP:** 35

Awoonor, Kofi, **WP:** 25

Balaban, John, **AP:** 81

Baraka, Amiri, **AP:** 89

Barańczak, Stanisław, **EP:** 77

Behn, Aphra, **BP:** 66

Berrigan, Daniel, **AP:** 137

Biermann, Wolf, **EP:** 119

Bly, Robert, **AP:** 188

Brecht, Bertolt, **EP:** 149

Breytenbach, Breyten, **EP:** 162

Brooks, Gwendolyn, **AP:** 247

Browning, Elizabeth Barrett, **BP:** 149

Butler, Samuel, **BP:** 180

Bynner, Witter, **AP:** 274

Cardenal, Ernesto, **WP:** 52

Catullus, **EP:** 197

Cervantes, Lorna Dee, **AP:** 298

Césaire, Aimé, **WP:** 56

Chartier, Alain, **EP:** 236

Clough, Arthur Hugh, **BP:** 266

Codrescu, Andrei, **AP:** 331

Coulette, Henri, **AP:** 362

Cowley, Malcolm, **AP:** 366

Crabbe, George, **BP:** 327

Darío, Rubén, **WP:** 71

Davies, Sir John, **BP:** 375

Day Lewis, Cecil, **BP:** 384

Dryden, John, **BP:** 433

Du Fu, **WP:** 84

Dugan, Alan, **AP:** 498

East German Poetry, **TE:** 87

Ehrhart, W. D., **AP:** 532

Enzensberger, Hans Magnus, **EP:** 323

Espada, Martín, **AP:** 559

Evans, Mari, **AP:** 563

Fanshawe, Sir Richard, **BP:** 481

Fenton, James, **BP:** 487

Ferlinghetti, Lawrence, **AP:** 593

Forché, Carolyn, **AP:** 611

Freneau, Philip, **AP:** 618

Giovanni, Nikki, **AP:** 692

Grass, Günter, **EP:** 418

Hafiz, **WP:** 108

Haines, John Meade, **AP:** 772

Harjo, Joy, **AP:** 789

Harrison, Tony, **BP:** 588

Herbert, Zbigniew, **EP:** 458

Hernández, José, **WP:** 114

Hikmet, Nazim, **WP:** 117

Holub, Miroslav, **EP:** 492

Illyés, Gyula, **EP:** 528

Johnson, James Weldon, **AP:** 972

Jordan, June, **AP:** 981

King, Henry, **BP:** 743

Kinnell, Galway, **AP:** 1033

Kizer, Carolyn, **AP:** 1046

Knight, Etheridge, **AP:** 1053

Ko Un, **WP:** 138

Kunze, Reiner, **EP:** 570

Lamb, Charles, **BP:** 768

Layton, Irving, **BP:** 808

Levertov, Denise, **AP:** 1111

Levine, Philip, **AP:** 1120

Li Qingzhao, **WP:** 157

Logue, Christopher, **BP:** 823

Lorde, Audre, **AP:** 1166

Lucan, **EP:** 621

Lydgate, John, **BP:** 832

McGrath, Thomas, **AP:** 1225

McKay, Claude, **AP:** 1234

MacLeish, Archibald, **AP:** 1244

Madhubuti, Haki R., **AP:** 1265

Malherbe, François de, **EP:** 639

Markham, Edwin, **AP:** 1274

Mayakovsky, Vladimir, **WP:** 176

Merwin, W. S., **AP:** 1331

Mickiewicz, Adam, **EP:** 702

Miles, Josephine, **AP:** 1340

Millay, Edna St. Vincent, **AP:** 1344

Miłosz, Czesław, **EP:** 709

Mitsui, James Masao, **AP:** 1354

Morris, William, **BP:** 924

Moss, Thylias, **AP:** 1380

Mura, David, **AP:** 1390

Murray, Les A., **BP:** 946

Neruda, Pablo, **WP:** 196

Ní Dhomhnaill, Nuala, **BP:** 964

Okigbo, Christopher, **WP:** 205

Olds, Sharon, **AP:** 1456

Olson, Charles, **AP:** 1469

Oppenheimer, Joel, **AP:** 1481

Otero, Blas de, **EP:** 757

Ovid, **EP:** 763

Paley, Grace, **AP:** 1506

Pasolini, Pier Paolo, **EP:** 776

Pavese, Cesare, **EP:** 783

Piercy, Marge, **AP:** 1532

Pinter, Harold, **BP:** 1001

Prévert, Jacques, **EP:** 861

Prior, Matthew, **BP:** 1026

Pushkin, Alexander, **WP:** 236

Queer Theory, **TE:** 774

Randall, Dudley, **AP:** 1595

Reed, Ishmael, **AP:** 1612

Rexroth, Kenneth, **AP:** 1621

Rich, Adrienne, **AP:** 1633

Ritsos, Yannis, **EP:** 904

Rodgers, Carolyn M., **AP:** 1668

Rolfe, Edwin, **AP:** 1682

Ruan Ji, **WP:** 250

Rukeyser, Muriel, **AP:** 1686

Sanchez, Sonia, **AP:** 1698

Seifert, Jaroslav, **EP:** 961

Senghor, Léopold, **WP:** 264

Skelton, John, **BP:** 1153

Słonimski, Antoni, **EP:** 968

Słowacki, Juliusz, **EP:** 972

Solomos, Dionysios, **EP:** 987

Soto, Gary, **AP:** 1862

Soyinka, Wole, **WP:** 276

Spenser, Edmund, **BP:** 1191

Statius, **EP:** 998

Swift, Jonathan, **BP:** 1218

Swir, Anna, **EP:** 1004

Szymborska, Wisława, **EP:** 1007

Tegnér, Esaias, **EP:** 1020

Thomson, James (1700-1748), **BP:** 1260

Tsvetayeva, Marina, **WP:** 293

Valentine, Jean, **AP:** 2024

Vergil, **EP:** 1080

Viereck, Peter, **AP:** 2042

Vörösmarty, Mihály, **EP:** 1112

Voznesensky, Andrei, **WP:** 311

Waldman, Anne, **AP:** 2076

Walker, Alice, **AP:** 2080

Walker, Margaret, **AP:** 2086

Waller, Edmund, **BP:** 1290

Walther von der Vogelweide, **EP:** 1119

Ważyk, Adam, **EP:** 1126

Weigl, Bruce, **AP:** 2102

Wheatley, Phillis, **AP:** 2114

Wheelwright, John, **AP:** 2126

Whittier, John Greenleaf, **AP:** 2144

Williams, C. K., **AP:** 2161

Wojahn, David, **AP:** 2190

Yamada, Mitsuye, **AP:** 2244

Yevtushenko, Yevgeny, **WP:** 339

Yosano Akiko, **WP:** 349

Zagajewski, Adam, **EP:** 1137

Zamora, Daisy, **WP:** 354

POSTCONFESSIONAL POETS

Abse, Dannie, **BP:** 1

Becker, Robin, **AP:** 110

Beer, Patricia, **BP:** 60

Bidart, Frank, **AP:** 162

Bishop, Elizabeth, **AP:** 169

Bukowski, Charles, **AP:** 264

Dennis, Carl, **AP:** 441

Derricotte, Toi, **AP:** 444

Dove, Rita, **AP:** 486

Dubie, Norman, **AP:** 493

Dunn, Stephen, **AP:** 517

Fennelly, Beth Ann, **AP:** 591

Flint, Roland, **AP:** 607

Gallagher, Tess, **AP:** 639

Glück, Louise, **AP:** 710

Gregg, Linda, **AP:** 735

Harper, Michael S., **AP:** 794

Hass, Robert, **AP:** 814

Hirsch, Edward, **AP:** 853

Hongo, Garrett Kaoru, **AP:** 900

Ignatow, David, **AP:** 941

Karr, Mary, **AP:** 993

Kunitz, Stanley, **AP:** 1083

Levine, Philip, **AP:** 1120

Matthews, William, **AP:** 1284

Mueller, Lisel, **AP:** 1383

Olds, Sharon, **AP:** 1456

Orr, Gregory, **AP:** 1485

Pastan, Linda, **AP:** 1514

Plumly, Stanley, **AP:** 1556

Ponsot, Marie, **AP:** 1569

Rankine, Claudia, **AP:** 1602

Rich, Adrienne, **AP:** 1633

Santos, Sherod, **AP:** 1711

Smith, Stevie, **BP:** 1164

Tate, James, **AP:** 1947

Wright, Charles, **AP:** 2207

Wright, James, **AP:** 2221

Zimmer, Paul, **AP:** 2261

POSTMODERNISM

Abse, Dannie, **BP:** 1

Achebe, Chinua, **WP:** 1

Alexie, Sherman, **AP:** 21

Angelou, Maya, **AP:** 46

Applewhite, James, **AP:** 51

Baker, David, **AP:** 77

Balaban, John, **AP:** 81

Beatty, Paul, **AP:** 107

Beckett, Samuel, **EP:** 87

Beer, Patricia, **BP:** 60

Belitt, Ben, **AP:** 114

Bernhard, Thomas, **EP:** 112

Bidart, Frank, **AP:** 162

Birney, Earle, **BP:** 86

Blackburn, Paul, **AP:** 180

Bly, Robert, **AP:** 188

Boland, Eavan, **BP:** 108

Bonnefoy, Yves, **EP:** 142

Bottoms, David, **AP:** 216

Bowers, Edgar, **AP:** 219

Brautigan, Richard, **AP:** 239

Brooks, Gwendolyn, **AP:** 247

Cardenal, Ernesto, **WP:** 52

Carson, Anne, **BP:** 225

Carver, Raymond, **AP:** 284

Cassity, Turner, **AP:** 291

Cervantes, Lorna Dee, **AP:** 298

Char, René, **EP:** 226

Cisneros, Sandra, **AP:** 318

Clampitt, Amy, **AP:** 322

Clifton, Lucille, **AP:** 326

Collier, Michael, **AP:** 336

Collins, Billy, **AP:** 341

Corso, Gregory, **AP:** 356

Creeley, Robert, **AP:** 392

Cruz, Victor Hernández, **AP:** 400

Cunningham, J. V., **AP:** 417

Dacey, Philip, **AP:** 425

Davie, Donald, **BP:** 367

Davison, Peter, **AP:** 437

Dorn, Edward, **AP:** 474

Dove, Rita, **AP:** 486

Dubie, Norman, **AP:** 493

Dugan, Alan, **AP:** 498

Duncan, Robert, **AP:** 509

Dunn, Stephen, **AP:** 517

Durrell, Lawrence, **BP:** 451

Eberhart, Richard, **AP:** 526

Everson, William, **AP:** 567

Fairchild, B. H., **AP:** 579

Feldman, Irving, **AP:** 588

Fenton, James, **BP:** 487

Ferlinghetti, Lawrence, **AP:** 593

Field, Edward, **AP:** 602

Follain, Jean, **EP:** 335

Fuller, Roy, **BP:** 500

Fulton, Alice, **AP:** 633

Galvin, Brendan, **AP:** 644

Gerstler, Amy, **AP:** 660

Gilbert, Jack, **AP:** 673

Ginsberg, Allen, **AP:** 677

Gioia, Dana, **AP:** 688

Giovanni, Nikki, **AP:** 692

Goldbarth, Albert, **AP:** 719

González Martínez, Enrique, **WP:** 101

Graham, Jorie, **AP:** 725

Grass, Günter, **EP:** 418

Gunn, Thom, **BP:** 560

Harper, Michael S., **AP:** 794

Harrison, Tony, **BP:** 588

Hass, Robert, **AP:** 814

Heaney, Seamus, **BP:** 594

Hébert, Anne, **BP:** 605

Herbert, Zbigniew, **EP:** 458

Heyen, William, **AP:** 841

Hill, Geoffrey, **BP:** 641

Hirsch, Edward, **AP:** 853

Hoffman, Daniel, **AP:** 863

Hogan, Linda, **AP:** 871

Hollander, John, **AP:** 877

Howard, Richard, **AP:** 909

Hughes, Ted, **BP:** 686

Ignatow, David, **AP:** 941

Johnson, Ronald, **AP:** 976

Justice, Donald, **AP:** 986

Kelly, Robert, **AP:** 1015

Kennedy, X. J., **AP:** 1020

Kinnell, Galway, **AP:** 1033

Kinsella, Thomas, **BP:** 751

Kunitz, Stanley, **AP:** 1083

Larkin, Philip, **BP:** 786

Lawrence, D. H., **BP:** 795

Lee, Li-Young, **AP:** 1102

Levertov, Denise, **AP:** 1111

Levine, Philip, **AP:** 1120

Levis, Larry, **AP:** 1127

Lifshin, Lyn, **AP:** 1136

Lindsay, Sarah, **AP:** 1143

Lorde, Audre, **AP:** 1166

MacBeth, George, **BP:** 841

McClure, Michael, **AP:** 1207

Macdonald, Cynthia, **AP:** 1211

McDonald, Walt, **AP:** 1215

McHugh, Heather, **AP:** 1230

Mackey, Nathaniel, **AP:** 1241

McMichael, James, **AP:** 1255

Matthews, William, **AP:** 1284

Meinke, Peter, **AP:** 1290

Merwin, W. S., **AP:** 1331

Miles, Josephine, **AP:** 1340

Miller, Vassar, **AP:** 1349

Miłosz, Czesław, **EP:** 709

Mitsui, James Masao, **AP:** 1354

Momaday, N. Scott, **AP:** 1358

Montague, John, **BP:** 914

Mueller, Lisel, **AP:** 1383

Muldoon, Paul, **BP:** 937

Murray, Les A., **BP:** 946

Neihardt, John G., **AP:** 1405

Nye, Naomi Shihab, **AP:** 1435

Olds, Sharon, **AP:** 1456

Olson, Charles, **AP:** 1469

Ondaatje, Michael, **BP:** 973

Oppenheimer, Joel, **AP:** 1481

Ortiz, Simon, **AP:** 1493

Paley, Grace, **AP:** 1506

Parra, Nicanor, **WP:** 216

Patchen, Kenneth, **AP:** 1520

Pavlović, Miodrag, **EP:** 786

Paz, Octavio, **WP:** 230

Peacock, Molly, **AP:** 1525

Piercy, Marge, **AP:** 1532

Pinsky, Robert, **AP:** 1538

Plumly, Stanley, **AP:** 1556

Ponge, Francis, **EP:** 848

Popa, Vasko, **EP:** 856

Reed, Ishmael, **AP:** 1612

Rukeyser, Muriel, **AP:** 1686

Sanchez, Sonia, **AP:** 1698

Seth, Vikram, **WP:** 272

Shapiro, Karl, **AP:** 1764

Silkin, Jon, **BP:** 1141

Sissman, L. E., **AP:** 1802

Smith, Dave, **AP:** 1817

Snyder, Gary, **AP:** 1840

Song, Cathy, **AP:** 1853

Sorrentino, Gilbert, **AP:** 1858

Soto, Gary, **AP:** 1862

Spender, Stephen, **BP:** 1183

Spicer, Jack, **AP:** 1868

Stafford, William, **AP:** 1872

Stern, Gerald, **AP:** 1893

Strand, Mark, **AP:** 1918

Structuralist and Poststructuralist Criticism, **TE:** 780

Stryk, Lucien, **AP:** 1927

Szymborska, Wisława, **EP:** 1007

Tate, James, **AP:** 1947

Tomlinson, Charles, **BP:** 1268

Transtr15mer, Tomas, **EP:** 1039

Tzara, Tristan, **EP:** 1044

Wakoski, Diane, **AP:** 2068

Warren, Robert Penn, **AP:** 2094

Whittemore, Reed, **AP:** 2140

Wilbur, Richard, **AP:** 2151

Williams, C. K., **AP:** 2161

Wright, Charles, **AP:** 2207

Wright, James, **AP:** 2221

Zimmer, Paul, **AP:** 2261

PRE-RAPHAELITES

Allingham, William, **BP:** 23

Morris, William, **BP:** 924

Patmore, Coventry, **BP:** 983

Rossetti, Christina, **BP:** 1060

Rossetti, Dante Gabriel, **BP:** 1065

Swinburne, Algernon Charles, **BP:** 1227

PRE-ROMANTICISM

Blake, William, **BP:** 91

Burns, Robert, **BP:** 173

Chatterton, Thomas, **BP:** 235

English Poetry in the Eighteenth Century, **TE:** 160

Gray, Thomas, **BP:** 542

Meredith, George, **BP:** 890

PROJECTIVIST SCHOOL. *See* BLACK MOUNTAIN POETS

PROSE POETRY

Alexander, Elizabeth, **AP:** 17

Alexie, Sherman, **AP:** 21

Baudelaire, Charles, **EP:** 80

Bernstein, Charles, **AP:** 132

Berrigan, Ted, **AP:** 143

Bly, Robert, **AP:** 188

Bonnefoy, Yves, **EP:** 142

Borges, Jorge Luis, **WP:** 39

Brautigan, Richard, **AP:** 239

Brooks, Gwendolyn, **AP:** 247

Carson, Anne, **BP:** 225

Cernuda, Luis, **EP:** 220

Char, René, **EP:** 226

Chatterton, Thomas, **BP:** 235

Claudel, Paul, **EP:** 244

Cliff, Michelle, **WP:** 61

Creeley, Robert, **AP:** 392

Cruz, Victor Hernández, **AP:** 400

Davies, Sir John, **BP:** 375

Eady, Cornelius, **AP:** 521

Éluard, Paul, **EP:** 313

Fairchild, B. H., **AP:** 579

Ferlinghetti, Lawrence, **AP:** 593

Flint, Roland, **AP:** 607

Follain, Jean, **EP:** 335

Forché, Carolyn, **AP:** 611

Gerstler, Amy, **AP:** 660

Gibran, Kahlil, **AP:** 663

Hahn, Kimiko, **AP:** 768

Harjo, Joy, **AP:** 789

Hass, Robert, **AP:** 814

Heaney, Seamus, **BP:** 594

Hejinian, Lyn, **AP:** 836

Herbert, Zbigniew, **EP:** 458

Hollander, John, **AP:** 877

Ignatow, David, **AP:** 941

Jarman, Mark, **AP:** 953

Jiménez, Juan Ramón, **EP:** 533

Jones, David, **BP:** 707

Justice, Donald, **AP:** 986

Kaufman, Bob, **AP:** 1002

Kelly, Brigit Pegeen, **AP:** 1012

Kunitz, Stanley, **AP:** 1083

Levis, Larry, **AP:** 1127

McGrath, Thomas, **AP:** 1225

McMichael, James, **AP:** 1255

Mallarmé, Stéphane, **EP:** 644

Matthews, William, **AP:** 1284

Meinke, Peter, **AP:** 1290

Merton, Thomas, **AP:** 1325

Middleton, Christopher, **BP:** 898

Momaday, N. Scott, **AP:** 1358

Moss, Thylias, **AP:** 1380

Mullen, Harryette, **AP:** 1387

Nye, Naomi Shihab, **AP:** 1435

Olds, Sharon, **AP:** 1456

Oliver, Mary, **AP:** 1463

Ondaatje, Michael, **BP:** 973

Ortiz Cofer, Judith, **AP:** 1499

Ostriker, Alicia Suskin, **AP:** 1502

Patchen, Kenneth, **AP:** 1520

Paz, Octavio, **WP:** 230

Poe, Edgar Allan, **AP:** 1561

Ponge, Francis, **EP:** 848

Rankine, Claudia, **AP:** 1602

Reverdy, Pierre, **EP:** 883

Sandburg, Carl, **AP:** 1704

Shapiro, Alan, **AP:** 1759

Simic, Charles, **AP:** 1785

Słowacki, Juliusz, **EP:** 972

Spicer, Jack, **AP:** 1868

Strand, Mark, **AP:** 1918

Tagore, Rabindranath, **WP:** 281

Tate, James, **AP:** 1947

Waldman, Anne, **AP:** 2076

Wright, C. D., **AP:** 2203

Young, Al, **AP:** 2248

REALISM

Dunbar, Paul Laurence, **AP:** 502

Frost, Robert, **AP:** 625

Masters, Edgar Lee, **AP:** 1278

Robinson, Edwin Arlington, **AP:** 1660

Sandburg, Carl, **AP:** 1704

RELIGIOUS POETRY. *See also* HYMNS

Ady, Endre, **EP:** 1

Arnold, Matthew, **BP:** 30

Berrigan, Daniel, **AP:** 137

Berry, Wendell, **AP:** 146

Bradstreet, Anne, **AP:** 223

Breton, Nicholas, **BP:** 124

Browning, Elizabeth Barrett, **BP:** 149

Cædmon, **BP:** 197

Calderón de la Barca, Pedro, **EP:** 170

Cardenal, Ernesto, **WP:** 52

Castro, Rosalía de, **EP:** 190

Christine de Pizan, **EP:** 240

Clarke, Austin, **BP:** 261

Claudel, Paul, **EP:** 244

Constable, Henry, **BP:** 301

Corn, Alfred, **AP:** 352

Cowper, William, **BP:** 320

Crashaw, Richard, **BP:** 337

Cruz, Sor Juana Inés de la, **WP:** 64

Cynewulf, **BP:** 344

Dennis, Carl, **AP:** 441

Dickinson, Emily, **AP:** 455

Donne, John, **BP:** 405

Dunbar, William, **BP:** 442

Eichendorff, Joseph von, **EP:** 299

Elytis, Odysseus, **EP:** 317

Everson, William, **AP:** 567

Garrett, George, **AP:** 656

Gezelle, Guido, **EP:** 384

Hafiz, **WP:** 108

Hampl, Patricia, **AP:** 785

Hemans, Felicia Dorothea, **BP:** 609

Herbert, George, **BP:** 617

Hill, Geoffrey, **BP:** 641

Hirshfield, Jane, **AP:** 858

Hopkins, Gerard Manley, **BP:** 666

Horton, George Moses, **AP:** 905

Hudgins, Andrew, **AP:** 924

Jarman, Mark, **AP:** 953

John of the Cross, Saint, **EP:** 539

Johnson, James Weldon, **AP:** 972

Jones, David, **BP:** 707

Judah ha-Levi, **EP:** 549

Karr, Mary, **AP:** 993

Kasdorf, Julia, **AP:** 996

Kavanagh, Patrick, **BP:** 726

Kelly, Brigit Pegeen, **AP:** 1012

Langland, William, **BP:** 780

Lee, Li-Young, **AP:** 1102

León, Luis de, **EP:** 597

Lydgate, John, **BP:** 832

McDonald, Walt, **AP:** 1215

Manger, Itzik, **EP:** 650

Manrique, Jorge, **EP:** 657

Manzoni, Alessandro, **EP:** 660

Marino, Giambattista, **EP:** 674

Markham, Edwin, **AP:** 1274

Menashe, Samuel, **AP:** 1302
Merton, Thomas, **AP:** 1325
Milton, John, **BP:** 905
Miyazawa, Kenji, **WP:** 191
Mora, Pat, **AP:** 1371
Morgenstern, Christian, **EP:** 727
Norris, Kathleen, **AP:** 1428
Ostriker, Alicia Suskin, **AP:** 1502
Pearl-Poet, **BP:** 991
Péguy, Charles-Pierre, **EP:** 791
Pope, Alexander, **BP:** 1005
Porter, Anne, **AP:** 1573
Price, Reynolds, **AP:** 1586
Prince, F. T., **BP:** 1021
Quarles, Francis, **BP:** 1031
Rogers, Pattiann, **AP:** 1679
Rossetti, Christina, **BP:** 1060
Ruan Ji, **WP:** 250
Rūmī, Jalāl al-Dīn, **WP:** 255
Saʿdi, **WP:** 260
Sassoon, Siegfried, **BP:** 1080
Smart, Christopher, **BP:** 1159
Solomos, Dionysios, **EP:** 987
Southwell, Robert, **BP:** 1178
Tagore, Rabindranath, **WP:** 281
Tasso, Torquato, **EP:** 1014
Taylor, Edward, **AP:** 1959
Thomas, R. S., **BP:** 1257
Thomson, James (1700-1748),
    BP: 1260
Traherne, Thomas, **BP:** 1277
Twichell, Chase, **AP:** 2002
Unamuno y Jugo, Miguel de, **EP:**
    1051
Vālmīki, **WP:** 308
Vaughan, Henry, **BP:** 1284
Vega Carpio, Lope de, **EP:** 1073
Verlaine, Paul, **EP:** 1093
Very, Jones, **AP:** 2039
Wang Wei, **WP:** 326
Watts, Isaac, **BP:** 1297
Wheatley, Phillis, **AP:** 2114
Whittier, John Greenleaf, **AP:**
    2144
Wright, Charles, **AP:** 2207

Wright, Franz, **AP:** 2217
Young, Edward, **BP:** 1349

RENAISSANCE
Camões, Luís de, **EP:** 180

RENAISSANCE, AMERICAN
Dickinson, Emily, **AP:** 455
Emerson, Ralph Waldo, **AP:** 544
English and American Poetry in
    the Nineteenth Century, **TE:**
    174
Holmes, Oliver Wendell, **AP:** 893
Longfellow, Henry Wadsworth,
    AP: 1157
Lowell, James Russell, **AP:** 1180
Melville, Herman, **AP:** 1294
Poe, Edgar Allan, **AP:** 1561
Thoreau, Henry David, **AP:** 1977
Whitman, Walt, **AP:** 2130

RENAISSANCE, CHICAGO.
See **CHICAGO**
RENAISSANCE

RENAISSANCE, ENGLISH
Breton, Nicholas, **BP:** 124
Campion, Thomas, **BP:** 202
Carew, Thomas, **BP:** 208
Chapman, George, **BP:** 228
Cowley, Abraham, **BP:** 312
Crashaw, Richard, **BP:** 337
Daniel, Samuel, **BP:** 352
Davenant, Sir William, **BP:** 362
Davies, Sir John, **BP:** 375
Dekker, Thomas, **BP:** 390
Donne, John, **BP:** 405
Drayton, Michael, **BP:** 417
Drummond of Hawthornden,
    William, **BP:** 424
Dunbar, William, **BP:** 442
English Poetry in the Seventeenth
    Century, **TE:** 144
English Poetry in the Sixteenth
    Century, **TE:** 130

Fanshawe, Sir Richard, **BP:** 481
Gascoigne, George, **BP:** 505
Greene, Robert, **BP:** 548
Greville, Fulke, **BP:** 555
Herbert, George, **BP:** 617
Heywood, John, **BP:** 635
Jonson, Ben, **BP:** 711
Lodge, Thomas, **BP:** 817
Marlowe, Christopher, **BP:** 870
Marvell, Andrew, **BP:** 877
Nashe, Thomas, **BP:** 953
Newcastle, Margaret Cavendish,
    duchess of, **BP:** 958
Prior, Matthew, **BP:** 1026
Ralegh, Sir Walter, **BP:** 1037
Sackville, Thomas, **BP:** 1074
Shakespeare, William, **BP:** 1105
Sidney, Sir Philip, **BP:** 1126
Sidney, Sir Robert, **BP:** 1135
Skelton, John, **BP:** 1153
Southwell, Robert, **BP:** 1178
Spenser, Edmund, **BP:** 1191
Suckling, Sir John, **BP:** 1206
Surrey, Henry Howard, earl of,
    BP: 1212
Traherne, Thomas, **BP:** 1277
Vaughan, Henry, **BP:** 1284
Waller, Edmund, **BP:** 1290

RENAISSANCE, FRENCH
Du Bellay, Joachim, **EP:** 289
Ronsard, Pierre de, **EP:** 912

RENAISSANCE, HARLEM.
See **HARLEM**
RENAISSANCE

RENAISSANCE, IRISH. *See*
IRISH LITERARY
REVIVAL

RENAISSANCE, ITALIAN
Ariosto, Ludovico, **EP:** 56
Bembo, Pietro, **EP:** 101
Boccaccio, Giovanni, **EP:** 131

Boiardo, Matteo Maria, **EP:** 135
Fracastoro, Girolamo, **EP:** 345
Michelangelo, **EP:** 694
Petrarch, **EP:** 828
Poliziano, **EP:** 841
Stampa, Gaspara, **EP:** 993
Tasso, Torquato, **EP:** 1014

RENAISSANCE, NATIVE AMERICAN. *See* NATIVE AMERICAN RENAISSANCE

RENAISSANCE, SCOTTISH
MacDiarmid, Hugh, **BP:** 846
Muir, Edwin, **BP:** 933

RENAISSANCE, SPANISH
Garcilaso de la Vega, **EP:** 362
John of the Cross, Saint, **EP:** 539
León, Luis de, **EP:** 597
Manrique, Jorge, **EP:** 657

RESTORATION
Behn, Aphra, **BP:** 66
Butler, Samuel, **BP:** 180
Carew, Thomas, **BP:** 208
Chatterton, Thomas, **BP:** 235
Congreve, William, **BP:** 296
Cotton, Charles, **BP:** 306
Cowley, Abraham, **BP:** 312
Davenant, Sir William, **BP:** 362
Dryden, John, **BP:** 433
English Poetry in the Seventeenth Century, **TE:** 144
Etherege, Sir George, **BP:** 476
Finch, Anne, **BP:** 491
King, Henry, **BP:** 743
Marvell, Andrew, **BP:** 877
Milton, John, **BP:** 905
Newcastle, Margaret Cavendish, duchess of, **BP:** 958
Oldham, John, **BP:** 969
Restoration Poetry, **TE:** 620
Rochester, John Wilmot, earl of, **BP:** 1048

Sedley, Sir Charles, **BP:** 1094
Vaughan, Henry, **BP:** 1284
Waller, Edmund, **BP:** 1290

RISORGIMENTO
Giusti, Giuseppe, **EP:** 391
Manzoni, Alessandro, **EP:** 660

ROMAN AUGUSTAN AGE. *See* AUGUSTAN AGE, ROMAN

ROMAN GOLDEN AGE. *See* GOLDEN AGE, ROMAN

ROMANTICISM. *See also* NEO-ROMANTICISM
Arany, János, **EP:** 42
Bécquer, Gustavo Adolfo, **EP:** 95
Beddoes, Thomas Lovell, **BP:** 56
Blake, William, **BP:** 91
Bowles, William Lisle, **BP:** 119
Brontë, Emily, **BP:** 137
Byron, Lord, **BP:** 186
Clare, John, **BP:** 254
Coleridge, Samuel Taylor, **BP:** 276
Corbière, Tristan, **EP:** 260
Crabbe, George, **BP:** 327
Darley, George, **BP:** 359
Eichendorff, Joseph von, **EP:** 299
English and American Poetry in the Nineteenth Century, **TE:** 174
English Poetry in the Eighteenth Century, **TE:** 160
Fireside Poets, **TE:** 633
Foscolo, Ugo, **EP:** 340
Gautier, Théophile, **EP:** 368
Goethe, Johann Wolfgang von, **EP:** 396
Heine, Heinrich, **EP:** 451
Hemans, Felicia Dorothea, **BP:** 609
Hölderlin, Friedrich, **EP:** 485

Hood, Thomas, **BP:** 650
Hugo, Victor, **EP:** 518
Hunt, Leigh, **BP:** 694
Keats, John, **BP:** 731
Lamartine, Alphonse de, **EP:** 591
Lamb, Charles, **BP:** 768
Landor, Walter Savage, **BP:** 774
Leopardi, Giacomo, **EP:** 607
Lermontov, Mikhail, **WP:** 142
Mallarmé, Stéphane, **EP:** 644
Mangan, James Clarence, **BP:** 866
Manzoni, Alessandro, **EP:** 660
Mickiewicz, Adam, **EP:** 702
Mörike, Eduard, **EP:** 732
Musset, Alfred de, **EP:** 736
Nerval, Gérard de, **EP:** 741
Novalis, **EP:** 748
Pushkin, Alexander, **WP:** 236
Romantic Poets, **TE:** 626
Scott, Sir Walter, **BP:** 1087
Shelley, Percy Bysshe, **BP:** 1112
Solomos, Dionysios, **EP:** 987
Southey, Robert, **BP:** 1171
Tegnér, Esaias, **EP:** 1020
Vigny, Alfred de, **EP:** 1099
Vörösmarty, Mihály, **EP:** 1112
Wordsworth, William, **BP:** 1310
Yosano Akiko, **WP:** 349

ROMANTICISM, AMERICAN. *See also* NEO-ROMANTICISM
Benét, William Rose, **AP:** 128
Bryant, William Cullen, **AP:** 259
Dennis, Carl, **AP:** 441
Emerson, Ralph Waldo, **AP:** 544
Freneau, Philip, **AP:** 618
Guest, Edgar A., **AP:** 748
Lanier, Sidney, **AP:** 1095
Longfellow, Henry Wadsworth, **AP:** 1157
Melville, Herman, **AP:** 1294
Poe, Edgar Allan, **AP:** 1561
Whitman, Walt, **AP:** 2130

Whittier, John Greenleaf, **AP:** 2144

Wylie, Elinor, **AP:** 2240

SATIRIC POETRY

Ariosto, Ludovico, **EP:** 56
Belloc, Hilaire, **BP:** 73
Betjeman, John, **BP:** 80
Boileau-Despréaux, Nicolas, **EP:** 138
Breton, Nicholas, **BP:** 124
Burns, Robert, **BP:** 173
Butler, Samuel, **BP:** 180
Bynner, Witter, **AP:** 274
Byron, Lord, **BP:** 186
Chappell, Fred, **AP:** 303
Chatterton, Thomas, **BP:** 235
Clarke, Austin, **BP:** 261
Coulette, Henri, **AP:** 362
Cowley, Abraham, **BP:** 312
Cummings, E. E., **AP:** 410
Davies, Sir John, **BP:** 375
Donne, John, **BP:** 405
Dryden, John, **BP:** 433
Du Bellay, Joachim, **EP:** 289
Dunbar, William, **BP:** 442
Etherege, Sir George, **BP:** 476
Feldman, Irving, **AP:** 588
Finch, Anne, **BP:** 491
Gascoigne, George, **BP:** 505
Gay, John, **BP:** 512
Giusti, Giuseppe, **EP:** 391
Heine, Heinrich, **EP:** 451
Hood, Thomas, **BP:** 650
Hope, A. D., **BP:** 660
Hugo, Victor, **EP:** 518
Hunt, Leigh, **BP:** 694
Johnson, Samuel, **BP:** 700
Jonson, Ben, **BP:** 711
Joyce, James, **BP:** 719
Juvenal, **EP:** 553
Kees, Weldon, **AP:** 1006
Kennedy, X. J., **AP:** 1020
Kinsella, Thomas, **BP:** 751
Kizer, Carolyn, **AP:** 1046

Kraus, Karl, **EP:** 563
Langland, William, **BP:** 780
Lodge, Thomas, **BP:** 817
Logue, Christopher, **BP:** 823
Lowell, James Russell, **AP:** 1180
Martial, **EP:** 678
Marvell, Andrew, **BP:** 877
Morgenstern, Christian, **EP:** 727
Nash, Ogden, **AP:** 1401
Oldham, John, **BP:** 969
Parra, Nicanor, **WP:** 216
Persius, **EP:** 806
Pope, Alexander, **BP:** 1005
Prior, Matthew, **BP:** 1026
Pushkin, Alexander, **WP:** 236
Reed, Ishmael, **AP:** 1612
Rexroth, Kenneth, **AP:** 1621
Rimbaud, Arthur, **EP:** 897
Rochester, John Wilmot, earl of, **BP:** 1048
Skelton, John, **BP:** 1153
Soyinka, Wole, **WP:** 276
Swift, Jonathan, **BP:** 1218
Updike, John, **AP:** 2016
Whittemore, Reed, **AP:** 2140
Wyatt, Sir Thomas, **BP:** 1322
Young, Edward, **BP:** 1349

SCHOOLROOM POETS. *See* **FIRESIDE POETS**

SCOTTISH RENAISSANCE. *See* **RENAISSANCE, SCOTTISH**

SOCIALIST REALISM

Aragon, Louis, **EP:** 35
Mayakovsky, Vladimir, **WP:** 176
Ważyk, Adam, **EP:** 1126
Yevtushenko, Yevgeny, **WP:** 339

SONGS

Allingham, William, **BP:** 23
Behn, Aphra, **BP:** 66
Biermann, Wolf, **EP:** 119

Blake, William, **BP:** 91
Burns, Robert, **BP:** 173
Camões, Luís de, **EP:** 180
Campion, Thomas, **BP:** 202
Carew, Thomas, **BP:** 208
Charles d'Orléans, **EP:** 230
Cohen, Leonard, **BP:** 272
Congreve, William, **BP:** 296
Davenant, Sir William, **BP:** 362
Donne, John, **BP:** 405
Dryden, John, **BP:** 433
Dunbar, Paul Laurence, **AP:** 502
Garcilaso de la Vega, **EP:** 362
Goethe, Johann Wolfgang von, **EP:** 396
Hartmann von Aue, **EP:** 441
Heine, Heinrich, **EP:** 451
Hemans, Felicia Dorothea, **BP:** 609
Johnson, James Weldon, **AP:** 972
Lear, Edward, **BP:** 812
Leopardi, Giacomo, **EP:** 607
Longfellow, Henry Wadsworth, **AP:** 1157
Machado, Antonio, **EP:** 633
Mörike, Eduard, **EP:** 732
Novalis, **EP:** 748
Poliziano, **EP:** 841
Prior, Matthew, **BP:** 1026
Rochester, John Wilmot, earl of, **BP:** 1048
Sappho, **EP:** 941
Sedley, Sir Charles, **BP:** 1094
Senghor, Léopold, **WP:** 264
Service, Robert W., **BP:** 1099
Sidney, Sir Robert, **BP:** 1135
Spenser, Edmund, **BP:** 1191
Stampa, Gaspara, **EP:** 993
Stevenson, Robert Louis, **BP:** 1201
Surrey, Henry Howard, earl of, **BP:** 1212
Swinburne, Algernon Charles, **BP:** 1227
Tagore, Rabindranath, **WP:** 281

Theognis, **EP:** 1029

Unamuno y Jugo, Miguel de, **EP:** 1051

Walther von der Vogelweide, **EP:** 1119

Watts, Isaac, **BP:** 1297

Wyatt, Sir Thomas, **BP:** 1322

Xie Lingyun, **WP:** 334

SONNETS. *See also*
PETRARCHAN SONNETS

Adams, Léonie, **AP:** 4

Anderson, Maggie, **AP:** 43

Auden, W. H., **BP:** 47

Baker, David, **AP:** 77

Belloc, Hilaire, **BP:** 73

Bembo, Pietro, **EP:** 101

Berrigan, Ted, **AP:** 143

Berryman, John, **AP:** 155

Boiardo, Matteo Maria, **EP:** 135

Bowles, William Lisle, **BP:** 119

Bridges, Robert, **BP:** 131

Brooke, Rupert, **BP:** 144

Brown, Sterling A., **AP:** 254

Browning, Elizabeth Barrett, **BP:** 149

Calderón de la Barca, Pedro, **EP:** 170

Camões, Luís de, **EP:** 180

Carew, Thomas, **BP:** 208

Cavalcanti, Guido, **EP:** 210

Clough, Arthur Hugh, **BP:** 266

Coleridge, Samuel Taylor, **BP:** 276

Collins, William, **BP:** 287

Constable, Henry, **BP:** 301

Coxe, Louis, **AP:** 375

Cruz, Sor Juana Inés de la, **WP:** 64

Dacey, Philip, **AP:** 425

Daniel, Samuel, **BP:** 352

Davies, Sir John, **BP:** 375

Dodson, Owen, **AP:** 471

Donne, John, **BP:** 405

Drayton, Michael, **BP:** 417

Drummond of Hawthornden, William, **BP:** 424

Du Bellay, Joachim, **EP:** 289

Dubie, Norman, **AP:** 493

Dučić, Jovan, **EP:** 292

Dunbar, Paul Laurence, **AP:** 502

Eberhart, Richard, **AP:** 526

Emanuel, James A., **AP:** 538

Fanshawe, Sir Richard, **BP:** 481

Foix, J. V., **EP:** 329

Foscolo, Ugo, **EP:** 340

Frost, Robert, **AP:** 625

Fuller, Roy, **BP:** 500

Garcilaso de la Vega, **EP:** 362

Gascoigne, George, **BP:** 505

Goethe, Johann Wolfgang von, **EP:** 396

Goldbarth, Albert, **AP:** 719

Góngora y Argote, Luis de, **EP:** 410

González Martínez, Enrique, **WP:** 101

Gray, Thomas, **BP:** 542

Greville, Fulke, **BP:** 555

Hacker, Marilyn, **AP:** 761

Hallam, Arthur Henry, **BP:** 575

Hardy, Thomas, **BP:** 579

Harrison, Tony, **BP:** 588

Hayden, Robert, **AP:** 820

Heaney, Seamus, **BP:** 594

Herbert, George, **BP:** 617

Hillyer, Robert, **AP:** 850

Hoffman, Daniel, **AP:** 863

Hollander, John, **AP:** 877

Hood, Thomas, **BP:** 650

Hopkins, Gerard Manley, **BP:** 666

Jiménez, Juan Ramón, **EP:** 533

Keats, John, **BP:** 731

King, Henry, **BP:** 743

Lamb, Charles, **BP:** 768

Lodge, Thomas, **BP:** 817

Logue, Christopher, **BP:** 823

Lowell, Amy, **AP:** 1172

Lowell, Robert, **AP:** 1187

McKay, Claude, **AP:** 1234

MacLeish, Archibald, **AP:** 1244

Marino, Giambattista, **EP:** 674

Masefield, John, **BP:** 885

Meinke, Peter, **AP:** 1290

Meredith, William, **AP:** 1308

Mickiewicz, Adam, **EP:** 702

Millay, Edna St. Vincent, **AP:** 1344

Milton, John, **BP:** 905

Mistral, Gabriela, **WP:** 185

Mörike, Eduard, **EP:** 732

Nashe, Thomas, **BP:** 953

Neruda, Pablo, **WP:** 196

Nerval, Gérard de, **EP:** 741

Nims, John Frederick, **AP:** 1421

Peacock, Molly, **AP:** 1525

Pessoa, Fernando, **EP:** 811

Petrarch, **EP:** 828

Ponsot, Marie, **AP:** 1569

Price, Reynolds, **AP:** 1586

Quarles, Francis, **BP:** 1031

Ralegh, Sir Walter, **BP:** 1037

Reese, Lizette Woodworth, **AP:** 1616

Rilke, Rainer Maria, **EP:** 889

Robinson, Edwin Arlington, **AP:** 1660

Ronsard, Pierre de, **EP:** 912

Rossetti, Dante Gabriel, **BP:** 1065

Saba, Umberto, **EP:** 925

Sarton, May, **AP:** 1714

Scott, Sir Walter, **BP:** 1087

Scott, Winfield Townley, **AP:** 1746

Seeger, Alan, **AP:** 1750

Seth, Vikram, **WP:** 272

Shakespeare, William, **BP:** 1105

Sidney, Sir Philip, **BP:** 1126

Sidney, Sir Robert, **BP:** 1135

Słonimski, Antoni, **EP:** 968

Solomos, Dionysios, **EP:** 987

Sorrentino, Gilbert, **AP:** 1858

Spenser, Edmund, **BP:** 1191

Stampa, Gaspara, **EP:** 993

Stern, Gerald, **AP:** 1893

Surrey, Henry Howard, earl of,
 BP: 1212
Swinburne, Algernon Charles,
 BP: 1227
Tasso, Torquato, **EP:** 1014
Taylor, Henry, **AP:** 1968
Teasdale, Sara, **AP:** 1974
Thomas, Dylan, **BP:** 1245
Trethewey, Natasha, **AP:** 1995
Tuckerman, Frederick Goddard,
 AP: 1998
Updike, John, **AP:** 2016
Vega Carpio, Lope de, **EP:** 1073
Verlaine, Paul, **EP:** 1093
Very, Jones, **AP:** 2039
Voigt, Ellen Bryant, **AP:** 2054
Wallace, Ronald, **AP:** 2090
Wheelwright, John, **AP:** 2126
Wilde, Oscar, **BP:** 1303
Williams, Miller, **AP:** 2168
Wojahn, David, **AP:** 2190
Wormser, Baron, **AP:** 2196
Wyatt, Sir Thomas, **BP:** 1322
Wylie, Elinor, **AP:** 2240

SOUTHERN AGRARIANS
Ransom, John Crowe, **AP:** 1605
Tate, Allen, **AP:** 1941
Warren, Robert Penn, **AP:** 2094

SPANISH GOLDEN AGE. *See*
GOLDEN AGE, SPANISH

SPANISH RENAISSANCE. *See*
RENAISSANCE, SPANISH

STORM AND STRESS. *See*
STURM UND DRANG

STURM UND DRANG
Goethe, Johann Wolfgang von,
 EP: 396
Schiller, Friedrich, **EP:** 949

SURREALIST POETS
Alberti, Rafael, **EP:** 6
Aleixandre, Vicente, **EP:** 12
Apollinaire, Guillaume, **EP:** 22
Aragon, Louis, **EP:** 35
Arp, Hans, **EP:** 62
Ashbery, John, **AP:** 55
Bly, Robert, **AP:** 188
Bonnefoy, Yves, **EP:** 142
Breton, André, **EP:** 157
Celan, Paul, **EP:** 214
Cernuda, Luis, **EP:** 220
Césaire, Aimé, **WP:** 56
Char, René, **EP:** 226
Cocteau, Jean, **EP:** 253
Codrescu, Andrei, **AP:** 331
Dubie, Norman, **AP:** 493
Ekelöf, Gunnar, **EP:** 306
Éluard, Paul, **EP:** 313
Elytis, Odysseus, **EP:** 317
García Lorca, Federico, **EP:** 355
Illyés, Gyula, **EP:** 528
Kaufman, Bob, **AP:** 1002
Neruda, Pablo, **WP:** 196
Reverdy, Pierre, **EP:** 883
Salinas, Pedro, **EP:** 936
Tate, James, **AP:** 1947
Tzara, Tristan, **EP:** 1044
Vallejo, César, **WP:** 300
Young, Dean, **AP:** 2257

SYMBOLIST POETS
Akhmatova, Anna, **WP:** 3
Annensky, Innokenty, **WP:** 21
Apollinaire, Guillaume, **EP:** 22
Baudelaire, Charles, **EP:** 80
Blok, Aleksandr, **WP:** 33
Borges, Jorge Luis, **WP:** 39
Corbière, Tristan, **EP:** 260
Crane, Stephen, **AP:** 387
Ekelöf, Gunnar, **EP:** 306
Eliot, T. S., **BP:** 458
Emerson, Ralph Waldo, **AP:** 544
French Symbolists, **TE:** 639
George, Stefan, **EP:** 377

Hofmannsthal, Hugo von, **EP:** 478
Jiménez, Juan Ramón, **EP:** 533
Khodasevich, Vladislav, **WP:** 133
Laforgue, Jules, **EP:** 584
Mallarmé, Stéphane, **EP:** 644
Pasternak, Boris, **WP:** 222
Rimbaud, Arthur, **EP:** 897
Salinas, Pedro, **EP:** 936
Seferis, George, **EP:** 957
Verhaeren, Émile, **EP:** 1089
Verlaine, Paul, **EP:** 1093

TOPOGRAPHICAL POETRY
Addison, Joseph, **BP:** 7
Betjeman, John, **BP:** 80
Bobrowski, Johannes, **EP:** 126
Booth, Philip, **AP:** 209
Bryant, William Cullen, **AP:** 259
Clare, John, **BP:** 254
Crabbe, George, **BP:** 327
Drayton, Michael, **BP:** 417
Freneau, Philip, **AP:** 618
Hughes, Ted, **BP:** 686
Hugo, Richard, **AP:** 934
Jonson, Ben, **BP:** 711
Pentzikis, Nikos, **EP:** 797
Pope, Alexander, **BP:** 1005
Spenser, Edmund, **BP:** 1191
Stevens, Wallace, **AP:** 1905
Waller, Edmund, **BP:** 1290
Whitman, Walt, **AP:** 2130
Wordsworth, William, **BP:** 1310

TRANSCENDENTALISM
Ammons, A. R., **AP:** 37
Dana, Robert, **AP:** 430
Dickinson, Emily, **AP:** 455
Emerson, Ralph Waldo, **AP:** 544
Holmes, Oliver Wendell, **AP:** 893
Longfellow, Henry Wadsworth,
 AP: 1157
Lowell, James Russell, **AP:** 1180
Thoreau, Henry David, **AP:** 1977
Very, Jones, **AP:** 2039

TUDOR AGE

English Poetry in the Fifteenth
Century, **TE:** 120
Heywood, John, **BP:** 635
Skelton, John, **BP:** 1153
Surrey, Henry Howard, earl of,
BP: 1212
Wyatt, Sir Thomas, **BP:** 1322

ULTRAISM

Neruda, Pablo, **WP:** 196
Vallejo, César, **WP:** 300

VERSE DRAMATISTS

Ariosto, Ludovico, **EP:** 56
Beddoes, Thomas Lovell, **BP:** 56
Byron, Lord, **BP:** 186
Calderón de la Barca, Pedro, **EP:**
170
Chatterton, Thomas, **BP:** 235
Coleridge, Samuel Taylor, **BP:**
276
Dodson, Owen, **AP:** 471
Dove, Rita, **AP:** 486
Eliot, T. S., **BP:** 458
Fanshawe, Sir Richard, **BP:** 481
Greene, Robert, **BP:** 548
Greville, Fulke, **BP:** 555
Hardy, Thomas, **BP:** 579
Harrison, Tony, **BP:** 588
Hugo, Victor, **EP:** 518
MacLeish, Archibald, **AP:** 1244
Millay, Edna St. Vincent, **AP:**
1344
Poe, Edgar Allan, **AP:** 1561
Rosenberg, Isaac, **BP:** 1055
Schwartz, Delmore, **AP:** 1738
Shakespeare, William, **BP:** 1105
Słowacki, Juliusz, **EP:** 972
Tasso, Torquato, **EP:** 1014

VICTORIAN ERA

Allingham, William, **BP:** 23
Arnold, Matthew, **BP:** 30
Bridges, Robert, **BP:** 131

Brontë, Emily, **BP:** 137
Browning, Elizabeth Barrett, **BP:**
149
Browning, Robert, **BP:** 158
Carroll, Lewis, **BP:** 213
Clough, Arthur Hugh, **BP:** 266
English and American Poetry in
the Nineteenth Century, **TE:**
174
Fireside Poets, **TE:** 633
FitzGerald, Edward, **BP:** 495
Hallam, Arthur Henry, **BP:** 575
Hardy, Thomas, **BP:** 579
Hemans, Felicia Dorothea, **BP:**
609
Hopkins, Gerard Manley, **BP:** 666
Housman, A. E., **BP:** 677
Hunt, Leigh, **BP:** 694
Kipling, Rudyard, **BP:** 760
Lear, Edward, **BP:** 812
Meredith, George, **BP:** 890
Mew, Charlotte, **BP:** 894
Morris, William, **BP:** 924
Patmore, Coventry, **BP:** 983
Rossetti, Christina, **BP:** 1060
Rossetti, Dante Gabriel, **BP:** 1065
Stevenson, Robert Louis, **BP:**
1201
Swinburne, Algernon Charles,
BP: 1227
Tennyson, Alfred, Lord, **BP:** 1236
Thomson, James (1834-1882),
BP: 1264
Wilde, Oscar, **BP:** 1303

VISIONARY POETRY

Baudelaire, Charles, **EP:** 80
Blake, William, **BP:** 91
Byron, Lord, **BP:** 186
Collins, William, **BP:** 287
Crane, Hart, **AP:** 379
Crashaw, Richard, **BP:** 337
Darío, Rubén, **WP:** 71
Eberhart, Richard, **AP:** 526
Ginsberg, Allen, **AP:** 677

Hayden, Robert, **AP:** 820
Kunitz, Stanley, **AP:** 1083
Layton, Irving, **BP:** 808
McClure, Michael, **AP:** 1207
Merwin, W. S., **AP:** 1331
Michaux, Henri, **EP:** 688
Neruda, Pablo, **WP:** 196
Novalis, **EP:** 748
Rilke Rainer Maria, **EP:** 889
Rimbaud, Arthur, **EP:** 897
Rūmī, Jalāl al-Dīn, **WP:** 255
Wormser, Baron, **AP:** 2196
Yeats, William Butler, **BP:** 1330

WAR POETS

Achebe, Chinua, **WP:** 1
Ady, Endre, **EP:** 1
Alberti, Rafael, **EP:** 6
Apollinaire, Guilaume, **EP:** 22
Aragon, Louis, **EP:** 35
Balaban, John, **AP:** 81
Blunden, Edmund, **BP:** 104
Brecht, Bertolt, **EP:** 149
Brooke, Rupert, **BP:** 144
Ehrhart, W. D., **AP:** 532
Freneau, Philip, **AP:** 618
Fuller, Roy, **BP:** 500
Gurney, Ivor, **BP:** 568
Jones, David, **BP:** 707
Logue, Christopher, **BP:** 823
McDonald, Walt, **AP:** 1215
Owen, Wilfred, **BP:** 977
Petőfi, Sándor, **EP:** 816
Reverdy, Pierre, **EP:** 883
Rosenberg, Isaac, **BP:** 1055
Sassoon, Siegfried, **BP:** 1080
Seeger, Alan, **AP:** 1750
Simpson, Louis, **AP:** 1793
Thomas, Edward, **BP:** 1252
Weigl, Bruce, **AP:** 2102

WOMEN POETS

Ackerman, Diane, **AP:** 1
Adams, Léonie, **AP:** 4
Ai, **AP:** 8

Akhmatova, Anna, **WP:** 3

Alegría, Claribel, **WP:** 9

Alexander, Elizabeth, **AP:** 17

Allen, Paula Gunn, **AP:** 27

Alvarez, Julia, **AP:** 31

Anderson, Maggie, **AP:** 43

Angelou, Maya, **AP:** 46

Atwood, Margaret, **BP:** 37

Ausländer, Rose, **AP:** 65

Bachmann, Ingeborg, **EP:** 72

Bang, Mary Jo, **AP:** 85

Barnard, Mary, **AP:** 100

Becker, Robin, **AP:** 110

Beer, Patricia, **BP:** 60

Behn, Aphra, **BP:** 66

Bishop, Elizabeth, **AP:** 169

Bogan, Louise, **AP:** 197

Boland, Eavan, **BP:** 108

Bradstreet, Anne, **AP:** 223

Brontë, Emily, **BP:** 137

Brooks, Gwendolyn, **AP:** 247

Browning, Elizabeth Barrett, **BP:** 149

Carson, Anne, **BP:** 225

Castro, Rosalía de, **EP:** 190

Cervantes, Lorna Dee, **AP:** 298

Chin, Marilyn, **AP:** 307

Christine de Pizan, **EP:** 240

Cisneros, Sandra, **AP:** 318

Clampitt, Amy, **AP:** 322

Cliff, Michelle, **WP:** 61

Clifton, Lucille, **AP:** 326

Cruz, Sor Juana Inés de la, **WP:** 64

Derricotte, Toi, **AP:** 444

Dickinson, Emily, **AP:** 455

Di Prima, Diane, **AP:** 464

Dove, Rita, **AP:** 486

Emerson, Claudia, **AP:** 541

Erdrich, Louise, **AP:** 553

Evans, Mari, **AP:** 563

Feminist Criticism, **TE:** 736

Fennelly, Beth Ann, **AP:** 591

Finch, Anne, **BP:** 491

Forché, Carolyn, **AP:** 611

Fulton, Alice, **AP:** 633

Gallagher, Tess, **AP:** 639

Gardner, Isabella, **AP:** 653

Gerstler, Amy, **AP:** 660

Gibson, Margaret, **AP:** 670

Giovanni, Nikki, **AP:** 692

Glancy, Diane, **AP:** 702

Glück, Louise, **AP:** 710

Graham, Jorie, **AP:** 725

Gregerson, Linda, **AP:** 732

Gregg, Linda, **AP:** 735

Guest, Barbara, **AP:** 745

H. D., **AP:** 754

Hacker, Marilyn, **AP:** 761

Hahn, Kimiko, **AP:** 768

Hampl, Patricia, **AP:** 785

Harjo, Joy, **AP:** 789

Hébert, Anne, **BP:** 605

Hejinian, Lyn, **AP:** 836

Hemans, Felicia Dorothea, **BP:** 609

Hirshfield, Jane, **AP:** 858

Hogan, Linda, **AP:** 871

Howe, Susan, **AP:** 913

Howes, Barbara, **AP:** 921

Hunt, Erica, **AP:** 938

Jacobsen, Josephine, **AP:** 950

Jordan, June, **AP:** 981

Karr, Mary, **AP:** 993

Kasdorf, Julia, **AP:** 996

Kasischke, Laura, **AP:** 999

Kelly, Brigit Pegeen, **AP:** 1012

Kenyon, Jane, **AP:** 1028

Kizer, Carolyn, **AP:** 1046

Kumin, Maxine, **AP:** 1073

Levertov, Denise, **AP:** 1111

Lewis, Janet, **AP:** 1132

Li Qingzhao, **WP:** 157

Lifshin, Lyn, **AP:** 1136

Lindsay, Sarah, **AP:** 1143

Lorde, Audre, **AP:** 1166

Lowell, Amy, **AP:** 1172

Loy, Mina, **AP:** 1200

Macdonald, Cynthia, **AP:** 1211

McGinley, Phyllis, **AP:** 1221

McHugh, Heather, **AP:** 1230

McPherson, Sandra, **AP:** 1258

Marie de France, **EP:** 666

Mew, Charlotte, **BP:** 894

Miles, Josephine, **AP:** 1340

Millay, Edna St. Vincent, **AP:** 1344

Miller, Vassar, **AP:** 1349

Mistral, Gabriela, **WP:** 185

Moore, Marianne, **AP:** 1364

Mora, Pat, **AP:** 1371

Moss, Thylias, **AP:** 1380

Mueller, Lisel, **AP:** 1383

Mullen, Harryette, **AP:** 1387

Muske, Carol, **AP:** 1396

Newcastle, Margaret Cavendish, duchess of, **BP:** 958

Ní Dhomhnaill, Nuala, **BP:** 964

Niedecker, Lorine, **AP:** 1415

Norris, Kathleen, **AP:** 1428

Notley, Alice, **AP:** 1431

Nye, Naomi Shihab, **AP:** 1435

Oates, Joyce Carol, **AP:** 1443

Olds, Sharon, **AP:** 1456

Oliver, Mary, **AP:** 1463

Ortiz Cofer, Judith, **AP:** 1499

Ostriker, Alicia Suskin, **AP:** 1502

Paley, Grace, **AP:** 1506

Parker, Dorothy, **AP:** 1509

Pastan, Linda, **AP:** 1514

Peacock, Molly, **AP:** 1525

Piercy, Marge, **AP:** 1532

Plath, Sylvia, **AP:** 1547

Ponsot, Marie, **AP:** 1569

Porter, Anne, **AP:** 1573

Rankine, Claudia, **AP:** 1602

Reese, Lizette Woodworth, **AP:** 1616

Rich, Adrienne, **AP:** 1633

Riding, Laura, **AP:** 1642

Rodgers, Carolyn M., **AP:** 1668

Rogers, Pattiann, **AP:** 1679

Rossetti, Christina, **BP:** 1060

Rukeyser, Muriel, **AP:** 1686

Sachs, Nelly, **EP:** 930

Sanchez, Sonia, **AP:** 1698

Sappho, **EP:** 941

Sarton, May, **AP:** 1714

Scalapino, Leslie, **AP:** 1724

Schnackenberg, Gjertrud, **AP:** 1728

Sexton, Anne, **AP:** 1753

Shomer, Enid, **AP:** 1769

Shore, Jane, **AP:** 1773

Silko, Leslie Marmon, **AP:** 1777

Sitwell, Edith, **BP:** 1145

Smith, Stevie, **BP:** 1164

Södergran, Edith, **EP:** 981

Song, Cathy, **AP:** 1853

Stampa, Gaspara, **EP:** 993

Stein, Gertrude, **AP:** 1885

Swensen, Cole, **AP:** 1931

Swenson, May, **AP:** 1934

Swir, Anna, **EP:** 1004

Szymborska, Wisława, **EP:** 1007

Teasdale, Sara, **AP:** 1974

Trethewey, Natasha, **AP:** 1995

Tsvetayeva, Marina, **WP:** 293

Twichell, Chase, **AP:** 2002

Valentine, Jean, **AP:** 2024

Van Duyn, Mona, **AP:** 2032

Voigt, Ellen Bryant, **AP:** 2054

Wakoski, Diane, **AP:** 2068

Waldman, Anne, **AP:** 2076

Walker, Alice, **AP:** 2080

Walker, Margaret, **AP:** 2086

Wheatley, Phillis, **AP:** 2114

Williams, Sherley Anne, **AP:** 2172

Wright, C. D., **AP:** 2203

Wylie, Elinor, **AP:** 2240

Yamada, Mitsuye, **AP:** 2244

Yosano Akiko, **WP:** 349

Zamora, Daisy, **WP:** 354

YOUNG ADULT POETRY. *See* **CHILDREN'S/YOUNG ADULT POETRY**

YOUNG VIENNA GROUP

Hofmannsthal, Hugo von, **EP:** 478

Zweig, Stefan, **EP:** 1141

Critical Survey of Poetry Series: Master List of Contents

The Critical Survey of Poetry, Fourth Edition, *profiles more than eight hundred poets in four subsets:* American Poets; *British, Irish, and Commonwealth Poets;* European Poets; *and* World Poets. *Although some individuals could have been included in more than one subset, each poet appears in only one subset. A fifth subset,* Topical Essays, *includes more than seventy overviews covering geographical areas, historical periods, movements, and critical approaches.*

AMERICAN POETS

Volume 1

Publisher's Note v
Contributors ix
Contents xv
Complete List of
  Contents xvii
Pronunciation Key xxiii

Diane Ackerman 1
Léonie Adams 4
Ai 8
Conrad Aiken 12
Elizabeth Alexander 17
Sherman Alexie 21
Agha Shahid Ali 24
Paula Gunn Allen 27
Julia Alvarez 31
A. R. Ammons 37
Maggie Anderson 43
Maya Angelou 46
James Applewhite 51
John Ashbery 55
Rose Ausländer 65

Jimmy Santiago Baca 71
David Baker 77
John Balaban 81
Mary Jo Bang 85
Amiri Baraka 89
Mary Barnard 100
Paul Beatty 107
Robin Becker 110
Ben Belitt 114

Marvin Bell 119
Stephen Vincent Benét . . . 124
William Rose Benét 128
Charles Bernstein 132
Daniel Berrigan 137
Ted Berrigan 143
Wendell Berry 146
John Berryman 155
Frank Bidart 162
Elizabeth Bishop 169
John Peale Bishop 177
Paul Blackburn 180
Robert Bly 188
Louise Bogan 197
Arna Bontemps 205
Philip Booth 209
David Bottoms 216
Edgar Bowers 219
Anne Bradstreet 223
Edward Kamau
  Brathwaite 228
Richard Brautigan 239
William Bronk 243
Gwendolyn Brooks 247
Sterling A. Brown 254
William Cullen Bryant 259
Charles Bukowski 264
Witter Bynner 274

Hayden Carruth 278
Raymond Carver 284
Turner Cassity 291
Lorna Dee Cervantes 298

Fred Chappell 303
Marilyn Chin 307
John Ciardi 312
Sandra Cisneros 318
Amy Clampitt 322
Lucille Clifton 326
Andrei Codrescu 331
Henri Cole 333
Michael Collier 336
Billy Collins 341
Cid Corman 347
Alfred Corn 352
Gregory Corso 356
Henri Coulette 362
Malcolm Cowley 366
Louis Coxe 375
Hart Crane 379
Stephen Crane 387
Robert Creeley 392
Victor Hernández Cruz . . . 400
Countée Cullen 404
E. E. Cummings 410
J. V. Cunningham 417

Philip Dacey 425
Robert Dana 430
Peter Davison 437
Carl Dennis 441
Toi Derricotte 444
James Dickey 448
Emily Dickinson 455
Diane di Prima 464
Owen Dodson 471

Edward Dorn 474
Mark Doty 481
Rita Dove 486
Norman Dubie 493
Alan Dugan 498
Paul Laurence Dunbar . . . 502
Robert Duncan 509
Stephen Dunn 517

Cornelius Eady 521
Richard Eberhart 526
W. D. Ehrhart 532
James A. Emanuel 538
Claudia Emerson 541
Ralph Waldo Emerson . . . 544
Louise Erdrich 553
Martín Espada 559
Mari Evans 563
William Everson 567

B. H. Fairchild 579
Kenneth Fearing 582
Irving Feldman 588
Beth Ann Fennelly 591
Lawrence Ferlinghetti . . . 593
Edward Field 602

Volume 2
Contents xxxi
Complete List of
    Contents xxxiii
Pronunciation Key xxxix

Roland Flint 607
Carolyn Forché 611
Philip Freneau 618
Robert Frost 625
Alice Fulton 633

Tess Gallagher 639
Brendan Galvin 644
Isabella Gardner 653
George Garrett 656
Amy Gerstler 660
Kahlil Gibran 663

Margaret Gibson 670
Jack Gilbert 673
Allen Ginsberg 677
Dana Gioia 688
Nikki Giovanni 692
Diane Glancy 702
Mel Glenn 706
Louise Glück 710
Albert Goldbarth 719
Jorie Graham 725
Linda Gregerson 732
Linda Gregg 735
Horace Gregory 738
Eamon Grennan 741
Barbara Guest 745
Edgar A. Guest 748

H. D. 754
Marilyn Hacker 761
Kimiko Hahn 768
John Meade Haines 772
Donald Hall 775
Patricia Hampl 785
Joy Harjo 789
Michael S. Harper 794
Jim Harrison 802
Robert Hass 814
Robert Hayden 820
Anthony Hecht 826
Lyn Hejinian 836
William Heyen 841
Robert Hillyer 850
Edward Hirsch 853
Jane Hirshfield 858
Daniel Hoffman 863
Linda Hogan 871
John Hollander 877
Anselm Hollo 887
Oliver Wendell Holmes . . . 893
Garrett Kaoru Hongo . . . 900
George Moses Horton . . . 905
Richard Howard 909
Susan Howe 913
Barbara Howes 921
Andrew Hudgins 924

Langston Hughes 927
Richard Hugo 934
Erica Hunt 938

David Ignatow 941

Josephine Jacobsen 950
Mark Jarman 953
Randall Jarrell 957
Robinson Jeffers 963
James Weldon Johnson . . . 972
Ronald Johnson 976
June Jordan 981
Donald Justice 986

Mary Karr 993
Julia Kasdorf 996
Laura Kasischke 999
Bob Kaufman 1002
Weldon Kees 1006
Brigit Pegeen Kelly 1012
Robert Kelly 1015
X. J. Kennedy 1020
Jane Kenyon 1028
Galway Kinnell 1033
David Kirby 1039
Lincoln Kirstein 1042
Carolyn Kizer 1046
Etheridge Knight 1053
Kenneth Koch 1058
Yusef Komunyakaa 1064
Ted Kooser 1070
Maxine Kumin 1073
Stanley Kunitz 1083

Sidney Lanier 1095
Li-Young Lee 1102
Brad Leithauser 1108
Denise Levertov 1111
Philip Levine 1120
Larry Levis 1127
Janet Lewis 1132
Lyn Lifshin 1136
Sarah Lindsay 1143
Vachel Lindsay 1146
John Logan 1153

Henry Wadsworth
    Longfellow 1157
Audre Lorde 1166
Amy Lowell 1172
James Russell Lowell . . . 1180
Robert Lowell 1187
Mina Loy 1200
Wing Tek Lum 1204

Volume 3
Contents xlvii
Complete List of
    Contents xlix
Pronunciation Key lv

Michael McClure 1207
Cynthia Macdonald 1211
Walt McDonald 1215
Phyllis McGinley 1221
Thomas McGrath 1225
Heather McHugh 1230
Claude McKay 1234
Nathaniel Mackey 1241
Archibald MacLeish 1244
James McMichael 1255
Sandra McPherson 1258
Haki R. Madhubuti 1265
Edwin Markham 1274
Edgar Lee Masters 1278
William Matthews 1284
Peter Meinke 1290
Herman Melville 1294
Samuel Menashe 1302
William Meredith 1308
James Merrill 1317
Thomas Merton 1325
W. S. Merwin 1331
Josephine Miles 1340
Edna St. Vincent Millay . . 1344
Vassar Miller 1349
James Masao Mitsui 1354
N. Scott Momaday 1358
Marianne Moore 1364
Pat Mora 1371
Howard Moss 1375

Thylias Moss 1380
Lisel Mueller 1383
Harryette Mullen 1387
David Mura 1390
Carol Muske 1396

Ogden Nash 1401
John G. Neihardt 1405
Howard Nemerov 1409
Lorine Niedecker 1415
John Frederick Nims . . . 1421
Kathleen Norris 1428
Alice Notley 1431
Naomi Shihab Nye 1435

Joyce Carol Oates 1443
Frank O'Hara 1451
Sharon Olds 1456
Mary Oliver 1463
Charles Olson 1469
George Oppen 1477
Joel Oppenheimer 1481
Gregory Orr 1485
Simon Ortiz 1493
Judith Ortiz Cofer 1499
Alicia Suskin Ostriker . . . 1502

Grace Paley 1506
Dorothy Parker 1509
Linda Pastan 1514
Kenneth Patchen 1520
Molly Peacock 1525
Carl Phillips 1529
Marge Piercy 1532
Robert Pinsky 1538
Sylvia Plath 1547
Stanley Plumly 1556
Edgar Allan Poe 1561
Marie Ponsot 1569
Anne Porter 1573
Ezra Pound 1577
Reynolds Price 1586

Carl Rakosi 1590
Dudley Randall 1595

Claudia Rankine 1602
John Crowe Ransom 1605
Ishmael Reed 1612
Lizette Woodworth
    Reese 1616
Kenneth Rexroth 1621
Charles Reznikoff 1627
Adrienne Rich 1633
Laura Riding 1642
James Whitcomb Riley . . . 1645
Alberto Ríos 1654
Tomás Rivera 1657
Edwin Arlington
    Robinson 1660
Carolyn M. Rodgers 1668
Theodore Roethke 1671
Pattiann Rogers 1679
Edwin Rolfe 1682
Muriel Rukeyser 1686

David St. John 1693
Sonia Sanchez 1698
Carl Sandburg 1704
Sherod Santos 1711
May Sarton 1714
Leslie Scalapino 1724
Gjertrud
    Schnackenberg 1728
James Schuyler 1732
Delmore Schwartz 1738
Winfield Townley
    Scott 1746
Alan Seeger 1750
Anne Sexton 1753
Alan Shapiro 1759
Karl Shapiro 1764
Enid Shomer 1769
Jane Shore 1773
Leslie Marmon Silko . . . 1777
Shel Silverstein 1781
Charles Simic 1785
Louis Simpson 1793
L. E. Sissman 1802
David Slavitt 1809
Dave Smith 1817

Volume 4

Contents lxi
Complete List of
    Contents lxiii
Pronunciation Key. lxix

William Jay Smith 1825
W. D. Snodgrass 1831
Gary Snyder 1840
Cathy Song 1853
Gilbert Sorrentino 1858
Gary Soto. 1862
Jack Spicer 1868
William Stafford 1872
Timothy Steele 1881
Gertrude Stein 1885
Gerald Stern 1893
Wallace Stevens 1905
James Still 1913
Mark Strand 1918
Lucien Stryk 1927
Cole Swensen 1931
May Swenson 1934

Allen Tate 1941
James Tate 1947
Edward Taylor 1959
Henry Taylor 1968
Sara Teasdale. 1974
Henry David Thoreau . . . 1977
Melvin B. Tolson. 1984
Jean Toomer 1988
Natasha Trethewey 1995
Frederick Goddard
    Tuckerman 1998
Chase Twichell 2002

Louis Untermeyer 2007
John Updike 2016

Jean Valentine 2024
Mark Van Doren 2027
Mona Van Duyn 2032
Jones Very 2039
Peter Viereck 2042
José García Villa 2048
Ellen Bryant Voigt 2054

David Wagoner. 2059
Diane Wakoski 2068
Anne Waldman. 2076
Alice Walker 2080
Margaret Walker 2086
Ronald Wallace. 2090
Robert Penn Warren . . . 2094
Bruce Weigl 2102
James Welch 2107
Philip Whalen 2111
Phillis Wheatley 2114
John Hall Wheelock . . . 2123
John Wheelwright 2126
Walt Whitman 2130
Reed Whittemore. 2140
John Greenleaf
    Whittier. 2144
Richard Wilbur. 2151
C. K. Williams 2161
Miller Williams 2168
Sherley Anne
    Williams 2172
William Carlos
    Williams 2175
Yvor Winters 2184

David Wojahn 2190
Baron Wormser 2196
C. D. Wright 2203
Charles Wright. 2207
Franz Wright 2217
James Wright. 2221
Jay Wright 2231
Elinor Wylie 2240

Mitsuye Yamada 2244
Al Young 2248
Dean Young 2257

Paul Zimmer 2261
Louis Zukofsky 2265

RESOURCES

Explicating Poetry 2273
Language and
    Linguistics 2282
Glossary of Poetical
    Terms 2294
Bibliography 2307
Guide to Online
    Resources. 2314
Time Line 2318
Major Awards 2321
Chronological List
    of Poets 2334

INDEXES

Categorized Index
    of Poets 2341
Master List of
    Contents. 2357
Subject Index. 2369

BRITISH, IRISH, AND COMMONWEALTH POETS

Volume 1

Publisher's Note v
Contributors ix
Contents xiii

Complete List of
    Contents xv
Pronunciation Key xix

Dannie Abse 1
Joseph Addison 7
Æ 13
Richard Aldington 17

William Allingham 23
Matthew Arnold 30
Margaret Atwood 37
W. H. Auden 47

Thomas Lovell Beddoes . . . 56
Patricia Beer 60
Aphra Behn 66
Hilaire Belloc 73
John Betjeman 80
Earle Birney 86
William Blake 91
Edmund Blunden 104
Eavan Boland 108
William Lisle Bowles 119
Nicholas Breton 124
Robert Bridges 131
Emily Brontë 137
Rupert Brooke 144
Elizabeth Barrett
    Browning 149
Robert Browning 158
Basil Bunting 168
Robert Burns 173
Samuel Butler 180
Lord Byron 186

Cædmon 197
Thomas Campion 202
Thomas Carew 208
Lewis Carroll 213
Anne Carson 225
George Chapman 228
Thomas Chatterton 235
Geoffrey Chaucer 243
John Clare 254
Austin Clarke 261
Arthur Hugh Clough . . . 266
Leonard Cohen 272
Samuel Taylor
    Coleridge 276
William Collins 287
Padraic Colum 292
William Congreve 296
Henry Constable 301

Charles Cotton 306
Abraham Cowley 312
William Cowper 320
George Crabbe 327
Richard Crashaw 337
Cynewulf 344

Samuel Daniel 352
George Darley 359
Sir William
    Davenant 362
Donald Davie 367
Sir John Davies 375
Cecil Day Lewis 384
Thomas Dekker 390
Walter de la Mare 398
John Donne 405
Michael Drayton 417
William Drummond of
    Hawthornden 424
John Dryden 433
William Dunbar 442
Lawrence Durrell 451

T. S. Eliot 458
William Empson 468
Sir George Etherege 476

Volume 2
Contents xxvii
Complete List of
    Contents xxix
Pronunciation Key xxxiii

Sir Richard Fanshawe 481
James Fenton 487
Anne Finch 491
Edward FitzGerald 495
Roy Fuller 500

George Gascoigne 505
John Gay 512
Oliver Goldsmith 520
John Gower 525

Robert Graves 534
Thomas Gray 542
Robert Greene 548
Fulke Greville 555
Thom Gunn 560
Ivor Gurney 568

Arthur Henry Hallam 575
Thomas Hardy 579
Tony Harrison 588
Seamus Heaney 594
Anne Hébert 605
Felicia Dorothea
    Hemans 609
Robert Henryson 612
George Herbert 617
Robert Herrick 626
John Heywood 635
Geoffrey Hill 641
Thomas Hood 650
A. D. Hope 660
Gerard Manley Hopkins . . . 666
A. E. Housman 677
Ted Hughes 686
Leigh Hunt 694

Samuel Johnson 700
David Jones 707
Ben Jonson 711
James Joyce 719

Patrick Kavanagh 726
John Keats 731
Henry King 743
Thomas Kinsella 751
Rudyard Kipling 760

Charles Lamb 768
Walter Savage Landor 774
William Langland 780
Philip Larkin 786
D. H. Lawrence 795
Layamon 803
Irving Layton 808
Edward Lear 812

Thomas Lodge. 817
Christopher Logue. 823
Richard Lovelace 827
John Lydgate 832

George MacBeth. 841
Hugh MacDiarmid. 846
Louis MacNeice 854
James Clarence Mangan. . . 866
Christopher Marlowe 870
Andrew Marvell 877
John Masefield 885
George Meredith 890
Charlotte Mew. 894
Christopher Middleton . . . 898
John Milton 905
John Montague 914
William Morris 924
Edwin Muir 933
Paul Muldoon 937
Les A. Murray. 946

Thomas Nashe. 953
Margaret Cavendish,
    duchess of Newcastle. . . 958
Nuala Ní Dhomhnaill 964

Volume 3
Contents xli
Complete List of
    Contents xliii
Pronunciation Key xlvii

John Oldham 969
Michael Ondaatje 973
Wilfred Owen 977

Coventry Patmore 983
Pearl-Poet 991
Harold Pinter 1001
Alexander Pope 1005
E. J. Pratt 1016

F. T. Prince 1021
Matthew Prior 1026

Francis Quarles. 1031

Sir Walter Ralegh 1037
Henry Reed. 1043
John Wilmot, earl of
    Rochester 1048
Isaac Rosenberg 1055
Christina Rossetti 1060
Dante Gabriel Rossetti . . . 1065

Thomas Sackville 1074
Siegfried Sassoon 1080
Sir Walter Scott 1087
Sir Charles Sedley 1094
Robert W. Service 1099
William Shakespeare. . . . 1105
Percy Bysshe Shelley . . . 1112
Sir Philip Sidney 1126
Sir Robert Sidney 1135
Jon Silkin. 1141
Edith Sitwell 1145
John Skelton 1153
Christopher Smart 1159
Stevie Smith 1164
Robert Southey. 1171
Robert Southwell. 1178
Stephen Spender 1183
Edmund Spenser 1191
Robert Louis
    Stevenson 1201
Sir John Suckling 1206
Henry Howard, earl of
    Surrey. 1212
Jonathan Swift 1218
Algernon Charles
    Swinburne 1227

Alfred, Lord Tennyson. . . 1236
Dylan Thomas 1245

Edward Thomas 1252
R. S. Thomas. 1257
James Thomson 1260
James Thomson 1264
Charles Tomlinson 1268
Thomas Traherne. 1277

Henry Vaughan. 1284

Edmund Waller. 1290
Isaac Watts 1297
Oscar Wilde 1303
William Wordsworth. . . . 1310
Sir Thomas Wyatt 1322

William Butler
    Yeats 1330
Edward Young 1349

RESOURCES
Explicating Poetry 1357
Language and
    Linguistics 1366
Glossary of Poetical
    Terms 1378
Bibliography 1391
Guide to Online
    Resources 1401
Time Line 1405
Major Awards 1408
Chronological List
    of Poets 1415

INDEXES
Geographical Index
    of Poets 1421
Categorized Index
    of Poets 1425
Master List of
    Contents. 1437
Subject Index. 1448

EUROPEAN POETS

Volume 1

Publisher's Note v
Contributors ix
Contents xiii
Complete List of Contents. . . xv
Pronunciation Key xix

Endre Ady 1
Rafael Alberti 6
Vicente Aleixandre 12
Anacreon 17
Guillaume Apollinaire 22
Apollonius Rhodius. 30
Louis Aragon 35
János Arany. 42
Archilochus. 50
Ludovico Ariosto 56
Hans Arp 62

Mihály Babits. 68
Ingeborg Bachmann 72
Stanisław Barańczak 77
Charles Baudelaire 80
Samuel Beckett 87
Gustavo Adolfo Bécquer . . . 95
Pietro Bembo 101
Gottfried Benn. 107
Thomas Bernhard 112
Wolf Biermann 119
Johannes Bobrowski. 126
Giovanni Boccaccio 131
Matteo Maria Boiardo. . . . 135
Nicolas
    Boileau-Despréaux. . . . 138
Yves Bonnefoy 142
Bertolt Brecht 149
André Breton 157
Breyten Breytenbach 162

Pedro Calderón de
    la Barca. 170
Callimachus 175
Luís de Camões 180

Giosuè Carducci. 185
Rosalía de Castro 190
Catullus 197
Constantine P. Cavafy . . . 204
Guido Cavalcanti 210
Paul Celan 214
Luis Cernuda 220
René Char 226
Charles d'Orléans 230
Alain Chartier 236
Christine de Pizan 240
Paul Claudel 244
Jean Cocteau. 253
Tristan Corbière 260

Gabriele D'Annunzio 264
Dante 270
Joachim du Bellay. 289
Jovan Dučić 292

Joseph von Eichendorff . . . 299
Gunnar Ekelöf 306
Paul Éluard 313
Odysseus Elytis 317
Hans Magnus
    Enzensberger. 323

J. V. Foix. 329
Jean Follain 335
Ugo Foscolo 340
Girolamo Fracastoro. 345

Federico García Lorca. . . . 355
Garcilaso de la Vega. 362
Théophile Gautier 368
Stefan George 377
Guido Gezelle 384
Giuseppe Giusti 391
Johann Wolfgang
    von Goethe. 396
Eugen Gomringer 405
Luis de Góngora
    y Argote 410

Gottfried von Strassburg. . . 415
Günter Grass. 418
Guillaume de Lorris
    and Jean de Meung . . . 424
Jorge Guillén 430

Volume 2

Contents xxvii
Complete List of
    Contents xxix
Pronunciation Key. xxxiii

Paavo Haavikko 435
Hartmann von Aue 441
Piet Hein. 447
Heinrich Heine 451
Zbigniew Herbert 458
Hesiod 465
Hermann Hesse 471
Hugo von Hofmannsthal. . . 478
Friedrich Hölderlin 485
Miroslav Holub 492
Arno Holz 497
Homer 502
Horace 510
Victor Hugo 518

Gyula Illyés 528

Juan Ramón Jiménez 533
Saint John of the Cross . . . 539
Judah ha-Levi 549
Juvenal. 553

Nikos Kazantzakis. 557
Karl Kraus 563
Reiner Kunze 570

Jean de La Fontaine 577
Jules Laforgue 584
Alphonse de Lamartine . . . 591
Luis de León. 597

Leonidas of Tarentum 602
Giacomo Leopardi. 607
Elias Lönnrot 617
Lucan 621
Lucretius. 627

Antonio Machado 633
François de Malherbe 639
Stéphane Mallarmé 644
Itzik Manger. 650
Jorge Manrique 657
Alessandro Manzoni. . . . 660
Marie de France 666
Giambattista Marino. . . . 674
Martial. 678
Harry Martinson. 681
Meleager. 685
Henri Michaux. 688
Michelangelo 694
Adam Mickiewicz. 702
Czesław Miłosz 709
Eugenio Montale 721
Christian Morgenstern. . . 727
Eduard Mörike. 732
Alfred de Musset 736

Gérard de Nerval 741
Novalis. 748

Blas de Otero 757
Ovid 763

Giovanni Pascoli. 771
Pier Paolo Pasolini 776
Cesare Pavese 783
Miodrag Pavlović 786
Charles-Pierre Péguy 791
Nikos Pentzikis 797
Saint-John Perse. 801
Persius. 806
Fernando Pessoa. 811
Sándor Petőfi 816
Petrarch 828
Pindar 836
Poliziano. 841

Francis Ponge 848
Vasko Popa 856

Volume 3
Contents xli
Complete List of
    Contents xliii
Pronunciation Key xlvii

Jacques Prévert 861
Sextus Propertius 866

Salvatore Quasimodo 873

Miklós Radnóti 879
Pierre Reverdy. 883
Rainer Maria Rilke 889
Arthur Rimbaud 897
Yannis Ritsos 904
Pierre de Ronsard 912
Tadeusz Różewicz. 917

Umberto Saba 925
Nelly Sachs 930
Pedro Salinas 936
Sappho. 941
Friedrich Schiller 949
George Seferis. 957
Jaroslav Seifert 961
Antoni Słonimski 968
Juliusz Słowacki. 972
Edith Södergran 981
Dionysios Solomos 987
Gaspara Stampa 993
Statius 998
Anna Swir 1004
Wisława Szymborska . . . 1007

Torquato Tasso 1014
Esaias Tegnér. 1020
Theocritus 1023
Theognis 1029
Georg Trakl 1033
Tomas Tranströmer. . . . 1039
Tristan Tzara 1044

Miguel de Unamuno
    y Jugo. 1051
Giuseppe Ungaretti. 1056

Paul Valéry. 1065
Lope de Vega Carpio. . . . 1073
Vergil. 1080
Émile Verhaeren 1089
Paul Verlaine 1093
Alfred de Vigny 1099
François Villon. 1106
Mihály Vörösmarty 1112
Walther von der
    Vogelweide 1119

Adam Ważyk. 1126
Wolfram von
    Eschenbach 1130

Adam Zagajewski 1137
Stefan Zweig 1141

RESOURCES
Explicating Poetry 1151
Language and
    Linguistics 1160
Glossary of Poetical
    Terms 1172
Bibliography 1185
Guide to Online
    Resources. 1199
Time Line 1202
Major Awards 1205
Chronological List
    of Poets 1211

INDEXES
Geographical Index
    of Poets 1217
Categorized Index
    of Poets 1220
Master List of
    Contents. 1229
Subject Index. 1240

WORLD POETS

Publisher's Note v
Contributors ix
Contents xi
Pronunciation Key xiii

Chinua Achebe 1
Anna Akhmatova 3
Claribel Alegría 9
Yehuda Amichai 14
Innokenty Annensky 21
Kofi Awoonor 25

Aleksandr Blok 33
Jorge Luis Borges 39
Joseph Brodsky 44

Ernesto Cardenal 52
Aimé Césaire 56
Michelle Cliff 61
Sor Juana Inés de la Cruz . . 64

Rubén Darío 71
Carlos Drummond de
  Andrade 76
Du Fu 84

Sergei Esenin 90

Firdusi 96

Enrique González
  Martínez 101

Hafiz 108
José Hernández 114
Nazim Hikmet 117

Issa 126

Vladislav Khodasevich . . . 133
Ko Un 138

Mikhail Lermontov 142
Li Bo 150
Li Qingzhao 157

Osip Mandelstam 163
Matsuo Bashō 170
Vladimir
  Mayakovsky 176
Meng Haoran 182
Gabriela Mistral 185
Kenji Miyazawa 191

Pablo Neruda 196

Christopher Okigbo 205
Omar Khayyám 208

Dan Pagis 213
Nicanor Parra 216
Boris Pasternak 222
Octavio Paz 230
Alexander Pushkin 236

Alfonso Reyes 245
Ruan Ji 250
Jalāl al-Dīn Rūmī 255

Saʿdi 260
Léopold Senghor 264
Vikram Seth 272
Wole Soyinka 276

Rabindranath Tagore . . . 281
Tao Qian 288
Marina Tsvetayeva 293

César Vallejo 300
Vālmīki 308
Andrei Voznesensky 311

Derek Walcott 317
Wang Wei 326

Xie Lingyun 334

Yevgeny Yevtushenko . . . 339
Yosano Akiko 349

Daisy Zamora 354

RESOURCES
Explicating Poetry 359
Language and
  Linguistics 368
Glossary of Poetical
  Terms 380
Bibliography 393
Guide to Online
  Resources 403
Time Line 406
Major Awards 408
Chronological List
  of Poets 413

INDEXES
Geographical Index
  of Poets 417
Categorized Index
  of Poets 419
Master List of
  Contents 423
Subject Index 434

TOPICAL ESSAYS

Volume 1

Publisher's Note v
Contributors ix
Contents xi
Complete List of
    Contents xiii

**POETRY AROUND
    THE WORLD**

African American Poetry 3
African Poetry 15
Asian American Poetry 21
Australian and New
    Zealand Poetry 30
Canadian Poetry 37
Caribbean Poetry 43
Catalan Poetry 48
Chinese Poetry 54
Croatian Poetry 71
Czech Poetry 78
East German Poetry 87
English and Continental
    Poetry in the
    Fourteenth Century 98
English Poetry in the
    Fifteenth Century 120
English Poetry in the
    Sixteenth Century 130
English Poetry in the
    Seventeenth Century . . . 144
English Poetry in the
    Eighteenth Century . . . 160
English and American
    Poetry in the
    Nineteenth Century . . . 174
English and American
    Poetry in the
    Twentieth Century 185
European Oral and Epic
    Traditions 214
French Poetry to 1700 232

French Poetry
    Since 1700 254
German Poetry to 1800 . . . 283
German Poetry: 1800 to
    Reunification 298
German Poetry Since
    Reunification 315
Greek Poetry in
    Antiquity 320
Greek Poetry
    Since 1820 331
Hungarian Poetry 352
Indian English Poetry 365
Italian Poetry to 1800 377
Italian Poetry
    Since 1800 393
Japanese Poetry
    to 1800 412
Japanese Poetry
    Since 1800 427
Latin American Poetry . . . 435
Latin Poetry 441
Latino Poetry 466

Volume 2

Contents xxi
Complete List
    of Contents xxiii

**POETRY AROUND
    THE WORLD** (*cont.*)

Macedonian Poetry 475
Native American Poetry . . . 478
Polish Poetry 489
Postcolonial Poetry 500
Russian Poetry 509
Scandinavian Poetry 526
Serbian Poetry 566
Slovak Poetry 573
Slovenian Poetry 579

Spanish Poetry
    to 1400 583
Spanish Poetry
    Since 1400 592
Tibetan Poetry 604

LITERARY MOVEMENTS

Metaphysical Poets 615
Restoration Poetry 620
Romantic Poets 626
Fireside Poets 633
French Symbolists 639
Imagists 644
Modernists 650
Harlem Renaissance 655
Beat Poets 661
Confessional Poets 668
New York School 674
Movement Poets 679
Black Mountain School . . . 684
Green Movement Poets . . . 690

CRITICISM AND THEORY

Criticism from Plato
    to Eliot 699
Archetypal and
    Psychological
    Criticism 719
Cultural Criticism 731
Feminist Criticism 736
Formalistic Criticism 743
Linguistic Criticism 750
Marxist Criticism 760
New Historicism 764
Postcolonial
    Criticism 769
Queer Theory 774
Structuralist and
    Poststructuralist
    Criticism 780

CUMULATIVE INDEXES

SUBJECT INDEX

All personages whose names appear in **boldface** *type in this index are the subjects of articles in* Critical Survey of Poetry, Fourth Edition. *The* **boldface** *letters that precede numbers in this index indicate the set in which the entry can be found:* **AP** = American Poets, **BP** = British, Irish, and Commonwealth Poets, **EP** = European Poets, **WP** = World Poets, **TE** = Topical Essays, *and* **CM** = Cumulative Indexes.

16 L.-P. (Sappho), **EP:** 945
94 L.-P. (Sappho), **EP:** 946
112 L.-P. (Sappho), **EP:** 948
357 P.; Anacreon, **EP:** 19
358 P.; Anacreon, **EP:** 20
359 P.; Anacreon, **EP:** 20
376 P.; Anacreon, **EP:** 21
396 P.; Anacreon, **EP:** 21
417 P.; Anacreon, **EP:** 21

"A" (Zukofsky), **AP:** 2269
"A Cristo crucificado." *See* "To Christ Crucified"
A la altura de las circunstancias. See *Clamor*
A la pintura. See *To Painting*
"A la vida religiosa" (León), **EP:** 601
"A Luigia Pallavicini caduta da cavallo." *See* "To Louise Pallavicini Fallen from a Horse"
A minden titkok verseiből. See *Of All Mysteries*
"A Santiago." *See* "To Santiago"
"A Víctor Hugo," **WP:** 73
"À Zurbarán" (Gautier), **EP:** 374
Abacus (Karr), **AP:** 994
Abdelazar (Behn), **BP:** 70
"Abduction, The" (Kunitz), **AP:** 1090
"Abend, Der." *See* "Evening"
"Abendland." *See* "Occident, The"
"Aboriginal Charter of Rights" (Walker), **TE:** 503
Aboriginal poetry, Australia, **TE:** 503
"Abou Ben Adhem" (Hunt), **BP:** 698
About Love (Montague), **BP:** 921
"About Marriage" (Levertov), **AP:** 1117

About That (Mayakovsky), **WP:** 179
About the House (Auden), **BP:** 53
Abraham's Knife, and Other Poems (Garrett), **AP:** 658
"Abrasive" (Everson), **AP:** 572
Absalom and Achitophel (Dryden), **BP:** 438, **TE:** 156, **TE:** 622
"Abschied." *See* "Departure"
Abse, Dannie, **BP:** 1-7; *Arcadia, One Mile*, **BP:** 4; "Funland," **BP:** 4; *New Selected Poems*, **BP:** 5; *Running Late*, **BP:** 4
Absences (Tate), **AP:** 1952
"Absent-Minded Beggar, The" (Kipling), **BP:** 765
"Absentia animi" (Ekelöf), **EP:** 309
Absolute Trust in the Goodness of the Earth (Walker), **AP:** 2084
Absurdist poets, **TE:** 522
Academy of American Poets Fellowship, **AP:** 2321, **CM:** 45, **TE:** 865
Accademia dell'Arcadia, **TE:** 387
Accentual meter, defined, **AP:** 2294, **BP:** 1378, **EP:** 1172, **TE:** 810, **WP:** 380
Accentual-syllabic meter, defined, **AP:** 2294, **BP:** 1378, **EP:** 1172, **TE:** 810, **WP:** 380
Accidental Weather (Santos), **AP:** 1713
"Accountability" (Dunbar), **AP:** 505
Acemeist poets. *See* Categorized Index
Achebe, Chinua, **TE:** 770, **WP:** 1-3; *Christmas in Biafra*, **WP:** 2; *Collected Poems*, **WP:** 2

"Achtzehnjährige, Der." *See* "Eighteen-Year-Old, The"
Ackerman, Diane, **AP:** 1-4; *Animal Sense*, **AP:** 3; *I Praise My Destroyer*, **AP:** 3; *Origami Bridges*, **AP:** 3; *Planets*, **AP:** 2
Acmeism, **TE:** 518
Acolytes (Giovanni), **AP:** 700
Acque e terre (Quasimodo), **EP:** 875
Actfive, and Other Poems (MacLeish), **AP:** 1252
Adam's Footprint (Miller), **AP:** 1350
Adams, Léonie, **AP:** 4-8; "Alas, Kind Element," **AP:** 7; *High Falcon, and Other Poems*, **AP:** 6; "The Reminder," **AP:** 8; *Those Not Elect*, **AP:** 6
Addison, Joseph, **BP:** 7-13, **TE:** 706; *The Campaign*, **BP:** 11; "A Letter from Italy," **BP:** 10
"Adieu." *See* "Farewell"
"Adlestrop" (Thomas), **BP:** 1255
Admit Impediment (Ponsot), **AP:** 1570
"Adolf Eichmann" (Carruth), **AP:** 279
Adonais (Shelley), **BP:** 1123
Adonais Prize for Poetry, **CM:** 46, **EP:** 1205, **TE:** 866, **WP:** 408
"Adónde te escondiste." *See* "Spiritual Canticle, The"
Adone, L' (Marino), **EP:** 677, **TE:** 386
Adonis (La Fontaine), **EP:** 579
"Adoration of the Magi, The" (Cernuda), **EP:** 225
Adorno, Theodor, **TE:** 311

Adult Bookstore (Shapiro), **AP:** 1768

"Adultery" (Dugan), **AP:** 499

Adventures in the Letter I (Simpson), **AP:** 1797

Ady, Endre, EP: 1-6, **TE:** 358; "Man in Inhumanity," **EP:** 5; *New Verses*, **EP:** 3; *Of All Mysteries*, **EP:** 4

Æ, **BP:** 13-17; *Homeward*, **BP:** 15

"Aella" (Chatterton), **BP:** 241

"Aeneas and Dido" (Brodsky), **WP:** 48

Aeneid (Vergil), **EP:** 1083

"Aeolian Harp, The" (Melville), **AP:** 1300

Aesthetic poets. *See* Categorized Index

Aetia (Callimachus), **EP:** 177

Affenfels und Barrikade (Biermann), **EP:** 124

Africa. *See* Geographical Index

Africa (Petrarch), **EP:** 833

"Africa Africa Africa" (Baraka), **AP:** 95

African American culture. *See* Categorized Index

African American poetry, **TE:** 3-14, **TE:** 209

"African Eclogues" (Chatterton), **BP:** 239

African poetry, **TE:** 15-20, **TE:** 506

Afro-Caribbean poetry, **TE:** 43

After (Hirshfield), **AP:** 862

"After a Reading at a Black College" (Derricotte), **AP:** 447

After All (Matthews), **AP:** 1288

After and Before the Lightning (Ortiz), **AP:** 1497

"After Apple-Picking" (Frost), **AP:** 627

After-Dinner Declarations (Parra), **WP:** 221

After Ikkyū, and Other Poems (Harrison), **AP:** 811

After Lorca (Spicer), **AP:** 1870

"After Our War" (Balaban), **AP:** 82

"After Speaking of One Who Died a Long Time Before" (Colum), **BP:** 295

After the Fall (Field), **AP:** 605

After the Killing (Randall), **AP:** 1600

After the Long Train (Mitsui), **AP:** 1356

After the Lost War (Hudgins), **AP:** 926

After the Reunion (Baker), **AP:** 79

After We Lost Our Way (Mura), **AP:** 1392

Afterlife, The (Levis), **AP:** 1130

"Against Fruition" (Suckling), **BP:** 1210

Against Love Poetry (Boland), **BP:** 116

Against the Falling Evil (McMichael), **AP:** 1255

Against the Silences (Blackburn), **AP:** 186

Age of Anxiety, The (Auden), **BP:** 52

"Agony" (Ungaretti), **EP:** 1059

Agua Santa/Holy Water (Mora), **AP:** 1373

Águila o sol?. See *Eagle or Sun?*

Ai, AP: 8-12; *Cruelty*, **AP:** 10; *Fate*, **AP:** 10; *Greed*, **AP:** 10; *Killing Floor*, **AP:** 10; *Vice*, **AP:** 11

Aiken, Conrad, AP: 12-17; *Changing Mind*, **AP:** 15; *The Charnel Rose*, **AP:** 15; *The Divine Pilgrim*, **AP:** 14; *The House of Dust*, **AP:** 15; *The Jig of Forslin*, **AP:** 15; *John Deth*, **AP:** 16; *A Little Who's Zoo of Mild Animals*, **AP:** 16; *The Morning Song of Lord Zero*, **AP:** 16; *The Pilgrimage of Festus*, **AP:** 15; "The Room," **AP:** 16; *Senlin*, **AP:** 15

"Airiños, airiños, aires" (Castro), **EP:** 194

"Airship Boys in Africa, The" (Cassity), **AP:** 294

Aitiōn. See *Aetia*

"Ajanta" (Rukeyser), **AP:** 1689

Åkesson, Sonja, **TE:** 555

Akhmatova, Anna, TE: 519, **WP:** 3-9; *Anno Domini MCMXXI*, **WP:** 6; *Belaya staya*, **WP:** 6; *Chetki*, **WP:** 5; *A Poem Without a Hero*, **WP:** 8; *Requiem*, **WP:** 7; *Vecher*, **WP:** 5

Alagherius, Durante. *See* Dante

Alaham (Greville), **BP:** 558

"Alas, Kind Element" (Adams), **AP:** 7

Alastor (Shelley), **BP:** 1117

Alaya (Hirshfield), **AP:** 860

Alberti, Rafael, EP: 6-12; "Ballad of the Lost Andalusian," **EP:** 11; *Cal y canto*, **EP:** 9; *Concerning the Angels*, **EP:** 9; "De los álamos y los sauces," **EP:** 10; *Entre el clavel y la espada*, **EP:** 10; *Marinero en tierra*, **EP:** 8; *Retornos de lo vivo lejano*, **EP:** 10; "Three Memories of Heaven," **EP:** 9; *To Painting*, **EP:** 11; *To See You and Not to See You*, **EP:** 9

"Albertus" (Gautier), **EP:** 373

Alcaeus, **TE:** 223, **TE:** 321

Alcayaga, Lucila Godoy. *See* Mistral, Gabriela

Alcman, **TE:** 224, **TE:** 322

Alcools (Apollinaire), **EP:** 27

Alcuin, **TE:** 462

Aldington, Edward Godfree. *See* Aldington, Richard

Aldington, Richard, BP: 17-23, **TE:** 188, **TE:** 646; "Choricos," **BP:** 20; "Eumenides," **BP:** 21; *A Fool i' the Forest*, **BP:** 21; *Pinorman*, **BP:** 19

Alegría, Claribel, WP: 9-14; *Casting Off*, **WP:** 13; *Flores del volcán/Flowers from the Volcano*, **WP:** 11; *Fugues*, **WP:** 12; *Luisa in Realityland*, **WP:** 11; *Sorrow*,

WP: 12; *Woman of the River,*
  WP: 12
Alehouse Sonnets (Dubie), **AP:** 495
Aleixandre, Vicente, EP: 12-17,
  TE: 600; *Ámbito,* **EP:** 15;
  Destruction or Love, **EP:** 15;
  Historia del corazón, **EP:** 16;
  Shadow of Paradise, **EP:** 16;
  Swords as if Lips, **EP:** 15
Aleksandrov, Josip Murn, **TE:** 580
Alepoudhelis, Odysseus. *See* Elytis,
  Odysseus
Aleramo, Sibilla, **TE:** 397
Alexander, Elizabeth, AP: 17-20;
  American Sublime, **AP:** 19;
  Antebellum Dream Book, **AP:** 19;
  Body of Life, **AP:** 19; *Praise Song
  for the Day,* **AP:** 20; *The Venus
  Hottentot,* **AP:** 18
Alexander, Margaret Walker. *See*
  Walker, Margaret
Alexander's Feast (Dryden), **BP:** 440
Alexandrian poets. *See* Categorized
  Index
Alexie, Sherman, AP: 21-24,
  TE: 486; *The Business of
  Fancydancing,* **AP:** 22; *Face,*
  AP: 23; *First Indian on the Moon,*
  AP: 23; *Old Shirts and New Skins,*
  AP: 23; *The Summer of Black
  Widows,* **AP:** 23
Alfieri, Vittorio, **TE:** 389
Alfred, Lord Tennyson. *See*
  Tennyson, Alfred, Lord
Algabal (George), **EP:** 381
Algarín, Miguel, **TE:** 467
Alguma poesia (Drummond de
  Andrade), **WP:** 80
Ali, Agha Shahid, AP: 24-27,
  TE: 374; *Call Me Ishmael
  Tonight,* **AP:** 27; *The Country
  Without a Post Office,* **AP:** 27;
  The Half-Inch Himalayas,
  AP: 26; *A Nostalgist's Map of
  America,* **AP:** 26

Alice's Adventures in Wonderland
  (Carroll), **BP:** 215
Alighieri, Dante. *See* Dante
Alive Together (Mueller), **AP:** 1386
All-American Girl (Becker), **AP:** 111
"All Choice Is Error" (Cunningham),
  AP: 420
"All-Knowing Rabbit" (Kennedy),
  AP: 1023
All My Pretty Ones (Sexton),
  AP: 1756, **TE:** 671
All of It Singing (Gregg), **AP:** 738
All Soul's Day (Esenin), **WP:** 93
"All the Soul Indrawn . . ."
  (Mallarmé), **EP:** 646
All the Whiskey in Heaven
  (Bernstein), **AP:** 135
All You Who Sleep Tonight (Seth),
  WP: 275
"Allant châtier la rebellion des
  Rochelois" (Malherbe), **EP:** 642
Allegiances (Stafford), **AP:** 1878
Allegory, defined, **AP:** 2294,
  BP: 1378, **EP:** 1172, **TE:** 810,
  WP: 380
Allegory, England, **TE:** 133
Allegria, L' (Ungaretti), **EP:** 1059
"Allegro, L'" (Milton), **BP:** 908
Allen, Paula Gunn, AP: 27-31,
  TE: 483; *A Cannon Between My
  Knees,* **AP:** 29; *Shadow Country,*
  AP: 30
Alleyne, Ellen. *See* Rossetti, Christina
Alligator Bride, The (Hall), **AP:** 779
Allingham, William, BP: 23-30;
  *Blackberries Picked Off Many
  Bushes,* **BP:** 29; "The Fairies,"
  BP: 23; *Laurence Bloomfield in
  Ireland,* **BP:** 28; *William
  Allingham,* **BP:** 27; "The Winding
  Banks of Erne," **BP:** 23
Alliteration, defined, **AP:** 2294,
  BP: 1378, **EP:** 1172, **TE:** 810,
  WP: 380
Alliterative revival, **TE:** 105

Allusion, defined, **AP:** 2294,
  BP: 1378, **EP:** 1172, **TE:** 810,
  WP: 380
Alonso, Dámaso, **TE:** 600
"Alpha" (Różewicz), **EP:** 923
"Altarwise by Owl-Light" (Thomas),
  BP: 1249
Alternate Means of Transport
  (Macdonald), **AP:** 1213
Altogether Different Language, An
  (Porter), **AP:** 1575
Álvarez, Juan de Yepes y. *See* John of
  the Cross, Saint
Alvarez, Julia, AP: 31-36, **TE:** 473;
  Homecoming, **AP:** 32; *The Other
  Side/El otro lado,* **AP:** 34; *The
  Woman I Kept to Myself,* **AP:** 35
Always, and Other Poems (Rivera),
  AP: 1659
"Always to Be Named" (Bobrowski),
  EP: 129
"Am I My Neighbor's Keeper?"
  (Eberhart), **AP:** 530
"Am Sonnabend Abend." *See* "On a
  Saturday Evening"
Ambarvalia (Clough), **BP:** 269
"Amber Bead, The" (Herrick),
  BP: 629
Ámbito (Aleixandre), **EP:** 15
Ambivalence, moral, **TE:** 193
Ambrogini, Angelo. *See* Poliziano
"America" (Angelou), **AP:** 50
America (Blake), **BP:** 99
America Was Promises (MacLeish),
  AP: 1252
American colonial poets. *See*
  Categorized Index
American early national poets. *See*
  Categorized Index
American Indian poetry. *See* Native
  American poetry
American Indian Poetry. See *Path on
  the Rainbow, The*
American naturalism. *See* Naturalism,
  American

American poetry; nineteenth century, **TE:** 174-184; twentieth century, **TE:** 185-213

American Primitive (Oliver), **AP:** 1466

"American Rhapsody (2)" (Fearing), **AP:** 584

American Scenes, and Other Poems (Tomlinson), **BP:** 1271

American Smooth (Dove), **AP:** 491

American Sublime (Alexander), **AP:** 19

American Takes a Walk, An (Whittemore), **AP:** 2141

American Way, The" (Corso), **AP:** 360

Americana, and Other Poems (Updike), **AP:** 2021

Americas Review (journal), **TE:** 466

Americus, Book I (Ferlinghetti), **AP:** 600

Amers. See Seamarks

Amichai, Yehuda, WP: 14-21; *Open Closed Open*, **WP:** 19

Amis, Aphara. *See* Behn, Aphra

Ammons, A. R., AP: 37-42; *A Coast of Trees*, **AP:** 41; *Collected Poems, 1951-1971*, **AP:** 39; *Corsons Inlet*, **AP:** 39; "Easter Morning," **AP:** 41; *Expressions of Sea Level*, **AP:** 38; *Garbage*, **AP:** 41; *Glare*, **AP:** 41; *Lake Effect Country*, **AP:** 40; *The Really Short Poems of A. R. Ammons*, **AP:** 41; *The Snow Poems*, **AP:** 40; *Sphere*, **AP:** 39; *Sumerian Vistas*, **AP:** 41; *Tape for the Turn of the Year*, **AP:** 39

"Among School Children" (Yeats), **BP:** 1342

"Among Tenses" (Morgenstern), **EP:** 730

Amores (Ovid), **EP:** 766

Amoretti (Spenser), **BP:** 1198

"Amoureuse, L'." *See* "Woman in Love, A"

Amours de Voyage (Clough), **BP:** 270

Amplitude (Gallagher), **AP:** 641

Amputations (Macdonald), **AP:** 1212

AM/TRAK (Baraka), **AP:** 96

"An ein fallendes Blatt." *See* "To a Falling Leaf"

"An Tieck." *See* "To Tieck"

Anabasis (Perse), **EP:** 804

Anacreon, EP: 17-22, **TE:** 322; 357 P., **EP:** 19; 358 P., **EP:** 20; 359 P., **EP:** 20; 376 P., **EP:** 21; 396 P., **EP:** 21; 417 P., **EP:** 21

Anacrusis, defined, **AP:** 2294, **BP:** 1378, **EP:** 1172, **TE:** 810, **WP:** 380

"Anaesthetic Criticism" (Crews), **TE:** 727

Anagnostakis, Manolis, **TE:** 348

Anakomidhi (Pentzikis), **EP:** 801

Anapest, defined, **AP:** 2294, **BP:** 1378, **EP:** 1172, **TE:** 810, **WP:** 380

Anaphora, defined, **AP:** 2294, **BP:** 1378, **EP:** 1172, **TE:** 810, **WP:** 380

Anathemata, The (Jones), **BP:** 709

Anatomy of Criticism (Frye), **TE:** 721

Anatomy of the World, An (Donne), **BP:** 414

Ancel, Paul. *See* Celan, Paul

Ancestors (Brathwaite), **AP:** 234

Ancia (Otero), **EP:** 761

Ancient Lights (Clarke), **BP:** 264

Ancient Rain, The (Kaufman), **AP:** 1005

And Come to Closure (Coulette), **AP:** 365

"And Death Shall Have No Dominion" (Thomas), **BP:** 1249

And Live Apart (Peacock), **AP:** 1527

And Morning (Flint), **AP:** 608

And Still Birds Sing (Stryk), **AP:** 1930

And the Stars Were Shining (Ashbery), **AP:** 62

Anderson, Maggie, AP: 43-46; *Cold Comfort*, **AP:** 44; *A Space Filled with Moving*, **AP:** 45

Andersson, Claes, **TE:** 560

Andrade, Carlos Drummond de. *See* Drummond de Andrade, Carlos

"Andrea del Sarto" (Browning), **BP:** 164

Andrei Bely Prize, **CM:** 47, **TE:** 867, **WP:** 409

Andrews, Claudia Emerson. *See* Emerson, Claudia

Andreyevna Gorenko, Anna. *See* Akhmatova, Anna

"Anecdotes, The" (Durrell), **BP:** 454

"Anfang." *See* "Beginning"

Angel Arms (Fearing), **AP:** 584

Ángel fieramente humano (Otero), **EP:** 761

Angel in the House, The (Patmore), **BP:** 987

Angel of History, The (Forché), **AP:** 616

Angelou, Maya, AP: 46-51; "America," **AP:** 50; "Song for the Old Ones," **AP:** 49; "Still I Rise," **AP:** 49

Angels and Earthly Creatures (Wylie), **AP:** 2242

Angels for the Burning (Mura), **AP:** 1394

Anglo-Mongrels and the Rose (Loy), **AP:** 1202

Anglophone poetry, Africa, **TE:** 16

Angry Penguin movement, **TE:** 32

Anhelli (Słowacki), **EP:** 978

Aniara (Martinson), **EP:** 683

Anile, Antonino, **TE:** 406

Animal de fondo (Jiménez), **EP:** 538

Animal Sense (Ackerman), **AP:** 3

"Animal, Vegetable, Mineral" (Bogan), **AP:** 202

Animals in That Country, The (Atwood), **BP:** 41

Ani-yun-wiya. *See* Glancy, Diane

Anna Snegina (Esenin), **WP:** 95

Annaeus Lucanus, Marcus. *See* Lucan

Annensky, Innokenty, TE: 518,
    WP: 21-25; "Depression," **WP:** 22;
    "The Double," **WP:** 22; "Poetry,"
    WP: 23; "The Steel Cicada,"
    WP: 24; "To a Poet," **WP:** 23

Annie Allen (Brooks), **AP:** 251

"Anniversary, The" (Pinsky), **AP:** 1546

Anno Domini MCMXXI (Akhmatova),
    WP: 6

Annunciations (Tomlinson), **BP:** 1274

Annus Mirabilis (Dryden), **BP:** 436

"Año lírico, El" (Darío), **WP:** 74

"Anonymous: Myself and Panguar"
    (Muldoon), **BP:** 942

Another Animal (Swenson), **AP:** 1936

Another Life (Walcott), **WP:** 320

"Anrufung des grossen Bären." *See*
    "Evocation of the Great Bear"

Antebellum Dream Book (Alexander),
    AP: 19

"Antéros" (Nerval), **EP:** 746

"Anthem" (Cohen), **BP:** 274

"Anthem for Doomed Youth" (Owen),
    BP: 982

Anthologie auf das Jahr 1782
    (Schiller), **EP:** 951

Anthology of New York Poets, A
    (anthology), **TE:** 675

Anthony, Florence. *See* Ai

Anti-Basilisk, The (Middleton),
    BP: 903

Anti-Platon (Bonnefoy), **EP:** 144

Antiquities of Rome, The (Du Bellay),
    EP: 291

Antschel, Paul. *See* Celan, Paul

Aphra Bayn. *See* Behn, Aphra

Apocalypse (Lawrence), **BP:** 801

Apollinaire, Guillaume, EP: 22-30,
    TE: 272; *Alcools*, **EP:** 27;
    Bestiary, **EP:** 27; *Calligrammes*,
    EP: 28; "The New Spirit and the
    Poets," **EP:** 23; poem about,
    EP: 1048

"Apollonius of Tyana" (Olson),
    AP: 1473

Apollonius Rhodius, EP: 30-35,
    TE: 328; *Argonautica*, **EP:** 31

"Apparently with no surprise"
    (Dickinson), **AP:** 461

Applause (Muske), **AP:** 1398

Apple That Astonished Paris, The
    (Collins), **AP:** 343

Applewhite, James, AP: 51-55; "A
    Conversation," **AP:** 54; *Daytime
    and Starlight*, **AP:** 54; *Following
    Gravity*, **AP:** 52; *Lessons in
    Soaring*, **AP:** 53; "A Place and a
    Voice," **AP:** 54; *River Writing*,
    AP: 52

"Apprehensions" (Duncan), **AP:** 514

Approaching Nada (Miller), **AP:** 1353

"Approaching Prayer" (Dickey),
    AP: 451

*Approximate Man, and Other
    Writings* (Tzara), **EP:** 1049

Approximate rhyme, defined,
    AP: 2294, **BP:** 1378, **EP:** 1172
    TE: 810, **WP:** 380,

April Galleons (Ashbery), **AP:** 62

Apuleius, Lucius, **TE:** 457

"Aquí." *See* "Here"

Arab (Słowacki), **EP:** 976

Aragon, Louis, EP: 35-42, **TE:** 274;
    "Elsa's Eyes," **EP:** 40; "Poem to
    Shout in the Ruins," **EP:** 39; "You
    Who Are the Rose," **EP:** 41

Arany, János, EP: 42-50, **TE:** 357;
    "Az elveszett alkótmany," **EP:** 44;
    The Death of King Buda, **EP:** 48;
    "Family Circle," **EP:** 46;
    "Midnight Duel," **EP:** 48;
    "Szondi's Two Pages," **EP:** 47;
    Toldi, **EP:** 44; "Török Bálint,"
    EP: 47; "The Welsh Bards,"
    EP: 47

Ararat (Glück), **AP:** 715

Arbor of Amorous Devices, The
    (Breton), **BP:** 127

Arcade (Hunt), **AP:** 939

Arcadia, One Mile (Abse), **BP:** 4

Archaeologist of Morning (Olsen),
    AP: 1475

Archeology of the Circle (Weigl),
    AP: 2104

Archer in the Marrow (Viereck),
    AP: 2046

Archetypal criticism, **TE:** 719-730

Archetype, **TE:** 192, **TE:** 719

Archetype, defined, **AP:** 2294,
    BP: 1378, **EP:** 1172, **TE:** 810,
    WP: 380

Archilochus, EP: 50-55, **TE:** 222,
    TE: 321; *Cologne Epode*, **EP:** 54;
    "On My Shield," **EP:** 53

Ardor (Bell), **AP:** 123

"Arfy i skripki" (Blok), **WP:** 36

Argentina. *See* Geographical Index

Argonautica (Apollonius Rhodius),
    EP: 31

Argote, Luis de Góngora y. *See*
    Góngora y Argote, Luis de

"Argument of His Book, The"
    (Herrick), **BP:** 628

Arias tristes (Jiménez), **EP:** 535

Aribau, Bonaventura Carles, **TE:** 51

Ariel (Plath), **TE:** 670

Ariosto, Ludovico, EP: 56-62,
    TE: 383; *Ariosto's Satyres*,
    EP: 60; *Orlando Furioso*, **EP:** 58,
    TE: 383

Ariosto's Satyres (Ariosto), **EP:** 60

Aristotle, **TE:** 700, **TE:** 743; *Poetics*,
    TE: 700

Ariwara no Narihira, **TE:** 416

Ark (Johnson), **AP:** 979

Arkansas Testament, The (Walcott),
    WP: 322

Armada of Thirty Whales, An
    (Hoffman), **AP:** 866

Arme Heinrich, Der (Hartmann),
    EP: 446

"Arms" (Beer), **BP:** 64

"Arms and the Boy" (Owen), **BP:** 981

Arnold, Matthew, BP: 30-37,
TE: 712; *Culture and Anarchy*,
TE: 731; "Dover Beach," **BP:** 35;
"The Scholar-Gipsy," **BP:** 34;
"Stanzas from the Grande
Chartreuse," **BP:** 35; "The Study
of Poetry," **TE:** 713; "Thyrsis,"
BP: 34; "To a Friend," **BP:** 33

Aronpuro, Kari, **TE:** 559

Arp, Hans, EP: 62-67; "I Am a
Horse," **EP:** 65; "In Space,"
EP: 66; "Kaspar Is Dead," **EP:** 65

Arrival of the Future, The (Fairchild),
AP: 580

Arrivants, The (Brathwaite), **AP:** 232

Arrivistes, The (Simpson), **AP:** 1795

Ars amatoria. See *Art of Love*

Ars poetica. See *Art of Poetry, The*
(Horace)

"Ars Poetica" (MacLeish), **AP:** 1250

"Art" (Gautier), **EP:** 375

Art for art's sake, **BP:** 721, **BP:** 1305,
EP: 82, **EP:** 88, **EP:** 296,
EP: 370, **TE:** 264; Italy, **TE:** 393;
Parnassians, **TE:** 639

Art of Blessing the Day, The (Piercy),
AP: 1535

Art of Drowning, The (Collins), **AP:** 344

Art of Love (Ovid), **EP:** 767

Art of Love, The (Koch), **AP:** 1061

"Art of Poetry, The" (Koch),
AP: 1062

Art of Poetry, The (Boileau-
Despréaux), **EP:** 140

Art of Poetry, The (Horace), **TE:** 702

Art of the Lathe, The (Fairchild),
AP: 581

Art poétique, L'. See *Art of Poetry,
The* (Boileau-Despréaux)

"Art poétique, L'" (Verlaine),
EP: 1095, **TE:** 642

*Arte nuevo de hacer comedias en este
tiempo, El.* See *New Art of
Writing Plays, The*

Artefactos (Parra), **WP:** 221

"Artémis" (Nerval), **EP:** 746

Arthurian legends, **TE:** 103, **TE:** 286

"Artist in the North, An"
(Tranströmer), **EP:** 1042

Arvon, Henri, **TE:** 761

"As I Walked Out One Evening"
(Auden), **BP:** 51

As If (Ciardi), **AP:** 316

As if It Matters (Grennan), **AP:** 743

"As the Team's Head-Brass"
(Thomas), **BP:** 1254

Ash Wednesday (Eliot), **BP:** 466

Ashbery, John, AP: 55-65, **TE:** 674;
And the Stars Were Shining,
AP: 62; *April Galleons*, **AP:** 62;
Houseboat Days, **AP:** 62; *Self-
Portrait in a Convex Mirror*,
AP: 60; *Some Trees*, **AP:** 57; *The
Tennis Court Oath*, **AP:** 59; *Three
Poems*, **AP:** 59; *A Wave*, **AP:** 62,
TE: 676; *Where Shall I Wander*,
AP: 63; *A Worldly Country*,
AP: 63; *Your Name Here*, **AP:** 63

"Ashes" (Saba), **EP:** 929

Ashes of Gramsci, The (Pasolini),
EP: 780

Asia Minor. See Geographical Index

Asian American culture. *See*
Categorized Index

Asian American poetry, **TE:** 21-29,
TE: 209

Asian-influenced poetry, **TE:** 192

"Ask Daddy, He Won't Know"
(Nash), **AP:** 1403

Ask Your Mama (Hughes), **AP:** 932

Aškerc, Anton, **TE:** 580

Aspects of Eve (Pastan), **AP:** 1515

Aspenström, Werner, **TE:** 549

Asphalt Georgics (Carruth), **AP:** 281

"Asphodel, That Greeny Flower"
(Williams), **AP:** 2182

"Associate Professor Delivers an
Exhortation to His Failing
Students, The" (Williams),
AP: 2170

Assumptions (Hacker), **AP:** 765

Astrea. *See* Behn, Aphra

Astronomers, The (Bowers), **AP:** 220

Astronomy of Love, The (Norris),
AP: 1430

Astrophel and Stella (Sidney),
BP: 1130

Astrov, Margot, **TE:** 481

Asylum in the Grasslands (Glancy),
AP: 704

At Redbones (Moss), **AP:** 1380

"At Rhodes" (Durrell), **BP:** 454

At Terror Street and Agony Way
(Bukowski), **AP:** 269

At the End of the Open Road
(Simpson), **AP:** 1796

"At the Executed Murderer's Grave"
(Wright), **AP:** 2226

"At the Great Wall of China"
(Blunden), **BP:** 107

"At the Theatre" (Cavafy), **EP:** 209

Atlantic Flyway (Galvin), **AP:** 647

"Atlantis" (Crane), **AP:** 386

Atlantis (Doty), **AP:** 483

Atoms, Soul Music, and Other Poems
(Wormser), **AP:** 2200

Atterbom, P. D. A., **TE:** 534

Atwood, Margaret, BP: 37-46,
TE: 40, **TE:** 502; *The Animals in
That Country*, **BP:** 41; *The Circle
Game*, **BP:** 40; *The Door*, **BP:** 45;
Interlunar, **BP:** 44; *The Journals
of Susanna Moodie*, **BP:** 41;
Morning in the Burned House,
BP: 45; *Power Politics*, **BP:** 43;
Procedures for Underground,
BP: 42; *True Stories*, **BP:** 44;
Two-Headed Poems, **BP:** 44; *You
Are Happy*, **BP:** 43

"Au beau demi-jour." *See* "In the
Lovely Half-light"

"Au lecteur." *See* "To the Reader"

"Au regard des divinités." *See* "In the
Eyes of the Gods"

"Aubade" (Empson), **BP:** 474

Aubade, defined, **AP:** 2294, **BP:** 1378, **EP:** 1172, **TE:** 810, **WP:** 380

Auden, W. H., **BP:** 47-55, **TE:** 653; *About the House*, **BP:** 53; *The Age of Anxiety*, **BP:** 52; "As I Walked Out One Evening," **BP:** 51; "Consider," **BP:** 50; "Herman Melville," **BP:** 52; "Lullaby," **BP:** 51; Stephen Spender, **BP:** 1185; "Tonight at Seven-Thirty," **BP:** 53

Auden, Wystan Hugh. *See* Auden, W. H.

Aue, Hartmann von. *See* Hartmann von Aue

Auf der Erde und in der Hölle (Bernhard), **EP:** 115

Auf eigene Hoffnung (Kunze), **EP:** 574

"August 19, Pad 19" (Swenson), **AP:** 1938

Augustan Age, English. *See* Categorized Index

Augustan Age, Roman, **TE:** 450. *See also* Categorized Index

Augustine, Saint, **TE:** 459

Aujourd'hui. See *Contemplations, Les*

Aunt Carmen's Book of Practical Saints (Mora), **AP:** 1374

Aurora Leigh (Browning), **BP:** 155

Ausländer, Rose, **AP:** 65-70

Ausonius, Decimus Magnus, **TE:** 460

Austerities (Simic), **AP:** 1788

Austin, J. L., **TE:** 757

Australia. *See* Geographical Index

Australian poetry, **TE:** 30-36, **TE:** 500

Austria. *See* Geographical Index

Autobiography of a Jukebox, The (Eady), **AP:** 524

Autobiography of Alice B. Toklas, The (Stein), **AP:** 1892

Autobiography of Red (Carson), **BP:** 227

Automatic writing, **EP:** 38

Autrefois. See *Contemplations, Les*

"Autumn Begins in Martins Ferry, Ohio" (Wright), **AP:** 2228

Autumn Grasses (Gibson), **AP:** 672

Autumn Journal (MacNeice), **BP:** 862

"Autumn Maneuvers" (Bachmann), **EP:** 75

"Autumnal, The" (Donne), **BP:** 411

Available Light (Booth), **AP:** 211

Available Light (Piercy), **AP:** 1534

Avant-garde poets; Italy, **TE:** 410; Japan, **TE:** 429. *See also* Categorized Index

"Ave Atque Vale" (Swinburne), **BP:** 1234

"Ave Maria" (Crane), **AP:** 382

Averno (Glück), **AP:** 717

Awakening (Stryk), **AP:** 1930

Awards, **AP:** 2321-2333, **BP:** 1408-1414, **CM:** 45-69, **EP:** 1205-1210, **TE:** 865-889, **WP:** 408-412

Awoonor, Kofi, **WP:** 25-32; *Latin American and Caribbean Notebook*, **WP:** 31; "The Sea Eats the Land at Home," **WP:** 29; "Songs of Sorrow," **WP:** 28; *Until the Morning After*, **WP:** 31; "We Have Found a New Land," **WP:** 30; "The Weaver Bird," **WP:** 29; "The Years Behind," **WP:** 30

Axe Handles (Snyder), **AP:** 1848

Axion Esti, The (Elytis), **EP:** 320, **TE:** 344

Ayala, Pedro López de, **TE:** 590

"Aye, There It Is! It Wakes To-night" (Brontë), **BP:** 142

"Az elveszett alkótmany" (Arany), **EP:** 44

Azorín, **TE:** 598

Azul (Darío), **WP:** 74

Azure (Esenin), **WP:** 94

"B Negative" (Kennedy), **AP:** 1022

"Babii Yar" (Yevtushenko), **WP:** 344

Babits, Mihály, **EP:** 68-72, **TE:** 359; *Jónás könyve*, **EP:** 71

Baca, Jimmy Santiago, **AP:** 71-76; *C-Train (Dream Boy's Story) and Thirteen Mexicans*, **AP:** 75; *Healing Earthquakes*, **AP:** 75; *Immigrants in Our Own Land, and Selected Earlier Poems*, **AP:** 73; *Martin & Meditations on the South Valley*, **AP:** 73; *Que linda la brisa*, **AP:** 74; *Set This Book on Fire*, **AP:** 74; *Spring Poems Along the Rio Grande*, **AP:** 75; *Winter Poems Along the Rio Grande*, **AP:** 75

"Bacchus" (Empson), **BP:** 473

Bachmann, Ingeborg, **EP:** 72-77, **TE:** 311; "Autumn Maneuvers," **EP:** 75; "Borrowed Time," **EP:** 75; "Curriculum Vitae," **EP:** 74; "Early Noon," **EP:** 74; "Evocation of the Great Bear," **EP:** 75; *Die Gestundete Zeit*, **EP:** 74

Backsass (Chappell), **AP:** 306

Backtalk (Becker), **AP:** 111

"Bad Blood" (Rimbaud), **EP:** 901

"Bad Time for Poetry" (Brecht), **EP:** 154

Bagel Shop Jazz (Kaufman), **AP:** 1004

Baggesen, Jens, **TE:** 533

Bai hua (Chinese vernacular), **TE:** 55

Bajza, Jozef Ignác, **TE:** 574

Baker, David, **AP:** 77-81; *After the Reunion*, **AP:** 79; *Laws of the Land*, **AP:** 78; *Midwest Eclogue*, **AP:** 79; *Sweet Home, Saturday Night*, **AP:** 78; *The Truth About Small Towns*, **AP:** 79

Bakhtin, Mikhail, **TE:** 760

Balaban, John, **AP:** 81-85; "After Our War," **AP:** 82; *Path, Crooked*

Path, **AP:** 83; "Sitting on Blue
Mountain . . .," **AP:** 83; "Words
for My Daughter," **AP:** 83
"Balada de la placeta." *See* "Ballad of
the Little Square"
Baladas de primavera (Jiménez),
EP: 536
"Balancing Act" (Pastan), **AP:** 1516
Balassi, Bálint, **TE:** 353
Balcony Tree, The (Middleton),
BP: 903
"Ballad" (Khodasevich), **WP:** 136
"Ballad of East and West, The"
(Kipling), **BP:** 765
Ballad of Reading Gaol, The (Wilde),
BP: 1308
"Ballad of the Children of the Czar,
The" (Schwartz), **AP:** 1741
"Ballad of the Despairing Husband"
(Creeley), **AP:** 396
"Ballad of the Harp-Weaver, The"
(Millay), **AP:** 1347
"Ballad of the Little Square" (García
Lorca), **EP:** 359
"Ballad of the Lost Andalusian"
(Alberti), **EP:** 11
"Ballad of the Oedipus Complex"
(Durrell), **BP:** 456
"Ballad of William Sycamore, The"
(Benét), **AP:** 126
"Ballad upon a Wedding, A"
(Suckling), **BP:** 1211
Ballade, **TE:** 244
Ballade, defined, **AP:** 2295,
BP: 1379, **EP:** 1173, **TE:** 811,
WP: 381
*Ballade at the Reverence of Our Lady,
Qwene of Mercy* (Lydgate),
BP: 837
*Ballades en jargon. See Poems in
Slang*
Ballads; England, **TE:** 167; fifteenth
century, **TE:** 125; Scandinavian,
TE: 528. *See also* Categorized
Index

Ballads (Stevenson), **BP:** 1204
Ballads, and Other Poems
(Longfellow), **AP:** 1161
Ballads, defined, **AP:** 2295,
BP: 1379, **EP:** 1173, **TE:** 811,
WP: 381
Ballistics (Collins), **AP:** 346
Balls for a One-Armed Juggler
(Layton), **BP:** 810
Balmont, Konstantin, **TE:** 517
Baltics (Tranströmer), **EP:** 1042
"Bananas" (Cervantes), **AP:** 302
Bandit, The (Hood), **BP:** 654
Bang, Mary Jo, AP: 85-89; *Elegy*,
AP: 88; *The Eye Like a Strange
Balloon*, **AP:** 87
"Banshee, The" (Morgenstern),
EP: 730
Banville, Théodore de, **TE:** 265
Baptism of Desire (Erdrich), **AP:** 556
Baraka, Amiri, AP: 89-100, **TE:** 3;
"Africa Africa Africa," **AP:** 95;
AM/TRAK, **AP:** 96; "Crow Jane,"
AP: 93; "Duncan Spoke of a
Process," **AP:** 92; "It's Nation
Time," **AP:** 95; "Leroy," **AP:** 93;
Un Poco Low Coup, **AP:** 98; "A
Poem Some People Will Have to
Understand," **AP:** 95; *Somebody
Blew Up America, and Other
Poems*, **AP:** 97
Barańczak, Stanisław, EP: 77-80;
The Weight of the Body, **EP:** 79
Barbarian in Asia, A (Michaux),
EP: 691
Barbarian Odes (Carducci), **EP:** 189
Barbour, John, **TE:** 109
Barca, Pedro Calderón de la. *See*
Calderón de la Barca, Pedro
"Bard, The" (Gray), **BP:** 547
Bard poetry, Russia, **TE:** 524
*Bar-do thos-sgrol. See Tibetan Book
of the Dead, The*
Bare Hills, The (Winters), **AP:** 2187
Bark (Popa), **EP:** 857

Barker, Jane, **TE:** 624
Barn Fever, and Other Poems
(Davison), **AP:** 440
Barnard, Mary, AP: 100-107;
Collected Poems, **AP:** 101; "Fable
from the Cayoosh Country,"
AP: 105; "Inheritance," **AP:** 104;
"Lethe," **AP:** 105; "Ondine,"
AP: 104; "Persephone," **AP:** 104;
"Playroom," **AP:** 101; "The
Rapids," **AP:** 103; "Shoreline,"
AP: 102; "The Spring," **AP:** 103;
Time and the White Tigress,
AP: 105; "Winter Evening,"
AP: 103
Barnes, Jim, **TE:** 692
Baron Buckhurst. *See* Sackville,
Thomas
Baronet Scott, First. *See* Scott, Sir
Walter
Baroque poetry, **TE:** 151; France,
TE: 251; Germany, **TE:** 292;
Hungary, **TE:** 353; Poland,
TE: 490; Sweden, **TE:** 530
"Barred Owl, A" (Wilbur), **AP:** 2158
Barrett, Elizabeth. *See* Browning,
Elizabeth Barrett
Barrons Wars, The (Drayton),
BP: 420
Base meter, defined, **AP:** 2295,
BP: 1379, **EP:** 1173, **TE:** 811,
WP: 381
Bashō. *See* Matsuo Bashō
Basoalto, Neftalí Ricardo Reyes. *See*
Neruda, Pablo
"Bateau ivre, Le." *See* "Drunken
Boat, The"
Batiushkov, Konstantin, **TE:** 511
Battaile of Agincourt, The (Drayton),
BP: 423
Battered Wife, and Other Poems, The
(Davie), **BP:** 374
"Battle-Piece" (Belitt), **AP:** 117
Battle-Pieces and Aspects of the War
(Melville), **AP:** 1297

Baudelaire, Charles, **EP:** 80-87,
TE: 266, TE: 640, TE: 753;
"Beacons," **EP:** 83; "A Carcass,"
EP: 83; "Correspondences,"
TE: 640; *Flowers of Evil*, **EP:** 82,
TE: 266;
"Heautontimoroumenos," **EP:** 86;
Paris Spleen, 1869, **EP:** 86; "The
Poor Child's Plaything," **EP:** 86;
"The Swan," **EP:** 85; "To the
Reader," **EP:** 83; "The Trip,"
EP: 86

Baudouin, Marcel and Pierre. *See*
Péguy, Charles-Pierre

"Beacons" (Baudelaire), **EP:** 83

Beastly Tales from Here and There
(Seth), **WP:** 275

Beat generation, TE: 203, TE: 661-
667

Beat poets. *See* Categorized Index

Beatnik, definition of, TE: 665

Beatty, Paul, **AP:** 107-110; *Big Bank
Take Little Bank*, **AP:** 108; *Joker,
Joker, Deuce*, **AP:** 109

"Beautiful, Pitiless Lady, The"
(Chartier), **EP:** 238

Beautiful Wreckage (Ehrhart),
AP: 535

"Beautiful Youth" (Benn), **EP:** 109

Beauty of the Husband, The (Carson),
BP: 227

Beauvoir, Simone de, TE: 774

"Because I could not stop for Death"
(Dickinson), **AP:** 463

Becher, Johannes R., TE: 307

Becker, Robin, **AP:** 110-114; *All-
American Girl*, **AP:** 111;
Backtalk, **AP:** 111; *Domain of
Perfect Affection*, **AP:** 113;
Giacometti's Dog, **AP:** 111; *The
Horse Fair*, **AP:** 113; *Personal
Effects*, **AP:** 111

Beckett, Samuel, **EP:** 87-95; *Echo's
Bones and Other Precipitates*,
EP: 92; "Enueg I," **EP:** 92;

"Sanies I," **EP:** 93; "Something
There," **EP:** 93; *Whoroscope*,
EP: 90

Bécquer, Gustavo Adolfo, **EP:** 95-
101, TE: 597; *The Rhymes*,
EP: 98; "Rime of the Swallows,"
EP: 100

Beddoes, Thomas Lovell, **BP:** 56-
60; *Bride's Tragedy, The*, **BP:** 58;
Death's Jest-Book, **BP:** 59;
"Dream Pedlary," **BP:** 59; *The
Improvisatore*, **BP:** 58; *The
Second Brother*, **BP:** 58

Bedford, Donald F. *See* Fearing,
Kenneth

Beer, Patricia, **BP:** 60-66; "Arms,"
BP: 64; "Called Home," **BP:** 63;
"The Clock," **BP:** 63; "Dilemma,"
BP: 62; *The Estuary*, **BP:** 64;
"The Eyes of the World," **BP:** 63;
"Female, Extinct," **BP:** 65;
"Home," **BP:** 65; *Selected Poems*,
BP: 62; "Self-Help," **BP:** 65

"Before an Old Painting of the
Crucifixion" (Momaday),
AP: 1360

Before Disaster (Winters), **AP:** 2189

Before It's Light (Lifshin), **AP:** 1140

Before Sleep (Booth), **AP:** 212

Before the Brave (Patchen), **AP:** 1523

Beforelife, The (Wright), **AP:** 2219

Begin Again (Paley), **AP:** 1508

"Beginning" (Novalis), **EP:** 752

Beginning and the End, The (Jeffers),
AP: 970

"Beginnings" (Hayden), **AP:** 823

Behind My Eyes (Lee), **AP:** 1106

Behn, Aphra, **BP:** 66-73, TE: 624;
Abdelazar, **BP:** 70; "The
Disappointment," **BP:** 71; "Love in
fantastic triumph sate," **BP:** 70;
"On the Death of Edmund Waller,"
BP: 71; "On the Death of the Late
Earl of Rochester," **BP:** 71

Bei Dao, TE: 67

Belaya staya (Akhmatova), **WP:** 6

*Belfry of Bruges, and Other Poems,
The* (Longfellow), **AP:** 1161

Belgium. *See* Geographical Index

"Believe It" (Logan), **AP:** 1156

Belinsky, Vissarion, TE: 515

Belitt, Ben, **AP:** 114-119; "Battle-
Piece," **AP:** 117; "Departures,"
AP: 116; *The Double Witness*,
AP: 117; *The Enemy Joy*,
AP: 117; *The Five-Fold Mesh*,
AP: 116; "The Habit of Angels,"
AP: 116; *Nowhere but Light*,
AP: 117; "The Orange Tree,"
AP: 117; *Possessions*, **AP:** 118;
"This Scribe My Hand," **AP:** 118;
"Walker," **AP:** 118; *Wilderness
Stair*, **AP:** 116

Bell, Ellis. *See* Brontë, Emily

Bell, Marvin, **AP:** 119-124; *Ardor*,
AP: 123; *The Book of the Dead
Man*, **AP:** 123; *Escape into You*,
AP: 122; *A Probable Volume of
Dreams*, **AP:** 122; *Residue of
Song*, **AP:** 122; *Stars Which See,
Stars Which Do Not See*, **AP:** 122;
These Green-Going-to-Yellow,
AP: 122

Bellay, Joachim du. *See* Du Bellay,
Joachim

"Belle Dame sans merci, La." *See*
"Beautiful, Pitiless Lady, The"

Bellman, Carl Michael, TE: 531

Belloc, Hilaire, **BP:** 73-79; "The End
of the Road," **BP:** 78; "Heroic
Poem in Praise of Wine," **BP:** 76;
"On a Dead Hostess," **BP:** 77; "To
Dives," **BP:** 78; "Your life is like a
little winter's day," **BP:** 78

Bellocq's Ophelia (Trethewey),
AP: 1996

"Bells for John Whiteside's
Daughter" (Ransom), **AP:** 1607

"Bells of San Blas, The"
(Longfellow), **AP:** 1161

Bellum civile. See *Pharsalia*

Beloved Infidel (Young), **AP:** 2259

Bembo, Pietro, **EP:** 101-107,
TE: 398; "A Curly Hair of Gold,"
EP: 105; "De Galeso et Maximo,"
EP: 106; *Gli Asolani*, **EP:** 104;
Rime, **EP:** 105

"Ben venga maggio." *See* "Oh,
Welcome May"

Bending the Bow (Duncan), **AP:** 515

"Beneath the Shadow of the Freeway"
(Cervantes), **AP:** 300

Benediktsson, Einar, **TE:** 541

Benét, Stephen Vincent, **AP:** 124-
128; "The Ballad of William
Sycamore," **AP:** 126; *John
Brown's Body*, **AP:** 126; "The
Mountain Whippoorwill,"
AP: 126; *Tiger Joy*, **AP:** 126;
Western Star, **AP:** 127

Benét, William Rose, **AP:** 128-132;
The Dust Which Is God, **AP:** 131;
Merchants from Cathay, **AP:** 131;
The Stairway of Surprise, **AP:** 131

Bengali poetry. *See* Indian English
poetry

Beniowski (Słowacki), **EP:** 978

Benjamin, David. *See* Slavitt, David

Benjamin, Walter, **TE:** 760

Benn, Gottfried, **EP:** 107-112,
TE: 307; "Beautiful Youth,"
EP: 109; "Departure," **EP:** 110;
"Lost Self," **EP:** 110; "One
Word," **EP:** 109

Bennett, Louise, **TE:** 44

"Bent Tree, The" (Manger), **EP:** 655

Beowulf, **TE:** 225

Berggren, Tobias, **TE:** 554

"Bernard and Sarah" (Taylor),
AP: 1971

Bernhard, Thomas, **EP:** 112-119;
Auf der Erde und in der Hölle,
EP: 115; *In hora mortis*, **EP:** 116;
Die Irren-die Häftlinge, **EP:** 117;
"Der Tag der Gesichter," **EP:** 115;

Unter dem Eisen des Mondes,
EP: 117

Bernolák, Antonín, **TE:** 574

Bernolák movement, **TE:** 574

Bernstein, Charles, **AP:** 132-136;
All the Whiskey in Heaven,
AP: 135; *Girly Man*, **AP:** 135;
Poetic Justice, **AP:** 134; *The
Sophist*, **AP:** 135; *With Strings*,
AP: 135

Berrigan, Daniel, **AP:** 137-143;
False Gods, Real Men, **AP:** 140;
Prison Poems, **AP:** 141; *Time
Without Number*, **AP:** 139

Berrigan, Ted, **AP:** 143-146;
Personal Poems, **AP:** 145; *The
Sonnets*, **AP:** 145

Berry, Wendell, **AP:** 146-155,
TE: 692; *The Broken Ground*,
AP: 149; *Clearing*, **AP:** 151; *The
Country of Marriage*, **AP:** 151;
Farming, **AP:** 151; *Findings*,
AP: 150; *Given*, **AP:** 153; *The
Kentucky River*, **AP:** 150;
Openings, **AP:** 151; *A Part*,
AP: 152; *Sabbaths*, **AP:** 152; *The
Wheel*, **AP:** 152

Berryman, John, **AP:** 155-162,
TE: 197; *Berryman's Sonnets*,
AP: 158; *The Dream Songs*,
AP: 160, **TE:** 198; *Homage to
Mistress Bradstreet*, **AP:** 159

Berryman's Sonnets (Berryman),
AP: 158

Bertin, Antoine, **TE:** 258

Beside the River Sar (Castro),
EP: 195

Best Hour of the Night, The
(Simpson), **AP:** 1798

Bestiary (Apollinaire), **EP:** 27

Betjeman, John, **BP:** 80-86; "Death
in Leamington," **BP:** 82; "Group
Life," **BP:** 84; "The Heart of
Thomas Hardy," **BP:** 83; "How to
Get on in Society," **BP:** 84;

"Ireland with Emily," **BP:** 83;
"The Olympic Girl," **BP:** 83

Betocchi, Carlo, **TE:** 406

Between Our Selves (Lorde),
AP: 1169

Beyond Silence (Hoffman), **AP:** 869

Bhatt, Sujata, **TE:** 375

Bicycles (Giovanni), **AP:** 700

Bidart, Frank, **AP:** 162-169; *The
Book of the Body*, **AP:** 164;
Desire, **AP:** 167; *Golden State*,
AP: 163; *In the Western Night*,
AP: 166; *Music Like Dirt*,
AP: 167; *The Sacrifice*, **AP:** 165;
Star Dust, **AP:** 168; *Watching the
Spring Festival*, **AP:** 168

Bidón, Luis Cernuda y. *See* Cernuda,
Luis

Biedermeier, **TE:** 299

Biermann, Wolf, **EP:** 119-126;
Affenfels und Barrikade, **EP:** 124;
Deutschland, **EP:** 123; *Für meine
Genossen*, **EP:** 123; *Heimat*,
EP: 125; *Mit Marx-und
Engelszungen*, **EP:** 123; *Paradies
uff Erden*, **EP:** 125; *Preussischer
Ikarus*, **EP:** 123; *Verdrehte Welt*,
EP: 124; *The Wire Harp*, **EP:** 122

Biernat of Lublin, **TE:** 489

Big Bank Take Little Bank (Beatty),
AP: 108

Big-Leg Music (Kirby), **AP:** 1041

Big Nose (Slavitt), **AP:** 1814

Bilingual Review (journal), **TE:** 466

Biographia Literaria (Coleridge),
TE: 710

Biography (Milarepa), **TE:** 609

Biography of Traman (Scott),
AP: 1748

"Bird, The" (Paz), **WP:** 232

Bird Catcher, The (Ponsot), **AP:** 1571

"Birdbrain" (Ginsberg), **AP:** 684

Birds (Perse), **EP:** 805

"Birds of Passage" (Longfellow),
AP: 1162

Birds, Beasts, and Flowers
　(Lawrence), **BP:** 799
Birmingham, Marie. *See* Ponsot,
　Marie
Birney, Earle, BP: 86-91; "David,"
　BP: 88; "For George Lamming,"
　BP: 90; "Trial of a City," **BP:** 89
Birthday Letters (Hughes), **BP:** 693,
　TE: 198
Bishop, Elizabeth, AP: 169-176;
　"The Fish," **AP:** 171; "In the
　Waiting Room," **AP:** 175; "The
　Man-Moth," **AP:** 172; "The Map,"
　AP: 174; "The Monument,"
　AP: 173; "Objects and
　Apparitions," **AP:** 172; "Over
　2000 Illustrations and a Complete
　Concordance," **AP:** 172;
　Questions of Travel, **AP:** 172;
　"The Riverman," **AP:** 173;
　"Sandpiper," **AP:** 171
Bishop, John Peale, AP: 177-180;
　"Fiametta," **AP:** 178; "The Hours,"
　AP: 179; "In the Dordogne,"
　AP: 178; "Metamorphoses of M,"
　AP: 178; *Now with His Love*,
　AP: 178; "Speaking of Poetry,"
　AP: 178; "A Subject of Sea
　Change," **AP:** 179; "Young Men
　Dead," **AP:** 178
"Bishop Blougram's Apology"
　(Browning), **BP:** 163
"Bishop Orders His Tomb at St.
　Praxed's Church, The"
　(Browning), **BP:** 162
Bitter Angel (Gerstler), **AP:** 661
Bitterfeld movement, **TE:** 88
Bjartmarsson, Sigfús, **TE:** 562
Björling, Gunnar, **TE:** 545
Bjørnson, Bjørnstjerne, **TE:** 538
Bjørnvig, Thorkild, **TE:** 551
Black Armour (Wylie), **AP:** 2242
Black Arts movement, **TE:** 6-7. *See
　also* Harlem Renaissance;
　Categorized Index

Black Christ, The (Cullen), **AP:** 408
Black Drum (Shomer), **AP:** 1771
Black Fire (anthology), **TE:** 7
Black Hair (Soto), **AP:** 1864
Black Heralds, The (Vallejo),
　WP: 303
Black Man Abroad (Emanuel),
　AP: 540
"Black Man Talks of Reaping, A"
　(Bontemps), **AP:** 208
Black Mountain poets. *See*
　Categorized Index
Black Mountain School, **TE:** 684-689
Black Pride (Madhubuti), **AP:** 1269
Black Skin, White Masks (Fanon),
　TE: 770
Black Unicorn, The (Lorde),
　AP: 1169
"Black Woman" (Senghor), **WP:** 269
Blackberries Picked Off Many Bushes
　(Allingham), **BP:** 29
Blackburn, Paul, AP: 180-188,
　TE: 688; *Against the Silences*,
　AP: 186; *Brooklyn-Manhattan
　Transit*, **AP:** 186; "Call It the
　Net," **AP:** 185; "December
　Journal: 1968," **AP:** 187; *Early
　Selected y Mas*, **AP:** 183; "How to
　Get Through Reality," **AP:** 184;
　"Lines, Trees, and Words,"
　AP: 185; "Mestrović and the
　Trees," **AP:** 184; "The Net of
　Moon," **AP:** 185; "The Purse
　Seine," **AP:** 185; *The Reardon
　Poems*, **AP:** 187; "Ritual I,"
　AP: 184; "Ritual IV," **AP:** 185
"Blackstone Rangers, The" (Brooks),
　AP: 252
Blake, Nicholas. *See* Day Lewis,
　Cecil
Blake, William, BP: 91-103,
　TE: 166, **TE:** 177, **TE:** 631;
　America, **BP:** 99; Beat generation,
　TE: 662; *The Book of Ahania*,
　BP: 100; *The Book of Los*,

BP: 100; *The Book of Thel*,
　BP: 96; *Europe*, **BP:** 99; *The
　First Book of Urizen*, **BP:** 100;
　The Four Zoas, **BP:** 101; *The
　French Revolution*, **BP:** 99;
　Jerusalem, **BP:** 102; *The
　Marriage of Heaven and Hell*,
　BP: 97; *Milton*, **BP:** 102; "The
　Sick Rose," **TE:** 720; *The Song of
　Los*, **BP:** 100; *Songs of Innocence
　and of Experience*, **BP:** 95;
　*Visions of the Daughters of
　Albion*, **BP:** 101
Blanco (Paz), **WP:** 234
Blank Verse (Lamb), **BP:** 771
Blank verse, defined, **AP:** 2295,
　BP: 1379, **EP:** 1173, **TE:** 811,
　WP: 381
"Blasphemies" (MacNeice), **BP:** 860
"Blazon" (Darío), **WP:** 75
"Blessed Damozel, The" (Rossetti),
　BP: 1068
"Blessing, The" (Kizer), **AP:** 1051
"Blessing, A" (Wright), **AP:** 2230
"Blessing of Women, A" (Kunitz),
　AP: 1090
Blessing the Boats (Clifton), **AP:** 329
Blizzard of One (Strand), **AP:** 1924
Blocks and Tackles (Murray),
　BP: 950
Blok, Aleksandr, TE: 518, **WP:** 33-
　39; "Arfy i skripki," **WP:** 36;
　"Gorod," **WP:** 36; "I Go into
　Darkened Temples," **WP:** 37; "I
　Have a Premonition of You,"
　WP: 37; *Nechayannaya radost*,
　WP: 37; *The Twelve*, **WP:** 38
Blood and Family (Kinsella), **BP:** 757
"Blood-birth" (Lorde), **AP:** 1169
Blood, Tin, Straw (Olds), **AP:** 1461
Bloodlines (Wright), **AP:** 2210
Bloomfield, Leonard, **TE:** 750
"Blow, The" (Seifert), **EP:** 966
Blowing of the Seed, The (Everson),
　AP: 573

Blue Garden (Howes), **AP:** 923

Blue Hour (Forché), **AP:** 616

Blue Juniata (Cowley), **AP:** 373

Blue Legends (Dučić), **EP:** 296

"Blue Meridian" (Toomer), **AP:** 1993

Blue Swallows, The (Nemerov),
    AP: 1413

Blue Wine, and Other Poems
    (Hollander), **AP:** 882

Blues (Giovanni), **AP:** 699

Blues Don't Change, The (Young),
    AP: 2254

Blues If You Want (Matthews),
    AP: 1288

Blunden, Edmund, BP: 104-108;
    "At the Great Wall of China,"
    BP: 107; *Poems, 1914-1930,*
    BP: 105; *The Shepherd, and
    Other Poems of Peace and War,*
    BP: 106; *Undertones of War,*
    BP: 107

Bly, Robert, AP: 188-197; *The Light
    Around the Body,* **AP:** 191; *Loving
    a Woman in Two Worlds,* **AP:** 194;
    The Man in the Black Coat Turns,
    AP: 194; *The Morning Glory,*
    AP: 192; *Morning Poems,*
    AP: 194; *My Sentence Was a
    Thousand Years of Joy,* **AP:** 195;
    *The Night Abraham Called to the
    Stars,* **AP:** 195; *Selected Poems,*
    AP: 194; *Silence in the Snowy
    Fields,* **AP:** 190; *Sleepers Joining
    Hands,* **AP:** 192; *This Body Is
    Made of Camphor and
    Gopherwood,* **AP:** 193; *This Tree
    Will Be Here for a Thousand
    Years,* **AP:** 193

Bo Juyi, **TE:** 62

Boat of Quiet Hours, The (Kenyon),
    AP: 1030

Bobrowski, Johannes, EP: 126-131;
    "Always to Be Named," **EP:** 129;
    "Language," **EP:** 129

Boccaccio, Giovanni, EP: 131-134,

TE: 102, **TE:** 380; *The Book of
Theseus,* **EP:** 134; *The Filostrato,*
    EP: 133

Bodmer, Johann Jakob, **TE:** 294

"Body" (Pinter), **BP:** 1004

Body of Life (Alexander), **AP:** 19

Boethius, **TE:** 461

Bogan, Louise, AP: 197-205;
    "Animal, Vegetable, Mineral,"
    AP: 202; "Exhortation," **AP:** 203;
    "Henceforth, from the Mind,"
    AP: 203; "Pain Has an Element of
    Blank," **AP:** 203; "Simple
    Autumnal," **AP:** 203; "Women,"
    AP: 199

"Bogland" (Heaney), **BP:** 597

Bohemia, **TE:** 78. *See also*
    Geographical Index

Boiardo, Matteo Maria, EP: 135-
    138, **TE:** 382; *Orlando
    Innamorato,* **EP:** 137, **TE:** 383;
    Trionfi, **EP:** 136

**Boileau-Despréaux, Nicolas,
    EP:** 138-141, **TE:** 251; *The Art of
    Poetry,* **EP:** 140; *Le Lutrin,*
    EP: 139; *Traité du sublime,*
    EP: 140

Boitempo (Drummond de Andrade),
    WP: 82

Boland, Eavan, BP: 108-119,
    TE: 210; *Against Love Poetry,*
    BP: 116; *Domestic Violence,*
    BP: 117; *In a Time of Violence,*
    BP: 116; *In Her Own Image,*
    BP: 111; *The Journey, and Other
    Poems,* **BP:** 114; *The Lost Land,*
    BP: 116; *Night Feed,* **BP:** 110

Boleros (Wright), **AP:** 2238

Bolivia. *See* Geographical Index

Bollingen Prize in Poetry, **AP:** 2322,
    CM: 47, **TE:** 867

"Bolond Istók" (Petőfi), **EP:** 825

Bond, Tess. *See* Gallagher, Tess

Bone Pallace Ballet (Bukowski),
    AP: 272

"Bonjour Monsieur Soutine" (Kiwus),
    TE: 316

Bonnefoy, Yves, EP: 142-149,
    TE: 280; *Anti-Platon,* **EP:** 144;
    Le Cœur-espace, **EP:** 147; *The
    Curved Planks,* **EP:** 147; *Hier
    régnant désert,* **EP:** 145; *La
    Longue chaîne de l'ancre,*
    EP: 148; *On the Motion and
    Immobility of Douve,* **EP:** 144;
    Poèmes, **EP:** 146; *Words in Stone,*
    EP: 146

Bontemps, Arna, AP: 205-209; "A
    Black Man Talks of Reaping,"
    AP: 208; "Golgotha Is a
    Mountain," **AP:** 207; "Nocturne at
    Bethesda," **AP:** 207; "The
    Return," **AP:** 207

Book of Ahania, The (Blake), **BP:** 100

Book of Exercises (Seferis), **EP:** 960

"Book of Four Ladies, The"
    (Chartier), **EP:** 238

Book of Gods and Devils, The
    (Simic), **AP:** 1789

Book of Good Love, The (Juan Ruiz),
    TE: 588

Book of Hours, The (Rilke), **EP:** 893

Book of Images, The (Rilke), **EP:** 893

Book of Life (Madhubuti), **AP:** 1272

Book of Longing, The (Cohen),
    BP: 275

Book of Los, The (Blake), **BP:** 100

Book of Medicines, The (Hogan),
    AP: 875

Book of My Nights (Lee), **AP:** 1106

Book of Songs (Heine), **EP:** 455

Book of Songs, The (anthology),
    TE: 56

Book of the Body, The (Bidart), **AP:** 164

Book of the Dead Man, The (Bell),
    AP: 123

Book of the Duchess (Chaucer), **BP:** 247

Book of the Green Man, The
    (Johnson), **AP:** 978

Book of Thel, The (Blake), **BP:** 96

Book of Theseus, The (Boccaccio),
EP: 134

Booke of Ayres, A (Campion),
BP: 206

"Boot, The" (Giusti), **EP:** 394

Booth, Philip, **AP:** 209-215;
Available Light, **AP:** 211; *Before
Sleep,* **AP:** 212; "Dreamscape,"
AP: 211; *Letter from a Distant
Land,* **AP:** 210; *Lifelines,*
AP: 215; "Not to Tell Lies,"
AP: 212; "The Question Poem,"
AP: 213; "Reach Road," **AP:** 215;
Relations, **AP:** 212; *Selves,*
AP: 214; *Weathers and Edges,*
AP: 211

Borchers, Elisabeth, **TE:** 312,
TE: 317

Borges, Jorge Luis, **WP:** 39-44;
Dream Tigers, **WP:** 42; *Fervor de
Buenos Aires,* **WP:** 42; *The Gold
of Tigers,* **WP:** 42

Born to Slow Horses (Brathwaite),
AP: 237

"Born Yesterday" (Larkin), **BP:** 790

Borough, The (Crabbe), **BP:** 333

"Borrowed Time" (Bachmann),
EP: 75

Boscán, Juan, **TE:** 592

Bosnia and Herzegovina. *See*
Geographical Index

Boss Cupid (Gunn), **BP:** 567

Bothie of Tober-na-Vuolich, The
(Clough), **BP:** 268

Bottoms, David, **AP:** 216-219; *In a
U-Haul North of Damascus,*
AP: 217; *Shooting Rats at the
Bibb County Dump,* **AP:** 217;
Under the Vulture-Tree, **AP:** 217;
Vagrant Grace, **AP:** 218; *Waltzing
Through the Endtime,* **AP:** 218

Bounty, The (Walcott), **WP:** 324

"Bouteille à la mer, La" (Vigny),
EP: 1105

"Bouzouki music" (Hollo), **AP:** 889

Bowers, Edgar, **AP:** 219-222; *The
Astronomers,* **AP:** 220; *Collected
Poems,* **AP:** 222; *For Louis
Pasteur,* **AP:** 221; *The Form of
Loss,* **AP:** 220; *Living Together,*
AP: 221

Bowge of Court, The (Skelton),
BP: 1155

Bowles, William Lisle, **BP:** 119-124;
and Samuel Taylor Coleridge,
BP: 121; *Monody, Written at
Matlock,* **BP:** 123; *The Picture,*
BP: 123; *The Spirit of Discovery,*
BP: 123

"Boy at the Window" (Wilbur),
AP: 2156

Boyd, Nancy. *See* Millay, Edna St.
Vincent

Boye, Karin, **TE:** 544

Boylan, Josephine. *See* Jacobsen,
Josephine

Boys Who Stole the Funeral, The
(Murray), **BP:** 948

Bracken, Thomas, **TE:** 35

Bradstreet, Anne, **AP:** 223-228,
TE: 153, **TE:** 200;
"Contemplations," **AP:** 224; poem
about, **AP:** 159; *The Tenth Muse
Lately Sprung Up in America,*
AP: 223

"Brahma" (Emerson), **AP:** 549

Braided Creek (Harrison), **AP:** 812

"Brain" (Pagis), **WP:** 215

Brandes, Georg, **TE:** 537

Brandt, Jørgen Gustava, **TE:** 563

Brant, Sebastian, **TE:** 288

Brathwaite, Edward Kamau,
AP: 228-239, **TE:** 45; *Ancestors,*
AP: 234; *The Arrivants,* **AP:** 232;
Born to Slow Horses, **AP:** 237;
"Caliban," **AP:** 231; *DS (2),*
AP: 236; *Middle Passages,*
AP: 236; *Mother Poem,* **AP:** 234;
Sun Poem, **AP:** 235; *X/Self,*
AP: 235

"Bratsk Station" (Yevtushenko),
WP: 344

Brautigan, Richard, **AP:** 239-243;
*Loading Mercury with a
Pitchfork,* **AP:** 242; *The Pill
Versus the Springhill Mine
Disaster,* **AP:** 241; *Rommel
Drives on Deep into Egypt,*
AP: 242

Braving the Elements (Merrill),
AP: 1319

Brazil. *See* Geographical Index

Bread Without Sugar (Stern),
AP: 1902

*Breaking of the Day, and Other
Poems, The* (Davison), **AP:** 439

"Breaking Silence" (Mirikitani),
TE: 23

Breath (Levine), **AP:** 1126

Breathing Room (Davison), **AP:** 440

Breathing Tokens (Sandburg),
AP: 1710

Brébeuf and His Brethren (Pratt),
BP: 1019

Brecht, Bertolt, **EP:** 149-157,
TE: 309; "Bad Time for Poetry,"
EP: 154; *Buckower Elegies,*
EP: 155; "In Dark Times,"
EP: 153; "Legend of the Origin of
the Book Tao-Tê-Ching on Lao-
tzû's Road into Exile," **EP:** 154;
"Of Poor B. B.," **EP:** 153;
"Remembering Marie A.,"
EP: 153; "Song of the Fort
Donald Railroad Gang," **EP:** 152;
Svendborg Poems, **EP:** 154

Breitinger, Johann Jakob, **TE:** 294

Brentano, Clemens, **TE:** 299

Breton, André, **EP:** 157-162,
TE: 274; *Communicating Vessels,*
EP: 159; *Fata Morgana,* **EP:** 161;
Free Union, **EP:** 161; "In the Eyes
of the Gods," **EP:** 160; "In the
Lovely Half-light," **EP:** 160;
Manifesto of Surrealism, **EP:** 159

Breton, Nicholas, **BP:** 124-131; *The Arbor of Amorous Devices,* **BP:** 127; *Brittons Bowre of Delights,* **BP:** 127; *The Countess of Pembroke's Passion,* **BP:** 128; *The Longing of a Blessed Heart,* **BP:** 129; *Pasquils Fooles-Cappe,* **BP:** 129; *Pasquils Mad-Cappe, Throwne at the Corruptions of These Times,* **BP:** 129; *The Passionate Shepheard,* **BP:** 128; *The Phoenix Nest,* **BP:** 127; *Pilgrimage to Paradise,* **BP:** 128; *A Solemne Passion of the Soules Love,* **BP:** 129; "A Sweet Lullabie," **BP:** 128

Breytenbach, Breyten, **EP:** 162-169; *Die Huis van die dowe,* **EP:** 165; *Kouevuur,* **EP:** 166; *Lotus,* **EP:** 167; *Met ander woorde,* **EP:** 167; *Oorblyfsels,* **EP:** 167; *Sinking Ship Blues,* **EP:** 167; *The True Confessions of an Albino Terrorist,* **EP:** 168; *Windcatcher,* **EP:** 168; *Die Ysterkoei moet sweet,* **EP:** 165

"Bridal Measure, A" (Dunbar), **AP:** 504

Bridel, Bedřich, **TE:** 80

Brides of Reason (Davie), **BP:** 369

"Bride's Prelude, The" (Rossetti), **BP:** 1068

Bride's Tragedy, The (Beddoes), **BP:** 58

Bridge, The (Crane), **AP:** 381, **TE:** 196

Bridges, Robert, **BP:** 131-137; *The Growth of Love,* **BP:** 133; "London Snow," **BP:** 132; "Low Barometer," **BP:** 133; *Milton's Prosody,* **BP:** 135; "On a Dead Child," **BP:** 133; *Poems, Third Series,* **BP:** 132; *Poetical Works of Robert Bridges,* **BP:** 134; *The Testament of Beauty,* **BP:** 135

Brief Candles (Taylor), **AP:** 1972

Briggflatts (Bunting), **BP:** 171

"Bringing Up" (Harrison), **BP:** 590

"Bristowe Tragedie" (Chatterton), **BP:** 240

Britting, Georg, **TE:** 309

Brittons Bowre of Delights (Breton), **BP:** 127

Brockport, New York (Heyen), **AP:** 847

Brodsky, Joseph, **TE:** 523, **WP:** 44-51; "Aeneas and Dido," **WP:** 48; Anna Akhmatova, **WP:** 8; "A Halt in the Wilderness," **WP:** 49; *A Part of Speech,* **WP:** 49; *So Forth,* **WP:** 50; "Sonnet," **WP:** 47; *To Urania,* **WP:** 50

Broken Ground, The (Berry), **AP:** 149

Bronk, William, **AP:** 243-246; *Death Is the Place,* **AP:** 246; *The World, the Worldless,* **AP:** 245

Brontë, Emily, **BP:** 137-143; "Aye, There It Is! It Wakes To-night," **BP:** 142; "Julian M. to A. G. Rochelle," **BP:** 142; "No Coward Soul Is Mine," **BP:** 142; "Oh Thy Bright Eyes Must Answer Now," **BP:** 141; "The Philosopher," **BP:** 141; "Rosina Alcona to Julius Brenzaida," **BP:** 141

Bronze Horseman, The (Pushkin), **WP:** 242

Brooke, Rupert, **BP:** 144-149; *1914, and Other Poems,* **BP:** 147; "The Old Vicarage, Grantchester," **BP:** 146

Brooklyn-Manhattan Transit (Blackburn), **AP:** 186

Brooks, Gwendolyn, **AP:** 247-254, **TE:** 6; *Annie Allen,* **AP:** 251; "The Blackstone Rangers," **AP:** 252; "Men of Careful Turns," **AP:** 251; "The Mother," **AP:** 250; "Sermons on the Warpland,"

AP: 251; *A Street in Bronzeville,* **AP:** 250; "We Real Cool," **AP:** 249

"Broom, The" (Leopardi), **EP:** 616

"Brooms" (Simic), **AP:** 1787

Brorson, Hans Adolph, **TE:** 531

Brother Louis. *See* Merton, Thomas

Brother to Dragons (Warren), **AP:** 2099

"Brotherhood of Men" (Eberhart), **AP:** 530

Brotherly Love (Hoffman), **AP:** 868

Brothers, I Loved You All (Carruth), **AP:** 280

Brown, James Willie. *See* Komunyakaa, Yusef

Brown, Sterling A., **AP:** 254-259; "Frankie and Johnnie," **AP:** 257; "The Last Ride of Wild Bill," **AP:** 257; "Memphis Blues," **AP:** 258; "Negro Characters as Seen by White Authors," **AP:** 256; "Remembering Nat Turner," **AP:** 258; "Sister Lou," **AP:** 258; "Slim Greer," **AP:** 257; *Southern Road,* **AP:** 256; "Strong Men," **AP:** 257

Browne, Felicia Dorothea. *See* Hemans, Felicia Dorothea

Browning, Elizabeth Barrett, **BP:** 149-157; *Aurora Leigh,* **BP:** 155; *Casa Guidi Windows,* **BP:** 154; "The Dead Pan," **BP:** 154; "A Drama of Exile," **BP:** 153; *Poems,* **BP:** 153; *Poems: New Edition,* **BP:** 154; "The Seraph and the Poet," **BP:** 156; *The Seraphim, and Other Poems,* **BP:** 153

Browning, Robert, **BP:** 158-167; "Andrea del Sarto," **BP:** 164; "Bishop Blougram's Apology," **BP:** 163; "The Bishop Orders His Tomb at St. Praxed's Church," **BP:** 162; "Childe Roland to the

Dark Tower Came," **BP:** 165; *Dramatic Lyrics*, **BP:** 161; *Dramatic Romances*, **BP:** 162; *Men and Women*, **BP:** 163; "My Last Duchess," **BP:** 162; *The Old Yellow Book*, **BP:** 165; "Porphyria's Lover," **BP:** 161; *The Ring and the Book*, **BP:** 165

Bruchac, Joseph, **TE:** 486

"Brunettina mia, La." *See* "My Brunette"

Brut (Layamon), **BP:** 805

Brutal Imagination (Eady), **AP:** 524

Brutus's Orchard (Fuller), **BP:** 502

Bryant, William Cullen, AP: 259-264, **TE:** 636; "A Forest Hymn," **AP:** 262; "The Prairies," **AP:** 262; "Thanatopsis," **AP:** 261

Buch der Lieder. See *Book of Songs* (Hcinc)

Buch von der deutschen Poeterey, Das (Opitz), **TE:** 292

Buchanan, George, **TE:** 463

Buckhurst, Baron. *See* Sackville, Thomas

Buckower Elegies (Brecht), **EP:** 155

Bucolic Comedies (Sitwell), **BP:** 1148

Budowałam barykadę. See *Building the Barricade*

Bufera, La. See *Storm, and Other Poems, The*

"Building, The" (Larkin), **BP:** 792

Building the Barricade (Swir), **EP:** 1006

Bukovina. *See* Geographical Index

Bukowski, Charles, AP: 264-274; *At Terror Street and Agony Way*, **AP:** 269; *Bone Pallace Ballet*, **AP:** 272; *A Bukowski Sampler*, **AP:** 269; *Burning in Water, Drowning in Flame*, **AP:** 270; *Cold Dogs in the Courtyard*, **AP:** 269; *Crucifix in a Deathhand*, **AP:** 268; *Dangling in the Tournefortia*, **AP:** 272; *The*

Days Run Away Like Wild Horses over the Hills, **AP:** 269; *Flower, Fist, and Bestial Wail*, **AP:** 267; *The Genius of the Crowd*, **AP:** 268; *It Catches My Heart in Its Hand*, **AP:** 268; *The Last Generation*, **AP:** 272; *Last Night of the Earth Poems*, **AP:** 272; *Longshot Poems for Broke Players*, **AP:** 268; *Love Is a Dog from Hell*, **AP:** 271; *Mockingbird Wish Me Luck*, **AP:** 270; *Open All Night*, **AP:** 273; *Play the Piano Drunk Like a Percussion Instrument Until the Fingers Begin to Bleed a Bit*, **AP:** 271; *Poems Written Before Jumping out of an Eight Story Window*, **AP:** 269; *Run with the Hunted*, **AP:** 268; "The Twins," **AP:** 267

Bukowski Sampler, A (Bukowski), **AP:** 269

"Buladelah-Taree Holiday Song Cycle, The" (Murray), **BP:** 948

Bull, Olaf, **TE:** 542

Bundle of Myrrh, A (Neihardt), **AP:** 1406

Bunting, Basil, BP: 168-173; *Briggflatts*, **BP:** 171; *The Spoils*, **BP:** 171; "Villon," **BP:** 170

"Burden of Itys, The" (Wilde), **BP:** 1307

Burguillos, Tomé de. *See* Vega Carpio, Lope de

"Burial of Orgaz, The" (Ritsos), **EP:** 909

Buried City (Moss), **AP:** 1378

"Burning Babe, The" (Southwell), **BP:** 1181

"Burning Bush" (Untermeyer), **AP:** 2012

Burning in Water, Drowning in Flame (Bukowski), **AP:** 270

Burning Perch, The (MacNeice), **BP:** 864

"Burning Poem, The" (MacBeth), **BP:** 844

Burning the Empty Nests (Orr), **AP:** 1487

Burning the Fence (McDonald), **AP:** 1217

Burns, Robert, BP: 173-180, **TE:** 170, **TE:** 177; "The Cotter's Saturday Night," **BP:** 176; *Poems*, **BP:** 178; "Tam O' Shanter," **BP:** 179

Business of Fancydancing, The (Alexie), **AP:** 22

Bustos Domecq, H. *See* Borges, Jorge Luis

Bustos, F. *See* Borges, Jorge Luis

Butcher's Dozen (Kinsella), **BP:** 756

Butler, Judith, **TE:** 774

Butler, Samuel, BP: 180-185, **TE:** 622; *Hudibras*, **BP:** 182, **TE:** 622

"Butterfly" (Sachs), **EP:** 934

"Butterfly Piece" (Hayden), **AP:** 823

"By Candlelight" (Plath), **AP:** 1553

By Lingual Wholes (Cruz), **AP:** 402

Bylina (poetic form), **TE:** 509

Bynner, Witter, AP: 274-277; "The Dead Loon," **AP:** 276; "Epithalamium and Elegy," **AP:** 276; *Grenstone Poems*, **AP:** 276; "An Ode to Harvard," **AP:** 275

Byron, Lord, BP: 186-196, **TE:** 178, **TE:** 631; *Childe Harold's Pilgrimage*, **BP:** 191; *Don Juan*, **BP:** 193; *English Bards and Scotch Reviewers*, **BP:** 190; *Hours of Idleness*, **BP:** 189; poem about, **EP:** 991; "Remembrance," **BP:** 190

"Byzantium" (Yeats), **BP:** 1345, **TE:** 193

C-Train (Dream Boy's Story) and Thirteen Mexicans (Baca), **AP:** 75

Cables to Rage (Lorde), **AP:** 1168

Cables to the Ace (Merton), **AP:** 1330

Cadence, defined, **AP:** 2295,
    BP: 1379, **EP:** 1173, **TE:** 811,
    WP: 381

Cadenus and Vanessa (Swift),
    BP: 1223

Cædmon, BP: 197-201, **TE:** 226;
    "Hymn," **BP:** 198

Caeiro, Alberto. *See* Pessoa,
    Fernando

Caelica (Greville), **BP:** 558

Caesar, **TE:** 449

Caesura, defined, **AP:** 2295,
    BP: 1379, **EP:** 1173, **TE:** 811,
    WP: 381

Caged Owl, The (Orr), **AP:** 1491

Cai Yan, **TE:** 59

Cal y canto (Alberti), **EP:** 9

Calderón de la Barca, Pedro,
    EP: 170-174; "Decima," **EP:** 173;
    "Lágrimas que vierte un alma
    arrepentida," **EP:** 173; *Psalle et
    sile*, **EP:** 173

"Caliban" (Brathwaite), **AP:** 231

Caliban in Blue, and Other Poems
    (McDonald), **AP:** 1217

"Call It the Net" (Blackburn),
    AP: 185

Call Me Ishmael Tonight (Ali), **AP:** 27

"Called Home" (Beer), **BP:** 63

Calligrammes (Apollinaire), **EP:** 28,
    TE: 273

Callimachus, EP: 175-180, **TE:** 328;
    Aetia, **EP:** 177; Epigram 2 M.,
    EP: 178; Epigram 30 M.,
    EP: 176; *Hecale*, **EP:** 178;
    Hymns, **EP:** 178; *Iambi*, **EP:** 178

Calling Myself Home (Hogan),
    AP: 873

Calpurnius Siculus, Titus, **TE:** 456

"Cambodia" (Fenton), **BP:** 489

Camerata dei Bardi, **TE:** 385

Camões, Luís de, **EP:** 180-185; *The
    Lusiads*, **EP:** 182

Camouflage (Muske), **AP:** 1396

Camp Notes, and Other Writings
    (Yamada), **AP:** 2247

Campana, Dino, **TE:** 402

Campbell, Dorothy Parker. *See*
    Parker, Dorothy

Campbell, Roy, **TE:** 501

Campion, Thomas, BP: 202-208; *A
    Booke of Ayres*, **BP:** 206; *Lord
    Hay's Masque*, **BP:** 205; *The
    Lord's Masque*, **BP:** 206; *The
    Somerset Masque*, **BP:** 206

Campos de Castilla. See *Castilian
    Camp, The*

Campos, Álvaro de. *See* Pessoa,
    Fernando

Canada. *See* Geographical Index

Canadian poetry, **TE:** 37-42, **TE:** 501

"Canadians" (Gurney), **BP:** 571

"Cancer Cells" (Pinter), **BP:** 1004

"Canción de jinete." *See* "Song of the
    Horseman, The"

Cancionero (Unamuno y Jugo),
    EP: 1054

Cancionero sin nombre (Parra),
    WP: 219

Canciones rusas (Parra), **WP:** 220

"Candle, A" (Suckling), **BP:** 1209

Cane (Toomer), **AP:** 1990

Cankar, Ivan, **TE:** 580

Cannon Between My Knees, A
    (Allen), **AP:** 29

"Canonization, The" (Donne),
    BP: 411, **TE:** 746

Cantar de mío Cid. See *Poem of the
    Cid*

Cantares gallegos (Castro), **EP:** 194

Canterbury Tales, The (Chaucer),
    BP: 250, **TE:** 113

Canti (Leopardi), **EP:** 611

Canti di Castelvecchio (Pascoli),
    EP: 775

Canticle (Guillén), **EP:** 432

Cántico. See *Canticle*

Cántico cósmico. See *Music of the
    Spheres, The*

Cántico espiritual (Otero), **EP:** 761

Cantigas (poetic form), **TE:** 584

"Canto ao homem do povo Charlie
    Chaplin." *See* "Song to the Man of
    the People C. C."

Canto General (Neruda), **WP:** 202

Canto novo (D'Annunzio), **EP:** 267

Cantos (Pound), **AP:** 1581, **TE:** 195

*Cantos de vida y esperanza, los
    cisnes, y otros poemas* (Darío),
    WP: 75

Canvas (Zagajewski), **EP:** 1139

Canzoniere, Il (Saba), **EP:** 927

Cao Zhi, **TE:** 59

Cap de Bonne-Espérance, Le
    (Cocteau), **EP:** 256

Capacity (McMichael), **AP:** 1256

"Cape Hatteras" (Crane), **AP:** 383

Captain's Verses, The (Neruda),
    WP: 202

Captivity (Derricotte), **AP:** 447

"Car, The" (Carver), **AP:** 288

"Carcass, A" (Baudelaire), **EP:** 83

Cardenal, Ernesto, WP: 52-56;
    "Marilyn Monroe," **WP:** 54; *The
    Music of the Spheres*, **WP:** 55;
    "Zero Hour," **WP:** 54

Carducci, Giosuè, EP: 185-190,
    TE: 393; *Barbarian Odes*,
    EP: 189; *Giambi ed epodi*,
    EP: 189; "Hymn to Satan,"
    EP: 188; *Juvenilia*, **EP:** 188;
    Levia gravia, **EP:** 189; *The Lyrics
    and Rhythms*, **EP:** 190; *Nuove
    poesie*, **EP:** 189; "Song of Love,"
    EP: 189

Carew, Thomas, BP: 208-213;
    "Disdaine returned," **BP:** 211;
    "An Elegie upon the Death of the
    Deane of Pauls, Dr. John Donne,"
    BP: 211; "Song, To my inconstant
    Mistress," **BP:** 210; "Upon some
    Alterations in my Mistress, after

my Departure into France,"
    BP: 210
"Cargoes" (Masefield), **BP:** 887
Caribbean poetry, **TE:** 43-47
Carlyle, Thomas, **TE:** 731
Carmen Deo Nostro (Crashaw),
    BP: 339
Carminalenia (Middleton), **BP:** 903
Carner, Josep, **TE:** 52
Carnivore, The (Slavitt), **AP:** 1811
Carol (lyric form), **TE:** 124
Caroline Age. *See* Categorized Index
Carolingian Revival, **TE:** 462
Carpelan, Bo, **TE:** 553
Carpio, Lope de Vega. *See* Vega
    Carpio, Lope de
"Carrefour" (Reverdy), **EP:** 885
Carrier of Ladders, The (Merwin),
    AP: 1335
"Carrion Comfort" (Hopkins), **BP:** 675
Carroll, Lewis, **BP:** 213-225; *Alice's
    Adventures in Wonderland*,
    BP: 215; *The Hunting of the
    Snark*, **BP:** 220; "Jabberwocky,"
    AP: 2288, **BP:** 218, **BP:** 1372,
    EP: 1166, **TE:** 804, **WP:** 374;
    *Through the Looking-Glass and
    What Alice Found There*, **BP:** 217
Carruth, Hayden, **AP:** 278-284;
    "Adolf Eichmann," **AP:** 279;
    Asphalt Georgics, **AP:** 281;
    Brothers, I Loved You All,
    AP: 280; *Doctor Jazz*, **AP:** 282;
    "Freedom and Discipline,"
    AP: 280; *From Snow and Rock,
    from Chaos*, **AP:** 280; *If You Call
    This Cry a Song*, **AP:** 281; "On a
    Certain Engagement South of
    Seoul," **AP:** 279; *Scrambled Eggs
    and Whiskey*, **AP:** 282; *The
    Sleeping Beauty*, **AP:** 281; *Tell Me
    Again How the White Heron
    Rises . . .*, **AP:** 282; *Toward the
    Distant Islands*, **AP:** 283
Carson, Anne, **BP:** 225-228, **TE:** 40;

Autobiography of Red, **BP:** 227;
    The Beauty of the Husband,
    BP: 227; *Plainwater*, **BP:** 226
Carthage (Wormser), **AP:** 2202
Carus, Titus Lucretius. *See* Lucretius
Carver, Raymond, **AP:** 284-291;
    "The Car," **AP:** 288; *Fires*,
    AP: 287; Tess Gallagher,
    AP: 639; "Near Klamath,"
    AP: 287; *A New Path to the
    Waterfall*, **AP:** 289; "NyQuil,"
    AP: 288; *Ultramarine*, **AP:** 287;
    "Winter Insomnia," **AP:** 287
Casa Guidi Windows (Browning),
    BP: 154
Casabianca (Hemans), **BP:** 611
Casal, Lourdes, **TE:** 471
Cascade Experiment (Fulton),
    AP: 636
Cassiodorus, **TE:** 462
Cassity, Turner, **AP:** 291-298; "The
    Airship Boys in Africa," **AP:** 294;
    The Defense of the Sugar Islands,
    AP: 295; *The Destructive
    Element*, **AP:** 296; *Devils and
    Islands*, **AP:** 297; "Gutenberg as
    Card Shark," **AP:** 293; *Hurricane
    Lamp*, **AP:** 295; "Mainstreaming,"
    AP: 295; *No Second Eden*,
    AP: 296; "Seven Destinations of
    Mayerling," **AP:** 293; *Silver Out
    of Shanghai*, **AP:** 295; "Soldiers
    of Orange," **AP:** 295; *Steeplejacks
    in Babel*, **AP:** 295; *Watchboy,
    What of the Night?*, **AP:** 294
"Castaway, The" (Cowper), **BP:** 323
Castaway, and Other Poems, The
    (Walcott), **WP:** 320
Castilian Camp, The (Machado),
    EP: 637
Casting of the Bells, The (Seifert),
    EP: 966
Casting Off (Alegría), **WP:** 13
Castle of Indolence, The (Thomson),
    BP: 1263

Castle Tzingal (Chappell), **AP:** 305
Castro, Rosalía de, **EP:** 190-196;
    "Airiños, airiños, aires," **EP:** 194;
    Beside the River Sar, **EP:** 195;
    Cantares gallegos, **EP:** 194;
    Follas novas, **EP:** 195; "I Used to
    Have a Nail," **EP:** 193; "Saint
    Scholastica," **EP:** 196; "They Say
    That Plants Do Not Speak,"
    EP: 195
"Cat, The" (Baudelaire), **TE:** 641
Catalan poetry, **TE:** 48-53
"Categories" (Kennedy), **AP:** 1025
Catharsis, defined, **TE:** 701
Cathay (Pound), **AP:** 1580
Cathedral, The (Lowell), **AP:** 1185
Catullus, **EP:** 197-203, **TE:** 449;
    Poem 64, **EP:** 201
Caudwell, Christopher, **TE:** 760
Cavafy, Constantine P., **EP:** 204-
    210, **TE:** 335; "At the Theatre,"
    EP: 209; "Craftsmen of Wine
    Bowls," **EP:** 209; "Exiles,"
    EP: 207; "Phihellene," **EP:** 208;
    "Pictured," **EP:** 209; "Waiting for
    the Barbarians," **EP:** 207;
    "Walls," **EP:** 209
Cavalcanti, Guido, **EP:** 210-214;
    "My Lady Asks Me," **EP:** 213
Cavalier poets. *See* Categorized Index
Cave Birds (Hughes), **BP:** 691
Cavendish, Margaret. *See* Newcastle,
    Margaret Cavendish, duchess of
Caviare at the Funeral (Simpson),
    AP: 1798
Čech, Svatopluk, **TE:** 82
Celan, Paul, **EP:** 214-220, **TE:** 311;
    Rose Ausländer, **AP:** 66; *Mohn
    und Gedächtnis*, **EP:** 217; *Die
    Niemandsrose*, **EP:** 218; *Speech-
    Grille*, **EP:** 218; *Von Schwelle zu
    Schwelle*, **EP:** 218
Cell, The (Hejinian), **AP:** 840
Cendrars, Blaise, **TE:** 270
"Ceneri." *See* "Ashes"

Ceneri de Gramsci, Le. See Ashes of Gramsci, The

Cent Ballades d'amant et de dame (Christine de Pizan), **EP:** 242

Centuries of Meditations (Traherne), **BP:** 1279

Cernuda, Luis, **EP:** 220-226; "The Adoration of the Magi," **EP:** 225; *Donde habite el olvido*, **EP:** 224; *Egloga, elegía, oda*, **EP:** 223; *Las nubes*, **EP:** 224; *Perfil del aire*, **EP:** 223; *Los placeres prohibidos*, **EP:** 223; *Un río, un amor*, **EP:** 223

Cervantes, Lorna Dee, **AP:** 298-303; "Bananas," **AP:** 302; "Beneath the Shadow of the Freeway," **AP:** 300; "Coffee," **AP:** 302; *Drive*, **AP:** 301; *Emplumada*, **AP:** 299; "Freeway 280," **AP:** 300; *From the Cables of Genocide*, **AP:** 301; "Oaxaca, 1974," **AP:** 300; "Poem for the Young White Man . . .," **AP:** 301; "Refugee Ship," **AP:** 299

Cervantes Prize. *See* Miguel de Cervantes Prize

Césaire, Aimé, **WP:** 56-61; *Return to My Native Land*, **WP:** 59; *Shackles*, **WP:** 59

"Chainsaw" (Everson), **AP:** 576

Chamber Music (Joyce), **BP:** 721

"Chambered Nautilus, The" (Holmes), **AP:** 898

Change of Address (Slavitt), **AP:** 1816

Change of World, A (Rich), **AP:** 1635

Changing Light at Sandover, The (Merrill), **AP:** 1322

Changing Mind (Aiken), **AP:** 15

"Channel Crossing" (Plath), **AP:** 1554

Channel Passage, and Other Poems, A (Swinburne), **BP:** 1233

Channing, Anne. *See* Porter, Anne

Chanson de Roland. See Song of Roland, The

Chansons de geste, **TE:** 233

Chant des morts, Le (Reverdy), **EP:** 888

Chants de Maldoror (Ducasse), **TE:** 266

Chants d'ombre (Senghor), **WP:** 268

Chants terrestres (Follain), **EP:** 337

Chapman, George, **BP:** 228-235; "A Coronet for His Mistress Philosophy," **BP:** 232; *Euthymiae Raptus*, **BP:** 233; *Hero and Leander*, **BP:** 232; *Ovid's Banquet of Sense*, **BP:** 231; *The Shadow of Night*, **BP:** 230

Chappell, Fred, **AP:** 303-307; *Backsass*, **AP:** 306; *Castle Tzingal*, **AP:** 305; *Family Gathering*, **AP:** 306; *First and Last Words*, **AP:** 305; *Midquest*, **AP:** 305; *Shadow Box*, **AP:** 306; *Spring Garden*, **AP:** 306

Char, René, **EP:** 226-230, **TE:** 279; "Commune présence," **EP:** 229

Charles d'Orléans, **EP:** 230-235, **TE:** 123, **TE:** 244; *Retenue d'amours*, **EP:** 233; *Songe en complainte*, **EP:** 233

Charnel Rose, The (Aiken), **AP:** 15

"Charogne, Une." *See* "Carcass, A"

Charon's Cosmology (Simic), **AP:** 1788

Chartier, Alain, **EP:** 236-240; "The Beautiful, Pitiless Lady," **EP:** 238; "The Book of Four Ladies," **EP:** 238; "The Excuse," **EP:** 238; "The Lay on Pleasure," **EP:** 237; "The Patriotic Debate," **EP:** 238

"Chat, Le." *See* "Cat, The"

Chattanooga (Reed), **AP:** 1614

Chatterton, Thomas, **BP:** 235-243, **TE:** 628; "Aella," **BP:** 241; "African Eclogues," **BP:** 239; "Bristowe Tragedie," **BP:** 240;

"An Excelente Balade of Charitie . . . ," **BP:** 240

Chattopadhyaya, Harindranath, **TE:** 371

Chaucer, Geoffrey, **BP:** 243-253, **EP:** 425, **TE:** 113, **TE:** 120; *Book of the Duchess*, **BP:** 247; *The Canterbury Tales*, **BP:** 250, **TE:** 113; *House of Fame*, **BP:** 247; *The Legend of Good Women*, **BP:** 248; *Parlement of Foules*, **BP:** 248; *Troilus and Criseyde*, **BP:** 249

Chaulieu, Guillaume Amfrye, Abbe de, **TE:** 255

Chedid, Andrée, **TE:** 280

Cheer, The (Meredith), **AP:** 1314

Chénier, André-Marie, **TE:** 258

Cherokee Lottery, The (Smith), **AP:** 1828

Chestnut Rain, The (Heyen), **AP:** 847

Chetki (Akhmatova), **WP:** 5

Chi, Juan. *See* Ruan Ji

Chiabrera, Gabriello, **TE:** 386

Chicago Poems (Sandburg), **AP:** 1709

Chicago Renaissance. *See* Categorized Index

Chicano poetry, **TE:** 466-474

Chief Joseph of the Nez Percé (Warren), **AP:** 2100

Childe Harold's Pilgrimage (Byron), **BP:** 191

"Childe Roland to the Dark Tower Came" (Browning), **BP:** 165

"Childhood" (Justice), **AP:** 990

Children's/young adult poetry, **TE:** 168. *See also* Categorized Index

Child's Garden of Verses, A (Stevenson), **BP:** 1203

Child's Play (Slavitt), **AP:** 1813

Chile. *See* Geographical Index

Chimeras, The (Nerval), **EP:** 745

Chin, Marilyn, **AP:** 307-312; *Dwarf Bamboo*, **AP:** 308; *The Phoenix Gone, the Terrace Empty*, **AP:** 309; *Rhapsody in Plain Yellow*, **AP:** 310

China. *See* Classical period, China, in Categorized Index; Geographical Index

China Trace (Wright), **AP:** 2211

Chinese American poetry, **TE:** 21

"Chinese Nightingale, The" (Lindsay), **AP:** 1151

Chinese poetry, **TE:** 54-70

"Chiocciola, La." *See* "Snail, The"

Choise of Valentines, The (Nashe), **BP:** 957

Chōka, **TE:** 413

Chomsky, Noam, **TE:** 753

Choral poetry, **TE:** 224

"Choricos" (Aldington), **BP:** 20

Chorus for Survival (Gregory), **AP:** 740

"Chorus of the Stones" (Sachs), **EP:** 933

Chosen by the Lion (Gregg), **AP:** 737

Chosen Light, A (Montague), **BP:** 917

Chrétien de Troyes, **TE:** 239

Christ of Velázquez, The (Unamuno y Jugo), **EP:** 1054

Christ II (Cynewulf), **BP:** 350

Christabel (Coleridge), **BP:** 283

Christensen, Inger, **TE:** 563

Christian Ethicks (Traherne), **BP:** 1280

Christine de Pizan, **EP:** 240-244; *Cent Ballades d'amant et de dame*, **EP:** 242; *The Tale of Joan of Arc*, **EP:** 243

Christmas in Biafra (Achebe), **WP:** 2

Christopher Brennan Award, **BP:** 1408, **CM:** 48, **TE:** 868

"Chronicle of Division, The" (Everson), **AP:** 573

Chronicle of the Cid. See *Poem of the Cid*

Chu ci (poetic form), **TE:** 58

"Church, The" (Herbert), **BP:** 623

"Church Going" (Larkin), **BP:** 791

Churchill, Charles, **TE:** 170

Chute d'un ange, La (Lamartine), **EP:** 595

Ciardi, John, **AP:** 312-318; *As If*, **AP:** 316; *Homeward to America*, **AP:** 316; *I Marry You*, **AP:** 316; *Live Another Day*, **AP:** 316; *Other Skies*, **AP:** 316; "Tenzone," **AP:** 317; *Thirty-nine Poems*, **AP:** 316; *This Strangest Everything*, **AP:** 317

Cicero, **TE:** 449

Cinq Grandes Odes. See *Five Great Odes*

Cinquain, defined, **AP:** 2295, **BP:** 1379, **EP:** 1173, **TE:** 811, **WP:** 381

"Cinque maggio, Il." *See* "Napoleonic Ode, The"

Cinto, Mossén. *See* Verdaguer, Jacint

Circle Game, The (Atwood), **BP:** 40

Circles on the Water (Piercy), **AP:** 1534

"Circus Performers, The" (Tzara), **EP:** 1049

Cisneros, Sandra, **AP:** 318-322; *Loose Woman*, **AP:** 320; *My Wicked, Wicked Ways*, **AP:** 320

Cistern, The (Seferis), **EP:** 959

"Cities and Thrones and Powers" (Kipling), **BP:** 764

Cities Burning (Randall), **AP:** 1599

"Cities, Plains, and People" (Durrell), **BP:** 454

"City in the Sea, The" (Poe), **AP:** 1566

"City of Dreadful Night, The" (Thomson), **BP:** 1267

City of Satisfactions, The (Hoffman), **AP:** 867

Civil Poems (Miles), **AP:** 1342

Civile Warres (Daniel), **BP:** 356

"Ck'o'yo medicine man, A" (Silko), **AP:** 1780

Claiming an Identity They Taught Me to Despise (Cliff), **WP:** 62

Claiming Kin (Voigt), **AP:** 2056

"Clamming" (Whittemore), **AP:** 2143

Clamor (Guillén), **EP:** 432

Clampitt, Amy, **AP:** 322-325; "A Hermit Thrush," **AP:** 324; "Imago," **AP:** 324; *The Isthmus*, **AP:** 323; "The Kingfisher," **AP:** 324; *Multitudes, Multitudes*, **AP:** 323

Clare, John, **BP:** 254-261; "Decay," **BP:** 259; "Gypsies," **BP:** 256; "The Mores," **BP:** 257; "Sand Martin," **BP:** 258

Clarel (Melville), **AP:** 1299

Clarke, Austin, **BP:** 261-266; *Ancient Lights*, **BP:** 264; *Mnemosyne Lay in Dust*, **BP:** 265; *Night and Morning*, **BP:** 263; *Pilgrimage, and Other Poems*, **BP:** 263

Claro enigma (Drummond de Andrade), **WP:** 81

Clasp, and Other Poems, The (Collier), **AP:** 338

Class Dismissed! (Glenn), **AP:** 708

Classic Ballroom Dances (Simic), **AP:** 1788

Classical period, ancient Greece, **TE:** 322

Classical period, China, **TE:** 55. *See also* Categorized Index

Classicism, **TE:** 149. *See also* Categorized Index

Classicism, defined, **AP:** 2295, **BP:** 1379, **EP:** 1173, **TE:** 811, **WP:** 381

Claudel, Paul, **EP:** 244-252, **TE:** 271; *The East I Know*, **EP:** 248; *Five Great Odes*, **EP:** 248, **TE:** 271; *La Messe là-bas, La*, **EP:** 250; "The Muse

Who Is Grace," **EP:** 249; "Within the House," **EP:** 249
Claudian, **TE:** 460
Claussen, Sophus, **TE:** 539
Clavijo Uva, **TE:** 470
Clean Slate (Zamora), **WP:** 355
Cleanness (Pearl-Poet), **BP:** 995
Clearing (Berry), **AP:** 151
Cleopatra (Daniel), **BP:** 356
"Cliff, The" (Lermontov), **WP:** 148
Cliff, Michelle, WP: 61-64;
   Claiming an Identity They Taught Me to Despise, **WP:** 62; *The Land of Look Behind*, **WP:** 63
Clifton, Lucille, AP: 326-331;
   Blessing the Boats, **AP:** 329;
   Good Times, **AP:** 328; *Good Woman*, **AP:** 328; *An Ordinary Woman*, **AP:** 328; *Quilting*,
   AP: 328; *The Terrible Stories*,
   AP: 329; *Two-Headed Woman*,
   AP: 328; *Voices*, **AP:** 329
Climbing the Divide (McDonald),
   AP: 1219
"Climbing the Peak of Mount Taibo" (Li Bo), **WP:** 153
"CLM" (Masefield), **BP:** 889
"Clock, The" (Beer), **BP:** 63
Clopinel, Jehan. *See* Jean de Meung
Close Chaplet, The (Riding),
   AP: 1643
Cloud in Pants, A (Mayakovsky),
   WP: 178
Cloud Moving Hands (Song),
   AP: 1856
Clouds (Petőfi), **EP:** 822
Clough, Arthur Hugh, BP: 266-272;
   Ambarvalia, **BP:** 269; *Amours de Voyage*, **BP:** 270; *The Bothie of Tober-na-Vuolich*, **BP:** 268;
   Dipsychus, **BP:** 269; *Mari Magno*,
   BP: 270; "The Questioning Spirit," **BP:** 269
"Clown" (Michaux), **EP:** 692
Coal (Lorde), **AP:** 1169

"Coal Fire" (Untermeyer), **AP:** 2014
Coast of Trees, A (Ammons), **AP:** 41
Coastal Nights and Inland Afternoons (Young), **AP:** 2255
Cocteau, Jean, EP: 253-259,
   TE: 275; *Le Cap de Bonne-Espérance*, **EP:** 256; *La Danse de Sophocle*, **EP:** 256; *Discours du grand sommeil*, **EP:** 257; *Opéra*,
   EP: 258; *Plain-Chant*, **EP:** 257;
   Poésies, 1917-1920, **EP:** 257; *Le Prince frivole*, **EP:** 256;
   Vocabulaire, **EP:** 257
Codrescu, Andrei, AP: 331-333; *The Forgiven Submarine*, **AP:** 332;
   Jealous Witness, **AP:** 332
Cœur-espace, Le (Bonnefoy),
   EP: 147
Cofer, Judith Ortiz. *See* Ortiz Cofer, Judith
"Coffee" (Cervantes), **AP:** 302
Cohen, Leonard, BP: 272-276;
   "Anthem," **BP:** 274; *The Book of Longing*, **BP:** 275; "Hallelujah,"
   BP: 275; *Stranger Music*,
   BP: 274; "Suzanne," **BP:** 274
Coins and Coffins (Wakoski),
   AP: 2070
Cold Calls (Logue), **BP:** 826
Cold Comfort (Anderson), **AP:** 44
Cold Dogs in the Courtyard (Bukowski), **AP:** 269
Cold Mountain Poems (Snyder),
   AP: 1846
Cole, Henri, AP: 333-336; *Middle Earth*, **AP:** 335; *The Visible Man*,
   AP: 335
Coleridge, Samuel Taylor, BP: 276-287, **TE:** 178, **TE:** 630, **TE:** 710;
   Biographia Lilteraria, **TE:** 710;
   Christabel, **BP:** 283; "Dejection,"
   BP: 284; "The Eolian Harp,"
   BP: 278; "Frost at Midnight,"
   BP: 280; "Kubla Khan," **BP:** 282;
   The Rime of the Ancient Mariner,

BP: 280; "This Lime-Tree Bower My Prison," **BP:** 279
Colin Clouts Come Home Againe (Spenser), **BP:** 1194
Collected Later Poems (Hecht),
   AP: 834
Collected Longer Poems, The (Rexroth), **AP:** 1625
Collected Poems (Achebe), **WP:** 2
Collected Poems, 1951-1971 (Ammons), **AP:** 39
Collected Poems (Barnard), **AP:** 101
Collected Poems (Bowers), **AP:** 222
Collected Poems, 1950-1970 (Davie),
   BP: 371
Collected Poems, 1936-1961 (Fuller),
   BP: 503
Collected Poems, 1947-1997 (Ginsberg), **AP:** 686
Collected Poems (Gregory), **AP:** 740
Collected Poems (Kenyon), **AP:** 1031
Collected Poems, 1956-2001 (Kinsella), **BP:** 758
Collected Poems, The (Kunitz), **AP:** 1092
Collected Poems (Larkin), **BP:** 793
Collected Poems, The (Merton), **AP:** 1330
Collected Poems (Middleton), **BP:** 904
Collected Poems, 1930-1983 (Miles),
   AP: 1343
Collected Poems, 1931-1987, The (Miłosz), **EP:** 717
Collected Poems (Montague), **BP:** 922
Collected Poems, 1935-1992 (Prince),
   BP: 1025
Collected Poems, 1948-1984 (Walcott), **WP:** 322
Collected Poems (Wilbur), **AP:** 2159
Collected Poems (Williams), **AP:** 2166
Collected Poems (Winters), **AP:** 2189
Collected Poems, 1952-1990, The (Yevtushenko), **WP:** 346

Collected Poems and Epigrams of J. V. Cunningham, The (Cunningham), **AP:** 419

Collected Poems of Frank O'Hara, The (O'Hara), **TE:** 676

Collected Poems of Howard Nemerov, The (Nemerov), **AP:** 1413

Collected Poems of Kenneth Koch, The (Koch), **TE:** 677

Collected Poetry of Nikki Giovanni, 1968-1998, The (Giovanni), **AP:** 699

Collected Shorter Poems, The (Rexroth), **AP:** 1624

Collected Works of Billy the Kid, The (Ondaatje), **BP:** 975

Collections of Ten Thousand Leaves, The. See Manyoshu, The

Collier, Michael, AP: 336-341; *The Clasp, and Other Poems,* **AP:** 338; *Dark Wild Realm,* **AP:** 340; *The Folded Heart,* **AP:** 338; *The Ledge,* **AP:** 339; *The Neighbor,* **AP:** 339

Collins, Billy, AP: 341-347; *The Apple That Astonished Paris,* **AP:** 343; *The Art of Drowning,* **AP:** 344; *Ballistics,* **AP:** 346; *Picnic, Lightning,* **AP:** 344; *Questions About Angels,* **AP:** 343; *Sailing Alone Around the Room,* **AP:** 345; *The Trouble with Poetry, and Other Poems,* **AP:** 345

Collins, William, BP: 287-291, **TE:** 169; "Ode on the Poetical Character," **BP:** 289; *An Ode on the Popular Superstitions of the Highlands of Scotland,* **BP:** 290; "Ode to Liberty," **BP:** 290; *Persian Eclogues,* **BP:** 289

Collyn Clout (Skelton), **BP:** 1157

Cologne Epode (Archilochus), **EP:** 54

Colonialism; Africa, **TE:** 15; beginning of, **TE:** 769; British, **TE:** 500; Caribbean, **TE:** 43

Colonna, Vittoria, **TE:** 386

Color Wheel, The (Steele), **AP:** 1883

Colors of Desire, The (Mura), **AP:** 1393

Colors Passing Through Us (Piercy), **AP:** 1535

Colum, Padraic, BP: 292-296; "After Speaking of One Who Died a Long Time Before," **BP:** 295; "A Cradle Song," **BP:** 294; "An Old Woman of the Roads," **BP:** 294; "Roger Casement," **BP:** 294

Columb, Patrick. *See* Colum, Padraic

Come Dance with Kitty Stobling, and Other Poems (Kavanagh), **BP:** 729

Comédie de la mort, La. See Drama of Death, The

Coming into Eighty (Sarton), **AP:** 1723

Coming to Terms (Miles), **AP:** 1342

Commonwealth Interregnum. *See* Categorized Index

Commonwealth literature, defined, **TE:** 500

Commonwealth studies. *See* Postcolonialism

"Commune présence" (Char), **EP:** 229

Communicating Vessels (Breton), **EP:** 159

"Communion" (Dunbar), **AP:** 507

"Complaint of Henry, Duke of Buckingham" (Sackville), **BP:** 1078

Complaint of the Black Knight (Lydgate), **BP:** 835

Complaintes, Les (Laforgue), **EP:** 587

Complaints (Spenser), **BP:** 1200

Complaynt of Rosamonde, The (Daniel), **BP:** 356

Complete Poems (Johnson), **AP:** 975

Complete Poems (Sandburg), **AP:** 1710

"Composed upon Westminster Bridge, September 3, 1802" (Wordsworth), **TE:** 746

Comus (Milton), **BP:** 908

Conceit, defined, **AP:** 2295, **BP:** 1379, **EP:** 1173, **TE:** 148, **TE:** 811, **WP:** 381

Conceptismo, **TE:** 594

Concerning the Angels (Alberti), **EP:** 9

Concerning the Book That Is the Body of the Beloved (Orr), **AP:** 1491

"Concord Hymn" (Emerson), **AP:** 551

Concrete poetry, **TE:** 317; Germany, **TE:** 312; Eugen Gomringer, **EP:** 406; Scandinavia, **TE:** 554. *See also* Categorized Index

Coney Island of the Mind, A (Ferlinghetti), **AP:** 597

Confederation poets (Canada), **TE:** 39

Confessio Amantis (Gower), **BP:** 531, **TE:** 112

"Confession, A" (MacBeth), **BP:** 844

Confession Stone, The (Dodson), **AP:** 473

Confessional poetry, **TE:** 200, **TE:** 668-673

Confessional poets. *See* Categorized Index

Confianza (Salinas), **EP:** 940

Congreve, William, BP: 296-301; "Song," **BP:** 297; "To the King, on the Taking of Namure," **BP:** 299

Conjure (Reed), **AP:** 1614

Connaissance de l'est. See East I Know, The

Connecting the Dots (Kumin), **AP:** 1079

Connotation, defined, **AP:** 2295, **BP:** 1379, **EP:** 1173, **TE:** 811, **WP:** 381

Conquistador (MacLeish), **AP:** 1251

Conscious and Verbal (Murray),
BP: 951

"Consider" (Auden), **BP:** 50

Considering How Exaggerated Music Is (Scalapino), **AP:** 1726

Consonance, defined, **AP:** 2296,
BP: 1380, **EP:** 1174, **TE:** 812,
WP: 382

Consonants, defined, **AP:** 2296,
BP: 1380, **EP:** 1174, **TE:** 812,
WP: 382

Constable, Henry, BP: 301-306;
Diana, **BP:** 303; *Spiritual Sonnets*, **BP:** 304

Constance (Kenyon), **AP:** 1031

Constant Defender (Tate), **AP:** 1953

Contemplado, El. See *Sea of San Juan, The*

"Contemplation on Night, A" (Gay),
BP: 517

"Contemplations" (Bradstreet),
AP: 224

Contemplations, Les (Hugo),
EP: 524, **TE:** 263

Contes et nouvelles en vers. See *Tales and Short Stories in Verse*

"Continent, The" (Duncan), **AP:** 514

Continental poetry; fourteenth century,
TE: 98-101, **TE:** 103-119

Continuous Life, The (Strand),
AP: 1923

Continuum (Evans), **AP:** 566

Contracted World, The (Meinke),
AP: 1293

Controlling image, defined,
AP: 2296, **BP:** 1380, **EP:** 1174,
TE: 812, **WP:** 382

Controlling metaphor, defined,
AP: 2296, **BP:** 1380, **EP:** 1174,
TE: 812, **WP:** 382

"Contumacious Poet, The"
(Corbière), **EP:** 262

"Conversation, A" (Applewhite),
AP: 54

"Conversation in Crisis" (Lorde),
AP: 1169

"Conversation in the Drawing Room,
The" (Kees), **AP:** 1009

Convivial Poems (Pascoli), **EP:** 775

"Cool Web, The" (Graves), **BP:** 537

Cool, Calm, and Collected (Kizer),
AP: 1052

"Cooled Heels Lament Against
Frivolity, the Mask of Despair"
(Dugan), **AP:** 500

Copacetic (Komunyakaa),
AP: 1067

Cope, Wendy, **TE:** 209

Coplas on the Death of His Father
(Manrique), **EP:** 658

"Copperline" (Price), **AP:** 1588

"Copulating Gods, The" (Kizer),
AP: 1049

Corbière, Tristan, EP: 260-263,
TE: 642; "The Contumacious
Poet," **EP:** 262; *Epitaph*, **EP:** 262;
"A Little Death to Make One
Laugh," **EP:** 262

"Corinna's Going A-Maying"
(Herrick), **BP:** 633

Corman, Cid, AP: 347-352; *Sun
Rock Man*, **AP:** 349

"Corn" (Lanier), **AP:** 1098

Corn, Alfred, AP: 352-356; "1992,"
AP: 355; *Notes from a Child of
Paradise*, **AP:** 354; "Poem in Four
Parts on New York City,"
AP: 354; *An Xmas Murder*,
AP: 355

Cornhuskers (Sandburg), **AP:** 1709

Corona trágica, La (Vega Carpio),
EP: 1078

"Coronet for His Mistress Philosophy,
A" (Chapman), **BP:** 232

"Correspondences" (Baudelaire),
TE: 640

Corso, Gregory, AP: 356-362; "The
American Way," **AP:** 360; *Elegiac
Feelings American*, **AP:** 360;

"Field Report," **AP:** 360;
Gasoline, **AP:** 359; *The Happy
Birthday of Death*, **AP:** 359;
Herald of the Autochthonic Spirit,
AP: 360; *Long Live Man*,
AP: 359; "Marriage," **AP:** 359;
Mindfield, **AP:** 360; "Window,"
AP: 360

Corsons Inlet (Ammons), **AP:** 39

Cosmic Canticle. See *Music of the
Spheres, The*

Cosmopolitan Greetings (Ginsberg),
AP: 685

Costa i Llobera, Miquel, **TE:** 51

Costumbrismo, **TE:** 598

"Cotter's Saturday Night, The"
(Burns), **BP:** 176

Cotton Candy on a Rainy Day
(Giovanni), **AP:** 697

Cotton, Charles, BP: 306-312;
Poems on Several Occasions,
BP: 311; *The Wonders of the
Peake*, **BP:** 310

"Cottonwood, Part Two" (Silko),
AP: 1780

Coulette, Henri, AP: 362-366; *And
Come to Closure*, **AP:** 365; *The
Family Goldschmitt*, **AP:** 364;
"The Junk Shop," **AP:** 362; *The
War of the Secret Agents, and
Other Poems*, **AP:** 362

Countess of Pembroke's Passion, The
(Breton), **BP:** 128

Country and the City, The (Williams),
TE: 734

Country Between Us, The (Forché),
AP: 615

*Country of a Thousand Years of
Peace, and Other Poems, The*
(Merrill), **AP:** 1318

Country of Marriage, The (Berry),
AP: 151

Country Without a Post Office, The
(Ali), **AP:** 27

Coup de dés jamais n'abolira le

hasard, Un. See *Dice Thrown Never Will Annul Chance*

Couplet, defined, **AP:** 2296, **BP:** 1380, **EP:** 1174, **TE:** 812, **WP:** 382

Course in General Linguistics (Saussure), **TE:** 750

"Course of a Particular, The" (Stevens), **AP:** 1911

Courtesy, The (Shapiro), **AP:** 1760

Courtly love, **TE:** 238

Courtship of Miles Standish, The (Longfellow), **AP:** 1163

"Courtship of the Yonghy-Bonghy-Bò, The" (Lear), **BP:** 815

Covenant (Shapiro), **AP:** 1761

Cowley, Abraham, **BP:** 312-319; *Davideis,* **BP:** 317; "Hymn to Light," **BP:** 317; *The Mistress,* **BP:** 316; "Ode to the Royal Society," **BP:** 318; *Pindarique Odes,* **BP:** 316; *Poems,* **BP:** 315; *Poeticall Blossomes,* **BP:** 315

Cowley, Malcolm, **AP:** 366-375; *Blue Juniata,* **AP:** 373; *The Dry Season,* **AP:** 372

Cowper, William, **BP:** 320-326, **TE:** 170; "The Castaway," **BP:** 323; "The Diverting History of John Gilpin," **BP:** 324; "On the Receipt of My Mother's Picture Out of Norfolk," **BP:** 322; "The Poplar Field," **BP:** 324; *The Task,* **BP:** 325

Coxe, Louis, **AP:** 375-378; *The Middle Passage,* **AP:** 377; *The Sea Faring, and Other Poems,* **AP:** 377

Crabbe, George, **BP:** 327-337, **TE:** 170; *The Borough,* **BP:** 333; *The Parish Register,* **BP:** 332; *Poems,* **BP:** 332; *Posthumous Tales,* **BP:** 336; *Tales in Verse,* **BP:** 334; *Tales of the Hall,* **BP:** 335; *The Village,* **BP:** 330

Crack in Everything, The (Ostriker), **AP:** 1504

Crackling of Thorns, A (Hollander), **AP:** 878

"Cradle Song, A" (Colum), **BP:** 294

"Craftsmen of Wine Bowls" (Cavafy), **EP:** 209

Crane, Hart, **AP:** 379-387, **TE:** 196; "Atlantis," **AP:** 386; "Ave Maria," **AP:** 382; *The Bridge,* **AP:** 381, **TE:** 196; "Cape Hatteras," **AP:** 383; "Cutty Sark," **AP:** 383; "The Dance," **AP:** 383; "For the Marriage of Faustus and Helen," **AP:** 381; "Indiana," **AP:** 383; poem about, **AP:** 955; "Powhatan's Daughter," **AP:** 382; "Quaker Hill," **AP:** 385; "The River," **AP:** 382; "Three Songs," **AP:** 384; "To Brooklyn Bridge," **AP:** 382; "The Tunnel," **AP:** 385; "Van Winkle," **AP:** 382

Crane, Stephen, **AP:** 387-392; "A man said to the universe," **AP:** 389

"Cranes of Ibycus, The" (Schiller), **EP:** 955

Crashaw, Richard, **BP:** 337-344; *Carmen Deo Nostro,* **BP:** 339; *Delights of the Muses,* **BP:** 339; "In the Holy Nativity of Our Lord," **BP:** 340; "Sainte Mary Magdalen," **BP:** 340; *Steps to the Temple,* **BP:** 339

Crazy Horse in Stillness (Heyen), **AP:** 848

Creeley, Robert, **AP:** 392-400, **TE:** 687; "Ballad of the Despairing Husband," **AP:** 396; *A Day Book,* **AP:** 397; "The Immoral Proposition," **AP:** 395; *Life and Death,* **AP:** 398; *Pieces,* **AP:** 397; *So There,* **AP:** 398; *Words,* **AP:** 397

Crepuscular poets, **TE:** 400

Crepusculario (Neruda), **WP:** 199

Crews, Frederick, **TE:** 726

"Cricket, The" (Tuckerman), **AP:** 2001

"Crin d'oro crespo." *See* "Curly Hair of Gold, A"

Crisis (Hesse), **EP:** 474

Cristo de Velázquez, El. See *Christ of Velázquez, The*

Criticism; archetypal, **TE:** 719-730; cultural, **TE:** 731-735; dialectical, **TE:** 761; England, **TE:** 132; feminist, **TE:** 736-742; formalist, **TE:** 743-749; history of, **TE:** 699-718; linguistic, **TE:** 750-759; Marxist, **TE:** 733, **TE:** 760-763; postcolonial, **TE:** 769-773; postmodern, **TE:** 733; poststructuralist, **TE:** 733, **TE:** 780-786; psychological, **TE:** 719-730; structuralist, **TE:** 780-786

Croatian poetry, **TE:** 71-77

Cronyn, George W., **TE:** 481

Crooked Inheritance, The (Piercy), **AP:** 1536

Crooked Lines of God, The (Everson), **AP:** 574

Crooked Run (Taylor), **AP:** 1972

Cross, Saint John of the. See John of the Cross, Saint

Cross Ties (Kennedy), **AP:** 1026

"Crossing Brooklyn Ferry" (Whitman), **AP:** 2136

Crossing to Sunlight (Zimmer), **AP:** 2263

Crossing to Sunlight Revisited (Zimmer), **AP:** 2263

Crow (Hughes), **BP:** 690, **TE:** 198

"Crow Jane" (Baraka), **AP:** 93

Crucifix in a Deathhand (Bukowski), **AP:** 268

Crucifixion in the Plaza de Armas (Espada), **AP:** 562

Cruelty (Ai), **AP:** 10

Cruz, Sor Juana Inés de la,
TE: 149, TE: 435, TE: 595,
WP: 64-70; "Esta tarde, mi bien,"
WP: 66; *First Dream*, WP: 68;
"Hombres necios," WP: 67
Cruz, Victor Hernández, AP: 400-
404; *By Lingual Wholes*, AP: 402;
Mainland, AP: 402; *Panoramas*,
AP: 403; *Red Beans*, AP: 403;
Rhythm, Content, and Flavor,
AP: 403; *Snaps*, AP: 401;
Tropicalization, AP: 402
Crystal, David, TE: 757
"Családi kör." *See* "Family Circle"
Csokonai Vitéz, Mihály, TE: 355
Csongor és Tünde (Vörösmarty),
EP: 1115
Csoori, Sandor, TE: 362
"Cuartilla." *See* "Sheet of Paper"
"Cuba" (Muldoon), BP: 940
Cuban American poetry, TE: 466-474
Cubism. *See* Categorized Index
Cueca larga, La (Parra), WP: 220
Cullen, Countée, AP: 404-410,
TE: 657; *The Black Christ*,
AP: 408; "From the Dark Tower,"
AP: 408; "Harlem Wine,"
AP: 408; "Heritage," AP: 407;
"Yet Do I Marvel," AP: 406
Culler, Jonathan, AP: 2305,
BP: 1389, EP: 1183, TE: 821,
WP: 391
Culteranismo, TE: 594
Cultural criticism, TE: 731-735
Cultural studies, TE: 733, TE: 760
Culture and Anarchy (Arnold),
TE: 731
Culture, defined, TE: 731
Cummings, E. E., AP: 410-417;
"r-p-o-p-h-e-s-s-a-g-r," AP: 413
Cunningham, J. V., AP: 417-424;
"All Choice Is Error," AP: 420;
*The Collected Poems and
Epigrams of J. V. Cunningham*,
AP: 419; "Haecceity," AP: 420;

"The Helmsman," AP: 421; *To
What Strangers, What Welcome*,
AP: 421
Cure for Love (Ovid), EP: 767
"Curly Hair of Gold, A" (Bembo),
EP: 105
Curnow, Allen, TE: 35
"Curriculum Vitae" (Bachmann),
EP: 74
Curtis, Natalie, TE: 481
Curved Planks, The (Bonnefoy),
EP: 147
Cuttlefish Bones (Montale), EP: 723
"Cutty Sark" (Crane), AP: 383
"Cycle des saisons, Le" (Ponge),
EP: 852
Cycle of the West, A (Neihardt),
AP: 1407
"Cygne, Le." *See* "Swan, The"
Cynewulf, BP: 344-351, TE: 226;
Christ II, BP: 350; *Elene*,
BP: 349; *The Fates of the
Apostles*, BP: 348; *Juliana*,
BP: 348
Cypresse Grove, A (Drummond),
BP: 431
Czech poetry, TE: 78-86
Czech Republic. *See* Geographical
Index
Czechowski, Heinz, TE: 317

Dacey, Philip, AP: 425-430; *The
Deathbed Playboy*, AP: 428;
"From the Front," AP: 428; *The
Man with Red Suspenders*,
AP: 427; *The Mystery of Max
Schmitt*, AP: 429; *The New York
Postcard Sonnets*, AP: 429; "The
Sleep," AP: 426; *Vertebrae
Rosaries*, AP: 429
Dactyl, defined, AP: 2296, BP: 1380,
EP: 1174, TE: 812, WP: 382
Dadaism, EP: 64, TE: 273, TE: 651.
See also Categorized Index
"Daddy" (Plath), AP: 1554

D'Aguiar, Fred, TE: 46
Dahlstierna, Gunno, TE: 530
Daily Horoscope (Gioia), AP: 690
Dainty Monsters, The (Ondaatje),
BP: 975
Dalai Lama, Sixth, TE: 609
"Dalaim" (Petőfi), EP: 824
Dalin, Olaf von, TE: 530
Damages, The (Howard), AP: 910
Dana, Robert, AP: 430-437; *In a
Fugitive Season*, AP: 434; *The
Morning of the Red Admirals*,
AP: 436; *The Power of the
Visible*, AP: 433; *Some Versions
of Silence*, AP: 433; *Starting Out
for the Difficult World*, AP: 434;
Summer, AP: 435; *Yes,
Everything*, AP: 435
"Dance, The" (Crane), AP: 383
Dance Most of All, The (Gilbert),
AP: 676
"Dance of the Sevin Deidly Synnis,
The" (Dunbar), BP: 448, TE: 128
"Dancer" (Sachs), EP: 934
Dancing (Young), AP: 2250
Dancing Bears, The (Merwin),
AP: 1334
*Dancing on the Grave of a Son of a
Bitch* (Wakoski), AP: 2073
Danger on Peaks (Snyder), AP: 1850
Dangers (McHugh), AP: 1232
Dangling in the Tournefortia
(Bukowski), AP: 272
Daniel, Samuel, BP: 352-358; *Civile
Warres*, BP: 356; *Cleopatra*,
BP: 356; *The Complaynt of
Rosamonde*, BP: 356; *Delia*,
BP: 355; *Musophilus*, BP: 357
D'Annunzio, Gabriele, EP: 264-
270, TE: 396; *Canto novo*,
EP: 267; *Intermezzo di rime*,
EP: 267; *Le laudi*, EP: 267;
Poema paradisiaco, EP: 267;
Primo vere, EP: 266
Danrin school, TE: 423

"Dans le vide." *See* "In Space"

Danse de Sophocle, La (Cocteau), **EP:** 256

Dante, EP: 270-289, **TE:** 101, **TE:** 378, **TE:** 464; *The Divine Comedy,* **EP:** 275

Darío, Rubén, TE: 436**WP:** 71-76; "A Víctor Hugo," **WP:** 73; "El Año lírico," **WP:** 74; *Azul,* **WP:** 74; "Blazon," **WP:** 75; *Cantos de vida y esperanza, los cisnes, y otros poemas,* **WP:** 75; *Prosas Profanas, and Other Poems,* **WP:** 74; "To Roosevelt," **WP:** 75

Dark and Splendid Mass, A (Evans), **AP:** 565

"Dark Eyes of Daughters, The" (Smith), **AP:** 1820

Dark Harbor (Strand), **AP:** 1924

Dark Horses (Kennedy), **AP:** 1026

Dark Houses, The (Hall), **AP:** 778

"Dark Night, The" (John), **EP:** 545

Dark Wild Realm (Collier), **AP:** 340

Darkening Water (Hoffman), **AP:** 869

Darker (Strand), **AP:** 1922

Darkness and the Light, The (Hecht), **AP:** 834

Darley, George, BP: 359-362; "It Is Not Beauty I Demand," **BP:** 360

"Darling, Let Us Go" (Ronsard), **EP:** 915

Darlington's Fall (Leithauser), **AP:** 1110

Daruwalla, Keki N., **TE:** 374

Das, Kamala, **TE:** 373, **TE:** 505

Dauber (Masefield), **BP:** 889

Dauenhauer, Nora Marks, **TE:** 482

Daughters, I Love You (Hogan), **AP:** 874

Davenant, Sir William, BP: 362-367; *Gondibert,* **BP:** 365; *Madagascar,* **BP:** 364; *The Preface to Gondibert with An Answer by Mr. Hobbes,* **BP:** 366; *Works,* **BP:** 365

Davičo, Oskar, **TE:** 570

"David" (Birney), **BP:** 88

Davideis (Cowley), **BP:** 317

Davie, Donald, BP: 367-375; *The Battered Wife, and Other Poems,* **BP:** 374; *Brides of Reason,* **BP:** 369; *Collected Poems, 1950-1970,* **BP:** 371; *Essex Poems, 1963-1967,* **BP:** 371; *Events and Wisdoms,* **BP:** 371; *In the Stopping Train, and Other Poems,* **BP:** 373; *A Sequence for Francis Parkman,* **BP:** 370; *The Shires,* **BP:** 372; *Six Epistles to Eva Hesse,* **BP:** 371

Davies, Sir John, BP: 375-384; *Epigrammes and Elegies,* **BP:** 379; *Hymnes of Astraea,* **BP:** 383; *Nosce Teipsum,* **BP:** 380; "Of Human Knowledge," **BP:** 380; *Orchestra,* **BP:** 381

Davison, Lawrence H. *See* Lawrence, D. H.

Davison, Peter, AP: 437-441; *Barn Fever, and Other Poems,* **AP:** 440; *The Breaking of the Day, and Other Poems,* **AP:** 439; *Breathing Room,* **AP:** 440; "Not Forgotten," **AP:** 439; *Pretending to Be Asleep,* **AP:** 439; *A Voice in the Mountain,* **AP:** 440; *Walking the Boundaries,* **AP:** 439; "Wordless Winter," **AP:** 440

Dawe, Bruce, **TE:** 33

"Day, The" (Kraus), **EP:** 567

Day After Chasing Porcupines (Welch), **AP:** 2110

Day Book, A (Creeley), **AP:** 397

Day by Day (Lowell), **AP:** 1198

"Day Cools . . ., The" (Södergran), **EP:** 985

"Day Lady Died, The" (O'Hara), **AP:** 1455

Day Lewis, Cecil, BP: 384-390;

From Feathers to Iron, **BP:** 387; *An Italian Visit,* **BP:** 388; *The Magnetic Mountain,* **BP:** 387; *Transitional Poem,* **BP:** 387

Day Sailing (Slavitt), **AP:** 1812

Day the Children Took Over, The (Welch), **AP:** 2110

"Day They Eulogized Mahalia, The" (Lorde), **AP:** 1169

"Daybreak" (Dickey), **AP:** 454

"Days" (Emerson), **AP:** 548

"Days of Foreboding" (Kunitz), **AP:** 1091

Days Run Away Like Wild Horses over the Hills, The (Bukowski), **AP:** 269

Daytime and Starlight (Applewhite), **AP:** 54

"De Galeso et Maximo" (Bembo), **EP:** 106

"De los álamos y los sauces" (Alberti), **EP:** 10

De nos oiseaux (Tzara), **EP:** 1048

De poetica. See *Poetics* (Aristotle)

De rerum natura. See *On the Nature of Things*

De un cancionero apócrifo (Machado), **EP:** 637

"Deacon's Masterpiece, The" (Holmes), **AP:** 897

Dead Alive and Busy, The (Shapiro), **AP:** 1762

Dead and the Living, The (Olds), **AP:** 1459

Dead Kingdom, The (Montague), **BP:** 920

"Dead Loon, The" (Bynner), **AP:** 276

"Dead Man's Dump" (Rosenberg), **BP:** 1058

"Dead Pan, The" (Browning), **BP:** 154

Dead Reckoning (Fearing), **AP:** 585

"Dead Soldiers" (Fenton), **BP:** 489

Dear Ghosts (Gallagher), **AP:** 642

Dear John, Dear Coltrane (Harper), **AP:** 797

Dear Men and Women (Wheelock), **AP:** 2125

Dear Past, and Other Poems, 1919-1994, The (Lewis), **AP:** 1135

Dearest Creature (Gerstler), **AP:** 662

"Death in Leamington" (Betjemen), **BP:** 82

Death Is the Place (Bronk), **AP:** 246

Death of a Naturalist (Heaney), **BP:** 596

"Death of a Poet, The" (Lermontov), **WP:** 147

"Death of a Son" (Silkin), **BP:** 1143

"Death of General Uncebunke, The" (Durrell), **BP:** 455

"Death of Guillaume Apollinaire, The" (Tzara), **EP:** 1048

Death of King Buda, The (Arany), **EP:** 48

Death of the Kapowsin Tavern (Hugo), **AP:** 935

Deathbed Playboy, The (Dacey), **AP:** 428

Death's Jest-Book (Beddoes), **BP:** 59

"Débat patriotique, Le." *See* "Patriotic Debate, The"

Debridement (Harper), **AP:** 798

Decadent poets, **TE:** 187, **TE:** 639; Czech, **TE:** 83; France, **TE:** 269; Poland, **TE:** 495; Russia, **TE:** 517. *See also* Categorized Index

"Decay" (Clare), **BP:** 259

"December Journal: 1968" (Blackburn), **AP:** 187

"Decima" (Calderón de la Barca), **EP:** 173

Declension in the Village of Chung Luong (Weigl), **AP:** 2105

De/Compositions (Snodgrass), **AP:** 1838

Deconstruction, **TE:** 208, **TE:** 782

Deconstruction, defined, **AP:** 2297, **BP:** 1381, **EP:** 1175, **TE:** 813, **WP:** 383

Decorum, defined, **TE:** 702

Deep Image poetry, **TE:** 191

Deep Image poets. *See* Categorized Index

Deepstep Come Shining (Wright), **AP:** 2205

"Deer Park" (Wang Wei), **WP:** 330

Defence and Illustration of the French Language, The (Du Bellay), **TE:** 248

Defence of Guenevere, and Other Poems, The (Morris), **BP:** 926

Defence of Poesie (Sidney), **TE:** 132, **TE:** 703

Defence of Poetry, A (Shelley), **TE:** 711

Défense et illustration de la langue française, La. See *Defence and Illustration of the French Language, The*

Defense of the Sugar Islands, The (Cassity), **AP:** 295

Deguy, Michel, **TE:** 280

Dei Sepolcri. See *On Sepulchers*

"Déjame" (Otero), **EP:** 760

"Dejection" (Coleridge), **BP:** 284

Dekker, His Dream (Dekker), **BP:** 396

Dekker, Thomas, BP: 390-398; *Dekker, His Dream*, **BP:** 396; *Old Fortunatus*, **BP:** 393; *The Shoemaker's Holiday*, **BP:** 394

De la Mare, Walter, BP: 398-405; "Haunted," **BP:** 402; "The Listeners," **BP:** 402; "The Slum Child," **BP:** 403; "The Traveller," **BP:** 403

"Delfica" (Nerval), **EP:** 746

Delia (Daniel), **BP:** 355

"Delight in Disorder" (Herrick), **BP:** 631

"Delight Song of Tsoai-talee, The" (Momaday), **AP:** 1360

Delights and Shadows (Kooser), **AP:** 1072

Delights of the Muses (Crashaw), **BP:** 339

"Delights of Winter at the Shore" (Whalen), **AP:** 2113

Delille, Jacques, **TE:** 257

"Deliria I" (Rimbaud), **EP:** 901

"Deliria II" (Rimbaud), **EP:** 901

Della Valle, Federico, **TE:** 387

De Mehun, Jean. *See* Jean de Meung

Demesne of the Swans, The (Tsvetayeva), **WP:** 297

Demetz, Peter, **TE:** 761

De Meung, Jean. *See* Jean de Meung

Demon, The (Lermontov), **WP:** 146

Demoticism (Greek vernacular), **TE:** 331

Denby, Edwin, **TE:** 674

Denmark. *See* Geographical Index

Denní služba (Holub), **EP:** 494

Dennis, Carl, AP: 441-444; *Practical Gods*, **AP:** 443; *Signs and Wonders*, **AP:** 443

Denotation, defined, **AP:** 2297, **BP:** 1381, **EP:** 1175, **TE:** 813, **WP:** 383

"Departure" (Benn), **EP:** 110

"Departures" (Belitt), **AP:** 116

Departures (Justice), **AP:** 989

Dependencies (Mueller), **AP:** 1384

Depressed foot, defined, **AP:** 2297, **BP:** 1381, **EP:** 1175, **TE:** 813, **WP:** 383

"Depression" (Annensky), **WP:** 22

Depth of Field (Heyen), **AP:** 843

Depth psychology, **TE:** 719

Derniers Vers de Jules Laforgue, Les (Laforgue), **EP:** 589

De Robertis, Giuseppe, **TE:** 401

Derozio, Henry, **TE:** 367

Derricotte, Toi, AP: 444-448; "After a Reading at a Black College," **AP:** 447; *Captivity*, **AP:** 447; *The Empress of the Death House*, **AP:** 446; "The Grandmother Poems," **AP:** 446; *Natural Birth*, **AP:** 446; *Tender*, **AP:** 447

Derrida, Jacques, **AP:** 2297,

BP: 1381, **EP:** 1175, **TE:** 775, **TE:** 782, **TE:** 813, **WP:** 383

XXXIII Kleengedichtjes (Gezelle), **EP:** 388

Derzhavin, Gavrila, **TE:** 511

Descending Figure (Glück), **AP:** 713

Descent of Alette, The (Notley), **AP:** 1433

Desconhort, Lo (Lull), **TE:** 49

"Description of a Salamander, The" (Swift), **BP:** 1222

"Desdichado, El" (Nerval), **EP:** 745

Desert Run (Yamada), **AP:** 2246

Deserted Village, The (Goldsmith), **BP:** 523

Desire (Bidart), **AP:** 167

Desmond, Gail Whang, **TE:** 24

Desnos, Robert, **TE:** 274

Desolación (Mistral), **WP:** 187

De Souza, Goan Eunice, **TE:** 373

Despréau, Monsieur. *See* Boileau-Despréaux, Nicolas

Destinées, Les (Vigny), **EP:** 1105

Destruction or Love (Aleixandre), **EP:** 15

Destructive Element, The (Cassity), **AP:** 296

Deutschland (Biermann), **EP:** 123

Deuxième Sexe, Le. See *Second Sex, The*

Devils and Islands (Cassity), **AP:** 297

Devil's Tour, The (Karr), **AP:** 995

Devotional Songs (Novalis), **EP:** 754

Dhomhnaill, Nuala Ní. *See* Ní Dhomhnaill, Nuala

Diachrony (linguistics), **TE:** 781

Dialect poetry. *See* Categorized Index

Dialectical criticism, **TE:** 761

"Dialectics of Love, The" (McGrath), **AP:** 1227

"Dialogue Between Mirth and Melancholy, A" (Newcastle), **BP:** 962

"Dialogue of Birds, A" (Newcastle), **BP:** 962

Dialogue of Proverbs, A (Heywood), **BP:** 637

Diamond Cutters, The (Rich), **AP:** 1635

Diana (Constable), **BP:** 303

Diana, Charles, and the Queen (Heyen), **AP:** 848

Diario de un poeta recién casado. See *Diary of a Newlywed Poet*

Diary of a Newlywed Poet (Jiménez), **EP:** 537

Dice Thrown Never Will Annul Chance (Mallarmé), **EP:** 649

"Dicen que no hablan las plantas." *See* "They Say That Plants Do Not Speak"

Dichtoefeningen (Gezelle), **EP:** 386

Dickey, James, AP: 448-455; "Approaching Prayer," **AP:** 451; "Daybreak," **AP:** 454; "Doorstep, Lightning, Waif-Dreaming," **AP:** 454; *Drowning with Others*, **AP:** 450; *The Eagle's Mile*, **AP:** 454; *Helmets*, **AP:** 451; *Into the Stone, and Other Poems*, **AP:** 450; "May Day Sermon," **AP:** 452; *Puella*, **AP:** 454; "Sleeping Out at Easter," **AP:** 450

Dickinson, Emily, AP: 455-464, **TE:** 191; "Apparently with no surprise," **AP:** 461; "Because I could not stop for Death," **AP:** 463; "I dreaded that first Robin, so," **AP:** 461; "I know that He exists," **AP:** 460; "I like to see it lap the Miles," **AP:** 458; "I started Early—Took my Dog," **AP:** 461; "I taste a liquor never brewed," **AP:** 461; "It sifts from Leaden Sieves," **AP:** 459; "It was not Death, for I stood up," **AP:** 459; "The Last Night that She lived," **AP:** 463; "A Narrow Fellow in the Grass," **AP:** 461; poem about, **AP:** 1025, **AP:** 1519

Diction, defined, **AP:** 2297, **BP:** 1381, **EP:** 1175, **TE:** 813, **WP:** 383

Didactic poetry, **TE:** 108; England, **TE:** 165; France, **TE:** 256

Diego, Gerardo, **TE:** 601

Dien Cai Dau (Komunyakaa), **AP:** 1067

Dieresis, defined, **AP:** 2297, **BP:** 1381, **EP:** 1175, **TE:** 813, **WP:** 383

Dieu (Hugo), **EP:** 526

Différance (literary term), **TE:** 783

Different Hours (Dunn), **AP:** 518

Different Ways to Pray (Nye), **AP:** 1438

Di Giacomo, Salvatore, **TE:** 398

Diktonius, Elmer, **TE:** 545

"Dilemma" (Beer), **BP:** 62

"Dimanches" (Laforgue), **EP:** 589

Dimensions of History (Wright), **AP:** 2236

Dimoula, Kiki, **TE:** 350

Dīn Rūmī, Jalāl al-. *See* Rūmī, Jalāl al-Dīn

Dinggedichte (Rilke), **EP:** 894

Dinners and Nightmares (Di Prima), **AP:** 467

Di Prima, Diane, AP: 464-471; *Dinners and Nightmares*, **AP:** 467; *Earthsong*, **AP:** 468; *Loba*, **AP:** 468; "Notes Toward a Poem of Revolution," **AP:** 469; *Revolutionary Letters*, **AP:** 469

Dipsychus (Clough), **BP:** 269

"Dirge, The" (King), **BP:** 749

"Disappointment, The" (Behn), **BP:** 71

Discontinuity; German expressionism, **TE:** 306; modernism, **TE:** 194

Discos visuales (Paz), **WP:** 234

Discours du grand sommeil (Cocteau), **EP:** 257

Discourse; gendered, **TE:** 739; New Historicism, **TE:** 767

Discourse of the Adventures Passed by Master F. J., The (Gascoigne), **BP:** 509

"Discovery" (Södergran), **EP:** 984

Discrepancies and Apparitions (Wakoski), **AP:** 2070

Discrete Series (Oppen), **AP:** 1479

Discursos de sobremesa. See After-Dinner Declarations

"Disdaine returned" (Carew), **BP:** 211

"Disillusionment of Ten O'Clock" (Stevens), **AP:** 1908

Disobedience (Notley), **AP:** 1434

"Displaced Orpheus, A" (Untermeyer), **AP:** 2014

Distance from Loved Ones (Tate), **AP:** 1954

Distance We Travel, The (Ehrhart), **AP:** 535

District and Circle (Heaney), **BP:** 603

Ditch, The (Voznesensky), **WP:** 314

Ditié de Jeanne d'Arc, Le. See Tale of Joan of Arc, The

"Diver, The" (Hayden), **AP:** 825

"Diverting History of John Gilpin, The" (Cowper), **BP:** 324

Divina commedia, La. See Divine Comedy, The

Divine Comedies (Merrill), **AP:** 1320

Divine Comedy, The (Dante), **EP:** 275

Divine Fancies (Quarles), **BP:** 1034

Divine Pilgrim, The (Aiken), **AP:** 14

Divine Tragedy, The (Longfellow), **AP:** 1164

Diving into the Wreck (Rich), **AP:** 1637

"Divorce of Lovers, A" (Sarton), **AP:** 1720

Dīwān över fursten av Emgión (Ekelöf), **EP:** 311

Dlatego żyjemy (Szymborska), **EP:** 1009

"Dockery and Son" (Larkin), **BP:** 791

Doctor Jazz (Carruth), **AP:** 282

Dodekalogos tou giftou, O. See Twelve Words of the Gypsy, The

Dodgson, Charles Lutwidge. *See* Carroll, Lewis

Dodson, Owen, **AP:** 471-474; *The Confession Stone*, **AP:** 473; *The Harlem Book of the Dead*, **AP:** 473; *Powerful Long Ladder*, **AP:** 472

Does Your House Have Lions? (Sanchez), **AP:** 1701

"Dog" (Ferlinghetti), **AP:** 598

Dog Fox Field (Murray), **BP:** 950

Dog Language (Twichell), **AP:** 2005

"Dog Named Ego, the Snowflakes as Kisses, A" (Schwartz), **AP:** 1743

Doha. See Tantric songs

Dolce stil nuovo, **TE:** 50, **TE:** 378. *See also* Categorized Index

Dolore, Il (Ungaretti), **EP:** 1062

Dolphin, The (Lowell), **AP:** 1197

Dőlt vitorla (Illyés), **EP:** 530

Domain of Perfect Affection (Becker), **AP:** 113

Domecq, H. Bustos. *See* Borges, Jorge Luis

Domesday Book (Masters), **AP:** 1282

Domestic Violence (Boland), **BP:** 117

Domestic Work (Trethewey), **AP:** 1996

Domin, Hilde, **TE:** 313

"Domination of Wallace Stevens" (Rakosi), **AP:** 1594

Don Juan (Byron), **BP:** 193

Donde habite el olvido (Cernuda), **EP:** 224

"Donna me prega." *See* "My Lady Asks Me"

Donne, John, **BP:** 405-417, **TE:** 144; *An Anatomy of the Word*, **BP:** 414; "The Autumnal," **BP:** 411; "The Canonization," **BP:** 411, **TE:** 746; "The Ecstasy," **BP:** 412; *Epithalamia*, **BP:** 414; "The

Flea," **BP:** 411; "Infinitati Sacrum," **BP:** 415; "Kind pity chokes my spleen," **BP:** 410; "A Nocturnal upon St. Lucy's Day, Being the Shortest Day," **BP:** 413; *Of the Progress of the Soule*, **BP:** 414; poem about, **BP:** 211; "To His Mistress Going to Bed," **BP:** 411; "Twickham Garden," **BP:** 413; "A Valediction," **BP:** 412

Don't Cry, Scream (Madhubuti), **AP:** 1270

Don't Let Me Be Lonely (Rankine), **AP:** 1604

Doolittle, Hilda. *See* H. D.

"Doom of a City, The" (Thomson), **BP:** 1266

Door, The (Atwood), **BP:** 45

Door (Viereck), **AP:** 2047

Door in the Mountain (Valentine), **AP:** 2025

Door in the Wall, The (Tomlinson), **BP:** 1275

Door into the Dark (Heaney), **BP:** 597

Doors of Stone, The (Prince), **BP:** 1024

"Doorstep, Lightning, Waif-Dreaming" (Dickey), **AP:** 454

Doren, Mark Van. *See* Van Doren, Mark

Dorn, Edward, **AP:** 474-481, **TE:** 687; *Gunslinger*, **AP:** 478; *Gunslinger Book III*, **AP:** 479; "The Rick of Green Wood," **AP:** 476; "Sousa," **AP:** 476; *The West*, **AP:** 476; "World Box-Score Cup," **AP:** 477

"Dorothy Q." (Holmes), **AP:** 896

Dorset, First Earl of. *See* Sackville, Thomas

Doty, Mark, **AP:** 481-486; *Atlantis*, **AP:** 483; *Fire to Fire*, **AP:** 485; *My Alexandria*, **AP:** 483; *Source*, **AP:** 484

"Double, The" (Annensky), **WP:** 22

"Double Axe, The" (Jeffers), **AP:** 968

Double Invention of Komo, The (Wright), **AP:** 2237

Double Witness, The (Belitt), **AP:** 117

Douglas, Gavin, **TE:** 128

Dove, Rita, **AP:** 486-493; *American Smooth*, **AP:** 491; *Grace Notes*, **AP:** 490; *Mother Love*, **AP:** 491; *Museum*, **AP:** 489; *On the Bus with Rosa Parks*, **AP:** 491; *Thomas and Beulah*, **AP:** 490; *The Yellow House on the Corner*, **AP:** 488

"Dover Beach" (Arnold), **BP:** 35

"Doves, The" (Ruan Ji), **WP:** 252

Down in My Heart (Stafford), **AP:** 1875

Downstream (Kinsella), **BP:** 755

Doyle, John. *See* Graves, Robert

Dozen Oranges, A (Sorrentino), **AP:** 1860

Dozens (Slavitt), **AP:** 1814

Drachmann, Holger, **TE:** 537

Draft of Light, A (Hollander), **AP:** 885

Drafts and Fragments of Cantos CX-CXVII (Pound), **AP:** 1584

Dragon and the Unicorn, The (Rexroth), **AP:** 1625

Dragontea, La (Vega Carpio), **EP:** 1077

Drahtharfe, Die. See Wire Harp, The

Drama of Death, The (Gautier), **EP:** 373

"Drama of Exile, A" (Browning), **BP:** 153

Dramatic dialogue, defined, **AP:** 2297, **BP:** 1381, **EP:** 1175, **TE:** 813, **WP:** 383

Dramatic Lyrics (Browning), **BP:** 161

Dramatic monologue, defined, **AP:** 2297, **BP:** 1381, **EP:** 1175, **TE:** 813, **WP:** 383

Dramatic monologues. *See* Categorized Index

Dramatic Romances (Browning), **BP:** 162

Drayton, Michael, **BP:** 417-424; *The Barrons Wars*, **BP:** 420; *The Battaile of Agincourt*, **BP:** 423; *Elegies upon Sundry Occasions*, **BP:** 423; *Endimion and Phoebe*, **BP:** 419; *Englands Heroicall Epistles*, **BP:** 420; *Idea*, **BP:** 422; *Ideas Mirrour*, **BP:** 419; *Mortimeriados*, **BP:** 419; *The Muses Elizium*, **BP:** 423; *Nimphidia*, **BP:** 423; *Poemes Lyrick and Pastorall*, **BP:** 420; *Poly-Olbion*, **BP:** 421; *Shepheards Sirena*, **BP:** 423

"Dream, The" (Hayden), **AP:** 823

Dream of a Common Language, The (Rich), **AP:** 1638

Dream of Governors, A (Simpson), **AP:** 1795

"Dream Pedlary" (Beddoes), **BP:** 59

Dream Songs, The (Berryman), **AP:** 160, **TE:** 198

Dream Tigers (Borges), **WP:** 42

Dream Work (Oliver), **AP:** 1466

"Dreamscape" (Booth), **AP:** 211

Driemaal XXXIII kleengedichtjes (Gezelle), **EP:** 389

"Drinkers, The" (Fearing), **AP:** 584

"Drinking Alone in the Moonlight" (Li Bo), **WP:** 154

Drive (Cervantes), **AP:** 301

Driver, Wilsonia Benita. *See* Sanchez, Sonia

"Driving Through Sawmill Towns" (Murray), **BP:** 948

Droste-Hülshoff, Annette von, **TE:** 300

"Drought and Zazen" (Miyazawa), **WP:** 193

Drowning with Others (Dickey), **AP:** 450

Drum-Taps (Whitman), **AP:** 2137

Drummond de Andrade, Carlos,

WP: 76-84; *Alguma poesia*, **WP:** 80; *Boitempo*, **WP:** 82; *Claro enigma*, **WP:** 81; *Fazendeiro do ar*, **WP:** 81; "In the Middle of the Road," **WP:** 80; "Isso é aquilo," **WP:** 82; *Lição de coisas*, **WP:** 82; "Poem of Seven Faces," **WP:** 80; "Residue," **WP:** 81; *A rosa do povo*, **WP:** 81; "Search for Poetry," **WP:** 81; *Sentimento do mundo*, **WP:** 81; "Song to the Man of the People C. C.," **WP:** 81

Drummond of Hawthornden, William, **BP:** 424-433; *A Cypresse Grove*, **BP:** 431; *The Entertainment*, **BP:** 431; *Flowres of Sion*, **BP:** 431; *A Pastorall Elegie*, **BP:** 432; *Poems*, **BP:** 430; *Teares, on the Death of Moeliades*, **BP:** 428

Drunk in the Furnace, The (Merwin), **AP:** 1334

Drunk Man Looks at the Thistle, A (MacDiarmid), **BP:** 848

"Drunken Boat, The" (Rimbaud), **EP:** 899, **TE:** 641

Dry Season, The (Cowley), **AP:** 372

Dry Sun, Dry Wind (Wagoner), **AP:** 2062

Dryden, John, **BP:** 433-442, **TE:** 144, **TE:** 622, **TE:** 705; *Absalom and Achitophel*, **BP:** 438, **TE:** 156, **TE:** 622; *Alexander's Feast*, **BP:** 440; *Annus Mirabilis*, **BP:** 436; *Mac Flecknoe*, **BP:** 437, **TE:** 622; "Preface to *Fables Ancient and Modern*," **TE:** 705; *Prologues and Epilogues*, **BP:** 437; *Religio Laici*, **BP:** 439; "A Song for St. Cecilia's Day," **BP:** 440; "To My Dear Friend Mr. Congreve," **BP:** 440; "To the Memory of Mr. Oldham," **BP:** 439, **BP:** 972

Drypoints of the Hasidim (Prince),
  BP: 1024
DS (2) (Brathwaite), **AP:** 236
Du Fu, **TE:** 61, **WP:** 84-89; "Moonlit
  Night," **WP:** 87; "The River by
  Our Village," **WP:** 88; "The
  Winding River," **WP:** 88
*Du mouvement et de l'immobilité de
  Douve. See On the Motion and
  Immobility of Douve*
Du Mu, **TE:** 62
Du Bellay, Joachim, **EP:** 289-292,
  TE: 248, **TE:** 463; *The
  Antiquities of Rome*, **EP:** 291; *The
  Defence and Illustration of the
  French Language*, **TE:** 248; *The
  Regrets*, **EP:** 291
Dubie, Norman, **AP:** 493-497;
  Alehouse Sonnets, **AP:** 495; *The
  Illustrations*, **AP:** 495; *In the
  Dead of the Night*, **AP:** 495;
  Insomniac Liar of Topo, **AP:** 496;
  The Mercy Seat, **AP:** 496;
  Ordinary Mornings of a Coliseum,
  AP: 496; *Selected and New
  Poems*, **AP:** 496; *The
  Springhouse*, **AP:** 496
Du Bouchet, André, **TE:** 279
Ducasse, Isidore-Lucien, **TE:** 266
Dučić, Jovan, **EP:** 292-298, **TE:** 569;
  Blue Legends, **EP:** 296
Dudley, Anne. *See* Bradstreet, Anne
Duffy, Carol Ann, **TE:** 210
"Dug Out, The" (Sassoon), **BP:** 1085
Dugan, Alan, **AP:** 498-502;
  "Adultery," **AP:** 499; "Cooled
  Heels Lament Against Frivolity,
  the Mask of Despair," **AP:** 500;
  "Fabrication of Ancestors,"
  AP: 499; "How We Heard the
  Name," **AP:** 499; "Letter to
  Donald Fall," **AP:** 500; "Love and
  Money," **AP:** 501; "Love Song,"
  AP: 500; "Night Scene Before
  Combat," **AP:** 501; "On a Seven-

Day Diary," **AP:** 500; "On Zero,"
  AP: 501; *Poems Seven*, **AP:** 501;
  Poems Six, **AP:** 501; "Take on
  Armageddon," **AP:** 501
Duino Elegies (Rilke), **EP:** 895
Dukes, Carol Muske. *See* Muske,
  Carol
"Dulce et Decorum Est" (Owen),
  BP: 980
"Duma." *See* "Meditation"
Dunbar, Paul Laurence, **AP:** 502-
  509, **TE:** 4; "Accountability,"
  AP: 505; "A Bridal Measure,"
  AP: 504; "Communion,"
  AP: 507; "Ere Sleep Comes
  Down to Soothe the Weary Eyes,"
  AP: 505; "In Summer," **AP:** 507;
  "Love and Grief," **AP:** 504;
  "Love's Humility," **AP:** 504;
  Lyrics of Love and Laughter,
  AP: 505; *Lyrics of Lowly Life*,
  AP: 505; *Lyrics of Sunshine and
  Shadow*, **AP:** 506; *Lyrics of the
  Hearthside*, **AP:** 504; "The Old
  Apple-Tree," **AP:** 508; "A Plea,"
  AP: 505; "Yesterday and To-
  morrow," **AP:** 506
Dunbar, William, **BP:** 442-450,
  TE: 127; "The Dance of the Sevin
  Deidly Synnis," **BP:** 448,
  TE: 128; "The Goldyn Targe,"
  BP: 445; "Lament for the
  Makaris," **BP:** 449; "The Tretis of
  the Tua Mariit Wemen and the
  Wedo," **BP:** 447
Duncan, Robert, **AP:** 509-517,
  TE: 687; "Apprehensions,"
  AP: 514; *Bending the Bow*,
  AP: 515; "The Continent,"
  AP: 514; "Food for Fire, Food for
  Thought," **AP:** 513; *Ground
  Work: Before the War*, **AP:** 515;
  The Opening of the Field,
  AP: 513; "Passages Poems,"
  AP: 515; "A Poem Beginning

with a Line by Pindar," **AP:** 513;
  Roots and Branches, **AP:** 514;
  "Sage Architect," **AP:** 514
"Duncan Spoke of a Process"
  (Baraka), **AP:** 92
Dunciad, The (Pope), **BP:** 1014
Dunlop, Eliza Hamilton, **TE:** 31
Dunn, Stephen, **AP:** 517-520;
  Different Hours, **AP:** 518;
  Everything Else in the World,
  AP: 519; *The Insistence of
  Beauty*, **AP:** 519; *Local
  Visitations*, **AP:** 519; *Not
  Dancing*, **AP:** 518
"Duns Scotus's Oxford" (Hopkins),
  BP: 674
Dupin, Jacques, **TE:** 279
Duration, defined, **AP:** 2297,
  BP: 1381, **EP:** 1175, **TE:** 813,
  WP: 383
Durrell, Lawrence, **BP:** 451-457;
  "The Anecdotes," **BP:** 454; "At
  Rhodes," **BP:** 454; "Ballad of the
  Oedipus Complex," **BP:** 456;
  "Cities, Plains, and People,"
  BP: 454; "The Death of General
  Uncebunke," **BP:** 455; "In
  Beirut," **BP:** 454; "Mareotis,"
  BP: 454; "Proffer the Loaves of
  Pain," **BP:** 455; "A Soliloquy of
  Hamlet," **BP:** 453; "Style,"
  BP: 453
"Dusk to Dusk" (Wheelwright),
  AP: 2129
Dust and Light (Wheelock), **AP:** 2124
Dust Which Is God, The (Benét),
  AP: 131
Dutt, Michael Madhusudan, **TE:** 368
Dutt, Toru, **TE:** 368
"Duty Was His Lodestar" (Smith),
  BP: 1168
Duyn, Mona Van. *See* Van Duyn,
  Mona
"Dvoinik." *See* "Double, The"
Dwarf Bamboo (Chin), **AP:** 308

"Dwelling Place in Heaven" (León), **EP:** 601

Dying (Sissman), **AP:** 1804

"Dying Goddess, The" (Kizer), **AP:** 1049

Dynamics of Literary Response, The (Holland), **TE:** 724

Dynasts, The (Hardy), **BP:** 586

Dziady. See Forefathers' Eve

"Each and All" (Emerson), **AP:** 550

Each in a Place Apart (McMichael), **AP:** 1256

Eady, Cornelius, **AP:** 521-526; *The Autobiography of a Jukebox*, **AP:** 524; *Brutal Imagination*, **AP:** 524; *The Gathering of My Name*, **AP:** 523; *Hardheaded Weather*, **AP:** 525; *Kartunes*, **AP:** 522; *Victims of the Latest Dance Craze*, **AP:** 523; *You Don't Miss Your Water*, **AP:** 523

Eagle or Sun? (Paz), **WP:** 233

Eagle's Mile, The (Dickey), **AP:** 454

Eagleton, Terry, **TE:** 761

Earl of Dorset, First. *See* Sackville, Thomas

Early Grrrl (Piercy), **AP:** 1535

"Early Noon" (Bachmann), **EP:** 74

Early Occult Memory Systems of the Lower Midwest (Fairchild), **AP:** 581

Early Selected y Mas (Blackburn), **AP:** 183

Earth Walk (Meredith), **AP:** 1313

Earthbound Zimmer (Zimmer), **AP:** 2262

Earthly Measures (Hirsch), **AP:** 856

Earthly Paradise, The (Morris), **BP:** 927

Earthquakes and Sunrise Missions (Madhubuti), **AP:** 1273

Earthsong (Di Prima), **AP:** 468

East German poetry, **TE:** 87-97, **TE:** 315

East I Know, The (Claudel), **EP:** 248

"Easter Morning" (Ammons), **AP:** 41

Easy (Flint), **AP:** 610

Eberhart, Richard, **AP:** 526-532, **TE:** 664; "Am I My Neighbor's Keeper?," **AP:** 530; "Brotherhood of Men," **AP:** 530; "Flux," **AP:** 531; "For a Lamb," **AP:** 529; "The Fury of Aerial Bombardment," **AP:** 530; "Grave Piece," **AP:** 531; "The Groundhog," **AP:** 528; "The Groundhog Revisiting," **AP:** 530; "New Hampshire, February," **AP:** 529; "1934," **AP:** 529; "Orchard," **AP:** 531; "Three Kids," **AP:** 531

"Ecce Puer" (Joyce), **BP:** 724

Echo's Bones and Other Precipitates (Beckett), **EP:** 92

"Éclair." *See* "Lightning"

Eclipse (Hogan), **AP:** 873

"Eclogue" (Lear), **BP:** 816

"Eclogue for Christmas, An" (MacNeice), **BP:** 861

Eclogues (Vergil), **EP:** 1082

Ecofeminism, **TE:** 693

Ecopoetry. *See* Categorized Index

"Ecstasy, The" (Donne), **BP:** 412

Ecuador (Michaux), **EP:** 691

Ed è subito sera (Quasimodo), **EP:** 876

Eddic poetry, **TE:** 227, **TE:** 526

Edge Effect (McPherson), **AP:** 1264

Edward Symmes, Robert. *See* Duncan, Robert

Edwardian Age. *See* Categorized Index

Edwards, Eli. *See* McKay, Claude

Effort at Speech (Meredith), **AP:** 1315

Egill Skallagrímsson, **TE:** 527

Egloga, elegía, oda (Cernuda), **EP:** 223

Ego psychology, **TE:** 723

Egy mondat a zsarnokságról. See One Sentence on Tyranny

Egypt. *See* Geographical Index

Ehrhart, W. D., **AP:** 532-537; *Beautiful Wreckage*, **AP:** 535; *The Distance We Travel*, **AP:** 535; *Empire*, **AP:** 534; *A Generation of Peace*, **AP:** 534; *Mostly Nothing Happens*, **AP:** 535; *Rootless*, **AP:** 534; *The Samisdat Poems*, **AP:** 534; *Sleeping with the Dead*, **AP:** 536; *To Those Who Have Gone Home Tired*, **AP:** 534

Eich, Günther, **TE:** 308

Eichendorff, Joseph von, **EP:** 299-306, **TE:** 299; "Moonlit Night," **EP:** 303

Eight Longer Poems (Slavitt), **AP:** 1815

"Eighteen-Year-Old, The" (Morgenstern), **EP:** 731

"Eighth Eclogue" (Radnóti), **EP:** 882

Eigner, Larry, **TE:** 687

"Ein Wort." *See* "One Word"

Einstein (MacLeish), **AP:** 1249

"Eisenhower's Visit to Franco, 1959" (Wright), **AP:** 2228

"Éjfeli párbaj." *See* "Midnight Duel"

Ekalē. See Hecale

Ekelöf, Gunnar, **EP:** 306-312, **TE:** 544; "Absentia animi," **EP:** 309; *Dīwān över fursten av Emgión*, **EP:** 311; *Färjesång*, **EP:** 309; *Guide to the Underworld*, **EP:** 312; "A July Night," **EP:** 310; *A Mölna Elegy*, **EP:** 311; *Non serviam*, **EP:** 309; "En Outsiders väg," **EP:** 308; "A Reality [dreamed]," **EP:** 310; *Sagan om Fatumeh*, **EP:** 312; *Sent på jorden*, **EP:** 308

Ekelund, Vilhelm, **TE:** 541

Ekphrastic poetry. *See* Categorized Index

El Salvador. *See* Geographical Index

Elaine's Book (Wright), **AP:** 2238

Electric Light (Heaney), **BP:** 603

Eleftheroi poliorkimenoi (Solomos), **EP:** 992

"Elegía a doña Juana la Loca" (García Lorca), **EP:** 358

"Elegía interrumpida." *See* "Interrupted Elegy"

Elegia na odejście. See *Elegy for the Departure, and Other Poems*

Elegiac Feelings American (Corso), **AP:** 360

"Elegie" (Walther), **EP:** 1125

"Elegie upon the Death of the Deane of Pauls, Dr. John Donne, An" (Carew), **BP:** 211

Elegies; ancient Greece, **TE:** 323; England, **TE:** 162. *See also* Categorized Index

Elegies (Propertius), **EP:** 869

Elegies for the Hot Season (McPherson), **AP:** 1259

Elegies for Toshiko (Miyazawa), **WP:** 193

Elegies upon Sundry Occasions (Drayton), **BP:** 423

Elegy (Bang), **AP:** 88

Elegy (Levis), **AP:** 1131

Elegy, defined, **AP:** 2297, **BP:** 1381, **EP:** 1175, **TE:** 813, **WP:** 383

Elegy for the Departure, and Other Poems (Herbert), **EP:** 464

Elegy on a Toy Piano (Young), **AP:** 2259

"Elegy Written in a Country Churchyard" (Gray), **BP:** 546

Elemental Odes, The (Neruda), **WP:** 202

"Elementary School Classroom in a Slum, An" (Spender), **BP:** 1188

Elements of San Joaquin, The (Soto), **AP:** 1863

Elene (Cynewulf), **BP:** 349

"11th: and last booke of the Ocean to Scinthia, The" (Ralegh), **BP:** 1041

"Eliduc" (Marie de France), **EP:** 672

Eliot, T. S., BP: 458-468, **TE:** 189, **TE:** 652, **TE:** 715; *Ash Wednesday*, **BP:** 466; Basil Bunting, **BP:** 168; *Four Quartets*, **BP:** 466; "Gerontion," **BP:** 463; "The Hollow Men," **BP:** 465; "The Love Song of J. Alfred Prufrock," **BP:** 462; *On Poetry and Poets*, **TE:** 715; *The Use of Poetry and the Use of Criticism*, **TE:** 715; *The Waste Land*, **BP:** 463

Elision, defined, **AP:** 2297, **BP:** 1381, **EP:** 1175, **TE:** 813, **WP:** 383

Elizabethan Age, **TE:** 136. *See also* Categorized Index

"Ellbee Novelty Company, Inc." (Goldbarth), **AP:** 722

Elmslie, Kenward, **TE:** 674

Éloges (Perse), **EP:** 804

Eloisa to Abelard (Pope), **BP:** 1011

"Elsa's Eyes" (Aragon), **EP:** 40

Éluard, Paul, EP: 313-317, **TE:** 274; "Enfermé, seul," **EP:** 316; "Première du monde," **EP:** 316; "A Woman in Love," **EP:** 316

Elytis, Odysseus, EP: 317-323, **TE:** 342; *The Axion Esti*, **EP:** 320, **TE:** 344; *Fotodhendro ke i dhekati tetarti omorfia, To*, **EP:** 321; *Ilios o protos, mazi me tis parallayies pano se mian ahtidha*, **EP:** 320; *Maria Nephele*, **EP:** 322; "The Passion," **EP:** 321; *Prosanatolizmi*, **EP:** 320

Emanuel, James A., AP: 538-541; *Black Man Abroad*, **AP:** 540; *Jazz from the Haiku King*, **AP:** 540; *Panther Man*, **AP:** 539; *The Treehouse, and Other Poems*, **AP:** 539; *Whole Grain*, **AP:** 540

Émaux et camées. See *Enamels and Cameos*

Embirikos, Andreas, **TE:** 342

Emblem poetry, **TE:** 149

Emblems of a Season of Fury (Merton), **AP:** 1329

Emerson, Claudia, AP: 541-544; *Late Wife*, **AP:** 543; *Pharaoh, Pharaoh*, **AP:** 542; *Pinion*, **AP:** 542

Emerson, Ralph Waldo, AP: 544-553, **TE:** 179; "Brahma," **AP:** 549; "Concord Hymn," **AP:** 551; "Days," **AP:** 548; "Each and All," **AP:** 550; "Give All to Love," **AP:** 550; "Hamatraya," **AP:** 549; "The Humble Bee," **AP:** 551; "Ode," **AP:** 551; "The Problem," **AP:** 549; "The Rhodora," **AP:** 550; "The Snow-Storm," **AP:** 549; Henry David Thoreau, **AP:** 1979; "Threnody," **AP:** 550; "Uriel," **AP:** 549; Jones Very, **AP:** 2040; "Woodnotes," **AP:** 551

Emily Dickinson in Southern California (Kennedy), **AP:** 1025

Empedocles, **TE:** 326

Emphasis, defined, **AP:** 2297, **BP:** 1381, **EP:** 1175, **TE:** 813, **WP:** 383

Empire (Ehrhart), **AP:** 534

"Empire of the Senseless, The" (Fenton), **BP:** 490

Emplumada (Cervantes), **AP:** 299

Empress of the Death House, The (Derricotte), **AP:** 446

Empson, William, BP: 468-476; "Aubade," **BP:** 474; "Bacchus," **BP:** 473; *The Gathering Storm*, **BP:** 474; "This Last Pain," **BP:** 473

En Castellano (Otero), **EP:** 761

"En una noche oscura." *See* "Dark Night, The"

Enamels and Cameos (Gautier), **EP:** 375

Enckell, Rabbe, **TE:** 546

End of Beauty, The (Graham), **AP:** 728

"End of Chronos, The" (Ungaretti), **EP:** 1061

End of the Alphabet, The (Rankine), **AP:** 1603

"End of the Road, The" (Belloc), **BP:** 78

End-stop, defined, **AP:** 2297, **BP:** 1381, **EP:** 1175, **TE:** 813, **WP:** 383

Endimion and Phoebe (Drayton), **BP:** 419

Endpoint, and Other Poems (Updike), **AP:** 2022

Enemy Joy, The (Belitt), **AP:** 117

"Enfermé, seul" (Éluard), **EP:** 316

"Enfin" (Reverdy), **EP:** 888

Engels, Friedrich, **TE:** 760

England. *See* Geographical Index

Englands Heroicall Epistles (Drayton), **BP:** 420

English Bards and Scotch Reviewers (Byron), **BP:** 190

English poetry; fourteenth century, **TE:** 98-101, **TE:** 103-119; fifteenth century, **TE:** 120-129; sixteenth century, **TE:** 130-143; seventeenth century, **TE:** 144-159; eighteenth century, **TE:** 160-173; nineteenth century, **TE:** 174-184; twentieth century, **TE:** 185-213

Engo (poetic technique), **TE:** 417

"Engraving" (Ritsos), **EP:** 908

Enlightenment; Hungary, **TE:** 354; Italy, **TE:** 388; Poland, **TE:** 492. *See also* Categorized Index

Ennius, Quintus, **TE:** 446

Entertainment, The (Drummond), **BP:** 431

Entre el clavel y la espada (Alberti), **EP:** 10

"Enueg I" (Beckett), **EP:** 92

Envoy, defined, **AP:** 2298, **BP:** 1382, **EP:** 1176, **TE:** 814, **WP:** 384

"Envy of Instinct, The" (Galvin), **AP:** 646

Enzensberger, Hans Magnus, **EP:** 323-328, **TE:** 311; *Lighter than Air*, **EP:** 326; *The Sinking of the Titanic*, **EP:** 325

"Eolian Harp, The" (Coleridge), **BP:** 278

Epic, defined, **AP:** 2298, **BP:** 1382, **EP:** 1176, **TE:** 814, **WP:** 384

Epic of Sheik Bedreddin, The (Hikmet), **WP:** 121

Epics; England, **TE:** 161; Europe, **TE:** 214-231; Poland, **TE:** 494; Scandinavia, **TE:** 529; Serbia, **TE:** 566; Tibet, **TE:** 607. *See also* Categorized Index

Epicureanism, **TE:** 453

Epigram 2 M. (Callimachus), **EP:** 178

Epigram 30 M. (Callimachus), **EP:** 176

Epigrammes and Elegies (Davies), **BP:** 379

Epigrams; ancient Greece, **TE:** 329; England, **TE:** 162; Martial, **TE:** 456. *See also* Categorized Index

Epigrams (Martial), **EP:** 680

Epipsychidion (Shelley), **BP:** 1121

"Episode" (Khodasevich), **WP:** 136

"Epistle to a Patron, An" (Prince), **BP:** 1023

Epistle to Dr. Arbuthnot (Pope), **BP:** 1014

Epistles; ancient Greece, **TE:** 453; England, **TE:** 162

Epistles (Horace), **EP:** 517

Epistles (Jarman), **AP:** 956

Epistolae metricae. See *Metrical Letters*

"Epistolary Essay from M. G. to O. B. upon their Mutual Poems, An" (Rochester), **BP:** 1054

Epitaph (Corbière), **EP:** 262

Epitaphios (Ritsos), **EP:** 908, **TE:** 345

Epitaphs and Occasions (Fuller), **BP:** 502

Epithalamia (Donne), **BP:** 414

Epithalamion (Spenser), **BP:** 1198

"Epithalamium and Elegy" (Bynner), **AP:** 276

Epodes (Horace), **EP:** 513

Epstein, Edmund L., **TE:** 751

"Equanimity" (Murray), **BP:** 949

"Equilibrists, The" (Ransom), **AP:** 1610

"Equitan" (Marie de France), **EP:** 671

Erb, Elke, **TE:** 315

Erba, Luciano, **TE:** 410

Erben, Karel Jaromír, **TE:** 81

Erdrich, Louise, **AP:** 553-559, **TE:** 484; *Baptism of Desire*, **AP:** 556; *Jacklight*, **AP:** 555; *Original Fire*, **AP:** 557

"Ere Sleep Comes Down to Soothe the Weary Eyes" (Dunbar), **AP:** 505

Erec (Hartmann), **EP:** 444

Erga kai Emerai. See *Works and Days*

Erika (Heyen), **AP:** 845

"Erinnerung an die Maria A." *See* "Remembering Marie A."

Erlingsson, Thorsteinn, **TE:** 537

Eroding Witness (Mackey), **AP:** 1242

"Eros Turannos" (Robinson), **AP:** 1664

Erosion (Graham), **AP:** 728

"Erosion" (Pratt), **BP:** 1017

Erotic poetry, **TE:** 293; England, **TE:** 137

Errancy, The (Graham), **AP:** 730

Escape into You (Bell), **AP:** 122

"Escargots" (Ponge), **EP:** 852

Eschenbach, Wolfram von. *See* Wolfram von Eschenbach

Esenin, Sergei, **TE:** 520, **WP:** 90-95; *All Soul's Day*, **WP:** 93; *Anna*

Snegina, **WP:** 95; *Azure*, **WP:** 94; "Inonia," **WP:** 94; *Moskva kabatskaia*, **WP:** 94; *Persidskie motivi*, **WP:** 95; *Pugachov*, **WP:** 94; "Strana negodiaev," **WP:** 94

Espada, Martín, **AP:** 559-563; *Crucifixion in the Plaza de Armas*, **AP:** 562; *Imagine the Angels of Bread*, **AP:** 561; *The Immigrant Iceboy's Bolero*, **AP:** 560; *A Mayan Astronomer in Hell's Kitchen*, **AP:** 561; *Rebellion Is the Circle of a Lover's Hands*, **AP:** 561; *The Republic of Poetry*, **AP:** 562; *Trumpets from the Islands of Their Eviction*, **AP:** 560

Espadas como labios. See *Swords as if Lips*

España. See *Spain, Take This Cup from Me*

España (Gautier), **EP:** 373

"Esprit nouveau et les poètes, L'." See "New Spirit and the Poets, The"

Espriu, Salvador, **TE:** 52

Espronceda, José de, **TE:** 597

Essay on Criticism, An (Pope), **BP:** 1008, **TE:** 163, **TE:** 706

Essay on Man, An (Pope), **BP:** 1011

"Essay on Psychiatrists" (Pinsky), **AP:** 1543

Essex Poems, 1963-1967 (Davie), **BP:** 371

"Esta tarde, mi bien" (Cruz), **WP:** 66

Estío (Jiménez), **EP:** 537

Esto no es un libro (Otero), **EP:** 762

"Estrellas y grillo." See "Stars and Cricket"

Estuary, The (Beer), **BP:** 64

"Et Maintenant" (Reverdy), **EP:** 888

Eternal Feminine, cult of, **WP:** 36

Etherege, Sir George, **BP:** 476-480, **TE:** 621; "The Imperfect Enjoyment," **BP:** 479; "A Prologue Spoken at the Opening of the Duke's New Playhouse," **BP:** 479; "Silvia," **BP:** 478; "Song: Ladies, though to your conquering eyes," **BP:** 479; "Song: To happy youths," **BP:** 479; "Songs," **BP:** 477; "To a Lady, Asking Him How Long He Would Love Her," **BP:** 478; "To a Very Young Lady," **BP:** 478; "Voiture's Urania," **BP:** 478

Éthiopiques (Senghor), **WP:** 269

Ethnopoetics, **TE:** 481

"Euclid Alone Has Looked on Beauty Bare" (Millay), **AP:** 1346

Eugen, Berthold. See Brecht, Bertolt

Eugene Onegin (Pushkin), **WP:** 241

"Eumenides" (Aldington), **BP:** 21

Europe (Blake), **BP:** 99

Euthymiae Raptus (Chapman), **BP:** 233

Evans, Mari, **AP:** 563-567, **TE:** 8; *Continuum*, **AP:** 566; *A Dark and Splendid Mass*, **AP:** 565; *I Am a Black Woman*, **AP:** 564; *Nightstar, 1973-1978*, **AP:** 565

Ève (Péguy), **EP:** 796

"Eve of St. Agnes, The" (Keats), **BP:** 737

"Eve Speaks" (Untermeyer), **AP:** 2011

"Evening" (Novalis), **EP:** 751

"Evening Land, The" (Lawrence), **BP:** 799

Events and Wisdoms (Davie), **BP:** 371

Everlasting Mercy, The (Masefield), **BP:** 888

Everson, William, **AP:** 567-578; "Abrasive," **AP:** 572; *The Blowing of the Seed*, **AP:** 573; "Chainsaw," **AP:** 576; "The Chronicle of Division," **AP:** 573; *The Crooked Lines of God*, **AP:** 574; "The Fictive Wish," **AP:** 573; "First Winter Storm," **AP:** 571; *The Hazards of Holiness*, **AP:** 574; "I Know It as the Sorrow," **AP:** 571; "The Illusion," **AP:** 572; *The Integral Years*, **AP:** 576; "The Kiss of the Cross," **AP:** 575; *Man-Fate*, **AP:** 575; *The Masculine Dead*, **AP:** 572; *The Masks of Drought*, **AP:** 576; "Moongate," **AP:** 576; "The Presence," **AP:** 572; *The Rose of Solitude*, **AP:** 575; "Saints," **AP:** 574; "The Screed of the Flesh," **AP:** 574; "The Sides of a Mind," **AP:** 572; *These Are the Ravens*, **AP:** 571; "Who Sees Through the Lens," **AP:** 571; *The Year's Declension*, **AP:** 574

"Everyone Sang" (Sassoon), **BP:** 1085

Everything Else in the World (Dunn), **AP:** 519

Everything Is Burning (Stern), **AP:** 1902

Eve's Striptease (Kasdorf), **AP:** 998

Evidence (Oliver), **AP:** 1468

"Evocation of the Great Bear" (Bachmann), **EP:** 75

"Evolution" (Morgenstern), **EP:** 731

Evropeiskaya noch' (Khodasevich), **WP:** 136

Ewald, Johannes, **TE:** 533

"Excelente Balade of Charitie . . . , An" (Chatterton), **BP:** 240

"Excuse, The (Chartier), **EP:** 238

"Exequy, The" (King), **BP:** 747

"Exhortation" (Bogan), **AP:** 203

"Exiles" (Cavafy), **EP:** 207

Exiles and Marriages (Hall), **AP:** 778

Existentialism, **TE:** 203; France, **TE:** 277

Exister (Follain), **EP:** 337

Expansive poetry. See Categorized Index

Expectation Days (McPherson), **AP:** 1264

"Experiment with a Rat, The" (Rakosi), **AP:** 1593

Experimental poets. *See* Categorized Index

"Expiation, L'" (Hugo), **EP:** 524

"Explanation, An" (Goldbarth), **AP:** 722

Explanation of America, An (Pinsky), **AP:** 1543

Explication process, **AP:** 2273-2281, **BP:** 1357-1365, **EP:** 1151-1159, **TE:** 789-797, **WP:** 359-367

Explications/Interpretations (Wright), **AP:** 2235

Expounding the Doubtful Points (Lum), **AP:** 1205

"Express, The" (Spender), **BP:** 1189

Expressionism, **TE:** 305. *See also* Categorized Index

Expressions of Sea Level (Ammons), **AP:** 38

Extended metaphor, defined, **AP:** 2298, **BP:** 1382, **EP:** 1176, **TE:** 814, **WP:** 384

Exteriorismo (poetic technique), **TE:** 438

Eye-Level (Shore), **AP:** 1774

Eye Like a Strange Balloon, The (Bang), **AP:** 87

Eye rhyme, defined, **AP:** 2298, **BP:** 1382, **EP:** 1176, **TE:** 814, **WP:** 384

"Eyes of the World, The" (Beer), **BP:** 63

Ezekiel, Nissim, **TE:** 372, **TE:** 506

Fable for Critics, A (Lowell), **AP:** 1184

"Fable from the Cayoosh Country" (Barnard), **AP:** 105

Fable of Polyphemus and Galatea (Góngora y Argote), **EP:** 413

"Fable of Pyramus and Thisbe, The" (Góngora y Argote), **EP:** 413

Fables; England, **TE:** 162; Spain,

TE: 596. *See also* Categorized Index

Fables (Gay), **BP:** 517

Fables (Henryson), **BP:** 614, **TE:** 127

Fables choisies, mises en vers. See *Fables Written in Verse*

Fables Written in Verse (La Fontaine), **EP:** 581, **TE:** 252

Fabliau, defined, **AP:** 2298, **BP:** 1382, **EP:** 1176, **TE:** 814, **WP:** 384

Fabliaux, **TE:** 240

"Fabrication of Ancestors" (Dugan), **AP:** 499

"Fábula de Píramo y Tisbe." *See* "Fable of Pyramus and Thisbe, The"

Fábula de Polifemo y Galatea. See *Fable of Polyphemus and Galatea*

Façade (Sitwell), **BP:** 1149

Faccio, Rina. *See* Aleramo, Sibilla

Face (Alexie), **AP:** 23

Face, The (St. John), **AP:** 1697

Facing the River (Miłosz), **EP:** 718

Facing the Tree (Ignatow), **AP:** 947

Faerie Queene, The (Spenser), **BP:** 1196

"Fair Chloris in a pigsty lay" (Rochester), **BP:** 1052

Fairchild, B. H., **AP:** 579-582; *The Arrival of the Future*, **AP:** 580; *The Art of the Lathe*, **AP:** 581; *Early Occult Memory Systems of the Lower Midwest*, **AP:** 581; *Local Knowledge*, **AP:** 581; *Usher*, **AP:** 581

"Fairies, The" (Allingham), **BP:** 23

"Faith" (Guest), **AP:** 753

Falkner, Gerhard, **TE:** 317

Fall of America, The (Ginsberg), **AP:** 684

Fall of Hyperion, The (Keats), **BP:** 736

Fall of Princes (Lydgate), **BP:** 838

Fallacy; affective, **TE:** 747; intentional, **TE:** 747

"Falling" (Różewicz), **EP:** 921

Falling from Silence (Slavitt), **AP:** 1815

Falling Hour, The (Wojahn), **AP:** 2194

Falling rhyme, defined, **AP:** 2298, **BP:** 1382, **EP:** 1176, **TE:** 814, **WP:** 384

Falling rhythm, defined, **AP:** 2298, **BP:** 1382, **EP:** 1176, **TE:** 814, **WP:** 384

Falling Up (Silverstein), **AP:** 1784

False Gods, Real Men (Berrigan), **AP:** 140

"Familiale" (Prévert), **EP:** 864

Familiar, The (Kinsella), **BP:** 758

"Family Circle" (Arany), **EP:** 46

Family Gathering (Chappell), **AP:** 306

Family Goldschmitt, The (Coulette), **AP:** 364

"Family Portrait, Three Generations" (Rakosi), **AP:** 1593

"Fancies" (Newcastle), **BP:** 960

"Fanny" (Kizer), **AP:** 1050

Fanon, Frantz, **TE:** 770

Fanshawe, Sir Richard, **BP:** 481-487; "An Ode upon Occasion of His Majesty's Proclamation in the Year 1630," **BP:** 483; "Presented to His Highness," **BP:** 484; "The Rose," **BP:** 484; "The Royalist," **BP:** 484; "The Saint's Encouragement," **BP:** 483

Far Field, The (Roethke), **AP:** 1677

"Far Rockaway" (Schwartz), **AP:** 1742

Far Rockaway of the Heart, A (Ferlinghetti), **AP:** 598

"Farewell" (Rimbaud), **EP:** 902

"Farewell, Go with God!" (Unamuno y Jugo), **EP:** 1053

"Farewell to Tobacco, A" (Lamb), **BP:** 772

"Farewell Without a Guitar" (Stevens), **AP:** 1911

　　　　　　　　　　　　　　　　　　　　　　　Critical Survey of Poetry

"Faris" (Mickiewicz), **EP:** 706

Färjesång (Ekelöf), **EP:** 309

Farmer's Bride, The (Mew), **BP:** 896

Farming (Berry), **AP:** 151

"Farys." *See* "Faris"

"Fast Break" (Hirsch), **AP:** 855

Fast Speaking Woman (Waldman), **AP:** 2078

"Fat" (Lifshin), **AP:** 1139

Fata Morgana (Breton), **EP:** 161

Fatal Interview (Millay), **AP:** 1347

Fate (Ai), **AP:** 10

Fate of the Jury, The (Masters), **AP:** 1282

Fate's Kite (Smith), **AP:** 1823

Fates of the Apostles, The (Cynewulf), **BP:** 348

Father, The (Olds), **AP:** 1460

"Father and Son" (Kunitz), **AP:** 1086

Father Guzman (Stern), **AP:** 1898

Father Louis. *See* Merton, Thomas

Father of the Plague-Stricken, The (Słowacki), **EP:** 977

Fazendeiro do ar (Drummond de Andrade), **WP:** 81

Fearing, Kenneth, AP: 582-587; "American Rhapsody (2)" (Fearing, **AP:** 584; *Angel Arms*, **AP:** 584; *Dead Reckoning*, **AP:** 585; "The Drinkers," **AP:** 584; "Flophouse," **AP:** 586; *Stranger at Coney Island*, **AP:** 586

Feel of Rock, The (Whittemore), **AP:** 2143

Feldman, Irving, AP: 588-591; *The Life and Letters*, **AP:** 590; *The Lost Originals*, **AP:** 589; *The Pripet Marshes, and Other Poems*, **AP:** 589

Felhok. See Clouds

"Female, Extinct" (Beer), **BP:** 65

Feminine rhyme, defined, **AP:** 2298, **BP:** 1382, **EP:** 1176, **TE:** 814, **WP:** 384

Feminist criticism, **TE:** 736-742

Feminist criticism, defined, **AP:** 2298, **BP:** 1382, **EP:** 1176, **TE:** 814, **WP:** 384

Feminist poets; Africa, **TE:** 17; Germany, **TE:** 316; India, **TE:** 374; Mexico, **TE:** 438; Scandinavia, **TE:** 555. *See also* Categorized Index

"Femme noire." *See* "Black Woman"

Fennelly, Beth Ann, AP: 591-593; *Open House*, **AP:** 592; *Tender Hooks*, **AP:** 592

Fenton, James, BP: 487-491; "Cambodia," **BP:** 489; "Dead Soldiers," **BP:** 489; "The Empire of the Senseless," **BP:** 490; "A German Requiem," **BP:** 489; "God, a Poem," **BP:** 489; "In a Notebook," **BP:** 489; *The Love Bomb, and Other Musical Pieces*, **BP:** 490; "Nothing," **BP:** 490; "Out of Danger," **BP:** 490; *Selected Poems*, **BP:** 490

Ferdowsī. *See See* Firdusi

Ferlin, Nils, **TE:** 543

Ferlinghetti, Lawrence, AP: 593-601, **TE:** 665; *Americus, Book I*, **AP:** 600; *A Coney Island of the Mind*, **AP:** 597; "Dog," **AP:** 598; *A Far Rockaway of the Heart*, **AP:** 598; *How to Paint Sunlight*, **AP:** 599

Fervor de Buenos Aires (Borges), **WP:** 42

Fêtes galantes. See Gallant Parties

Feuilles d'automne, Les (Hugo), **EP:** 523

"Fiametta" (Bishop), **AP:** 178

"Fictive Wish, The" (Everson), **AP:** 573

Fidelity (Paley), **AP:** 1508

Field, Barron, **TE:** 30

Field, Edward, AP: 602-606; *After the Fall*, **AP:** 605; *A Frieze for a Temple of Love*, **AP:** 604; *A Full Heart*, **AP:** 604; *Stand Up, Friend, with Me*, **AP:** 603; *Variety Photoplays*, **AP:** 604

Field Guide (Hass), **AP:** 816

"Field Report" (Corso), **AP:** 360

Field Work (Heaney), **BP:** 601

Fields of Learning (Miles), **AP:** 1342

Fifty Minute Mermaid, The (Ní Dhomhnaill), **BP:** 966

Fifty Poems (Meleager). *See Garland*

Fifty Years, and Other Poems (Johnson), **AP:** 974

Fig for Momus, A (Lodge), **BP:** 820

Fighting Terms (Gunn), **BP:** 562

Figured Wheel, The (Pinsky), **AP:** 1545

Figurehead, and Other Poems (Hollander), **AP:** 884

Figures for an Apocalypse (Merton), **AP:** 1328

Figures of the Human (Ignatow), **AP:** 946

Filipino American poetry, **TE:** 25

Filostrato, The (Boccaccio), **EP:** 133

Fin de Satan, La (Hugo), **EP:** 525

"Fin du Globe" (MacBeth), **BP:** 842

Finch, Anne, BP: 491-495; "The Introduction," **BP:** 492; "A Nocturnal Reverie," **BP:** 493; "The Petition for an Absolute Retreat," **BP:** 493; "The Spleen," **BP:** 494; "To the Nightingale," **BP:** 494; "The Tree," **BP:** 493

"Finding Fault with My Sons" (Tao Qian), **WP:** 290

Findings (Berry), **AP:** 150

Findings (Howard), **AP:** 911

Fine! (Mayakovsky), **WP:** 180

"Fine di Crono." *See* "End of Chronos, The"

Fink, Diane. *See* Ackerman, Diane

Finland. *See* Geographical Index

Firdusi, WP: 96-100; *Sah-name*, **WP:** 98

Fire and Flower (Kasischke), **AP:** 1001

"Fire and Ice" (Frost), **AP:** 631

Fire Screen, The (Merrill), **AP:** 1319

Fire to Fire (Doty), **AP:** 485

Firefall (Van Duyn), **AP:** 2037

Fires (Carver), **AP:** 287

Fireside poets, **TE:** 633-638. *See also* Categorized Index

First and Last Words (Chappell), **AP:** 305

First Book of Urizen, The (Blake), **BP:** 100

First Cities, The (Lorde), **AP:** 1168

"First Confession" (Kennedy), **AP:** 1023

"First Death" (Justice), **AP:** 990

First Dream (Cruz), **WP:** 68

First Earl of Dorset. *See* Sackville, Thomas

"First Eclogue" (Garcilaso de la Vega), **EP:** 366

First Fruits of Australian Poetry (Field), **TE:** 30

First Indian on the Moon (Alexie), **AP:** 23

"First Letter to Calumpang" (Weigl), **AP:** 2104

First Love, and Other Poems (Rolfe), **AP:** 1684

First Morning, The (Viereck), **AP:** 2045

First person, defined, **AP:** 2298, **BP:** 1382, **EP:** 1176, **TE:** 814, **WP:** 384

First Poems (Merrill), **AP:** 1318

"First Song" (Kinnell), **AP:** 1034

First Will and Testament (Patchen), **AP:** 1523

"First Winter Storm" (Everson), **AP:** 571

Firstborn (Glück), **AP:** 712

Fischer, Ernst, **TE:** 761

"Fisches Nachtgesang." *See* "Fish's Lullaby"

"Fish, The" (Bishop), **AP:** 171

Fishman, Solomon. *See* Rolfe, Edwin

"Fish's Lullaby" (Morgenstern), **EP:** 730

"Fitz Adams' Story" (Lowell), **AP:** 1184

FitzGerald, Edward, BP: 495-500; *Rubáiyát of Omar Kháyyám,* **BP:** 497

"Fiumi, I." *See* "Rivers, The"

Five-Fold Mesh, The (Belitt), **AP:** 116

Five Great Odes (Claudel), **EP:** 248, **TE:** 271

"Fix" (Fulton), **AP:** 634

Flaccus, Aulus Persius. *See* Persius

Flanders. *See* Geographical Index

"Flea, The" (Donne), **BP:** 411

"Fleeing" (Sachs), **EP:** 934

Flesh and Blood (Williams), **AP:** 2165

Fletcher, Giles, **TE:** 152

Fletcher, John Gould, **TE:** 647

Fleurs de bonne volonté, Des (Laforgue), **EP:** 588

Fleurs du mal, Les. See Flowers of Evil

Flight of Swans, A (Tagore), **WP:** 285

Flint, F. S., **TE:** 648

Flint, Roland, AP: 607-611; *And Morning,* **AP:** 608; *Easy,* **AP:** 610; "Heads of the Children," **AP:** 608; "A Letter Home," **AP:** 609; "Little Men Who Come Blindly," **AP:** 610; *Pigeon,* **AP:** 609; *Say It,* **AP:** 608; "Sicily," **AP:** 609; *Stubborn,* **AP:** 609

Flood (Matthews), **AP:** 1287

Flood, The (Tomlinson), **BP:** 1274

"Flophouse" (Fearing), **AP:** 586

Flores del volcán/Flowers from the Volcano (Alegría), **WP:** 11

"Flower-Fed Buffaloes, The" (Lindsay), **AP:** 1152

Flower, Fist, and Bestial Wail (Bukowski), **AP:** 267

Flowers and Insects (Hughes), **BP:** 693

Flowers from theVolcano. See Flores del volcán/Flowers from the Volcano

Flowers of Evil (Baudelaire), **EP:** 82, **TE:** 266

Flowers of Unceasing Coincidence, The (Kelly), **AP:** 1018

Flowres of Sion (Drummond), **BP:** 431

"Flux" (Eberhart), **AP:** 531

Flying at Night (Kooser), **AP:** 1072

Foix, J. V., EP: 329-335, **TE:** 52; "I Was Riding at Full Gallop Around the City Walls, Pursued by a Throng of Superstitious Coalmongers," **EP:** 334; "The Partisans of the Sun," **EP:** 333; *Sol, i de dol,* **EP:** 333; "Without Symbolism," **EP:** 332

Folded Heart, The (Collier), **AP:** 338

Folding Cliffs, The (Merwin), **AP:** 1337

Folk poetry; China, **TE:** 56; Croatia, **TE:** 73; Czech, **TE:** 80; Germany, **TE:** 295; Greece, **TE:** 332; Hungary, **TE:** 356; India, **TE:** 370; Macedonia, **TE:** 475; and Adam Mickiewicz, **TE:** 493; Russia, **TE:** 520; Scandinavia, **TE:** 528; Serbia, **TE:** 566; Tibet, **TE:** 608

Follain, Jean, EP: 335-340; *Chants terrestres,* **EP:** 337; *Exister,* **EP:** 337; *La Main chaude,* **EP:** 336

Follas novas (Castro), **EP:** 195

Following Gravity (Applewhite), **AP:** 52

Fontaine, Jean de La. *See* La Fontaine, Jean de

"Food for Fire, Food for Thought" (Duncan), **AP:** 513

"Food of Love" (Kizer), **AP:** 1051

Fool I' the Forest, A (Aldington),
BP: 21

Foot/feet, defined, **AP:** 2298,
BP: 1382, **EP:** 1176, **TE:** 814,
WP: 384

"For a Freshman Reader" (Justice),
AP: 988

"For a Lamb" (Eberhart), **AP:** 529

For a Limited Time Only (Wallace),
AP: 2093

"For Artaud" (McClure), **AP:** 1209

"For C." (Whalen), **AP:** 2112

"For George Lamming" (Birney),
BP: 90

"For God in My Sorrows"
(McDonald), **AP:** 1219

"For Koras and Balafong" (Senghor),
WP: 268

For Louis Pasteur (Bowers), **AP:** 221

For My Brother Jesus (Layton),
BP: 811

"For My Daughter" (Kees), **AP:** 1009

For My People (Walker), **AP:** 2088

"For the Marriage of Faustus and
Helen" (Crane), **AP:** 381

For the Sleepwalkers (Hirsch),
AP: 855

For the Unfallen (Hill), **BP:** 642

For the Union Dead (Lowell),
AP: 1193

Force of Religion, The (Young),
BP: 1351

"Forced March" (Radnóti), **EP:** 882

Forces of Plenty, The (Voigt),
AP: 2056

Forché, Carolyn, AP: 611-618; *The
Angel of History*, **AP:** 616; *Blue
Hour*, **AP:** 616; *The Country
Between Us*, **AP:** 615; *Gathering
the Tribes*, **AP:** 613

Forefathers' Eve, part 3 (Mickiewicz),
EP: 706

Forefathers' Eve, parts 2 and 4
(Mickiewicz), **EP:** 705

Forerunner, The (Gibran), **AP:** 667

Foreseeable Futures (Matthews),
AP: 1288

"Forest Hymn, A" (Bryant), **AP:** 262

"Forest Lake" (Södergran), **EP:** 985

Forgiven Submarine, The (Codrescu),
AP: 332

Form, defined, **AP:** 2299, **BP:** 1383,
EP: 1177, **TE:** 815, **WP:** 385

Form of Loss, The (Bowers), **AP:** 220

Formalism, Russian, defined,
AP: 2299, **BP:** 1383, **EP:** 1177,
TE: 815, **WP:** 385

Formalist criticism, **TE:** 743-749

Forms of Exile (Montague), **BP:** 916

"Forsaken Garden, A" (Swinburne),
BP: 1234

Forssell, Lars, **TE:** 550

Fort, Paul, **TE:** 270

Fortunate Traveller, The (Walcott),
WP: 321

Fortunatus, Venantius, **TE:** 462

Foscolo, Ugo, EP: 340-345; *Le
Grazie*, **EP:** 344; *On Sepulchers*,
EP: 343; "Perhaps Because of the
Fateful Quiet," **EP:** 343;
"Sonetti," **EP:** 342; "To Louise
Pallavicini Fallen from a Horse,"
EP: 343; "To the Healed Friend,"
EP: 343; "You Nurturer of the
Muses," **EP:** 342

Foster, Joy. *See* Harjo, Joy

*Fotodhendro ke i dhekati tetarti
omorfia, To* (Elytis), **EP:** 321

Foucault, Michel, **TE:** 766, **TE:** 776

Found poetry, defined, **AP:** 2299,
BP: 1383, **EP:** 1177, **TE:** 815,
WP: 385

Fountain in Kentucky, A (Nims),
AP: 1424

Four Good Things (McMichael),
AP: 1256

Four Quartets (Eliot), **BP:** 466

Four Zoas, The (Blake), **BP:** 101

Fowler, Roger, **TE:** 758

Fox (Rich), **AP:** 1640

Fracastoro, Girolamo, EP: 345-354;
*Naugerius sive de poetica
dialogus*, **EP:** 352; *Syphilis*,
EP: 349

Frameless Windows, Squares of Light
(Song), **AP:** 1855

France. *See* Geographical Index

France, Marie de. *See* Marie de
France

Francis, Paula Marie. *See* Allen,
Paula Gunn

Francophone poetry; Africa, **TE:** 16;
Canada, **TE:** 37

Frank, Joseph, **TE:** 780

"Frankie and Johnnie" (Brown),
AP: 257

Franzén, Frans Mikael, **TE:** 532

Fray Luis. *See* León, Luis de

Frazer, Sir James George, **TE:** 719

Fredmans epistlar (Bellman),
TE: 532

Fredmans sånger (Bellman), **TE:** 532

Fredy Neptune (Murray), **BP:** 951

Free Union (Breton), **EP:** 161

Free verse, defined, **AP:** 2299,
BP: 1383, **EP:** 1177, **TE:** 815,
WP: 385

"Freedom and Discipline" (Carruth),
AP: 280

"Freeway 280" (Cervantes), **AP:** 300

"Fremdling, Der." *See* Stranger, The

French poetry; origins to seventeenth
century, **TE:** 232-253; eighteenth
century to present, **TE:** 254-282

French Revolution, The (Blake), **BP:** 99

Freneau, Philip, AP: 618-625; "On
the Universality and Other
Attributes of the God of Nature,"
AP: 622

Frescoes for Mr. Rockefeller's City
(MacLeish), **AP:** 1252

Freud, Sigmund, **TE:** 720

"Friendship" (Thoreau), **AP:** 1982

Frieze for a Temple of Love, A (Field),
AP: 604

Frithiof's Saga (Tegnér), **EP:** 1022

Fröding, Gustaf, **TE:** 538

From a Land Where Other People Live (Lorde), **AP:** 1169

From a Three-Cornered World (Mitsui), **AP:** 1357

"From an Old House in America" (Rich), **AP:** 1638

From Feathers to Iron (Day Lewis), **BP:** 387

"From House to Home" (Rossetti), **BP:** 1062

From Room to Room (Kenyon), **AP:** 1030

From Snow and Rock, from Chaos (Carruth), **AP:** 280

"From Stone to Steel" (Pratt), **BP:** 1018

From the Cables of Genocide (Cervantes), **AP:** 301

"From the Dark Tower" (Cullen), **AP:** 408

"From the Front" (Dacey), **AP:** 428

From the Joke Shop (Fuller), **BP:** 503

"From Yellow Lake" (Van Duyn), **AP:** 2033

Fronto, Marcus Cornelius, **TE:** 457

Frost, Robert, **AP:** 625-633, **TE:** 653; "After Apple-Picking," **AP:** 627; Peter Davison, **AP:** 438; "Fire and Ice," **AP:** 631; Lyn Lifshin, **AP:** 1138; "Mending Wall," **AP:** 631

"Frost at Midnight" (Coleridge), **BP:** 280

Frost Medal, **AP:** 2322, **CM:** 50, **TE:** 870

Frostenson, Katarina, **TE:** 556

Frühen Kränze, Die (Zweig), **EP:** 1145

"Früher Mittag." *See* "Early Noon"

Frye, Northrop, **AP:** 2294, **BP:** 1378, **EP:** 1172, **TE:** 719, **TE:** 810, **WP:** 380

Fu (poetic form), **TE:** 58

Fu, Du. *See* Du Fu

Fudo Trilogy, The (Snyder), **AP:** 1847

Fuel (Nye), **AP:** 1439

Fugitive poets. *See* Categorized Index

Fugues (Alegría), **WP:** 12

Führer Bunker, The (Snodgrass), **AP:** 1837

Fujiwara Teika, **TE:** 419

Full Heart, A (Field), **AP:** 604

Fuller, Roy, **BP:** 500-504; *Brutus's Orchard*, **BP:** 502; *Collected Poems, 1936-1961*, **BP:** 503; *Epitaphs and Occasions*, **BP:** 502; *From the Joke Shop*, **BP:** 503; "To M. S. Killed in Spain," **BP:** 501; "To My Brother," **BP:** 501

Fulton, Alice, **AP:** 633-638; *Cascade Experiment*, **AP:** 636; "Fix," **AP:** 634; "Fuzzy Feelings," **AP:** 635; "The Orthodox Waltz," **AP:** 635

"Funeral Ode on the Death of the Princess Charlotte" (Southey), **BP:** 1176

"Funland" (Abse), **BP:** 4

"Funnels, The" (Morgenstern), **EP:** 730

Für meine Genossen (Biermann), **EP:** 123

"Furious Versions" (Lee), **AP:** 1105

Furtado, Joseph, **TE:** 372

"Fury of Aerial Bombardment, The" (Eberhart), **AP:** 530

Futurism, **TE:** 651; Italy, **TE:** 401; Poland, **TE:** 497; Russia, **TE:** 520. *See also* Categorized Index

"Fuzzy Feelings" (Fulton), **AP:** 635

Gadanie po knige (Voznesensky), **WP:** 315

Gadara, Meleager of. *See* Meleager

Galgenlieder. See Gallows Songs, The

Gallagher, Tess, **AP:** 639-643;

Amplitude, **AP:** 641; and Raymond Carver, **AP:** 286; *Dear Ghosts*, **AP:** 642; *Instructions to the Double*, **AP:** 640; *Moon Crossing Bridge*, **AP:** 642; *My Black Horse*, **AP:** 642; *Under Stars*, **AP:** 641; *Willingly*, **AP:** 641

Gallant Parties (Verlaine), **EP:** 1096

Gallery of Harlem Portraits, A (Tolson), **AP:** 1986

Gallows Songs, The (Morgenstern), **EP:** 729

Gallus, **TE:** 451

Galvin, Brendan, **AP:** 644-653; *Atlantic Flyway*, **AP:** 647; "The Envy of Instinct," **AP:** 646; *Great Blue*, **AP:** 649; *Habitat*, **AP:** 651; *Hotel Malabar*, **AP:** 650; *The Minutes No One Owns*, **AP:** 649; *No Time for Good Reasons*, **AP:** 648; *Place Keepers*, **AP:** 650; "Running," **AP:** 647; *Saints in Their Ox-Hide Boat*, **AP:** 649; *Seals in the Inner Harbor*, **AP:** 649; *Sky and Island Light*, **AP:** 650; *The Strength of a Named Thing*, **AP:** 650; *Winter Oysters*, **AP:** 649; "The Winter Runner," **AP:** 647

"Ganymed" (Goethe), **EP:** 402

Garbage (Ammons), **AP:** 41

García Lorca, Federico, **EP:** 355-362, **TE:** 600; "Ballad of the Little Square," **EP:** 359; "Elegía a doña Juana la Loca," **EP:** 358; *The Gypsy Ballads of García Lorca*, **EP:** 359; *Lament for the Death of a Bullfighter*, **EP:** 360; *Poet in New York*, **EP:** 360; "Somnambule Ballad," **EP:** 359; "The Song of the Horseman," **EP:** 359

Garcilaso de la Vega, **EP:** 362-368, **TE:** 593; "First Eclogue,"

EP: 366; "Second Eclogue,"
  EP: 365
"Garden, The" (Whalen), AP: 2113,
  BP: 880
"Garden Note" (Lewis), AP: 1135
"Garden of Proserpine, The"
  (Swinburne), BP: 1232
Gardening in the Dark (Kasischke),
  AP: 1001
Gardner, Isabella, AP: 653-656;
  *Isabella Gardner: The Collected
  Poems*, AP: 656; *The Looking
  Glass*, AP: 654; *That Was Then*,
  AP: 655; *West of Childhood*,
  AP: 655
Gardons, S. S. *See* Snodgrass, W. D.
Garland (Meleager), EP: 686, TE: 329
Garlande of Laurell, The (Skelton),
  BP: 1157
Garrett, George, AP: 656-660;
  *Abraham's Knife, and Other
  Poems*, AP: 658; *Luck's Shining
  Child*, AP: 659; *The Reverend
  Ghost*, AP: 658
Gascoigne, George, BP: 505-512,
  TE: 136; *The Discourse of the
  Adventures Passed by Master F. J.*,
  BP: 509; "Gascoignes Good
  Morrow," BP: 511; "Gascoignes
  Memories," BP: 508; *A Hundreth
  Sundrie Flowres Bounde Up in
  One Small Poesie*, BP: 511; *The
  Steele Glas, a Satyre*, BP: 510
"Gascoignes Good Morrow"
  (Gascoigne), BP: 511
"Gascoignes Memories" (Gascoigne),
  BP: 508
Gasoline (Corso), AP: 359
"Gates, The" (Rukeyser), AP: 1691
Gathering of My Name, The (Eady),
  AP: 523
Gathering Storm, The (Empson),
  BP: 474
Gathering the Bones Together (Orr),
  AP: 1488

Gathering the Tribes (Forché),
  AP: 613
Gatomachia (Vega Carpio), EP: 1078
Gaucho Martin Fierro, The
  (Hernández), WP: 116
Gaudete (Hughes), BP: 691
Gautier, Théophile, EP: 368-377,
  TE: 264; "À Zurbarán," EP: 374;
  "Albertus," EP: 373; "Art,"
  EP: 375; *The Drama of Death*,
  EP: 373; *Enamels and Cameos*,
  EP: 375; *España*, EP: 373; "In
  deserto," EP: 373; *Poésies*,
  EP: 372; "Symphony in White
  Major," EP: 375
Gawain poems, TE: 104
Gawain-Poet. *See* Pearl-Poet
Gay and lesbian culture. *See*
  Categorized Index
Gay, John, BP: 512-520; "A
  Contemplation on Night,"
  BP: 517; *Fables*, BP: 517;
  "Proem to the Courteous Reader,"
  BP: 516; "The Ravens, the
  Sexton, and the Earth-Worm,"
  BP: 518; *The Shepherd's Week*,
  BP: 516; *Trivia*, BP: 517; *Wine*,
  BP: 516
"Gazing at Yellow Crane Mountain"
  (Li Bo), WP: 154
Gdzie wschodzi słońce i kędy zapada
  (Miłosz), EP: 717
Ge-sar epic, TE: 607
Gebir (Landor), BP: 778
"Gedicht, Das." *See* "Poem, The"
Gedichte und lyrische Dramen. See
  Poems and Verse Plays
Gedichten, gezangen, en gebeden
  (Gezelle), EP: 387
"Geese, The" (Graham), AP: 726
Geijer, Erik Gustaf, TE: 535
Geistliche Lieder. See *Devotional
  Songs*
Gellius, Aulus, TE: 457
Gender; feminist criticism, TE: 736;

performance of, TE: 777; queer
  theory, TE: 774; social
  construction of, TE: 777
"General William Booth Enters into
  Heaven" (Lindsay), AP: 1149
Generation of '98, TE: 598. *See also*
  Categorized Index
Generation of '27, TE: 598. *See also*
  Categorized Index
Generation of '68, TE: 498. *See also*
  Categorized Index
Generation of Peace, A (Ehrhart),
  AP: 534
"Generations" (Gurney), BP: 570
Generations (Rogers), AP: 1681
Genezis z ducha (Słowacki), EP: 979
Genius of the Crowd, The
  (Bukowski), AP: 268
Genius versus wit, TE: 166
"Gentle Reader" (Jacobsen), AP: 952
Gentle Weight Lifter, The (Ignatow),
  AP: 944
Geocentric (Rogers), AP: 1680
Geography of Lograire, The (Merton),
  AP: 1330
Geography of the Near Past (Young),
  AP: 2253
Georg Büchner Prize, CM: 49,
  EP: 1206, TE: 869
George Washington Poems, The
  (Wakoski), AP: 2071
George, Stefan, EP: 377-384,
  TE: 304; *Algabal*, EP: 381; *The
  Seventh Ring*, EP: 383; *The Year
  of the Soul*, EP: 382
Georgian poetry, TE: 187
Georgian poets. *See* Categorized Index
Georgics (Vergil), EP: 1083
German Democratic Republic poetry.
  See East German poetry
German poetry; origins to nineteenth
  century, TE: 283-297; nineteenth
  century to Reunification,
  TE: 298-314; Reunification to
  present, TE: 315-319

"German Requiem, A" (Fenton),
  BP: 489
Germany. *See* Geographical Index
"Gerontion" (Eliot), **BP:** 463
Gerstler, Amy, AP: 660-663; *Bitter
  Angel,* **AP:** 661; *Dearest
  Creature,* **AP:** 662; *Ghost Girl,*
  AP: 662; *The True Bride,* **AP:** 661
Gerusalemme conquistata. See
  Jerusalem Conquered
Gerusalemme liberata. See *Jerusalem
  Delivered*
Gesammelten Gedichte, (Zweig),
  EP: 1145
"Gestundete Zeit, Die." *See*
  "Borrowed Time"
Gestundete Zeit, Die (Bachmann),
  EP: 74
Gesualdo (Hejinian), **AP:** 839
Gezelle, Guido, EP: 384-391;
  XXXIII Kleengedichtjes, **EP:** 388;
  Dichtoefeningen, **EP:** 386;
  Driemaal XXXIII kleengedichtjes,
  EP: 389; *Gedichten, gezangen, en
  gebeden,* **EP:** 387; *Rijmsnoer,*
  EP: 390; *Tijdkrans,* **EP:** 389
Ghana. *See* Geographical Index
Ghazal, defined, **AP:** 2299, **BP:** 1383,
  EP: 1177, **TE:** 815, **WP:** 385
Ghazals. *See* Categorized Index
Ghose, Sri Aurobindo, **TE:** 369
Ghose, Kasiprasad, **TE:** 367
Ghose, Manmohan, **TE:** 371
Ghost Girl (Gerstler), **AP:** 662
Ghost of Eden, The (Twichell),
  AP: 2003
Ghost Soldiers, The (Tate), **AP:** 1958
Giacometti's Dog (Becker), **AP:** 111
Giambi ed epodi (Carducci), **EP:** 189
Giant Night (Waldman), **AP:** 2078
Gibran, Kahlil, AP: 663-670; *The
  Forerunner,* **AP:** 667; *The
  Procession,* **AP:** 667; *The
  Prophet,* **AP:** 667; *Sand and
  Foam,* **AP:** 668

Gibson, Margaret, AP: 670-673;
  Autumn Grasses, **AP:** 672;
  Memories of the Future, **AP:** 672;
  Signs, **AP:** 671
"Gift, The" (Lee), **AP:** 1104
Gift, A (Slavitt), **AP:** 1815
Gilbert, Anne Hart, **TE:** 43
Gilbert, Jack, AP: 673-676; *The
  Dance Most of All,* **AP:** 676; *The
  Great Fires,* **AP:** 675; *Monolithos,*
  AP: 675; *Refusing Heaven,*
  AP: 676; *Views of Jeopardy,*
  AP: 675
Gilbert, Nicolas-Joseph-Laurent,
  TE: 257
Gilded Lapse of Time, A
  (Schnackenberg), **AP:** 1730
Ginsberg, Allen, AP: 677-688,
  TE: 662; "Birdbrain," **AP:** 684;
  Collected Poems, 1947-1997,
  AP: 686; *Cosmopolitan
  Greetings,* **AP:** 685; *The Fall of
  America,* **AP:** 684; "Howl,"
  AP: 680, **TE:** 663; "Kaddish,"
  AP: 681; "Kral Majales,"
  AP: 682; *Mind Breaths,* **AP:** 684;
  Plutonian Ode, **AP:** 684; *White
  Shroud,* **AP:** 684; "Witchita
  Vortex Sutra," **AP:** 683
Gioia, Dana, AP: 688-692; *Daily
  Horoscope,* **AP:** 690; *The Gods of
  Winter,* **AP:** 690; *Interrogations at
  Noon,* **AP:** 691
Giovanni, Nikki, AP: 692-702,
  TE: 11; *Acolytes,* **AP:** 700;
  Bicycles, **AP:** 700; *Blues,* **AP:** 699;
  *The Collected Poetry of Nikki
  Giovanni, 1968-1998,* **AP:** 699;
  Cotton Candy on a Rainy Day,
  AP: 697; *Love Poems,* **AP:** 699;
  My House, **AP:** 696; "Nikki-Rosa,"
  TE: 11; *The Selected Poems of
  Nikki Giovanni,* **AP:** 699
Giovanni, Yolande Cornelia. *See*
  Giovanni, Nikki

Giraffe (Plumly), **AP:** 1558
Girl in Glass, The (Smith), **AP:** 1828
Girly Man (Bernstein), **AP:** 135
Gitanjali Song Offerings (Tagore),
  WP: 285
Giusti, Giuseppe, EP: 391-396; "The
  Boot," **EP:** 394; "In Sant'
  Ambrogio's," **EP:** 395; "The Land
  of the Dead," **EP:** 394; *Notable
  scherzi,* **EP:** 394; "The Snail,"
  EP: 395; "The Trifler," **EP:** 395
"Give All to Love" (Emerson),
  AP: 550
Given (Berry), **AP:** 153
Given Sugar, Given Salt (Hirshfield),
  AP: 861
Gjuzel, Bogomil, **TE:** 476
Glancy, Diane, AP: 702-706; *Asylum
  in the Grasslands,* **AP:** 704; *Iron
  Woman,* **AP:** 705; *The Relief of
  America,* **AP:** 705; *Rooms,*
  AP: 706
Glare (Ammons), **AP:** 41
Glass Face in the Rain, A (Stafford),
  AP: 1878
Glass Hammer, The (Hudgins),
  AP: 926
Glassworks (Wojahn), **AP:** 2191
Glatter, Miklós. *See* Radnóti, Miklós
Glenn, Mel, AP: 706-710; *Class
  Dismissed!,* **AP:** 708; *Jump Ball,*
  AP: 709; *Split Image,* **AP:** 709;
  Who Killed Mr. Chippendale?,
  AP: 708
Gli Asolani (Bembo), **EP:** 104
Glu (poetic form), **TE:** 608
Glück, Louise, AP: 710-719; *Ararat,*
  AP: 715; *Averno,* **AP:** 717;
  Descending Figure, **AP:** 713;
  Firstborn, **AP:** 712; *The House on
  Marshland,* **AP:** 713;
  Meadowlands, **AP:** 716;
  "October," **AP:** 717; *The Triumph
  of Achilles,* **AP:** 714; *A Village
  Life,* **AP:** 718; *Vita Nova,* **AP:** 716

Gnomes and Occasions (Nemerov),
    AP: 1413
Gnomic verse, defined, **AP:** 2299,
    BP: 1383, **EP:** 1177, **TE:** 815,
    WP: 385
"Go, Lovely Rose" (Waller),
    BP: 1295
"Goblin Market" (Rossetti), **BP:** 1062
"God" (Lawrence), **BP:** 801
"God, a Poem" (Fenton), **BP:** 489
God Defend New Zealand (Bracken),
    TE: 35
God of Indeterminacy, The
    (McPherson), **AP:** 1264
Godfrey of Strawbourg. *See* Gottfried
    von Strassburg
Godhead (Kinsella), **BP:** 758
"Godhead as Lynx, The" (Sarton),
    AP: 1720
"Gods of Greece, The" (Schiller),
    EP: 954
Gods of Winter, The (Gioia), **AP:** 690
God's Silence (Wright), **AP:** 2220
God's Trombones (Johnson), **AP:** 974
Godzinna myśli (Słowacki), **EP:** 976
Goethe, age of. *See* Categorized
    Index
Goethe, Johann Wolfgang von,
    EP: 396-405, **TE:** 295;
    "Ganymed," **EP:** 402;
    "Prometheus," **EP:** 402; *Roman
    Elegies*, **EP:** 402; "Welcome and
    Farewell," **EP:** 401; *West-Eastern
    Divan*, **EP:** 403
"Going, Going" (Larkin), **BP:** 792
Going Back to the River (Hacker),
    AP: 767
Going for the Rain (Ortiz), **AP:** 1496
Gold Cell, The (Olds), **AP:** 1460
Gold Coast Customs (Sitwell),
    BP: 1151
Gold of Tigers, The (Borges), **WP:** 42
Goldbarth, Albert, AP: 719-725;
    "Ellbee novelty Company, Inc.,"
    AP: 722; "An Explanation,"

AP: 722; "Khirbet Shema,"
    AP: 721; "Song for Longing,"
    AP: 722; "The Story of
    Civilization," **AP:** 721; "The Two
    Domains," **AP:** 723
Golden age, China, **TE:** 60
Golden Age, Latin. *See* Categorized
    Index
Golden Age, Roman. *See* Categorized
    Index
Golden Age, Spanish. *See*
    Categorized Index
Golden Bough, The (Frazer), **TE:** 719
Golden Gate, The (Seth), **WP:** 274
Golden Legend, The (Longfellow),
    AP: 1164
Golden State (Bidart), **AP:** 163
Golden Wreath Award, **CM:** 51,
    EP: 1207, **TE:** 871, **WP:** 410
Goldsmith, Oliver, BP: 520-525,
    TE: 169; *The Deserted Village*,
    BP: 523; *The Traveller*, **BP:** 522
"Goldyn Targe, The" (Dunbar),
    BP: 445
"Golf Links, The" (Cleghorn),
    TE: 762
"Golgotha Is a Mountain"
    (Bontemps), **AP:** 207
Golob, Zvonimir, **TE:** 76
Goluben'. See See *Azure*
Gomringer, Eugen, EP: 405-410;
    *Poesie als Mittel der
    Umweltgestaltung*, **EP:** 406;
    Worte sind Schatten, **EP:** 408
Goncourt Prize in Poetry, **CM:** 52,
    EP: 1208, **TE:** 872
Gondibert (Davenant), **BP:** 365
Góngora y Argote, Luis de,
    EP: 410-415, **TE:** 594, **TE:** 618;
    Fable of Polyphemus and Galatea,
    EP: 413; "The Fable of Pyramus
    and Thisbe," **EP:** 413; *The
    Solitudes*, **EP:** 414
Gongorism, **TE:** 594, **TE:** 618
Gonzaga, Russell, **TE:** 26

Gonzales, Rodolfo, **TE:** 468
González Martínez, Enrique,
    WP: 101-107; *Lirismos*,
    WP: 104; *La muerte del cisne*,
    WP: 106; *Preludios*, **WP:** 104;
    Los senderos ocultos, **WP:** 105;
    Silénter, **WP:** 105; "Wring the
    Swan's Neck," **WP:** 104
Gonzalo de Berceo, **TE:** 586
Good Fight, The (Kinsella), **BP:** 756
Good Journey, A (Ortiz), **AP:** 1497
Good Morning, America (Sandburg),
    AP: 1709
Good Morning and Good Night
    (Wagoner), **AP:** 2066
*Good News of Death, and Other
    Poems* (Simpson), **AP:** 1795
*Good Night, Willie Lee, I'll See You in
    the Morning* (Walker), **AP:** 2083
Good Time Was Had by All, A
    (Smith), **BP:** 1167
Good Times (Clifton), **AP:** 328
Good Trembling (Wormser),
    AP: 2199
Good Woman (Clifton), **AP:** 328
Goodside, Grace. *See* Paley, Grace
Googe, Barnabe, **TE:** 135
Gordon, Adam Lindsay, **TE:** 31
Gordon, George. *See* Byron, Lord
Gorenko, Anna Andreyevna. *See*
    Akhmatova, Anna
"Gorod" (Blok), **WP:** 36
"Gospel of Beauty, The" (Lindsay),
    AP: 1150
Gothic literature, **TE:** 167
Gotovac, Vlado, **TE:** 76
Gottfried von Strassburg, EP: 415-
    418; *Tristan and Isolde*, **EP:** 416
Gottsched, Johann Christoph,
    TE: 294
Gourmont, Remy de, **TE:** 640
Governor General's Literary Awards
    (English-language poetry),
    CM: 52, **TE:** 872
Governor General's Literary Awards

(French-language poetry),
CM: 52, **TE:** 872
Governor-General's Award in Poetry
(English), **BP:** 1409
Governor-General's Award in Poetry
(French), **BP:** 1409
Govoni, Corrado, **TE:** 400
Gower, John, BP: 525-533;
Confessio Amantis, **BP:** 531,
TE: 112; *Mirour de l'Omme*,
BP: 528; *Vox Clamantis*, **BP:** 529
Gozzano, Guido, **TE:** 400
Grace Leven Prize for Poetry,
BP: 1410, **CM:** 56, **TE:** 876
Grace Notes (Dove), **AP:** 490
Graham, Jorie, AP: 725-731; *The
End of Beauty*, **AP:** 728; *Erosion*,
AP: 728; *The Errancy*, **AP:** 730;
"The Geese," **AP:** 726; *Hybrids of
Plants and of Ghosts*, **AP:** 727;
Region of Unlikeness, **AP:** 730;
Swarm, **AP:** 730
Grainger, James, **TE:** 43
Grammar and language, **TE:** 753
Gramsci, Antonio, **TE:** 760
*Grand Testament, Le. See Great
Testament, The*
"Grandmother Poems, The"
(Derricotte), **AP:** 446
Grass, Günter, EP: 418-424; *Letzte
Tänze*, **EP:** 421; *Novemberland*,
EP: 421
"Grasshopper, The" (Lovelace), **BP:** 829
Grave of the Right Hand, The
(Wright), **AP:** 2209
"Grave Piece" (Eberhart), **AP:** 531
Graves, Robert, BP: 534-542; "The
Cool Web," **BP:** 537; "The Legs,"
BP: 538; "The Naked and the
Nude," **BP:** 537; "The
Philosopher," **BP:** 538; "The Pier-
Glass," **BP:** 538; "Return of the
Goddess," **BP:** 540; "The Sweet
Shop Around the Corner,"
BP: 540

"Graveyard by the Sea, The" (Valéry),
EP: 1069
Graveyard school, **TE:** 628. *See also*
Categorized Index
Gray, Thomas, BP: 542-548,
TE: 169; "The Bard," **BP:** 547;
"Elegy Written in a Country
Churchyard," **BP:** 546; "Hymn to
Adversity," **BP:** 545; "Ode on a
Distant Prospect of Eton College,"
BP: 545; "Ode on the Spring,"
BP: 544; "The Progress of Poesy,"
BP: 547
Grazie, Le (Foscolo), **EP:** 344
Grażyna (Mickiewicz), **EP:** 705
Great Bird of Love, The (Zimmer),
AP: 2263
Great Blue (Galvin), **AP:** 649
"Great Blue Heron, The" (Kizer),
AP: 1051
Great Britain. *See* Geographical Index
Great Cloak, The (Montague),
BP: 919
Great Enigma, The (Transtfömer),
EP: 1043
Great Fires, The (Gilbert), **AP:** 675
Great Hunger, The (Kavanagh),
BP: 729
Great Testament, The (Villon),
EP: 1109
Greatcoat, Dai. *See* Jones, David
Greece. *See* Geographical Index
Greed (Ai), **AP:** 10
Greed (Wakoski), **AP:** 2074
Greek Anthology (Leonidas), **EP:** 604
Greek Anthology, The (Meleager),
EP: 687
Greek poetry; antiquity, **TE:** 215,
TE: 320-330; since 1820,
TE: 331-351
Green Dark, The (Ponsot), **AP:** 1570
Green movement, **TE:** 690-695
"Green Springs the Tree" (Taylor),
AP: 1972
Green Wall, The (Wright), **AP:** 2224

Greenblatt, Stephen, **TE:** 764
Greene, Robert, BP: 548-555; *A
Maiden's Dream*, **BP:** 553
Gregerson, Linda, AP: 732-735;
Magnetic North, **AP:** 734;
Waterborne, **AP:** 733; *The Woman
Who Died in Her Sleep*, **AP:** 733
Gregg, Linda, AP: 735-738; *All of It
Singing*, **AP:** 738; *Chosen by the
Lion*, **AP:** 737; *In the Middle
Distance*, **AP:** 737; *The
Sacraments of Desire*, **AP:** 737;
Things and Flesh, **AP:** 737; *Too
Bright to See*, **AP:** 736
Gregorčič, Simon, **TE:** 580
Gregorius (Hartmann), **EP:** 445
Gregory, Horace, AP: 738-741;
Chelsea Rooming House,
AP: 740; *Chorus for Survival*,
AP: 740; *Collected Poems*,
AP: 740
Grennan, Eamon, AP: 741-744; *As
if It Matters*, **AP:** 743; *Relations*,
AP: 743; *Still Life with Waterfall*,
AP: 743
Grenstone Poems (Bynner), **AP:** 276
Greville, Fulke, BP: 555-560;
Alaham, **BP:** 558; *Caelica*,
BP: 558; *Mustapha*, **BP:** 558
Grieg, Nordahl, **TE:** 547
Grieve, Christopher Murray. *See*
MacDiarmid, Hugh
"Grifel' naia oda." *See* "Slate Ode"
Griffin Poetry Prize, **AP:** 2323,
BP: 1410, **CM:** 53, **TE:** 873
Grindel, Eugène. *See* Éluard, Paul
Grooks (Hein), **EP:** 450
Ground Work: Before the War
(Duncan), **AP:** 515
"Groundhog, The" (Eberhart),
AP: 528
"Groundhog Revisiting, The"
(Eberhart), **AP:** 530
"Group Life" (Betjemen), **BP:** 84
Grove Day, A., **TE:** 481

Growing into Love (Kennedy),
    AP: 1023
Growth of Love, The (Bridges),
    BP: 133
Gruk. See Grooks
Grünbein, Durs, **TE:** 318
Grundtvig, N. F. S., **TE:** 534
Gruppe. *See* Categorized Index
Gryphius, Andreas, **TE:** 292
Guadalupe. *See* Geographical Index
"Guardador de rebanhos, O." *See*
    "Keeper of Flocks, The"
Guarini, Battista, **TE:** 385
Gucio zaczarowany (Miłosz),
    EP: 716
"Guerre" (Reverdy), **EP:** 886
Guest, Barbara, **AP:** 745-748,
    TE: 674; *Miniatures, and Other
    Poems*, **AP:** 746; *The Red Gaze*,
    AP: 747; *Symbiosis*, **AP:** 746
Guest, Edgar A., **AP:** 748-753;
    "Faith," **AP:** 753; "Home,"
    AP: 752
Guests of Space (Hollo), **AP:** 892
Guide to the Ruins (Nemerov),
    AP: 1411
Guide to the Underworld (Ekelöf),
    EP: 312
Guillaume de Lorris, **EP:** 424-430;
    The Romance of the Rose,
    EP: 426, **TE:** 240
Guillén, Jorge, **EP:** 430-434;
    Canticle, **EP:** 432; *Clamor*,
    EP: 432; *Homage*, **EP:** 433
Guitar and Concertina (Fröding),
    TE: 538
Gujarati poetry. *See* Indian English
    poetry
Gulf Music (Pinsky), **AP:** 1546
Gulf, and Other Poems, The
    (Walcott), **WP:** 320
Gullberg, Hjalmar, **TE:** 543
Gumilyov, Nikolay, **TE:** 518
Gundulić, Ivan, **TE:** 72
"Gunga Din" (Kipling), **BP:** 765

Gunn, Thom, **BP:** 560-568; *Boss
    Cupid*, **BP:** 567; *Fighting Terms*,
    BP: 562; *Jack Straw's Castle, and
    Other Poems*, **BP:** 565; *The Man
    with Night Sweats*, **BP:** 567;
    Moly, **BP:** 565; *My Sad Captains,
    and Other Poems*, **BP:** 563; *The
    Passages of Joy*, **BP:** 566;
    Positives, **BP:** 564; *The Sense of
    Movement*, **BP:** 563; *Touch*,
    BP: 564; *Undesirables*, **BP:** 566
Gunnarsson, Pétur, **TE:** 561
Gunslinger (Dorn), **AP:** 478
Gunslinger Book III (Dorn), **AP:** 479
Gurney, Ivor, **BP:** 568-574;
    "Canadians," **BP:** 571;
    "Generations," **BP:** 570; "To His
    Love," **BP:** 570
Gushi (poetic form), **TE:** 59
Gustafsson, Lars, **TE:** 555
"Gutenberg as Card Shark" (Cassity),
    AP: 293
Guthmundsson, Tómas, **TE:** 548
Gynocriticism, **TE:** 736
Gyöngyösi, István, **TE:** 354
"Gypsies" (Clare), **BP:** 256
Gypsy Ballads of García Lorca, The
    (García Lorca), **EP:** 359
"Gyrtt in my giltlesse gowne"
    (Surrey), **BP:** 1215

H. D., **AP:** 754-760, **TE:** 188,
    TE: 647; "Oread," **AP:** 756
Ha-Ha, The (Kirby), **AP:** 1041
Haavikko, Paavo, **EP:** 435-441,
    TE: 552; *Neljätoista hallitsijaa*,
    EP: 440; *One and Twenty*,
    EP: 440; *The Winter Palace*,
    EP: 438
Haavio, Martti. *See* Mustapää, P.
"Habit of Angels, The" (Belitt),
    AP: 116
Habitat (Galvin), **AP:** 651
Hacedor, El. See Dream Tigers
Hacker, Marilyn, **AP:** 761-768;

Assumptions, **AP:** 765; *Going
    Back to the River*, **AP:** 767;
    Presentation Piece, **AP:** 762;
    Separations, **AP:** 764; *Squares
    and Courtyards*, **AP:** 767; *Taking
    Notice*, **AP:** 764; *Winter Numbers*,
    AP: 767
"Haecceity" (Cunningham), **AP:** 420
Hafiz, **WP:** 108-113
Hagedorn, Jessica, **TE:** 25
Hagiwara Sakutarō, **TE:** 429
Hahn, Kimiko, **AP:** 768-772;
    Mosquito and Ant, **AP:** 770; *The
    Narrow Road to the Interior*,
    AP: 771; *Toxic Flora*, **AP:** 771;
    The Unbearable Heart, **AP:** 770;
    Volatile, **AP:** 770
Hahn, Ulla, **TE:** 316
Haikai no renga (poetic form),
    TE: 422
Haiku, **TE:** 420, **TE:** 427. *See also*
    Categorized Index
Haiku, defined, **AP:** 2299, **BP:** 1383,
    EP: 1177, **TE:** 815, **WP:** 385
Haines, John Meade, **AP:** 772-775;
    "I am a Tree, Very Quiet are My
    Leaves," **AP:** 773; *The Owl in the
    Mask of the Dreamer*, **AP:** 775;
    "Pickers," **AP:** 774
"Hair" (Lifshin), **AP:** 1140
Håkansson, Björn, **TE:** 554
Ha-Levi, Judah. *See* Judah ha-Levi
Halevi, Yehuda. *See* Judah ha-Levi
Half-Inch Himalayas, The (Ali),
    AP: 26
Halfway (Kumin), **AP:** 1075
Hall, Donald, **AP:** 775-785; *The
    Alligator Bride*, **AP:** 779; *The
    Dark Houses*, **AP:** 778; *Exiles and
    Marriages*, **AP:** 778; *The Happy
    Man*, **AP:** 781; *Jane Kenyon*,
    AP: 1028; *Kicking the Leaves*,
    AP: 780; *The Museum of Clear
    Ideas*, **AP:** 782; *Old and New
    Poems*, **AP:** 782; *The Old Life*,

AP: 782; *The One Day*, AP: 781;
The Painted Bed, AP: 783; *A Roof
of Tiger Lilies*, AP: 779; *The
Town of Hill*, AP: 779; *White
Apples and the Taste of Stone*,
AP: 784; *Without*, AP: 783; *The
Yellow Room*, AP: 779

Hall, Helen Diane. *See* Glancy, Diane

Hall, Lyn. *See* Hejinian, Lyn

Hallam, Arthur Henry, BP: 575-
579; *Remains, in Verse and Prose*,
BP: 576

"Halleluja" (Sachs), EP: 933

"Hallelujah" (Cohen), BP: 275

Halliday, M. A. K., TE: 755

"Halt in the Wilderness, A"
(Brodsky), WP: 49

"Hamatraya" (Emerson), AP: 549

Hamlet of A. MacLeish, The
(MacLeish), AP: 1249

Hammer of the Village, The (Petőfi),
EP: 821

Hampl, Patricia, AP: 785-789;
Resort, and Other Poems,
AP: 787; *Woman Before an
Aquarium*, AP: 787

Hamri, Thorsteinn frá, TE: 561

Han Yu, TE: 62

Handwriting (Ondaatje), BP: 976

Hangover Mass (Kennedy), AP: 1026

Haoran, Meng. *See* Meng Haoran

"Happily Neighing, the Herds Graze"
(Mandelstam), WP: 165

Happy as a Dog's Tail (Swir),
EP: 1006

Happy Birthday of Death, The
(Corso), AP: 359

Happy Childhood, A (Matthews),
AP: 1287

Happy Family (Shore), AP: 1776

Happy Hour (Shapiro), AP: 1760

Happy Man, The (Hall), AP: 781

Happy Marriage, The (MacLeish),
AP: 1248

Hara Shirō, TE: 433

Hard Freight (Wright), AP: 2209

Hard Hours, The (Hecht), AP: 829

Hard Labor (Pavese), EP: 784

"Hard Rock Returns to Prison from
the Hospital for the Criminal
Insane" (Knight), AP: 1055

Hardenberg, Friedrich von. *See*
Novalis

Hardheaded Weather (Eady),
AP: 525

Harding, Gunnar, TE: 555

Hardy, Thomas, BP: 579-588,
TE: 190; *The Dynasts*, BP: 586;
*Moments of Vision and
Miscellaneous Verses*, BP: 586;
poem about, BP: 83; *Poems of the
Past and Present*, BP: 584; *Satires
of Circumstance*, BP: 585; *Time's
Laughingstocks, and Other Verses*,
BP: 585; *Wessex Poems, and
Other Verses*, BP: 584

Harjo, Joy, AP: 789-794, TE: 484,
TE: 694; *How We Became
Human*, AP: 792; *In Mad Love
and War*, AP: 792; *A Map to the
Next World*, AP: 792; *Secrets from
the Center of the World*, AP: 791;
She Had Some Horses, AP: 791;
What Moon Drove Me to This?,
AP: 790; *The Woman Who Fell
from the Sky*, AP: 792

Harlem Book of the Dead, The
(Dodson), AP: 473

Harlem Gallery (Tolson), AP: 1986

Harlem Renaissance, TE: 5,
TE: 655-660. *See also*
Categorized Index

"Harlem Wine" (Cullen), AP: 408

Harmonies poétiques et religieuses
(Lamartine), EP: 594

Harp Lake (Hollander), AP: 883

Harper, Michael S., AP: 794-802;
Dear John, Dear Coltrane,
AP: 797; *Debridement*, AP: 798;
Healing Song for the Inner Ear,

AP: 798; *History Is Your Own
Heartbeat*, AP: 797; *Images of
Kin*, AP: 798; *Nightmare Begins
Responsibility*, AP: 798; *Song*,
AP: 798; *Songlines in
Michaeltree*, AP: 799; *Use
Trouble*, AP: 799

Harping On (Kizer), AP: 1052

Harpur, Charles, TE: 30

Harris, Max, TE: 32

Harrison, Jim, AP: 802-814; *After
Ikkyū, and Other Poems*, AP: 811;
Braided Creek, AP: 812; *Letters
to Yesenin*, AP: 807; *Locations*,
AP: 805; *Natural World*, AP: 810;
Outlyer and Ghazals, AP: 806;
Plain Song, AP: 804; *Returning to
Earth*, AP: 808; *Saving Daylight*,
AP: 812; *Selected and New
Poems, 1961-1981*, AP: 809; *The
Shape of the Journey*, AP: 811;
*The Theory and Practice of
Rivers*, AP: 810

Harrison, Tony, BP: 588-594;
"Bringing Up," BP: 590;
"Laureate's Block," BP: 593; *The
Loiners*, BP: 590; "The School of
Eloquence," BP: 591; *V., and
Other Poems*, BP: 592

Hart sisters, TE: 43

Hartmann von Aue, EP: 441-447,
TE: 286; *Der Arme Heinrich*,
EP: 446; *Erec*, EP: 444;
Gregorius, EP: 445; *Iwein*,
EP: 444; *The Lament*, EP: 443

Haru to shura. See *Spring and Asura*

Harvard aesthetes. *See* Categorized
Index

Harvest Poems, 1910-1960
(Sandburg), AP: 1710

"Harvest Song" (Toomer), AP: 1992

"Harvests" (Pagis), WP: 216

Harvey, Anne Gray. *See* Sexton, Anne

Hass, Robert, AP: 814-819; *Field
Guide*, AP: 816; *Human Wishes*,

AP: 816; *Praise*, AP: 816; *Sun Under Wood*, AP: 817; *Time and Materials*, AP: 817; *Twentieth Century Pleasures*, AP: 816

Hauge, Olav H., TE: 556

Haugen, Paal-Helge, TE: 558

Hault, Jean du. *See* Éluard, Paul

"Haunted" (De la Mare), BP: 402

"Haunted House, The" (Hood), BP: 658

"Haunted Palace, The" (Poe), AP: 1567

Have Come, Am Here (Villa), AP: 2051

Havlíček Borovský, Karel, TE: 81

Haw Lantern, The (Heaney), BP: 602

Hawk in the Rain, The (Hughes), BP: 688

Hawkes, Terence, TE: 751

Hawthornden, William Drummond of. *See* Drummond of Hawthornden, William

Hayden, Robert, AP: 820-826, TE: 11; "Beginnings," AP: 823; "Butterfly Piece," AP: 823; "The Diver," AP: 825; "The Dream," AP: 823; "An Inference of Mexico," AP: 824; "Middle Passage," AP: 823; "Monet's 'Waterlilies'," AP: 823

Haynes, Florence. *See* Ai

Hazard, the Painter (Meredith), AP: 1313

Hazards of Holiness, The (Everson), AP: 574

"Heads of the Children" (Flint), AP: 608

Healing Earthquakes (Baca), AP: 75

Healing Song for the Inner Ear (Harper), AP: 798

Heaney, Seamus, BP: 594-605, TE: 199; "Bogland," BP: 597; *Death of a Naturalist*, BP: 596; *District and Circle*, BP: 603; *Door into the Dark*, BP: 597;

Electric Light, BP: 603; *Field Work*, BP: 601; *The Haw Lantern*, BP: 602; *North*, BP: 599, TE: 199; *Opened Ground*, BP: 603; *Seeing Things*, BP: 603; *The Spirit Level*, BP: 603; *Station Island*, BP: 602; *Stations*, BP: 599; *Sweeney Astray*, BP: 601; *Wintering Out*, BP: 598

Heart as Ever Green, The (Rodgers), AP: 1670

"Heart of Thomas Hardy, The" (Betjemen), BP: 83

Heartlove (Madhubuti), AP: 1273

Heart's Garden, the Garden's Heart, The (Rexroth), AP: 1625

Heart's Needle (Snodgrass), AP: 1833, TE: 201, TE: 669

"Heautontimoroumenos" (Baudelaire), EP: 86

Heavensgate (Okigbo), WP: 206

"Heavy Bear Who Goes with Me, The" (Schwartz), AP: 1743

Hebbel, Friedrich, TE: 302

Hébert, Anne, BP: 605-608; *Mystery of the Verb*, BP: 607; *Les Songes en équilibre*, BP: 607; *The Tombs of the Kings*, BP: 607

Hecale (Callimachus), EP: 178

Hecht, Anthony, AP: 826-836; *Collected Later Poems*, AP: 834; *The Darkness and the Light*, AP: 834; *The Hard Hours*, AP: 829; *Millions of Strange Shadows*, AP: 832; *A Summoning of Stones*, AP: 828; *The Transparent Man*, AP: 833; *The Venetian Vespers*, AP: 832

Heidenstam, Verner von, TE: 538

Heimat (Biermann), EP: 125

Hein, Piet, EP: 447-451; *Grooks*, EP: 450; *Den Tiende Muse*, EP: 450

Heine, Heinrich, EP: 451-458, TE: 301; Gustavo Adolfo

Bécquer, EP: 97; *Book of Songs*, EP: 455; *Last of the Romantics*, EP: 455; *New Poems*, EP: 456; *Romanzero*, EP: 457

Hejinian, Lyn, AP: 836-841; *The Cell*, AP: 840; *Gesualdo*, AP: 839; *My Life*, AP: 839; *Oxota*, AP: 840; *Writing Is an Aid to Memory*, AP: 839

Hellaakoski, Aaro, TE: 546

Hellenistic poets, TE: 328. *See also* Categorized Index

Hello, Darkness (Sissman), AP: 1806

Helmets (Dickey), AP: 451

"Helmsman, The" (Cunningham), AP: 421

Helység-kalapácsa, A. See Hammer of the Village, The

Hemans, Felicia Dorothea, BP: 609-612; *Casabianca*, BP: 611; *Lays of Many Lands*, BP: 611; *Records of Women, with Other Poems*, BP: 611; *The Siege of Valencia*, BP: 611

"Henceforth, from the Mind" (Bogan), AP: 203

Henryson, Robert, BP: 612-617, TE: 127; *Fables*, BP: 614, TE: 127; *Tale of Orpheus*, BP: 616; *The Testament of Cresseid*, BP: 614

Her Blue Body Everything We Know (Walker), AP: 2084

"Her Pure Fingernails on High Offering Their Onyx" (Mallarmé), EP: 647

Herald of the Autochthonic Spirit (Corso), AP: 360

Heraldos negros, Los. See Black Heralds, The

Herbert, George, BP: 617-626; "The Church," BP: 623; "Love," BP: 624; *The Temple*, BP: 620

Herbert, Zbigniew, EP: 458-465; *Elegy for the Departure, and*

Other Poems, **EP:** 464; *Hermes, pies i gwiazda*, **EP:** 463; *Mr. Cogito*, **EP:** 463; *Napis*, **EP:** 463; *Report from the Besieged City, and Other Poems*, **EP:** 463; *Studium przedmiotu*, **EP:** 463

"Herbstmanöver." *See* "Autumn Maneuvers"

Herder, Johann Gottfried, **TE:** 295

"Here" (Salinas), **EP:** 938

Heredia, José-Maria de (French poet), **TE:** 265

"Heritage" (Cullen), **AP:** 407

"Herman Melville" (Auden), **BP:** 52

Hermes, pies i gwiazda (Herbert), **EP:** 463

Hermeticism; Germany, **TE:** 311; Italy, **TE:** 405. *See also* Categorized Index

"Hermit Thrush, A" (Clampitt), **AP:** 324

Hermodsson, Elisabet, **TE:** 555

Hernández, José, WP: 114-117, **TE:** 435; *The Gaucho Martin Fierro*, **WP:** 116; *The Return of Martin Fierro*, **WP:** 116

Hernández, Miguel, **TE:** 601

Hero and Leander (Chapman), **BP:** 232

"Hero and Leander" (Hood), **BP:** 655

Hero and Leander (Marlowe), **BP:** 873

Herodias (Mallarmé), **EP:** 648

Heroes and Heroines (Whittemore), **AP:** 2141

"Heroic Poem in Praise of Wine" (Belloc), **BP:** 76

Herrick, Robert, BP: 626-635, **TE:** 150; "The Amber Bead," **BP:** 629; "The Argument of His Book," **BP:** 628; "Corinna's Going A-Maying," **BP:** 633; "Delight in Disorder," **BP:** 631; "Julia's Petticoat," **BP:** 630; *Noble Numbers*, **BP:** 633; "The

Pillar of Fame," **BP:** 634; "To Blossoms," **BP:** 634; "To the Virgins, to make much of Time," **BP:** 632

Hervent, Maurice. *See* Éluard, Paul

Hesiod, EP: 465-471, **TE:** 221, **TE:** 320; *Theogony*, **EP:** 468, **TE:** 222; *Works and Days*, **EP:** 469, **TE:** 222

Hesse, Hermann, EP: 471-478; *Crisis*, **EP:** 474; *Poems*, **EP:** 474

"Hester" (Lamb), **BP:** 772

Heyduk, Adolf, **TE:** 82

Heyen, William, AP: 841-849; *Brockport, New York*, **AP:** 847; *The Chestnut Rain*, **AP:** 847; *Crazy Horse in Stillness*, **AP:** 848; *Depth of Field*, **AP:** 843; *Diana, Charles, and the Queen*, **AP:** 848; *Erika*, **AP:** 845; *Long Island Light*, **AP:** 844; *Lord Dragonfly*, **AP:** 846; *Noise in the Trees*, **AP:** 844; *Pterodactyl Rose*, **AP:** 848; *Ribbons*, **AP:** 848; *Shoah Train*, **AP:** 848; *The Swastika Poems*, **AP:** 845

Heym, Georg, **TE:** 306

Heywood, John, BP: 635-640; *A Dialogue of Proverbs*, **BP:** 637; *The Spider and the Fly*, **BP:** 638

"Hi, Kuh" (Zukofsky), **AP:** 2267

Hier régnant désert (Bonnefoy), **EP:** 145

High Falcon, and Other Poems (Adams), **AP:** 6

High Malady (Pasternak), **WP:** 226

High Windows (Larkin), **BP:** 792

Highgrade (Whalen), **AP:** 2113

Hikmet, Nazim, WP: 117-125; *The Epic of Sheik Bedreddin*, **WP:** 121; *Human Landscapes*, **WP:** 122; *Jokond ile Si-Ya-U*, **WP:** 121; *Rubaiyat*, **WP:** 122; *Taranta Babu'ya mektuplar*, **WP:** 121

Hill, Archibald A., **TE:** 751

Hill, Geoffrey, BP: 641-650, **TE:** 198; *For the Unfallen*, **BP:** 642; *King Log*, **BP:** 643; *Mercian Hymns*, **BP:** 645, **TE:** 198; *The Mystery of the Charity of Charles Péguy*, **BP:** 647; *The Orchards of Syon*, **BP:** 648; *Tenebrae*, **BP:** 646; *A Treatise of Civil Power*, **BP:** 649; *The Triumph of Love*, **BP:** 647, **TE:** 199

Hillyer, Robert, AP: 850-853; *A Letter to Robert Frost and Others*, **AP:** 852; *Pattern of a Day*, **AP:** 852; *The Seventh Hill*, **AP:** 851

Hindi poetry. *See* Indian English poetry

Hinge and Sign (McHugh), **AP:** 1233

Hirsch, Edward, AP: 853-858; *Earthly Measures*, **AP:** 856; "Fast Break," **AP:** 855; *For the Sleepwalkers*, **AP:** 855; *Lay Back the Darkness*, **AP:** 857; *The Night Parade*, **AP:** 856; "Omen," **AP:** 855; *On Love*, **AP:** 856; "Skywriting," **AP:** 855; *Special Orders*, **AP:** 857; *Wild Gratitude*, **AP:** 855

Hirshfield, Jane, AP: 858-863; *After*, **AP:** 862; *Alaya*, **AP:** 860; *Given Sugar, Given Salt*, **AP:** 861; *The Lives of the Heart*, **AP:** 861; *The October Palace*, **AP:** 860; *Of Gravity and Angels*, **AP:** 860

Historia del corazón (Aleixandre), **EP:** 16

Historical criticism, defined, **AP:** 2299, **BP:** 1383, **EP:** 1177, **TE:** 815, **WP:** 385

Historical poetry; England, **TE:** 140; Middle English, **TE:** 109; modern Greek, **TE:** 336

History (Lowell), **AP:** 1196

History Is Your Own Heartbeat
(Harper), **AP:** 797
History of My Heart (Pinsky),
AP: 1544
Hitomaro. *See* Kakinomoto Hitomaro
H'm (Thomas), **BP:** 1259
Hobbes, Thomas, **TE:** 153
Hoccleve, Thomas, **TE:** 122
Hoddis, Jakob von, **TE:** 306
Hododarje (Pavlović), **EP:** 789
Hoffman, Daniel, AP: 863-871; *An
Armada of Thirty Whales,*
AP: 866; *Beyond Silence,*
AP: 869; *Brotherly Love,*
AP: 868; *The City of
Satisfactions*, **AP:** 867; *Darkening
Water*, **AP:** 869; *A Little Geste,
and Other Poems*, **AP:** 867;
Middens of the Tribe, **AP:** 868
Hofmannsthal, Hugo von, EP: 478-
484, **TE:** 304; "Der Jüngling und
die Spinne," **EP:** 483; *Poems and
Verse Plays*, **EP:** 482; "Stanzas in
Terza Rima," **EP:** 481; "Where I
Near and Where I Land . . . ,"
EP: 483; "Zum Gedächtnis des
Schauspielers Mitterwurzer,"
EP: 482
Hofmannswaldau, Christian Hofmann
von, **TE:** 293
Hogan, Linda, AP: 871-876,
TE: 485, **TE:** 692; *The Book of
Medicines*, **AP:** 875; *Calling
Myself Home*, **AP:** 873; *Daughters,
I Love You*, **AP:** 874; *Eclipse*,
AP: 873; *Savings*, **AP:** 875; *Seeing
Through the Sun*, **AP:** 874
Hogan, Richard Franklin. *See* Hugo,
Richard
Hoggart, Richard, **TE:** 733
Hokku (poetic form), **TE:** 424
Holan, Vladimír, **TE:** 85
Holberg, Ludvig, **TE:** 530
Hölderlin, Friedrich, EP: 485-492,
TE: 296; *Nachtgesänge*, **EP:** 489

"Hole in the Floor, A" (Wilbur),
AP: 2155
Hollander, John, AP: 877-886; *Blue
Wine, and Other Poems*, **AP:** 882;
A Crackling of Thorns, **AP:** 878;
A Draft of Light, **AP:** 885;
Figurehead, and Other Poems,
AP: 884; *Harp Lake*, **AP:** 883; *In
Time and Place*, **AP:** 883;
Jiggery-Pokery, **AP:** 880; *Movie-
going, and Other Poems*, **AP:** 879;
The Night Mirror, **AP:** 880;
Picture Window, **AP:** 884; *Powers
of Thirteen*, **AP:** 882; *Reflections
on Espionage*, **AP:** 880; *Spectral
Emanations*, **AP:** 881; *Tales Told
of the Fathers*, **AP:** 881; *Town and
Country Matters*, **AP:** 880; *Types
of Shape*, **AP:** 879; *Visions from
the Ramble*, **AP:** 879
Hollo, Anselm, AP: 887-893;
"Bouzouki music," **AP:** 889;
Guests of Space, **AP:** 892;
"Manifest destiny," **AP:** 889;
*Notes on the Possibilities and
Attractions of Existence*, **AP:** 891;
"Old space cadet speaking,"
AP: 890; *Rue Wilson Monday*,
AP: 890
"Hollow Men, The" (Eliot), **BP:** 465
Holmes, Oliver Wendell, AP: 893-
899, **TE:** 637; "The Chambered
Nautilus," **AP:** 898; "The
Deacon's Masterpiece," **AP:** 897;
"Dorothy Q.," **AP:** 896; "The Last
Leaf," **AP:** 896; "The Living
Temple," **AP:** 898; "Old
Ironsides," **AP:** 896
Holmsen, Bjarne P. *See* Holz, Arno
Holocaust (Reznikoff), **AP:** 1631
Holub, Miroslav, EP: 492-497;
Denní služba, **EP:** 494; *Intensive
Care*, **EP:** 496; *Interferon,*
EP: 495; *Poems Before and After,*
EP: 495; *The Rampage*, **EP:** 496;

Sagittal Section, **EP:** 494;
Vanishing Lung Syndrome,
EP: 495
*Holy Water. See Agua Santa/Holy
Water*
Holz, Arno, EP: 497-502, **TE:** 303;
Phantasus, 1898, **EP:** 498;
Phantasus, 1929, **EP:** 499;
Phantasus, 1961, **EP:** 501
Homage (Guillén), **EP:** 433
"Homage to Clotho" (Sissman),
AP: 1807
Homage to Mistress Bradstreet
(Berryman), **AP:** 159
Homage to Sextus Propertius
(Pound), **AP:** 1580
"Hombres necios" (Cruz), **WP:** 67
"Home" (Guest), **AP:** 752, **BP:** 65
Home Course in Religion (Soto),
AP: 1866
Homecoming (Alvarez), **AP:** 32
Homecoming Singer, The (Wright),
AP: 2234
Homegirls and Handgrenades
(Sanchez), **AP:** 1700
Homenaje. See Homage
Homer, EP: 502-510, **TE:** 217,
TE: 320; *Iliad*, **EP:** 506, **TE:** 217;
Odyssey, **EP:** 508, **TE:** 217
Homeward (Æ), **BP:** 15
Homeward to America (Ciardi), **AP:** 316
*Homme approximatif, L'. See
Approximate Man, and Other
Writings*
"Homme paisible, Un." *See
"Tractable Man, A"*
"Honest Lover whosoever"
(Suckling), **BP:** 1210
Honey and Salt (Sandburg), **AP:** 1710
Honeybee (Nye), **AP:** 1440
Hongo, Garrett Kaoru, AP: 900-
905; *The River of Heaven,*
AP: 904; *Yellow Light*, **AP:** 902
Honkadori (poetic technique),
TE: 418

Hood, Thomas, **BP:** 650-660; *The Bandit*, **BP:** 654; "The Haunted House," **BP:** 658; "Hero and Leander," **BP:** 655; "Lycus the Centaur," **BP:** 655; *Miss Kilmansegg and Her Precious Leg*, **BP:** 657; *Odes and Addresses to Great People*, **BP:** 656; "The Plea of the Midsummer Fairies," **BP:** 655; "The Sea of Death," **BP:** 655; "The Song of the Shirt," **BP:** 658; *Whims and Oddities*, **BP:** 656

"Hook" (Wright), **AP:** 2230

Hope of Liberty, The (Horton), **AP:** 907

Hope, A. D., **BP:** 660-666, **TE:** 502; "Imperial Adam," **BP:** 664; *Orpheus*, **BP:** 665; *The Wandering Islands*, **BP:** 663

Hopkins, Gerard Manley, **BP:** 666-677; "Carrion Comfort," **BP:** 675; "Duns Scotus's Oxford," **BP:** 674; "Pied Beauty," **BP:** 674; "The Windhover," **BP:** 671; "The Wreck of the *Deutschland*," **BP:** 669

"Hora cero, La." *See* "Zero Hour"

Horace, **EP:** 510-518, **TE:** 451, **TE:** 702; *The Art of Poetry*, **TE:** 702; *Epistles*, **EP:** 517; *Epodes*, **EP:** 513; *Odes*, **EP:** 515; *Satires*, **EP:** 514

Horae Lyricae (Watts), **BP:** 1300

Horse Fair, The (Becker), **AP:** 113

Horse Latitudes (Muldoon), **BP:** 944

"Horses in Central Park" (Swenson), **AP:** 1936

Horses Make a Landscape Look More Beautiful (Walker), **AP:** 2083

"Horseshoe Finder, The" (Mandelstam), **WP:** 168

Horton, George Moses, **AP:** 905-908; *The Hope of Liberty*, **AP:** 907; *Naked Genius*, **AP:** 908;

The Poetical Works of George M. Horton, **AP:** 907

"Horus" (Nerval), **EP:** 746

Hosties noires (Senghor), **WP:** 269

Hotel Malabar (Galvin), **AP:** 650

"Hound of Ulster, The" (Smith), **BP:** 1167

"Hours, The" (Bishop), **AP:** 179

Hours of Idleness (Byron), **BP:** 189

House of Dust, The (Aiken), **AP:** 15

House of Fame (Chaucer), **BP:** 247

House of Life, The (Rossetti), **BP:** 1070

House of Song, The (Wagoner), **AP:** 2065

House on Marshland, The (Glück), **AP:** 713

Houseboat Days (Ashbery), **AP:** 62

Housekeeping in a Dream (Kasischke), **AP:** 1001

Housman, A. E., **BP:** 677-685; *Last Poems*, **BP:** 682; *More Poems*, **BP:** 682; *A Shropshire Lad*, **BP:** 682; "With rue my heart is laden," **BP:** 682

"How Annandale Went Out" (Robinson), **AP:** 1667

How Beautiful the Beloved (Orr), **AP:** 1492

How I Came to Drink My Grandmother's Piano (Norris), **AP:** 1429

How I Got Ovah (Rodgers), **AP:** 1670

How the Plains Indians Got Horses (Plumly), **AP:** 1558

"How to Eat an Orange" (MacBeth), **BP:** 843

"How to Get on in Society" (Betjeman), **BP:** 84

"How to Get Through Reality" (Blackburn), **AP:** 184

How to Paint Sunlight (Ferlinghetti), **AP:** 599

How We Became Human (Harjo), **AP:** 792

"How We Heard the Name" (Dugan), **AP:** 499

Howard, Henry, earl of Surrey. *See* Surrey, Henry Howard, earl of

Howard, Richard, **AP:** 909-913; *The Damages*, **AP:** 910; *Findings*, **AP:** 911; *Like Most Revelations*, **AP:** 911; *Lining Up*, **AP:** 911; *Misgivings*, **AP:** 911; *No Traveller*, **AP:** 911; *Quantities*, **AP:** 910; *Trappings*, **AP:** 912; *Two-Part Inventions*, **AP:** 911; *Untitled Subjects*, **AP:** 911

Howe, Susan, **AP:** 913-921; *The Midnight*, **AP:** 918; *The Nonconformist's Memorial*, **AP:** 918; *Pierce-Arrow*, **AP:** 918; *Pythagorean Silence*, **AP:** 916; *Souls of the Labadie Tract*, **AP:** 919; *The Liberties*, **AP:** 916

Howes, Barbara, **AP:** 921-924; *Blue Garden*, **AP:** 923; *In the Cold Country*, **AP:** 922; *Light and Dark*, **AP:** 922; *Looking up at the Leaves*, **AP:** 922; *The Undersea Farmer*, **AP:** 922

"Howl" (Ginsberg), **AP:** 680, **TE:** 663

Howling at the Moon (Hagiwara), **TE:** 429

Hoyt, Elinor Morton. *See* Wylie, Elinor

Hsieh K'ang-lo. *See* Xie Lingyun

Huchel, Peter, **TE:** 308

Hudgins, Andrew, **AP:** 924-927; *After the Lost War*, **AP:** 926; *The Glass Hammer*, **AP:** 926; *Saints and Strangers*, **AP:** 925

Hudibras (Butler), **BP:** 182, **TE:** 622

Hugging the Jukebox (Nye), **AP:** 1439

Hugh Selwyn Mauberley (Pound), **AP:** 1581, **TE:** 195

Hughes, Edward James. *See* Hughes, Ted

Hughes, Langston, **AP:** 927-933,
TE: 658; *Ask Your Mama*,
AP: 932; *The Panther and the
Lash*, **AP:** 932; *The Weary Blues*,
AP: 930

Hughes, Ted, **BP:** 686-694, **TE:** 198;
Birthday Letters, **BP:** 693,
TE: 198; *Cave Birds*, **BP:** 691;
Crow, **BP:** 690, **TE:** 198; *Flowers
and Insects*, **BP:** 693; *Gaudete*,
BP: 691; *The Hawk in the Rain*,
BP: 688; *Lupercal*, **BP:** 688;
Moortown, **BP:** 692; *Remains of
Elmet*, **BP:** 692; *Season Songs*,
BP: 692; *Wodwo*, **BP:** 689;
Wolfwatching, **BP:** 693

Hugo, Richard, **AP:** 934-937; *Death
of the Kapowsin Tavern*, **AP:** 935;
*The Lady in Kicking Horse
Reservoir*, **AP:** 936; *Making
Certain It Goes On*, **AP:** 937; *The
Right Madness on Skye*, **AP:** 936;
A Run of Jacks, **AP:** 935; *What
Thou Lovest Well, Remains
American*, **AP:** 936

Hugo, Victor, **EP:** 518-527, **TE:** 262;
Les Contemplations, **EP:** 524,
TE: 263; *Dieu*, **EP:** 526;
"L'Expiation'," **EP:** 524; *Les
Feuilles d'automne*, **EP:** 523; *La
Fin de Satan*, **EP:** 525; *The
Legend of the Centuries*, **EP:** 525;
Odes et ballades, **EP:** 522; *Les
Orientales*, **EP:** 523; *Les Rayons
et les ombres*, **EP:** 523

Huis van die dowe, Die
(Breytenbach), **EP:** 165

Huldén, Lars, **TE:** 560

Human Fantasy, The (Whalen),
AP: 2124

Human Landscapes (Hikmet),
WP: 122

Human Poems (Vallejo), **WP:** 305

Human Wishes (Hass), **AP:** 816

Humanism, **TE:** 733; Germany,

TE: 290; Italy, **TE:** 381; Spain,
TE: 592

Humble Administrator's Garden, The
(Seth), **WP:** 274

"Humble Bee, The" (Emerson), **AP:** 551

Hundred-Thousand Songs (Milarepa),
TE: 609

*Hundreth Sundrie Flowres Bounde
Up in One Small Poesie, A*
(Gascoigne), **BP:** 511

Hungarian poetry, **TE:** 352-364

Hungary. *See* Geographical Index

"Hungerfield" (Jeffers), **AP:** 969

Hunt, Erica, **AP:** 938-940; *Arcade*,
AP: 939; *Local History*, **AP:** 938;
Piece Logic, **AP:** 940

Hunt, Leigh, **BP:** 694-699; "Abou
Ben Adhem," **BP:** 698; *The Story
of Rimini*, **BP:** 697

"Hunting of the Hare, The"
(Newcastle), **BP:** 962

Hunting of the Snark, The (Carroll),
BP: 220

Hurricane Lamp (Cassity), **AP:** 295

"Hurricane Watch" (Pastan),
AP: 1516

"Huswifery" (Taylor), **AP:** 1961

Hybrids of Plants and of Ghosts
(Graham), **AP:** 727

"Hymn" (Cædmon), **BP:** 198

"Hymn of Man" (Swinburne),
BP: 1233

"Hymn to Adversity" (Gray),
BP: 545

"Hymn to Death" (Ronsard), **EP:** 916

"Hymn to Intellectual Beauty"
(Shelley), **BP:** 1121

Hymn to Liberty, The (Solomos),
EP: 990, **TE:** 332

"Hymn to Light" (Cowley), **BP:** 317

"Hymn to St. Geryon, I" (McClure),
AP: 1209

"Hymn to Satan" (Carducci), **EP:** 188

"Hymne de la mort." *See* "Hymn to
Death"

Hymnen an die Nacht. See *Hymns to
the Night*

Hymnes of Astraea (Davies), **BP:** 383

Hymni. See *Hymns*

Hymns; England, **TE:** 168; Germany,
TE: 291; Homeric, **TE:** 217,
TE: 320; Hungary, **TE:** 352;
Latin, **TE:** 460; Scandinavia,
TE: 529; Slovakia, **TE:** 573;
Spain, **TE:** 586. *See also*
Categorized Index

Hymns (Callimachus), **EP:** 178

Hymns to Lenin (MacDiarmid),
BP: 850

Hymns to the Night (Novalis),
EP: 753, **TE:** 298

Hyperbole, defined, **AP:** 2299,
BP: 1383, **EP:** 1177, **TE:** 815,
WP: 385

Hyperion (Keats), **BP:** 734

"I always called her Aunt Susie"
(Silko), **AP:** 1780

I Am a Black Woman (Evans), **AP:** 564

"I Am a Horse" (Arp), **EP:** 65

"I Am a Realist" (Różewicz),
EP: 922

"I am a Tree, Very Quiet are My
Leaves" (Haines), **AP:** 773

"I Am Goya" (Voznesensky),
WP: 314

I Am Joaquín/Yo soy Joaquín
(Gonzales), **TE:** 468

I Am the Bitter Name (Williams),
AP: 2163

*I Am Writing to You from a Far-Off
Country* (Michaux), **EP:** 691

I Apologize for the Eyes in My Head
(Komunyakaa), **AP:** 1067

"I Cannot Know . . ." (Radnóti),
EP: 881

I Can't Remember (Macdonald),
AP: 1214

"I dreaded that first Robin, so"
(Dickinson), **AP:** 461

"I Go into Darkened Temples" (Blok), **WP:** 37

"I Have a Premonition of You" (Blok), **WP:** 37

"I Have a Rendezvous with Death" (Seeger), **AP:** 1752

"I Know It as the Sorrow" (Everson), **AP:** 571

"I know that He exists" (Dickinson), **AP:** 460

"I like to see it lap the Miles" (Dickinson), **AP:** 458

I Marry You (Ciardi), **AP:** 316

I Praise My Destroyer (Ackerman), **AP:** 3

"I Remember, I Remember" (Larkin), **BP:** 790

"I Screamed in the Night" (Róż ewicz), **EP:** 920

"I See the Mad" (Różewicz), **EP:** 919

"I skuchno i grustno . . ." *See* "It's Boring and Sad . . ."

"I started Early—Took my Dog" (Dickinson), **AP:** 461

"I taste a liquor never brewed" (Dickinson), **AP:** 461

"I Used to Have a Nail" (Castro), **EP:** 193

"I Walk Out Alone onto the Road . . ." (Lermontov), **WP:** 148

"I Was Riding at Full Gallop Around the City Walls, Pursued by a Throng of Superstitious Coalmongers" (Foix), **EP:** 334

"I Was Sitting upon a Rock" (Walther), **EP:** 1124

Iamb, defined, **AP:** 2299, **BP:** 1383, **EP:** 1177, **TE:** 815, **WP:** 385

Iambi (Callimachus), **EP:** 178

Iambic pentameter, defined, **AP:** 2299, **BP:** 1383, **EP:** 1177, **TE:** 815, **WP:** 385

"Ich bin ein Pferd." *See* "I Am a Horse"

"Ich saz ûf eine Steine." *See* "I Was Sitting upon a Rock"

"Ichabod" (Whittier), **AP:** 2148

"Ichinaka wa." *See* "In the City"

Iconographs (Swenson), **AP:** 1937

"¡Id con Dios!" *See* "Farewell, Go with God!"

Idanre, and Other Poems (Soyinka), **WP:** 278

Idea (Drayton), **BP:** 422

"Idea of Ancestry, The" (Knight), **AP:** 1056

Ideas Mirrour (Drayton), **BP:** 419

Identical rhyme, defined, **AP:** 2299, **BP:** 1383, **EP:** 1177, **TE:** 815, **WP:** 385

Ideology, **TE:** 761; of art, **TE:** 304; cultural criticism, **TE:** 764; defined, **TE:** 760

Idylls (Theocritus), **EP:** 1024

Idylls of the King (Tennyson), **BP:** 1242

If Birds Build with Your Hair (Snodgrass), **AP:** 1837

If I Could Sleep Deeply Enough (Miller), **AP:** 1352

If I Had Wheels or Love (Miller), **AP:** 1353

"If We Must Die" (McKay), **AP:** 1238, **TE:** 44

If You Call This Cry a Song (Carruth), **AP:** 281

Ifekandu Okigbo, Christopher. *See* Okigbo, Christopher

Igitur (Mallarmé), **EP:** 649

Ignatow, David, AP: 941-949; *Facing the Tree,* **AP:** 947; *Figures of the Human,* **AP:** 946; *The Gentle Weight Lifter,* **AP:** 944; *Poems,* **AP:** 944; *Rescue the Dead,* **AP:** 946; *Say Pardon,* **AP:** 945; *Tread the Dark,* **AP:** 947; *Whisper to the Earth,* **AP:** 948

Ihara Saikaku, **TE:** 423

Ikones (Pentzikis), **EP:** 799

Iliad (Homer), **EP:** 506, **TE:** 217

Ilić, Vojislav, **TE:** 569

Ilios o protos, mazi me tis parallayies pano se mian ahtidha (Elytis), **EP:** 320

Ill Lit (Wright), **AP:** 2219

Illuminations (Rimbaud), **EP:** 902, **TE:** 268

"Illusion, The" (Everson), **AP:** 572

Illusion and Reality (Caudwell), **TE:** 760

Illustrations, The (Dubie), **AP:** 495

Illyés, Gyula, EP: 528-532, **TE:** 361; *Dőlt vitorla,* **EP:** 530; *Kézfogások,* **EP:** 530; *Nehéz föld,* **EP:** 530; *One Sentence on Tyranny,* **EP:** 531; *Sarjúrendek,* **EP:** 530

Illyrian movement, **TE:** 73

"I'm a Shepherd" (Pessoa), **EP:** 814

"Im Winter." *See* "In Winter"

Image and the Law, The (Nemerov), **AP:** 1411

Imagery, defined, **AP:** 2299, **BP:** 1383, **EP:** 1177, **TE:** 815, **WP:** 385

Images of Kin (Harper), **AP:** 798

Imaginative truth, **TE:** 626

Imagine the Angels of Bread (Espada), **AP:** 561

Imaginism, **WP:** 92

Imagism, **TE:** 187, **TE:** 644-649, **TE:** 652. *See also* Categorized Index

Imagistes, Des (anthology), **AP:** 1175, **TE:** 645, **TE:** 652

"Imago" (Clampitt), **AP:** 324

Imitation de Notre-Dame la lune, L' (Laforgue), **EP:** 588

"Immer zu benennen." *See* "Always to Be Named"

Immigrant Iceboy's Bolero, The (Espada), **AP:** 560

Immigrants in Our Own Land, and Selected Earlier Poems (Baca), **AP:** 73

Immobile Wind, The (Winters),
   AP: 2187
"Immoral Proposition, The"
   (Creeley), **AP:** 395
"Immrama" (Muldoon), **BP:** 940
Imnos is tin eleftheria. See *Hymn to
   Liberty, The*
"Imperfect Enjoyment, The"
   (Etherege), **BP:** 479
"Imperial Adam" (Hope), **BP:** 664
Impermanence, **TE:** 417
"Impossible, The" (Rimbaud),
   EP: 902
Impressionism. *See* Categorized
   Index
Improvisatore, The (Beddoes), **BP:** 58
"In a Dark Time" (Roethke),
   AP: 1677
In a Free State (Naipaul), **TE:** 772
In a Fugitive Season (Dana), **AP:** 434
In a Green Night (Walcott), **WP:** 319
"In a Notebook" (Fenton), **BP:** 489
In a Time of Violence (Boland),
   BP: 116
In a U-Haul North of Damascus
   (Bottoms), **AP:** 217
"In Beirut" (Durrell), **BP:** 454
"In Bertram's Garden" (Justice),
   AP: 988
In Broken Country (Wagoner), **AP:** 2064
"In Church with Hart Crane"
   (Jarman), **AP:** 955
"In Dark Times" (Brecht), **EP:** 153
In den Wohnungen des Todes (Sachs),
   EP: 932
"In der blauen Ferne." *See* "In the
   Blue Distance"
"In der Flucht." *See* "Fleeing"
"In deserto" (Gautier), **EP:** 373
"In Distrust of Merits" (Moore),
   AP: 1368
"In finsteren Zeiten." *See* "In Dark
   Times"
In Her Own Image (Boland), **BP:** 111
In hora mortis (Bernhard), **EP:** 116

In Mad Love and War (Harjo),
   AP: 792
In Memoriam (Tennyson), **BP:** 1242
In Memoriam James Joyce
   (MacDiarmid), **BP:** 852
"In Memory of the Unknown Poet,
   Robert Boardman Vaughn"
   (Justice), **AP:** 990
"In morte di Carlo Imbonati"
   (Manzoni), **EP:** 664
In Other Words (Swenson), **AP:** 1939
In Parenthesis (Jones), **BP:** 709
"In Sant' Ambrogio's" (Giusti),
   EP: 395
"In Space" (Arp), **EP:** 66
"In Summer" (Dunbar), **AP:** 507
In Switzerland (Słowacki), **EP:** 977
In the Bear's House (Momaday),
   AP: 1362
"In the Blue Distance" (Sachs),
   EP: 934
"In the City" (Matsuo Bashō),
   WP: 174
In the Cold Country (Howes),
   AP: 922
"In the Crevice of Time" (Jacobsen),
   AP: 952
In the Dead of the Night (Dubie),
   AP: 495
"In the Dordogne" (Bishop), **AP:** 178
"In the Eyes of the Gods" (Breton),
   EP: 160
"In the Grave No Flower" (Millay),
   AP: 1348
"In the Holy Nativity of Our Lord"
   (Crashaw), **BP:** 340
"In the Lovely Half-light" (Breton),
   EP: 160
In the Middle Distance (Gregg),
   AP: 737
"In the Middle of the Road"
   (Drummond de Andrade), **WP:** 80
"In the Mountains" (Li Bo), **WP:** 154
"In the Naked Bed, in Plato's Cave"
   (Schwartz), **AP:** 1742

In the Outer Dark (Plumly),
   AP: 1557
In the Pines (St. John), **AP:** 1696
"In the Room" (Thomson), **BP:** 1266
In the Room of Never Grieve
   (Waldman), **AP:** 2079
In the Room We Share (Simpson),
   AP: 1799
*In the Stopping Train, and Other
   Poems* (Davie), **BP:** 373
"In the Waiting Room" (Bishop),
   AP: 175
In the Western Night (Bidart),
   AP: 166
In Time and Place (Hollander),
   AP: 883
"In Time of Grief" (Reese), **AP:** 1619
"In Winter" (Trakl), **EP:** 1035
"Incantata" (Muldoon), **BP:** 942
"Incidents in the Life of My Uncle
   Arly" (Lear), **BP:** 816
India. *See* Geographical Index
Indian English poetry, **TE:** 365-376
Indian poetry, **TE:** 505-506
"Indiana" (Crane), **AP:** 383
Indians' Book, The (anthology),
   TE: 481
Indians in the Woods, The (Lewis),
   AP: 1134
Indigenous poetry; Canada, **TE:** 504;
   Commonwealth, **TE:** 503
"Induction" (Sackville), **BP:** 1077
Inés de la Cruz, Sor Juana. *See* Cruz,
   Sor Juana Inés de la
"Inference of Mexico, An" (Hayden),
   AP: 824
"Infinitati Sacrum" (Donne), **BP:** 415
"Ingenting." *See* "Nothing"
"Inheritance" (Barnard), **AP:** 104
"Iniquity of the Fathers, upon the
   Children, The" (Rossetti),
   BP: 1063
Inner Room, The (Merrill), **AP:** 1323
Inni sacri. See *Sacred Hymns, The*
"Inonia" (Esenin), **WP:** 94

Inside the Blood Factory (Wakoski), **AP:** 2071

Inside the Onion (Nemerov), **AP:** 1414

Insistence of Beauty, The (Dunn), **AP:** 519

Insomniac Liar of Topo (Dubie), **AP:** 496

"Instructions for Crossing the Border" (Pagis), **WP:** 215

"Instructions to a Painter" (Waller), **BP:** 1296

Instructions to the Double (Gallagher), **AP:** 640

Integral Years, The (Everson), **AP:** 576

Intellectual Things (Kunitz), **AP:** 1086

Intensive Care (Holub), **EP:** 496

Interferon (Holub), **EP:** 495

Interior monologue, defined, **AP:** 2300, **BP:** 1384, **EP:** 1178, **TE:** 816, **WP:** 386

Interlunar (Atwood), **BP:** 44

Intermezzo di rime (D'Annunzio), **EP:** 267

Interrogation Palace (Wojahn), **AP:** 2195

"Interrogations" (Lee), **AP:** 1105

Interrogations at Noon (Gioia), **AP:** 691

"Interrupted Elegy" (Paz), **WP:** 233

Into the Stone, and Other Poems (Dickey), **AP:** 450

"Introduction, The" (Finch), **BP:** 492

Invisible Threads (Yevtushenko), **WP:** 345

"Invocation" (McKay), **AP:** 1237

"Invocation to Kali, An" (Sarton), **AP:** 1721

Iovis (Waldman), **AP:** 2078

Iran. *See* Geographical Index

Ireland. *See* Geographical Index

"Ireland with Emily" (Betjemen), **BP:** 83

Irene (Johnson), **BP:** 705

Irigaray, Luce, **TE:** 774

Iris (Jarman), **AP:** 955

Irish Literary Revival. *See* Categorized Index

Irish poetry, **TE:** 210

Iron Pastoral, The (Nims), **AP:** 1423

Iron Woman (Glancy), **AP:** 705

Irony, defined, **AP:** 2300, **BP:** 1384, **EP:** 1178, **TE:** 816, **WP:** 386

Irren-die Häftlinge, Die (Bernhard), **EP:** 117

Is ton Thanato tou Lord Byron (Solomos), **EP:** 991

Isabella Gardner: The Collected Poems (Gardner), **AP:** 656

Ishikawa Takuboku, **TE:** 428

Isidro, El (Vega Carpio), **EP:** 1077

Iskandariya (Kelly), **AP:** 1014

Israel. *See* Geographical Index

Issa, WP: 126-132

"Isso é aquilo" (Drummond de Andrade), **WP:** 82

Isthmus, The (Clampitt), **AP:** 323

It Catches My Heart in Its Hand (Bukowski), **AP:** 268

"It Is Crying in My Heart" (Verlaine), **EP:** 1097

"It Is Not Beauty I Demand" (Darley), **BP:** 360

"It may be good, like it who list" (Wyatt), **BP:** 1326

"It sifts from Leaden Sieves" (Dickinson), **AP:** 459

"It was not Death, for I stood up" (Dickinson), **AP:** 459

Italian poetry; origins to nineteenth century, **TE:** 377-392; nineteenth century to present, **TE:** 393-411

Italian Visit, An (Day Lewis), **BP:** 388

Italy. *See* Geographical Index

"It's Boring and Sad . . ." (Lermontov), **WP:** 148

"It's Nation Time" (Baraka), **AP:** 95

Ivanovskiye sitsi (Yevtushenko), **WP:** 345

Iwein (Hartmann), **EP:** 444

Iyengar, K. R. Srinivasa, **TE:** 367

"Jabberwocky" (Carroll), **AP:** 2288, **BP:** 218, **BP:** 1372, **EP:** 1166, **TE:** 804, **WP:** 374

Jaccottet, Philippe, **TE:** 280

Jack, and Other New Poems (Kumin), **AP:** 1080

Jack Straw's Castle, and Other Poems (Gunn), **BP:** 565

Jacklight (Erdrich), **AP:** 555

Jackson, Laura Riding. *See* Riding, Laura

Jackstraws (Simic), **AP:** 1790

"Jacob" (Reyes), **WP:** 249

Jacob, Max, **TE:** 275

Jacobean Age. *See* Categorized Index

Jacobsen, Jens Peter, **TE:** 537

Jacobsen, Josephine, AP: 950-953; "Gentle Reader," **AP:** 952; "In the Crevice of Time," **AP:** 952; "Let Each Man Remember," **AP:** 952; "Lines to a Poet," **AP:** 952; "The Monosyllable," **AP:** 952; "Reading on the Beach," **AP:** 952; "The Shade-Seller," **AP:** 952; "Softly," **AP:** 952

Jacobsen, Rolf, **TE:** 551

Jahier, Piero, **TE:** 401

Jahr der Seele, Das. *See Year of the Soul, The*

Jakobson, Roman, **AP:** 2304, **BP:** 1388, **EP:** 1182, **TE:** 751, **TE:** 781, **TE:** 820, **WP:** 390

Jalāl al-Dīn Rūmī. *See* Rūmī, Jalāl al-Dīn

Jamaica. *See* Geographical Index

James I, **TE:** 122

James Laughlin Award, **AP:** 2324, **CM:** 55, **TE:** 875

Jameson, Fredric, **TE:** 761

Jammes, Francis, **TE:** 270

"Janet Waking" (Ransom), **AP:** 1608

Janevski, Slavko, **TE:** 476

János the Hero (Petőfi), **EP:** 821

Japan. *See* Geographical Index

Japanese American poetry, **TE:** 22

Japanese poetry; origins to nineteenth century, **TE:** 412-426; nineteenth century to present, **TE:** 427-434

Jardines lejanos (Jiménez), **EP:** 536

Jarman, Mark, **AP:** 953-956; *Epistles*, **AP:** 956; "In Church with Hart Crane," **AP:** 955; *Iris*, **AP:** 955; *North Sea*, **AP:** 954

Jarrell, Randall, **AP:** 957-963; *Little Friend, Little Friend*, **AP:** 959; *The Lost World*, **AP:** 961; *The Seven-League Crutches*, **AP:** 960; "The Woman at the Washington Zoo," **AP:** 961

Jazz from the Haiku King (Emanuel), **AP:** 540

Jazz poetry, **TE:** 11

Jazz poets. *See* Categorized Index

Jeake, Samuel, Jr. *See* Aiken, Conrad

Jealous Witness (Codrescu), **AP:** 332

Jean de Meung, **EP:** 424-429; *The Romance of the Rose*, **EP:** 426, **TE:** 240

Jeanne d'Arc (Péguy), **EP:** 794

Jechai do Lwówa (Zagajewski), **EP:** 1139

Jeffers, Robinson, **AP:** 963-971; *The Beginning and the End*, **AP:** 970; "The Double Axe," **AP:** 968; and William Everson, **AP:** 568; "Hungerfield," **AP:** 969; "The Place for No Story," **AP:** 969; *Tamar*, **AP:** 967; *The Women at Point Sur*, **AP:** 968

Jenko, Simon, **TE:** 580

"Jenny" (Rossetti), **BP:** 1069

Jensen, Johannes V., **TE:** 542

Jerry, Bongo, **TE:** 46

Jersey Rain (Pinsky), **AP:** 1545

Jerusalem (Blake), **BP:** 102

Jerusalem Conquered (Tasso), **EP:** 1019

Jerusalem Delivered (Tasso), **EP:** 1017, **TE:** 384

Jerusalén conquistada (Vega Carpio), **EP:** 1077

"Jesse Helms" (Lorde), **AP:** 1171

Jewish culture. *See* Categorized Index

Jews in Babylonia (Reznikoff), **AP:** 1631

Ji, Ruan. *See* Ruan Ji

Jig of Forslin, The (Aiken), **AP:** 15

Jiggery-Pokery (Hollander), **AP:** 880

Jigme, Hortsang, **TE:** 610

Jiménez, Juan Ramón, **EP:** 533-539, **TE:** 599; *Animal de fondo*, **EP:** 538; *Arias tristes*, **EP:** 535; *Baladas de primavera*, **EP:** 536; *Diary of a Newlywed Poet*, **EP:** 537; *Estío*, **EP:** 537; *Jardines lejanos*, **EP:** 536; *Pastorales*, **EP:** 536; *La Soledad sonora*, **EP:** 536; *Spiritual Sonnets*, **EP:** 537

Jindyworobak movement, **TE:** 32

"Jinny the Just" (Prior), **BP:** 1029

Jnanpith Award, **CM:** 54, **TE:** 874, **WP:** 411

Jocelyn (Lamartine), **EP:** 595

Johannesen, Georg, **TE:** 557

John Brown's Body (Benét), **AP:** 126

John Deth (Aiken), **AP:** 16

John of the Cross, Saint, **EP:** 539-548; "The Dark Night," **EP:** 545; "The Living Flame of Love," **EP:** 547; "The Spiritual Canticle," **EP:** 546

Johnson, Age of. *See* Categorized Index

Johnson, Aphra. *See* Behn, Aphra

Johnson, Bengt Emil, **TE:** 554

Johnson, Colin. *See* Narogin, Mudrooroo

Johnson, James Weldon, **AP:** 972-975, **TE:** 4, **TE:** 659; *Complete Poems*, **AP:** 975; *Fifty Years, and Other Poems*, **AP:** 974; *God's Trombones*, **AP:** 974; *Lift Every Voice and Sing*, **AP:** 973; *Saint Peter Relates an Incident*, **AP:** 974

Johnson, Marguerite Annie. *See* Angelou, Maya

Johnson, Ronald, **AP:** 976-981; *Ark*, **AP:** 979; *The Book of the Green Man*, **AP:** 978; *RADI OS I-IV*, **AP:** 979; *Songs of the Earth*, **AP:** 978; *To Do as Adam Did*, **AP:** 980; *Valley of the Many-Colored Grasses*, **AP:** 977

Johnson, Samuel, **BP:** 700-707, **TE:** 169, **TE:** 706; *Irene*, **BP:** 705; *The Lives of the Poets*, **TE:** 706; *London*, **BP:** 703; *The Vanity of Human Wishes*, **BP:** 704

Joker, Joker, Deuce (Beatty), **AP:** 109

Jokond ile Si-Ya-U (Hikmet), **WP:** 121

Jokotoba (poetic technique), **TE:** 417

Jónás könyve (Babits), **EP:** 71

Jónasson, Jóhannes B. *See* Kötlum, Jóhannes úr

Jones, David, **BP:** 707-710; *The Anathemata*, **BP:** 709; *In Parenthesis*, **BP:** 709; *The Sleeping Lord, and Other Fragments*, **BP:** 710

Jones, LeRoi. *See* Baraka, Amiri

Jones, Sir William, **TE:** 365

Jonson, Ben, **BP:** 711-719, **TE:** 149; *Timber*, **BP:** 713; "To Penshurst," **BP:** 716

Jonsson, Thorsteinn. *See* Hamri, Thorsteinn frá

Jordan, June, **AP:** 981-985; *Kissing God Goodbye*, **AP:** 984; *Naming Our Destiny*, **AP:** 984; *Some Changes*, **AP:** 983

Jørgensen, Johannes, **TE:** 539

"Joujou du pauvre, Le." *See* "Poor Child's Plaything, The"

"Journal for My Daughter" (Kunitz), **AP:** 1088

Journal of the Sun (Mitsui), **AP:** 1355

Journals of Susanna Moodie, The (Atwood), **BP:** 41

Journey, and Other Poems, The (Boland), **BP:** 114

Journey, and Other Poems, The (Winters), **AP:** 2188

"Journey Beyond the Hills" (Still), **AP:** 1917

"Journey Toward Poetry" (Sarton), **AP:** 1719

Journeys and Places (Muir), **BP:** 935

Joyce, James, **BP:** 719-725; and Samuel Beckett, **EP:** 89; *Chamber Music*, **BP:** 721; "Ecce Puer," **BP:** 724; *Pomes Penyeach*, **BP:** 723

József, Attila, **TE:** 360

Juan Chi. *See* Ruan Ji

Juan Rulfo Prize for Latin American and Caribbean Literature, **CM:** 64, **TE:** 884, **WP:** 412

Juana, Sor. *See* Cruz, Sor Juana Inés de la

Jubilation (Tomlinson), **BP:** 1275

Judah ha-Levi, **EP:** 549-553; "Ode to Zion," **EP:** 551

Jueju (poetic form), **TE:** 60

Jugendstil, **TE:** 303. *See also* Categorized Index

Jugo, Miguel de Unamuno y. *See* Unamuno y Jugo, Miguel de

Juhász, Gyula, **TE:** 359

Julian and Maddalo (Shelley), **BP:** 1116

"Julian M. to A. G. Rochelle" (Brontë), **BP:** 142

Juliana (Cynewulf), **BP:** 348

"Julia's Petticoat" (Herrick), **BP:** 630

"Julinatt, En." *See* "July Night, A"

"July Night, A" (Ekelöf), **EP:** 310

Jump Ball (Glenn), **AP:** 709

"June 1940" (Spender), **BP:** 1187

Jung, Carl, **AP:** 2294, **BP:** 1378, **EP:** 1172, **TE:** 719, **TE:** 810; literary criticism, **TE:** 719, **WP:** 380

"Jüngling und die Spinne, Der" (Hofmannsthal), **EP:** 483

Junk Shop, The" (Coulette), **AP:** 362

Justice, Donald, **AP:** 986-988, **AP:** 990-992; "Childhood," **AP:** 990; *Departures*, **AP:** 989; "First Death," **AP:** 990; "For a Freshman Reader," **AP:** 988; "In Bertram's Garden," **AP:** 988; "In Memory of the Unknown Poet, Robert Boardman Vaughn," **AP:** 990; "A Letter," **AP:** 989; *New and Selected Poems*, **AP:** 990; *Night Light*, **AP:** 988; "Presences," **AP:** 989; *Selected Poems*, **AP:** 990; "Sonatina in Green," **AP:** 989; "Sonnet to My Father," **AP:** 987; *The Summer Anniversaries*, **AP:** 987; "Tales from a Family Album," **AP:** 987; "The Telephone Number of the Muse," **AP:** 989; "To the Hawks," **AP:** 988

Juvenal, **EP:** 553-556, **TE:** 456; *Satire 3*, **EP:** 556; *Satire 10*, **EP:** 556

Juvenilia (Carducci), **EP:** 188

Kabaphes, Konstantionos Petrou. *See* Cavafy, Constantine P.

Ka-bzhas (poetic form), **TE:** 610

"Kaddish" (Ginsberg), **AP:** 681

Kaichōon, **TE:** 428

Kaila, Tiina, **TE:** 559

Kailas, Uuno, **TE:** 546

Kain, Saul. *See* Sassoon, Siegfried

Kakekotoba (poetic technique), **TE:** 417

Kakinomoto Hitomaro, **TE:** 413

Kaksikymmentä ja yksi. See *One and Twenty*

Kalevala (Lönnrot), **EP:** 619

Kallimachos. *See* Callimachus

Kalvos, Andreas, **TE:** 333

Kamen. See *Stone*

Kanshi (poetic form), **TE:** 429

Kantemir, Antioch, **TE:** 510

"Karintha" (Toomer), **AP:** 1991

Karlfeldt, Erik Axel, **TE:** 539

Karouzos, Nikos, **TE:** 349

Karr, Mary, **AP:** 993-996; *Abacus*, **AP:** 994; *The Devil's Tour*, **AP:** 995; *Sinners Welcome*, **AP:** 995; *Viper Rum*, **AP:** 995

Kartunes (Eady), **AP:** 522

Karyotakis, Kostas, **TE:** 339

Karyotakism, **TE:** 339

Kasdorf, Julia, **AP:** 996-999; *Eve's Striptease*, **AP:** 998; *Sleeping Preacher*, **AP:** 998

Kasischke, Laura, **AP:** 999-1002; *Fire and Flower*, **AP:** 1001; *Gardening in the Dark*, **AP:** 1001; *Housekeeping in a Dream*, **AP:** 1001; *Lilies Without*, **AP:** 1001; *Wild Brides*, **AP:** 1000

"Kaspar Is Dead" (Arp), **EP:** 65

"Katastrophi ton Psaron" (Solomos), **EP:** 991

"Kathaleen Ny-Houlahan" (Mangan), **BP:** 869

Katolická Moderna, **TE:** 83

Kaufman, Bob, **AP:** 1002-1006; *The Ancient Rain*, **AP:** 1005; *Bagel Shop Jazz*, **AP:** 1004

Kavanagh, Patrick, **BP:** 726-731; *Come Dance with Kitty Stobling, and Other Poems*, **BP:** 729; *The Great Hunger*, **BP:** 729; "Lines Written on a Seat on the Grand Canal," **BP:** 730; *Recent Poems*, **BP:** 729; "Shancoduff," **BP:** 728

Kazantzakis, Nikos, **EP:** 557-562, **TE:** 346; *The Odyssey*, **EP:** 560

Kazinczy, Ferenc, **TE:** 354

Keats, John, **BP:** 731-743, **TE:** 178,

TE: 630, **TE:** 712; "The Eve of St. Agnes," **BP:** 737; *The Fall of Hyperion*, **BP:** 736; *Hyperion*, **BP:** 734; *Lamia*, **BP:** 738; "Ode on a Grecian Urn," **BP:** 741; "Ode on Indolence," **BP:** 736; "Ode on Melancholy," **BP:** 740; "Ode to a Nightingale," **BP:** 739; "On Seeing the Elgin Marbles," **BP:** 736; "On Sitting Down to Read King Lear Once Again," **BP:** 735; "To Autumn," **BP:** 740

"Keeper of Flocks, The" (Pessoa), **EP:** 814

Kees, Weldon, **AP:** 1006-1012; "The Conversation in the Drawing Room," **AP:** 1009; "For My Daughter," **AP:** 1009; "Robinson," **AP:** 1009; "A Salvo for Hans Hofmann," **AP:** 1010; "The Turtle," **AP:** 1010

Kellgren, Johann Henrik, **TE:** 532

Kelly, Brigit Pegeen, **AP:** 1012-1014; *Iskandariya*, **AP:** 1014; *The Orchard*, **AP:** 1013; *Song*, **AP:** 1013; *To the Place of Trumpets*, **AP:** 1013

Kelly, Robert, **AP:** 1015-1019; *The Flowers of Unceasing Coincidence*, **AP:** 1018; *The Loom*, **AP:** 1018

Kennedy, X. J., **AP:** 1020-1028; "All-Knowing Rabbit," **AP:** 1023; "B Negative," **AP:** 1022; "Categories," **AP:** 1025; *Cross Ties*, **AP:** 1026; *Dark Horses*, **AP:** 1026; *Emily Dickinson in Southern California*, **AP:** 1025; "First Confession," **AP:** 1023; *Growing into Love*, **AP:** 1023; *Hangover Mass*, **AP:** 1026; *Nude Descending a Staircase*, **AP:** 1022; "On Being Accused of Wit," **AP:** 1026

Kenny, Maurice, **TE:** 485

Kentucky River, The (Berry), **AP:** 150

Kenyon, Jane, **AP:** 1028-1033; *The Boat of Quiet Hours*, **AP:** 1030; *Collected Poems*, **AP:** 1031; *Constance*, **AP:** 1031; *From Room to Room*, **AP:** 1030; Donald Hall, **AP:** 777; *Let Evening Come*, **AP:** 1030; *Otherwise*, **AP:** 1031

Kerouac, Jack, **TE:** 206, **TE:** 661; *Mexico City Blues*, **TE:** 665

Kette, Dragotin, **TE:** 580

Key-Åberg, Sandro, **TE:** 550

Kézfogások (Illyés), **EP:** 530

Kharjas (poetic form), **TE:** 583

Khayyám, Omar. *See* Omar Khayyám

"Khirbet Shema" (Goldbarth), **AP:** 721

Khodasevich, Vladislav, **WP:** 133-138; "Ballad," **WP:** 136; "Episode," **WP:** 136; *Evropeiskaya noch'*, **WP:** 136; *Molodost'*, **WP:** 134; *Putem zerna*, **WP:** 135; *Shchastlivy domik*, **WP:** 135; *Tyazhelaya lira*, **WP:** 136

Khorosho! See *Fine!*, **WP:** 413

Khumish Lider (Manger), **EP:** 656

Ki no Tsurayuki, **TE:** 415

Kicking the Leaves (Hall), **AP:** 780

Killigrew, Anne, **TE:** 624

Killing Floor (Ai), **AP:** 10

Killing Memory, Seeking Ancestors (Madhubuti), **AP:** 1273

"Kilroy" (Viereck), **AP:** 2044

Kim Tong Il, **TE:** 24

Kincaid, Jamaica, **TE:** 772

"Kind pity chokes my spleen" (Donne), **BP:** 410

Kinds of Affection (Miles), **AP:** 1342

King, Henry, **BP:** 743-751; "The Dirge," **BP:** 749; "The Exequy," **BP:** 747; "The Labyrinth," **BP:** 749; "Sic Vita," **BP:** 748

King Log (Hill), **BP:** 643

"King of Asine, The" (Seferis), **EP:** 960

"King of the River" (Kunitz), **AP:** 1087

"Kingdom, The" (MacNeice), **BP:** 860

"Kingfisher, The" (Clampitt), **AP:** 324

"Kingfishers, The" (Olson), **AP:** 1474

Kingo, Thomas, **TE:** 530

Kingsley Tufts Poetry Award, **AP:** 2331, **CM:** 66, **TE:** 886

Kinnell, Galway, **AP:** 1033-1039; "First Song," **AP:** 1034; *Strong Is Your Hold*, **AP:** 1037; "That Silent Evening," **AP:** 1036; "Vapor Trail Reflected in the Frog Pond," **AP:** 1036

Kinsella, Thomas, **BP:** 751-760; *Blood and Family*, **BP:** 757; *Butcher's Dozen*, **BP:** 756; *Collected Poems, 1956-2001*, **BP:** 758; *Downstream*, **BP:** 755; *The Familiar*, **BP:** 758; *Godhead*, **BP:** 758; *The Good Fight*, **BP:** 756; *The Messenger*, **BP:** 757; *Nightwalker, and Other Poems*, **BP:** 755; *Notes from the Land of the Dead, and Other Poems*, **BP:** 755; *The Pen Shop*, **BP:** 758; *Poems from Centre City*, **BP:** 757; *A Selected Life*, **BP:** 756

Kipling, Rudyard, **BP:** 760-767; "The Absent-Minded Beggar," **BP:** 765; "The Ballad of East and West," **BP:** 765; "Cities and Thrones and Powers," **BP:** 764; "Gunga Din," **BP:** 765; "The Last of the Light Brigade," **BP:** 763; "Loot," **BP:** 763; "The Way Through the Woods," **BP:** 764

Kirby, David, **AP:** 1039-1042; *Big-Leg Music*, **AP:** 1041; *The Ha-Ha*, **AP:** 1041; *My Twentieth Century*, **AP:** 1041; *Sarah Bernhardt's Leg*, **AP:** 1041; *Saving the Young Men of Vienna*, **AP:** 1041

The Collected Poems, **AP:** 1092; "Days of Foreboding," **AP:** 1091; "Father and Son," **AP:** 1086; *Intellectual Things*, **AP:** 1086; "Journal for My Daughter," **AP:** 1088; "King of the River," **AP:** 1087; "The Knot," **AP:** 1089; "The Lincoln Relics," **AP:** 1090; *Next-to-Last Things*, **AP:** 1090; "Open the Gates," **AP:** 1087; *Passing Through*, **AP:** 1091; *Passport to the War*, **AP:** 1086; *The Poems of Stanley Kunitz, 1928-1978*, **AP:** 1089; "Robin Redbreast," **AP:** 1088; *Selected Poems, 1928-1958*, **AP:** 1087; *The Testing-Tree*, **AP:** 1087; "The Wellfleet Whale," **AP:** 1091
Kunze, Reiner, **EP:** 570-576; *Aug eigene Hoffnung*, **EP:** 574; *Ein Tag auf dieser Erde*, **EP:** 575
Kynewulf. *See* Cynewulf
Kyrie (Voigt), **AP:** 2057

Laboratories of the Spirit (Thomas), **BP:** 1259
Labrunie, Gérard. *See* Nerval, Gérard de. *See* Nerval, Gérard de
"Labyrinth, The" (King), **BP:** 749
Labyrinth, The (Muir), **BP:** 935
"Lac, Le." *See* "Lake, The"
Lacan, Jacques, **TE:** 725
La Cour, Paul, **TE:** 548
Lady in Kicking Horse Reservoir, The (Hugo), **AP:** 936
"Lady Lazarus" (Plath), **AP:** 1554
Lady of the Lake, The (Scott), **BP:** 1091
"Lady Xi" (Wang Wei), **WP:** 329
La Fontaine, Jean de, **EP:** 577-583, **TE:** 252; *Adonis*, **EP:** 579; *Fables Written in Verse*, **EP:** 581, **TE:** 252; *The Loves of Cupid and Psyche*, **EP:** 580; *Le Songe de Vaux*, **EP:** 580; *Tales and Short*

Stories in Verse, **EP:** 580
Laforgue, Jules, **EP:** 584-590, **TE:** 269; *Les Complaintes*, **EP:** 587; *Les Derniers Vers de Jules Laforgue*, **EP:** 589; "Dimanches," **EP:** 589; *Des Fleurs de bonne volonté*, **EP:** 588; *L'Imitation de Notre-Dame la lune*, **EP:** 588
Lagar (Mistral), **WP:** 189
Lagerkvist, Pär, **TE:** 543
"Lágrimas que vierte un alma arrepentida" (Calderón de la Barca), **EP:** 173
Laguna Woman (Silko), **AP:** 1779
"Lai de plaisance, Le." *See* "Lay on Pleasure, The"
Lais, Le. See Legacy, The
"Lake, The" (Lamartine), **EP:** 593
Lake Effect Country (Ammons), **AP:** 40
"Lake Isle of Innisfree, The" (Yeats), **BP:** 1336
Lake poets. *See* Categorized Index
Lakoff, Robin, **TE:** 739
"Lamarck Elaborated" (Wilbur), **AP:** 2154
Lamartine, Alphonse de, **EP:** 591-597, **TE:** 260; *La Chute d'un ange*, **EP:** 595; *Harmonies poétiques et religieuses*, **EP:** 594; *Jocelyn*, **EP:** 595; "The Lake," **EP:** 593; *Nouvelles méditations poétiques*, **EP:** 594; *Poetical Meditations*, **EP:** 593, **TE:** 260; "Les Revolutions," **EP:** 595; "Tristesse," **EP:** 594; "The Valley," **EP:** 594
Lamb, Charles, **BP:** 768-774; *Blank Verse*, **BP:** 771; "A Farewell to Tobacco," **BP:** 772; "Hester," **BP:** 772; "The Old Familiar Faces," **BP:** 772; "On an Infant Dying as Soon as Born," **BP:** 773; *The Poetical Works of Charles*

Lamb, **BP:** 772; *Satan in Search of a Wife*, **BP:** 773; "Written at Cambridge," **BP:** 772
Lambro, powstańca grecki (Słowacki), **EP:** 976
Lambros (Solomos), **EP:** 991
Lament, The (Hartmann), **EP:** 443
Lament for the Death of a Bullfighter (García Lorca), **EP:** 360
"Lament for the Makaris" (Dunbar), **BP:** 449
"Lamentación de Navidad" (Reyes), **WP:** 249
Lamia (Keats), **BP:** 738
Lamplit Answer, The (Schnackenberg), **AP:** 1729
Land of Bliss, The (Song), **AP:** 1856
Land of Look Behind, The (Cliff), **WP:** 63
"Land of the Dead, The" (Giusti), **EP:** 394
Landfall (Wagoner), **AP:** 2064
Landor, Walter Savage, **BP:** 774-779; *Gebir*, **BP:** 778; *The Siege of Ancona*, **BP:** 778
"Landscape with Tractor" (Taylor), **AP:** 1972
Langgässer, Elisabeth, **TE:** 309
Langland, William, **BP:** 780-786; *The Vision of William, Concerning Piers the Plowman*, **BP:** 781, **TE:** 110
Language, **AP:** 2282-2293, **BP:** 1366-1377, **EP:** 129, **EP:** 1160-1171, **TE:** 798-809, **WP:** 368-379; feminist criticism, **TE:** 737
Language (Spicer), **AP:** 1870
Language and Woman's Place (Lakoff), **TE:** 739
Language poetry, **TE:** 208. *See also* Categorized Index
Langue (linguistics), **TE:** 750
Langue d'oc (poetic form), **TE:** 237
Lanier, Sidney, **AP:** 1095-1102;

"Corn," **AP:** 1098; "The Marshes of Glynn," **AP:** 1100; "Song of the Chattahoochee," **AP:** 1099; "Thar's More in the Man than Thar Is in the Land," **AP:** 1098

"Lanval" (Marie de France), **EP:** 670

Lap of Honour, A (MacDiarmid), **BP:** 852

"Large Red Man Reading" (Stevens), **AP:** 1908

"Lark Ascending, The" (Meredith), **BP:** 892

Larkin, Philip, **BP:** 786-794, **TE:** 203, **TE:** 682; "Born Yesterday," **BP:** 790; "The Building," **BP:** 792; "Church Going," **BP:** 791; *Collected Poems*, **BP:** 793; "Dockery and Son," **BP:** 791; "Going, Going," **BP:** 792; *High Windows*, **BP:** 792; "I Remember, I Remember," **BP:** 790; *The Less Deceived*, **BP:** 790; "The Mower," **BP:** 793; *The North Ship*, **BP:** 789; *The Whitsun Weddings*, **BP:** 791

Larsen, Marianne, **TE:** 564

Larsson, Stig, **TE:** 556

Lasker-Schüler, Else, **TE:** 306

Last Attachment, A (Prince), **BP:** 1024

"Last Confession, A" (Rossetti), **BP:** 1069

Last Generation, The (Bukowski), **AP:** 272

"Last Leaf, The" (Holmes), **AP:** 896

Last Night of the Earth Poems (Bukowski), **AP:** 272

"Last Night that She lived, The" (Dickinson), **AP:** 463

"Last of the Light Brigade, The" (Kipling), **BP:** 763

Last of the Romantics (Heine), **EP:** 455

Last Poems (Housman), **BP:** 682

Last Poems (Lawrence), **BP:** 801

"Last Ride of Wild Bill, The" (Brown), **AP:** 257

"Last Stop" (Seferis), **EP:** 961

Late Empire (Wojahn), **AP:** 2193

Late Settings (Merrill), **AP:** 1322

Late Wife (Emerson), **AP:** 543

"Lately, Alas, I Knew a Gentle Boy" (Thoreau), **AP:** 1982

Latin America. *See* Geographical Index

Latin American and Caribbean Notebook (Awoonor), **WP:** 31

Latin American poetry, **TE:** 435-440

Latin Deli, The (Ortiz Cofer), **AP:** 1501

Latin poetry, **TE:** 441-465

Latino culture. *See* Categorized Index

Latino poetry, **TE:** 466-474

Laudi, Le (D'Annunzio), **EP:** 267

Laughing Time (Smith), **AP:** 1827

"Laureate's Block" (Harrison), **BP:** 593

Laurel de Apolo (Vega Carpio), **EP:** 1078

Laurence Bloomfield in Ireland (Allingham), **BP:** 28

Lautréamont. *See* Ducasse, Isidore-Lucien

Lavorare stanca. See *Hard Labor*

"Law" (Radnóti), **EP:** 880

Lawman. *See* Layamon

Lawrence, D. H., **BP:** 795-803, **TE:** 648; *Apocalypse*, **BP:** 801; *Birds, Beasts, and Flowers*, **BP:** 799; "The Evening Land," **BP:** 799; "God," **BP:** 801; *Last Poems*, **BP:** 801; *Look! We Have Come Through!*, **BP:** 799; *Nettles*, **BP:** 800; *Pansies*, **BP:** 800; "Rhyming Poems," **BP:** 798; "The Ship of Death," **BP:** 801; "Snake," **BP:** 800; "13,000 People," **BP:** 800

Laws of Ice, The (Price), **AP:** 1588

Laws of the Land (Baker), **AP:** 78

Lawson, Henry, **TE:** 32

Lay Back the Darkness (Hirsch), **AP:** 857

Lay of the Last Minstrel, The (Scott), **BP:** 1090

"Lay on Pleasure, The" (Chartier), **EP:** 237

Layamon, **BP:** 803-807; *Brut*, **BP:** 805

Lays of Many Lands (Hemans), **BP:** 611

Layton, Irving, **BP:** 808-811; *Balls for a One-Armed Juggler*, **BP:** 810; *For My Brother Jesus*, **BP:** 811; *A Red Carpet for the Sun*, **BP:** 810; *A Wild Peculiar Joy*, **BP:** 811

Lazarus, Henry. *See* Slavitt, David

Lde'u, **TE:** 607

"LDMN Analysis of Thomas Nashe's 'Song'" (MacBeth), **BP:** 842

Leaf and the Cloud, The (Oliver), **AP:** 1467

Leaflets (Rich), **AP:** 1636

Lear, Edward, **BP:** 812-817; "The Courtship of the Yonghy-Bonghy-Bò," **BP:** 815; "Eclogue," **BP:** 816; "Incidents in the Life of My Uncle Arly," **BP:** 816; "Mr. and Mrs. Discobbolos," **BP:** 816; "The Pelican Chorus," **BP:** 816; "The Quangle Wangle's Hat," **BP:** 817

Leaves of Grass (Whitman), **AP:** 2133

"Leaving Seoul" (Lew), **TE:** 24

Leavis, F. R., **TE:** 732, **TE:** 743

Lebediny stan. See *Demesne of the Swans, The*

Lebrun, Ponce-Denis Écouchard, **TE:** 257

Leconte de Lisle, Charles-Marie, **TE:** 265

"Leda and the Swan" (Yeats), **BP:** 1337

Ledge, The (Collier), **AP:** 339

Lee, Cynthia. *See* Macdonald, Cynthia

Lee, Don L. *See* Madhubuti, Haki R.

Lee, Li-Young, **AP:** 1102-1108, **TE:** 27; *Behind My Eyes*, **AP:** 1106; *Book of My Nights*, **AP:** 1106; "Furious Versions," **AP:** 1105; "The Gift," **AP:** 1104; "Interrogations," **AP:** 1105; "Persimmons," **AP:** 1104; "Visions and Interpretations," **AP:** 1105

Legacy, The (Villon), **EP:** 1108

Legend of Good Women, The (Chaucer), **BP:** 248

Legend of the Centuries, The (Hugo), **EP:** 525

"Legend of the Origin of the Book Tao-Tê-Ching on Lao-tzû's Road into Exile" (Brecht), **EP:** 154

Legendary Performance (Rogers), **AP:** 1680

Légende des siècles, La. See *Legend of the Centuries, The*

"Legende von der Entstehung des Buches Taoteking." *See* "Legend of the Origin of the Book Tao-Tê-Ching on Lao-tzû's Road into Exile"

Léger, Alexis Saint-Léger. *See* Perse, Saint-John

"Legs, The" (Graves), **BP:** 538

Lehmann, Wilhelm, **TE:** 309

Leichter als Luft. See *Lighter than Air*

Leino, Eino, **TE:** 540

Leithauser, Brad, **AP:** 1108-1111; *Darlington's Fall*, **AP:** 1110

Lenau, Nikolaus, **TE:** 301

"Leningrad" (Mandelstam), **WP:** 168

Lenngren, Anna Maria, **TE:** 532

Lenore Marshall Poetry Prize, **AP:** 2325, **CM:** 57, **TE:** 877

León, Luis de, **EP:** 597-602; "A la vida religiosa," **EP:** 601;

"Dwelling Place in Heaven," **EP:** 601; *The Perfect Wife*, **EP:** 600; "To Christ Crucified," **EP:** 600; "To Santiago," **EP:** 600

Léonard, Nicolas-Germain, **TE:** 258

Leonidas of Tarentum, **EP:** 602-607; *Greek Anthology*, **EP:** 604

Leopardi, Giacomo, **EP:** 607-617; "The Broom," **EP:** 616; *Canti*, **EP:** 611; "Night Song of a Nomadic Shepherd in Asia," **EP:** 614; "Sappho's Last Song," **EP:** 613; "To Italy," **EP:** 611; "The Younger Brutus," **EP:** 613

Lermontov, Mikhail, **TE:** 513, **WP:** 142-150; "The Cliff," **WP:** 148; "The Death of a Poet," **WP:** 147; *The Demon*, **WP:** 146; "I Walk Out Alone onto the Road . . . ," **WP:** 148; "It's Boring and Sad . . . ," **WP:** 148; "Meditation," **WP:** 147; "The Sail," **WP:** 145

"Leroy" (Baraka), **AP:** 93

Lesbos. *See* Geographical Index

Leśmian, Bolesław, **TE:** 496

Less Deceived, The (Larkin), **BP:** 790

Lessons in Soaring (Applewhite), **AP:** 53

"Lessons of the War" (Reed), **BP:** 1046

"Let Each Man Remember" (Jacobsen), **AP:** 952

Let Evening Come (Kenyon), **AP:** 1030

"Let Me Tell You" (Williams), **AP:** 2170

"Lethe" (Barnard), **AP:** 105

"Letter, A" (Justice), **AP:** 989

Letter from a Distant Land (Booth), **AP:** 210

"Letter from Italy, A" (Addison), **BP:** 10

"Letter Home, A" (Flint), **AP:** 609

"Letter to Donald Fall" (Dugan), **AP:** 500

Letter to Robert Frost and Others, A (Hillyer), **AP:** 852

"Letter, Unposted" (Rukeyser), **AP:** 1690

"Letters and Other Worlds" (Ondaatje), **BP:** 975

Letters from a Father, and Other Poems (Van Duyn), **AP:** 2036

Letters from Maine (Sarton), **AP:** 1722

Letters to Yesenin (Harrison), **AP:** 807

Letzte Tänze (Grass), **EP:** 421

"Levél Várady Antalhoz" (Petőfi), **EP:** 824

Levertov, Denise, **AP:** 1111-1120, **TE:** 687; "About Marriage," **AP:** 1117; "Listening to Distant Guns," **AP:** 1116; "On the Edge of Darkness," **AP:** 1116; "Those Who Want Out," **AP:** 1114; "To the Muse," **AP:** 1115

Levi, Judah ha-. *See* Judah ha-Levi

Lévi-Strauss, Claude, **TE:** 753

Levia gravia (Carducci), **EP:** 189

Levin, Samuel, **TE:** 754

Levine, Philip, **AP:** 1120-1127; *Breath*, **AP:** 1126; *The Mercy*, **AP:** 1126; *Not This Pig*, **AP:** 1122; *On the Edge*, **AP:** 1122; *The Simple Truth*, **AP:** 1126; *Sweet Will*, **AP:** 1124; *They Feed They Lion*, **AP:** 1123; *A Walk with Tom Jefferson*, **AP:** 1124; *What Work Is*, **AP:** 1125

Levis, Larry, **AP:** 1127-1132; *The Afterlife*, **AP:** 1130; *Elegy*, **AP:** 1131; "A Poem of Horses," **AP:** 1130; *The Widening Spell of the Leaves*, **AP:** 1130; *Wrecking Crew*, **AP:** 1130

Levstik, Fran, **TE:** 580

Lew, Walter, **TE:** 24

Lewis, Cecil Day. *See* Day Lewis, Cecil

Lewis, Janet, **AP:** 1132-1136; *The Dear Past, and Other Poems, 1919-1994*, **AP:** 1135; "Garden Note," **AP:** 1135; *The Indians in the Woods*, **AP:** 1134; *Poems Old and New, 1918-1978*, **AP:** 1135; "The Reader," **AP:** 1134

Li Bo, **TE:** 60, **WP:** 150-157; "Climbing the Peak of Mount Taibo," **WP:** 153; "Drinking Alone in the Moonlight," **WP:** 154; "Gazing at Yellow Crane Mountain," **WP:** 154; "In the Mountains," **WP:** 154; "The Road to Shu Is Hard," **WP:** 155; "Wandering About Mount Tai," **WP:** 153

Li Ch'ing-chao. *See* Li Qingzhao

Li Pai. *See* Li Bo

Li Po. *See* Li Bo

Li Qingzhao, **TE:** 63, **WP:** 157-162; "To the Tune," **WP:** 159; "Tune," **WP:** 159

Li Sao, The (Qu Yuan), **TE:** 58

Li Shangyin, **TE:** 62

Li Taibo. *See* Li Bo

Li T'ai-pai. *See* Li Bo

Li T'ai-po. *See* Li Bo

Li-Young Lee. *See* Lee, Li-Young

Liberation poetry, Africa, **TE:** 16

Liberties, The (Howe), **AP:** 916

Liberty (Thomson), **BP:** 1262

Libretto for the Republic of Liberia (Tolson), **AP:** 1986

Libro de buen amor. See *Book of Good Love, The*

Libya. *See* Geographical Index

Lição de coisas (Drummond de Andrade), **WP:** 82

Lice, The (Merwin), **AP:** 1335

Lichtenstein, Alfred, **TE:** 308

Licorice Daughter, The (Lifshin), **AP:** 1141

"Lie, The" (Ralegh), **BP:** 1042

Lies (Williams), **AP:** 2163

"Lies Lovingly Told" (Oates), **AP:** 1447

Lieutenant Schmidt (Pasternak), **WP:** 227

Life and Death (Creeley), **AP:** 398

Life and Death of Jason, The (Morris), **BP:** 927

Life and Letters, The (Feldman), **AP:** 590

Life Studies (Lowell), **AP:** 1192, **TE:** 201, **TE:** 668

Lifelines (Booth), **AP:** 215

Lifshin, Lyn, **AP:** 1136-1143; *Before It's Light*, **AP:** 1140; "Fat," **AP:** 1139; "Hair," **AP:** 1140; *The Licorice Daughter*, **AP:** 1141; *92 Rapple Drive*, **AP:** 1142; *Persephone*, **AP:** 1142; *Upstate Madonna*, **AP:** 1139; "You Understand the Requirements," **AP:** 1140

Lift Every Voice and Sing (Johnson), **AP:** 973

"Light" (Ondaatje), **BP:** 975

Light and Dark (Howes), **AP:** 922

Light Around the Body, The (Bly), **AP:** 191

Light in the Attic, A (Silverstein), **AP:** 1784

Light verse. *See* Categorized Index

Lighter than Air (Enzensberger), **EP:** 326

"Lightning" (Rimbaud), **EP:** 902

"Like a Bull" (Radnóti), **EP:** 881

Like a Bulwark (Moore), **AP:** 1369

Like Most Revelations (Howard), **AP:** 911

Liliencron, Detlev von, **TE:** 303

Lilies Without (Kasischke), **AP:** 1001

Lim, Genny, **TE:** 22

Limerick, defined, **AP:** 2300, **BP:** 1384, **EP:** 1178, **TE:** 816, **WP:** 386

"Lincoln Relics, The" (Kunitz), **AP:** 1090

"Lincoln, the Man of the People" (Markham), **AP:** 1276

Lindegren, Erik, **TE:** 549

Lindsay, Sarah, **AP:** 1143-1146; *Mount Clutter*, **AP:** 1145; *Primate Behavior*, **AP:** 1144; *Twigs and Knucklebones*, **AP:** 1145

Lindsay, Vachel, **AP:** 1146-1153; "The Chinese Nightingale," **AP:** 1151; "The Flower-Fed Buffaloes," **AP:** 1152; "General William Booth Enters into Heaven," **AP:** 1149; "The Gospel of Beauty," **AP:** 1150; Sara Teasdale, **AP:** 1975

Line, defined, **AP:** 2300, **BP:** 1384, **EP:** 1178, **TE:** 816, **WP:** 386

Lines at Intersection (Miles), **AP:** 1341

"Lines Composed a Few Miles Above Tintern Abbey" (Wordsworth), **BP:** 1314

Lines from Neuchatel (Meinke), **AP:** 1291

"Lines to a Poet" (Jacobsen), **AP:** 952

"Lines, Trees, and Words" (Blackburn), **AP:** 185

"Lines Written in Anticipation . . ." (Sassoon), **BP:** 1085

"Lines Written on a Seat on the Grand Canal" (Kavanagh), **BP:** 730

Linguistic criticism, **TE:** 750-759

Linguistics, **AP:** 2282-2293, **BP:** 1366-1377, **EP:** 1160-1171, **TE:** 798-809, **WP:** 368-379

Lining Up (Howard), **AP:** 911

Liquid Paper (Meinke), **AP:** 1292

Lirismos (González Martínez), **WP:** 104

List (Zagajewski), **EP:** 1139

"Listeners, The" (De la Mare), **BP:** 402

"Listening to Distant Guns" (Levertov), **AP:** 1116

Litany of Friends, A (Randall),
    AP: 1600
Literature as "criticism of life," **TE:** 713
Literature as Social Discourse
    (Fowler), **TE:** 758
Lithuania. *See* Geographical Index
Little Boat (Valentine), **AP:** 2026
"Little Death to Make One Laugh, A"
    (Corbière), **EP:** 262
"Little Duck Bathes, A" (Radnóti),
    EP: 882
Little Friend, Little Friend (Jarrell),
    AP: 959
Little Geste, and Other Poems, A
    (Hoffman), **AP:** 867
Little Henrietta (Reese), **AP:** 1620
"Little Men Who Come Blindly"
    (Flint), **AP:** 610
"Little Orphant Annie" (Riley),
    AP: 1651
"Little Song About Charity, A"
    (McGrath), **AP:** 1227
Little Space, The (Ostriker), **AP:** 1504
"Little Town in Siberia" (Tzara),
    EP: 1048
Little Who's Zoo of Mild Animals, A
    (Aiken), **AP:** 16
Littlefoot (Wright), **AP:** 2215
Live Another Day (Ciardi), **AP:** 316
Live or Die (Sexton), **AP:** 1756
"Lives" (Rukeyser), **AP:** 1689
*Lives of Saints Edmund and Fremund,
    The* (Lydgate), **BP:** 837
Lives of the Heart, The (Hirshfield),
    AP: 861
Lives of the Poets, The (Johnson),
    TE: 706
"Living Flame of Love, The" (John),
    EP: 547
"Living Temple, The" (Holmes),
    AP: 898
Living Together (Bowers), **AP:** 221
Livius Andronicus, Lucius, **TE:** 446
"Livre des quatre dames, Le." *See*
    "Book of Four Ladies, The"

Livy, **TE:** 452
"Llama de amor viva." *See* "Living
    Flame of Love, The"
Llanto por Ignacio Sánchez Mejías.
    See *Lament for the Death of a
    Bullfighter*
Loading Mercury with a Pitchfork
    (Brautigan), **AP:** 242
Loba (Di Prima), **AP:** 468
Local History (Hunt), **AP:** 938
Local Knowledge (Fairchild),
    AP: 581
Local Measures (Miles), **AP:** 1341
Local Visitations (Dunn), **AP:** 519
Locations (Harrison), **AP:** 805
Locked House, A (Snodgrass),
    AP: 1838
Lodge, Thomas, BP: 817-823; *A Fig
    for Momus,* **BP:** 820; *Phillis with
    the Tragical Complaynt of Elstred,*
    BP: 820; *Scillaes Metamorphosis,*
    BP: 821
Loerke, Oskar, **TE:** 309
Logan, John, AP: 1153-1157;
    "Believe It," **AP:** 1156; "Poem for
    My Brother," **AP:** 1155; *Poem in
    Progress,* **AP:** 1155; *The Zig-Zag
    Walk,* **AP:** 1155
Logbook II (Seferis), **EP:** 960
Loges, François des. *See* Villon,
    François
Logue, Christopher, BP: 823-826;
    Cold Calls, **BP:** 826; *New
    Numbers,* **BP:** 825; *Selected
    Poems,* **BP:** 825
Loiners, The (Harrison), **BP:** 590
Lomonosov, Mikhail, **TE:** 510
London (Johnson), **BP:** 703
"London Fête, A" (Patmore), **BP:** 986
"London, has thou accused me"
    (Surrey), **BP:** 1216
"London Snow" (Bridges), **BP:** 132
Lonely Suppers of W. V. Balloon, The
    (Middleton), **BP:** 901
Long Island Light (Heyen), **AP:** 844

Long Live Man (Corso), **AP:** 359
Long Marriage, The (Kumin),
    AP: 1080
Longfellow, Henry Wadsworth,
    AP: 1157-1165, **TE:** 633;
    Ballads, and Other Poems,
    AP: 1161; *The Belfry of Bruges,
    and Other Poems,* **AP:** 1161; "The
    Bells of San Blas," **AP:** 1161;
    "Birds of Passage," **AP:** 1162;
    The Courtship of Miles Standish,
    AP: 1163; *The Divine Tragedy,*
    AP: 1164; *The Golden Legend,*
    AP: 1164; *The New England
    Tragedies,* **AP:** 1164; "A Psalm of
    Life," **TE:** 761; *The Seaside and
    the Fireside,* **AP:** 1161; *The Song
    of Hiawatha,* **AP:** 1163
Longing of a Blessed Heart, The
    (Breton), **BP:** 129
Longinus, **TE:** 702; *On the Sublime,*
    TE: 702
Longshot Poems for Broke Players
    (Bukowski), **AP:** 268
Longue chaîne de l'ancre, La
    (Bonnefoy), **EP:** 148
Lönnrot, Elias, EP: 617-621,
    TE: 529; *Kalevala,* **EP:** 619
"Look, The" (Teasdale), **AP:** 1976
Look! We Have Come Through!
    (Lawrence), **BP:** 799
Looking Glass, The (Gardner),
    AP: 654
Looking up at the Leaves (Howes),
    AP: 922
Loom, The (Kelly), **AP:** 1018
Loose Woman (Cisneros), **AP:** 320
"Loot" (Kipling), **BP:** 763
Lorca, Federico García. *See* García
    Lorca, Federico
Lord, Albert B., **TE:** 218
Lord Dragonfly (Heyen), **AP:** 846
Lord Hay's Masque (Campion), **BP:** 205
"Lord, I've seen too much" (Shapiro),
    AP: 1767

Lord Tennyson, Alfred. *See* Tennyson, Alfred, Lord

Lord Weary's Castle (Lowell), **AP:** 1190

Lorde, Audre, AP: 1166-1172, **TE:** 8; *Between Our Selves*, **AP:** 1169; *The Black Unicorn*, **AP:** 1169; "Blood-birth," **AP:** 1169; *Cables to Rage*, **AP:** 1168; *Coal*, **AP:** 1169; "Conversation in Crisis," **AP:** 1169; "The Day They Eulogized Mahalia," **AP:** 1169; *The First Cities*, **AP:** 1168; *From a Land Where Other People Live*, **AP:** 1169; "Jesse Helms," **AP:** 1171; *The Marvelous Arithmetics of Distance*, **AP:** 1171; "October," **AP:** 1170; *Our Dead Behind Us*, **AP:** 1169; "Outside," **AP:** 1169; "Power," **AP:** 1169; *Undersong*, **AP:** 1170

Lord's Masque, The (Campion), **BP:** 206

Lorris, Guillaume de. *See* Guillaume de Lorris

"Lost Dancer, The" (Toomer), **AP:** 1993

Lost Generation. *See* Categorized Index

Lost Land, The (Boland), **BP:** 116

Lost Lunar Baedeker, The (Loy), **AP:** 1203

Lost Originals, The (Feldman), **AP:** 589

Lost Pilot, The (Tate), **AP:** 1949

Lost River (Tate), **AP:** 1957

"Lost Self" (Benn), **EP:** 110

Lost World, The (Jarrell), **AP:** 961

"Lotos-Eaters, The" (Tennyson), **BP:** 1238

Lotus (Breytenbach), **EP:** 167

Lotus Flowers, The (Voigt), **AP:** 2057

Louis, Brother. *See* Merton, Thomas

"Louise" (Smith), **BP:** 1168

Loury, Guillaume de. *See* Guillaume de Lorris

"Love" (Herbert), **BP:** 624

"Love and Grief" (Dunbar), **AP:** 504

"Love and Money" (Dugan), **AP:** 501

Love as Love, Death as Death (Riding), **AP:** 1644

Love Bomb, and Other Musical Pieces, The (Fenton), **BP:** 490

"Love in fantastic triumph sate" (Behn), **BP:** 70

"Love in the Valley" (Meredith), **BP:** 892

Love Is a Dog from Hell (Bukowski), **AP:** 271

Love Is Enough (Morris), **BP:** 929

Love Letter from an Impossible Land (Meredith), **AP:** 1310

Love Letters of Phyllis McGinley, The (McGinley), **AP:** 1223

Love of Fame, the Universal Passion (Young), **BP:** 1352

Love Poems (Giovanni), **AP:** 699

Love Poems (Sexton), **AP:** 1757

Love poetry. *See* Categorized Index

"Love Song" (Dugan), **AP:** 500

"Love Song of J. Alfred Prufrock, The" (Eliot), **BP:** 462

"Love Songs of the Sixth Dalai Lama," **TE:** 609

"Love Sonnet" (Updike), **AP:** 2019

Love You (Randall), **AP:** 1600

Løveid, Cecilie, **TE:** 558

Lovelace, Richard, BP: 827-832; "The Grasshopper," **BP:** 829

Lover's Familiar, The (McMichael), **AP:** 1255

"Love's Humility" (Dunbar), **AP:** 504

Loves of Cupid and Psyche, The (La Fontaine), **EP:** 580

Lovesick (Stern), **AP:** 1901

Loving a Woman in Two Worlds (Bly), **AP:** 194

"Low Barometer" (Bridges), **BP:** 133

Low Ceiling (Kirstein), **AP:** 1044

Lowell, Amy, AP: 1172-1179, **TE:** 648, **TE:** 652; "On Looking at a Copy of Alice Meynell's Poems," **AP:** 1177

Lowell, James Russell, AP: 1180-1186, **TE:** 634; *The Cathedral*, **AP:** 1185; *A Fable for Critics*, **AP:** 1184; "Fitz Adams' Story," **AP:** 1184; "The Unhappy Lot of Mr. Knott," **AP:** 1184

Lowell, Robert, AP: 1187-1199, **TE:** 201, **TE:** 668; *Day by Day*, **AP:** 1198; *The Dolphin*, **AP:** 1197; *For the Union Dead*, **AP:** 1193; *History*, **AP:** 1196; *Life Studies*, **AP:** 1192, **TE:** 201, **TE:** 668; *Lord Weary's Castle*, **AP:** 1190; *The Mills of the Kavanaughs*, **AP:** 1191; *Near the Ocean*, **AP:** 1194; *Notebook, 1967-1968*, **AP:** 1195

"Lower East Side Poem, A" (Piñero), **TE:** 469

"Lowest Room, The" (Rossetti), **BP:** 1063

Lowy, Mina. *See* Loy, Mina

Loy, Mina, AP: 1200-1203; *Anglo-Mongrels and the Rose*, **AP:** 1202; *The Lost Lunar Baedeker*, **AP:** 1203; "Parturition," **AP:** 1202; *Songs to Joannes*, **AP:** 1202

Lu You, **TE:** 63

Lucan, EP: 621-626; *Pharsalia*, **EP:** 623

Lucas, Margaret. *See* Newcastle, Margaret Cavendish, duchess of

Lucas, Victoria. *See* Plath, Sylvia

Lucidor, Lasse, **TE:** 530

"Lucifer in Starlight" (Meredith), **BP:** 893

Lucilius, Gaius, **TE:** 446

Luck's Shining Child (Garrett), **AP:** 659

Lucky Life (Stern), **AP:** 1895

Lucky Poet (MacDiarmid), **BP:** 851
Lucretius, **EP:** 627-632, **TE:** 449;
  On the Nature of Things, **EP:** 628
*Ludzie na moście. See People on a
  Bridge*
Luis, Fray. *See* León, Luis de
Luisa in Realityland (Alegría),
  WP: 11
Lukáč, Emil Boleslav, **TE:** 576
Lukács, Georg, **TE:** 760
"Luke Havergal" (Robinson),
  AP: 2273, **BP:** 1357, **EP:** 1151,
  TE: 789, **WP:** 359
Lull, Raymond, **TE:** 48
"Lullaby" (Auden), **BP:** 51
Lum, Wing Tek, **AP:** 1204-1206;
  Expounding the Doubtful Points,
  AP: 1205; *What the Kite Thinks*,
  AP: 1206
Lundkvist, Artur, **TE:** 544
Lupercal (Hughes), **BP:** 688
Lushi (poetic form), **TE:** 60
Lusiads, The (Camões), **EP:** 182
Lusophone poetry, Africa, **TE:** 16
Lutrin, Le (Boileau-Despréaux),
  EP: 139
Lutwidge Dodgson, Charles. *See*
  Carroll, Lewis
Luzán, Ignacio de, **TE:** 595
Luzi, Mario, **TE:** 406
"Lycidas" (Milton), **BP:** 908
"Lycus the Centaur" (Hood), **BP:** 655
Lydgate, John, **BP:** 832-840,
  TE: 121; *Ballade at the
  Reverence of Our Lady, Qwene of
  Mercy*, **BP:** 837; *Complaint of the
  Black Knight*, **BP:** 835; *Fall of
  Princes*, **BP:** 838; *The Lives of
  Saints Edmund and Fremund*,
  BP: 837
Lying Down in the Olive Press
  (Shore), **AP:** 1774
"Lying in a Hammock at William
  Duffy's Farm in Pine Island,
  Minnesota" (Wright), **AP:** 2223

Lynch, B. Suárez. *See* Borges, Jorge
  Luis
"Lynching, The" (McKay), **AP:** 1239
Lyre, Pinchbeck. *See* Sassoon,
  Siegfried
Lyric poetry; English, **TE:** 162;
  French, **TE:** 237; German,
  TE: 287; Indian, **TE:** 372; Italian,
  TE: 377; Native American,
  TE: 478; Restoration, **TE:** 620;
  Serbian, **TE:** 566. *See also*
  Categorized Index
Lyric poetry, defined, **AP:** 2300,
  BP: 1384, **EP:** 1178, **TE:** 816,
  WP: 386
Lyrical Ballads (Wordsworth), **BP:** 1312
Lyrics, Middle English, **TE:** 107,
  TE: 123
Lyrics and Rhythms, The (Carducci),
  EP: 190
Lyrics of Love and Laughter
  (Dunbar), **AP:** 505
Lyrics of Lowly Life (Dunbar),
  AP: 505
Lyrics of Sunshine and Shadow
  (Dunbar), **AP:** 506
Lyrics of the Hearthside (Dunbar),
  AP: 504
*Lyutenant Shmidt. See Lieutenant
  Schmidt*

"Ma Rainey" (Brown), **TE:** 12
Mac Flecknoe (Dryden), **BP:** 437,
  TE: 622
McAuley, James, **TE:** 33
MacBeth, George, **BP:** 841-846;
  "The Burning Poem," **BP:** 844;
  "A Confession," **BP:** 844; "Fin du
  Globe," **BP:** 842; "How to Eat an
  Orange," **BP:** 843; "LDMN
  Analysis of Thomas Nashe's
  'Song'," **BP:** 842; "A Poet's Life,"
  BP: 843; "The Red Herring,"
  BP: 845; "Scissor-Man," **BP:** 845;
  "The Ski Murders," **BP:** 842;

"Two Experiments," **BP:** 842;
  "What Metre Is," **BP:** 843
McClure, Michael, **AP:** 1207-1211;
  "For Artaud," **AP:** 1209; "Hymn
  to St. Geryon, I," **AP:** 1209;
  "Peyote Poem, Part I," **AP:** 1209;
  "The Robe," **AP:** 1209; "The
  Rug," **AP:** 1209; *Selected Poems*,
  AP: 1210
MacDiarmid, Hugh, **BP:** 846-854; *A
  Drunk Man Looks at the Thistle*,
  BP: 848; *Hymns to Lenin*,
  BP: 850; *In Memoriam James
  Joyce*, **BP:** 852; *A Lap of Honour*,
  BP: 852; *Lucky Poet*, **BP:** 851; *A
  Moment in Eternity*, **BP:** 848; "On
  a Raised Beach," **BP:** 851; *Penny
  Wheep*, **BP:** 848; *Sangschaw*,
  BP: 848; *Stony Limits, and Other
  Poems*, **BP:** 851; *To Circumjack
  Cencrastus*, **BP:** 850
Macdonald, Cynthia, **AP:** 1211-
  1215; *Alternate Means of
  Transport*, **AP:** 1213;
  Amputations, **AP:** 1212; *I Can't
  Remember*, **AP:** 1214;
  Transplants, **AP:** 1213
McDonald, Walt, **AP:** 1215-1221;
  Burning the Fence, **AP:** 1217;
  *Caliban in Blue, and Other
  Poems*, **AP:** 1217; *Climbing the
  Divide*, **AP:** 1219; "For God in
  My Sorrows," **AP:** 1219; *A
  Thousand Miles of Stars*,
  AP: 1220
Macedonian poetry, **TE:** 475-477
McGinley, Phyllis, **AP:** 1221-1225;
  *The Love Letters of Phyllis
  McGinley*, **AP:** 1223; *A Short
  Walk from the Station*, **AP:** 1223;
  Stones from a Glass House,
  AP: 1223; *Times Three*, **AP:** 1224
McGrath, Thomas, **AP:** 1225-1230;
  "The Dialectics of Love,"
  AP: 1227; "A Little Song About

Charity," **AP:** 1227; "You Can Start the Poetry Now," **AP:** 1228

McGuckian, Medbh, **TE:** 210

Mácha, Karel Hynek, **TE:** 81

Machado, Antonio, EP: 633-638, **TE:** 598; *The Castilian Camp*, **EP:** 637; *De un cancionero apócrifo*, **EP:** 637; *Nuevas canciones*, **EP:** 637; *Proverbios y canciones*, **EP:** 637; *Soledades*, **EP:** 636

Machar, Josef Svatopluk, **TE:** 83

McHugh, Heather, AP: 1230-1233; *Dangers*, **AP:** 1232; *Hinge and Sign*, **AP:** 1233; *A World of Difference*, **AP:** 1232

McKay, Claude, AP: 1234-1240, **TE:** 44, **TE:** 658; "If We Must Die," **AP:** 1238, **TE:** 44; "Invocation," **AP:** 1237; "The Lynching," **AP:** 1239; "The Tropics in New York," **AP:** 1237; "We Wear the Mask," **AP:** 1238

Mackey, Nathaniel, AP: 1241-1244; *Eroding Witness*, **AP:** 1242; *School of Udhra*, **AP:** 1242; *Splay Anthem*, **AP:** 1243; *Whatsaid Serif*, **AP:** 1243

MacLeish, Archibald, AP: 1244-1254; *Actfive, and Other Poems*, **AP:** 1252; *America Was Promises*, **AP:** 1252; "Ars Poetica," **AP:** 1250; *Conquistador*, **AP:** 1251; *Einstein*, **AP:** 1249; *Frescoes for Mr. Rockefeller's City*, **AP:** 1252; *The Hamlet of A. MacLeish*, **AP:** 1249; *The Happy Marriage*, **AP:** 1248; *New and Collected Poems, 1917-1976*, **AP:** 1248; *New Found Land*, **AP:** 1250; "Old Man's Journey," **AP:** 1253; *The Pot of Earth*, **AP:** 1248; *Public Speech*, **AP:** 1252; *Streets in the Moon*, **AP:** 1249

McMichael, James, AP: 1255-1257; *Against the Falling Evil*, **AP:** 1255; *Capacity*, **AP:** 1256; *Each in a Place Apart*, **AP:** 1256; *Four Good Things*, **AP:** 1256; *The Lover's Familiar*, **AP:** 1255

MacNeice, Louis, BP: 854-866; *Autumn Journal*, **BP:** 862; "Blasphemies," **BP:** 860; *The Burning Perch*, **BP:** 864; "An Eclogue for Christmas," **BP:** 861; "The Kingdom," **BP:** 860; *Solstices*, **BP:** 864; "To Hedli," **BP:** 860; *Visitations*, **BP:** 864

Macpherson, James; *Ossian*, **TE:** 628

McPherson, Sandra, AP: 1258-1265; *Edge Effect*, **AP:** 1264; *Elegies for the Hot Season*, **AP:** 1259; *Expectation Days*, **AP:** 1264; *The God of Indeterminacy*, **AP:** 1264; *Patron Happiness*, **AP:** 1262; *Radiation*, **AP:** 1260; *The Spaces Between Birds*, **AP:** 1264; *Streamers*, **AP:** 1263; *The Year of Our Birth*, **AP:** 1261

Macrobius, Ambrosius Theodosius, **TE:** 459

Mad-song, defined, **AP:** 2300, **BP:** 1384, **EP:** 1178, **TE:** 816, **WP:** 386

Madagascar (Davenant), **BP:** 364

Madame de Staël, **TE:** 259

Madhubuti, Haki R., AP: 1265-1274; *Black Pride*, **AP:** 1269; *Book of Life*, **AP:** 1272; *Don't Cry, Scream*, **AP:** 1270; *Earthquakes and Sunrise Missions*, **AP:** 1273; *Heartlove*, **AP:** 1273; *Killing Memory, Seeking Ancestors*, **AP:** 1273; *Think Black*, **AP:** 1269; *We Walk the Way of the New World*, **AP:** 1271

Madoc (Muldoon), **BP:** 941, **TE:** 210

Magellanic Clouds, The (Wakoski), **AP:** 2072

Magnetic Mountain, The (Day Lewis), **BP:** 387

Magnetic North (Gregerson), **AP:** 734

"Maiden Song" (Rossetti), **BP:** 1063

Maiden's Dream, A (Greene), **BP:** 553

Main chaude, La (Follain), **EP:** 336

"Main-Morte" (Reverdy), **EP:** 887

Mainland (Cruz), **AP:** 402

"Mainstreaming" (Cassity), **AP:** 295

"Maison fermée, La." *See* "Within the House"

Máj. See *May*

Makars, **TE:** 126

"Making an End" (Oates), **AP:** 1447

Making Certain It Goes On (Hugo), **AP:** 937

Makings of Happiness, The (Wallace), **AP:** 2092

Makurakotoba (poetic technique), **TE:** 414

Mal du siècle, **TE:** 260

Malherbe, François de, EP: 639-644, **TE:** 251; "Allant châtier la rebellion des Rochelois," **EP:** 642; "Récit d'un berger," **EP:** 641

Malinowski, Ivan, **TE:** 562

Mallarmé, Stéphane, EP: 644-650, **TE:** 268, **TE:** 643; "All the Soul Indrawn . . . ," **EP:** 646; Paul Claudel, **EP:** 247; *Dice Thrown Never Will Annul Chance*, **EP:** 649; "Her Pure Fingernails on High Offering Their Onyx," **EP:** 647; *Herodias*, **EP:** 648; *Igitur*, **EP:** 649; "My Old Books Closed at the Name of Paphos," **EP:** 647

Mallorcan school, **TE:** 51

Malone, Louis. *See* MacNeice, Louis

Malory, Sir Thomas, **TE:** 125

Man and Camel (Strand), **AP:** 1924

Man-Fate (Everson), **AP:** 575

"Man in Inhumanity" (Ady), **EP:** 5

Man in the Black Coat Turns, The (Bly), **AP:** 194

Man in the Divided Sea, A (Merton), **AP:** 1328

"Man-Moth, The" (Bishop), **AP:** 172

"Man said to the universe, A" (Crane), **AP:** 389

Man Song (Neihardt), **AP:** 1407

Man Who Shook Hands, The (Wakoski), **AP:** 2074

Man with Night Sweats, The (Gunn), **BP:** 567

Man with Red Suspenders, The (Dacey), **AP:** 427

"Man with the Hoe, The" (Markham), **AP:** 1276

Manatee/Humanity (Waldman), **AP:** 2079

Manathi poetry. *See* Indian English poetry

Mandela's Earth, and Other Poems (Soyinka), **WP:** 279

Mandelstam, Osip, TE: 519, **WP:** 163-170; "Happily Neighing, the Herds Graze," **WP:** 165; "The Horseshoe Finder," **WP:** 168; "Leningrad," **WP:** 168; *Poems,* **WP:** 168; "Slate Ode," **WP:** 168; *Stone,* **WP:** 166; *Tristia,* **WP:** 167

Mangan, James Clarence, BP: 866-870; "Kathaleen Ny-Houlahan," **BP:** 869; "The Nameless One," **BP:** 870; "O'Hussey's Ode to the Maguire," **BP:** 869

Manger, Itzik, EP: 650-657; "The Bent Tree," **EP:** 655; *Khumish Lider,* **EP:** 656

"Manifest destiny" (Hollo), **AP:** 889

Manifesto of Surrealism (Breton), **EP:** 159

Maninbo. See Ten Thousand Lives

Manner, Eeva-Liisa, **TE:** 552

Manninen, Otto, **TE:** 540

Manrique, Jorge, EP: 657-660; *Coplas on the Death of His Father,* **EP:** 658

Man ṣūr, Abū ol-Qāsen. *See* Firdusi

"Mantis" (Zukofsky), **AP:** 2267

Many Named Beloved, The (Menashe), **AP:** 1303

Many Voices (Villa), **AP:** 2051

Manyoshu, The (anthology), **TE:** 412

Manzoni, Alessandro, EP: 660-666; "In morte di Carlo Imbonati," **EP:** 664; "Marzo 1821," **EP:** 665; "The Napoleonic Ode," **EP:** 665; "The Pentecost," **EP:** 665; *The Sacred Hymns,* **EP:** 664; "Il trionfo della libertà," **EP:** 663

Maoist poetry, **TE:** 67

Maori poets, **TE:** 504

"Map, The" (Bishop), **AP:** 174

Map of the Night, A (Wagoner), **AP:** 2066

"Map of Verona, A" (Reed), **BP:** 1045

Map to the Next World, A (Harjo), **AP:** 792

Mappings (Seth), **WP:** 274

Maragall, Juan, **TE:** 51

March, Ausiàs, **TE:** 50

Mare, Walter de la. *See* De la Mare, Walter

Maremágnum. See Clamor

"Mareotis" (Durrell), **BP:** 454

Marginalization and literary works, **TE:** 734

Mari Magno (Clough), **BP:** 270

Maria Nephele (Elytis), **EP:** 322

Marian poems, **TE:** 124

Marie de France, EP: 666-674; "Eliduc," **EP:** 672; "Equitan," **EP:** 671; "Lanval," **EP:** 670; "The Two Lovers," **EP:** 670

"Marilyn Monroe" (Cardenal), **WP:** 54

Marinero en tierra (Alberti), **EP:** 8

Marinetti, Filippo Tommaso, **TE:** 401

Marinismo, **TE:** 386, **TE:** 618

Marino, Giambattista, EP: 674-678, **TE:** 386, **TE:** 618; *L'Adone,* **EP:** 677, **TE:** 386

Markham, Edwin, AP: 1274-1277; "Lincoln, the Man of the People," **AP:** 1276; "The Man with the Hoe," **AP:** 1276; "Our Israfel," **AP:** 1276; "Walt Whitman," **AP:** 1277

"Marks" (Pastan), **AP:** 1517

Marlowe, Christopher, BP: 870-876; *Hero and Leander,* **BP:** 873; "The Passionate Shepherd to His Love," **BP:** 873

Marmon, Leslie. *See* Silko, Leslie Marmon

Maro, Publius Vergilius. *See* Vergil

Marot, Clément, **TE:** 247

"Marriage" (Corso), **AP:** 359

Marriage (Waldman), **AP:** 2078

Marriage in the Trees, The (Plumly), **AP:** 1560

Marriage of Heaven and Hell, The (Blake), **BP:** 97

"Marshes of Glynn, The" (Lanier), **AP:** 1100

Martial, EP: 678-681, **TE:** 456; *Epigrams,* **EP:** 680

Martian poetry, **TE:** 208

Martin, Egbert, **TE:** 44

Martin; & Meditations on the South Valley (Baca), **AP:** 73

Martínez, Enrique González. *See* González Martínez, Enrique

Martínez, Ernesto Cardenal. *See* Cardenal, Ernesto

Martinique. *See* Geographical Index

Martinson, Harry, EP: 681-685, **TE:** 544; *Aniara,* **EP:** 683; *Passad,* **EP:** 683

Marulić, Marko, **TE:** 71

Marvell, Andrew, BP: 877-884; "The Garden," **BP:** 880; "To His Coy Mistress," **BP:** 880; "Upon Appleton House," **BP:** 882

Marvelous Arithmetics of Distance, The (Lorde), **AP:** 1171

Marx, Karl, **TE:** 760

Marxism and Form (Jameson), **TE:** 761

Marxist criticism, **TE:** 733, **TE:** 760-763

Marxist criticism, defined, **AP:** 2300, **BP:** 1384, **EP:** 1178, **TE:** 816, **WP:** 386

"Mary's Song" (Plath), **AP:** 1552

"Marzo 1821" (Manzoni), **EP:** 665

Mas, Josep Arseni Vicenç Foix i. *See* Foix, J. V.

Masaoka Shiki, **TE:** 428

Masaoka Shiki International Haiku Prize, **CM:** 58, **TE:** 878, **WP:** 411

Masculine Dead, The (Everson), **AP:** 572

Masculine rhyme, defined, **AP:** 2300, **BP:** 1384, **EP:** 1178, **WP:** 386, **TE:** 816

Masefield, John, **BP:** 885-890; "Cargoes," **BP:** 887; "CLM," **BP:** 889; *Dauber*, **BP:** 889; *The Everlasting Mercy*, **BP:** 888

Mask for Janus, A (Merwin), **AP:** 1334

Masks of Drought, The (Everson), **AP:** 576

Masters, Edgar Lee, **AP:** 1278-1284; *Domesday Book*, **AP:** 1282; *The Fate of the Jury*, **AP:** 1282; *The New Spoon River*, **AP:** 1280; *Spoon River Anthology*, **AP:** 1279

Materials, The (Oppen), **AP:** 1479

Matevski, Mateja, **TE:** 476

Mathnavī of Jalālu'ddīn Rūmī, The (Rūmī), **WP:** 257

"Matin." *See* "Morning"

Matsunaga Teitoku, **TE:** 422

Matsuo Bashō, **TE:** 423, **WP:** 170-176; "In the City," **WP:** 174; *The Narrow Road to the Deep North*, **WP:** 175

Matthews, William, **AP:** 1284-1289; *After All*, **AP:** 1288; *Blues If You Want*, **AP:** 1288; *Flood*, **AP:** 1287; *Foreseeable Futures*, **AP:** 1288; *A Happy Childhood*, **AP:** 1287; *Rising and Falling*, **AP:** 1286; *Ruining the New Road*, **AP:** 1286; *Sleek for the Long Flight*, **AP:** 1286; *Sticks and Stones*, **AP:** 1286; *Time and Money*, **AP:** 1288

Maud (Tennyson), **BP:** 1242

"Maudlin" (Plath), **AP:** 1552

Maulānā. *See* Rūmī, Jalāl al-Dīn

"Mauvais Sang." *See* "Bad Blood"

Max. *See* Kumin, Maxine

Maximus Poems, The (Olson), **AP:** 1475, **TE:** 197

May (Mácha), **TE:** 81

"May Day Sermon" (Dickey), **AP:** 452

"May Night" (Musset), **EP:** 737

Mayakovsky, Vladimir, **TE:** 520, **WP:** 176-182; *About That*, **WP:** 179; *A Cloud in Pants*, **WP:** 178; *Fine!*, **WP:** 180; *150,000,000*, **WP:** 179; *Ya*, **WP:** 178

Mayan Astronomer in Hell's Kitchen, A (Espada), **AP:** 561

Mažuranić, Ivan, **TE:** 73

Meadowlands (Glück), **AP:** 716

Medici, Lorenzo de', **TE:** 381

Medieval poetry, Latin, **TE:** 461

"Meditation" (Lermontov), **WP:** 147

"Meditation 8" (Taylor), **AP:** 1962

"Meditation 39" (Taylor), **AP:** 1961

"Meditation 56" (Taylor), **AP:** 1963

Méditations poétiques. See *Poetical Meditations*

"Mediterranean, The" (Tate), **AP:** 1943

Megara, Theognis of. *See* Theognis

Mehren, Stein, **TE:** 556

Mehun, Jean de. *See* Jean de Meung

Meinke, Peter, **AP:** 1290-1294; *The Contracted World*, **AP:** 1293; *Lines from Neuchatel*, **AP:** 1291; *Liquid Paper*, **AP:** 1292; *The Night Train and the Golden Bird*, **AP:** 1291; *Night Watch on the Chesapeake*, **AP:** 1292; *Scars*, **AP:** 1293; *Trying to Surprise God*, **AP:** 1292; *Underneath the Lantern*, **AP:** 1292; *Zinc Fingers*, **AP:** 1293

Meleager, **EP:** 685-688, **TE:** 329; *Garland*, **EP:** 686, **TE:** 329; *The Greek Anthology*, **EP:** 687

"Melusine, If Your Well Had Not" (Sachs), **EP:** 933

Melville, Herman, **AP:** 1294-1301; "The Aeolian Harp," **AP:** 1300; *Battle-Pieces and Aspects of the War*, **AP:** 1297; *Clarel*, **AP:** 1299; "Misgivings," **AP:** 1297; "Shiloh, a Requiem," **AP:** 1299

Memleketimden insan manzaralari. See *Human Landscapes*

Memoir of the Hawk (Tate), **AP:** 1957

"Mémoire" (Reverdy), **EP:** 887

Memoirs in Oxford (Prince), **BP:** 1024

Memories of the Future (Gibson), **AP:** 672

"Memphis Blues" (Brown), **AP:** 258

Men and Women (Browning), **BP:** 163

"Men of Careful Turns" (Brooks), **AP:** 251

Menashe, Samuel, **AP:** 1302-1308; *The Many Named Beloved*, **AP:** 1303; *New and Selected Poems*, **AP:** 1307; *The Niche Narrows*, **AP:** 1306; *No Jerusalem but This*, **AP:** 1303; *To Open*, **AP:** 1305

"Mending Wall" (Frost), **AP:** 631

Meng Hao-jan (Meng Haoran), **WP:** 184

Meng Haoran, WP: 182-185; *Meng Hao-jan*, **WP:** 184; *The Mountain Poems of Meng Hao-jan*, **WP:** 184
Mensagem. See Message
"Menses" (Millay), **AP:** 1348
Merchants from Cathay (Benét), **AP:** 131
Mercian Hymns (Hill), **BP:** 645, **TE:** 198
Mercy, The (Levine), **AP:** 1126
Mercy Seat, The (Dubie), **AP:** 496
Meredith, George, BP: 890-894; "The Lark Ascending," **BP:** 892; "Love in the Valley," **BP:** 892; "Lucifer in Starlight," **BP:** 893; "Modern Love," **BP:** 893
Meredith, Louisa Anne, **TE:** 31
Meredith, William, AP: 1308-1317; *The Cheer*, **AP:** 1314; *Earth Walk*, **AP:** 1313; *Effort at Speech*, **AP:** 1315; *Hazard, the Painter*, **AP:** 1313; *Love Letter from an Impossible Land*, **AP:** 1310; *The Open Sea, and Other Poems*, **AP:** 1311; *Partial Accounts*, **AP:** 1315; *Ships and Other Figures*, **AP:** 1311; *The Wreck of the Thresher, and Other Poems*, **AP:** 1312
Merezhkovsky, Dmitri, **TE:** 516
Merrill, James, AP: 1317-1325; *Braving the Elements*, **AP:** 1319; *The Changing Light at Sandover*, **AP:** 1322; *The Country of a Thousand Years of Peace, and Other Poems*, **AP:** 1318; *Divine Comedies*, **AP:** 1320; *The Fire Screen*, **AP:** 1319; *First Poems*, **AP:** 1318; *The Inner Room*, **AP:** 1323; *Late Settings*, **AP:** 1322; *Mirabell*, **AP:** 1320; *Nights and Days*, **AP:** 1319; *A Scattering of Salts*, **AP:** 1323; *Scripts for the Pageant*, **AP:** 1321; *Water Street*, **AP:** 1318

Merry Gang. *See* Categorized Index
Merton, Thomas, AP: 1325-1331; *Cables to the Ace*, **AP:** 1330; *The Collected Poems*, **AP:** 1330; *Emblems of a Season of Fury*, **AP:** 1329; *Figures for an Apocalypse*, **AP:** 1328; *The Geography of Lograire*, **AP:** 1330; *A Man in the Divided Sea*, **AP:** 1328; *Original Child Bomb*, **AP:** 1329; *The Strange Islands*, **AP:** 1329; *The Tears of the Blind Lions*, **AP:** 1329; *Thirty Poems*, **AP:** 1328
Merwin, W. S., AP: 1331-1339; *The Carrier of Ladders*, **AP:** 1335; *The Dancing Bears*, **AP:** 1334; *The Drunk in the Furnace*, **AP:** 1334; *The Folding Cliffs*, **AP:** 1337; *The Lice*, **AP:** 1335; *A Mask for Janus*, **AP:** 1334; *Migration*, **AP:** 1337; *Opening the Hand*, **AP:** 1336; *Present Company*, **AP:** 1337; *The Pupil*, **AP:** 1337; *The Rain in the Trees*, **AP:** 1336; *The River Sound*, **AP:** 1337; *The Shadow of Sirius*, **AP:** 1338; *Travels*, **AP:** 1336; *The Vixen*, **AP:** 1336
"Mes bouquins refermés sur le nom de Paphos." *See* "My Old Books Closed at the Name of Paphos"
Mess là-bas, La (Claudel), **EP:** 250
Message (Pessoa), **EP:** 813
Messenger (Voigt), **AP:** 2057
Messenger, The (Kinsella), **BP:** 757
"Mestrović and the Trees" (Blackburn), **AP:** 184
Met ander woorde (Breytenbach), **EP:** 167
Metamorphoses (Ovid), **EP:** 768
"Metamorphoses of M" (Bishop), **AP:** 178
Metamorphosis (Sitwell), **BP:** 1150
Metaphor, defined, **AP:** 2300,

BP: 1384, **EP:** 1178, **TE:** 816, **WP:** 386
Metaphysical poetry, **TE:** 147, **TE:** 615-619, **TE:** 708, **TE:** 744; twentieth century, **TE:** 189
Metaphysical poets. *See* Categorized Index
Metapoem, **TE:** 278
Metastasio, Pietro, **TE:** 387
Meter, defined, **AP:** 2301, **BP:** 1385, **EP:** 1179, **TE:** 817, **WP:** 387
Metonymy, defined, **AP:** 2301, **BP:** 1385, **EP:** 1179, **TE:** 817, **WP:** 387
Metrical Letters (Petrarch), **EP:** 834
Meung, Jean de. *See* Jean de Meung
Mew, Charlotte, BP: 894-897; *The Farmer's Bride*, **BP:** 896; *The Rambling Sailor*, **BP:** 897
Mexico. *See* Geographical Index
Mexico City Blues (Kerouac), **TE:** 665
Meyer, Conrad Ferdinand, **TE:** 302
Meyer, Lynn. *See* Slavitt, David
"Mezzogiorno d'inverno." *See* "Winter Noon"
Mgur (poetic form), **TE:** 608
Miasto bez imienia (Miłosz), **EP:** 716
"Michael" (Wordsworth), **BP:** 1316
Michaux, Henri, EP: 688-694, **TE:** 277; *A Barbarian in Asia*, **EP:** 691; "Clown," **EP:** 692; *Ecuador*, **EP:** 691; *I Am Writing to You from a Far-Off Country*, **EP:** 691; "My King," **EP:** 692; "A Tractable Man," **EP:** 692
Michelangelo, EP: 694-702
Mickiewicz, Adam, EP: 702-709, **TE:** 493; "Faris," **EP:** 706; *Forefathers' Eve*, parts 2 and 4, **EP:** 705; *Forefathers' Eve*, part 3, **EP:** 706; *Grażyna*, **EP:** 705; *Konrad Wallenrod*, **EP:** 706; *Pan Tadeusz*, **EP:** 707, **TE:** 494; *Sonnets from the Crimea*, **EP:** 705

Midaregami. See *Tangled Hair*

Middens of the Tribe (Hoffman),
    AP: 868

Middle Earth (Cole), **AP:** 335

Middle English period. *See*
    Categorized Index

Middle High German period. *See*
    Categorized Index

Middle Passage, The (Coxe), **AP:** 377

"Middle Passage" (Hayden), **AP:** 823

Middle Passages (Brathwaite),
    AP: 236

Middleton, Christopher, **BP:** 898-
    905; *The Anti-Basilisk*, **BP:** 903;
    The Balcony Tree, **BP:** 903;
    Carminalenia, **BP:** 903; *Collected
    Poems*, **BP:** 904; *The Lonely
    Suppers of W. V. Balloon*,
    BP: 901; *Nonsequences/
    Selfpoems*, **BP:** 900; *Our Flowers
    and Nice Bones*, **BP:** 901;
    Pataxanadu, and Other Prose,
    BP: 902; *The Tenor on
    Horseback*, **BP:** 904; *Torse Three*,
    BP: 900

Midnight, The (Howe), **AP:** 918

Midnight, Mary. *See* Smart,
    Christopher

"Midnight Duel" (Arany), **EP:** 48

Midnight Salvage (Rich), **AP:** 1640

"Midnight Special" (Sorrentino),
    AP: 1859

"Midpoint" (Updike), **AP:** 2019

Midquest (Chappell), **AP:** 305

Midsummer (Walcott), **WP:** 322

Midwest Eclogue (Baker), **AP:** 79

Mientras (Otero), **EP:** 762

"Mignonne, allons voir si la rose."
    See "Darling, Let Us Go"

Migration (Merwin), **AP:** 1337

Miguel de Cervantes Prize, **CM:** 49,
    EP: 1207, **TE:** 869, **WP:** 410

Mihalić, Slavko, **TE:** 75

"M'ijo no mira nada" (Rivera),
    AP: 1659

Milarepa, **TE:** 609

Miles, Josephine, **AP:** 1340-1343;
    Civil Poems, **AP:** 1342; *Collected
    Poems, 1930-1983*, **AP:** 1343;
    Coming to Terms, **AP:** 1342;
    Fields of Learning, **AP:** 1342;
    Kinds of Affection, **AP:** 1342;
    Lines at Intersection, **AP:** 1341;
    Local Measures, **AP:** 1341;
    Poems, 1930-1960, **AP:** 1342;
    Poems on Several Occasions,
    AP: 1341; *Prefabrications*,
    AP: 1341; *To All Appearances*,
    AP: 1342

Miljković, Branko, **TE:** 571

"Mill, The" (Verhaeren), **EP:** 1091

Millay, Edna St. Vincent, **AP:** 1344-
    1349; "The Ballad of the Harp-
    Weaver," **AP:** 1347; "Euclid
    Alone Has Looked on Beauty
    Bare," **AP:** 1346; *Fatal Interview*,
    AP: 1347; "In the Grave No
    Flower," **AP:** 1348; "Menses,"
    AP: 1348

Miller, J. Hillis, **AP:** 2302, **BP:** 1386,
    EP: 1180, **TE:** 818, **WP:** 388

Miller, Vassar, **AP:** 1349-1354;
    Adam's Footprint, **AP:** 1350;
    Approaching Nada, **AP:** 1353; *If I
    Could Sleep Deeply Enough*,
    AP: 1352; *If I Had Wheels or
    Love*, **AP:** 1353; *My Bones Being
    Wiser*, **AP:** 1352; *Onions and
    Roses*, **AP:** 1352; *Struggling to
    Swim on Concrete*, **AP:** 1353;
    Wage War on Silence, **AP:** 1351

Millevoye, Charles-Hubert, **TE:** 258

Millions of Strange Shadows (Hecht),
    AP: 832

Mills of the Kavanaughs, The
    (Lowell), **AP:** 1191

Miłosz, Czesław, **EP:** 709-721; *The
    Collected Poems, 1931-1987*,
    EP: 717; *Facing the River*,
    EP: 718; *Gdzie wschodzi słońce i*

kędy zapada, **EP:** 717; *Gucio
    zaczarowany*, **EP:** 716; *Król
    Popiel i inne wiersze*, **EP:** 716;
    Miasto bez imienia, **EP:** 716;
    Ocalenie, **EP:** 715; *Poemat o
    czasie zastygłym*, **EP:** 714;
    Second Space, **EP:** 718; *Selected
    Poems, 1931-2004*, **EP:** 719;
    Światło dzienne, **EP:** 715; *A
    Treatise on Poetry*, **EP:** 715; *Trzy
    zimy*, **EP:** 715; "You Who Have
    Wronged," **EP:** 717

Milton (Blake), **BP:** 102

Milton, John, **BP:** 905-914,
    TE: 623; "L'Allegro," **BP:** 908;
    Comus, **BP:** 908; "Lycidas,"
    BP: 908; "On the Morning of
    Christ's Nativity," **BP:** 907;
    Paradise Lost, **BP:** 909, **TE:** 623;
    Paradise Regained, **BP:** 911; "Il
    Penseroso," **BP:** 908; *Samson
    Agonistes*, **BP:** 912

Milton's Prosody (Bridges), **BP:** 135

Mimesis, **TE:** 699, **TE:** 701

"Mimosa, Le" (Ponge), **EP:** 853

Mind Breaths (Ginsberg), **AP:** 684

"Mind-Reader, The" (Wilbur),
    AP: 2158

Mindfield (Corso), **AP:** 360

Miniatures, and Other Poems (Guest),
    AP: 746

Minimalist poetry. *See* Categorized
    Index

Minjian poets, **TE:** 68

Minne (poetic form), **TE:** 287

"Minneapolis Poem, The" (Wright),
    AP: 2229

Minstrelsy of the Scottish Border, The
    (Scott), **BP:** 1090

Mint Snowball (Nye), **AP:** 1440

Minute Hand, The (Shore), **AP:** 1775

Minutes No One Owns, The (Galvin),
    AP: 649

Mir zur Feier (Rilke), **EP:** 892

Mirabell (Merrill), **AP:** 1320

Miracle Fair (Szymborska), **EP:** 1012

Mirikitani, Janice, **TE:** 23

Mirour de l'Omme (Gower), **BP:** 528

Mirror (Roig), **TE:** 50

Mirror for Magistrates, A (Sackville), **BP:** 1076

Mirrors and Windows (Nemerov), **AP:** 1412

Mirrors of Venus (Wheelwright), **AP:** 2128

Misgivings (Howard), **AP:** 911

"Misgivings" (Melville), **AP:** 1297

Miss Kilmansegg and Her Precious Leg (Hood), **BP:** 657

Mistral, Gabriela, WP: 185-190; *Desolación,* **WP:** 187; *Lagar,* **WP:** 189; *Poema de Chile,* **WP:** 190; *Tala,* **WP:** 188; *Ternura,* **WP:** 189

Mistress, The (Cowley), **BP:** 316

Misty poetry, **TE:** 67

Mit Marx-und Engelszungen (Biermann), **EP:** 123

Mitsui, James Masao, AP: 1354-1357; *After the Long Train,* **AP:** 1356; *From a Three-Cornered World,* **AP:** 1357; *Journal of the Sun,* **AP:** 1355

Mixed Company (Shapiro), **AP:** 1761

Miyazawa Kenji, TE: 430, **WP:** 191-195; "Drought and Zazen," **WP:** 193; *Elegies for Toshiko,* **WP:** 193; "Shigoto," **WP:** 194; *Spring and Asura,* **WP:** 192

Mleko iskoni (Pavlović), **EP:** 788

Mnemonic verse, defined, **AP:** 2301, **BP:** 1385, **EP:** 1179, **TE:** 817, **WP:** 387

Mnemosyne Lay in Dust (Clarke), **BP:** 265

Mockingbird Wish Me Luck (Bukowski), **AP:** 270

"Modern Love" (Meredith), **BP:** 893

Modern Poetry and the Tradition (Brooks), **TE:** 744

Moderna, **TE:** 74, **TE:** 575

Modernism, **TE:** 12, **TE:** 185, **TE:** 650-654; Canadian, **TE:** 39; Catalan, **TE:** 51; Croatian, **TE:** 74; Czech, **TE:** 83; Finno-Swedish, **TE:** 545; German, **TE:** 310; Indian English, **TE:** 372; Russian, **TE:** 516; Slovenian, **TE:** 580. *See also* Categorized Index

Modernism, defined, **AP:** 2301, **BP:** 1385, **EP:** 1179, **TE:** 817, **WP:** 387

Modernismo, **TE:** 435, **TE:** 598, **WP:** 73, **WP:** 80, **WP:** 103. *See also* Categorized Index

Mohn und Gedächtnis (Celan), **EP:** 217

"Moïse" (Vigny), **EP:** 1103, **TE:** 261

Mokichi. *See* Saitō Mokichi

Mölna Elegy, A (Ekelöf), **EP:** 311

Molodost' (Khodasevich), **WP:** 134

Moly (Gunn), **BP:** 565

Momaday, N. Scott, AP: 1358-1364, **TE:** 482; "Before an Old Painting of the Crucifixion," **AP:** 1360; "The Delight Song of Tsoai-talee," **AP:** 1360; *In the Bear's House,* **AP:** 1362; *The Way to Rainy Mountain,* **AP:** 1361

Moment in Eternity, A (MacDiarmid), **BP:** 848

Moments of Vision and Miscellaneous Verses (Hardy), **BP:** 586

"Mon Roi." *See* "My King"

"Mondnacht." *See* "Moonlit Night"

"Monet's 'Waterlilies'" (Hayden), **AP:** 823

"Monkey" (Ruan Ji), **WP:** 253

Monody, Written at Matlock (Bowles), **BP:** 123

Monolithos (Gilbert), **AP:** 675

"Monosyllable, The" (Jacobsen), **AP:** 952

Monroe, Harriet, **BP:** 18

Mont Blanc (Shelley), **BP:** 1119

"Mont des Oliviers, Le" (Vigny), **EP:** 1103

Montague, John, BP: 914-923; *About Love,* **BP:** 921; *A Chosen Light,* **BP:** 917; *Collected Poems,* **BP:** 922; *The Dead Kingdom,* **BP:** 920; *Forms of Exile,* **BP:** 916; *The Great Cloak,* **BP:** 919; *Mount Eagle,* **BP:** 921; *Poisoned Lands, and Other Poems,* **BP:** 916; *The Rough Field,* **BP:** 918; *Selected Poems,* **BP:** 920; *A Slow Dance,* **BP:** 919; *Smashing the Piano,* **BP:** 922; *Tides,* **BP:** 917; *Time in Armagh,* **BP:** 922

Montale, Eugenio, EP: 721-727, **TE:** 403; *Cuttlefish Bones,* **EP:** 723; *The Occasions,* **EP:** 724; *Satura,* **EP:** 726; *The Storm, and Other Poems,* **EP:** 725

Montcorbier, François de. *See* Villon, François

Montenegro. *See* Geographical Index

Monti, Vincenzo, **TE:** 390

"Monument, The" (Bishop), **AP:** 173

Moon Crossing Bridge (Gallagher), **AP:** 642

"Moongate" (Everson), **AP:** 576

Moonlight Sonata, The (Ritsos), **EP:** 910, **TE:** 346

"Moonlit Night" (Eichendorff), **EP:** 303, **WP:** 87

Moore, Marianne, AP: 1364-1371, **TE:** 653; "In Distrust of Merits," **AP:** 1368; *Like a Bulwark,* **AP:** 1369; "Nevertheless," **AP:** 1368; *The Pangolin, and Other Verse,* **AP:** 1368; *Selected Fables of La Fontaine,* **AP:** 1369; *Tell Me, Tell Me,* **AP:** 1369; "What Are Years?," **AP:** 1368

Moortown (Hughes), **BP:** 692

Mora, Pat, AP: 1371-1375, **TE:** 471; *Agua Santa/Holy Water,*

AP: 1373; *Aunt Carmen's Book of Practical Saints*, **AP:** 1374

"Morada del cielo." *See* "Dwelling Place in Heaven"

Moraes, Dom, **TE:** 374

Morall Fabillis of Esope, the Phrygian, The. See Fables (Henryson)

Moratín, Nicolás Fernández de, **TE:** 595

More, Henry, **TE:** 149

"More a Man Has the More a Man Wants, The" (Muldoon), **BP:** 941

"More About People" (Nash), **AP:** 1403

More Poems (Housman), **BP:** 682

Moréas, Jean, **TE:** 639

"Mores, The" (Clare), **BP:** 257

Morgan, Emanuel. *See* Bynner, Witter

Morgenstern, Christian, EP: 727-732; "Among Tenses," **EP:** 730; "The Banshee," **EP:** 730; "The Eighteen-Year-Old," **EP:** 731; "Evolution," **EP:** 731; "Fish's Lullaby," **EP:** 730; "The Funnels," **EP:** 730; *The Gallows Songs*, **EP:** 729; "Korf's Clock," **EP:** 730

Mori Ōgai, **TE:** 428

Mörike, Eduard, EP: 732-735, **TE:** 300; "On a Christmas Rose," **EP:** 734; "A Visit to the Charterhouse," **EP:** 734

Morley, Hilda, **TE:** 689

"Morning" (Rimbaud), **EP:** 902

Morning Glory, The (Bly), **AP:** 192

Morning in the Burned House (Atwood), **BP:** 45

"Morning of the Poem, The" (Schuyler), **AP:** 1735

Morning of the Red Admirals, The (Dana), **AP:** 436

Morning Poems (Bly), **AP:** 194

Morning Song of Lord Zero, The (Aiken), **AP:** 16

Morový sloup. See Plague Column, The

Morris, William, BP: 924-933; *The Defence of Guenevere, and Other Poems*, **BP:** 926; *The Earthly Paradise*, **BP:** 927; *The Life and Death of Jason*, **BP:** 927; *Love Is Enough*, **BP:** 929; *The Story of Sigurd the Volsung and the Fall of the Niblungs*, **BP:** 930

"Mort du loup, La" (Vigny), **EP:** 1104

Mortimeriados (Drayton), **BP:** 419

Moses (Rosenberg), **BP:** 1057

Moskva kabatskaia (Esenin), **WP:** 94

Mosquito and Ant (Hahn), **AP:** 770

Moss, Howard, AP: 1375-1379; *Buried City*, **AP:** 1378; *Notes from the Castle*, **AP:** 1378; *Rules of Sleep*, **AP:** 1378; *A Winter Come, A, Summer Gone*, **AP:** 1377

Moss, Thylias, AP: 1380-1382; *At Redbones*, **AP:** 1380; *Slave Moth*, **AP:** 1381; *Small Congregations*, **AP:** 1381; *Tokyo Butter*, **AP:** 1382

Mossén Cinto. *See* Verdaguer, Jacint

Most Delightful History of Reynard the Fox. See Roman de Renart

Mostly Nothing Happens (Ehrhart), **AP:** 535

"Mother, The" (Brooks), **AP:** 250

Mother, and Other Poems, The (Sitwell), **BP:** 1148

Mother/Child Papers, The (Ostriker), **AP:** 1503

Mother Love (Dove), **AP:** 491

Mother Poem (Brathwaite), **AP:** 234

"Mother's Hearse, A" (Smith), **BP:** 1166

Motorcycle Betrayal Poems, The (Wakoski), **AP:** 2072

"Moulin, Le." *See* "Mill, The"

Moulton, Elizabeth Barrett. *See* Browning, Elizabeth Barrett

Mount Clutter (Lindsay), **AP:** 1145

Mount Eagle (Montague), **BP:** 921

Mountain Poems of Meng Hao-jan, The (Meng Haoran), **WP:** 184

"Mountain Whippoorwill, The" (Benét), **AP:** 126

Mountains and Rivers Without End (Snyder), **AP:** 1849

Movement poets, **TE:** 203, **TE:** 679-683; William Empson, **BP:** 470. *See also* Categorized Index

Movie-going, and Other Poems (Hollander), **AP:** 879

"Moving Through the Silent Crowd" (Spender), **BP:** 1186

"Mower, The" (Larkin), **BP:** 793

Mówię do swego ciała. See Talking to My Body

Moy Sand and Gravel (Muldoon), **BP:** 943

"Mr. and Mrs. Discobbolos" (Lear), **BP:** 816

Mr. Cogito (Herbert), **EP:** 463

Mueller, Lisel, AP: 1383-1387; *Alive Together*, **AP:** 1386; *Dependencies*, **AP:** 1384; *The Need to Hold Still*, **AP:** 1385; *The Private Life*, **AP:** 1384; *Second Language*, **AP:** 1386; *Waving from Shore*, **AP:** 1386

Muerte del cisne, La (González Martínez), **WP:** 106

Muir, Edwin, BP: 933-937; *Journeys and Places*, **BP:** 935; *The Labyrinth*, **BP:** 935; *One Foot in Eden*, **BP:** 936

Mujer del rio Sumpul, La. See Woman of the River

Muldoon, Paul, BP: 937-946, **TE:** 209; "Anonymous: Myself and Panguar," **BP:** 942; "Cuba," **BP:** 940; *Horse Latitudes*, **BP:** 944; "Immrama," **BP:** 940; "Incantata," **BP:** 942; *Madoc*, **BP:** 941, **TE:** 210; "The More a Man Has the More a Man Wants," **BP:** 941; *Moy Sand and Gravel*,

BP: 943; *Mules,* **BP:** 940; *New Weather,* **BP:** 939; *Poems, 1968-1998,* **BP:** 942; "Why Brownlee Left," **BP:** 940
Mules (Muldoon), **BP:** 940
Mullen, Harryette, **AP:** 1387-1390; *Muse and Drudge,* **AP:** 1389; *Sleeping with the Dictionary,* **AP:** 1389; *S*PeRM**K*T,* **AP:** 1388; *Trimmings,* **AP:** 1388
Mulroney and Others (Wormser), **AP:** 2201
Multiculturalism, defined, **AP:** 2301, **BP:** 1385, **EP:** 1179, **TE:** 817, **WP:** 387
Multitudes (Clampitt), **AP:** 323
Muñoz, Blas de Otero. *See* Otero, Blas de
Mura, David, **AP:** 1390-1395; *After We Lost Our Way,* **AP:** 1392; *Angels for the Burning,* **AP:** 1394; *The Colors of Desire,* **AP:** 1393
Murray, Les A., **BP:** 946-952, **TE:** 33, **TE:** 502; *Blocks and Tackles,* **BP:** 950; *The Boys Who Stole the Funeral,* **BP:** 948; "The Buladelah-Taree Holiday Song Cycle," **BP:** 948; *Conscious and Verbal,* **BP:** 951; *Dog Fox Field,* **BP:** 950; "Driving Through Sawmill Towns," **BP:** 948; "Equanimity," **BP:** 949; *Fredy Neptune,* **BP:** 951; "The Quality of Sprawl," **BP:** 949; *Subhuman Redneck Poems,* **BP:** 950; *The Vernacular Republic,* **BP:** 949
Muse and Drudge (Mullen), **AP:** 1389
"Muse as Medusa, The" (Sarton), **AP:** 1721
"Muse Who Is Grace, The" (Claudel), **EP:** 249
Muses Elizium, The (Drayton), **BP:** 423
Museum (Dove), **AP:** 489

Museum of Clear Ideas, The (Hall), **AP:** 782
Music Like Dirt (Bidart), **AP:** 167
Music Minus One (Shore), **AP:** 1775
Music of the Spheres, The (Cardenal), **WP:** 55
Muske, Carol, **AP:** 1396-1400; *Applause,* **AP:** 1398; *Camouflage,* **AP:** 1396; *An Octave Above Thunder,* **AP:** 1399; *Red Trousseau,* **AP:** 1398; *Skylight,* **AP:** 1397; *Sparrow,* **AP:** 1399; *Wyndmere,* **AP:** 1397
Musophilus (Daniel), **BP:** 357
Musset, Alfred de, **EP:** 736-740, **TE:** 262; "May Night," **EP:** 737; "On a Dead Woman," **EP:** 739; "A Wasted Evening," **EP:** 738
Mustapää, P., **TE:** 546
Mustapha (Greville), **BP:** 558
My Alexandria (Doty), **AP:** 483
My Black Horse (Gallagher), **AP:** 642
My Bones Being Wiser (Miller), **AP:** 1352
"My Brunette" (Poliziano), **EP:** 846
"My Familiar Dream" (Verlaine), **EP:** 1095
"My Heat" (O'Hara), **AP:** 1453
My House (Giovanni), **AP:** 696
"My King" (Michaux), **EP:** 692
"My Lady Asks Me" (Cavalcanti), **EP:** 213
"My Last Duchess" (Browning), **BP:** 162
My Life (Hejinian), **AP:** 839
"My mother's maids, when they did sew and spin" (Wyatt), **BP:** 1328
My Noiseless Entourage (Simic), **AP:** 1790
"My Old Books Closed at the Name of Paphos" (Mallarmé), **EP:** 647
"My Religion" (Unamuno y Jugo), **EP:** 1053
My Sad Captains, and Other Poems (Gunn), **BP:** 563

My Sentence Was a Thousand Years of Joy (Bly), **AP:** 195
My Sister, Life (Pasternak), **WP:** 226
"My Sisters, O My Sisters" (Sarton), **AP:** 1718
My Twentieth Century (Kirby), **AP:** 1041
My Voice Because of You (Salinas), **EP:** 939
My Wicked, Wicked Ways (Cisneros), **AP:** 320
Myricae (Pascoli), **EP:** 774
"Myrtho" (Nerval), **EP:** 746
Myrtle, Marmaduke. *See* Addison, Joseph
Mystère de la charité de Jeanne d'Arc, Le. See Mystery of the Charity of Joan of Arc, The
Mystère des saints innocents, Le. See Mystery of the Holy Innocents, and Other Poems, The
Mystery of Max Schmitt, The (Dacey), **AP:** 429
Mystery of Small Houses (Notley), **AP:** 1434
Mystery of the Charity of Charles Péguy, The (Hill), **BP:** 647
Mystery of the Charity of Joan of Arc, The (Péguy), **EP:** 794
Mystery of the Holy Innocents, and Other Poems, The (Péguy), **EP:** 795
Mystery of the Verb (Hébert), **BP:** 607
Mystery Train (Wojahn), **AP:** 2192
Mysticism, Germany, **TE:** 289
Myth, **TE:** 192
Myth, defined, **AP:** 2301, **BP:** 1385, **EP:** 1179, **TE:** 817, **WP:** 387
Myth criticism, defined, **AP:** 2301, **BP:** 1385, **EP:** 1179, **TE:** 817, **WP:** 387
Mythistorema (Seferis), **EP:** 960, **TE:** 340
Myths and Texts (Snyder), **AP:** 1845

Nachtgesänge (Hölderlin), **EP:** 489

"Nächtliche Stunde." *See* "Nocturnal Hour"

Naevius, Gnaeus, **TE:** 446

Naidu, Sarojini, **TE:** 369, **TE:** 505

Naipaul, V. S., **TE:** 772

"Naked and the Nude, The" (Graves), **BP:** 537

Naked Genius (Horton), **AP:** 908

"Nameless One, The" (Mangan), **BP:** 870

Naming Our Destiny (Jordan), **AP:** 984

Napis (Herbert), **EP:** 463

"Napoleonic Ode, The" (Manzoni), **EP:** 665

Narihira. *See* Ariwara no Narihira

Narogin, Mudrooroo, **TE:** 504

Narrative poetry. *See* Categorized Index

Narrator, defined, **AP:** 2301, **BP:** 1385, **EP:** 1179, **TE:** 817, **WP:** 387

"Narrow Fellow in the Grass, A" (Dickinson), **AP:** 461

Narrow Road to the Deep North, The (Matsuo Bashō), **WP:** 175

Narrow Road to the Interior, The (Hahn), **AP:** 771

Nash, Ogden, **AP:** 1401-1405; "Ask Daddy, He Won't Know," **AP:** 1403; "More About People," **AP:** 1403; "A Necessary Dirge," **AP:** 1403; "Spring Comes to Murray Hill," **AP:** 1403; *There's Always Another Windmill*, **AP:** 1404; *Versus*, **AP:** 1403

Nashe, Thomas, **BP:** 953-958; *The Choise of Valentines*, **BP:** 957

"Nashedshii podkovu." *See* "Horseshoe Finder, The"

Naso, Publius Ovidius. *See* Ovid

National Book Award in Poetry, **AP:** 2326, **CM:** 58, **TE:** 878

National Socialism, **TE:** 310

Native American culture. *See* Categorized Index

Native American poetry, **TE:** 209, **TE:** 478-488

Native American Renaissance. *See* Categorized Index

Native Guard (Trethewey), **AP:** 1997

Natsume Sōseki, **TE:** 429

Natural Birth (Derricotte), **AP:** 446

Natural Man, A (Soto), **AP:** 1866

Natural World (Harrison), **AP:** 810

Naturalism, **TE:** 182; Germany, **TE:** 303; Russia, **TE:** 515; Scandinavia, **TE:** 537. *See also* Categorized Index

Naturalism, American. *See* Categorized Index

"Nature and Free Animals" (Smith), **BP:** 1166

Nature of Things, The. See Taking the Side of Things

Nature poetry; Denmark, **TE:** 531; East Germany, **TE:** 93; England, **TE:** 165, **TE:** 628; France, **TE:** 260; Germany, **TE:** 308; United States, **TE:** 180. *See also* Categorized Index

Nature with Man (Silkin), **BP:** 1142

Naugerius sive de poetica dialogus (Fracastoro), **EP:** 352

Nazor, Vladimir, **TE:** 74

Neal, Larry, **TE:** 7

Near Changes (Van Duyn), **AP:** 2036

"Near Klamath" (Carver), **AP:** 287

Near the Ocean (Lowell), **AP:** 1194

"Necessary Dirge, A" (Nash), **AP:** 1403

Necessities of Life (Rich), **AP:** 1636

Necessity of Art, The (Fischer), **TE:** 761

Nechayannaya radost (Blok), **WP:** 37

Need to Hold Still, The (Mueller), **AP:** 1385

Negative Blue (Wright), **AP:** 2214

Negri, Ada, **TE:** 407

Negritude, **TE:** 16, **WP:** 59. *See also* Categorized Index

"Negro Characters as Seen by White Authors" (Brown), **AP:** 256

"Négy-ökrös szekér, A" (Petőfi), **EP:** 823

Nehéz föld (Illyés), **EP:** 530

"Neige, La." *See* "Snow, The"

Neighbor, The (Collier), **AP:** 339

Neihardt, John G., **AP:** 1405-1409; *A Bundle of Myrrh*, **AP:** 1406; *A Cycle of the West*, **AP:** 1407; *Man Song*, **AP:** 1407; *The Stranger at the Gate*, **AP:** 1407

Nekrasov, Nikolai, **TE:** 515

Neljätoista hallitsijaa (Haavikko), **EP:** 440

Nemerov, Howard, **AP:** 1409-1415; *The Blue Swallows*, **AP:** 1413; *The Collected Poems of Howard Nemerov*, **AP:** 1413; *Gnomes and Occasions*, **AP:** 1413; *Guide to the Ruins*, **AP:** 1411; *The Image and the Law*, **AP:** 1411; *Inside the Onion*, **AP:** 1414; *Mirrors and Windows*, **AP:** 1412; *The Next Room of the Dream*, **AP:** 1412; "Runes," **AP:** 1413; *The Salt Garden*, **AP:** 1412; *Sentences*, **AP:** 1414; *War Stories*, **AP:** 1414

Nemesianus, **TE:** 457

"Nemzeti dal" (Petőfi), **EP:** 826

Neoclassical poets. *See* Categorized Index

Neoclassicism, **TE:** 156; criticism, **TE:** 705; Italy, **TE:** 391; Latin America, **TE:** 435

Neo-Hermeticism, **TE:** 409

Neon Vernacular (Komunyakaa), **AP:** 1068

Neoplatonism. *See* Categorized Index

Neorealism. *See* Categorized Index

Neorealism, Italy, **TE:** 409

Neo-Romanticism. *See* Categorized Index

Neoterics, **TE:** 450

Nepočin-polje. See *Unrest-Field*

Nepos, Cornelius, **TE:** 449

Neruda, Jan, **TE:** 82

Neruda, Pablo, **WP:** 196-204; *Canto General*, **WP:** 202; *The Captain's Verses*, **WP:** 202; *Crepuscularino*, **WP:** 199; *The Elemental Odes*, **WP:** 202; *Residence on Earth, and Other Poems*, **WP:** 200; *Tentativa del hombre infinito*, **WP:** 200; *Twenty Love Poems and a Song of Despair*, **WP:** 199; *Las Uvas y el viento*, **WP:** 202

Nerval, Gérard de, **EP:** 741-748, **TE:** 265; "Antéros," **EP:** 746; "Artémis," **EP:** 746; *The Chimeras*, **EP:** 745; "Delfica," **EP:** 746; "El Desdichado," **EP:** 745; "Horus," **EP:** 746; "Myrtho," **EP:** 746; "Vers dorés," **EP:** 747

"Net of Moon, The" (Blackburn), **AP:** 185

Nets to Catch the Wind (Wylie), **AP:** 2242

Nettles (Lawrence), **BP:** 800

Neumann, Lisel. See Mueller, Lisel

Neustadt International Prize, **BP:** 1411, **CM:** 59, **EP:** 1208, **TE:** 879, **WP:** 411

"Nevertheless" (Moore), **AP:** 1368

New Addresses (Koch), **AP:** 1063

New and Collected Poems, 1917-1976 (MacLeish), **AP:** 1248

New and Selected Poems (Justice), **AP:** 990

New and Selected Poems (Menashe), **AP:** 1307

New and Selected Poems (Oliver), **AP:** 1466

New and Selected Poems (Scott), **AP:** 1748

New and Selected Poems (Smith), **AP:** 1828

New and Selected Things Taking Place (Swenson), **AP:** 1938

New Art of Writing Plays, The (Vega Carpio), **EP:** 1077

"New Birth, The" (Very), **AP:** 2041

New Black Renaissance. *See* Black Arts movement

New Criticism, **TE:** 193, **TE:** 715, **TE:** 733

New Criticism, defined, **AP:** 2301, **BP:** 1385, **EP:** 1179, **TE:** 817, **WP:** 387

New England Tragedies, The (Longfellow), **AP:** 1164

New Formalism. *See* Categorized Index

New Found Land (MacLeish), **AP:** 1250

"New Hampshire, February" (Eberhart), **AP:** 529

New Historicism, **TE:** 764-768

New Humanism, **TE:** 732

New Lines (anthology), **TE:** 681

New Narrative poetry. *See* Categorized Index

New Negro movement. *See* Harlem Renaissance

New Numbers (Logue), **BP:** 825

New Path to the Waterfall, A (Carver), **AP:** 289

New Poems (Heine), **EP:** 456

New Poems (Rilke), **EP:** 894

New Poetry, The (anthology), **TE:** 682

New populists, Hungary, **TE:** 361

New School of Athens, **TE:** 334

New Science, **TE:** 154

New Selected Poems (Abse), **BP:** 5

New Selected Poems (Strand), **AP:** 1925

New Simplicity, **TE:** 553

"New Spirit and the Poets, The" (Apollinaire), **EP:** 23

New Spoon River, The (Masters), **AP:** 1280

New Subjectivity, **TE:** 312

New Verses (Ady), **EP:** 3

New Weather (Muldoon), **BP:** 939

New York Intellectuals, **TE:** 732

New York Postcard Sonnets, The (Dacey), **AP:** 429

New York School, **TE:** 191, **TE:** 674-678. *See also* Categorized Index

New Zealand. *See* Geographical Index

New Zealand poetry, **TE:** 30-36, **TE:** 502

Newcastle, Margaret Cavendish, duchess of, **BP:** 958-964; "A Dialogue Between Mirth and Melancholy," **BP:** 962; "A Dialogue of Birds," **BP:** 962; "Fancies," **BP:** 960; "The Hunting of the Hare," **BP:** 962; *Philosophicall Fancies*, **BP:** 961; "A World in an Eare-Ring," **BP:** 961

Next Room of the Dream, The (Nemerov), **AP:** 1412

Next-to-Last Things (Kunitz), **AP:** 1090

Nezval, Vítězslav, **TE:** 85

Ngugi Wa Thiong'o, **TE:** 771

Ní Dhomhnaill, Nuala, **BP:** 964-968; *The Fifty Minute Mermaid*, **BP:** 966; *Pharaoh's Daughter*, **BP:** 966; *Selected Poems*, **BP:** 966

Niatum, Duane, **TE:** 482

Nibelungenlied, **TE:** 228, **TE:** 286

Nicaragua. *See* Geographical Index

Niche Narrows, The (Menashe), **AP:** 1306

Nichols, Grace, **TE:** 46

"Nick and the Candlestick" (Plath), **AP:** 1553

Niedecker, Lorine, **AP:** 1415-1421; "Paean to Place," **AP:** 1419

Niemandsrose, Die (Celan), **EP:** 218

Nigeria. *See* Geographical Index

Night Abraham Called to the Stars,
    The (Bly), **AP:** 195
"Night and Day" (Rosenberg),
    BP: 1057
Night and Morning (Clarke), **BP:** 263
Night Feed (Boland), **BP:** 110
"Night Fishing for Blues" (Smith),
    AP: 1821
"Night in Hell" (Rimbaud), **EP:** 901
Night Light (Justice), **AP:** 988
Night Mirror, The (Hollander),
    AP: 880
Night Parade, The (Hirsch), **AP:** 856
Night Picnic (Simic), **AP:** 1790
"Night Scene Before Combat"
    (Dugan), **AP:** 501
"Night Song of a Nomadic Shepherd
    in Asia" (Leopardi), **EP:** 614
Night-Thoughts (Young), **BP:** 1352
Night Train and the Golden Bird, The
    (Meinke), **AP:** 1291
Night Watch on the Chesapeake
    (Meinke), **AP:** 1292
Nightmare Begins Responsibility
    (Harper), **AP:** 798
"Nightmare by Day" (Frost),
    AP: 2012
"Nightpiece" (Sorrentino), **AP:** 1859
Nights and Days (Merrill), **AP:** 1319
Nightstar, 1973-1978 (Evans),
    AP: 565
Nightwalker, and Other Poems
    (Kinsella), **BP:** 755
Nike Award, **EP:** 1209, **CM:** 60,
    TE: 880
"Nikki-Rosa" (Giovanni), **TE:** 11
Nimphidia (Drayton), **BP:** 423
Nims, John Frederick, AP: 1421-
    1428; *A Fountain in Kentucky,*
    AP: 1424; *The Iron Pastoral,*
    AP: 1423; *The Kiss,* **AP:** 1425;
    Knowledge of the Evening,
    AP: 1425; *Of Flesh and Bone,*
    AP: 1425; *The Powers of Heaven*
    and Earth, **AP:** 1427

1914, and Other Poems (Brooke),
    BP: 147
"1992" (Corn), **AP:** 355
"1934" (Eberhart), **AP:** 529
92 Rapple Drive (Lifshin), **AP:** 1142
Nishiwaki Junsaburō, **TE:** 429
Nishiyama Sōin, **TE:** 423
Njegoš, Petar Petrović, **TE:** 567
"No Coward Soul Is Mine" (Brontë),
    BP: 142
No Heaven (Ostriker), **AP:** 1505
No Heaven (St. John), **AP:** 1695
No Jerusalem but This (Menashe),
    AP: 1303
"No meio do caminho." *See* "In the
    Middle of the Road"
"No One So Much as You" (Thomas),
    BP: 1255
No Second Eden (Cassity), **AP:** 296
No Time for Good Reasons (Galvin),
    AP: 648
No Traveller (Howard), **AP:** 911
No Voyage, and Other Poems
    (Oliver), **AP:** 1465
Nobel Prize in Literature, **AP:** 2327,
    BP: 1412, **CM:** 60, **EP:** 1209,
    TE: 880, **WP:** 412
Noble Numbers (Herrick), **BP:** 633
"Nocturnal Hour" (Kraus), **EP:** 567
"Nocturnal Reverie, A" (Finch),
    BP: 493
"Nocturnal upon St. Lucy's Day,
    Being the Shortest Day, A"
    (Donne), **BP:** 413
"Nocturne at Bethesda" (Bontemps),
    AP: 207
Nocturnes (Senghor), **WP:** 270
Noël, Bernard, **TE:** 280
Noise in the Trees (Heyen), **AP:** 844
Non serviam (Ekelöf), **EP:** 309
Nonconformist's Memorial, The
    (Howe), **AP:** 918
Nonsense verse, **BP:** 215
Nonsequences/Selfpoems
    (Middleton), **BP:** 900

Noonuccal, Oodgeroo. *See* Walker,
    Kath
Nordbrandt, Henrik, **TE:** 564
Norden, Charles. *See* Durrell,
    Lawrence
Nordenflycht, Hedvig Charlotta,
    TE: 531
Nordic poetry. *See* Scandinavian
    poetry
Norén, Lars, **TE:** 555
Norris, Kathleen, AP: 1428-1431;
    The Astronomy of Love,
    AP: 1430; *How I Came to Drink*
    My Grandmother's Piano,
    AP: 1429
North (Heaney), **BP:** 599, **TE:** 199
North Sea (Jarman), **AP:** 954
North Ship, The (Larkin), **BP:** 789
Northern Ireland. *See* Geographical
    Index
Norwid, Kamil, **TE:** 494
Nosce Teipsum (Davies), **BP:** 380
"Nostalgia" (Viereck), **AP:** 2045
Nostalgist's Map of America, A (Ali),
    AP: 26
Not Dancing (Dunn), **AP:** 518
"Not Forgotten" (Davison), **AP:** 439
Not So Deep as a Well (Parker),
    AP: 1511
Not This Pig (Levine), **AP:** 1122
"Not to Tell Lies" (Booth), **AP:** 212
"Not Waving but Drowning" (Smith),
    BP: 1170
Notable scherzi (Giusti), **EP:** 394
Notebook, 1967-1968 (Lowell),
    AP: 1195
Notes from a Child of Paradise
    (Corn), **AP:** 354
Notes from the Castle (Moss),
    AP: 1378
Notes from the Land of the Dead, and
    Other Poems (Kinsella), **BP:** 755
Notes on the Possibilities and
    Attractions of Existence (Hollo),
    AP: 891

"Notes Toward a Poem of
Revolution" (Di Prima), **AP:** 469
"Nothin' to Say" (Riley), **AP:** 1650
"Nothing" (Fenton), **BP:** 490,
EP: 986
Nothing in Nature Is Private
(Rankine), **AP:** 1603
Notley, Alice, AP: 1431-1435; *The
Descent of Alette*, **AP:** 1433;
Disobedience, **AP:** 1434; *Mystery
of Small Houses*, **AP:** 1434
Nouvelles méditations poétiques
(Lamartine), **EP:** 594
Nova Skitija (Pavlović), **EP:** 789
Novak, Helga M., **TE:** 317
Novalis, EP: 748-756, **TE:** 298;
"Beginning," **EP:** 752; *Devotional
Songs*, **EP:** 754; "Evening,"
EP: 751; *Hymns to the Night*,
EP: 753, **TE:** 298; "On a
Saturday Evening," **EP:** 752;
"The Poem," **EP:** 754; *The
Stranger*, **EP:** 752; "To a Falling
Leaf," **EP:** 751; "To Tieck,"
EP: 754
Novemberland (Grass), **EP:** 421
Novísimos, **TE:** 601
*Now That My Father Lies Down
Beside Me* (Plumly), **AP:** 1560
"Now the Sky" (Van Doren),
AP: 2030
Now with His Love (Bishop), **AP:** 178
Nowhere but Light (Belitt), **AP:** 117
Nubes, Las (Cernuda), **EP:** 224
Nude Descending a Staircase
(Kennedy), **AP:** 1022
Nuevas canciones; (Machado),
EP: 637
"Nuit de l'enfer." *See* "Night in Hell"
"Nuit de mai, La." *See* "May Night"
"Numbers" (Smith), **BP:** 1169
Nuove poesie (Carducci), **EP:** 189
Nurture (Kumin), **AP:** 1078
Nuyorican poetry, **TE:** 466-474
Nye, Naomi Shihab, AP: 1435-1442;

Different Ways to Pray, **AP:** 1438;
Fuel, **AP:** 1439; *Honeybee*,
AP: 1440; *Hugging the Jukebox*,
AP: 1439; *Mint Snowball*,
AP: 1440; *Red Suitcase*,
AP: 1439; *Words Under the
Words*, **AP:** 1440; *Yellow Glove*,
AP: 1439
"NyQuil" (Carver), **AP:** 288

Oaten, Edward Farley, **TE:** 366
Oates, Joyce Carol, AP: 1443-1450;
"Lies Lovingly Told," **AP:** 1447;
"Making an End," **AP:** 1447;
*Women Whose Lives Are Food,
Men Whose Lives Are Money*,
AP: 1446
"Oaxaca, 1974" (Cervantes), **AP:** 300
Object poem, **TE:** 305
Object-relations theory, **TE:** 725
Objectivism. *See* Categorized Index
"Objects and Apparitions" (Bishop),
AP: 172
Oblako v shtanakh. See *Cloud in
Pants, A*
Oblivion Ha-Ha, The (Tate),
AP: 1951
Obrestad, Tor, **TE:** 557
Ocalenie (Miłosz), **EP:** 715
Occasional verse, **AP:** 2301,
BP: 1385, **EP:** 1179, **TE:** 817,
WP: 387. *See also* Categorized
Index
Occasions, The (Montale), **EP:** 724
"Occident, The" (Trakl), **EP:** 1035
Octave Above Thunder, An (Muske),
AP: 1399
Octave, defined, **AP:** 2302, **BP:** 1386,
EP: 1180, **TE:** 818, **WP:** 388
"October" (Glück), **AP:** 717,
AP: 1170, **AP:** 1938
October Palace, The (Hirshfield),
AP: 860
Oda do wielości (Zagajewski),
EP: 1139

"Ode" (Emerson), **AP:** 551
"Ode in Memory of the American
Volunteers Fallen for France"
(Seeger), **AP:** 1751
"Ode: Intimations of Immortality
from Recollections of Early
Childhood" (Wordsworth),
BP: 1317
"Ode on a Distant Prospect of Eton
College" (Gray), **BP:** 545
"Ode on a Grecian Urn" (Keats),
BP: 741
"Ode on Indolence" (Keats), **BP:** 736
"Ode on Melancholy" (Keats),
BP: 740
"Ode on the Poetical Character"
(Collins), **BP:** 289
*Ode on the Popular Superstitions of
the Highlands of Scotland, An*
(Collins), **BP:** 290
"Ode on the Spring" (Gray), **BP:** 544
"Ode to a Nightingale" (Keats),
BP: 739
"Ode to Anactoria" (Sappho),
EP: 945
"Ode to Aphrodite" (Sappho),
EP: 944
"Ode to George Haldane, Governor of
the Island of Jamaica, An"
(Williams), **TE:** 43
"Ode to Harvard, An" (Bynner),
AP: 275
"Ode to Liberty" (Collins), **BP:** 290
"Ode to the Confederate Dead"
(Tate), **AP:** 1944
"Ode to the Royal Society" (Cowley),
BP: 318
"Ode to the West Wind" (Shelley),
BP: 1122
"Ode to Zion" (Judah ha-Levi),
EP: 551
"Ode upon Occasion of His Majesty's
Proclamation in the Year 1630,
An" (Fanshawe), **BP:** 483
"Ode, Written during the

Negotiations with Buonaparte, in January 1814" (Southey), **BP:** 1176

Odes, **AP:** 2302, **BP:** 1386, **EP:** 1180, **TE:** 818, **WP:** 388. *See also* Categorized Index

Odes (Horace), **EP:** 515

Odes and Addresses to Great People (Hood), **BP:** 656

Odes et ballades (Hugo), **EP:** 522

Odes, England, **TE:** 161

Odlévání zvonů. See Casting of the Bells, The

Odyssey (Homer), **EP:** 508, **TE:** 217

Odyssey, The (Kazantzakis), **EP:** 560

Oehlenschläger, Adam Gottlob, **TE:** 533

Of All Mysteries (Ady), **EP:** 4

Of Being Numerous (Oppen), **AP:** 1480

Of Flesh and Bone (Nims), **AP:** 1425

Of Gravity and Angels (Hirshfield), **AP:** 860

"Of His Majesty's Receiving the News of the Duke of Buckingham's Death" (Waller), **BP:** 1293

"Of Human Knowledge" (Davies), **BP:** 380

"Of Modern Poetry" (Stevens), **AP:** 1907

"Of Poor B. B." (Brecht), **EP:** 153

"Of the Lady Who Can Sleep When She Pleases" (Waller), **BP:** 1294

"Of the Last Verses in the Book" (Waller), **BP:** 1296

"Of the Muse" (Sarton), **AP:** 1722

Of the Progress of the Soule (Donne), **BP:** 414

"Offering for Mr. Bluehart, An" (Wright), **AP:** 2225

Ogawa, Pelorhanke Ai. *See* Ai

Ogun Abibiman (Soyinka), **WP:** 279

"Oh Thy Bright Eyes Must Answer Now" (Brontë), **BP:** 141

"Oh, Welcome May" (Poliziano), **EP:** 846

O'Hara, Frank, **AP:** 1451-1456, **TE:** 674; *The Collected Poems of Frank O'Hara*, **TE:** 676; "The Day Lady Died," **AP:** 1455; "My Heat," **AP:** 1453; "Poem (Lana Turner has collapsed!)," **AP:** 1455; "Savoy," **AP:** 1454

"O'Hussey's Ode to the Maguire" (Mangan), **BP:** 869

Oiseaux. See Birds

Ojciec zadżumionych. See Father of the Plague-Stricken, The

Okigbo, Christopher, **WP:** 205-207, **TE:** 507; *Heavensgate*, **WP:** 206; *Path of Thunder*, **WP:** 207

Økland, Einar, **TE:** 557

Oktave (Pavlović), **EP:** 788

Okura. *See* Yamanoe Okura

Old and New Poems (Hall), **AP:** 782

"Old Apple-Tree, The" (Dunbar), **AP:** 508

"Old Familiar Faces, The" (Lamb), **BP:** 772

Old Fortunatus (Dekker), **BP:** 393

Old Heart (Plumly), **AP:** 1560

"Old Ironsides" (Holmes), **AP:** 896

Old Life, The (Hall), **AP:** 782

"Old Man and Jim, The" (Riley), **AP:** 1650

"Old Man's Journey" (MacLeish), **AP:** 1253

Old Shirts and New Skins (Alexie), **AP:** 23

"Old space cadet speaking" (Hollo), **AP:** 890

"Old Swimmin'-Hole, The" (Riley), **AP:** 1652

"Old Vicarage, Grantchester, The" (Brooke), **BP:** 146

"Old Woman of the Roads, An" (Colum), **BP:** 294

Old Yellow Book, The (Browning), **BP:** 165

Oldham, John, **BP:** 969-973; poem about, **BP:** 439; *Satyrs upon the Jesuits*, **BP:** 970

Olds, Sharon, **AP:** 1456-1463; *Blood, Tin, Straw*, **AP:** 1461; *The Dead and the Living*, **AP:** 1459; *The Father*, **AP:** 1460; *The Gold Cell*, **AP:** 1460; *One Secret Thing*, **AP:** 1462; *Satan Says*, **AP:** 1458; *Strike Sparks*, **AP:** 1461; *The Wellspring*, **AP:** 1461

Olenic, Linda. *See* Pastan, Linda

Oliver, Mary, **AP:** 1463-1469; *American Primitive*, **AP:** 1466; *Dream Work*, **AP:** 1466; *Evidence*, **AP:** 1468; *The Leaf and the Cloud*, **AP:** 1467; *New and Selected Poems*, **AP:** 1466; *No Voyage, and Other Poems*, **AP:** 1465; *Red Bird*, **AP:** 1468; *Thirst*, **AP:** 1467; *Twelve Moons*, **AP:** 1466; *Why I Wake Early*, **AP:** 1467

Olor Iscanus (Vaughan), **BP:** 1286

Olson, Charles, **AP:** 1469-1476, **TE:** 197, **TE:** 686; "Apollonius of Tyana," **AP:** 1473; *Archaeologist of Morning*, **AP:** 1475; "The Kingfishers," **AP:** 1474; *The Maximus Poems*, **AP:** 1475, **TE:** 197; "Projective Verse," **TE:** 205

Olympian Ode 1 (Pindar), **EP:** 840

"Olympic Girl, The" (Betjemen), **BP:** 83

Omar Khayyám, **WP:** 208-212; *The Rubáiyát*, **WP:** 211

"Omen" (Hirsch), **AP:** 855

Omeros (Walcott), **WP:** 323

"On a Certain Engagement South of Seoul" (Carruth), **AP:** 279

"On a Christmas Rose" (Mörike), **EP:** 734

"On a Dead Child" (Bridges), **BP:** 133

"On a Dead Hostess" (Belloc),
    BP: 77

"On a Dead Woman" (Musset),
    EP: 739

"On a Raised Beach" (MacDiarmid),
    BP: 851

"On a Saturday Evening" (Novalis),
    EP: 752

"On a Seven-Day Diary" (Dugan),
    AP: 500

"On an Infant Dying as Soon as
    Born" (Lamb), **BP:** 773

"On Being Accused of Wit"
    (Kennedy), **AP:** 1026

"On Looking at a Copy of Alice
    Meynell's Poems" (Lowell),
    AP: 1177

On Love (Hirsch), **AP:** 856

"On My Shield" (Archilochus), **EP:** 53

On Occasion (Oppenheimer),
    AP: 1483

On Poetry (Swift), **BP:** 1224

On Poetry and Poets (Eliot), **TE:** 715

"On Receiving News of the War"
    (Rosenberg), **BP:** 1057

"On Seeing the Elgin Marbles"
    (Keats), **BP:** 736

On Sepulchers (Foscolo), **EP:** 343

"On Sitting Down to Read King Lear
    Once Again" (Keats), **BP:** 735

"On the Abolition of the English
    Department" (Ngugi Wa Thiong'o
    et al.), **TE:** 771

"On the Anniversary of Her Grace"
    (Weigl), **AP:** 2104

On the Bus with Rosa Parks (Dove),
    AP: 491

"On the Death of Edmund Waller"
    (Behn), **BP:** 71

"On the Death of the Late Earl of
    Rochester" (Behn), **BP:** 71

On the Edge (Koch), **AP:** 1062

On the Edge (Levine), **AP:** 1122

"On the Edge of Darkness"
    (Levertov), **AP:** 1116

"On the Morning of Christ's Nativity"
    (Milton), **BP:** 907

*On the Motion and Immobility of
    Douve* (Bonnefoy), **EP:** 144

On the Nature of Things (Lucretius),
    EP: 628

"On the Receipt of My Mother's
    Picture Out of Norfolk" (Cowper),
    BP: 322

On the Sublime (Longinus), **TE:** 702

"On the Universality and Other
    Attributes of the God of Nature"
    (Freneau), **AP:** 622

"On Zero" (Dugan), **AP:** 501

Once (Walker), **AP:** 2083

Ondaatje, Michael, BP: 973-977,
    TE: 40; *The Collected Works of
    Billy the Kid,* **BP:** 975; *The
    Dainty Monsters,* **BP:** 975;
    Handwriting, **BP:** 976; "Letters
    and Other Worlds," **BP:** 975;
    "Light," **BP:** 975; *Secular Love,*
    BP: 976

"Ondine" (Barnard), **AP:** 104

One and Twenty (Haavikko), **EP:** 440

One Big Self (Wright), **AP:** 2206

One Day, The (Hall), **AP:** 781

One Foot in Eden (Muir), **BP:** 936

150,000,000 (Mayakovsky), **WP:** 179

One Secret Thing (Olds), **AP:** 1462

One Sentence on Tyranny (Illyés),
    EP: 531

"One Word" (Benn), **EP:** 109

Onions and Roses (Miller), **AP:** 1352

Ono no Komachi, **TE:** 416

Onofri, Arturo, **TE:** 401

Oorblyfsels (Breytenbach), **EP:** 167

Open All Night (Bukowski), **AP:** 273

Open Closed Open (Amichai),
    WP: 19

Open House (Fennelly), **AP:** 592

Open House (Roethke), **AP:** 1674

Open Sea, and Other Poems, The
    (Meredith), **AP:** 1311

"Open the Gates" (Kunitz), **AP:** 1087

"Open Window, The" (Tranströmer),
    EP: 1041

Opened Ground (Heaney), **BP:** 603

Opening of the Field, The (Duncan),
    AP: 513

Opening the Hand (Merwin),
    AP: 1336

Openings (Berry), **AP:** 151

Opéra (Cocteau), **EP:** 258

Opitz, Martin, **TE:** 292

Oppen, George, AP: 1477-1481;
    Discrete Series, **AP:** 1479; *The
    Materials,* **AP:** 1479; *Of Being
    Numerous,* **AP:** 1480; *Primitive,*
    AP: 1480; *Seascape,* **AP:** 1480;
    This in Which, **AP:** 1479

Oppenheimer, Joel, AP: 1481-1485,
    TE: 688; *On Occasion,* **AP:** 1483;
    The Woman Poems, **AP:** 1484

"Öppna fönstret, Det." *See* "Open
    Window, The"

"Opportunity" (Sill), **TE:** 762

"Oración por Marilyn Monroe." *See*
    "Marilyn Monroe"

Oral tradition; Africa, **TE:** 15;
    Croatia, **TE:** 218; Europe,
    TE: 214-231; Native American,
    TE: 478; Russia, **TE:** 509; Serbia,
    TE: 218. *See also* Categorized
    Index

"Orange Tree, The" (Belitt), **AP:** 117

Orangery, The (Sorrentino),
    AP: 1860

"Orchard" (Eberhart), **AP:** 531

Orchard, The (Kelly), **AP:** 1013

Orchard, The (Saʿdi), **WP:** 261

Orchards of Syon, The (Hill), **BP:** 648

Orchestra (Davies), **BP:** 381

Ordinary Mornings of a Coliseum
    (Dubie), **AP:** 496

Ordinary Woman, An (Clifton),
    AP: 328

"Oread" (H. D.), **AP:** 756

Oregon Message, An (Stafford),
    AP: 1879

Orfeo (Poliziano), **EP:** 844

Organic form, **TE:** 743

Orientales, Les (Hugo), **EP:** 523

Orientalism (Said), **TE:** 769

Origami Bridges (Ackerman), **AP:** 3

Original Child Bomb (Merton),
　AP: 1329

Original Fire (Erdrich), **AP:** 557

Original Love (Peacock), **AP:** 1528

Orlando Furioso (Ariosto), **EP:** 58,
　TE: 383

Orlando Innamorato (Boiardo),
　EP: 137, **TE:** 383

Orléans, Charles d'. *See* Charles
　d'Orléans

Ørnsbo, Jess, **TE:** 562

Oro de los tigres, El. See *Gold of
　Tigers, The*

Orpheus (Hope), **BP:** 665

Orpheus and Eurydice (Orr),
　AP: 1490

Orr, Gregory, AP: 1485-1493;
　Burning the Empty Nests,
　AP: 1487; *The Caged Owl,*
　AP: 1491; *Concerning the Book
　That Is the Body of the Beloved,*
　AP: 1491; *Gathering the Bones
　Together,* **AP:** 1488; *How
　Beautiful the Beloved,* **AP:** 1492;
　Orpheus and Eurydice, **AP:** 1490;
　The Red House, **AP:** 1489

Országh-Hviezdoslav, Pavol, **TE:** 575

Ortega y Gasset, José, **TE:** 599

"Orthodox Waltz, The" (Fulton),
　AP: 635

Ortiz Cofer, Judith, AP: 1499-1502;
　The Latin Deli, **AP:** 1501; *The
　Year of Our Revolution,* **AP:** 1501

Ortiz, Simon, AP: 1493-1499,
　TE: 483; *After and Before the
　Lightning,* **AP:** 1497; *Going for
　the Rain,* **AP:** 1496; *A Good
　Journey,* **AP:** 1497; *Out There
　Somewhere,* **AP:** 1497

87 pesama (Pavlović), **EP:** 788

Osman (Gundulić), **TE:** 72

Ossi di seppia. See *Cuttlefish Bones*

Ossian (Macpherson), **TE:** 628

"Ostanovka v pustyne." *See* "Halt in
　the Wilderness, A"

Östersjöar. See *Baltics*

Ostriker, Alicia Suskin, AP: 1502-
　1505; *The Crack in Everything,*
　AP: 1504; *The Little Space,*
　AP: 1504; *The Mother/Child
　Papers,* **AP:** 1503; *No Heaven,*
　AP: 1505; *The Volcano Sequence,*
　AP: 1504

Otero, Blas de, EP: 757-763; *Ancia,*
　EP: 761; *Ángel fieramente
　humano,* **EP:** 761; *Cántico
　espiritual,* **EP:** 761; "Déjame,"
　EP: 760; *En Castellano,* **EP:** 761;
　Esto no es un libro, **EP:** 762;
　Mientras, **EP:** 762; *Pido la paz y
　la palabra,* **EP:** 761; *Que trata de
　España,* **EP:** 762; *Redoble de
　conscientcia,* **EP:** 761

Other Side/El otro lado, The
　(Alvarez), **AP:** 34

Other Side of the River, The (Wright),
　AP: 2213

Other Skies (Ciardi), **AP:** 316

Otherwise (Kenyon), **AP:** 1031

Ōtomo Tabito, **TE:** 415

Ōtomo Yakamochi, **TE:** 415

Otro lado, El. See *Other Side/El otro
　lado, The*

Ottava rima, defined, **AP:** 2302,
　BP: 1386, **EP:** 1180, **TE:** 818,
　WP: 388

"Otto tone" (Walther), **EP:** 1124

Ottoman Empire. *See* Geographical
　Index

"Our Bog Is Dood" (Smith),
　BP: 1169

Our Dead Behind Us (Lorde),
　AP: 1169

Our Flowers and Nice Bones
　(Middleton), **BP:** 901

"Our Israfel" (Markham), **AP:** 1276

Ours (Swensen), **AP:** 1933

Out of Danger (Fenton), **BP:** 490

"Out of Lycophron" (Sedley),
　BP: 1096

Out-of-the-Body Travel (Plumly),
　AP: 1559

"Out of the Cradle Endlessly
　Rocking" (Whitman), **AP:** 2136

Out There Somewhere (Ortiz),
　AP: 1497

Outlyer and Ghazals (Harrison),
　AP: 806

"Outside" (Lorde), **AP:** 1169

"Outsiders väg, En" (Ekelöf),
　EP: 308

Ouwe, Hartmann von. *See* Hartmann
　von Aue

Ouyang Xiu, **TE:** 62

"Over Sir John's Hill" (Thomas),
　BP: 1250

"Over 2000 Illustrations and a
　Complete Concordance" (Bishop),
　AP: 172

Øverland, Arnulf, **TE:** 546

Ovid, EP: 763-770; *Amores,*
　EP: 766; *Art of Love,* **EP:** 767;
　Cure for Love, **EP:** 767;
　Metamorphoses, **EP:** 768

Ovid's Banquet of Sense (Chapman),
　BP: 231

Owen, Wilfred, BP: 977-982;
　"Anthem for Doomed Youth,"
　BP: 982; "Arms and the Boy,"
　BP: 981; "Dulce et Decorum Est,"
　BP: 980; "Strange Meeting,"
　BP: 981; "To Poesy," **BP:** 980

Owl in the Mask of the Dreamer, The
　(Haines), **AP:** 775

Owner of the House, The (Simpson),
　AP: 1800

Owuor-Anyumba, Henry, **TE:** 771

Oxford Movement. *See* Categorized
　Index

Oxota (Hejinian), **AP:** 840

Oxymoron, defined, **AP:** 2302,
  BP: 1386, **EP:** 1180, **TE:** 818,
  WP: 388
"Oza" (Voznesensky), **WP:** 314

Padmasambhava, **TE:** 605
"Paean to Place" (Niedecker),
  AP: 1419
Pagis, Dan, **WP:** 213-216; "Brain,"
  WP: 215; "Harvests," **WP:** 216;
  "Instructions for Crossing the
  Border," **WP:** 215; *Poems by Dan
  Pagis*, **WP:** 214; *Points of
  Departure*, **WP:** 214
"Pain Has an Element of Blank"
  (Bogan), **AP:** 203
Painted Bed, The (Hall), **AP:** 783
"Pájaro, El." *See* "Bird, The"
Palamas, Kostis, **TE:** 334
Paley, Grace, **AP:** 1506-1509; *Begin
  Again*, **AP:** 1508; *Fidelity*,
  AP: 1508
Palm, Göran, **TE:** 554
Palmiro Vicarion, Count. *See* Logue,
  Christopher
Pálsson, Sigurður, **TE:** 561
Paludan-Müller, Frederik, **TE:** 535
Pan Tadeusz (Mickiewicz), **EP:** 707,
  TE: 494
"Panegyrick to My Lord Protector, A"
  (Waller), **BP:** 1295
Pangolin, and Other Verse, The
  (Moore), **AP:** 1368
Pannonius, Janus, **TE:** 353
Panoramas (Cruz), **AP:** 403
Pansies (Lawrence), **BP:** 800
"Panther, The" (Rilke), **EP:** 895
Panther and the Lash, The (Hughes),
  AP: 932
Panther Man (Emanuel), **AP:** 539
Pantoum, defined, **AP:** 2302,
  BP: 1386, **EP:** 1180, **TE:** 818,
  WP: 388
"Papa Love Baby" (Smith), **BP:** 1167
Paper Soul (Rodgers), **AP:** 1669

"Parabolic Ballad" (Voznesensky),
  WP: 314
Paradies uff Erden (Biermann),
  EP: 125
Paradise Lost (Milton), **BP:** 909,
  TE: 623
Paradise Poems (Stern), **AP:** 1900
Paradise Regained (Milton), **BP:** 911
Paradox, defined, **AP:** 2302,
  BP: 1386, **EP:** 1180, **TE:** 818,
  WP: 388
Parallelism, **TE:** 752
"Pardon, The" (Wilbur), **AP:** 2157
Parini, Giuseppe, **TE:** 388
"Paris in Snow" (Senghor), **WP:** 269
Paris Spleen, 1869 (Baudelaire),
  EP: 86
Parish Register, The (Crabbe),
  BP: 332
Parker, Dorothy, **AP:** 1509-1513;
  Not So Deep as a Well, **AP:** 1511
Parlement of Foules (Chaucer),
  BP: 248
Parmenides, **TE:** 325
Parnassianism, **EP:** 970, **TE:** 264,
  TE: 639. *See also* Categorized
  Index
Parny, Évariste-Désiré de Forges de,
  TE: 258
Parole (linguistics), **TE:** 750
Paros, Archilochus of. *See*
  Archilochus
Parra, Nicanor, **WP:** 216-222,
  TE: 438; *After-Dinner
  Declarations*, **WP:** 221;
  Artefactos, **WP:** 221; *Cancionero
  sin nombre*, **WP:** 219; *Canciones
  rusas*, **WP:** 220; *La Cueca larga*,
  WP: 220; *Versos de salón*,
  WP: 220
Parry, Miilman, **TE:** 218
Part, A (Berry), **AP:** 152
Part of Speech, A (Brodsky), **WP:** 49
Parti pris des choses, Le. See *Taking
  the Side of Things*

Partial Accounts (Meredith),
  AP: 1315
"Partisans of the Sun, The" (Foix),
  EP: 333
"Parturition" (Loy), **AP:** 1202
Parun, Vesna, **TE:** 75
"Parus." *See* "Sail, The"
Parzival (Wolfram von Eschenbach),
  EP: 1132, **TE:** 287
Pascarella, Cesare, **TE:** 399
Pascoli, Giovanni, **EP:** 771-776,
  TE: 395; *Canti di Castelvecchio*,
  EP: 775; *Convivial Poems*,
  EP: 775; *Myricae*, **EP:** 774;
  Poemetti, **EP:** 775
Pasolini, Pier Paolo, **EP:** 776-782,
  TE: 400; *The Ashes of Gramsci*,
  EP: 780; *Poesia in forma di rosa*,
  EP: 781; *Poesie a Casarsa*,
  EP: 779; *La Religione del mio
  tempo*, **EP:** 781; *Trasumanar e
  organizzar*, **EP:** 781
Pasquils Fooles-Cappe (Breton),
  BP: 129
*Pasquils Mad-Cappe, Throwne at the
  Corruptions of These Times*
  (Breton), **BP:** 129
Passad (Martinson), **EP:** 683
"Passage to India" (Whitman),
  AP: 2138
Passages of Joy, The (Gunn), **BP:** 566
"Passages Poems" (Duncan), **AP:** 515
Passing Through (Kunitz), **AP:** 1091
"Passion, The" (Elytis), **EP:** 321
Passionate Shepheard, The (Breton),
  BP: 128
"Passionate Shepherd to His Love,
  The" (Marlowe), **BP:** 873
Passport to the War (Kunitz),
  AP: 1086
Passwords (Stafford), **AP:** 1879
Past, the Future, the Present, The
  (Whittemore), **AP:** 2143
Pastan, Linda, **AP:** 1514-1520;
  Aspects of Eve, **AP:** 1515;

"Balancing Act," **AP:** 1516; "Hurricane Watch," **AP:** 1516; "Marks," **AP:** 1517; "Prosody 101," **AP:** 1517

Pasternak, Boris, **TE:** 521, **WP:** 222-229; *High Malady*, **WP:** 226; *Lieutenant Schmidt*, **WP:** 227; *My Sister, Life*, **WP:** 226; *The Poems of Doctor Zhivago*, **WP:** 227; "Prince Potemkin," **WP:** 227; *Spektorsky*, **WP:** 227; Andrei Voznesensky, **WP:** 312; *The Year 1905*, **WP:** 227

Pastoral poets. *See* Categorized Index

Pastorales (Jiménez), **EP:** 536

Pastorall Elegie, A (Drummond), **BP:** 432

Pataxanadu, and Other Prose (Middleton), **BP:** 902

Patchen, Kenneth, **AP:** 1520-1525; *Before the Brave*, **AP:** 1523; *First Will and Testament*, **AP:** 1523

Pater, Walter, **BP:** 1304

Paterson (Williams), **AP:** 2178, **TE:** 196

Path, Crooked Path (Balaban), **AP:** 83

Path of Thunder (Okigbo), **WP:** 207

Path on the Rainbow, The (anthology), **TE:** 481

Patience (Pearl-Poet), **BP:** 994

Patmore, Coventry, **BP:** 983-991; *The Angel in the House*, **BP:** 987; "A London Fête," **BP:** 986; *The Unknown Eros, and Other Odes*, **BP:** 989; *The Victories of Love*, **BP:** 988

Patraput (Tagore), **WP:** 286

"Pàtria, La" (Aribau), **TE:** 51

"Patriotic Debate, The" (Chartier), **EP:** 238

Patriotic verse, German, **TE:** 299

Patron Happiness (McPherson), **AP:** 1262

Pattern of a Day (Hillyer), **AP:** 852

Pattern poets. *See* Categorized Index

Patuah sagur patuah. See *Open Closed Open*

Pavese, Cesare, **EP:** 783-786; *Hard Labor*, **EP:** 784; *Verrà la morte e avrà i tuoi occhi*, **EP:** 785

Pavlović, Miodrag, **EP:** 786-791, **TE:** 570; *Hododarje*, **EP:** 789; *Mleko iskoni*, **EP:** 788; *Nova Skitija*, **EP:** 789; *Oktave*, **EP:** 788; *87 pesama*, **EP:** 788; *Stub sećanja*, **EP:** 788; *Svetli i tamni praznici*, **EP:** 789; *Velika Skitija*, **EP:** 789

Pavlovski, Radovan, **TE:** 476

"Paysans, Les." *See* "Peasants, The"

Paz, Octavio, **TE:** 438, **WP:** 230-236; "The Bird," **WP:** 232; *Blanco*, **WP:** 234; *Discos visuales*, **WP:** 234; *Eagle or Sun?*, **WP:** 233; "Interrupted Elegy," **WP:** 233; "Poetry," **WP:** 232; *Renga*, **WP:** 234; "Snapshots," **WP:** 234; "Stars and Cricket," **WP:** 232; *Sun Stone*, **WP:** 233

P'Bitek, Okot, **TE:** 507

"Peach Blossom Spring" (Tao Qian), **WP:** 292

Peacock, Molly, **AP:** 1525-1528; *And Live Apart*, **AP:** 1527; *Original Love*, **AP:** 1528; *Raw Heaven*, **AP:** 1527; *Take Heart*, **AP:** 1527

Peacock Poems, The (Williams), **AP:** 2173

Pearl (Pearl-Poet), **BP:** 997, **TE:** 108

Pearl-Poet, **BP:** 991-1001, **TE:** 108; *Cleanness*, **BP:** 995; *Patience*, **BP:** 994; *Pearl*, **BP:** 997, **TE:** 108; *Sir Gawain and the Green Knight*, **BP:** 999, **TE:** 111

"Peasants, The" (Verhaeren), **EP:** 1090

Peau noire, masques blancs. See *Black Skin, White Masks*

Peeslake, Gaffer. *See* Durrell, Lawrence

Péguy, Charles-Pierre, **EP:** 791-797, **TE:** 271; *Ève*, **EP:** 796; *Jeanne d'Arc*, **EP:** 794; *The Mystery of the Charity of Joan of Arc*, **EP:** 794; *The Mystery of the Holy Innocents, and Other Poems*, **EP:** 795; *The Portico of the Mystery of the Second Virtue*, **EP:** 795; *La Tapisserie de Notre-Dame*, **EP:** 796; *La Tapisserie de sainte Geneviève et de Jeanne d'Arc*, **EP:** 796

"Pelican Chorus, The" (Lear), **BP:** 816

Pelorhanke Ai Ogawa. *See* Ai

Pen Shop, The (Kinsella), **BP:** 758

PEN/Voelcker Award for Poetry, **AP:** 2327, **CM:** 61, **TE:** 881

Penny Wheep (MacDiarmid), **BP:** 848

"Penseroso, Il" (Milton), **BP:** 908

Pentameter, defined, **AP:** 2302, **BP:** 1386, **EP:** 1180, **TE:** 818, **WP:** 388

"Pentecost, The" (Manzoni), **EP:** 665

Pentzikis, Nikos, **EP:** 797-801; *Anakomidhi*, **EP:** 801; *Ikones*, **EP:** 799

People and Dog in the Sun (Wallace), **AP:** 2092

People Live Here (Simpson), **AP:** 1798

People on a Bridge (Szymborska), **EP:** 1011

People, Yes, The (Sandburg), **AP:** 1709

Peopled Landscape, A (Tomlinson), **BP:** 1271

Pérez Firmat, Gustavo, **TE:** 472

Perfect Fiction, The (Sorrentino), **AP:** 1860

Perfect Wife, The (León), **EP:** 600

Perfil del aire (Cernuda), **EP:** 223

Performance poetry, **TE:** 27. *See also* Categorized Index

"Perhaps Because of the Fateful Quiet" (Foscolo), **EP:** 343

Peri hypsous. See On the Sublime

Periphrasis, defined, **AP:** 2302, **BP:** 1386, **EP:** 1180, **TE:** 818, **WP:** 388

Perishing, The (Santos), **AP:** 1714

Perlmutter, Andrei. *See* Codrescu, Andrei

Permit Me Refuge (Rolfe), **AP:** 1684

Perse, Saint-John, **EP:** 801-806, **TE:** 277; *Anabasis*, **EP:** 804; *Birds*, **EP:** 805; *Éloges*, **EP:** 804; *Seamarks*, **EP:** 804

"Persephone" (Barnard), **AP:** 104

Persephone (Lifshin), **AP:** 1142

Persia. *See* Geographical Index

Persian Eclogues (Collins), **BP:** 289

Persidskie motivi (Esenin), **WP:** 95

Persimmon Tree, The (Viereck), **AP:** 2045

"Persimmons" (Lee), **AP:** 1104

Persius, **EP:** 806-810, **TE:** 456; *Satires*, **EP:** 807

Personal Effects (Becker), **AP:** 111

Personal Poems (Berrigan), **AP:** 145

Peru. *See* Geographical Index

Pessoa, Fernando, **EP:** 811-816; "I'm a Shepherd," **EP:** 814; "The Keeper of Flocks," **EP:** 814; *Message*, **EP:** 813; "The Roses of the Gardens of Adonis," **EP:** 815; "Stations of the Cross," **EP:** 813; "Tobacco-Shop," **EP:** 814

Peter Lazarovitch, Irving. *See* Layton, Irving

Petersen, Nis, **TE:** 548

"Petit Mort pour rire." *See* "Little Death to Make One Laugh, A"

Petit Testament, Le. See Legacy, The

"Petite Ville en Sibérie." *See* "Little Town in Siberia"

"Petition for an Absolute Retreat, The" (Finch), **BP:** 493

Petits Poèmes en prose. See Paris Spleen, 1869

Petőfi, Sándor, **EP:** 816-828, **TE:** 357; "Bolond Istók," **EP:** 825; *Clouds*, **EP:** 822; "Dalaim," **EP:** 824; *The Hammer of the Village*, **EP:** 821; *János the Hero*, **EP:** 821; "Levél Várady Antalhoz," **EP:** 824; "A Négyökrös szekér," **EP:** 823; "Nemzeti dal," **EP:** 826; "Reszket a bokor, mert," **EP:** 824; "Rózsabokor a domboldalon," **EP:** 825; "Szeptember végen," **EP:** 824; "Szeretlek, kedvesem," **EP:** 825; "Tündérálom," **EP:** 823

Petrarch, **EP:** 828-836, **TE:** 102, **TE:** 379; *Africa*, **EP:** 833; *Metrical Letters*, **EP:** 834; *Triumphs*, **EP:** 833

Petrarchan sonnets, **TE:** 136. *See also* Categorized Index

Petri, György, **TE:** 362

Petrou Kabaphes, Konstantionos. *See* Cavafy, Constantine P.

Pétursson, Hannes, **TE:** 553

"Peyote Poem, Part I" (McClure), **AP:** 1209

Phaedrus, **TE:** 456

Phallocentricism, **TE:** 737

Phantasus, 1898 (Holz), **EP:** 498

Phantasus, 1929 (Holz), **EP:** 499

Phantasus, 1961 (Holz), **EP:** 501

Pharaoh, Pharaoh (Emerson), **AP:** 542

Pharaoh's Daughter (Ní Dhomhnaill), **BP:** 966

"Phares, Les." *See* "Beacons"

Pharsalia (Lucan), **EP:** 623

Phenomenological criticism, defined, **AP:** 2302, **BP:** 1386, **EP:** 1180, **TE:** 818, **WP:** 388

Phenomenological psychology, **TE:** 727

"Phihellene" (Cavafy), **EP:** 208

Philips, Katherine, **TE:** 624

Phillips, Carl, **AP:** 1529-1532; *Quiver of Arrows*, **AP:** 1530

Phillis with the Tragical Complaynt of Elstred (Lodge), **BP:** 820

Philoktetes (Ritsos), **EP:** 910

"Philosopher, The" (Brontë), **BP:** 141, **BP:** 538

Philosophes, **TE:** 254

Philosophical poetry, ancient Greece, **TE:** 324

Philosophicall Fancies (Newcastle), **BP:** 961

"Philosophy" (Thomson), **BP:** 1266

Phoenix and the Tortoise, The (Rexroth), **AP:** 1625

Phoenix and the Turtle, The (Shakespeare), **BP:** 1106

Phoenix Gone, the Terrace Empty, The (Chin), **AP:** 309

Phoenix Nest, The (Breton), **BP:** 127

Phyllyp Sparowe (Skelton), **BP:** 1156

Pian wen (poetic form), **TE:** 60

"Piano Kissed by a Fragile Hand, The" (Verlaine), **EP:** 1097

"Piano que baise une main frêle, La." *See* "Piano Kissed by a Fragile Hand, The"

"Piazza Piece" (Ransom), **AP:** 1609

"Pickers" (Haines), **AP:** 774

Picnic, Lightning (Collins), **AP:** 344

Picture, The (Bowles), **BP:** 123

Picture Bride (Song), **AP:** 1854

Picture Window (Hollander), **AP:** 884

"Pictured" (Cavafy), **EP:** 209

Pido la paz y la palabra (Otero), **EP:** 761

Piece Logic (Hunt), **AP:** 940

Pieces (Creeley), **AP:** 397

"Pied Beauty" (Hopkins), **BP:** 674

Piedra de sol. See Sun Stone

"Pier-Glass, The" (Graves), **BP:** 538

Pierce-Arrow (Howe), **AP:** 918

Piercy, Marge, **AP:** 1532-1538; *The Art of Blessing the Day,*

AP: 1535; *Available Light,*
AP: 1534; *Circles on the Water,*
AP: 1534; *Colors Passing
Through Us,* AP: 1535; *The
Crooked Inheritance,* AP: 1536;
Early Grrrl, AP: 1535
Pierre écrite. See Words in Stone
*Piers Plowman. See Vision of
William, Concerning Piers the
Plowman, The*
"Pietà, La." *See* "Pity"
Pietri, Pedro, TE: 470
Pigeon (Flint), AP: 609
Pilgrimage, and Other Poems
(Clarke), BP: 263
Pilgrimage of Festus, The (Aiken),
AP: 15
Pilgrimage to Paradise (Breton),
BP: 128
*Pill Versus the Springhill Mine
Disaster, The* (Brautigan),
AP: 241
"Pillar of Fame, The" (Herrick),
BP: 634
Pilot Star Elegies, The (Santos),
AP: 1713
Pindar, EP: 836-841, TE: 327;
Olympian Ode 1, EP: 840;
Pythian Ode 8, EP: 840; *Pythian
Ode* 10, EP: 839
Pindarique Odes (Cowley), BP: 316
Pindaros. *See* Pindar
Pindarus. *See* Pindar
Piñero, Miguel, TE: 466
Pinion (Emerson), AP: 542
Pinorman (Aldington), BP: 19
Pinsky, Robert, AP: 1538-1547;
"The Anniversary," AP: 1546;
"Essay on Psychiatrists,"
AP: 1543; *An Explanation of
America,* AP: 1543; *The Figured
Wheel,* AP: 1545; *Gulf Music,*
AP: 1546; *History of My Heart,*
AP: 1544; *Jersey Rain,* AP: 1545;
"Poem of Disconnected Parts,"

AP: 1546; *Sadness and
Happiness,* AP: 1540; "Waiting,"
AP: 1541; *The Want Bone,*
AP: 1545
Pinson, Barbara Ann. *See* Guest,
Barbara
Pinta, Harold. *See* Pinter, Harold
Pinter, Harold, BP: 1001-1005;
"Body," BP: 1004; "Cancer
Cells," BP: 1004; "Requiem for
1945," BP: 1003; "To My Wife,"
BP: 1004; *War,* BP: 1003
Pisan Cantos, The (Pound), AP: 1583
"Pity" (Ungaretti), EP: 1061
Pizan, Christine de. *See* Christine de
Pizan
"Place and a Voice, A" (Applewhite),
AP: 54
"Place for No Story, The" (Jeffers),
AP: 969
Place Keepers (Galvin), AP: 650
Placeres prohibidos, Los (Cernuda),
EP: 223
Plague Column, The (Seifert),
EP: 966
*Plague Monument, The. See Plague
Column, The*
Plain-Chant (Cocteau), EP: 257
Plain Song (Harrison), AP: 804
Plain style, TE: 134
Plainwater (Carson), BP: 226
*Planches courbes, Les. See Curved
Planks, The*
Planets (Ackerman), AP: 2
Plath, Sylvia, AP: 1547-1555,
TE: 202, TE: 670; *Ariel,*
TE: 670; "By Candlelight,"
AP: 1553; "Channel Crossing,"
AP: 1554; "Daddy," AP: 1554;
"Lady Lazarus," AP: 1554;
"Mary's Song," AP: 1552;
"Maudlin," AP: 1552; "Nick and
the Candlestick," AP: 1553;
"Words," AP: 1554
Plato, TE: 700; *Republic,* TE: 700

Plave legende. See Blue Legends
*Play the Piano Drunk Like a
Percussion Instrument Until the
Fingers Begin to Bleed a Bit*
(Bukowski), AP: 271
"Playroom" (Barnard), AP: 101
"Plea, A" (Dunbar), AP: 505
"Plea of the Midsummer Fairies"
(Hood), BP: 655
Pleasure Dome (Komunyakaa),
AP: 1068
*Pleasures of Peace, and Other Poems,
The* (Koch), AP: 1061
Pléiade poets, TE: 248, TE: 463. *See
also* Categorized Index
Pleynet, Marcelin, TE: 278
PLOT (Rankine), AP: 1603
Płótno. See Canvas
"Pluie" (Ponge), EP: 853
Plumly, Stanley, AP: 1556-1561;
Giraffe, AP: 1558; *How the
Plains Indians Got Horses,*
AP: 1558; *In the Outer Dark,*
AP: 1557; *The Marriage in the
Trees,* AP: 1560; *Now That My
Father Lies Down Beside Me,*
AP: 1560; *Old Heart,* AP: 1560;
Out-of-the-Body Travel,
AP: 1559; *Summer Celestial,*
AP: 1560
Plums, Stones, Kisses, and Hooks
(Wallace), AP: 2091
Plutonian Ode (Ginsberg), AP: 684
Poco Low Coup, Un (Baraka), AP: 98
Podjavorinská, Ludmila, TE: 575
Podróż na wschód (Słowacki),
EP: 978
Poe, Edgar Allan, AP: 1561-1569;
"The City in the Sea," AP: 1566;
French reception of, EP: 82; "The
Haunted Palace," AP: 1567;
"Romance," AP: 1564; "Sonnet—
To Science," AP: 1564;
"Ulalume," AP: 1565
"Poem, The" (Novalis), EP: 754

Poem Beginning "The" (Zukofsky),
    AP: 2268
"Poem Beginning with a Line by
    Pindar, A" (Duncan), **AP:** 513
Poem Counterpoem (Randall),
    AP: 1598
"Poem for Adults" (Ważyk),
    EP: 1129
"Poem for My Brother" (Logan),
    AP: 1155
"Poem for Myself, A" (Knight),
    AP: 1056
"Poem for the Young White Man . . ."
    (Cervantes), **AP:** 301
"Poem in Four Parts on New York
    City" (Corn), **AP:** 354
Poem in Progress (Logan), **AP:** 1155
"Poem (Lana Turner has collapsed!)"
    (O'Hara), **AP:** 1455
"Poem of Disconnected Parts"
    (Pinsky), **AP:** 1546
"Poem of Horses, A" (Levis),
    AP: 1130
"Poem of Seven Faces" (Drummond
    de Andrade), **WP:** 80
Poem of the Cid (anonymous),
    TE: 584
"Poem on St. James' Park as Lately
    Improved by His Majesty, A"
    (Waller), **BP:** 1295
Poem on the Last Day, A (Young),
    BP: 1351
Poem sequence, **TE:** 194
Poem 64 (Catullus), **EP:** 201
"Poem Some People Will Have to
    Understand, A" (Baraka), **AP:** 95
"Poem to Shout in the Ruins"
    (Aragon), **EP:** 39
Poem Traveled Down My Arm, A
    (Walker), **AP:** 2085
Poem Without a Hero, A
    (Akhmatova), **WP:** 8
Poema bez geroya. See *Poem Without
    a Hero, A*
Poema de Chile (Mistral), **WP:** 190

Poema de Fernán González
    (anonymous), **TE:** 588
"Poema de sete faces." *See* "Poem of
    Seven Faces"
Poema paradisiaco (D'Annunzio),
    EP: 267
Poemas humanos. See *Human Poems*
Poemat o czasie zastygłym (Miłosz),
    EP: 714
"Poème à crier dans les ruines." *See*
    "Poem to Shout in the Ruins"
Poèmes (Bonnefoy), **EP:** 146
Poemes Lyrick and Pastorall
    (Drayton), **BP:** 420
Poèmes saturniens (Verlaine),
    EP: 1095
Poemetti (Pascoli), **EP:** 775
Poemi conviviali. See *Convivial
    Poems*
Poems (Bécquer). *See Rhymes, The*
Poems, 1914-1930 (Blunden),
    BP: 105
Poems (Browning), **BP:** 153
Poems (Burns), **BP:** 178
Poems (Cowley), **BP:** 315
Poems (Crabbe), **BP:** 332
Poems (Drummond), **BP:** 430
Poems (Hesse), **EP:** 474
Poems (Ignatow), **AP:** 944
Poems (Mandelstam), **WP:** 168
Poems, 1930-1960 (Miles), **AP:** 1342
Poems, 1968-1998 (Muldoon),
    BP: 942
Poems (Rich), **AP:** 1637
Poems, 1947-1957 (Smith), **AP:** 1827
Poems and Ballads (Swinburne),
    BP: 1232
Poems and Ballads: Second Series
    (Swinburne), **BP:** 1234
Poems and Verse Plays
    (Hofmannsthal), **EP:** 482
Poems Before and After (Holub),
    EP: 495
Poems by Dan Pagis (Pagis),
    WP: 214

Poems by Doveglion (Villa),
    AP: 2051
Poems from Centre City (Kinsella),
    BP: 757
Poems in Prose (Baudelaire). *See
    Paris Spleen, 1869*
Poems in Prose (Wilde), **BP:** 1309
Poems in Slang (Villon), **EP:** 1111
*Poems: New and Collected, 1957-
    1997* (Szymborska), **EP:** 1011
Poems, New and Selected
    (Whittemore), **AP:** 2143
Poems: New Edition (Browning),
    BP: 154
Poems of Doctor Zhivago, The
    (Pasternak), **WP:** 227
Poems of Lincoln Kirstein, The
    (Kirstein), **AP:** 1045
"Poems of Our Climate" (Stevens),
    AP: 1908
*Poems of Stanley Kunitz, 1928-1978,
    The* (Kunitz), **AP:** 1089
Poems of the Past and Present
    (Hardy), **BP:** 584
Poems Old and New, 1918-1978
    (Lewis), **AP:** 1135
Poems on Several Occasions
    (Cotton), **BP:** 311
Poems on Several Occasions (Miles),
    AP: 1341
Poems Seven (Dugan), **AP:** 501
Poems Six (Dugan), **AP:** 501
Poems, Third Series (Bridges),
    BP: 132
Poems to Stella (Swift), **BP:** 1223
*Poems Written Before Jumping out of
    an Eight Story Window*
    (Bukowski), **AP:** 269
"Poesía." *See* "Poetry" (Paz)
Poesia in forma di rosa (Pasolini),
    EP: 781
Poesie a Casarsa (Pasolini), **EP:** 779
*Poesie als Mittel der
    Umweltgestaltung* (Gomringer),
    EP: 406

Poésies (Gautier), **EP:** 372

Poésies, 1917-1920 (Cocteau),
    EP: 257

"Poet" (Viereck), **AP:** 2044

Poet, Pearl. *See* Pearl-Poet

Poet in New York (García Lorca),
    EP: 360

Poet Laureate Consultant in Poetry,
    AP: 2327, **CM:** 61, **TE:** 881

Poet Laureate of the United Kingdom
    of Great Britain and Northern
    Ireland, **BP:** 1413, **CM:** 62,
    TE: 882

*Poeta en Nueva York. See Poet in New
    York*

"Poète contumace, Le." *See*
    "Contumacious Poet, The"

Poetic diction, **TE:** 709

Poetic Edda, **TE:** 226

Poetic function, **TE:** 781

Poetic Justice (Bernstein), **AP:** 134

Poetical Meditations (Lamartine),
    EP: 593, **TE:** 260

Poetical terms, **AP:** 2294-2306,
    BP: 1378-1390, **EP:** 1172-1184,
    TE: 810-822, **WP:** 380-392

Poetical Works of Charles Lamb, The
    (Lamb), **BP:** 772

*Poetical Works of George M. Horton,
    The* (Horton), **AP:** 907

Poetical Works of Robert Bridges
    (Bridges), **BP:** 134

Poeticall Blossomes (Cowley),
    BP: 315

Poetics; defined, **TE:** 700; France,
    TE: 276; German Enlightenment,
    TE: 294; Marxist criticism,
    TE: 761; modern, **TE:** 194,
    TE: 715, **TE:** 750; Octavio Paz,
    TE: 438; Romanticism, **TE:** 298;
    Scandinavia, **TE:** 554; Spain,
    TE: 595; Symbolism, **TE:** 643

Poetics (Aristotle), **TE:** 700, **TE:** 743

"Poetry" (Annensky), **WP:** 23,
    WP: 232; literary canon,

TE: 734; as literature, **TE:** 703;
    psychology, **TE:** 744; science,
    TE: 744

"Poetry" (Paz), **WP:** 232

Poetry (magazine), **TE:** 645

Poetry (periodical), **BP:** 18

"Poetry and Grammar" (Stein),
    AP: 1891

"Poets and the Rain" (Sarton),
    AP: 1719

"Poet's Life, A" (MacBeth), **BP:** 843

"Poetu." *See* "To a Poet"

"Poeziia." *See* "Poetry" (Annensky)

Poiesis, **TE:** 701

Point of view, defined, **AP:** 2302,
    BP: 1386, **EP:** 1180, **TE:** 818,
    WP: 388

Points of Departure (Pagis), **WP:** 214

Points of View (Reed), **AP:** 1614

Poisoned Lands, and Other Poems
    (Montague), **BP:** 916

Poland. *See* Geographical Index

Poli, Umberto. *See* Saba, Umberto

Polish poetry, **TE:** 489-499

Politeia. See Republic (Plato)

Politian. *See* Poliziano

Political poetry; China, **TE:** 56; East
    Germany, **TE:** 91; Germany,
    TE: 299, **TE:** 311; postwar Japan,
    TE: 431; Middle English,
    TE: 109; nineteenth century
    Poland, **TE:** 493; Serbia,
    TE: 569; Soviet Union, **TE:** 524;
    Sweden, **TE:** 554

Political poets. *See* Categorized Index

Political Self-Portrait, 1919-1939
    (Wheelwright), **AP:** 2128

Poliziano, **EP:** 841-848, **TE:** 381,
    TE: 463; "My Brunette,"
    EP: 846; "Oh, Welcome May,"
    EP: 846; *Orfeo*, **EP:** 844; *Stanze*,
    EP: 845

Poltava (Pushkin), **WP:** 242

Poly-Olbion (Drayton), **BP:** 421

Pomes Penyeach (Joyce), **BP:** 723

Pondicherry school, **TE:** 372

Ponge, Francis, **EP:** 848-855,
    TE: 278; "Le Cycle des saisons,"
    EP: 852; "Escargots," **EP:** 852;
    "Le Mimosa," **EP:** 853; "Pluie,"
    EP: 853; *Taking the Side of
    Things*, **EP:** 851

Ponsot, Marie, **AP:** 1569-1573;
    Admit Impediment, **AP:** 1570; *The
    Bird Catcher*, **AP:** 1571; *The
    Green Dark*, **AP:** 1570; *Springing*,
    AP: 1572; *True Minds*, **AP:** 1570

"Poor Child's Plaything, The"
    (Baudelaire), **EP:** 86

Popa, Vasko, **EP:** 856-860, **TE:** 570;
    Bark, **EP:** 857; *Kuća nasred
    druma*, **EP:** 859; *Raw Flesh*,
    EP: 859; *Secondary Heaven*,
    EP: 858; *Unrest-Field*, **EP:** 857;
    Wolf Salt, **EP:** 859

Pope, Alexander, **BP:** 1005-1016,
    TE: 163, **TE:** 706; *The Dunciad*,
    BP: 1014; *Eloisa to Abelard*,
    BP: 1011; *Epistle to Dr.
    Arbuthnot*, **BP:** 1014; *An Essay on
    Criticism*, **BP:** 1008, **TE:** 706; *An
    Essay on Man*, **BP:** 1011; *The
    Rape of the Lock*, **BP:** 1010

Popiól i wiatr (Słonimski), **EP:** 971

"Poplar Field, The" (Cowper), **BP:** 324

*Porche du mystère de la deuxième
    vertu, Le. See Portico of the
    Mystery of the Second Virtue, The*

Porphyras (Solomos), **EP:** 992

"Porphyria's Lover" (Browning),
    BP: 161

Porter, Anne, **AP:** 1573-1576; *An
    Altogether Different Language*,
    AP: 1575

Porter, Countée LeRoy. *See* Cullen,
    Countée

*Portico of the Mystery of the Second
    Virtue, The* (Péguy), **EP:** 795

Portraits and Elegies
    (Schnackenberg), **AP:** 1729

Portugal. *See* Geographical Index

"Poshchechina obshchestvennomu vkusu." *See* "Slap in the Face of the Public Taste, A"

Positives (Gunn), **BP:** 564

Possessions (Belitt), **AP:** 118

"Postcard from the Volcano, A" (Stevens), **AP:** 1910

Postcolonial criticism, **TE:** 769-773

Postcolonial poetry, **TE:** 211, **TE:** 500-508; Africa, **TE:** 16, **TE:** 770; Caribbean, **TE:** 46, **TE:** 772; India, **TE:** 772; Pakistan, **TE:** 772

Postcolonialism, defined, **AP:** 2302, **BP:** 1386, **EP:** 1180, **TE:** 818, **WP:** 388

Postconfessional poets. *See* Categorized Index

Posthumous Tales (Crabbe), **BP:** 336

Postmodernism, **TE:** 207; Canada, **TE:** 40; Latin America, **TE:** 436; Scandinavia, **TE:** 556. *See also* Categorized Index

Postmodernism, defined, **AP:** 2302, **BP:** 1386, **EP:** 1180, **TE:** 818, **WP:** 388

Poststructuralism, **TE:** 784

Poststructuralist criticism, **TE:** 733, **TE:** 780-786

Pot of Earth, The (MacLeish), **AP:** 1248

Poulet, Georges, **AP:** 2302, **BP:** 1386, **EP:** 1180, **TE:** 818, **WP:** 388

Pound, Ezra, **AP:** 1577-1586, **BP:** 168, **TE:** 188, **TE:** 652, **TE:** 784; *Cantos*, **AP:** 1581, **TE:** 195; *Cathay*, **AP:** 1580; *Drafts and Fragments of Cantos CX-CXVII*, **AP:** 1584; and H. D., **AP:** 755; *Homage to Sextus Propertius*, **AP:** 1580, **TE:** 195; *Hugh Selwyn Mauberley*, **AP:** 1581, **TE:** 195; *The Pisan Cantos*, **AP:** 1583

"Power" (Lorde), **AP:** 1169

Power of the Visible, The (Dana), **AP:** 433

Power Politics (Atwood), **BP:** 43

Powerful Long Ladder (Dodson), **AP:** 472

Powers of Heaven and Earth, The (Nims), **AP:** 1427

Powers of Thirteen (Hollander), **AP:** 882

"Powhatan's Daughter" (Crane), **AP:** 382

Practical Gods (Dennis), **AP:** 443

Pragnienie (Zagajewski), **EP:** 1140

"Prairies, The" (Bryant), **AP:** 262

Praise (Hass), **AP:** 816

Praise poetry, **TE:** 15

Praise Song for the Day (Alexander), **AP:** 20

Pratt, E. J., **BP:** 1016-1021; *Brébeuf and His Brethren*, **BP:** 1019; "Erosion," **BP:** 1017; "From Stone to Steel," **BP:** 1018; *The Roosevelt and the Antinoe*, **BP:** 1019; "The Shark," **BP:** 1018; *The Titanic*, **BP:** 1019; *Towards the Last Spike*, **BP:** 1020

Pratt, Mary Louise, **TE:** 758

"Prayer of Columbus" (Whitman), **AP:** 2139

Précieux poets, **TE:** 251

Prefabrications (Miles), **AP:** 1341

"Preface to *Fables Ancient and Modern*" (Dryden), **TE:** 705

Preface to Gondibert with An Answer by Mr. Hobbes, The (Davenant), **BP:** 366

Preface to *Lyrical Ballads* (Wordsworth), **TE:** 708

Prelude, The (Wordsworth), **BP:** 1318

Preludios (González Martínez), **WP:** 104

"Première du monde" (Éluard), **EP:** 316

Pre-Raphaelites, **TE:** 183. *See also* Categorized Index

Pre-Romanticism; France, **TE:** 258. *See also* Categorized Index

"Presence, The" (Everson), **AP:** 572

"Presences" (Justice), **AP:** 989

Present Company (Merwin), **AP:** 1337

Presentation Piece (Hacker), **AP:** 762

"Presented to His Highness" (Fanshawe), **BP:** 484

Prešeren, France, **TE:** 579

Pretending to Be Asleep (Davison), **AP:** 439

Preussischer Ikarus (Biermann), **EP:** 123

Prévert, Jacques, **EP:** 861-866, **TE:** 275; "Familiale," **EP:** 864

Price, Reynolds, **AP:** 1586-1589; "Copperline," **AP:** 1588; *The Laws of Ice*, **AP:** 1588; *The Use of Fire*, **AP:** 1588; *Vital Provisions*, **AP:** 1588

Prima, Diane Di. *See* Di Prima, Diane

Primate Behavior (Lindsay), **AP:** 1144

Primele Poème (Tzara), **EP:** 1047

Primero sueño. See First Dream

Primitive (Oppen), **AP:** 1480

Primitive Mentor (Young), **AP:** 2259

Primitivism, **TE:** 168; Sweden, **TE:** 544

Primo vere (D'Annunzio), **EP:** 266

Prince, F. T., **BP:** 1021-1026; *Collected Poems, 1935-1992*, **BP:** 1025; *The Doors of Stone*, **BP:** 1024; *Drypoints of the Hasidim*, **BP:** 1024; "An Epistle to a Patron," **BP:** 1023; *A Last Attachment*, **BP:** 1024; *Memoirs in Oxford*, **BP:** 1024; "Soldiers Bathing," **BP:** 1023; "To a Man on His Horse," **BP:** 1023

Prince frivole, Le (Cocteau), **EP:** 256

"Prince Potemkin" (Pasternak), **WP:** 227

"Prince's Progress, The" (Rossetti), **BP:** 1062

Princess, The (Tennyson), **BP:** 1242
Prior, Matthew, **BP:** 1026-1030; "Jinny the Just," **BP:** 1029; *Solomon on the Vanity of the World*, **BP:** 1029
Pripet Marshes, and Other Poems, The (Feldman), **AP:** 589
Prism (St. John), **AP:** 1696
Prison Poems (Berrigan), **AP:** 141
Private Life, The (Mueller), **AP:** 1384
"Pro Femina" (Kizer), **AP:** 1049
Probable Volume of Dreams, A (Bell), **AP:** 122
"Problem, The" (Emerson), **AP:** 549
Procedures for Underground (Atwood), **BP:** 42
Procession, The (Gibran), **AP:** 667
"Procura da poesia." *See* "Search for Poetry"
"Prodigal Son, The" (Różewicz), **EP:** 920
"Proem to the Courteous Reader" (Gay), **BP:** 516
"Proffer the Loaves of Pain" (Durrell), **BP:** 455
Profil group, **TE:** 557
"Progress of Poesy, The" (Gray), **BP:** 547
Projective verse, **TE:** 197
"Projective Verse" (Olson), **TE:** 205
Prolegomenon to a Theodicy, A (Rexroth), **AP:** 1625
Proletarian poetry, **TE:** 84
"Prologue Spoken at the Opening of the Duke's New Playhouse, A" (Etherege), **BP:** 479
Prologues and Epilogues (Dryden), **BP:** 437
"Prometheus" (Goethe), **EP:** 402
Prometheus Unbound (Shelley), **BP:** 1119
Promises (Warren), **AP:** 2098
Proof, The (Winters), **AP:** 2188
Propertius, Sextus, **EP:** 866-872; *Elegies*, **EP:** 869

Prophet, The (Gibran), **AP:** 667
Prophets for a New Day (Walker), **AP:** 2089
Prosanatolizmi (Elytis), **EP:** 320
Prosas Profanas, and Other Poems (Darío), **WP:** 74
Prose poem, defined, **AP:** 2302, **BP:** 1386, **EP:** 1180, **TE:** 818, **WP:** 388
Prose poetry, **TE:** 266. *See also* Categorized Index
"Prosody 101" (Pastan), **AP:** 1517
Protagoras (Simonides), **TE:** 325
"Prothalamion" (Schwartz), **AP:** 1743
Provençal poetry, **TE:** 48
Proverbios y canciones (Machado), **EP:** 637
Prudhomme, René François Armand. *See* Prudhomme, Sully
Prudhomme, Sully, **TE:** 265
PS3569.L3: Poems (Slavitt), **AP:** 1815
Psalle et sile (Calderón de la Barca), **EP:** 173
"Psalm of Life, A" (Longfellow), **TE:** 761
Psalmes of David, The (Sidney), **BP:** 1130
Psappho. *See* Sappho
Psychoanalysis, **TE:** 722
Psychological criticism, **TE:** 719-730
Psychological criticism, defined, **AP:** 2303, **BP:** 1387, **EP:** 1181, **TE:** 819, **WP:** 389
Pterodactyl Rose (Heyen), **AP:** 848
Public Speech (MacLeish), **AP:** 1252
Puella (Dickey), **AP:** 454
Puerto Rican Obituary (Pietri), **TE:** 470
Puerto Rican poetry. *See* Nuyorican poetry
Pueyrredón, José Rafael Hernández y. *See* Hernández, José
Pugachov (Esenin), **WP:** 94
Pulci, Luigi, **TE:** 382

Pulitzer Prize in Poetry, **AP:** 2328, **CM:** 62, **TE:** 882
Pun, defined, **AP:** 2303, **BP:** 1387, **EP:** 1181, **TE:** 819, **WP:** 389
Punjabi poetry. *See* Indian English poetry
Pupil, The (Merwin), **AP:** 1337
Purdy, Al, **TE:** 502
"Pure and Impure Poetry" (Warren), **TE:** 744
"Purse Seine, The" (Blackburn), **AP:** 185
Pushkin, Alexander, **TE:** 512, **WP:** 236-244; *The Bronze Horseman*, **WP:** 242; *Eugene Onegin*, **WP:** 241; *Poltava*, **WP:** 242; *Ruslan and Liudmila*, **WP:** 240
Putem zerna (Khodasevich), **WP:** 135
Pyrrhus, defined, **AP:** 2303, **BP:** 1387, **EP:** 1181, **TE:** 819, **WP:** 389
Pythagorean Silence (Howe), **AP:** 916
Pythian Ode 8 (Pindar), **EP:** 840
Pythian Ode 10 (Pindar), **EP:** 839

Qu Yuan, **TE:** 58
"Quaker Hill" (Crane), **AP:** 385
"Quality of Sprawl, The" (Murray), **BP:** 949
"Quangle Wangle's Hat, The" (Lear), **BP:** 817
Quantities (Howard), **AP:** 910
Quarles, Francis, **BP:** 1031-1036; *Divine Fancies*, **BP:** 1034
Quasimodo, Salvatore, **EP:** 873-878, **TE:** 404; *Acque e terre*, **EP:** 875; *Ed è subito sera*, **EP:** 876; *To Give and to Have*, **EP:** 877
Quatrain, defined, **AP:** 2303, **BP:** 1387, **EP:** 1181, **TE:** 819, **WP:** 389
Que linda la brisa (Baca), **AP:** 74
Que trata de España (Otero), **EP:** 762

Que van a dar en el mar. See *Clamor*

Queen's Gold Medal for Poetry, **BP:** 1413, **CM:** 63, **TE:** 883

Queer, defined, **TE:** 775

Queer theory, **TE:** 774-779

"Question Poem, The" (Booth), **AP:** 213

"Questioning Spirit, The" (Clough), **BP:** 269

Questions About Angels (Collins), **AP:** 343

Questions of Travel (Bishop), **AP:** 172

Quevedo y Villegas, Francisco Gómez de, **TE:** 594

Quilting (Clifton), **AP:** 328

Quintilian, **TE:** 455

Quiver of Arrows (Phillips), **AP:** 1530

Racin, Kosta, **TE:** 475

Racine, Louis, **TE:** 256

RADI OS I-IV (Johnson), **AP:** 979

Radiation (McPherson), **AP:** 1260

Radishchev, Aleksandr, **TE:** 511

Radnóti, Miklós, EP: 879-883, **TE:** 360; "Eighth Eclogue," **EP:** 882; "Forced March," **EP:** 882; "I Cannot Know . . .," **EP:** 881; "Law," **EP:** 880; "Like a Bull," **EP:** 881; "A Little Duck Bathes," **EP:** 882; "Razglednicas," **EP:** 883; "Second Eclogue," **EP:** 881; "Song," **EP:** 882; "War Diary," **EP:** 881

Radunitsa. See *All Soul's Day*

"Raggedy Man, The" (Riley), **AP:** 1651

Raičković, Stevan, **TE:** 571

Rain in the Trees, The (Merwin), **AP:** 1336

Raine, Craig, **TE:** 208

Rakić, Milan, **TE:** 569

Rakosi, Carl, AP: 1590-1595; "Domination of Wallace Stevens,"

AP: 1594; "The Experiment with a Rat," **AP:** 1593; "Family Portrait, Three Generations," **AP:** 1593; "A Retrospect," **AP:** 1592; "The Review," **AP:** 1594; "VI Dirge," **AP:** 1594

Ralegh, Sir Walter, BP: 1037-1043; "The 11th: and last booke of the Ocean to Scinthia," **BP:** 1041; "The Lie," **BP:** 1042

Ramal, Walter. *See* De la Mare, Walter

Ramayana, The (Vālmīki), **WP:** 310

"Ramble in St. James's Park, A" (Rochester), **BP:** 1052

Rambling Sailor, The (Mew), **BP:** 897

Rambouillet, marquise de, **TE:** 251

Rampage, The (Holub), **EP:** 496

Randall, Dudley, AP: 1595-1602; *After the Killing,* **AP:** 1600; *Cities Burning,* **AP:** 1599; *A Litany of Friends,* **AP:** 1600; *Love You,* **AP:** 1600; *Poem Counterpoem,* **AP:** 1598

Rankine, Claudia, AP: 1602-1605; *Don't Let Me Be Lonely,* **AP:** 1604; *The End of the Alphabet,* **AP:** 1603; *Nothing in Nature Is Private,* **AP:** 1603; *PLOT,* **AP:** 1603

Ransom, John Crowe, AP: 1605-1612; "Bells for John Whiteside's Daughter," **AP:** 1607; "The Equilibrists," **AP:** 1610; "Janet Waking," **AP:** 1608; "Piazza Piece," **AP:** 1609

Rape of Lucrece, The (Shakespeare), **BP:** 1106

Rape of the Lock, The (Pope), **BP:** 1010

"Rapids, The" (Barnard), **AP:** 103

Raport z oblężonego miasta i inne wiersze. See *Report from the Besieged City, and Other Poems*

Ravenna (Wilde), **BP:** 1305

"Ravens, the Sexton, and the Earth-Worm, The" (Gay), **BP:** 518

Raw Flesh (Popa), **EP:** 859

Raw Heaven (Peacock), **AP:** 1527

Rayons et les ombres, Les (Hugo), **EP:** 523

"Razglednicas" (Radnóti), **EP:** 883

"Reach Road" (Booth), **AP:** 215

"Reader, The" (Lewis), **AP:** 1134

"Reading on the Beach" (Jacobsen), **AP:** 952

Realism; Croatia, **TE:** 74; Germany, **TE:** 302; Scandinavia, **TE:** 537. *See also* Categorized Index

Realism, defined, **AP:** 2303, **BP:** 1387, **EP:** 1181, **TE:** 819, **WP:** 389

"Reality [*dreamed*], A" (Ekelöf), **EP:** 310

Really Short Poems of A. R. Ammons, The (Ammons), **AP:** 41

Reardon Poems, The (Blackburn), **AP:** 187

Reasons for Moving (Strand), **AP:** 1921

Rebellion Is the Circle of a Lover's Hands (Espada), **AP:** 561

Rèbora, Clemente, **TE:** 406

Recent Poems (Kavanagh), **BP:** 729

"Récit d'un berger" (Malherbe), **EP:** 641

Reckoner (Tate), **AP:** 1954

Records of Women, with Other Poems (Hemans), **BP:** 611

Recycling (Różewicz), **EP:** 923

Red Beans (Cruz), **AP:** 403

Red Bird (Oliver), **AP:** 1468

Red Carpet for the Sun, A (Layton), **BP:** 810

Red Coal, The (Stern), **AP:** 1897

Red Gaze, The (Guest), **AP:** 747

"Red Herring, The" (MacBeth), **BP:** 845

Red House, The (Orr), **AP:** 1489

Red Leaves of Night, The (St. John), **AP:** 1696

Red Suitcase (Nye), **AP:** 1439

Red Trousseau (Muske), **AP:** 1398

Redoble de consciencia (Otero),
EP: 761

Reed, E. *See* Evans, Mari

Reed, Henry, **BP:** 1043-1048;
"Lessons of the War," **BP:** 1046;
"A Map of Verona," **BP:** 1045;
"Tintagel," **BP:** 1046; "Triptych,"
BP: 1046

Reed, Ishmael, **AP:** 1612-1616;
Chattanooga, **AP:** 1614; *Conjure*,
AP: 1614; *Points of View*,
AP: 1614

Reese, Lizette Woodworth,
AP: 1616-1621; "In Time of
Grief," **AP:** 1619; *Little Henrietta*,
AP: 1620; *Spicewood*, **AP:** 1619;
"Tears," **AP:** 1619; *Wild Cherry*,
AP: 1619

Reflections on Espionage (Hollander),
AP: 880

"Refrigerium" (Tuckerman),
AP: 2000

"Refugee Ship" (Cervantes), **AP:** 299

Refusing Heaven (Gilbert), **AP:** 676

Regarding Wave (Snyder), **AP:** 1847

Region of Unlikeness (Graham),
AP: 730

Regional poetry, Italy, **TE:** 397

Régnier, Henri de, **TE:** 269

Regrets, The (Du Bellay), **EP:** 291

Regular meter, defined, **AP:** 2303,
BP: 1387, **EP:** 1181, **TE:** 819,
WP: 389

Reichenthal, Laura. *See* Riding, Laura

Reis, Ricardo. *See* Pessoa, Fernando

Rej, Mikolaj, **TE:** 489

Rejoicings (Stern), **AP:** 1895

Relations (Booth), **AP:** 212

Relations (Grennan), **AP:** 743

"Relationship of the Poet to
Daydreaming, The" (Freud),
TE: 722

Relative stress, defined, **AP:** 2303,

BP: 1387, **EP:** 1181, **TE:** 819,
WP: 389

Relief of America, The (Glancy),
AP: 705

Religio Laici (Dryden), **BP:** 439

Religione del mio tempo, La
(Pasolini), **EP:** 781

Religious poetry; England, **TE:** 138,
TE: 149, **TE:** 168; France,
TE: 256; Hungary, **TE:** 353;
Iceland, **TE:** 527; Italy, **TE:** 377,
TE: 406; Poland, **TE:** 489. *See
also* Categorized Index

Reliquiae Juveniles (Watts), **BP:** 1301

Remains, in Verse and Prose
(Hallam), **BP:** 576

Remains of Elmet (Hughes), **BP:** 692

Remedia amoris. *See Cure for Love*

"Remembering Marie A." (Brecht),
EP: 153

"Remembering Nat Turner" (Brown),
AP: 258

"Remembrance" (Byron), **BP:** 190

"Remembrance from a Dream in
1963" (Różewicz), **EP:** 922

"Reminder, The" (Adams), **AP:** 8

Renaissance. *See* Categorized Index

Renaissance; Catalan, **TE:** 49;
criticism, **TE:** 703; Croatia,
TE: 72; England, **TE:** 145;
France, **TE:** 245; Hungary,
TE: 352; Italy, **TE:** 381; Latin
poetry, **TE:** 463; Poland, **TE:** 489

Renaixença, **TE:** 51

Rendezvous with America (Tolson),
AP: 1986

"Renegade Wants Words, The"
(Welch), **AP:** 2109

Renga (Paz), **WP:** 234

Renga (poetic form), **TE:** 420

Renga (Tomlinson et al.), **TE:** 200

Repair (Williams), **AP:** 2166

"Reply to Matthew Arnold of My
Fifth Day in Fano, A" (Wright),
AP: 2230

*Report from the Besieged City, and
Other Poems* (Herbert), **EP:** 463

"Repression of War Experience"
(Sassoon), **BP:** 1084

Republic (Plato), **TE:** 700

Republic of Poetry, The (Espada),
AP: 562

Requiem (Akhmatova), **WP:** 7

"Requiem for 1945" (Pinter),
BP: 1003

Rerum natura, De. *See On the Nature
of Things*

Rescue the Dead (Ignatow), **AP:** 946

Rescued Year, The (Stafford), **AP:** 1877

Residence on Earth, and Other Poems
(Neruda), **WP:** 200

Residencia en la tierra. *See
Residence on Earth, and Other
Poems*

"Residue" (Drummond de Andrade),
WP: 81

Residue of Song (Bell), **AP:** 122

"Resíduo." *See* "Residue"

Resistance poetry; Italy, **TE:** 407

Resolution, defined, **AP:** 2303,
BP: 1387, **EP:** 1181, **TE:** 819,
WP: 389

Resort, and Other Poems (Hampl),
AP: 787

*Résponce aux injures et calomnies de
je ne sçay quels prédicans et
ministres de Genève* (Ronsard),
EP: 916

Restoration. *See* Categorized Index

Restoration poetry, **TE:** 620-625

Restorative poetry, Native American,
TE: 479

"Reszket a bokor, mert" (Petőfi),
EP: 824

Retenue d'amours (Charles
d'Orléans), **EP:** 233

Retornos de lo vivo lejano (Alberti),
EP: 10

Retrieval System, The (Kumin),
AP: 1077

"Retrospect, A" (Rakosi), **AP:** 1592

"Return, The" (Bontemps), **AP:** 207

Return, The (Tomlinson), **BP:** 1274

"Return of Aphrodite, The" (Sarton), **AP:** 1720

Return of Martin Fierro, The (Hernández), **WP:** 116

"Return of the Goddess" (Graves), **BP:** 540

Return to My Native Land (Césaire), **WP:** 59

Return to the City of White Donkeys (Tate), **AP:** 1958

Returning to Earth (Harrison), **AP:** 808

Reuterswärd, Carl Fredrik, **TE:** 554

Revard, Carter, **TE:** 485

Reverdy, Pierre, **EP:** 883-889, **TE:** 275; "Carrefour," **EP:** 885; *Le Chant des morts*, **EP:** 888; "Enfin," **EP:** 888; "Et Maintenant," **EP:** 888; "Guerre," **EP:** 886; "Main-Morte," **EP:** 887; "Mémoire," **EP:** 887

Reverend Ghost, The (Garrett), **AP:** 658

Reviczky, Gyula, **TE:** 358

"Review, The" (Rakosi), **AP:** 1594

Revista Bilingüe, La (journal), **TE:** 466

Revista Chicano-Riqueña (journal), **TE:** 466

Revolutionary Letters (Di Prima), **AP:** 469

Revolutionary Petunias, and Other Poems (Walker), **AP:** 2083

"Revolutions, Les" (Lamartine), **EP:** 595

Rexroth, Kenneth, **AP:** 1621-1627, **TE:** 663; *The Collected Longer Poems*, **AP:** 1625; *The Collected Shorter Poems*, **AP:** 1624; *The Dragon and the Unicorn*, **AP:** 1625; *The Heart's Garden, the Garden's Heart*, **AP:** 1625;

The Phoenix and the Tortoise, **AP:** 1625; *A Prolegomenon to a Theodicy*, **AP:** 1625

Reyes, Alfonso, **WP:** 245-250; "Jacob," **WP:** 249; "Lamentación de Navidad," **WP:** 249; "Sopa," **WP:** 249

Reznikoff, Charles, **AP:** 1627-1632; *Holocaust*, **AP:** 1631; *Jews in Babylonia*, **AP:** 1631; *Testimony*, **AP:** 1631

Rhapsody in Plain Yellow (Chin), **AP:** 310

Rhetorical poetry, **TE:** 292

Rhétoriqueurs, **TE:** 247

Rhodius, Apollonius. *See* Apollonius Rhodius

"Rhodora, The" (Emerson), **AP:** 550

"Rhotruda" (Tuckerman), **AP:** 2000

Rhyme, **TE:** 752

Rhyme, defined, **AP:** 2303, **BP:** 1387, **EP:** 1181, **TE:** 819, **WP:** 389

Rhyme scheme, defined, **AP:** 2303, **BP:** 1387, **EP:** 1181, **TE:** 819, **WP:** 389

Rhymes, The (Bécquer), **EP:** 98

Rhymes (Petrarch), **TE:** 380

Rhymes of a Pfc (Kirstein), **AP:** 1044

"Rhyming Poems" (Lawrence), **BP:** 798

Rhythm, Content, and Flavor (Cruz), **AP:** 403

Riba, Carles, **TE:** 52

Ribbons (Heyen), **AP:** 848

Rich, Adrienne, **AP:** 1633-1641; *A Change of World*, **AP:** 1635; *The Diamond Cutters*, **AP:** 1635; *Diving into the Wreck*, **AP:** 1637; *The Dream of a Common Language*, **AP:** 1638; *Fox*, **AP:** 1640; "From an Old House in America," **AP:** 1638; *Leaflets*, **AP:** 1636; *Midnight Salvage*, **AP:** 1640; *Necessities of Life*,

AP: 1636; *Poems*, **AP:** 1637; *Snapshots of a Daughter-in-Law*, **AP:** 1635; *Time's Power*, **AP:** 1639; "Transcendental Etude," **AP:** 1639; *A Wild Patience Has Taken Me This Far*, **AP:** 1639; *The Will to Change*, **AP:** 1637; *Your Native Land, Your Life*, **AP:** 1639

Rich, Barbara. *See* Riding, Laura

"Rick of Green Wood, The" (Dorn), **AP:** 476

Riding, Laura, **AP:** 1642-1645; *The Close Chaplet*, **AP:** 1643; *Love as Love, Death as Death*, **AP:** 1644

"Riding a One-Eyed Horse" (Taylor), **AP:** 1971

Riding Jackson, Laura. *See* Riding, Laura

Rifbjerg, Klaus, **TE:** 562

Riffaterre, Michael, **TE:** 752

Right Madness on Skye, The (Hugo), **AP:** 936

Rijmsnoer (Gezelle), **EP:** 390

Riley, James Whitcomb, **AP:** 1645-1653; "Knee-Deep in June," **AP:** 1650; "Little Orphant Annie," **AP:** 1651; "Nothin' to Say," **AP:** 1650; "The Old Man and Jim," **AP:** 1650; "The Old Swimmin'-Hole," **AP:** 1652; "The Raggedy Man," **AP:** 1651; "When the Frost Is on the Punkin," **AP:** 1650

Rilke, Rainer Maria, **EP:** 889-897, **TE:** 304; *The Book of Hours*, **EP:** 893; *The Book of Images*, **EP:** 893; *Dinggedichte*, **EP:** 894; *Duino Elegies*, **EP:** 895; *Mir zur Feier*, **EP:** 892; *New Poems*, **EP:** 894; "The Panther," **EP:** 895; *Sonnets to Orpheus*, **EP:** 895

Rimado de palaçio (Ayala), **TE:** 590

Rimas. See *Rhymes, The*

Rimbaud, Arthur, **EP:** 897-904,

TE: 268, TE: 641; "Bad Blood,"
    EP: 901; Paul Claudel, EP: 247;
    "Deliria I," EP: 901; "Deliria II,"
    EP: 901; "The Drunken Boat,"
    EP: 899; "Farewell," EP: 902;
    Illuminations, EP: 902, TE: 268;
    "The Impossible," EP: 902;
    "Lightning," EP: 902; "Morning,"
    EP: 902; "Night in Hell,"
    EP: 901; *A Season in Hell*,
    EP: 900, TE: 268; "Seer Letter,"
    EP: 899; "Vowels," EP: 900
Rime (Bembo), EP: 105
Rime (Stampa), EP: 995
Rime of the Ancient Mariner, The
    (Coleridge), BP: 280
"Rime of the Swallows" (Bécquer),
    EP: 100
Rime royal, defined, AP: 2304,
    BP: 1388, EP: 1182, TE: 820,
    WP: 390
Rímur (poetic form), TE: 529
Rinaldo (Tasso), EP: 1017
Ring and the Book, The (Browning),
    BP: 165
Río, un amor, Un (Cernuda), EP: 223
Ríos, Alberto, AP: 1654-1657; *The*
    Smallest Muscle in the Human
    Body, AP: 1655; *The Theater of*
    Night, AP: 1656; *Whispering to*
    Fool the Wind, AP: 1655
Riprap (Snyder), AP: 1845
Rising and Falling (Matthews),
    AP: 1286
Risorgimento. *See* Categorized Index
Ritsos, Yannis, EP: 904-911,
    TE: 345; "The Burial of Orgaz,"
    EP: 909; "Engraving," EP: 908;
    Epitaphios, EP: 908, TE: 345;
    The Moonlight Sonata, EP: 910,
    TE: 346; *Philoktetes*, EP: 910; *To*
    Tragoudi tes adelphes mou,
    EP: 908
"Ritual I" (Blackburn), AP: 184
"Ritual IV" (Blackburn), AP: 185

Ritual poetry, Native American,
    TE: 479
Riven Doggeries (Tate), AP: 1953
"River, The" (Crane), AP: 382
River at Wolf, The (Valentine),
    AP: 2026
"River by Our Village, The" (Du Fu),
    WP: 88
River of Heaven, The (Hongo),
    AP: 904
River Sound, The (Merwin),
    AP: 1337
River Writing (Applewhite), AP: 52
Rivera, Tomás, AP: 1657-1660;
    Always, and Other Poems,
    AP: 1659; "M'ijo no mira nada,"
    AP: 1659; "The Searchers,"
    AP: 1659
"Riverman, The" (Bishop), AP: 173
"Rivers, The" (Ungaretti), EP: 1060
"Road to Shu Is Hard, The" (Li Bo),
    WP: 155
"Robe, The" (McClure), AP: 1209
"Robin Redbreast" (Kunitz),
    AP: 1088
"Robinson" (Kees), AP: 1009
Robinson, Edwin Arlington,
    AP: 1660-1668; "Eros Turannos,"
    AP: 1664; "How Annandale Went
    Out," AP: 1667; "Luke Havergal,"
    AP: 2273, BP: 1357, EP: 1151,
    TE: 789, WP: 359; "The Whip,"
    AP: 1666
Rochester, John Wilmot, earl of,
    BP: 1048-1055, TE: 620; "An
    Epistolary Essay from M. G. to
    O. B. upon their Mutual Poems,"
    BP: 1054; "Fair Chloris in a
    pigsty lay," BP: 1052; "A Ramble
    in St. James's Park," BP: 1052; "A
    Satire Against Mankind,"
    BP: 1053; "A Song," BP: 1051;
    "Timon," BP: 1052
Rock and Shell (Wheelwright),
    AP: 2128

Rock-Tree Boy. See Momaday,
    N. Scott
Roderick, the Last of the Goths
    (Southey), BP: 1175
Rodgers, Carolyn M., AP: 1668-
    1671; *The Heart as Ever Green*,
    AP: 1670; *How I Got Ovah*,
    AP: 1670; *Paper Soul*, AP: 1669;
    Songs of a Blackbird, AP: 1670
Roethke, Theodore, AP: 1671-1679;
    The Far Field, AP: 1677; "In a
    Dark Time," AP: 1677; *Open*
    House, AP: 1674; *Sequence,*
    Sometimes Metaphysical,
    AP: 1677; "The Visitant,"
    AP: 1674; and David Wagoner,
    AP: 2059; *The Waking*, AP: 1675;
    Words for the Wind, AP: 1676
"Roger Casement" (Colum), BP: 294
Rogers, Pattiann, AP: 1679-1682;
    Generations, AP: 1681;
    Geocentric, AP: 1680; *Legendary*
    Performance, AP: 1680; *Spitting*
    and Binding, AP: 1680
Roiç de Corella, Joan, TE: 50
Roig, Jaume, TE: 50
Roland, Alan, TE: 726
Rolfe, Edwin, AP: 1682-1686; *First*
    Love, and Other Poems,
    AP: 1684; *Permit Me Refuge*,
    AP: 1684; *To My*
    Contemporaries, AP: 1683
Roman de la rose. See Romance of
    the Rose, The
Roman de Renart, TE: 241
Roman Elegies (Goethe), EP: 402
Roman Empire. *See* Geographical
    Index
Roman period, Greece, TE: 329
"Romance" (Poe), AP: 1564
Romance of the Rose, The (Guillaume
    de Lorris and Jean de Meung),
    EP: 426, TE: 240
"Romance sonambulo." *See*
    "Somnambule Ballad"

Romancero gitano. See Gypsy
Ballads of García Lorca, The
Romances; England, **TE:** 124;
France, **TE:** 239; Germany,
TE: 286; Middle English,
TE: 105
Romances sans paroles. See
Romances Without Words
Romances Without Words (Verlaine),
EP: 1097, **TE:** 268
Romania. *See* Geographical Index
Romano, Enotrio. *See* Carducci,
Giosuè
Romanticism; criticism, **TE:** 708;
Croatian, **TE:** 73; Czech poetry,
TE: 81; definition of, **TE:** 298;
England, **TE:** 176, **TE:** 626-632;
France, **TE:** 258; Germany,
TE: 298; Hungary, **TE:** 355;
Poland, **TE:** 492; Scandinavia,
TE: 533; Serbia, **TE:** 567;
Slovakia, **TE:** 574; Spain,
TE: 597; twentieth century,
TE: 191. *See also* Categorized
Index
Romanticism, American. *See*
Categorized Index
Romanticism, defined, **AP:** 2304,
BP: 1388, **EP:** 1182, **TE:** 820,
WP: 390
Romanzero (Heine), **EP:** 457
Romero, Alberto, **TE:** 471
*Römische Elegien. See Roman
Elegies*
Rommel Drives on Deep into Egypt
(Brautigan), **AP:** 242
Rondeau, defined, **AP:** 2304,
BP: 1388, **EP:** 1182, **TE:** 820,
WP: 390
Rondel. *See* Rondeau
Rondisti, **TE:** 407
Ronsard, Pierre de, **EP:** 912-917,
TE: 247; "Darling, Let Us Go,"
EP: 915; "Hymn to Death,"
EP: 916; *Résponce aux injures et*

*calomnies de je ne sçay quels
prédicans et ministres de Genève*,
EP: 916; "When You Are Old,"
EP: 916
Roof of Tiger Lilies, A (Hall),
AP: 779
"Room, The" (Aiken), **AP:** 16
Room of One's Own, A (Woolf),
TE: 738
Rooms (Glancy), **AP:** 706
Roosevelt and the Antinoe, The
(Pratt), **BP:** 1019
Rootless (Ehrhart), **AP:** 534
Roots and Branches (Duncan),
AP: 514
Rosa do povo, A; Drummond de
Andrade, **WP:** 81
*Rosa profunda, La. See Gold of
Tigers, The*
"Rosas amo dos jardins do Adónis,
As." *See* "Roses of the Gardens of
Adonis, The"
"Rose, The" (Fanshawe), **BP:** 484
Rose, Wendy, **TE:** 485
Rose Garden, The (Saʿdi), **WP:** 262
Rose of Solitude, The (Everson),
AP: 575
Rosenberg, Isaac, **BP:** 1055-1059;
"Dead Man's Dump," **BP:** 1058;
Moses, **BP:** 1057; "Night and
Day," **BP:** 1057; "On Receiving
News of the War," **BP:** 1057;
Youth, **BP:** 1057
Rosenstock, Sami. *See* Tzara, Tristan
"Roses of the Gardens of Adonis,
The" (Pessoa), **EP:** 815
"Rosina Alcona to Julius Brenzaida"
(Brontë), **BP:** 141
Rossetti, Christina, **BP:** 1060-1065;
"From House to Home,"
BP: 1062; "Goblin Market,"
BP: 1062; "The Iniquity of the
Fathers, upon the Children,"
BP: 1063; "The Lowest Room,"
BP: 1063; "Maiden Song,"

BP: 1063; "The Prince's
Progress," **BP:** 1062
Rossetti, Dante Gabriel, **BP:** 1065-
1073, **TE:** 183; "The Blessed
Damozel," **BP:** 1068; "The
Bride's Prelude," **BP:** 1068; *The
House of Life*, **BP:** 1070; "Jenny,"
BP: 1069; "A Last Confession,"
BP: 1069; "The Stream's Secret,"
BP: 1070
Rossi, Matti, **TE:** 559
Rothschild, Dorothy. *See* Parker,
Dorothy
Roucher, Jean-Antoine, **TE:** 257
Rough Field, The (Montague),
BP: 918
Rounding the Horn (Slavitt), **AP:** 1813
Rousseau, Jean-Baptiste, **TE:** 255
Roux, Paul-Pierre. *See* Saint-Pol-
Roux
Rov. See Ditch, The
"Royalist, The" (Fanshawe), **BP:** 484
Różewicz, Tadeusz, **EP:** 917-924;
"Alpha," **EP:** 923; "Falling,"
EP: 921; "I Am a Realist,"
EP: 922; "I Screamed in the
Night," **EP:** 920; "I See the Mad,"
EP: 919; "The Prodigal Son,"
EP: 920; *Recycling*, **EP:** 923;
"Remembrance from a Dream in
1963," **EP:** 922; "To the Heart,"
EP: 922
"Rózsabokor a dombodalon"
(Petőfi), **EP:** 825
"r-p-o-p-h-e-s-s-a-g-r" (Cummings),
AP: 413
Ruan Ji, **TE:** 59, **WP:** 250-254; "The
Doves," **WP:** 252; "Monkey,"
WP: 253
Rubailer. See Rubaiyat
Rubaiyat (Hikmet), **WP:** 122
Rubáiyát, The (Omar Khayyám),
WP: 211
Rubáiyát of Omar Kháyyám
(FitzGerald), **BP:** 497

Rubaiyat stanza, defined, **AP:** 2304, **BP:** 1388, **EP:** 1182, **TE:** 820, **WP:** 390

Rue Wilson Monday (Hollo), **AP:** 890

Rúfus, Milan, **TE:** 577

"Rug, The" (McClure), **AP:** 1209

Ruining the New Road (Matthews), **AP:** 1286

Ruiz, José Martínez. *See* Azorín

Rukeyser, Muriel, **AP:** 1686-1692; "Ajanta," **AP:** 1689; "The Gates," **AP:** 1691; "Letter, Unposted," **AP:** 1690; "Lives," **AP:** 1689; *The Speed of Darkness*, **AP:** 1690; *Theory of Flight*, **AP:** 1688; *A Turning Wind*, **AP:** 1688; *U.S. 1*, **AP:** 1688

Rules of Sleep (Moss), **AP:** 1378

Rulfo Prize for Latin American and Caribbean Literature. *See* Juan Rulfo Prize for Latin American and Caribbean Literature

Rūmī, Jalāl al-Dīn, **WP:** 255-259; *The Mathnavī of Jalālu'ddīn Rūmī*, **WP:** 257; *The Sufi Path of Love*, **WP:** 257

Run of Jacks, A (Hugo), **AP:** 935

Run with the Hunted (Bukowski), **AP:** 268

"Runagate Runagate" (Hayden), **TE:** 11

"Runes" (Nemerov), **AP:** 1413

Runius, Johan, **TE:** 530

"Running" (Galvin), **AP:** 647, **AP:** 2155

Running Late (Abse), **BP:** 4

Rushdie, Salman, **TE:** 772

Ruskin, John, **TE:** 731

Ruslan and Liudmila (Pushkin), **WP:** 240

Russell, George William. *See* Æ

Russia. *See* Geographical Index

Russian poetry, **TE:** 509-525

Ruth Lilly Poetry Prize, **AP:** 2325, **CM:** 57, **TE:** 877

"S veselym rzhaniem pasutsia tabuny." *See* "Happily Neighing, the Herds Graze"

Saarikoski, Pentti, **TE:** 558

Saavedra, Ángel de, **TE:** 597

Saba, Umberto, **EP:** 925-930, **TE:** 404; "Ashes," **EP:** 929; *Il canzoniere*, **EP:** 927; "Ulysses," **EP:** 929; "Winter Noon," **EP:** 929

Sabbaths (Berry), **AP:** 152

Sachs, Leonie. *See* Sachs, Nelly

Sachs, Nelly, **EP:** 930-935; "Butterfly," **EP:** 934; "Chorus of the Stones," **EP:** 933; "Dancer," **EP:** 934; "Fleeing," **EP:** 934; "Halleluja," **EP:** 933; *In den Wohnungen des Todes*, **EP:** 932; "In the Blue Distance," **EP:** 934; "Melusine, If Your Well Had Not," **EP:** 933; "She Dances," **EP:** 934; *Sternverdunkelung*, **EP:** 933

Sackville, Charles, earl of Dorset, **TE:** 620

Sackville, Thomas, **BP:** 1074-1080; "Complaint of Henry, Duke of Buckingham," **BP:** 1078; "Induction," **BP:** 1077; *A Mirror for Magistrates*, **BP:** 1076

Sacraments of Desire, The (Gregg), **AP:** 737

Sacred Hymns, The (Manzoni), **EP:** 664

Sacrifice, The (Bidart), **AP:** 165

Sa'di, **WP:** 260-264; *The Orchard*, **WP:** 261; *The Rose Garden*, **WP:** 262

Sadness and Happiness (Pinsky), **AP:** 1540

Sagan om Fatumeh (Ekelöf), **EP:** 312

"Sage Architect" (Duncan), **AP:** 514

"Sage in the Sierra, The" (Van Doren), **AP:** 2030

Sagesse (Verlaine), **EP:** 1097

Sagittal Section (Holub), **EP:** 494

Sah-name (Firdusi), **WP:** 98

Sahtouris, Miltos, **TE:** 349

Said, Edward W., **TE:** 769

Saikaku. *See* Ihara Saikaku

"Sail, The" (Lermontov), **WP:** 145

Sailing Alone Around the Room (Collins), **AP:** 345

"Sailing to Byzantium" (Yeats), **BP:** 1345, **TE:** 193

St. John, David, **AP:** 1693-1698; *The Face*, **AP:** 1697; *In the Pines*, **AP:** 1696; *No Heaven*, **AP:** 1695; *Prism*, **AP:** 1696; *The Red Leaves of Night*, **AP:** 1696; *The Shore*, **AP:** 1695; *Study for the World's Body*, **AP:** 1696; *Terraces of Rain*, **AP:** 1696

Saint John of the Cross. *See* John of the Cross, Saint

Saint Judas (Wright), **AP:** 2225

Saint-Lambert, Jean-François, marquis de, **TE:** 256

St. Lucia. *See* Geographical Index

Saint Peter Relates an Incident (Johnson), **AP:** 974

Saint Peter's Complaint (Southwell), **BP:** 1181

Saint-Pol-Roux, **TE:** 270

"Saint Scholastica" (Castro), **EP:** 196

St. Vincent Millay, Edna. *See* Millay, Edna St. Vincent

"Sainte Mary Magdalen" (Crashaw), **BP:** 340

"Saints" (Everson), **AP:** 574

Saints and Strangers (Hudgins), **AP:** 925

"Saint's Encouragement, The" (Fanshawe), **BP:** 483

Saints in Their Ox-Hide Boat (Galvin), **AP:** 649

Saitō Mokichi, **TE:** 428

Salamancan poets, **TE:** 593

Salinas, Pedro, **EP:** 936-941, **TE:** 600; *Confianza*, **EP:** 940; "Here," **EP:** 938; *My Voice*

Because of You, **EP:** 939; *The Sea of San Juan*, **EP:** 940; "Sheet of Paper," **EP:** 938; *Todo más claro, y otros poemas*, **EP:** 940; "Yes, Too Much of Everything," **EP:** 939

Salt Garden, The (Nemerov), **AP:** 1412

Salustri, Carlo Alberto, **TE:** 399

"Salvo for Hans Hofmann, A" (Kees), **AP:** 1010

Samarkand and Other Markets I Have Known (Soyinka), **WP:** 279

Samisdat Poems, The (Ehrhart), **AP:** 534

Samson Agonistes (Milton), **BP:** 912

Samyro, S. *See* Tzara, Tristan

San Francisco Renaissance, **TE:** 663

Sanchez, Carol Lee, **TE:** 483

Sánchez, Ricardo, **TE:** 468

Sanchez, Sonia, **AP:** 1698-1703; *Does Your House Have Lions?*, **AP:** 1701; *Homegirls and Handgrenades*, **AP:** 1700; *Shake Loose My Skin*, **AP:** 1702; *We a BaddDDD People*, **AP:** 1701

Sand and Foam (Gibran), **AP:** 668

"Sand Martin" (Clare), **BP:** 258

Sandburg, Carl, **AP:** 1704-1711; *Breathing Tokens*, **AP:** 1710; *Chicago Poems*, **AP:** 1709; *Complete Poems*, **AP:** 1710; *Cornhuskers*, **AP:** 1709; *Good Morning, America*, **AP:** 1709; *Harvest Poems, 1910-1960*, **AP:** 1710; *Honey and Salt*, **AP:** 1710; *The People, Yes*, **AP:** 1709; *Slabs of the Sunburnt West*, **AP:** 1709; *Smoke and Steel*, **AP:** 1709

Sanders, Ed, **TE:** 675

"Sandpiper" (Bishop), **AP:** 171

Sangschaw (MacDiarmid), **BP:** 848

"Sanies I" (Beckett), **EP:** 93

Sannazzaro, Jacopo, **TE:** 382

Sanqu, **TE:** 64

Sant Jordi, Jordi de, **TE:** 49

"Santa Escolástica." *See* "Saint Scholastica"

Santillana, Juana Inés de Asbaje y Ramírez de. *See* Cruz, Sor Juana Inés de la

Santos, Sherod, **AP:** 1711-1714; *Accidental Weather*, **AP:** 1713; *The Perishing*, **AP:** 1714; *The Pilot Star Elegies*, **AP:** 1713; *The Southern Reaches*, **AP:** 1713

Sapphics Against Anger, and Other Poems (Steele), **AP:** 1883

Sappho, **EP:** 941-949, **TE:** 223, **TE:** 321; 16 L.-P., **EP:** 945; 94 L.-P., **EP:** 946; 112 L.-P., **EP:** 948; "Ode to Anactoria," **EP:** 945; "Ode to Aphrodite," **EP:** 944

"Sappho's Last Song" (Leopardi), **EP:** 613

Sarah Bernhardt's Leg (Kirby), **AP:** 1041

Sarjúrendek (Illyés), **EP:** 530

Sarmiento, Félix Rubén García. *See* Darío, Rubén

Saroyan, Aram, **TE:** 675

Sarton, Eléanore Marie. *See* Sarton, May

Sarton, May, **AP:** 1714-1724; *Coming into Eighty*, **AP:** 1723; "A Divorce of Lovers," **AP:** 1720; "The Godhead as Lynx," **AP:** 1720; "An Invocation to Kali," **AP:** 1721; "Journey Toward Poetry," **AP:** 1719; *Letters from Maine*, **AP:** 1722; "The Muse as Medusa," **AP:** 1721; "My Sisters, O My Sisters," **AP:** 1718; "Of the Muse," **AP:** 1722; "Poets and the Rain," **AP:** 1719; "The Return of Aphrodite," **AP:** 1720; *The Silence Now*, **AP:** 1723; "These Images Remain," **AP:** 1720

Sartorius, Joachim, **TE:** 317

Sarvig, Ole, **TE:** 550

Sashun, Sigmund. *See* Sassoon, Siegfried

Sa-skya Pandita, **TE:** 608

Sassoon, Siegfried, **BP:** 1080-1087; "The Dug Out," **BP:** 1085; "Everyone Sang," **BP:** 1085; "Lines Written in Anticipation . . . ," **BP:** 1085; "Repression of War Experience," **BP:** 1084; *Sequences*, **BP:** 1086; "They," **BP:** 1084

Satan in Search of a Wife (Lamb), **BP:** 773

Satan Says (Olds), **AP:** 1458

Satire (Ariosto). *See* Ariostos Satyres

"Satire Against Mankind, A" (Rochester), **BP:** 1053

Satire 3 (Juvenal), **EP:** 556

Satire 10 (Juvenal), **EP:** 556

Satires (Horace), **EP:** 514

Satires (Persius), **EP:** 807

Satires of Circumstance (Hardy), **BP:** 585

Satiric poetry; England, **TE:** 138, **TE:** 161; Latin, **TE:** 456; Restoration, **TE:** 156, **TE:** 621. *See also* Categorized Index

Satirical poetry; England, **TE:** 163

Satura (Montale), **EP:** 726

Satura (poetic form), **TE:** 443

Saturae. *See* *Satires* (Persius)

Satyrs upon the Jesuits (Oldham), **BP:** 970

Sauser, Frédéric. *See* Cendrars, Blaise

Saussure, Ferdinand de, **TE:** 750, **TE:** 775, **TE:** 780

Save the Last Dance (Stern), **AP:** 1903

Saving Daylight (Harrison), **AP:** 812

Saving the Young Men of Vienna (Kirby), **AP:** 1041

Savings (Hogan), **AP:** 875

"Savoy" (O'Hara), **AP:** 1454

Say It (Flint), **AP:** 608

Say Pardon (Ignatow), **AP:** 945

Sayles, Thelma Lucille. *See* Clifton, Lucille

Scalapino, Leslie, AP: 1724-1727; *Considering How Exaggerated Music Is*, **AP:** 1726; *Way*, **AP:** 1726; *Zither and Autobiography*, **AP:** 1727

Scandinavian poetry, **TE:** 526-565

Scansion, defined, **AP:** 2304, **BP:** 1388, **EP:** 1182, **TE:** 820, **WP:** 390

Scapigliatura movement, **TE:** 393

Scar literature (China), **TE:** 67

Scar Tissue (Wright), **AP:** 2215

Scars (Meinke), **AP:** 1293

Scattered Chapters (Wormser), **AP:** 2202

Scattered Returns (Sissman), **AP:** 1805

Scattering of Salts, A (Merrill), **AP:** 1323

Schade, Jens August, **TE:** 548

Scherzer, Rosalie Beatrice Ruth. *See* Ausländer, Rose

Schiller, Friedrich, EP: 949-956, **TE:** 296; *Anthologie auf das Jahr 1782*, **EP:** 951; "The Cranes of Ibycus," **EP:** 955; "The Gods of Greece," **EP:** 954; "The Song of the Bell," **EP:** 955

Schionatulander and Sigune (Wolfram von Eschenbach), **EP:** 1133

Schlauch, Margaret, **TE:** 761

"Schlechte Zeit für Lyrik." *See* "Bad Time for Poetry"

Schnackenberg, Gjertrud, AP: 1728-1732; *A Gilded Lapse of Time*, **AP:** 1730; *The Lamplit Answer*, **AP:** 1729; *Portraits and Elegies*, **AP:** 1729; *Supernatural Love*, **AP:** 1731; *The Throne of Labdacus*, **AP:** 1730

"Scholar-Gipsy, The" (Arnold), **BP:** 34

"Schöne Jugend." *See* "Beautiful Youth"

School Figures (Song), **AP:** 1855

"School of Eloquence, The" (Harrison), **BP:** 591

School of Udhra (Mackey), **AP:** 1242

Schuyler, James, AP: 1732-1738, **TE:** 674; "The Morning of the Poem," **AP:** 1735; "Song," **AP:** 1735

Schwartz, Delmore, AP: 1738-1746, **TE:** 669; "The Ballad of the Children of the Czar," **AP:** 1741; "A Dog Named Ego, the Snowflakes as Kisses," **AP:** 1743; "Far Rockaway," **AP:** 1742; "The Heavy Bear Who Goes with Me," **AP:** 1743; "In the Naked Bed, in Plato's Cave," **AP:** 1742; "Prothalamion," **AP:** 1743; "Seurat's Sunday Afternoon Along the Seine," **AP:** 1744; *Summer Knowledge*, **AP:** 1744; "Tired and Unhappy, You Think of Houses," **AP:** 1742

Scillaes Metamorphosis (Lodge), **BP:** 821

"Scissor-Man" (MacBeth), **BP:** 845

Scotland. *See* Geographical Index

Scott, First Baronet. *See* Scott, Sir Walter

Scott, Sir Walter, BP: 1087-1093, **TE:** 178, **TE:** 629; *The Lady of the Lake*, **BP:** 1091; *The Lay of the Last Minstrel*, **BP:** 1090; *The Minstrelsy of the Scottish Border*, **BP:** 1090

Scott, Winfield Townley, AP: 1746-1749; *Biography of Traman*, **AP:** 1748; *New and Selected Poems*, **AP:** 1748; *Scrimshaw*, **AP:** 1748; *To Marry Strangers*, **AP:** 1748

Scrambled Eggs and Whiskey (Carruth), **AP:** 282

"Screed of the Flesh, The" (Everson), **AP:** 574

Scribleruls Club, **TE:** 163

Scrimshaw (Scott), **AP:** 1748

Scripts for the Pageant (Merrill), **AP:** 1321

Scudéry, Madeleine de, **TE:** 252

"Sea Eats the Land at Home, The" (Awooner), **WP:** 29

Sea Faring, and Other Poems, The (Coxe), **AP:** 377

Sea Grapes (Walcott), **WP:** 320

"Sea of Death, The" (Hood), **BP:** 655

Sea of San Juan, The (Salinas), **EP:** 940

Seals in the Inner Harbor (Galvin), **AP:** 649

Seamarks (Perse), **EP:** 804

Search, Alexander. *See* Pessoa, Fernando

"Search for Poetry" (Drummond de Andrade), **WP:** 81

"Searchers, The" (Rivera), **AP:** 1659

Searching for the Ox (Simpson), **AP:** 1797

Searle, John R., **TE:** 757

Seascape (Oppen), **AP:** 1480

Seaside and the Fireside, The (Longfellow), **AP:** 1161

Season in Hell, A (Rimbaud), **EP:** 900, **TE:** 268

Season Songs (Hughes), **BP:** 692

"Seasons, The" (Koch), **AP:** 1063

Seasons, The (Thomson), **BP:** 1262, **TE:** 165

"Seasons of the Soul" (Tate), **AP:** 1944

"Sechzigjährige dankt, Der" (Zweig), **EP:** 1146

Second Brother, The (Beddoes), **BP:** 58

"Second Coming, The" (Yeats), **BP:** 1339

"Second Eclogue" (Garcilaso de la Vega), **EP:** 365, **EP:** 881

Second Language (Mueller), **AP:** 1386

Second Sex, The (Beauvoir), **TE:** 737

Second Space (Miłosz), **EP:** 718

Second Vanguard, **TE:** 497

Secondary Heaven (Popa), **EP:** 858

Secrets from the Center of the World (Harjo), **AP:** 791

Secular Love (Ondaatje), **BP:** 976

Sedgwick, Eve Kosofsky, **TE:** 774

Sedley, Sir Charles, **BP:** 1094-1099; "Out of Lycophron," **BP:** 1096; "To Liber," **BP:** 1096

Seed on the Wind, A (Zimmer), **AP:** 2262

Seeger, Alan, **AP:** 1750-1753; "I Have a Rendezvous with Death," **AP:** 1752; "Ode in Memory of the American Volunteers Fallen for France," **AP:** 1751

Seeing Is Believing (Tomlinson), **BP:** 1271

Seeing Things (Heaney), **BP:** 603

Seeing Through the Sun (Hogan), **AP:** 874

"Seer Letter" (Rimbaud), **EP:** 899

Seferiades, Giorgos Stylianou. *See* Seferis, George

Seferis, George, **EP:** 957-961, **TE:** 340; *Book of Exercises*, **EP:** 960; *The Cistern*, **EP:** 959; "The King of Asine," **EP:** 960; "Last Stop," **EP:** 961; *Logbook II*, **EP:** 960; *Mythistorema*, **EP:** 960; *Turning Point*, **EP:** 959

Seguidilla, defined, **AP:** 2304, **BP:** 1388, **EP:** 1182, **TE:** 820, **WP:** 390

Segundo volumen de las obras. See *First Dream*

Seifert, Jaroslav, **EP:** 961-968, **TE:** 85; "The Blow," **EP:** 966; *The Casting of the Bells*, **EP:** 966; *The Plague Column*, **EP:** 966

Selected and New Poems (Dubie), **AP:** 496

Selected and New Poems, 1961-1981 (Harrison), **AP:** 809

Selected Fables of La Fontaine (Moore), **AP:** 1369

Selected Life, A (Kinsella), **BP:** 756

Selected Poems (Beer), **BP:** 62

Selected Poems (Bly), **AP:** 194

Selected Poems (Fenton), **BP:** 490

Selected Poems (Justice), **AP:** 990

Selected Poems, 1928-1958 (Kunitz), **AP:** 1087

Selected Poems (Logue), **BP:** 825

Selected Poems (McClure), **AP:** 1210

Selected Poems, 1931-2004 (Miłosz), **EP:** 719

Selected Poems (Montague), **BP:** 920

Selected Poems (Ní Dhomhnaill), **BP:** 966

Selected Poems (Shapiro), **AP:** 1762

Selected Poems (Simpson), **AP:** 1797

Selected Poems (Strand), **AP:** 1923

Selected Poems (Van Duyn), **AP:** 2037

Selected Poems and New (Villa), **AP:** 2053

Selected Poems from the Divani Shamsi Tabrīz. See *Sufi Path of Love, The*

Selected Poems of Nikki Giovanni, The (Giovanni), **AP:** 699

"Self and the Weather, The" (Whittemore), **AP:** 2143

"Self-Help" (Beer), **BP:** 65

Self-Portrait in a Convex Mirror (Ashbery), **AP:** 60

Selves (Booth), **AP:** 214

Sem Tov, Rabbi, **TE:** 590

Semiotics, defined, **AP:** 2304, **BP:** 1388, **EP:** 1182, **TE:** 820, **WP:** 390

Semonides, **TE:** 321

Senderos ocultos, Los (González Martínez), **WP:** 105

Senegal. *See* Geographical Index

Senghor, Léopold, **WP:** 264-272; "Black Woman," **WP:** 269; and Aimé Césaire, **WP:** 57; *Chants d'ombre*, **WP:** 268; *Éthiopiques*, **WP:** 269; "For Koras and Balafong," **WP:** 268; *Hosties noires*, **WP:** 269; *Nocturnes*, **WP:** 270; "Paris in Snow," **WP:** 269

Senlin (Aiken), **AP:** 15

Sense of Movement, The (Gunn), **BP:** 563

"Sense simbolisme." *See* "Without Symbolism"

Sensibility movement, **TE:** 165

Sent på jorden (Ekelöf), **EP:** 308

Sentences (Nemerov), **AP:** 1414

Sentimento del tempo (Ungaretti), **EP:** 1060

Sentimento do mundo; Drummond de Andrade, **WP:** 81

Separations (Hacker), **AP:** 764

Sepolcri, Dei. See *On Sepulchers*

Sequence for Francis Parkman, A (Davie), **BP:** 370

Sequence, Sometimes Metaphysical (Roethke), **AP:** 1677

Sequences (Sassoon), **BP:** 1086

"Seraph and the Poet, The" (Browning), **BP:** 156

Seraphim, and Other Poems, The (Browning), **BP:** 153

Serbia. *See* Geographical Index

Serbian poetry, **TE:** 566-572

"Sermon 14" (Taylor), **AP:** 1963

"Sermons on the Warpland" (Brooks), **AP:** 251

Service, Robert W., **BP:** 1099-1104; *Songs of a Sourdough*, **BP:** 1103

"Ses purs ongles trés haut dédiant leur onyx." *See* "Her Pure Fingernails on High Offering Their Onyx"

Sestet (Wright), **AP:** 2216

Sestet, defined, **AP:** 2304, **BP:** 1388, **EP:** 1182, **TE:** 820, **WP:** 390

Sestina, defined, **AP:** 2304, **BP:** 1388, **EP:** 1182, **TE:** 820, **WP:** 390

Sestra moia zhizn'. See *My Sister, Life*

Set This Book on Fire (Baca), **AP:** 74

Seth, Vikram, TE: 374, **WP:** 272-276; *All You Who Sleep Tonight*, **WP:** 275; *Beastly Tales from Here and There*, **WP:** 275; *The Golden Gate*, **WP:** 274; *The Humble Administrator's Garden*, **WP:** 274; *Mappings*, **WP:** 274

Sette giornate del mondo creato, Le (Tasso), **EP:** 1016

Settler poets, **TE:** 500

"Seurat's Sunday Afternoon Along the Seine" (Schwartz), **AP:** 1744

Seven Deadly Sins, and Other Poems, The (Slavitt), **AP:** 1816

"Seven Destinations of Mayerling" (Cassity), **AP:** 293

Seven-League Crutches, The (Jarrell), **AP:** 960

"Seven Songs for an Old Voice" (Wagoner), **AP:** 2063

Seventh Hill, The (Hillyer), **AP:** 851

Seventh Ring, The (George), **EP:** 383

Several Poems Compiled with Great Variety of Wit and Learning, Full of Delight. See *Tenth Muse Lately Sprung Up in America*

Sevillan poets, **TE:** 593

Sexton, Anne, AP: 1753-1759, **TE:** 671; *All My Pretty Ones*, **AP:** 1756, **TE:** 671; *Live or Die*, **AP:** 1756; *Love Poems*, **AP:** 1757; *To Bedlam and Part Way Back*, **AP:** 1755; *Transformations*, **AP:** 1757

Seymour, Arthur J., **TE:** 45

Sgrung, **TE:** 607

Shackles (Césaire), **WP:** 59

"Shade-Seller, The" (Jacobsen), **AP:** 952

Shadow Box (Chappell), **AP:** 306

Shadow Country (Allen), **AP:** 30

Shadow of Heaven (Voigt), **AP:** 2057

Shadow of Night, The (Chapman), **BP:** 230

Shadow of Paradise (Aleixandre), **EP:** 16

Shadow of Sirius, The (Merwin), **AP:** 1338

Shaft, The (Tomlinson), **BP:** 1274

Shahnamah. See *Sah-name*

Shake Loose My Skin (Sanchez), **AP:** 1702

Shakespeare, William, BP: 1105-1112; *The Phoenix and the Turtle*, **BP:** 1106; *The Rape of Lucrece*, **BP:** 1106; *Venus and Adonis*, **BP:** 1106

Shakespearean Negotiations (Greenblatt), **TE:** 764

Shams al Dīn Muḥammed of Shīrāz. *See* Hafiz

"Shancoduff" (Kavanagh), **BP:** 728

Shape of the Journey, The (Harrison), **AP:** 811

Shapiro, Alan, AP: 1759-1764; *The Courtesy*, **AP:** 1760; *Covenant*, **AP:** 1761; *The Dead Alive and Busy*, **AP:** 1762; *Happy Hour*, **AP:** 1760; *Mixed Company*, **AP:** 1761; *Selected Poems*, **AP:** 1762; *Song and Dance*, **AP:** 1762; *Tantalus in Love*, **AP:** 1763

Shapiro, Karl, AP: 1764-1769; *Adult Bookstore*, **AP:** 1768; "Lord, I've seen too much," **AP:** 1767

"Shark, The" (Pratt), **BP:** 1018

Shaykh. *See* Sa'di

Shchastlivy domik (Khodasevich), **WP:** 135

"She Dances" (Sachs), **EP:** 934

She Had Some Horses (Harjo), **AP:** 791

"Sheet of Paper" (Salinas), **EP:** 938

Sheffey, Asa Bundy. *See* Hayden, Robert

Shelley, Percy Bysshe, BP: 1112-1125, **TE:** 178, **TE:** 630, **TE:** 711; *Adonais*, **BP:** 1123; *Alastor*, **BP:** 1117; *A Defence of Poetry*, **TE:** 711; *Epipsychidion*, **BP:** 1121; "Hymn to Intellectual Beauty," **BP:** 1121; *Julian and Maddalo*, **BP:** 1116; *Mont Blanc*, **BP:** 1119; "Ode to the West Wind," **BP:** 1122; *Prometheus Unbound*, **BP:** 1119

Shelley Memorial Award, **AP:** 2329, **CM:** 64, **TE:** 884

Shelton, John. *See* Skelton, John

Shemuel ha-Levi, Yehuda ben. *See* Judah ha-Levi

Shepheardes Calender, The (Spenser), **BP:** 1194

Shepheards Sirena (Drayton), **BP:** 423

Shepherd, and Other Poems of Peace and War, The (Blunden), **BP:** 106

Shepherd's Week, The (Gay), **BP:** 516

Shi (poetic form), **TE:** 59

"Shigoto" (Miyazawa), **WP:** 194

Shijing. See *Book of Songs, The*

Shiki. *See* Masaoka Shiki

"Shiloh, a Requiem" (Melville), **AP:** 1299

Shinkokinshū (anthology), **TE:** 418

Shintaisho (anthology), **TE:** 427

"Ship of Death, The" (Lawrence), **BP:** 801

Ships and Other Figures (Meredith), **AP:** 1311

Shiraishi Kazuko, **TE:** 432

Shiraz, Shams al-Din Muhammad of. *See* Hafiz

Shires, The (Davie), **BP:** 372

Shoah Train (Heyen), **AP:** 848

Shoemaker's Holiday, The (Dekker), **BP:** 394

Shōfū, **TE:** 423

241

Shomer, Enid, **AP:** 1769-1773; *Black Drum*, **AP:** 1771; *Stars at Noon*, **AP:** 1771; *This Close to the Earth*, **AP:** 1770

Shooting Rats at the Bibb County Dump (Bottoms), **AP:** 217

Shore, The (St. John), **AP:** 1695

Shore, Jane, **AP:** 1773-1776; *Eye-Level*, **AP:** 1774; *Happy Family*, **AP:** 1776; *Lying Down in the Olive Press*, **AP:** 1774; *The Minute Hand*, **AP:** 1775; *Music Minus One*, **AP:** 1775; *A Yes-or-No Answer*, **AP:** 1776

"Shoreline" (Barnard), **AP:** 102

"Short History, A" (Wilbur), **AP:** 2158

Short Walk from the Station, A (McGinley), **AP:** 1223

Showalter, Elaine C., **TE:** 736

"Shrapnel Shards on Blue Water" (Thuy), **TE:** 27

Shropshire Lad, A (Housman), **BP:** 682

Shroud of the Gnome (Tate), **AP:** 1956

Shuttle in the Crypt, A (Soyinka), **WP:** 278

"¡Sí, todo con exceso!" *See* "Yes, Too Much of Everything"

Sia, Beau, **TE:** 22

"Sic Vita" (H. King), **BP:** 748

Sicilian school, **TE:** 378

Sicily. *See* Geographical Index

"Sicily" (Flint), **AP:** 609

"Sick Rose, The" (Blake), **TE:** 720

"Sides of a Mind, The" (Everson), **AP:** 572

Sidney, Mary, **BP:** 1136

Sidney, Sir Philip, **BP:** 1126-1135; *Astrophel and Stella*, **BP:** 1130; *Defence of Poesie*, **TE:** 132, **TE:** 703; *The Psalmes of David*, **BP:** 1130

Sidney, Sir Robert, **BP:** 1135-1141

"Sie tanzt." *See* "She Dances"

Siebente Ring, Der. See Seventh Ring, The

Siege of Ancona, The (Landor), **BP:** 778

Siege of Valencia, The (Hemans), **BP:** 611

"Siegfriedslage" (Kirstein), **AP:** 1045

Signifiers and signifieds, **TE:** 726, **TE:** 775, **TE:** 780

Signs (Gibson), **AP:** 671

Signs and Wonders (Dennis), **AP:** 443

Sigurthsson, Stefán, **TE:** 548

Sikelianos, Angelos, **TE:** 337

Silence in the Snowy Fields (Bly), **AP:** 190

Silence Now, The (Sarton), **AP:** 1723

Silénter (González Martínez), **WP:** 105

Silex Scintillans (Vaughan), **BP:** 1287

Silkin, Jon, **BP:** 1141-1145; "Death of a Son," **BP:** 1143; *Nature with Man*, **BP:** 1142

Silko, Leslie Marmon, **AP:** 1777-1781, **TE:** 483; "A Ck'o'yo medicine man," **AP:** 1780; "Cottonwood, Part Two," **AP:** 1780; "I always called her Aunt Susie," **AP:** 1780; *Laguna Woman*, **AP:** 1779; *Storyteller*, **AP:** 1779

Silvae (Statius), **EP:** 1000

Silver Age; Latin poetry, **TE:** 453; Russian, **TE:** 516

Silver Out of Shanghai (Cassity), **AP:** 295

Silverstein, Shel, **AP:** 1781-1785; *Falling Up*, **AP:** 1784; *A Light in the Attic*, **AP:** 1784; *Where the Sidewalk Ends*, **AP:** 1783

Silverstein, Shelby. *See* Silverstein, Shel

"Silvia" (Etherege), **BP:** 478

Sima Xiangru, **TE:** 59

Simavne Kadisi oğu Şeyh Bedreddin

destanı. See Epic of Sheik Bedreddin, The

Šimić, Antun Branko, **TE:** 75

Simic, Charles, **AP:** 1785-1793; *Austerities*, **AP:** 1788; *The Book of Gods and Devils*, **AP:** 1789; "Brooms," **AP:** 1787; *Charon's Cosmology*, **AP:** 1788; *Classic Ballroom Dances*, **AP:** 1788; *Jackstraws*, **AP:** 1790; *My Noiseless Entourage*, **AP:** 1790; *Night Picnic*, **AP:** 1790; *Sixty Poems*, **AP:** 1791; *That Little Something*, **AP:** 1791; *Unending Blues*, **AP:** 1788; *Walking the Black Cat*, **AP:** 1790; *White*, **AP:** 1788; *The World Doesn't End*, **AP:** 1789

Simić, Dušan. *See* Simic, Charles

Simile, defined, **AP:** 2304, **BP:** 1388, **EP:** 1182, **TE:** 820, **WP:** 390

Simoni, Michelangelo di Lodovico Buonarroti. *See* Michelangelo

Simonides, **TE:** 325

"Simple Autumnal" (Bogan), **AP:** 203

Simple Plan, A (Soto), **AP:** 1866

Simple Truth, The (Levine), **AP:** 1126

Simpson, Louis, **AP:** 1793-1802; *Adventures in the Letter I*, **AP:** 1797; *The Arrivistes*, **AP:** 1795; *At the End of the Open Road*, **AP:** 1796; *The Best Hour of the Night*, **AP:** 1798; *Caviare at the Funeral*, **AP:** 1798; *A Dream of Governors*, **AP:** 1795; *Good News of Death, and Other Poems*, **AP:** 1795; *In the Room We Share*, **AP:** 1799; *The Owner of the House*, **AP:** 1800; *People Live Here*, **AP:** 1798; *Searching for the Ox*, **AP:** 1797; *Selected Poems*, **AP:** 1797

Sinclair, John, **TE:** 756

Singing, The (Williams), **AP:** 2166

Sinisgalli, Leonardo, **TE:** 406

Sinking of the Titanic, The (Enzensberger), **EP:** 325

Sinking Ship Blues (Breytenbach), **EP:** 167

Sinners Welcome (Karr), **AP:** 995

Sinopoulos, Takis, **TE:** 347

Sir Gawain and the Green Knight (Pearl-Poet), **BP:** 999, **TE:** 111

Sishui (Wen Yidou), **TE:** 66

Sissman, L. E., AP: 1802-1809; *Dying,* **AP:** 1804; *Hello, Darkness,* **AP:** 1806; "Homage to Clotho," **AP:** 1807; *Scattered Returns,* **AP:** 1805; "Two Encounters," **AP:** 1804

"Sister Lou" (Brown), **AP:** 258

Sister My Life. See My Sister, Life

"Sitting on Blue Mountain . . ." (Balaban), **AP:** 83

Sitwell, Edith, BP: 1145-1153, **TE:** 187; *Bucolic Comedies,* **BP:** 1148; *Façade,* **BP:** 1149; *Gold Coast Customs,* **BP:** 1151; *Metamorphosis,* **BP:** 1150; *The Mother, and Other Poems,* **BP:** 1148

Sitwellian poetry, **TE:** 187

"VI Dirge" (Rakosi), **AP:** 1594

Six Epistles to Eva Hesse (Davie), **BP:** 371

Sixty Poems (Simic), **AP:** 1791

Sjöberg, Birger, **TE:** 543

Skaldic poetry, **TE:** 527

Skamander, **TE:** 496

Skelton, John, BP: 1153-1159, **TE:** 133; *The Bowge of Court,* **BP:** 1155; *Collyn Clout,* **BP:** 1157; *The Garlande of Laurell,* **BP:** 1157; *Phyllyp Sparowe,* **BP:** 1156; *Speke, Parrot,* **BP:** 1156; *Ware the Hawk,* **BP:** 1156; *Why Come Ye Nat to Courte,* **BP:** 1157

"Ski Murders, The" (MacBeth), **BP:** 842

Sklepy mięsne (Zagajewski), **EP:** 1139

"Skogssjön." *See* "Forest Lake"

Skolia, **TE:** 323

Skryt. See Sinking Ship Blues

Sky and Island Light (Galvin), **AP:** 650

Skylight (Muske), **AP:** 1397

"Skywriting" (Hirsch), **AP:** 855

Slabs of the Sunburnt West (Sandburg), **AP:** 1709

Sládkovič, Andrej, **TE:** 575

Slamnig, Ivan, **TE:** 76

"Slap in the Face of Public Taste, A" (Russian Futurist manifesto), **WP:** 177

"Slate Ode" (Mandelstam), **WP:** 168

Slave Moth (Moss), **AP:** 1381

Slaviček, Milivoj, **TE:** 75

Slavitt, David, AP: 1809-1817; *Big Nose,* **AP:** 1814; *The Carnivore,* **AP:** 1811; *Change of Address,* **AP:** 1816; *Child's Play,* **AP:** 1813; *Day Sailing,* **AP:** 1812; *Dozens,* **AP:** 1814; *Eight Longer Poems,* **AP:** 1815; *Falling from Silence,* **AP:** 1815; *A Gift,* **AP:** 1815; *PS3569.L3: Poems,* **AP:** 1815; *Rounding the Horn,* **AP:** 1813; *The Seven Deadly Sins, and Other Poems,* **AP:** 1816; *Suits for the Dead,* **AP:** 1810; *Vital Signs,* **AP:** 1813; *The Walls of Thebes,* **AP:** 1814; *William Henry Harrison, and Other Poems,* **AP:** 1816

Slávy dcera (Kollár), **TE:** 81

Sleek for the Long Flight (Matthews), **AP:** 1286

"Sleep, The" (Dacey), **AP:** 426

Sleepers Joining Hands (Bly), **AP:** 192

Sleeping Beauty, The (Carruth), **AP:** 281

Sleeping Lord, and Other Fragments, The (Jones), **BP:** 710

"Sleeping Out at Easter" (Dickey), **AP:** 450

Sleeping Preacher (Kasdorf), **AP:** 998

Sleeping with One Eye Open (Strand), **AP:** 1921

Sleeping with the Dead (Ehrhart), **AP:** 536

Sleeping with the Dictionary (Mullen), **AP:** 1389

Slessor, Kenneth, **TE:** 32

"Slim Greer" (Browning), **AP:** 257

Słonimski, Antoni, EP: 968-972; *Popiól i wiatr,* **EP:** 971

Slovak poetry, **TE:** 573-578

Slovenian poetry, **TE:** 579-582

Slovo o polku Igoreve. See Tale of the Armament of Igor, The

Slow Dance, A (Montague), **BP:** 919

Słowacki, Juliusz, EP: 972-981, **TE:** 494; *Anhelli,* **EP:** 978; *Arab,* **EP:** 976; *Beniowski,* **EP:** 978; *The Father of the Plague-Stricken,* **EP:** 977; *Genezis z ducha,* **EP:** 979; *Godzinna myśli,* **EP:** 976; *In Switzerland,* **EP:** 977; *Król-Duch,* **EP:** 979; *Lambro, powstańca grecki,* **EP:** 976; *Podróż na wschód ,* **EP:** 978; *Wacław,* **EP:** 977; *Żmija,* **EP:** 976

"Slum Child, The" (De la Mare), **BP:** 403

Small Congregations (Moss), **AP:** 1381

"Small Tantric Sermon" (Whalen), **AP:** 2113

Smallest Muscle in the Human Body, The (Ríos), **AP:** 1655

Smart, Christopher, BP: 1159-1163; *A Song to David,* **BP:** 1161

Smashing the Piano (Montague), **BP:** 922

"Smert poeta." *See* "Death of a Poet, The"

Smith, Dave, AP: 1817-1824; "The

Dark Eyes of Daughters,"
AP: 1820; *Fate's Kite*, **AP:** 1823;
"Night Fishing for Blues,"
AP: 1821; "Southern Crescent,"
AP: 1823; "The Tire Hangs in the
Woods," **AP:** 1822
Smith, Florence Margaret. *See* Smith,
Stevie
Smith, Henry Lee, Jr., **TE:** 750
Smith, John Allyn. *See* Berryman,
John
Smith, Rosamond. *See* Oates, Joyce
Carol
Smith, Stevie, **BP:** 1164-1171; "Duty
Was His Lodestar," **BP:** 1168; *A
Good Time Was Had by All*,
BP: 1167; "The Hound of Ulster,"
BP: 1167; "Louise," **BP:** 1168;
"A Mother's Hearse," **BP:** 1166;
"Nature and Free Animals,"
BP: 1166; "Not Waving but
Drowning," **BP:** 1170;
"Numbers," **BP:** 1169; "Our Bog
Is Dood," **BP:** 1169; "Papa Love
Baby," **BP:** 1167; "To Carry the
Child," **BP:** 1169; "The
Wanderer," **BP:** 1166; "The Zoo,"
BP: 1166
Smith, William Jay, **AP:** 1825-1830;
The Cherokee Lottery, **AP:** 1828;
The Girl in Glass, **AP:** 1828;
Laughing Time, **AP:** 1827; *New
and Selected Poems*, **AP:** 1828;
Poems, 1947-1957, **AP:** 1827; *The
Tin Can, and Other Poems*,
AP: 1828; *Words by the Water*,
AP: 1829
Smoke and Steel (Sandburg),
AP: 1709
Smrek, Ján, **TE:** 576
Smudging (Wakoski), **AP:** 2073
"Snail, The" (Giusti), **EP:** 395
"Snake" (Lawrence), **BP:** 800
Snaps (Cruz), **AP:** 401
"Snapshots" (Paz), **WP:** 234

Snapshots of a Daughter-in-Law
(Rich), **AP:** 1635
Snodgrass, W. D., **AP:** 1831-1840,
TE: 201, **TE:** 669; *De/
Compositions*, **AP:** 1838; *The
Führer Bunker*, **AP:** 1837; *Heart's
Needle*, **AP:** 1833, **TE:** 201,
TE: 669; *If Birds Build with Your
Hair*, **AP:** 1837; *A Locked House*,
AP: 1838
Snoilsky, Carl, **TE:** 536
"Snow, The" (Verhaeren), **EP:** 1092
"Snow-Bound" (Whittier), **AP:** 2149
Snow Poems, The (Ammons), **AP:** 40
"Snow-Storm, The" (Emerson),
AP: 549
Snow Watcher, The (Twichell),
AP: 2004
Snyder, Gary, **AP:** 1840-1852,
TE: 206; *Axe Handles*, **AP:** 1848;
Cold Mountain Poems, **AP:** 1846;
Danger on Peaks, **AP:** 1850; *The
Fudo Trilogy*, **AP:** 1847;
*Mountains and Rivers Without
End*, **AP:** 1849; *Myths and Texts*,
AP: 1845; *Regarding Wave*,
AP: 1847; *Riprap*, **AP:** 1845;
Turtle Island, **AP:** 1847
So Forth (Brodsky), **WP:** 50
So There (Creeley), **AP:** 398
Soares, Bernardo. *See* Pessoa,
Fernando
Sobre los ángeles. See *Concerning
the Angels*
Social Realism, China, **TE:** 66
Socialist Realism, **TE:** 84; Hungary,
TE: 361. *See also* Categorized
Index
Society of the Temple, **TE:** 255
Sociolinguistics, **TE:** 758
Södergran, Edith, **EP:** 981-987,
TE: 545; "The Day Cools . . .,"
EP: 985; "Discovery," **EP:** 984;
"Forest Lake," **EP:** 985;
"Nothing," **EP:** 986

"Softly" (Jacobsen), **AP:** 952
Sōgi, **TE:** 421
"Soirée perdue, Une." *See* "Wasted
Evening, A"
Sól (Szymborska), **EP:** 1010
Sol, i de dol (Foix), **EP:** 333
"Soldiers Bathing" (Prince),
BP: 1023
"Soldiers of Orange" (Cassity),
AP: 295
Soledad primera. See *Solitudes, The*
Soledad segunda. See *Solitudes, The*
Soledad sonora, La (Jiménez),
EP: 536
Soledades. See *Solitudes, The*
Soledades (Machado), **EP:** 636
*Solemne Passion of the Soules Love,
A* (Breton), **BP:** 129
"Soliloquy of Hamlet, A" (Durrell),
BP: 453
"Solitary, The" (Teasdale), **AP:** 1976
Solitudes, The (Góngora y Argote),
EP: 414; **TE:** 594
*Solitudes of Don Luis de Góngora,
The*. See *Solitudes, The*
Šoljan, Antun, **TE:** 76
Solomon on the Vanity of the World
(Prior), **BP:** 1029
Solomos, Dionysios, **EP:** 987-993,
TE: 331; *Eleftheroi
poliorkimenoi*, **EP:** 992; *The
Hymn to Liberty*, **EP:** 990; *Is ton
Thanato tou Lord Byron*, **EP:** 991;
"Katastrophi ton Psaron,"
EP: 991; *To Kritikos*, **EP:** 991;
Lambros, **EP:** 991; *Porphyras*,
EP: 992
Solon, **TE:** 224
Solovyov, Vladimir, **TE:** 517
Solstices (MacNeice), **BP:** 864
Sombra del paraíso. See *Shadow of
Paradise*
Some Changes (Jordan), **AP:** 983
"Some General Instructions" (Koch),
AP: 1062

Some One Sweet Angel Chile
(Williams), **AP:** 2174

Some Trees (Ashbery), **AP:** 57

Some Versions of Silence (Dana),
AP: 433

*Somebody Blew Up America, and
Other Poems* (Baraka), **AP:** 97

Someday, Maybe (Stafford),
AP: 1878

Somerset Masque, The (Campion),
BP: 206

Something About the Blues (Young),
AP: 2256

"Something There" (Beckett), **EP:** 93

"Somnambule Ballad" (García
Lorca), **EP:** 359

"Son du cor, Le." *See* "Sound of the
Hunting Horn, The"

"Sonatina in Green" (Justice),
AP: 989

Sonetos espirituales. See *Spiritual
Sonnets*

"Sonetti" (Foscolo), **EP:** 342

Sonety krymskie. See *Sonnets from the
Crimea*

Song (Harper), **AP:** 798

Song (Kelly), **AP:** 1013

"Song" (Schuyler), **AP:** 1735,
BP: 297, **BP:** 1051, **EP:** 882

Song, Cathy, **AP:** 1853-1858,
TE: 24; *Cloud Moving Hands*,
AP: 1856; *Frameless Windows,
Squares of Light*, **AP:** 1855; *The
Land of Bliss*, **AP:** 1856; *Picture
Bride*, **AP:** 1854; *School Figures*,
AP: 1855

Song and Dance (Shapiro), **AP:** 1762

"Song and Story" (Voigt), **AP:** 2056

Song at the Year's Turning (Thomas),
BP: 1259

Song ci, **TE:** 58

"Song for Longing" (Goldbarth),
AP: 722

"Song for St. Cecilia's Day, A"
(Dryden), **BP:** 440

"Song for the Old Ones" (Angelou),
AP: 49

"Song: Ladies, though to your
conquering eyes" (Etherege),
BP: 479

Song of Hiawatha, The (Longfellow),
AP: 1163

Song of Los, The (Blake), **BP:** 100

"Song of Love" (Carducci), **EP:** 189

"Song of Myself" (Whitman),
AP: 2133

"Song of Napalm" (Weigl), **AP:** 2104

Song of Roland, The (anonymous),
TE: 229, **TE:** 234

"Song of the Bell, The" (Schiller),
EP: 955

"Song of the Chattahoochee"
(Lanier), **AP:** 1099

"Song of the Fort Donald Railroad
Gang" (Brecht), **EP:** 152

"Song of the Horseman, The" (García
Lorca), **EP:** 359

"Song of the Shirt, The" (Hood),
BP: 658

Song to David, A (Smart), **BP:** 1161

"Song: To happy youths" (Etherege),
BP: 479

"Song, To my inconstant Mistress"
(Carew), **BP:** 210

"Song to the Man of the People C. C."
(Drummond de Andrade), **WP:** 81

Song Turning Back into Itself, The
(Young), **AP:** 2252

Songe de Vaux, Le (La Fontaine),
EP: 580

Songe en complainte (Charles
d'Orléans), **EP:** 233

Songes en équilibre, Les (Hébert),
BP: 607

Songlines in Michaeltree (Harper),
AP: 799

Songs, **BP:** 477; Native American,
TE: 478; Soviet Russia, **TE:** 524;
Swedish, **TE:** 531. *See also*
Categorized Index

Songs Before Sunrise (Swinburne),
BP: 1233

Songs for Tomorrow (Ko Un),
WP: 140

Songs of a Blackbird (Rodgers),
AP: 1670

Songs of a Sourdough (Service),
BP: 1103

Songs of Innocence and of Experience
(Blake), **BP:** 95

"Songs of Sorrow" (Awooner),
WP: 28

Songs of the Earth (Johnson),
AP: 978

Songs to Joannes (Loy), **AP:** 1202

Sonne, Jørgen, **TE:** 562

"Sonnet" (Brodsky), **WP:** 47;
England, **TE:** 137

Sonnet, defined, **AP:** 2304, **BP:** 1388,
EP: 1182, **TE:** 820, **WP:** 390

Sonnet X (Tuckerman), **AP:** 2000

"Sonnet to My Father" (Justice),
AP: 987

"Sonnet—To Science" (Poe),
AP: 1564

Sonnets. *See* Categorized Index

Sonnets, The (Berrigan), **AP:** 145

Sonnets from the Crimea
(Mickiewicz), **EP:** 705

Sonnets to Orpheus (Rilke), **EP:** 895

Sonnevi, Göran, **TE:** 554

Soothsayers and Omens (Wright),
AP: 2235

"Sopa" (Reyes), **WP:** 249

Sophist, The (Bernstein), **AP:** 135

Sophists, **TE:** 325

Šopov, Aco, **TE:** 476

Sor Juana. *See* Cruz, Sor Juana Inés
de la

Sorgegondolen. See *Sorrow Gondola*

Sorrentino, Gilbert, **AP:** 1858-1861;
A Dozen Oranges, **AP:** 1860;
"Midnight Special," **AP:** 1859;
"Nightpiece," **AP:** 1859; *The
Orangery*, **AP:** 1860; *The Perfect*

Fiction, **AP:** 1860; *White Sail*,
AP: 1860

Sorrow (Alegría), **WP:** 12

Sorrow Gondola (Tranströmer),
EP: 1042

Sōseki. *See* Natsume Sōseki

Soto, Gary, **AP:** 1862-1868,
TE: 471; *Black Hair*, **AP:** 1864;
The Elements of San Joaquin,
AP: 1863; *Home Course in
Religion*, **AP:** 1866; *A Natural
Man*, **AP:** 1866; *A Simple Plan*,
AP: 1866; *The Tale of Sunlight*,
AP: 1864; *Where Sparrows Work
Hard*, **AP:** 1864; *Who Will Know
Us?*, **AP:** 1865

Souls of the Labadie Tract (Howe),
AP: 919

Sound of Dreams Remembered, The
(Young), **AP:** 2255

"Sound of the Hunting Horn, The"
(Verlaine), **EP:** 1098

Source (Doty), **AP:** 484

"Sousa" (Dorn), **AP:** 476

South Africa. *See* Geographical Index

South African poetry, **TE:** 504

South Korea. *See* Geographical Index

Southeast Asian American poetry,
TE: 26

Southern Agrarians. *See* Categorized
Index

"Southern Crescent" (Smith), **AP:** 1823

Southern Cross, The (Wright),
AP: 2212

Southern Reaches, The (Santos),
AP: 1713

Southern Road (Brown), **AP:** 256

Southey, Robert, **BP:** 1171-1178;
"Funeral Ode on the Death of the
Princess Charlotte," **BP:** 1176;
"Ode, Written during the
Negotiations with Buonaparte, in
January 1814," **BP:** 1176;
Roderick, the Last of the Goths,
BP: 1175

Southwell, Robert, **BP:** 1178-1183;
"The Burning Babe," **BP:** 1181;
Saint Peter's Complaint,
BP: 1181; "A Vale of teares,"
BP: 1180

"Souvenirs" (Hagedorn), **TE:** 25

Soyinka, Wole, **TE:** 506, **WP:** 276-
280; *Idanre, and Other Poems*,
WP: 278; *Mandela's Earth, and
Other Poems*, **WP:** 279; *Ogun
Abibiman*, **WP:** 279; *Samarkand
and Other Markets I Have Known*,
WP: 279; *A Shuttle in the Crypt*,
WP: 278

Space Filled with Moving, A
(Anderson), **AP:** 45

Spaces Between Birds, The
(McPherson), **AP:** 1264

Spain. *See* Geographical Index

Spain, Take This Cup from Me
(Vallejo), **WP:** 307

Spanish poetry; origins to fifteenth
century, **TE:** 583-591; fifteenth
century to present, **TE:** 592-603

Sparrow (Muske), **AP:** 1399

"Spatial Form in Modern Literature"
(Frank), **TE:** 780

Spatiality, **TE:** 780, **TE:** 783

"Speaking of Poetry" (Bishop),
AP: 178

Special Orders (Hirsch), **AP:** 857

Spectral Emanations (Hollander),
AP: 881

Speech act theory, **TE:** 757

Speech-Grille (Celan), **EP:** 218

Speed of Darkness, The (Rukeyser),
AP: 1690

Speke, Parrot (Skelton), **BP:** 1156

Spektorsky (Pasternak), **WP:** 227

Spender, Stephen, **BP:** 1183-1191;
"An Elementary School
Classroom in a Slum," **BP:** 1188;
"The Express," **BP:** 1189; "June
1940," **BP:** 1187; "Moving
Through the Silent Crowd,"

BP: 1186; "Ultima Ratio Regum,"
BP: 1187

Spenser, Edmund, **BP:** 1191-1201,
EP: 425, **TE:** 139, **TE:** 146;
Amoretti, **BP:** 1198; *Colin Clouts
Come Home Againe*, **BP:** 1194;
Complaints, **BP:** 1200;
Epithalamion, **BP:** 1198; *The
Faerie Queene*, **BP:** 1196; *The
Shepheardes Calender*, **BP:** 1194

S*PeRM**K*T (Mullen), **AP:** 1388

Sphere (Ammons), **AP:** 39

Sphinx, The (Wilde), **BP:** 1308

Spicer, Jack, **AP:** 1868-1871; *After
Lorca*, **AP:** 1870; *Language*,
AP: 1870; "A Textbook of
Poetry," **AP:** 1870

Spicewood (Reese), **AP:** 1619

Spicher Kasdorf, Julia. *See* Kasdorf,
Julia

Spider and the Fly, The (Heywood),
BP: 638

Spill o llibre de les dones. See Mirror

Spirit Cabinet (Wojahn), **AP:** 2194

Spirit Level, The (Heaney), **BP:** 603

Spirit of Discovery, The (Bowles),
BP: 123

"Spiritual Canticle, The" (John),
EP: 546

Spiritual Sonnets (Constable),
BP: 304

Spiritual Sonnets (Jiménez), **EP:** 537

Spitting and Binding (Rogers),
AP: 1680

Spivak, Gayatri Chakravorty, **TE:** 739

Splay Anthem (Mackey), **AP:** 1243

"Spleen, The" (Finch), **BP:** 494

*Spleen de Paris, Le. See Paris Spleen,
1869*

Split foot, defined, **AP:** 2305,
BP: 1389, **EP:** 1183, **TE:** 821,
WP: 391

Split Image (Glenn), **AP:** 709

Spoils, The (Bunting), **BP:** 171

Spondee, defined, **AP:** 2305,

BP: 1389, **EP:** 1183, **TE:** 821, **WP:** 391

Spoon River Anthology (Masters), **AP:** 1279

Sporedno nebo. See *Secondary Heaven*

"Sprache." *See* "Language"

"Spring, The" (Barnard), **AP:** 103

Spring and Asura (Miyazawa), **WP:** 192

"Spring Comes to Murray Hill" (Nash), **AP:** 1403

Spring Garden (Chappell), **AP:** 306

"Spring on Troublesome Creek" (Still), **AP:** 1917

Spring Poems Along the Rio Grande (Baca), **AP:** 75

Springhouse, The (Dubie), **AP:** 496

Springing (Ponsot), **AP:** 1572

Sprung rhythm, defined, **AP:** 2305, **BP:** 1389, **EP:** 1183, **TE:** 821, **WP:** 391

Squares and Courtyards (Hacker), **AP:** 767

Sri Lanka. *See* Geographical Index

Stadler, Ernst, **TE:** 307

Stafford, William, AP: 1872-1880; *Allegiances*, **AP:** 1878; *Down in My Heart*, **AP:** 1875; *A Glass Face in the Rain*, **AP:** 1878; *An Oregon Message*, **AP:** 1879; *Passwords*, **AP:** 1879; *The Rescued Year*, **AP:** 1877; *Someday, Maybe*, **AP:** 1878; *Stories That Could Be True*, **AP:** 1878; *Traveling Through the Dark*, **AP:** 1875; *West of Your City*, **AP:** 1875

Stagnelius, Erik Johan, **TE:** 534

Stairway of Surprise, The (Benét), **AP:** 131

"Stalnaia cikada." *See* "Steel Cicada, The"

Stampa, Gaspara, EP: 993-997, **TE:** 386; *Rime*, **EP:** 995

Stand Up, Friend, with Me (Field), **AP:** 603

Stanza, defined, **AP:** 2305, **BP:** 1389, **EP:** 1183, **TE:** 821, **WP:** 391

"Stanzas from the Grande Chartreuse" (Arnold), **BP:** 35

Stanzas in Meditation (Stein), **AP:** 1891

"Stanzas in Terza Rima" (Hofmannsthal), **EP:** 481

Stanze (Poliziano), **EP:** 845

Star-Apple Kingdom, The (Walcott), **WP:** 321

Star Dust (Bidart), **AP:** 168

"Stars and Cricket" (Paz), **WP:** 232

Stars at Noon (Shomer), **AP:** 1771

Stars Which See, Stars Which Do Not See (Bell), **AP:** 122

Starting Out for the Difficult World (Dana), **AP:** 434

"Stateside" (Kirstein), **AP:** 1044

Station Island (Heaney), **BP:** 602

Stations (Heaney), **BP:** 599

"Stations of the Cross" (Pessoa), **EP:** 813

Statius, EP: 998-1004; *Silvae*, **EP:** 1000; *Thebaid*, **EP:** 1001

"Steel Cicada, The" (Annensky), **WP:** 24

Steele, Timothy, AP: 1881-1885; *The Color Wheel*, **AP:** 1883; *Sapphics Against Anger, and Other Poems*, **AP:** 1883; *Toward the Winter Solstice*, **AP:** 1884; *Uncertainties and Rest*, **AP:** 1882

Steele Glas, a Satyre, The (Gascoigne), **BP:** 510

Steeplejacks in Babel (Cassity), **AP:** 295

Stéfan, Jude, **TE:** 280

Stefánsson, Davíth, **TE:** 548

Stein, Gertrude, AP: 1885-1893; *The Autobiography of Alice B. Toklas*, **AP:** 1892; "Poetry and Grammar," **AP:** 1891; and Leslie

Scalapino, **AP:** 1726; *Stanzas in Meditation*, **AP:** 1891; *Tender Buttons*, **AP:** 1890; *Things as They Are*, **AP:** 1889; *Three Lives*, **AP:** 1890

Steinarr, Steinn, **TE:** 553

Steiu, Andrei. *See* Codrescu, Andrei

Stephanos. See *Garland*

Stephansson, Stephan G., **TE:** 541

Steps to the Temple (Crashaw), **BP:** 339

Stern, Gerald, AP: 1893-1905; *Bread Without Sugar*, **AP:** 1902; *Everything Is Burning*, **AP:** 1902; *Father Guzman*, **AP:** 1898; *Lovesick*, **AP:** 1901; *Lucky Life*, **AP:** 1895; *Paradise Poems*, **AP:** 1900; *The Red Coal*, **AP:** 1897; *Rejoicings*, **AP:** 1895; *Save the Last Dance*, **AP:** 1903

Sternverdunkelung (Sachs), **EP:** 933

Stevens, Wallace, AP: 1905-1913, **TE:** 653; "The Course of a Particular," **AP:** 1911; "Disillusionment of Ten O'Clock," **AP:** 1908; "Farewell Without a Guitar," **AP:** 1911; "Large Red Man Reading," **AP:** 1908; "Of Modern Poetry," **AP:** 1907; "Poems of Our Climate," **AP:** 1908; "A Postcard from the Volcano," **AP:** 1910; and Carl Rakosi, **AP:** 1594; "Sunday Morning," **AP:** 1909

Stevenson, Robert Louis, BP: 1201-1206; *Ballads*, **BP:** 1204; *A Child's Garden of Verses*, **BP:** 1203; "To Any Reader," **BP:** 1203; *Underwoods*, **BP:** 1204

Stewart, Harold, **TE:** 33

Sticks and Stones (Matthews), **AP:** 1286

Stikhotvoreniya. See *Poems* (Mandelstam)

Still, James, AP: 1913-1918; "Journey Beyond the Hills,"

AP: 1917; "Spring on Troublesome Creek," AP: 1917
"Still I Rise" (Angelou), AP: 49
Still Life with Waterfall (Grennan), AP: 743
Still to Mow (Kumin), AP: 1081
"Stivale, Lo." *See* "Boot, The"
Sto pociech (Szymborska), EP: 1010
Stone (Mandelstam), WP: 166
Stones from a Glass House (McGinley), AP: 1223
Stony Limits, and Other Poems (MacDiarmid), BP: 851
Stories That Could Be True (Stafford), AP: 1878
Storm, Theodor, TE: 302
Storm, and Other Poems, The (Montale), EP: 725
"Story of Civilization, The" (Goldbarth), AP: 721
Story of Our Lives, The (Strand), AP: 1922
"Story of Phoebus and Daphne, Applied, The" (Waller), BP: 1294
Story of Rimini, The (Hunt), BP: 697
Story of Sigurd the Volsung and the Fall of the Niblungs, The (Morris), BP: 930
Storyteller (Silko), AP: 1779
Straits (Koch), AP: 1063
Stramm, August, TE: 308
"Strana negodiaev" (Esenin), WP: 94
Strand, Mark, AP: 1918-1927; *Blizzard of One*, AP: 1924; *The Continuous Life*, AP: 1923; *Dark Harbor*, AP: 1924; *Darker*, AP: 1922; *Man and Camel*, AP: 1924; *New Selected Poems*, AP: 1925; *Reasons for Moving*, AP: 1921; *Selected Poems*, AP: 1923; *Sleeping with One Eye Open*, AP: 1921; *The Story of Our Lives*, AP: 1922
Strange Islands, The (Merton, AP: 1329

"Strange Meeting" (Owen), BP: 981
Stranger, The (Novalis), EP: 752
Stranger at Coney Island (Fearing), AP: 586
Stranger at the Gate, The (Neihardt), AP: 1407
Stranger Music (Cohen), BP: 274
Strawbourg, Godfrey of. *See* Gottfried von Strassburg
Streamers (McPherson), AP: 1263
"Stream's Secret, The" (Rossetti), BP: 1070
Street in Bronzeville, A (Brooks), AP: 250
Streets in the Moon (MacLeish), AP: 1249
Strength of a Named Thing, The (Galvin), AP: 650
Strike Sparks (Olds), AP: 1461
String Light (Wright), AP: 2205
Stritar, Josip, TE: 580
Strong Is Your Hold (Kinnell), AP: 1037
"Strong Men" (Brown), AP: 257
Strophe, TE: 299
Structuralism, defined, AP: 2305, BP: 1389, EP: 1183, TE: 780, TE: 821, WP: 391
Structuralist criticism, TE: 780-786
Struggling to Swim on Concrete (Miller), AP: 1353
Stryk, Lucien, AP: 1927-1931; *And Still Birds Sing*, AP: 1930; *Awakening*, AP: 1930
Stub, Ambrosius, TE: 531
Stub sećanja (Pavlović), EP: 788
Stubborn (Flint), AP: 609
Studium przedmiotu (Herbert), EP: 463
Study for the World's Body (St. John), AP: 1696
"Study of Poetry, The" (Arnold), TE: 713
Štúr, Ludovít, TE: 574
Sturm und drang. *See* Categorized Index

"Style" (Durrell), BP: 453
Style in Language (Sebeok), TE: 751
Stylistic analysis, TE: 756
Stylistic devices, TE: 753
Stylistics, TE: 750
Su Dongpo, TE: 63
Suárez Lynch, B. *See* Borges, Jorge Luis
Subhasitaratnanidhi (Sa-skya Pandita), TE: 608
Subhuman Redneck Poems (Murray), BP: 950
Subject Matter (Wormser), AP: 2201
"Subject of Sea Change, A" (Bishop), AP: 179
Substitution, defined, AP: 2305, BP: 1389, EP: 1183, TE: 821, WP: 391
"Such hap as I am happed in" (Wyatt), BP: 1327
Such Rich Hour (Swensen), AP: 1933
Suckling, Sir John, BP: 1206-1212; "Against Fruition," BP: 1210; "A Ballad upon a Wedding," BP: 1211; "A Candle," BP: 1209; "Honest Lover whosoever," BP: 1210; "Upon my Lady Carliles walking in Hampton-Court garden," BP: 1209; "The Wits," BP: 1211
Sufi Path of Love, The (Rūmī), WP: 257
Sugar-Cane, The (Grainger), TE: 43
Suhrawardy, Shahid, TE: 372
Suits for the Dead (Slavitt), AP: 1810
Sumerian Vistas (Ammons), AP: 41
Summer (Dana), AP: 435
Summer Anniversaries, The (Justice), AP: 987
Summer Celestial (Plumly), AP: 1560
Summer Knowledge (Schwartz), AP: 1744
Summer of Black Widows, The (Alexie), AP: 23
Summoning of Stones, A (Hecht), AP: 828

"Summons, The" (Vörösmarty),
     EP: 1116
Sun Poem (Brathwaite), **AP:** 235
Sun Rock Man (Corman), **AP:** 349
Sun Stone (Paz), **WP:** 233
Sun Under Wood (Hass), **AP:** 817
"Sunday" (Tzara), **EP:** 1048
"Sunday Morning" (Stevens),
     AP: 1909
Supernatural Love (Schnackenberg),
     AP: 1731
Supervielle, Jules, **TE:** 275
Supreme Yoga, The (Vālmīki),
     WP: 310
"Sur une morte." *See* "On a Dead
     Woman"
Surrealism, **TE:** 191; Czech, **TE:** 84;
     definition of, **TE:** 273; France,
     TE: 273; Greece, **TE:** 342;
     Scandinavia, **TE:** 555; Slovakia,
     TE: 576
Surrealist poets. *See* Categorized
     Index
Surrey, Henry Howard, earl of,
     BP: 1212-1218; "Gyrtt in my
     giltlesse gowne," **BP:** 1215;
     "London, has thou accused me,"
     BP: 1216; "Wyatt resteth here,
     that quick could never rest,"
     BP: 1215
Suskin, Alicia. *See* Ostriker, Alicia
     Suskin
Sutton, Henry. *See* Slavitt, David
"Suzanne" (Cohen), **BP:** 274
Svendborg Poems (Brecht), **EP:** 154
Svetli i tamni praznici (Pavlović),
     EP: 789
Swabia. *See* Geographical Index
"Swan, The" (Baudelaire), **EP:** 85
Swarm (Graham), **AP:** 730
Swastika Poems, The (Heyen), **AP:** 845
Sweden. *See* Geographical Index
Sweeney Astray (Heaney), **BP:** 601
Sweet Home, Saturday Night (Baker),
     AP: 78

"Sweet Lullabie, A" (Breton),
     BP: 128
"Sweet Shop Around the Corner,
     The" (Graves), **BP:** 540
Sweet Will (Levine), **AP:** 1124
Swensen, Cole, **AP:** 1931-1934;
     Ours, **AP:** 1933; *Such Rich Hour*,
     AP: 1933
Swenson, May, **AP:** 1934-1940;
     Another Animal, **AP:** 1936;
     "August 19, Pad 19," **AP:** 1938;
     "Horses in Central Park,"
     AP: 1936; *Iconographs*,
     AP: 1937; *In Other Words*,
     AP: 1939; *New and Selected
     Things Taking Place*, **AP:** 1938;
     "October," **AP:** 1938; "A Thank-
     You Letter," **AP:** 1939
Światło dzienne (Miłosz), **EP:** 715
Swift, Jonathan, **BP:** 1218-1226;
     Cadenus and Vanessa, **BP:** 1223;
     "The Description of a
     Salamander," **BP:** 1222; *On
     Poetry*, **BP:** 1224; *Poems to Stella*,
     BP: 1223; *Verses on the Death of
     Dr. Swift, D.S.P.D.*, **BP:** 1224;
     "Verses wrote in a Lady's Ivory
     Table-Book," **BP:** 1222
Swinburne, Algernon Charles,
     BP: 1227-1235; "Ave Atque
     Vale," **BP:** 1234; *A Channel
     Passage, and Other Poems*,
     BP: 1233; "A Forsaken Garden,"
     BP: 1234; "The Garden of
     Proserpine," **BP:** 1232; "Hymn of
     Man," **BP:** 1233; *Poems and
     Ballads*, **BP:** 1232; *Poems and
     Ballads: Second Series*, **BP:** 1234;
     Songs Before Sunrise, **BP:** 1233;
     "A Vision of Spring in Winter,"
     BP: 1234
Swir, Anna, **EP:** 1004-1007;
     Building the Barricade, **EP:** 1006;
     Happy as a Dog's Tail, **EP:** 1006;
     Talking to My Body, **EP:** 1006

Switzerland. *See* Geographical Index
Swords as if Lips (Aleixandre), **EP:** 15
Syllabic meter, defined, **AP:** 2305,
     BP: 1389, **EP:** 1183, **TE:** 821,
     WP: 391
Symbiosis (Guest), **AP:** 746
Symbol, defined, **AP:** 2305,
     BP: 1389, **EP:** 1183, **TE:** 821,
     WP: 391
Symbolism, **TE:** 188, **TE:** 267,
     TE: 639-643; Denmark, **TE:** 539;
     Germany, **TE:** 304; Russia,
     TE: 518
*Symbolist Movement in Literature,
     The* (Symons), **TE:** 189
Symbolist poets. *See* Categorized
     Index
Symons, Arthur, **TE:** 189
"Symphony in White Major"
     (Gautier), **EP:** 375
Synchrony (linguistics), **TE:** 781
Syndrom mizející plíce. *See* Vanishing
     Lung Syndrome
Synecdoche, defined, **AP:** 2306,
     BP: 1390, **EP:** 1184, **TE:** 822,
     WP: 392
Synesthesia and Symbolist poetry,
     TE: 641
Syntactic Structures (Chomsky),
     TE: 753
Syphilis (Fracastoro), **EP:** 349
Syracuse, Theocritus of. *See*
     Theocritus
Syria. *See* Geographical Index
Syruć, J. *See* Miłosz, Czesław
Szabó, Lőrinc, **TE:** 360
Szarzyński, Mikolaj Sep, **TE:** 490
"Szeptember végen" (Petőfi),
     EP: 824
"Szeretlek, kedvesem" (Petőfi),
     EP: 825
"Szondi két apródja." *See* "Szondi's
     Two Pages"
"Szondi's Two Pages" (Arany),
     EP: 47

"Szózat." *See* "Summons, The"

Szymborska, Wisława, **EP:** 1007-
1013, **TE:** 498; *Dlatego żyjemy*,
EP: 1009; *Koniec i początek*,
EP: 1011; *Miracle Fair*,
EP: 1012; *People on a Bridge*,
EP: 1011; *Poems: New and
Collected, 1957-1997*, **EP:** 1011;
Sól, **EP:** 1010; *Sto pociech*,
EP: 1010; *Wielka liczba*,
EP: 1011; *Wołanie do Yeti*,
EP: 1011; *Wszelki wypadek*,
EP: 1010

T. S. Eliot Prize, **BP:** 1408, **CM:** 50,
TE: 870

"Tabacaria." *See* "Tobacco-Shop"

Taban lo Liyong, **TE:** 771

Tabermann, Tommy, **TE:** 559

Tabito. *See* Ōtomo Tabito

Taeuber, Sophie, **EP:** 64

"Tag, Der." *See* "Day, The"

Tag auf dieser Erde, Ein (Kunze),
EP: 575

"Tag der Gesichter, Der" (Bernhard),
EP: 115

Tagore, Rabindranath, **TE:** 371,
WP: 281-288; *A Flight of Swans*,
WP: 285; *Gitanjali Song
Offerings*, **WP:** 285; *Patraput*,
WP: 286

Takamura Kōtarō, **TE:** 430

Take Heart (Peacock), **AP:** 1527

"Take on Armageddon" (Dugan),
AP: 501

Taking Notice (Hacker), **AP:** 764

Taking the Side of Things (Ponge),
EP: 851

Takuboku. *See* Ishikawa Takuboku

Tala (Mistral), **WP:** 188

Tale of Joan of Arc, The (Christine de
Pizan), **EP:** 243

Tale of Orpheus (Henryson), **BP:** 616

Tale of Sunlight, The (Soto),
AP: 1864

Tale of the Armament of Igor, The
(anonymous), **TE:** 509

Tales and Short Stories in Verse (La
Fontaine), **EP:** 580

"Tales from a Family Album"
(Justice), **AP:** 987

Tales in Verse (Crabbe), **BP:** 334

Tales of the Hall (Crabbe), **BP:** 335

Tales Told of the Fathers (Hollander),
AP: 881

Talking Dirty to the Gods
(Komunyakaa), **AP:** 1068

Talking to My Body (Swir), **EP:** 1006

Tall, Pattiann. *See* Rogers, Pattiann

Taller generation, **TE:** 438

Talvipalatsi. See *Winter Palace, The*

"Tam O' Shanter" (Burns), **BP:** 179

Tamar (Jeffers), **AP:** 967

Tamil poetry. *See* Indian English
poetry

Tangled Hair (Yosano Akiko),
WP: 352

Tanikawa Shuntarō, **TE:** 431

Tanka, **TE:** 413

Tantalus in Love (Shapiro), **AP:** 1763

Tantric songs, **TE:** 608

"Tänzerin." *See* "Dancer"

Tao Qian, **TE:** 60, **WP:** 288-293;
"Finding Fault with My Sons,"
WP: 290; "Peach Blossom
Spring," **WP:** 292

Tape for the Turn of the Year
(Ammons), **AP:** 39

Tapisserie de Notre-Dame, La
(Péguy), **EP:** 796

*Tapisserie de sainte Geneviève et de
Jeanne d'Arc, La* (Péguy),
EP: 796

Tar (Williams), **AP:** 2165

Taranta Babu'ya mektuplar (Hikmet),
WP: 121

Tarentum, Leonidas of. *See* Leonidas
of Tarentum

Task, The (Cowper), **BP:** 325

Tasso, Torquato, **EP:** 1014-1020,

TE: 384; *Jerusalem Conquered*,
EP: 1019; *Jerusalem Delivered*,
EP: 1017; *Rinaldo*, **EP:** 1017; *Le
sette giornate del mondo creato*,
EP: 1016

Tate, Allen, **AP:** 1941-1947; "The
Mediterranean," **AP:** 1943; "Ode
to the Confederate Dead,"
AP: 1944; "Seasons of the Soul,"
AP: 1944; "Tension in Poetry,"
TE: 744

Tate, James, **AP:** 1947-1959;
Absences, **AP:** 1952; *Constant
Defender*, **AP:** 1953; *Distance
from Loved Ones*, **AP:** 1954; *The
Ghost Soldiers*, **AP:** 1958; *The
Lost Pilot*, **AP:** 1949; *Lost River*,
AP: 1957; *Memoir of the Hawk*,
AP: 1957; *The Oblivion Ha-Ha*,
AP: 1951; *Reckoner*, **AP:** 1954;
*Return to the City of White
Donkeys*, **AP:** 1958; *Riven
Doggeries*, **AP:** 1953; *Shroud of
the Gnome*, **AP:** 1956; *Viper Jazz*,
AP: 1953; *Worshipful Company of
Fletchers*, **AP:** 1955

Taylor, Edward, **AP:** 1959-1968;
"Huswifery," **AP:** 1961;
"Meditation 8," **AP:** 1962;
"Meditation 39," **AP:** 1961;
"Meditation 56," **AP:** 1963;
"Sermon 14," **AP:** 1963

Taylor, Henry, **AP:** 1968-1974;
"Bernard and Sarah," **AP:** 1971;
Brief Candles, **AP:** 1972; *Crooked
Run*, **AP:** 1972; "Green Springs
the Tree," **AP:** 1972; "Landscape
with Tractor," **AP:** 1972; "Riding
a One-Eyed Horse," **AP:** 1971

Teares, on the Death of Moeliades
(Drummond), **BP:** 428

"Tears" (Reese), **AP:** 1619

Tears of the Blind Lions, The
(Merton), **AP:** 1329

Teasdale, Sara, **AP:** 1974-1977;

"The Look," **AP:** 1976; "The Solitary," **AP:** 1976

Tegnér, Esaias, EP: 1020-1023, **TE:** 535; *Frithiof's Saga,* **EP:** 1022

Teitoku. *See* Matsunaga Teitoku

"Telephone Number of the Muse, The" (Justice), **AP:** 989

Tell Me Again How the White Heron Rises . . . (Carruth), **AP:** 282

Tell Me, Tell Me (Moore), **AP:** 1369

Telquelistes, **TE:** 276

Temple, The (Herbert), **BP:** 620

Temporality, **TE:** 780, **TE:** 783

Ten Thousand Leaves, The. See *Manyoshu, The*

Ten Thousand Lives (Ko Un), **WP:** 140

Tender (Derricotte), **AP:** 447

Tender Buttons (Stein), **AP:** 1890

Tender Hooks (Fennelly), **AP:** 592

Tenebrae (Hill), **BP:** 646

Tennis Court Oath, The (Ashbery), **AP:** 59

Tennyson, Alfred, Lord, BP: 1236-1244, **TE:** 180; Arthur Henry Hallam, **BP:** 578; *Idylls of the King,* **BP:** 1242; *In Memoriam,* **BP:** 1242; "The Lotos-Eaters," **BP:** 1238; *Maud,* **BP:** 1242; *The Princess,* **BP:** 1242; "Ulysses," **BP:** 1239

Tenor on Horseback, The (Middleton), **BP:** 904

"Tension in Poetry" (Tate), **TE:** 744

Tentativa del hombre infinito (Neruda), **WP:** 200

Tenth Muse Lately Sprung Up in America, The (Bradstreet), **AP:** 223

"Tenzone" (Ciardi), **AP:** 317

Tercet, defined, **AP:** 2306, **BP:** 1390, **EP:** 1184, **TE:** 822, **WP:** 392

Ternura (Mistral), **WP:** 189

"Terra dei morti, La." *See* "Land of the Dead, The"

Terra promessa, La (Ungaretti), **EP:** 1062

Terraces of Rain (St. John), **AP:** 1696

Terrible Stories, The (Clifton), **AP:** 329

Terror and Decorum (Viereck), **AP:** 2044

Terza rima, defined, **AP:** 2306, **BP:** 1390, **EP:** 1184, **TE:** 822, **WP:** 392

"Terzinen." *See* "Stanzas in Terza Rima"

Teseida delle nozze d'Emilia. See *Book of Theseus, The*

Testament of Beauty, The (Bridges), **BP:** 135

Testament of Cresseid, The (Henryson), **BP:** 614

Testimony (Reznikoff), **AP:** 1631

Testing-Tree, The (Kunitz), **AP:** 1087

"Textbook of Poetry, A" (Spicer), **AP:** 1870

Thakur, Rabindranath. *See* Tagore, Rabindranath

Thalia Rediviva (Vaughan), **BP:** 1288

"Thanatopsis" (Bryant), **AP:** 261

"Thank-You Letter, A" (Swenson), **AP:** 1939

"Thar's More in the Man than Thar Is in the Land" (Lanier), **AP:** 1098

That Little Something (Simic), **AP:** 1791

"That Silent Evening" (Kinnell), **AP:** 1036

That Was Then (Gardner), **AP:** 655

Theater of Night, The (Ríos), **AP:** 1656

Thebaid (Statius), **EP:** 1001

Theme, defined, **AP:** 2306, **BP:** 1390, **EP:** 1184, **TE:** 822, **WP:** 392

Theocritus, EP: 1023-1029; *Idylls,* **EP:** 1024

Theognidea (Theognis), **EP:** 1030

Theognis, EP: 1029-1033, **TE:** 224, **TE:** 322; *Theognidea,* **EP:** 1030

Theogony (Hesiod), **EP:** 468, **TE:** 222

Theory and Practice of Rivers, The (Harrison), **AP:** 810

Theory of Flight (Rukeyser), **AP:** 1688

Theory of Literature (Wellek and Warren), **TE:** 746

There's Always Another Windmill (Nash), **AP:** 1404

These Are the Ravens (Everson), **AP:** 571

These Green-Going-to-Yellow (Bell), **AP:** 122

"These Images Remain" (Sarton), **AP:** 1720

"They" (Sassoon), **BP:** 1084

They Feed They Lion (Levine), **AP:** 1123

"They flee from me, that sometime did me seek" (Wyatt), **BP:** 1326

"They Say That Plants Do Not Speak" (Castro), **EP:** 195

Thieves of Paradise (Komunyakaa), **AP:** 1068

Things and Flesh (Gregg), **AP:** 737

Things as They Are (Stein), **AP:** 1889

Think Black (Madhubuti), **AP:** 1269

Third person, defined, **AP:** 2306, **BP:** 1390, **EP:** 1184, **TE:** 822, **WP:** 392

Thirst (Oliver), **AP:** 1467

"13,000 People" (Lawrence), **BP:** 800

Thirty-nine Poems (Ciardi), **AP:** 316

Thirty Poems (Merton), **AP:** 1328

This Blessed Earth (Wheelock), **AP:** 2125

This Body Is Made of Camphor and Gopherwood (Bly), **AP:** 193

This Close to the Earth (Shomer), **AP:** 1770

This in Which (Oppen), **AP:** 1479

"This Last Pain" (Empson), **BP:** 473

"This Lime-Tree Bower My Prison" (Coleridge), **BP:** 279

"This Pleasing Anxious Being" (Wilbur), **AP:** 2158

"This Scribe My Hand" (Belitt), **AP:** 118

This Strangest Everything (Ciardi), **AP:** 317

This Tree Will Be Here for a Thousand Years (Bly), **AP:** 193

Thomas, Antoine-Léonard, **TE:** 257

Thomas, Dylan, **BP:** 1245-1252; "Altarwise by Owl-Light," **BP:** 1249; "And Death Shall Have No Dominion," **BP:** 1249; "Over Sir John's Hill," **BP:** 1250

Thomas, Edward, **BP:** 1252-1256; "Adlestrop," **BP:** 1255; "As the Team's Head-Brass," **BP:** 1254; "No One So Much as You," **BP:** 1255

Thomas, R. S., **BP:** 1257-1260; *H'm*, **BP:** 1259; *Laboratories of the Spirit*, **BP:** 1259; *Song at the Year's Turning*, **BP:** 1259

Thomas and Beulah (Dove), **AP:** 490

Thomsen, Søren Ulrik, **TE:** 564

Thomson, James (1700-1748), **BP:** 1260-1264, **TE:** 165; *The Castle of Indolence*, **BP:** 1263; *Liberty*, **BP:** 1262; *The Seasons*, **BP:** 1262, **TE:** 165

Thomson, James (1834-1882), **BP:** 1264-1268; "The City of Dreadful Night," **BP:** 1267; "The Doom of a City," **BP:** 1266; "In the Room," **BP:** 1266; "Philosophy," **BP:** 1266; "A Voice from the Nile," **BP:** 1267

Thoreau, Henry David, **AP:** 1977-1984; "Friendship," **AP:** 1982; "Lately, Alas, I Knew a Gentle Boy," **AP:** 1982

Thorild, Thomas, **TE:** 532

Thorne, J. P., **TE:** 754

Those Not Elect (Adams), **AP:** 6

"Those Who Want Out" (Levertov), **AP:** 1114

Thousand Miles of Stars, A (McDonald), **AP:** 1220

"Three Kids" (Eberhart), **AP:** 531

Three Lives (Stein), **AP:** 1890

"Three Memories of Heaven" (Alberti), **EP:** 9

Three Poems (Ashbery), **AP:** 59

"Three Songs" (Crane), **AP:** 384

"Threnody" (Emerson), **AP:** 550

Throne of Labdacus, The (Schnackenberg), **AP:** 1730

Through the Looking-Glass and What Alice Found There (Carroll), **BP:** 217

Thuy, Le Thi Diem, **TE:** 26

Thwaites, Elizabeth Hart, **TE:** 43

"Thyrsis" (Arnold), **BP:** 34

Tibetan Book of the Dead, The (Padmasambhava), **TE:** 605

Tibetan poetry, **TE:** 604-611

Tibullinus. *See* Parny, Évariste-Désiré de Forges de

Tide and Continuities (Viereck), **AP:** 2046

Tides (Montague), **BP:** 917

Tiende Muse, Den (Hein), **EP:** 450

Tiepolo's Hound (Walcott), **WP:** 324

Tiger Joy (Benét), **AP:** 126

Tijdkrans (Gezelle), **EP:** 389

Timber (Jonson), **BP:** 713

Time and Materials (Hass), **AP:** 817

Time and Money (Matthews), **AP:** 1288

Time and the White Tigress (Barnard), **AP:** 105

Time in Armagh (Montague), **BP:** 922

Time of Bees, A (Van Duyn), **AP:** 2034

Time Without Number (Berrigan), **AP:** 139

Time's Fancy (Wallace), **AP:** 2093

Time's Laughingstocks, and Other Verses (Hardy), **BP:** 585

Time's Power (Rich), **AP:** 1639

Times Three (McGinley), **AP:** 1224

"Timon" (Rochester), **BP:** 1052

Tin Can, and Other Poems, The (Smith), **AP:** 1828

Tin Ujević Award, **CM:** 66, **EP:** 1210, **TE:** 886

"Tintagel" (Reed), **BP:** 1046

"Tire Hangs in the Woods, The" (Smith), **AP:** 1822

"Tired and Unhappy, You Think of Houses" (Schwartz), **AP:** 1742

Tish poets, **TE:** 40

Titanic, The (Pratt), **BP:** 1019

Titurel. See Schionatulander and Sigune

"To a Defeated Savior" (Wright), **AP:** 2224

"To a Falling Leaf" (Novalis), **EP:** 751

"To a Friend" (Arnold), **BP:** 33

"To a Lady, Asking Him How Long He Would Love Her" (Etherege), **BP:** 478

"To a Man on His Horse" (Prince), **BP:** 1023

"To a Poet" (Annensky), **WP:** 23

"To a Very Young Lady" (Etherege), **BP:** 478

To All Appearances (Miles), **AP:** 1342

"To Any Reader" (Stevens), **BP:** 1203

"To Autumn" (Keats), **BP:** 740

To Bedlam and Part Way Back (Sexton), **AP:** 1755

"To Blossoms" (Herrick), **BP:** 634

"To Brooklyn Bridge" (Crane), **AP:** 382

"To Carry the Child" (Smith), **BP:** 1169

"To Christ Crucified" (León), **EP:** 600

To Circumjack Cencrastus (MacDiarmid), **BP:** 850

"To Dives" (Belloc), **BP:** 78

To Do as Adam Did (Johnson), **AP:** 980

To Give and to Have (Quasimodo), **EP:** 877

"To Hedli" (MacNeice), **BP:** 860

"To His Coy Mistress" (Marvell), **BP:** 880

"To His Love" (Gurney), **BP:** 570

"To His Mistress Going to Bed" (Donne), **BP:** 411

"To Italy" (Leopardi), **EP:** 611

"To Liber" (Sedley), **BP:** 1096

"To Louise Pallavicini Fallen from a Horse" (Foscolo), **EP:** 343

"To M. S. Killed in Spain" (Fuller), **BP:** 501

To Marry Strangers (Scott), **AP:** 1748

"To My Brother" (Fuller), **BP:** 501

To My Contemporaries (Rolfe), **AP:** 1683

"To My Dear Friend Mr. Congreve" (Dryden), **BP:** 440

"To My Godson, on His Christening" (Van Duyn), **AP:** 2034

"To My Wife" (Pinter), **BP:** 1004

To Open (Menashe), **AP:** 1305

To Painting (Alberti), **EP:** 11

"To Penshurst" (Jonson), **BP:** 716

"To Poesy" (Owen), **BP:** 980

"To Roosevelt" (Darío), **WP:** 75

"To Santiago" (León), **EP:** 600

To See, To Take (Van Duyn), **AP:** 2035

To See You and Not to See You (Alberti), **EP:** 9

"To the Hawks" (Justice), **AP:** 988

"To the Healed Friend" (Foscolo), **EP:** 343

"To the Heart" (Różewicz), **EP:** 922

"To the King, on the Taking of Namure" (Congreve), **BP:** 299

"To the Memory of Mr. Oldham" (Dryden), **BP:** 439, **BP:** 972

"To the Muse" (Levertov), **AP:** 1115

"To the Nightingale" (Finch), **BP:** 494

To the Place of Trumpets (Kelly), **AP:** 1013

"To the Reader" (Baudelaire), **EP:** 83

"To the Tune" (Li Qingzhao), **WP:** 159

"To the Virgins, to make much of Time" (Herrick), **BP:** 632

To Those Who Have Gone Home Tired (Ehrhart), **AP:** 534

"To Tieck" (Novalis), **EP:** 754

To Urania (Brodsky), **WP:** 50

To What Strangers, What Welcome (J. V. Cunningham), **AP:** 421

"Tobacco-Shop" (Pessoa), **EP:** 814

Todo más claro, y otros poemas (Salinas), **EP:** 940

Tokyo Butter (Moss), **AP:** 1382

Toldi (Arany), **EP:** 44

Tolson, Melvin B., **AP:** 1984-1988; *A Gallery of Harlem Portraits*, **AP:** 1986; *Harlem Gallery*, **AP:** 1986; *Libretto for the Republic of Liberia*, **AP:** 1986; *Rendezvous with America*, **AP:** 1986

Tombs of the Kings, The (Hébert), **BP:** 607

Tomlinson, Charles, **BP:** 1268-1277; *American Scenes, and Other Poems*, **BP:** 1271; *Annunciations*, **BP:** 1274; *The Door in the Wall*, **BP:** 1275; *The Flood*, **BP:** 1274; *Jubilation*, **BP:** 1275; *A Peopled Landscape*, **BP:** 1271; *Renga*, **TE:** 200; *The Return*, **BP:** 1274; *Seeing Is Believing*, **BP:** 1271; *The Shaft*, **BP:** 1274; *The Vineyard Above the Sea*, **BP:** 1275; *The Way In, and Other Poems*, **BP:** 1273; *The Way of a World*, **BP:** 1272; *Written on Water*, **BP:** 1273

Tone, defined, **AP:** 2306, **BP:** 1390, **EP:** 1184, **TE:** 822, **WP:** 392

"Tonight at Seven-Thirty" (Auden), **BP:** 53

Too Bright to See (Gregg), **AP:** 736

Toomer, Jean, **AP:** 1988-1994; "Blue Meridian," **AP:** 1993; *Cane*, **AP:** 1990; "Harvest Song," **AP:** 1992; "Karintha," **AP:** 1991; "The Lost Dancer," **AP:** 1993

Topographical poetry. *See* Categorized Index

"Török Bálint" (Alany), **EP:** 47

Torse Three (Middleton), **BP:** 900

"Toska." *See* "Depression"

Tóth, Árpád, **TE:** 359

Tottel's Miscellany (anthology), **TE:** 134

Touch (Gunn), **BP:** 564

"Toute l'âme résumée . . ." *See* "All the Soul Indrawn . . ."

Toward a Speech Act Theory of Literary Discourse (Pratt), **TE:** 758

Toward the Distant Islands (Carruth), **AP:** 283

Toward the Winter Solstice (Steele), **AP:** 1884

Towards the Last Spike (Pratt), **BP:** 1020

Town and Country Matters (Hollander), **AP:** 880

Town of Hill, The (Hall), **AP:** 779

Toxic Flora (Hahn), **AP:** 771

"Tractable Man, A" (Michaux), **EP:** 692

Tragoudi tes adelphes mou, To (Ritsos), **EP:** 908

Traherne, Thomas, **BP:** 1277-1283; *Centuries of Meditations*, **BP:** 1279; *Christian Ethicks*, **BP:** 1280; *Traherne's Poems of Felicity*, **BP:** 1281

Traherne's Poems of Felicity (Traherne), **BP:** 1281

Traité du sublime (Boileau-Despréaux), **EP:** 140

Trakl, Georg, **EP:** 1033-1039, **TE:** 306; "In Winter," **EP:** 1035; "The Occident," **EP:** 1035

Traktat poetycki. See Treatise on Poetry, A

"Transcendental Etude" (Rich), **AP:** 1639

Transcendentalism, **TE:** 179. *See also* Categorized Index

Transfigurations (Wright), **AP:** 2239

Transformational poetry, Native American, **TE:** 480

Transformations (Sexton), **AP:** 1757

Transitional Poem (Day Lewis), **BP:** 387

Translation; Indian English poetry, **TE:** 369; Native American poetry, **TE:** 481

Transparent Man, The (Hecht), **AP:** 833

Transplants (Macdonald), **AP:** 1213

Tranströmer, Tomas, EP: 1039-1044, **TE:** 550; "An Artist in the North," **EP:** 1042; *Baltics,* **EP:** 1042; *The Great Enigma,* **EP:** 1043; "The Open Window," **EP:** 1041; *Sorrow Gondola,* **EP:** 1042

Trapassi, Pietro. *See* Metastasio, Pietro

Trappings (Howard), **AP:** 912

Trasumanar e organizzar (Pasolini), **EP:** 781

Traveling Light (Wagoner), **AP:** 2065

Traveling Through the Dark (Stafford), **AP:** 1875

"Traveller, The" (De la Mare), **BP:** 403

Traveller, The (Goldsmith), **BP:** 522

Travels (Merwin), **AP:** 1336

Traverseger, George L., **TE:** 750

Tread the Dark (Ignatow), **AP:** 947

Treatise of Civil Power, A (Hill), **BP:** 649

Treatise on Poetry, A (Miłosz), **EP:** 715

"Tree, The" (Finch), **BP:** 493

Tree Witch, The (Viereck), **AP:** 2046

Treehouse, and Other Poems, The (Emanuel), **AP:** 539

Trembecki, Stanisław, **TE:** 492

Trethewey, Natasha, AP: 1995-1998; *Bellocq's Ophelia,* **AP:** 1996; *Domestic Work,* **AP:** 1996; *Native Guard,* **AP:** 1997

"Tretis of the Tua Mariit Wemen and the Wedo, The" (Dunbar), **BP:** 447

"Trial of a City" (Birney), **BP:** 89

Tribe of Ben, **TE:** 150

"Trichter, Die." *See* "Funnels, The"

"Trifler, The" (Giusti), **EP:** 395

Trilce (Vallejo), **WP:** 304

Trilling, Lionel, **TE:** 732

Trimmings (Mullen), **AP:** 1388

Triolet, Elsa, **EP:** 37

Trionfi (Boiardo), **EP:** 136

Trionfi (Petrarch). *See Triumphs*

"Trionfo della libertà, Il" (Manzoni), **EP:** 663

"Trip, The" (Baudeliare), **EP:** 86

"Triptych" (Reed), **BP:** 1046

Tristan, T. *See* Tzara, Tristan

Tristan and Isolde (Gottfried von Strassburg, **EP:** 416

"Tristesse" (Lamartine), **EP:** 594

Tristia (Mandelstam), **WP:** 167

Triumph of Achilles, The (Glück), **AP:** 714

Triumph of Love, The (Hill), **BP:** 647, **TE:** 199

Triumphs (Petrarch), **EP:** 833

Trivia (Gay), **BP:** 517

Trivial Breath (Wylie), **AP:** 2242

Trochee, defined, **AP:** 2306, **BP:** 1390, **EP:** 1184, **TE:** 822, **WP:** 392

Troilus and Criseyde (Chaucer), **BP:** 249

Tropicalization (Cruz), **AP:** 402

"Tropics in New York, The" (McKay), **AP:** 1237

Troubador poetry, **TE:** 237

Trouble with Poetry, and Other Poems, The (Collins), **AP:** 345

Trouvères (poetic style), **TE:** 239

True Bride, The (Gerstler), **AP:** 661

True Confessions of an Albino Terrorist, The (Breytenbach), **EP:** 168

True Minds (Ponsot), **AP:** 1570

True Stories (Atwood), **BP:** 44

Trumpets from the Islands of Their Eviction (Espada), **AP:** 560

Truncation, defined, **AP:** 2306, **BP:** 1390, **EP:** 1184, **TE:** 822, **WP:** 392

Truth About Small Towns, The (Baker), **AP:** 79

Trying to Surprise God (Meinke), **AP:** 1292

Trzy zimy (Miłosz), **EP:** 715

Tsangyang Gyatso. *See* Dalai Lama, Sixth

Tsoai-talee. *See* Momaday, N. Scott

Tsuki ni hoeru. See Howling at the Moon

Tsvetayeva, Marina, TE: 521, **WP:** 293-299; *The Demesne of the Swans,* **WP:** 297; *Vecherny albom,* **WP:** 297; *Versty I,* **WP:** 297; *Volshebny fonar,* **WP:** 297

Tu Fu. *See* Du Fu

"Tu ti spezzisti." *See* "You Shattered"

Tuckerman, Frederick Goddard, AP: 1998-2002; "The Cricket," **AP:** 2001; "Refrigerium," **AP:** 2000; "Rhotruda," **AP:** 2000; Sonnet X, **AP:** 2000

Tudor age. *See* Categorized Index

Tullin, Christian Braunmann, **TE:** 531

"Tündéralom" (Petőfi), **EP:** 823

"Tune" (Li Qingzhao), **WP:** 159

Tunes for Bears to Dance To (Wallace), **AP:** 2091

"Tunnel, The" (Crane), **AP:** 385

Turberville, George, **TE:** 136

Turkey. *See* Geographical Index

Turning Point (Seferis), **EP:** 959

Turning Wind, A (Rukeyser),
    AP: 1688

Turoldo, David Maria, **TE:** 407

"Turtle, The" (Kees), **AP:** 1010

Turtle Island (Snyder), **AP:** 1847

Tuscany. *See* Geographical Index

Tuwhare, Hone, **TE:** 34

Twelve, The (Blok), **WP:** 38

Twelve Moons (Oliver), **AP:** 1466

Twelve Words of the Gypsy, The
    (Palamas), **TE:** 335

Twentieth Century Pleasures (Hass),
    AP: 816

*Twenty Love Poems and a Song of
    Despair* (Neruda), **WP:** 199

Twichell, Chase, **AP:** 2002-2006;
    Dog Language, **AP:** 2005; *The
    Ghost of Eden*, **AP:** 2003; *The
    Snow Watcher*, **AP:** 2004

"Twickham Garden" (Donne),
    BP: 413

Twigs and Knucklebones (Lindsay),
    AP: 1145

"Twins, The" (Bukowski), **AP:** 267

"Two Domains, The" (Goldbarth),
    AP: 723

"Two Encounters" (Sissman),
    AP: 1804

"Two Experiments" (MacBeth),
    BP: 842

"Two Hangovers" (Wright),
    AP: 2227

Two-Headed Poems (Atwood),
    BP: 44

Two-Headed Woman (Clifton),
    AP: 328

"Two Lovers, The" (Marie de
    France), **EP:** 670

Two-Part Inventions (Howard),
    AP: 911

Two Trees (Voigt), **AP:** 2057

Tyazhelaya lira (Khodasevich),
    WP: 136

Types of Shape (Hollander), **AP:** 879

Tyutchev, Fyodor, **TE:** 515

Tzara, Tristan, **EP:** 1044-1050;
    *Approximate Man, and Other
    Writings*, **EP:** 1049; "The Circus
    Performers," **EP:** 1049; *De nos
    oiseaux*, **EP:** 1048; "The Death of
    Guillaume Apollinaire,"
    EP: 1048; "Little Town in
    Siberia," **EP:** 1048; *Primele
    Poème*, **EP:** 1047; "Sunday,"
    EP: 1048; *Vingt-cinq Poèmes*,
    EP: 1048

"Uder." *See* "Blow, The"

Ueda Bin, **TE:** 428

Új versek. See *New Verses*

Ujević, Tin, **TE:** 75

Ukraine. *See* Geographical Index

"Ulalume" (Poe), **AP:** 1565

"Ultima Ratio Regum" (Spender),
    BP: 1187

Ultraism. *See* Categorized Index

Ultraísmo, **TE:** 437

Ultramarine (Carver), **AP:** 287

"Ulysses" (Tennyson), **BP:** 1239,
    EP: 929

Un, Ko. *See* Ko Un

"Una-ha vez tiven un cravo." *See* "I
    Used to Have a Nail"

Unamuno y Jugo, Miguel de,
    EP: 1051-1056, **TE:** 598;
    Cancionero, **EP:** 1054; *The Christ
    of Velázquez*, **EP:** 1054;
    "Farewell, Go with God!,"
    EP: 1053; "My Religion,"
    EP: 1053

Unbearable Heart, The (Hahn),
    AP: 770

Uncertainties and Rest (Steele),
    AP: 1882

"Under Ben Bulben" (Yeats),
    BP: 1347

Under Stars (Gallagher), **AP:** 641

Under the Vulture-Tree (Bottoms),
    AP: 217

Underneath the Lantern (Meinke),
    AP: 1292

Undersea Farmer, The (Howes),
    AP: 922

Undersong (Lorde), **AP:** 1170

Undertones of War (Blunden),
    BP: 107

Underwoods (Stevenson), **BP:** 1204

Undesirables (Gunn), **BP:** 566

Unending Blues (Simic), **AP:** 1788

Ungaretti, Giuseppe, **EP:** 1056-
    1064, **TE:** 402; "Agony,"
    EP: 1059; *L'allegria*, **EP:** 1059; *Il
    dolore*, **EP:** 1062; "The End of
    Chronos," **EP:** 1061; "Pity,"
    EP: 1061; "The Rivers,"
    EP: 1060; *Sentimento del tempo*,
    EP: 1060; *La terra promessa*,
    EP: 1062; "You Shattered,"
    EP: 1062

Ungrateful Garden, The (Kizer),
    AP: 1048

"Unhappy Lot of Mr. Knott, The"
    (Lowell), **AP:** 1184

United States. *See* Geographical
    Index

Unknown Eros, and Other Odes, The
    (Patmore), **BP:** 989

Unraveling Strangeness, The (Weigl),
    AP: 2105

Unrest-Field (Popa), **EP:** 857

Unter dem Eisen des Mondes
    (Bernhard), **EP:** 117

"Unter Zeiten." *See* "Among Tenses"

Untergang der Titanic, Der. See
    Sinking of the Titanic, The

Untermeyer, Louis, **AP:** 2007-2015;
    "Burning Bush," **AP:** 2012; "Coal
    Fire," **AP:** 2014; "A Displaced
    Orpheus," **AP:** 2014; "Eve
    Speaks," **AP:** 2011; "Nightmare
    by Day," **AP:** 2012

Until the Morning After (Awoonor), **WP:** 31

Untitled Subjects (Howard), **AP:** 911

Up Country (Kumin), **AP:** 1076

Updike, John, **AP:** 2016-2023; *Americana, and Other Poems*, **AP:** 2021; *Endpoint, and Other Poems*, **AP:** 2022; "Love Sonnet," **AP:** 2019; "Midpoint," **AP:** 2019

"Upon Appleton House" (Marvell), **BP:** 882

"Upon my Lady Carliles walking in Hampton-Court garden" (Suckling), **BP:** 1209

"Upon some Alterations in my Mistress, after my Departure into France" (Carew), **BP:** 210

"Upptäckt." *See* "Discovery"

Upstate Madonna (Lifshin), **AP:** 1139

Urdu poetry. *See* Indian English poetry

"Uriel" (Emerson), **AP:** 549

U.S. 1 (Rukeyser), **AP:** 1688

Use of Fire, The (Price), **AP:** 1588

Use of Poetry and the Use of Criticism, The (Eliot), **TE:** 715

Use Trouble (Harper), **AP:** 799

Uses of Adversity, The (Wallace), **AP:** 2093

Usher (Fairchild), **AP:** 581

"Utyos." *See* "Cliff, The"

Uvas y el viento, Las (Neruda), **WP:** 202

V., and Other Poems (Harrison), **BP:** 592

Vagrant Grace (Bottoms), **AP:** 218

Vägvisare till underjorden. See Guide to the Underworld

Vajda, János, **TE:** 358

Vakalo, Eleni, **TE:** 349

"Vale of teares, A" (Southwell), **BP:** 1180

"Valediction, A" (Donne), **BP:** 412

Valentine, Jean, **AP:** 2024-2027; *Door in the Mountain*, **AP:** 2025; *Little Boat*, **AP:** 2026; *The River at Wolf*, **AP:** 2026

Valentines (Kooser), **AP:** 1073

"Valentines to the Wide World" (Van Duyn), **AP:** 2033

Valéry, Paul, **EP:** 1065-1073, **TE:** 272, **TE:** 639; "The Graveyard by the Sea," **EP:** 1069

Vallejo, César, **WP:** 300-308; *The Black Heralds*, **WP:** 303; *Human Poems*, **WP:** 305; *Spain, Take This Cup from Me*, **WP:** 307; *Trilce*, **WP:** 304

"Valley, The" (Lamartine), **EP:** 594

Valley of the Many-Colored Grasses (Johnson), **AP:** 977

"Vallon, Le." *See* "Valley, The"

Vālmīki, **WP:** 308-311; *The Ramayana*, **WP:** 310; *The Supreme Yoga*, **WP:** 310

Van Doren, Mark, **AP:** 2027-2031; and John Berryman, **AP:** 157; "Now the Sky," **AP:** 2030; "The Sage in the Sierra," **AP:** 2030; "A Winter Diary," **AP:** 2029

Van Duyn, Mona, **AP:** 2032-2038; *Firefall*, **AP:** 2037; "From Yellow Lake," **AP:** 2033; *Letters from a Father, and Other Poems*, **AP:** 2036; *Near Changes*, **AP:** 2036; *Selected Poems*, **AP:** 2037; *A Time of Bees*, **AP:** 2034; "To My Godson, on His Christening," **AP:** 2034; *To See, To Take*, **AP:** 2035; "Valentines to the Wide World," **AP:** 2033

Vanishing Lung Syndrome (Holub), **EP:** 495

Vanity of Human Wishes, The (Johnson), **BP:** 704

"Van Winkle" (Crane), **AP:** 382

"Vapor Trail Reflected in the Frog Pond" (Kinnell), **AP:** 1036

Vara, Madeleine. *See* Riding, Laura

Varela, Luis de León. *See* León, Luis de

Variety Photoplays (Field), **AP:** 604

Varnalis, Kostas, **TE:** 338

Varro, **TE:** 449

Vaughan, Henry, **BP:** 1284-1289; *Olor Iscanus*, **BP:** 1286; *Silex Scintillans*, **BP:** 1287; *Thalia Rediviva*, **BP:** 1288

Vecher (Akhmatova), **WP:** 5

Vecherny albom (Tsvetayeva), **WP:** 297

Vega, Garcilaso de la. *See* Garcilaso de la Vega

Vega Carpio, Lope de, **EP:** 1073-1080, **TE:** 594; *La corona trágica*, **EP:** 1078; *La Dragontea*, **EP:** 1077; *Gatomachia*, **EP:** 1078; *El Isidro*, **EP:** 1077; *Jerusalén conquistada*, **EP:** 1077; *Laurel de Apolo*, **EP:** 1078; *The New Art of Writing Plays*, **EP:** 1077

Veinte poemas de amor y una canción desesperada. See Twenty Love Poems and a Song of Despair

Velika Skitija (Pavlović), **EP:** 789

Venetian Vespers, The (Hecht), **AP:** 832

Venison, Alfred. *See* Pound, Ezra

Vennberg, Karl, **TE:** 549

Venus and Adonis (Shakespeare), **BP:** 1106

Venus Hottentot, The (Alexander), **AP:** 18

Verdaguer, Jacint, **TE:** 51

Verdrehte Welt (Biermann), **EP:** 124

Vergil, **EP:** 1080-1089, **TE:** 451; *Aeneid*, **EP:** 1083; *Eclogues*, **EP:** 1082; *Georgics*, **EP:** 1083

Verhaeren, Émile, **EP:** 1089-1092, **TE:** 269; "The Mill," **EP:** 1091; "The Peasants," **EP:** 1090; "The Snow," **EP:** 1092; *Les Villages illusoires*, **EP:** 1092

Verismo, **TE:** 393

"Verklighet [*drömd*], En." *See*
 "Reality [*dreamed*], A"

Verlaine, Paul, **EP:** 1093-1099,
 TE: 267, **TE:** 642; "L'Art
 poétique," **EP:** 1095; *Gallant
 Parties*, **EP:** 1096; "It Is Crying in
 My Heart," **EP:** 1097; "My
 Familiar Dream," **EP:** 1095; "The
 Piano Kissed by a Fragile Hand,"
 EP: 1097; *Poèmes saturniens*,
 EP: 1095; *Romances Without
 Words*, **EP:** 1097, **TE:** 268;
 Sagesse, **EP:** 1097; "The Sound
 of the Hunting Horn," **EP:** 1098

"Verlorenes Ich." *See* "Lost Self"

Vernacular poetry; England, **TE:** 131;
 Italy, **TE:** 377; Latin, **TE:** 464

Vernacular Republic, The (Murray),
 BP: 949

Verrà la morte e avrà i tuoi occhi
 (Pavese), **EP:** 785

"Vers dorés" (Nerval), **EP:** 747

Verse, defined, **AP:** 2306, **BP:** 1390,
 EP: 1184, **TE:** 822, **WP:** 392

Verse drama, defined, **AP:** 2306,
 BP: 1390, **EP:** 1184, **TE:** 822,
 WP: 392

Verse dramatists. *See* Categorized
 Index

Verse paragraph, defined, **AP:** 2306,
 BP: 1390, **EP:** 1184, **TE:** 822,
 WP: 392

*Verses on the Death of Dr. Swift,
 D.S.P.D.* (Swift), **BP:** 1224

"Verses wrote in a Lady's Ivory
 Table-Book" (Swift), **BP:** 1222

Verset claudélien, **TE:** 271

Versos de salón (Parra), **WP:** 220

Versty I (Tsvetayeva), **WP:** 297

Versus (Nash), **AP:** 1403

Versus fescennini, **TE:** 443

Versus saturnius, **TE:** 443

*Verte y no verte. See To You and Not
 to You*

Vertebrae Rosaries (Dacey), **AP:** 429

Vertical Man (Kinsella), **BP:** 756

Very, Jones, **AP:** 2039-2042; "The
 New Birth," **AP:** 2041; "The
 Wind-Flower," **AP:** 2041

Vesaas, Tarjei, **TE:** 551

Vicarion, Count Palmiro. *See* Logue,
 Christopher

Vice (Ai), **AP:** 11

Victims of the Latest Dance Craze
 (Eady), **AP:** 523

Victor, Comte de Vigny, Alfred. *See*
 Vigny, Alfred de

Victorian era, **BP:** 764, **TE:** 180;
 criticism, **TE:** 712; reaction
 against, **TE:** 186. *See also*
 Categorized Index

Victories of Love, The (Patmore),
 BP: 988

Victory odes, **TE:** 327

Vides, Claribel Isabel Alegría. *See*
 Alegría, Claribel

Viereck, Peter, **AP:** 2042-2048;
 Archer in the Marrow, **AP:** 2046;
 Door, **AP:** 2047; *The First
 Morning*, **AP:** 2045; "Kilroy,"
 AP: 2044; "Nostalgia," **AP:** 2045;
 The Persimmon Tree, **AP:** 2045;
 "Poet," **AP:** 2044; *Terror and
 Decorum*, **AP:** 2044; *Tide and
 Continuities*, **AP:** 2046; *The Tree
 Witch*, **AP:** 2046

Vietnam War; John Balaban, **AP:** 81;
 Daniel Berrigan, **AP:** 138; Robert
 Bly, **AP:** 190; W. D. Ehrhart,
 AP: 533; Yusef Komunyakaa,
 AP: 1067; Denise Levertov,
 AP: 1116; Bruce Weigl,
 AP: 2103; C. K. Williams,
 AP: 2163

Views of Jeopardy (Gilbert), **AP:** 675

Vigil, The (Williams), **AP:** 2165

Vigny, Alfred de, **EP:** 1099-1106,
 TE: 261; "La Bouteille à la mer,"
 EP: 1105; *Les Destinées*,

EP: 1105; "Moïse," **EP:** 1103,
 TE: 261; "Le Mont des Oliviers,"
 EP: 1103; "La Mort du loup,"
 EP: 1104

Villa, José García, **AP:** 2048-2054,
 TE: 25; *Have Come, Am Here*,
 AP: 2051; *Many Voices*,
 AP: 2051; *Poems by Doveglion*,
 AP: 2051; *Selected Poems and
 New*, **AP:** 2053; *Volume Two*,
 AP: 2052

Village, The (Crabbe), **BP:** 330

Village Life, A (Glück), **AP:** 718

Villages illusoires, Les (Verhaeren),
 EP: 1092

Villancicos, **TE:** 584

Villanelle, defined, **AP:** 2306,
 BP: 1390, **EP:** 1184, **TE:** 822,
 WP: 392

Villion, François, **TE:** 244

"Villon" (Bunting), **BP:** 170

Villon, François, **EP:** 1106-1112;
 The Great Testament, **EP:** 1109;
 The Legacy, **EP:** 1108; *Poems in
 Slang*, **EP:** 1111

Vincent Millay, Edna St. *See* Millay,
 Edna St. Vincent

Vineyard Above the Sea, The
 (Tomlinson), **BP:** 1275

Vingt-cinq Poèmes (Tzara), **EP:** 1048

Violent Foam, The (Zamora),
 WP: 355

*Violenta espuma, La. See Violent
 Foam, The*

Viper Jazz (Tate), **AP:** 1953

Viper Rum (Karr), **AP:** 995

Virgil. *See* Vergil

*Virtuoso Literature for Two and Four
 Hands* (Wakoski), **AP:** 2073

Visible Man, The (Cole), **AP:** 335

"Vision of Spring in Winter, A"
 (Swinburne), **BP:** 1234

*Vision of William, Concerning Piers
 the Plowman, The* (Langland),
 BP: 781, **TE:** 110

Visionary poetry. *See* Categorized Index

"Visions and Interpretations" (Lee), **AP:** 1105

Visions from the Ramble (Hollander), **AP:** 879

Visions of the Daughters of Albion (Blake), **BP:** 101

"Visit to the Charterhouse, A" (Mörike), **EP:** 734

"Visitant, The" (Roethke), **AP:** 1674

Visitations (MacNeice), **BP:** 864

"Visiting the Temple of Gathered Fragrance" (Wang Wei), **WP:** 330

Vita Nova (Glück), **AP:** 716

Vital Provisions (Price), **AP:** 1588

Vital Signs (Slavitt), **AP:** 1813

Vixen, The (Merwin), **AP:** 1336

Vizenor, Gerald R., **TE:** 484

Vocabulaire (Cocteau), **EP:** 257

Vociani, **TE:** 401

Vodnik, Valentin, **TE:** 579

Vogelweide, Walther von der. *See* Walther von der Vogelweide

"Voice from the Nile, A" (Thomson), **BP:** 1267

Voice in the Mountain, A (Davison), **AP:** 440

Voices (Clifton), **AP:** 329

Voigt, Ellen Bryant, AP: 2054-2058; *Claiming Kin*, **AP:** 2056; *The Forces of Plenty*, **AP:** 2056; *Kyrie*, **AP:** 2057; *The Lotus Flowers*, **AP:** 2057; *Messenger*, **AP:** 2057; *Shadow of Heaven*, **AP:** 2057; "Song and Story," **AP:** 2056; *Two Trees*, **AP:** 2057

"Voiture's Urania" (Etherege), **BP:** 478

Volatile (Hahn), **AP:** 770

Volcano Sequence, The (Ostriker), **AP:** 1504

Vold, Jan Erik, **TE:** 557

Volkslied, **TE:** 289

Volshebny fonar (Tsvetayeva), **WP:** 297

Voltaire, **TE:** 255

Volume Two (Villa), **AP:** 2052

"Vom armen B. B." *See* "Of Poor B. B."

Von Aue, Hartmann. *See* Hartmann von Aue

Von Hofmannsthal, Hugo. *See* Hofmannsthal, Hugo von

Von Schwelle zu Schwelle (Celan), **EP:** 218

Vormärz, **TE:** 300

Vörösmarty, Mihály, EP: 1112-1118, **TE:** 356; *Csongor és Tünde*, **EP:** 1115; "The Summons," **EP:** 1116; *Zalán futása*, **EP:** 1114

"Vowels" (Rimbaud), **EP:** 900

Vox Clamantis (Gower), **BP:** 529

"Voyage, Le." *See* "Trip, The"

Voz a tí debida, La. See *My Voice Because of You*

Voznesensky, Andrei, TE: 522, **WP:** 311-316; *The Ditch*, **WP:** 314; *Gadanie po knige*, **WP:** 315; "I Am Goya," **WP:** 314; "Oza," **WP:** 314; "Parabolic Ballad," **WP:** 314

Vrchlický, Jaroslav, **TE:** 83

Vučja so. See *Wolf Salt*

"Vykhozhu odin ya na dorogu . . ." *See* "I Walk Out Alone onto the Road . . ."

Vysokaya bolezn'. See *High Malady*

W Szwajcarii. See *In Switzerland*

Wacław (Słowacki), **EP:** 977

Wage War on Silence (Miller), **AP:** 1351

Wagoner, David, AP: 2059-2067; *Dry Sun, Dry Wind*, **AP:** 2062; *Good Morning and Good Night*, **AP:** 2066; *The House of Song*, **AP:** 2065; *In Broken Country*, **AP:** 2064; *Landfall*, **AP:** 2064; *A Map of the Night*, **AP:** 2066;

"Seven Songs for an Old Voice," **AP:** 2063; *Traveling Light*, **AP:** 2065; *Walt Whitman Bathing*, **AP:** 2064; *Who Shall Be the Sun?*, **AP:** 2063

"Waiting" (Pinsky), **AP:** 1541

"Waiting for the Barbarians" (Cavafy), **EP:** 207

Waiting for the King of Spain (Wakoski), **AP:** 2074

Waking, The (Roethke), **AP:** 1675

Wakoski, Diane, AP: 2068-2076; *Coins and Coffins*, **AP:** 2070; *Dancing on the Grave of a Son of a Bitch*, **AP:** 2073; *Discrepancies and Apparitions*, **AP:** 2070; *The George Washington Poems*, **AP:** 2071; *Greed*, **AP:** 2074; *Inside the Blood Factory*, **AP:** 2071; *The Magellanic Clouds*, **AP:** 2072; *The Man Who Shook Hands*, **AP:** 2074; *The Motorcycle Betrayal Poems*, **AP:** 2072; *Smudging*, **AP:** 2073; *Virtuoso Literature for Two and Four Hands*, **AP:** 2073; *Waiting for the King of Spain*, **AP:** 2074

Walcott, Derek, TE: 45, **TE:** 211, **TE:** 505, **WP:** 317-326; *Another Life*, **WP:** 320; *The Arkansas Testament*, **WP:** 322; *The Bounty*, **WP:** 324; *The Castaway, and Other Poems*, **WP:** 320; *Collected Poems, 1948-1984*, **WP:** 322; *The Fortunate Traveller*, **WP:** 321; *The Gulf, and Other Poems*, **WP:** 320; *In a Green Night*, **WP:** 319; *Midsummer*, **WP:** 322; *Omeros*, **WP:** 323; *Sea Grapes*, **WP:** 320; *The Star-Apple Kingdom*, **WP:** 321; *Tiepolo's Hound*, **WP:** 324

Waldman, Anne, AP: 2076-2080; *Fast Speaking Woman*, **AP:** 2078; *Giant Night*, **AP:** 2078; *In the*

Room of Never Grieve, **AP:** 2079; *Iovis*, **AP:** 2078; *Manatee/ Humanity*, **AP:** 2079; *Marriage*, **AP:** 2078

Wales. *See* Geographical Index

"Walesi bardok, A." *See* "Welsh Bards, The"

Walk on the Ledge (Yevtushenko), **WP:** 346

Walk with Tom Jefferson, A (Levine), **AP:** 1124

"Walker" (Belitt), **AP:** 118

Walker, Alice, **AP:** 2080-2086; *Absolute Trust in the Goodness of the Earth*, **AP:** 2084; *Good Night, Willie Lee, I'll See You in the Morning*, **AP:** 2083; *Her Blue Body Everything We Know*, **AP:** 2084; *Horses Make a Landscape Look More Beautiful*, **AP:** 2083; *Once*, **AP:** 2083; *A Poem Traveled Down My Arm*, **AP:** 2085; *Revolutionary Petunias, and Other Poems*, **AP:** 2083

Walker, Kath, **TE:** 503

Walker, Margaret, **AP:** 2086-2090; *For My People*, **AP:** 2088; *Prophets for a New Day*, **AP:** 2089

Walking the Black Cat (Simic), **AP:** 1790

Walking the Boundaries (Davison), **AP:** 439

Walking to Martha's Vineyard (Wright), **AP:** 2220

"Walking to Sleep" (Wilbur), **AP:** 2157

Wallace, Ronald, **AP:** 2090-2094; *For a Limited Time Only*, **AP:** 2093; *The Makings of Happiness*, **AP:** 2092; *People and Dog in the Sun*, **AP:** 2092; *Plums, Stones, Kisses, and Hooks*, **AP:** 2091; *Time's Fancy*,

AP: 2093; *Tunes for Bears to Dance To*, **AP:** 2091; *The Uses of Adversity*, **AP:** 2093

Wallace Stevens Award, **AP:** 2330, **CM:** 65, **TE:** 885

Waller, Edmund, **BP:** 1290-1297, **TE:** 150; "Go, Lovely Rose," **BP:** 1295; "Instructions to a Painter," **BP:** 1296; "Of His Majesty's Receiving the News of the Duke of Buckingham's Death," **BP:** 1293; "Of the Lady Who Can Sleep When She Pleases," **BP:** 1294; "Of the Last Verses in the Book," **BP:** 1296; "A Panegyrick to My Lord Protector," **BP:** 1295; "A Poem on St. James' Park as Lately Improved by His Majesty," **BP:** 1295; "The Story of Phoebus and Daphne, Applied," **BP:** 1294

"Walls" (Cavafy), **EP:** 209

Walls of Thebes, The (Slavitt), **AP:** 1814

"Walt Whitman" (Markham), **AP:** 1277

Walt Whitman Award, **AP:** 2331, **CM:** 67, **TE:** 887

Walt Whitman Bathing (Wagoner), **AP:** 2064

Walther von der Vogelweide, **EP:** 1119-1126, **TE:** 287; "Elegie," **EP:** 1125; "I Was Sitting upon a Rock," **EP:** 1124; "Otto tone," **EP:** 1124

Waltzing Through the Endtime (Bottoms), **AP:** 218

"Wanderer, The" (Smith), **BP:** 1166

"Wandering About Mount Tai" (Li Bo), **WP:** 153

Wandering Islands, The (Hope), **BP:** 663

Wang Anshi, **TE:** 63

Wang Wei, **TE:** 60, **TE:** 62, **WP:** 326-333; "Deer Park,"

WP: 330; "Lady Xi," **WP:** 329; "Visiting the Temple of Gathered Fragrance," **WP:** 330

Want Bone, The (Pinsky), **AP:** 1545

War (Pinter), **BP:** 1003

"War Diary" (Radnóti), **EP:** 881

War of the Secret Agents, and Other Poems, The (Coulette), **AP:** 362

War poetry; ancient Greece, **TE:** 324; France, **TE:** 271; Greece, **TE:** 344; Norway, **TE:** 547

War poets. *See* Categorized Index

War Stories (Nemerov), **AP:** 1414

Ward, Mary Jo. *See* Bang, Mary Jo

Ware the Hawk (Skelton), **BP:** 1156

Warren, Austin, **TE:** 746

Warren, Robert Penn, **AP:** 2094-2101; *Brother to Dragons*, **AP:** 2099; *Chief Joseph of the Nez Percé*, **AP:** 2100; *Promises*, **AP:** 2098; "Pure and Impure Poetry," **TE:** 744; *You, Emperors, and Others*, **AP:** 2099

Waste Land, The (Eliot), **BP:** 463, **TE:** 189

"Wasted Evening, A" (Musset), **EP:** 738

Watchboy, What of the Night? (Cassity), **AP:** 294

Watching the Spring Festival (Bidart), **AP:** 168

Water Street (Merrill), **AP:** 1318

Waterborne (Gregerson), **AP:** 733

Watts, Isaac, **BP:** 1297-1303, **TE:** 168; *Horae Lyricae*, **BP:** 1300; *Reliquiae Juveniles*, **BP:** 1301

Wave, A (Ashbery), **AP:** 62, **TE:** 676

Waving from Shore (Mueller), **AP:** 1386

Way (Scalapino), **AP:** 1726

Way In, and Other Poems, The (Tomlinson), **BP:** 1273

Way of a World, The (Tomlinson), **BP:** 1272

"Way Through the Woods, The" (Kipling), **BP:** 764

Way to Rainy Mountain, The (Momaday), **AP:** 1361

Ważyk, Adam, EP: 1126-1130; "Poem for Adults," **EP:** 1129

We a BaddDDD People (Sanchez), **AP:** 1701

"We Have Found a New Land" (Awooner), **WP:** 30

"We Real Cool" (Brooks), **AP:** 249

We Walk the Way of the New World (Madhubuti), **AP:** 1271

"We Wear the Mask" (McKay), **AP:** 1238

Weary Blues, The (Hughes), **AP:** 930

Weather Central (Kooser), **AP:** 1071

Weathers and Edges (Booth), **AP:** 211

"Weaver Bird, The" (Awooner), **WP:** 29

Weight of the Body, The (Barańczak), **EP:** 79

Weigl, Bruce, AP: 2102-2107; *Archeology of the Circle,* **AP:** 2104; *Declension in the Village of Chung Luong,* **AP:** 2105; "First Letter to Calumpang," **AP:** 2104; "On the Anniversary of Her Grace," **AP:** 2104; "Song of Napalm," **AP:** 2104; *The Unraveling Strangeness,* **AP:** 2105

Welch, James, AP: 2107-2111; *Day After Chasing Porcupines,* **AP:** 2110; *The Day the Children Took Over,* **AP:** 2110; "Knives," **AP:** 2109; "The Renegade Wants Words," **AP:** 2109

"Welcome and Farewell" (Goethe), **EP:** 401

Welhaven, Johan Sebastian, **TE:** 536

Wellek, René, **TE:** 746

"Wellfleet Whale, The" (Kunitz), **AP:** 1091

Wellspring, The (Olds), **AP:** 1461

"Welsh Bards, The" (Arany), **EP:** 47

Wen Yiduo, **TE:** 66

Wenli (classical Chinese writing), **TE:** 55

"Wenn nicht dein Brunnen, Melusine." *See* "Melusine, If Your Well Had Not"

Wenyan (literary Chinese writing), **TE:** 55

Werfel, Franz, **TE:** 307

Wergeland, Henrik, **TE:** 536

"Werwolf, Der." *See* "Banshee, The"

Wessex Poems, and Other Verses (Hardy), **BP:** 584

West, The (Dorn), **AP:** 476

West-Eastern Divan (Goethe), **EP:** 403

West Indian poetry. *See* Caribbean poetry

West Indies. *See* Geographical Index

West of Childhood (Gardner), **AP:** 655

West of Your City (Stafford), **AP:** 1875

Western Star (Benét), **AP:** 127

Westöstlicher Divan. See West-Eastern Divan

Whalen, Philip, AP: 2111-2114; "Delights of Winter at the Shore," **AP:** 2113; "For C.," **AP:** 2112; "The Garden," **AP:** 2113; *Highgrade,* **AP:** 2113; *The Human Fantasy,* **AP:** 2124; "Small Tantric Sermon," **AP:** 2113

What? (Ko Un), **WP:** 140

"What Are Years?" (Moore), **AP:** 1368

"What Metre Is" (MacBeth), **BP:** 843

What Moon Drove Me to This? (Harjo), **AP:** 790

What the Kite Thinks (Lum), **AP:** 1206

What Thou Lovest Well, Remains American (Hugo), **AP:** 936

What Work Is (Levine), **AP:** 1125

Whatsaid Serif (Mackey), **AP:** 1243

Wheatley, Phillis, AP: 2114-2122, **TE:** 3

Wheel, The (Berry), **AP:** 152

Wheeling Motel (Wright), **AP:** 2220

Wheelock, John Hall, AP: 2123-2126; *Dear Men and Women,* **AP:** 2125; *Dust and Light,* **AP:** 2124; *This Blessed Earth,* **AP:** 2125

Wheelwright, John, AP: 2126-2130; "Dusk to Dusk," **AP:** 2129; *Mirrors of Venus,* **AP:** 2128; *Political Self-Portrait, 1919-1939,* **AP:** 2128; *Rock and Shell,* **AP:** 2128

When (Wormser), **AP:** 2201

"When Lilacs Last in the Dooryard Bloom'd" (Whitman), **AP:** 2138

"When the Frost Is on the Punkin" (Riley), **AP:** 1650

"When You Are Old" (Ronsard), **EP:** 916

"Where I Near and Where I Land . . ." (Hofmannsthal), **EP:** 483

Where Shall I Wander (Ashbery), **AP:** 63

Where Sparrows Work Hard (Soto), **AP:** 1864

Where the Sidewalk Ends (Silverstein), **AP:** 1783

Whims and Oddities (Hood), **BP:** 656

"Whip, The" (Robinson), **AP:** 1666

Whisper to the Earth (Ignatow), **AP:** 948

Whispering to Fool the Wind (Ríos), **AP:** 1655

White (Simic), **AP:** 1788

White Apples and the Taste of Stone (Hall), **AP:** 784

White Sail (Sorrentino), **AP:** 1860

White Shroud (Ginsberg), **AP:** 684

White Words, The (Wormser), **AP:** 2198

Whitehall, Harold, **TE:** 751

Whitman, Walt, AP: 2130-2140,
　　TE: 190; Beat generation,
　　TE: 205; "Crossing Brooklyn
　　Ferry," **AP:** 2136; *Drum-Taps*,
　　AP: 2137; and Kenneth Koch,
　　AP: 1061; *Leaves of Grass*,
　　AP: 2133; "Out of the Cradle
　　Endlessly Rocking," **AP:** 2136;
　　"Passage to India," **AP:** 2138;
　　poem about, **AP:** 1277; "Prayer of
　　Columbus," **AP:** 2139; and
　　Theodore Roethke, **AP:** 1674;
　　"Song of Myself," **AP:** 2133; and
　　Henry David Thoreau, **AP:** 1980;
　　"When Lilacs Last in the
　　Dooryard Bloom'd," **AP:** 2138
Whitsun Weddings, The (Larkin),
　　BP: 791
Whittemore, Reed, AP: 2140-2144;
　　An American Takes a Walk,
　　AP: 2141; "Clamming,"
　　AP: 2143; *The Feel of Rock*,
　　AP: 2143; *Heroes and Heroines*,
　　AP: 2141; *The Past, the Future,
　　the Present*, **AP:** 2143; *Poems,
　　New and Selected*, **AP:** 2143;
　　"The Self and the Weather,"
　　AP: 2143
Whittier, John Greenleaf,
　　AP: 2144-2151, **TE:** 635;
　　"Ichabod," **AP:** 2148; "Snow-
　　Bound," **AP:** 2149
Who Killed Mr. Chippendale?
　　(Glenn), **AP:** 708
"Who Sees Through the Lens"
　　(Everson), **AP:** 571
Who Shall Be the Sun? (Wagoner),
　　AP: 2063
Who Will Know Us? (Soto), **AP:** 1865
Whole Grain (Emanuel), **AP:** 540
Whoroscope (Beckett), **EP:** 90
"Whoso list to hunt" (Wyatt),
　　BP: 1325
"Why Brownlee Left" (Muldoon),
　　BP: 940

Why Come Ye Nat to Courte
　　(Skelton), **BP:** 1157
Why I Wake Early (Oliver), **AP:** 1467
Widening Spell of the Leaves, The
　　(Levis), **AP:** 1130
Wielka liczba (Szymborska),
　　EP: 1011
Wieners, John, **TE:** 688
Wilbur, Richard, AP: 2151-2161; "A
　　Barred Owl," **AP:** 2158; "Boy at
　　the Window," **AP:** 2156;
　　Collected Poems, **AP:** 2159; "A
　　Hole in the Floor," **AP:** 2155;
　　"Lamarck Elaborated," **AP:** 2154;
　　"The Mind-Reader," **AP:** 2158;
　　"The Pardon," **AP:** 2157;
　　"Running," **AP:** 2155; "A Short
　　History," **AP:** 2158; "This
　　Pleasing Anxious Being,"
　　AP: 2158; "Walking to Sleep,"
　　AP: 2157
Wild Brides (Kasischke), **AP:** 1000
Wild Cherry (Reese), **AP:** 1619
Wild Gratitude (Hirsch), **AP:** 855
*Wild Patience Has Taken Me This Far,
　　A* (Rich), **AP:** 1639
Wild Peculiar Joy, A (Layton),
　　BP: 811
Wilde, Oscar, BP: 1303-1310; *The
　　Ballad of Reading Gaol*,
　　BP: 1308; "The Burden of Itys,"
　　BP: 1307; *Poems in Prose*,
　　BP: 1309; *Ravenna*, **BP:** 1305;
　　The Sphinx, **BP:** 1308
Wilderness Stair (Belitt), **AP:** 116
Will to Change, The (Rich), **AP:** 1637
Willehalm (Wolfram von
　　Eschenbach), **EP:** 1134
William Allingham (Allingham),
　　BP: 27
*William Henry Harrison, and Other
　　Poems* (Slavitt), **AP:** 1816
Williams, C. K., AP: 2161-2168;
　　Collected Poems, **AP:** 2166; *Flesh
　　and Blood*, **AP:** 2165; *I Am the*

Bitter Name, **AP:** 2163; *Lies*,
　　AP: 2163; *Repair*, **AP:** 2166; *The
　　Singing*, **AP:** 2166; *Tar*,
　　AP: 2165; *The Vigil*, **AP:** 2165;
　　With Ignorance, **AP:** 2164
Williams, Francis, **TE:** 43
Williams, Jonathan, **TE:** 688
Williams, Miller, AP: 2168-2171;
　　"The Associate Professor Delivers
　　an Exhortation to His Failing
　　Students You," **AP:** 2170; "Let
　　Me Tell You," **AP:** 2170
Williams, Raymond, **TE:** 734,
　　TE: 761
Williams, Sherley Anne, AP: 2172-
　　2175; *The Peacock Poems*,
　　AP: 2173; *Some One Sweet Angel
　　Chile*, **AP:** 2174
Williams, William Carlos,
　　AP: 2175-2184, **TE:** 196,
　　TE: 653; "Asphodel, That Greeny
　　Flower," **AP:** 2182; *Paterson*,
　　AP: 2178, **TE:** 196
Willingly (Gallagher), **AP:** 641
"Willkommen und Abschied." *See*
　　"Welcome and Farewell"
Wilmot, John, earl of Rochester. *See*
　　Rochester, John Wilmot, earl of
"Wind-Flower, The" (Very),
　　AP: 2041
Windcatcher (Breytenbach), **EP:** 168
"Windhover, The" (Hopkins),
　　BP: 671
"Winding Banks of Erne, The"
　　(Allingham), **BP:** 23
"Winding River, The" (Du Fu), **WP:** 88
"Window" (Corso), **AP:** 360
Wine (Gay), **BP:** 516
Wing Tek Lum. *See* Lum, Wing Tek
Winokur, Maxine. *See* Kumin,
　　Maxine
Winter Come, A, Summer Gone, A
　　(Moss), **AP:** 1377
"Winter Diary, A" (Van Doren),
　　AP: 2029

"Winter Evening" (Barnard), **AP:** 103

"Winter Insomnia" (Carver), **AP:** 287

Winter Morning Walks (Kooser),
　AP: 1072

"Winter Noon" (Saba), **EP:** 929

Winter Numbers (Hacker), **AP:** 767

Winter Oysters (Galvin), **AP:** 649

Winter Palace, The (Haavikko),
　EP: 438

Winter Poems Along the Rio Grande
　(Baca), **AP:** 75

"Winter Runner, The" (Galvin),
　AP: 647

Wintering Out (Heaney), **BP:** 598

Winters, Yvor, AP: 2184-2190; *The*
　Bare Hills, **AP:** 2187; *Before*
　Disaster, **AP:** 2189; *Collected*
　Poems, **AP:** 2189; *The Immobile*
　Wind, **AP:** 2187; *The Journey, and*
　Other Poems, **AP:** 2188; *The*
　Proof, **AP:** 2188

Winther, Christian, **TE:** 535

Wire Harp, The (Biermann), **EP:** 122

Wit, defined, **TE:** 708

"Witchita Vortex Sutra" (Ginsberg),
　AP: 683

With Ignorance (Williams), **AP:** 2164

"With rue my heart is laden"
　(Housman), **BP:** 682

With Strings (Bernstein), **AP:** 135

"Within the House" (Claudel),
　EP: 249

Without (Hall), **AP:** 783

"Without Symbolism" (Foix),
　EP: 332

"Wits, The" (Suckling), **BP:** 1211

Wivallius, Lars, **TE:** 529

"Wo ich nahe, wo ich lande . . ." *See*
　"Where I Near and Where I
　Land . . ."

Wodwo (Hughes), **BP:** 689

Wojahn, David, AP: 2190-2196; *The*
　Falling Hour, **AP:** 2194;
　Glassworks, **AP:** 2191;
　Interrogation Palace, **AP:** 2195;

Late Empire, **AP:** 2193; *Mystery*
　Train, **AP:** 2192; *Spirit Cabinet*,
　AP: 2194

Wołanie do Yeti (Szymborska),
　EP: 1009

Wolf Salt (Popa), **EP:** 859

Wolfram von Eschenbach,
　EP: 1130-1136, **TE:** 286;
　Parzival, **EP:** 1132, **TE:** 287;
　Schionatulander and Sigune,
　EP: 1133; *Willehalm*, **EP:** 1134

Wolfwatching (Hughes), **BP:** 693

"Woman at the Washington Zoo,
　The" (Jarrell), **AP:** 961

Woman Before an Aquarium (Hampl),
　AP: 787

Woman I Kept to Myself, The
　(Alvarez), **AP:** 35

"Woman in Love, A" (Éluard),
　EP: 316

Woman of the River (Alegría), **WP:** 12

Woman Poems, The (Oppenheimer),
　AP: 1484

Woman Who Died in Her Sleep, The
　(Gregerson), **AP:** 733

Woman Who Fell from the Sky, The
　(Harjo), **AP:** 792

"Women" (Bogan), **AP:** 199

Women at Point Sur, The (Jeffers),
　AP: 968

Women poets, **TE:** 210; Africa,
　TE: 18; Australia, **TE:** 31;
　Germany, **TE:** 312; India,
　TE: 373; Italy, **TE:** 386. *See also*
　Categorized Index

Women Whose Lives Are Food, Men
　Whose Lives Are Money (Oates),
　AP: 1446

Wonders of the Peake, The (Cotton),
　BP: 310

"Woodnotes" (Emerson), **AP:** 551

Woolf, Virginia; *A Room of One's*
　Own, **TE:** 738

"Wordless Winter" (Davison),
　AP: 440

Words (Creeley), **AP:** 397

"Words" (Plath), **AP:** 1554

Words by the Water (Smith),
　AP: 1829

"Words for My Daughter" (Balaban),
　AP: 83

Words for the Wind (Roethke),
　AP: 1676

Words in Stone (Bonnefoy), **EP:** 146

Words Under the Words (Nye),
　AP: 1440

Wordsworth, William, BP: 1310-
　1321, **TE:** 177, **TE:** 628,
　TE: 708; "Composed upon
　Westminster Bridge, September 3,
　1802," **TE:** 746; "Lines
　Composed a Few Miles Above
　Tintern Abbey," **BP:** 1314; *Lyrical*
　Ballads, **BP:** 1312; "Michael,"
　BP: 1316; "Ode: Intimations of
　Immortality from Recollections of
　Early Childhood," **BP:** 1317;
　Preface to *Lyrical Ballads*,
　TE: 708; *The Prelude*, **BP:** 1318;
　and Henry David Thoreau,
　AP: 1981

"Work" (Cook), **TE:** 762

Works (Davenant), **BP:** 365

Works and Days (Hesiod), **EP:** 469,
　TE: 222

World Anthology, The (anthology),
　TE: 675

"World Box-Score Cup" (Dorn),
　AP: 477

World Doesn't End, The (Simic),
　AP: 1789

"World in an Eare-Ring, A"
　(Newcastle), **BP:** 961

World of Difference, A (McHugh),
　AP: 1232

World of Ten Thousand Things, The
　(Wright), **AP:** 2214

World, the Worldless, The (Bronk),
　AP: 245

World War I; Richard Aldington,

BP: 20; Guillaume Apollinaire,
　EP: 28; Mihály Babits, **EP:** 70;
　John Peale Bishop, **AP:** 178;
　Edmund Blunden, **BP:** 105
World War II; Anna Akhmatova,
　WP: 7; Rose Ausländer, **AP:** 67;
　Ingeborg Bachmann, **EP:** 74;
　Lincoln Kirstein, **AP:** 1044;
　Kenneth Koch, **AP:** 1063; Denise
　Levertov, **AP:** 1116
Worldly Country, A (Ashbery),
　AP: 63
Wormser, Baron, AP: 2196-2203;
　*Atoms, Soul Music, and Other
　Poems,* **AP:** 2200; *Carthage,*
　AP: 2202; *Good Trembling,*
　AP: 2199; *Mulroney and Others,*
　AP: 2201; *Scattered Chapters,*
　AP: 2202; *Subject Matter,*
　AP: 2201; *When,* **AP:** 2201; *The
　White Words,* **AP:** 2198
Worshipful Company of Fletchers
　(Tate), **AP:** 1955
Worte in Versen (Kraus), **EP:** 567
Worte sind Schatten (Gomringer),
　EP: 408
"Wreck of the *Deutschland,* The"
　(Hopkins), **BP:** 669
*Wreck of the Thresher, and Other
　Poems, The* (Meredith), **AP:** 1312
Wrecking Crew (Levis), **AP:** 1130
Wright, C. D., AP: 2203-2206;
　Deepstep Come Shining,
　AP: 2205; *One Big Self,*
　AP: 2206; *String Light,* **AP:** 2205
Wright, Charles, AP: 2207-2217;
　Bloodlines, **AP:** 2210; *China
　Trace,* **AP:** 2211; *The Grave of
　the Right Hand,* **AP:** 2209; *Hard
　Freight,* **AP:** 2209; *Littlefoot,*
　AP: 2215; *Negative Blue,*
　AP: 2214; *The Other Side of the
　River,* **AP:** 2213; *Scar Tissue,*
　AP: 2215; *Sestet,* **AP:** 2216; *The
　Southern Cross,* **AP:** 2212; *The

World of Ten Thousand Things,
　AP: 2214; *Zone Journals,*
　AP: 2213
Wright, Franz, AP: 2217-2221; *The
　Beforelife,* **AP:** 2219; *God's
　Silence,* **AP:** 2220; *Ill Lit,*
　AP: 2219; *Walking to Martha's
　Vineyard,* **AP:** 2220; *Wheeling
　Motel,* **AP:** 2220
Wright, James, AP: 2221-2231; "At
　the Executed Murderer's Grave,"
　AP: 2226; "Autumn Begins in
　Martins Ferry, Ohio," **AP:** 2228;
　"A Blessing," **AP:** 2230;
　"Eisenhower's Visit to Franco,
　1959," **AP:** 2228; *The Green Wall,*
　AP: 2224; "Hook," **AP:** 2230;
　"Lying in a Hammock at William
　Duffy's Farm in Pine Island,
　Minnesota," **AP:** 2223; "The
　Minneapolis Poem," **AP:** 2229;
　"An Offering for Mr. Bluehart,"
　AP: 2225; "A Reply to Matthew
　Arnold of My Fifth Day in Fano,"
　AP: 2230; *Saint Judas,* **AP:** 2225;
　"To a Defeated Savior,"
　AP: 2224; "Two Hangovers,"
　AP: 2227
Wright, Jay, AP: 2231-2240;
　Boleros, **AP:** 2238; *Dimensions of
　History,* **AP:** 2236; *The Double
　Invention of Komo,* **AP:** 2237;
　Elaine's Book, **AP:** 2238;
　Explications/Interpretations,
　AP: 2235; *The Homecoming
　Singer,* **AP:** 2234; *Soothsayers
　and Omens,* **AP:** 2235;
　Transfigurations, **AP:** 2239
Wright, Judith, **TE:** 33, **TE:** 502
"Wring the Swan's Neck" (González
　Martínez), **WP:** 104
Writing Is an Aid to Memory
　(Hejinian), **AP:** 839
"Written at Cambridge" (Lamb),
　BP: 772

Written on Water (Tomlinson),
　BP: 1273
Wszelki wypadek (Szymborska),
　EP: 1010
Wyatt, Sir Thomas, BP: 1322-1329;
　"It may be good, like it who list,"
　BP: 1326; "My mother's maids,
　when they did sew and spin,"
　BP: 1328; "Such hap as I am
　happed in," **BP:** 1327; "They flee
　from me, that sometime did me
　seek," **BP:** 1326; "Whoso list to
　hunt," **BP:** 1325
"Wyatt resteth here, that quick could
　never rest" (Surrey), **BP:** 1215
Wylie, Elinor, AP: 2240-2243;
　Angels and Earthly Creatures,
　AP: 2242; *Black Armour,*
　AP: 2242; *Nets to Catch the
　Wind,* **AP:** 2242; *Trivial Breath,*
　AP: 2242
Wyndmere (Muske), **AP:** 1397

X/Self (Brathwaite), **AP:** 235
Xie Lingyun, WP: 334-338
Xin yuefu, **TE:** 62
Xmas Murder, An (Corn), **AP:** 355

Ya (Mayakovsky), **WP:** 178
Yakamochi. *See* Ōtomo Yakamochi
Yale Series of Younger Poets,
　AP: 2332, **CM:** 67, **TE:** 887
Yamada, Mitsuye, AP: 2244-2248;
　Camp Notes, and Other Writings,
　AP: 2247; *Desert Run,* **AP:** 2246
Yamanoe Okura, **TE:** 414
Year 1905, The (Pasternak), **WP:** 227
Year of Our Birth, The (McPherson),
　AP: 1261
Year of Our Revolution, The (Ortiz
　Cofer), **AP:** 1501
Year of the Soul, The (George),
　EP: 382
"Years Behind, The" (Awooner),
　WP: 30

Year's Declension, The (Everson), **AP:** 574

Yeats, William Butler, BP: 1330-1349, **TE:** 652; William Allingham, **BP:** 24; "Among School Children," **BP:** 1342; "Byzantium," **BP:** 1345, **TE:** 193; "The Lake Isle of Innisfree," **BP:** 1336; "Leda and the Swan," **BP:** 1337; "Sailing to Byzantium," **BP:** 1345, **TE:** 193; "The Second Coming," **BP:** 1339; "Under Ben Bulben," **BP:** 1347

Yellow Glove (Nye), **AP:** 1439

Yellow House on the Corner, The (Dove), **AP:** 488

Yellow Light (Hongo), **AP:** 902

Yellow Room, The (Hall), **AP:** 779

Yes, Everything (Dana), **AP:** 435

Yes-or-No Answer, A (Shore), **AP:** 1776

"Yes, Too Much of Everything" (Salinas), **EP:** 939

"Yesterday and To-morrow" (Dunbar), **AP:** 506

"Yet Do I Marvel" (Cullen), **AP:** 406

"Yeux d'Elsa, Les." *See* "Elsa's Eyes"

Yevtushenko: Selected Poems (Yevtushenko), **WP:** 348

Yevtushenko, Yevgeny, TE: 522, **WP:** 339-348; "Babii Yar," **WP:** 344; "Bratsk Station," **WP:** 344; *The Collected Poems, 1952-1990,* **WP:** 346; *Invisible Threads,* **WP:** 345; *Ivanovskiye sitsi,* **WP:** 345; *Walk on the Ledge,* **WP:** 346; *Yevtushenko: Selected Poems,* **WP:** 348; "Zima Junction," **WP:** 343

Yo soy Joaquín. See I Am Joaquín/Yo soy Joaquín

Yoga Vāsiṣṭha. See Supreme Yoga, The

Yonghuai shi, **TE:** 59

Yosano Akiko, TE: 428, **WP:** 349-353; *Tangled Hair,* **WP:** 352

You Are Happy (Atwood), **BP:** 43

"You Can Start the Poetry Now" (McGrath), **AP:** 1228

You Don't Miss Your Water (Eady), **AP:** 523

You, Emperors, and Others (Warren), **AP:** 2099

"You Nurturer of the Muses" (Foscolo), **EP:** 342

"You Shattered" (Ungaretti), **EP:** 1062

"You Understand the Requirements" (Lifshin), **AP:** 1140

"You Who Are the Rose" (Aragon), **EP:** 41

"You Who Have Wronged" (Miłosz), **EP:** 717

Young, Al, AP: 2248-2257; *The Blues Don't Change,* **AP:** 2254; *Coastal Nights and Inland Afternoons,* **AP:** 2255; *Dancing,* **AP:** 2250; *Geography of the Near Past,* **AP:** 2253; *Something About the Blues,* **AP:** 2256; *The Song Turning Back into Itself,* **AP:** 2252; *The Sound of Dreams Remembered,* **AP:** 2255

Young, Dean, AP: 2257-2260; *Beloved Infidel,* **AP:** 2259; *Elegy on a Toy Piano,* **AP:** 2259; *Primitive Mentor,* **AP:** 2259

Young, Edward, BP: 1349-1353; *The Force of Religion,* **BP:** 1351; *Love of Fame, the Universal Passion,* **BP:** 1352; *Night-Thoughts,* **BP:** 1352; *A Poem on the Last Day,* **BP:** 1351

Young, Richard. *See* Young, Dean

Young adult poetry. *See* Children's/young adult poetry in Categorized Index

"Young Men Dead" (Bishop), **AP:** 178

Young Poland poetry, **TE:** 495

Young Vienna Group. *See* Categorized Index

"Younger Brutus, The" (Leopardi), **EP:** 613

"Your life is like a little winter's day" (Belloc), **BP:** 78

Your Name Here (Ashbery), **AP:** 63

Your Native Land, Your Life (Rich), **AP:** 1639

Youth (Rosenberg), **BP:** 1057

Ysterkoei moet sweet, Die (Breytenbach), **EP:** 165

Yuan Zhen, **TE:** 62

Yuefu, **TE:** 59

Yūgen, **TE:** 419

Yugloslavia. *See* Geographical Index

Zagajewski, Adam, EP: 1137-1141; *Canvas,* **EP:** 1139; *Jechai do Lwówa,* **EP:** 1139; *Komunikat,* **EP:** 1139; *List,* **EP:** 1139; *Oda do wielości,* **EP:** 1139; *Pragnienie,* **EP:** 1140; *Sklepy mięsne,* **EP:** 1139; *Ziemia Ognista,* **EP:** 1139

Zalán futása (Vörösmarty), **EP:** 1114

Zamora, Daisy, WP: 354-356; *Clean Slate,* **WP:** 355; *The Violent Foam,* **WP:** 355

Zanzotto, Andrea, **TE:** 409

Zepeda, Ofelia, **TE:** 486

"Zero Hour" (Cardenal), **WP:** 54

Zhukovsky, Vasily, **TE:** 511

Ziemia Ognista (Zagajewski), **EP:** 1139

Zig-Zag Walk, The (Logan), **AP:** 1155

"Zima Junction" (Yevtushenko), **WP:** 343

Zimmer, Paul, AP: 2261-2265; *Crossing to Sunlight,* **AP:** 2263; *Crossing to Sunlight Revisited,* **AP:** 2263; *Earthbound Zimmer,* **AP:** 2262; *The Great Bird of Love,* **AP:** 2263; *A Seed on the Wind,* **AP:** 2262

Zinc Fingers (Meinke), **AP:** 1293

"Zionide." *See* "Ode to Zion"

Zither and Autobiography (Scalapino), **AP:** 1727

Živo meso. See Raw Flesh

Zmaj, Jovan Jovanović, **TE:** 568

Żmija (Słowacki), **EP:** 976

Zone Journals (Wright), **AP:** 2213

"Zoo, The" (Smith), **BP:** 1166

Zrínyi, Miklós, **TE:** 353

Zukofsky, Louis, AP: 2265-2270; "A," **AP:** 2269; "Hi, Kuh," **AP:** 2267; "Mantis," **AP:** 2267; *Poem Beginning "The,"* **AP:** 2268

"Zum Gedächtnis des Schauspielers Mitterwurzer" (Hofmannsthal), **EP:** 482

Župančič, Oton, **TE:** 581

Zweig, Stefan, **EP:** 1141-1147; *Die Frühen Kränze*, **EP:** 1145; *Gesammelten Gedichte*, **EP:** 1145; "Der Sechzigjährige dankt," **EP:** 1146